Springer Texts in Business and Economics

More information about this series at http://www.springer.com/series/10099

Jan Ubøe

Introductory Statistics for Business and Economics

Theory, Exercises and Solutions

Springer

Jan Ubøe
Department of Business
and Management Science
Norwegian School of Economics
Bergen, Norway

ISSN 2192-4333 ISSN 2192-4341 (electronic)
Springer Texts in Business and Economics
ISBN 978-3-319-70935-2 ISBN 978-3-319-70936-9 (eBook)
https://doi.org/10.1007/978-3-319-70936-9

Library of Congress Control Number: 2017960422

Printed on acid-free paper

This Springer imprint is published by Springer Nature
The registered company is Springer International Publishing AG
The registered company address is: Gewerbestrasse 11, 6330 Cham, Switzerland

Electronic Supplementary Material The online version of this book (https://doi.org/10.1007/978-3-319-70936-9) contains supplementary material, which is available to authorized users.

To Bernt Øksendal who taught me everything I know about probability theory, and Jostein Lillestøl who taught me all I know about statistics.

Preface

This book has a traditional yet modern approach to teaching statistics. When combined with my newly developed system for collaborate learning, it is well suited for modern teaching formats like flipped classrooms, but it also serves well if the lecturer prefers a more traditional approach.

My system for collaborative learning can be downloaded from the book's website. The files are available for lecturers only and contain supplementary problems with separate solution files for each chapter. The system is particularly targeted at the average student, and my own students like it a lot. Many of them report back that it is great fun!

I strongly believe that the best way to learn statistics is by doing. As a consequence of this, the main body of each chapter is shorter than what has been common. The idea is to let students work with exercises as soon as possible, and most of my efforts have been invested in developing interesting, relevant, and to some extent challenging exercises. The exercises are divided into two parts. The exercises in the first part of each chapter are straightforward. From my experience even excellent students struggle a lot when they study new material, and to quickly gain momentum it is necessary that the first few exercises are very simple. Only when the basic framework is in place is it time to move on to more interesting problems.

As a motivation for further studies, students need to see interesting applications from the start. Throughout the book I have picked bits and pieces of theory that are usually taught on a much higher level and organized them such that they are suitable for beginners. These exercises are all equipped with a short label providing lecturers with hints of what type of theory/issues they discuss. My approach is much appreciated by students, who at an early stage see that statistics is essential to any serious study of economics. In the beginning of the book there are only a few such problems, but as we learn more there is more room for relevant applications. Some of these exercises are challenging, but complexity was never a goal. Nontrivial problems tend to have nontrivial solutions, but my intent is to present theory in the simplest possible way. The labeled exercises are not always difficult. Indeed, some of the exercises that have given me the most pleasure have a very simple solution.

My book is one of the very few that makes some use of nonlinear theory, in particular theory related to logarithms and exponential functions. I have often heard that such theory should be avoided since it is too difficult for students, but from my experience this is not true. Why at all do we teach beginner courses in mathematics, if none of this theory is to be used later? To keep things simple, however, I have mainly included computations that would have been considered straightforward when encountered in a beginner course in mathematics.

Many textbooks now focus on software applications. Statistical software is an indispensable tool once the theory is understood. Very often, however, the users do not properly understand the limitations of the theory, and misinterpretations are all too common. The problem is increasing at all levels in science. I refer to and use software applications only sparingly throughout the book. To hedge various forms of malpractice, I discuss several pitfalls I have come across, in the exercises.

A lot of people have contributed to this book, and I will mention only a few. First of all I wish to thank all my former students at Norwegian School of Economics. These students have been my fortune in life, and few of the exercises in this book would ever materialized had it not been for such abundance of ability and talent. Second I should thank Per Oscar Andersen for his never ending encouragement for the Norwegian edition and Arve Michaelsen for endless hours of typesetting and preparation of figures. Bernt Øksendal deserves a special thanks for teaching me probability theory and for being a constant source of inspiration. Jostein Lillestøl deserves a special thanks for teaching me statistics, and Jostein's brilliant textbook in statistics has no doubt served as a template for my own presentation. Jonas Andersson deserves a special thanks for the many times he clarified points I did not fully understand.

Last I wish to thank the editorial staff at Springer for a very positive, swift, and professional handling of my manuscript.

Bergen, Norway
October 2017

Jan Ubøe

Contents

Descriptive Statistics

1

Abstract

In this chapter we will look at very basic statistical concepts. The material is facilitated to make it available to a wide audience and does not require any prerequisites. For some readers this will mean that they are already familiar with the contents and it may be sufficient to browse quickly through the chapter before continuing to the next chapters. Otherwise it can be necessary to study the material in detail, and it might be wise to invest some time on the exercises.

1.1 Population and Samples

Most statistical surveys start out with a collection of numbers in some form. We can imagine that we collect data for a poll, or that we collect data to examine the earnings of a company, the possibilities are endless. Such collection of data can, however, be done in two principally different ways.

One option is that we collect all the relevant information. In a poll this means that we ask everybody, or that we examine every single earning of a company. The task for a statistician is then to find a good way to present the numbers to make the contents easy to interpret for everyone.

In many cases it may not be practical or even possible to collect all the information. In such cases we must settle with a sample. In a poll this means that we only ask a part of the population, and in accounting we might only check some randomly selected earnings. This puts the statistician in a different position. He or she must examine the results, but in addition judge if the effects within the sample can be generalized to the rest of the population. How much confidence can we have in the effects seen in the sample? The problem is that elements in the sample may differ from the rest of the population in a systematic way. We call such differences selection bias.

J. Ubøe, *Introductory Statistics for Business and Economics*, Springer Texts in Business and Economics, https://doi.org/10.1007/978-3-319-70936-9_1

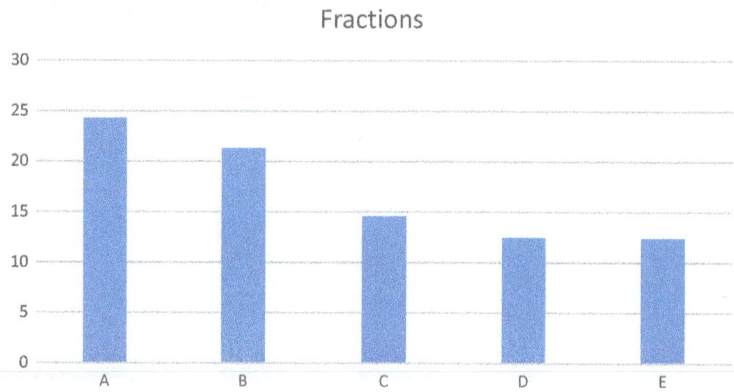

Fig. 1.1 A bar chart

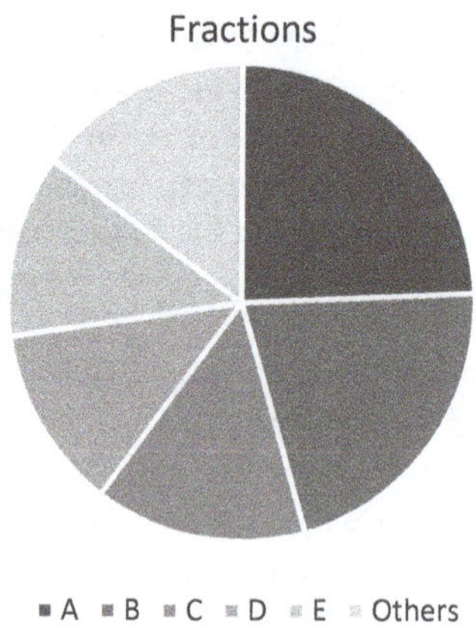

Fig. 1.2 A pie chart

Example 1.1 During an election a total of 2,521,879 votes were cast. Party A received 612,632 votes, party B received 534,852 votes, party C received 369,236 votes, party D received 316,456 votes, and party E received 312,839 votes. These numbers are facts. How can we present them in a transparent fashion?

A common solution is to transfer the numbers into percentages, i.e.

A 24.3% B 21.3% C 14.6% D 12.5% E 12.4%

A graphical display in terms of a bar chart gives a better overview, see Fig. 1.1.

When we have sorted the numbers such that the biggest number comes first with the other numbers following in descending order, it is usual to call the graph a Pareto chart. This makes the information easy to read and is often a good idea. Alternatively we may display the numbers in terms of a pie chart, see Fig. 1.2.

In a pie chart the size of the numbers is represented by the area of the pie. That gives a visual impression of the numbers. We can, e.g., see that parties A and B did not receive a majority of the votes together.

We have seen that it is possible to display the same information in several different ways. There is, however, no reason to question the numbers. The facts are undisputed and give the exact outcome of the election. In this case there is no selection bias.

Example 1.2 In a poll we have asked 1000 randomly chosen people what party they would prefer if there was an election today. 203 would have voted A, 201 B, 160 C, 134 D, and 120 E.

It is of course possible to display these numbers as in Example 1.1, but there is a principal difference. What would have happened if we asked somebody else? To what extent does the poll generalize to the whole population? These are important questions for a statistician. In a poll we run the risk of selection bias, and a statistician must be able to judge the size of this bias. The answers to these questions will have to wait, but we will return to them later in the book.

In a statistical survey we use the word population to denote all possible alternatives that could have been examined, while the word sample is used to signify only those alternatives that were in fact examined. In a poll the population is typically all the people with the right to vote, while the sample is those people who were in fact asked about their opinion. Since it is quite important to distinguish the two notions, we will throughout the book use the uppercase letter N when we talk about the whole population, while the lowercase letter n refers to the number of observations in a sample.

In most applications we only have information on the sample, but wish to make decisions based on the properties of the population. In the book we will see how properties of the sample can be used to compute what properties we are likely to find in the population. This is a central topic in statistics and has a special name: statistical inference. Statistical inference is central to any decision process. We have to ask if the probability is sufficiently large to make a decision. The process prior to a decision can be displayed as shown in Fig. 1.3.

It is important to keep in mind that the sample should represent the population. The selection needs to be random, and we should seek to avoid that the members of the sample influence each other. We should, for example, not ask members of a protest march as those people may have opinions that are not typical for the population.

When we ask questions, it is important that formulations are neutral. In many situations it may be important that the members of the sample are anonymous. If we forget to take such matters into account, chances are that the answers are affected by the way we carried out the survey.

When we have collected all the data, we need to analyze them. We can rarely be sure of what the population means. Sometimes the tendency is so weak that we are unable to draw any conclusions. In other cases tendencies are so strong that they probably apply to the population.

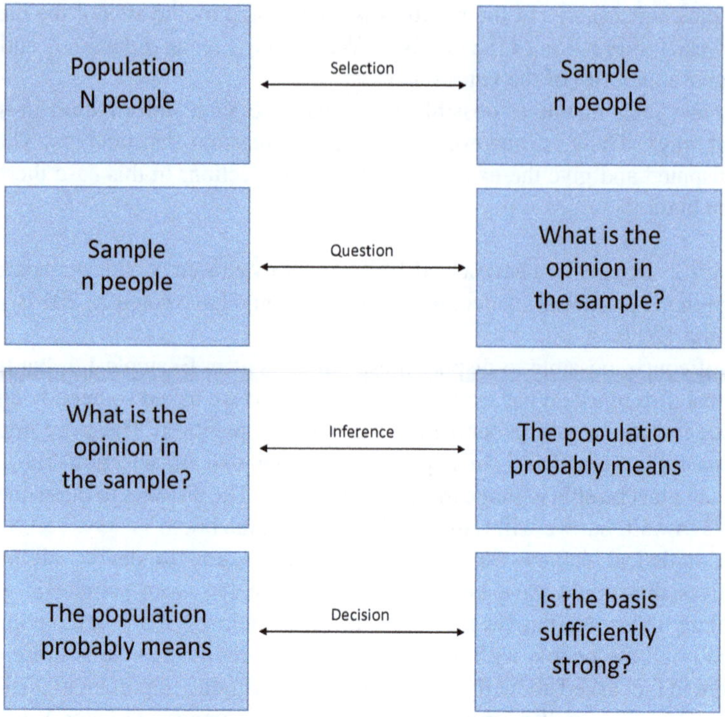

Fig. 1.3 The process prior to a decision

When the statistical analysis is ready, we have to determine if the basis is strong enough to make a decision. This is something that should be discussed prior to the survey. When we are planning a survey, we should think through if we are likely to end up with a clear conclusion. If it later becomes clear that our data are insufficient, we are not free to simply repeat the survey. If we repeat a survey sufficiently many times, we are likely to obtain results supporting quite divergent views. In such cases it is necessary to consider all examinations in conjunction, and we are not free to pick out a single observation set supporting a particular point of view. Violations of this principle are considered to be scientific fraud, but mistakes are common among people with insufficient knowledge of statistics. It is a serious problem that people unintentionally misinterpret statistical findings, and later in the book we will discuss several common pitfalls.

1.2 The Median

When we have collected data, it is important to present the findings in a transparent fashion. Let us assume that we have collected data on the return of 7 different stocks. The numbers we collected were as follows:

$$2.7\%, \quad 9.2\%, \quad 11.4\%, \quad 4.6\%, \quad 5.2\%, \quad 5.6\%, \quad -2.4\%.$$

This gives a rather messy picture of the data. The picture becomes more clear if we sort the numbers in ascending order:

$$-2.4\%, \quad 2.7\%, \quad 3.6\%, \quad 5.2\%, \quad 5.6\%, \quad 9.2\%, \quad 11.4\%.$$

We are now able to conclude that the returns varied from −2.4% to 11.4%. We can proceed in this way to describe the extremes in the data. The extremes do not necessarily give a good picture of the entire dataset. It can very well happen that the extremes are somewhat special and not really typical for the data. We need other concepts which offer more precise information. The median is an example of this kind and is roughly defined as a number such that half of the observations are smaller while the second half are larger. The median for the dataset above is hence 5.2%. This number tells us that half of the unit trusts performed at 5.2% or better, and that the other half performed at 5.2% or worse. The precise definition of the median is as follows:

Definition 1.1 The median of a collection of n numbers/observations ordered in ascending order is:

- Observation number $\frac{n+1}{2}$ if n is an odd number.
- The midpoint between observation $\frac{n}{2}$ and observation $\frac{n}{2} + 1$ if n is even.

Example 1.3 Find the median of the numbers

$$1.5\%, \quad 2.3\%, \quad -3.4\%, \quad -5.6\%, \quad 0.3\%, \quad -3.4\%, \quad 3.2\% \quad 2.2\%.$$

Solution: We first write these numbers in ascending order

$$-5.6\%, \quad -3.4\%, \quad -3.4\%, \quad 0.3\%, \quad 1.5\%, \quad 2.2\%, \quad 2.3\%, \quad 3.2\%.$$

In this case we have $n = 8$ observations. Since n is even, the median is the midpoint between observation 4 and 5, i.e.

$$\text{Median} = \frac{0.3\% + 1.5\%}{2} = 0.9\%.$$

Strictly speaking there is no need to process the numbers when we have just a few observations. The situation is quite different if we have a huge number of data. We can for example imagine that we have collected data from 1451 different unit trusts. It serves no purpose to print out all these numbers. If it turns out that the returns vary from −11.9% to 7.7% with a median of −10.5%, we can quickly form an image of the data. We can conclude that at least half of these trusts performed quite badly, i.e., not better than −10.5%. We do not, however, possess a clear picture of how many trusts had a good performance. Was the trust with 7.7% return a rare exception or did many trusts perform at that level? To answer such questions, we need information beyond the median.

1.3 Quartiles and Mode

Quartiles provide additional information about the data. Roughly speaking we find the quartiles when we divide the numbers (sorted in ascending order) into four equally large groups. We call the transition between the first two groups as the first quartile, the transition between the two groups in the middle is the median, and the transition between the last two groups is the third quartile.

If $n+1$ is divisible by 4, the first quartile is observation number $\frac{n+1}{4}$ and the third quartile is observation number $\frac{3(n+1)}{4}$. The general definition is a bit cumbersome, see Exercise 1.15, but the computations are fully automated in computer programs and there is no reason to study this in detail. The concept provides only a rough picture of the data anyway, and the roughness does not change if we focus the details.

We return to the example above where we observed the return of 1451 unit trusts. If we sort the returns in ascending order, we get

$$\frac{1451+1}{4} = 363 \qquad \text{and} \qquad \frac{3(1451+1)}{4} = 1089.$$

The first quartile is hence observation number 363 and the third quartile is observation 1089. As an example let us assume that the first quartile is −10.7% and that the third quartile is −9.8%. We then know that about half of the trusts are performing between these two levels. This improves the picture compared with the case where we only knew the median. We are also able to conclude that at most one quarter of the funds (those above the third quartile) are performing well. This shows us that information on the quartiles clarifies the major trends in our data.

The distance between the first and third quartile is called the interquartile range. If the interquartile range is small, we know that about half of the data are close to each other. The interquartile range is one of several examples of how to measure the spread in our data. We have seen that the quartiles make it possible to get a better overview of the data, but certainly not a full solution. We can always proceed to present more details. The challenge is to focus the main features of the dataset without entering into too much detail.

In some connections we are likely to observe the same number multiple times. It can then be useful to know which observation is the most frequent. The most frequent observation is called the mode.

Table 1.1 The length of stay at an hotel

Days	1	2	3	4	5	6	7	8	9	10
Frequency	419	609	305	204	177	156	103	105	62	35

Example 1.4 We have collected data from $n = 2175$ visitors at an hotel. Table 1.1 shows the number of days people stayed.

Find the mode, median, and first and third quartiles for this observation set.

Solution: The most frequent observation is 2 days, which is registered 609 times. The mode is hence 2 days. The median is observation number 1088. We see that the sum of the two first categories is 1028, hence the median must be in category 3, i.e., the median is 3 days. To find the first and third quartiles we compute

$$\frac{2175 + 1}{4} = 544 \qquad 3 \cdot 544 = 1632.$$

We see that observation number 544 must be in category 2, the first quartile is hence 2 days. If we compute the sum of the first 4 categories, we see that they sum to 1537. That means that the third quartile must be in category 5. Third quartile is hence 5 days.

1.4 Relative Frequency and Histograms

Instead of frequencies we can compute how many percent of the observations we find in each category. We call these numbers relative frequencies. In general we define relative frequency as follows:

$$\text{Relative frequency} = \frac{\text{Number of observations within a group}}{\text{Number of observations in total}}.$$

In Example 1.4 we had 2175 observations in total. We find the relative frequencies if we divide the numbers in Table 1.1 by 2175. The results are displayed in Table 1.2.

In cases where there are lots of different outcomes, it may be beneficial to aggregate data in groups. It is then possible to make a new frequency table with the relative frequencies of each group. If we use the data from Example 1.4, we get Table 1.3.

Table 1.2 The length of stay at an hotel

Days	1	2	3	4	5	6	7	8	9	10
Relative frequency	0.19	0.28	0.14	0.09	0.08	0.07	0.05	0.05	0.03	0.02

Table 1.3 The length of stay at an hotel

Days	1–2	3–4	5–6	7 or more
Relative frequency	0.47	0.23	0.15	0.15

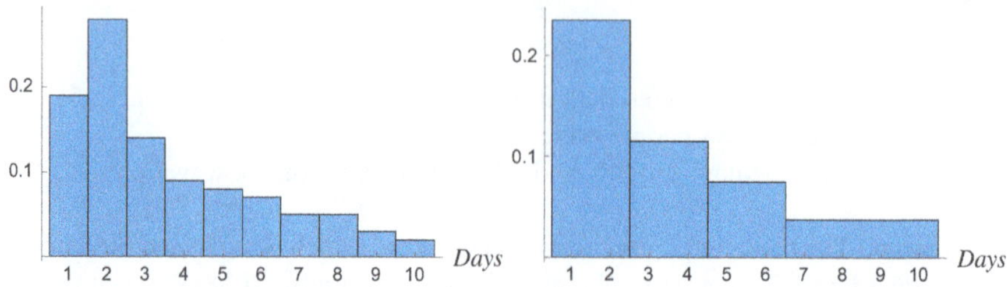

Fig. 1.4 Histograms

Tables of relative frequencies are often displayed by histograms. When we make histograms, we divide the sorted data into a number of nonoverlapping intervals and find relative frequencies within each interval. The result is displayed in a bar chart where:

- Each bar has a width equal to the width of the corresponding data.
- Each bar has a height defined by

$$\text{Height of bar} = \frac{\text{Relative frequency}}{\text{Width of interval}}.$$

- All bars are adjacent.

It is possible to make several different histograms from the same dataset. Most common is to divide the range of the data into 5–15 equally spaced intervals. Figure 1.4 shows two different histograms using the data from Example 1.4.

From the expressions above we see that

$$\text{Area of bar} = \text{Width of interval} \cdot \frac{\text{Relative frequency}}{\text{Width of interval}} = \text{Relative frequency}.$$

The area of each bar shows how big fraction of the observations that are related to the bar. In particular we note that the sum of the areas is 1, i.e., 100%. That is a property common to all probability densities, a concept we will study in detail later.

1.5 The Mean

The mean is probably the single most important concept in statistics, and we will return to this concept several times throughout this book. We first consider a simple example.

Example 1.5 What is the mean of the numbers

$$0, 1, 2, 3, 4, 5, 6, 7, 8, 9, 10, 11, 12, 13, 14, 15, 16, 17, 17, 18, 19, 20?$$

Solution: The mean is the middle value of the numbers, and even though we have not yet formulated a precise definition, it is clear that the answer must be 10.

One reason why the mean is so central to statistics is that it is suited to describe large datasets. If we compute the mean of the numbers

$$0, 100, 200, 300, \ldots, 1800, 1900, 2000,$$

the answer is 1000. Even if we did not know the numbers behind the computations, it is easy to understand that numbers with mean 10 must be very different from numbers with mean 1000; in the latter case most of the numbers need to be considerably larger. In many statistical surveys there are enormous amounts of data behind the computations. The purpose of using means is to present basic findings in the simplest possible way. It is, however, important to understand that the usefulness is limited. The use of means is a crude simplification that by far does not say everything about the data in question.

We find the arithmetic mean of a series of numbers/observations when we add the numbers and divide the result by the number of observations. We can imagine that we observe the values X of a stock on 5 consecutive days. If we find

$$X_1 = 2, \qquad X_2 = 3, \qquad X_3 = 2, \qquad X_4 = 1, \qquad X_5 = 2,$$

the mean is

$$\overline{X} = \frac{1}{5}(2 + 3 + 2 + 1 + 2) = 2.$$

This principle is true in general as the mean is defined as follows:

Definition 1.2 Given n observations of a variable X, the mean $\overline{X}$ is defined by

$$\overline{X} = \frac{1}{n}(X_1 + X_2 + \cdots + X_n) = \frac{1}{n}\sum_{i=1}^{n} X_i.$$

In this definition we have made use of the mathematical symbol $\sum$. That does not present any complications since it simply means we should sum all the numbers indicated by the indices marked out at the top/bottom of the symbol. If we use this definition on the numbers we considered in Example 1.5, we have 21 numbers in total. If we sum all these numbers, we find

$$X_1 + X_2 + \cdots + X_{21} = 0 + 1 + \cdots + 21 = 210.$$

The mean is hence

$$\overline{X} = \frac{1}{21} \cdot 210 = 10.$$

This corresponds well with the more intuitive approach above. As we already mentioned, the mean is far from containing all the relevant information. If we consider the two sequences:

$$1.8 \quad 2 \quad 2.2 \tag{1.1}$$

$$1 \quad 2 \quad 3, \tag{1.2}$$

both have mean 2. As the spread of the sequences are quite different, it is clear that we need more information to separate them.

1.6 Sample Variance and Sample Standard Deviation

In statistics we usually make use of the sample variance and the sample standard deviation to quantify the spread in a dataset. When it is clear from context that we speak about a sample, we sometimes drop the prefix sample and talk about variance and standard deviation. The purpose of these quantities is to measure how much the numbers deviate from the mean. Using these measures we will see that the spreads in (1.1) and (1.2) are quite different.

Definition 1.3 The sample variance S_X^2 of a series of numbers/observations is defined by the formula

$$S_X^2 = \frac{1}{n-1}\left((X_1 - \overline{X})^2 + \cdots + (X_n - \overline{X})^2\right) = \frac{1}{n-1}\sum_{i=1}^{n}(X_i - \overline{X})^2.$$

The formula is a bit complicated but this is of no consequence in practical applications. Computations of this sort are almost exclusively carried out by computer software, see the section on Excel at the end of this chapter. The formula is abstract, and it is definitely possible to misinterpret it. It is important to understand that the order of the operations is crucial, and that only one order provides the correct answer.

Table 1.4 Sum of squared errors

i	X_i	$(X_i - \overline{X})$	$(X_i - \overline{X})^2$
1	1	−6	36
2	8	1	1
3	10	3	9
4	4	−3	9
5	7	0	0
6	12	5	25
Sum		0	80

Example 1.6 Assume that $X_1 = 1, X_2 = 8, X_3 = 10, X_4 = 4, X_5 = 7, X_6 = 12$. It is easy to see that $\overline{X} = 7$. The sample variance can then be computed as in Table 1.4.

In the third column in Table 1.4 we see how much the observations deviate from the mean. We see that the sum of the deviations is zero. This is in fact true for any dataset, which explains why the sum of the deviations is useless as a measure of spread. When we square the deviations, we make sure that all the terms contribute to the sum. When we have computed the sum of squares, we use the formula from the definition to see that

$$S_X^2 = \frac{1}{5}\sum_{i=1}^{n}(X_i - \overline{X})^2 = \frac{1}{5} \cdot 80 = 16.$$

From the definition we see that the sample variance is small when all the deviations from the mean value are small, and that the sample variance is large when several terms are positioned far from the mean. Small sample variance is hence the same as small spread in the data, while the sample variance will be large if the observed values are far apart.

The size of the sample variance is often difficult to interpret. We often report the spread in terms of the sample standard deviation S_X which is defined as follows:

$$S_X = \sqrt{S_X^2}.$$

The advantage of the standard deviation is that it usually has a more transparent interpretation. We often think of the standard deviation as the typical spread around the mean value, see the exercises where we elaborate further on this interpretation. For the dataset reported in Example 1.6, we get

$$S_X = \sqrt{16} = 4,$$

and we interpret that the deviation from the mean 7 is typically 4. From the table above we see that some deviations are smaller than 4 and some are bigger, but 4 is roughly the right size of the deviations.

Table 1.5 Sum of squared errors

i	X_i	$(X_i - \overline{X})$	$(X_i - \overline{X})^2$
1	5	0	0
2	2	−3	9
3	4	−1	1
4	4	−1	1
5	10	5	25
Sum		0	36

If we return to the numbers

$$1.8 \quad 2 \quad 2.2$$

$$1 \quad 2 \quad 3,$$

we see that the first series has variance $S_X^2 = 0.04$ and standard deviation $S_X = 0.2$, while the second series has variance $S_X^2 = 1$ and standard deviation $S_X = 1$. The standard deviation is hence 5 times bigger for the second series. This makes good sense since the distance between the numbers is 5 times bigger. A large standard deviation means that the numbers are far apart, while a small value indicates that the values are approximately equal. A special case occurs when the standard deviation is zero. This can only happen when all the values are identical.

Example 1.7 Let $X_1 = 5, X_2 = 2, X_3 = 4, X_4 = 4, X_5 = 10$. Find the mean, the sample variance, and the sample standard deviation.

Solution: We use the formulas to see that

$$\overline{X} = \frac{1}{5}(5 + 2 + 4 + 4 + 10) = 5,$$

$$S_X^2 = \frac{1}{4} \cdot 36 = 9, \qquad S_X = \sqrt{9} = 3. \text{ See Table 1.5.}$$

1.7 Sample Covariance and Coefficient of Variation

The sample variance is used whenever we want to measure the spread within a sample. Often, however, we need to compare two different samples.

Example 1.8 Table 1.6 shows corresponding values of X and Y.

If we take a brief look at the numbers in Table 1.6, we see that they correspond. There is a clear tendency that small X-values are found together with small Y-values, and that large X-values are found together with large Y-values. Figure 1.5 displays the corresponding pairs.

Table 1.6 The data for Example 1.8

X_1	X_2	X_3	X_4	X_5	X_6	X_7	X_8	X_9	X_{10}
2	12	1	1	10	25	3	9	27	2
Y_1	Y_2	Y_3	Y_4	Y_5	Y_6	Y_7	Y_8	Y_9	Y_{10}
3	11	3	1	12	21	6	4	31	2

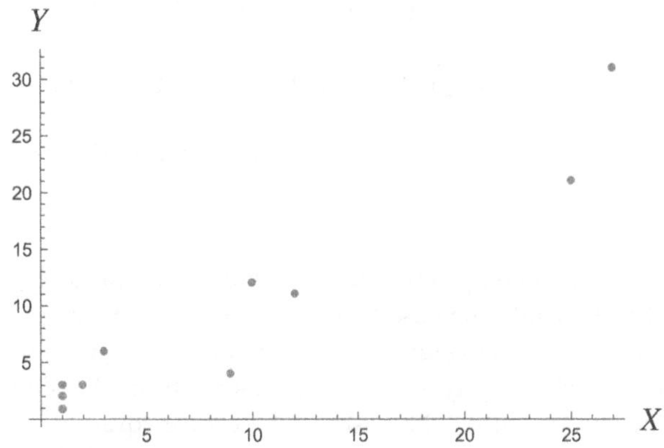

Fig. 1.5 Corresponding values

There are some exceptions that do not have a clear interpretation, but the main tendency appears to be clear. The question is then if we can find a method to measure how strongly the values correspond to each other. The sample covariance turns out to be useful in this respect, and we can use this quantity to judge if two samples pull in the same direction.

Definition 1.4 If our two samples are $X_1, \ldots, X_n$ and $Y_1, \ldots, Y_n$, the sample covariance S_{XY} is defined by

$$\begin{aligned} S_{XY} &= \frac{1}{n-1}\left((X_1-\overline{X})(Y_1-\overline{Y}) + \cdots + (X_n-\overline{X})(Y_n-\overline{Y})\right) \\ &= \frac{1}{n-1}\sum_{i=1}^{n}(X_i-\overline{X})(X_i-\overline{X}). \end{aligned}$$

It is interesting to note that if the two samples happen to be equal, then the sample covariance equals the variance. When it is clear from context that we speak about samples, we sometimes drop the prefix sample and speak about covariance.

Example 1.9 Let $X_1 = 242, X_2 = 266, X_3 = 218, X_4 = 234$ and $Y_1 = 363, Y_2 = 399, Y_3 = 327, Y_4 = 351$. Find S_{XY}.

Solution: We first compute $\overline{X} = 240$ and $\overline{Y} = 360$. We then use the formula to see that

$$\begin{aligned}
S_{XY} &= \frac{1}{3}\big((X_1 - \overline{X})(Y_1 - \overline{Y}) + (X_2 - \overline{X})(Y_2 - \overline{Y}) \\
&\quad + (X_3 - \overline{X})(Y_3 - \overline{Y}) + (X_4 - \overline{X})(Y_4 - \overline{Y})\big) \\
&= \frac{1}{3}\big((242 - 240)(363 - 360) + (266 - 240)(399 - 360) \\
&\quad + (218 - 240)(327 - 360) + (234 - 240)(351 - 360)\big) \\
&= 600.
\end{aligned}$$

The main purpose of the covariance is to measure how two variables correspond. If it is mainly the case that a large value of X (large here means bigger than the mean) is found together with a large value of Y, while small values (smaller than the mean) of X largely are found together with small values of Y, most of the terms in the covariance will be positive. A positive covariance indicates that the terms pull in the same direction. We call this positive covariation. The opposite will happen if small X is usually found together with large Y and large X usually are together with small Y. When this happens most terms in the covariance will be negative, often leading to a negative total value. With negative covariance the terms pull in opposite directions, and we call this negative covariation. A borderline case happens if the covariance is zero. There is then no tendency in any direction, and we say that the results are uncorrelated.

Even though the sign of the covariance is quite informative, the size is more difficult to interpret. What is big depends to a great extent on the context. In some cases a covariance of 1,000,000 may be big, but not always. If we, e.g., consider distances in space measured in km, a covariance of 1,000,000 may be approximately zero. There is, however, a simple way to measure the impact of the covariance; the coefficient of variation.

Maximum linear covariation is obtained whenever the observation pairs are on a line with nonzero slope. When the slope is positive, an increase in one variable will always lead to an increase in the other variable, this is positive covariation. If the slope is negative, an increase in one variable will always lead to a decrease in the other variable, this is negative covariation. The coefficient of variation measures the amount of linear covariation.

Definition 1.5 The coefficient of variation R_{XY} is defined by

$$R_{XY} = \frac{S_{XY}}{S_X \cdot S_Y}.$$

In this formula we must compute the standard deviations S_X and S_Y separately. It is possible to prove that for any pair of samples, then

$$-1 \leq R_{XY} \leq 1.$$

If we return to Example 1.9 and compute S_X and S_Y, we get

$$R_{XY} = \frac{600}{20 \cdot 30} = 1.$$

This means that in this case the linear covariation is maximal. If we look closer at the numbers, it is easy to see why. For any i, we have

$$Y_i = \frac{3}{2} \cdot X_i.$$

Even in cases with few observations, a relation of this sort is by no means easy to detect. This shows that the coefficient of variation is an efficient tool to reveal such relations, in particular if the number of observations is large.

The values -1 and 1 are extremes, and such values can only be obtained in special cases. It is possible to show that $R_{XY} = 1$ if and only if there is a constant $k > 0$ and another constant K such that

$$X_i = k \cdot Y_i + K, \qquad \text{for all } i = 1, 2, \ldots, n,$$

and that $R_{XY} = -1$ if and only if there is a constant $k < 0$ and another constant K such that

$$X_i = k \cdot Y_i + K, \qquad \text{for all } i = 1, 2, \ldots, n.$$

In both cases the observations (X_i, Y_i) are confined to a straight line, and this is the only way we can obtain maximum linear covariation. If we return to Example 1.8, we can compute

$$R_{XY} = 0.96.$$

We see that this value is close to maximum positive covariation, and we have thus confirmed the tendency that we saw in the dataset.

Example 1.10 Assume that we have observed the values of 4 different stocks, A, B, C, and D at 100 different point in time. We wonder if there is a connection between the stock price of A and any of the other stock prices. To see if there is a connection between A and B, we plot the numbers $(A_1, B_1), (A_2, B_2), \ldots, (A_{100}, B_{100})$ in the same figure. We do the same with A and C and with A and D. The results are shown in Fig. 1.6.

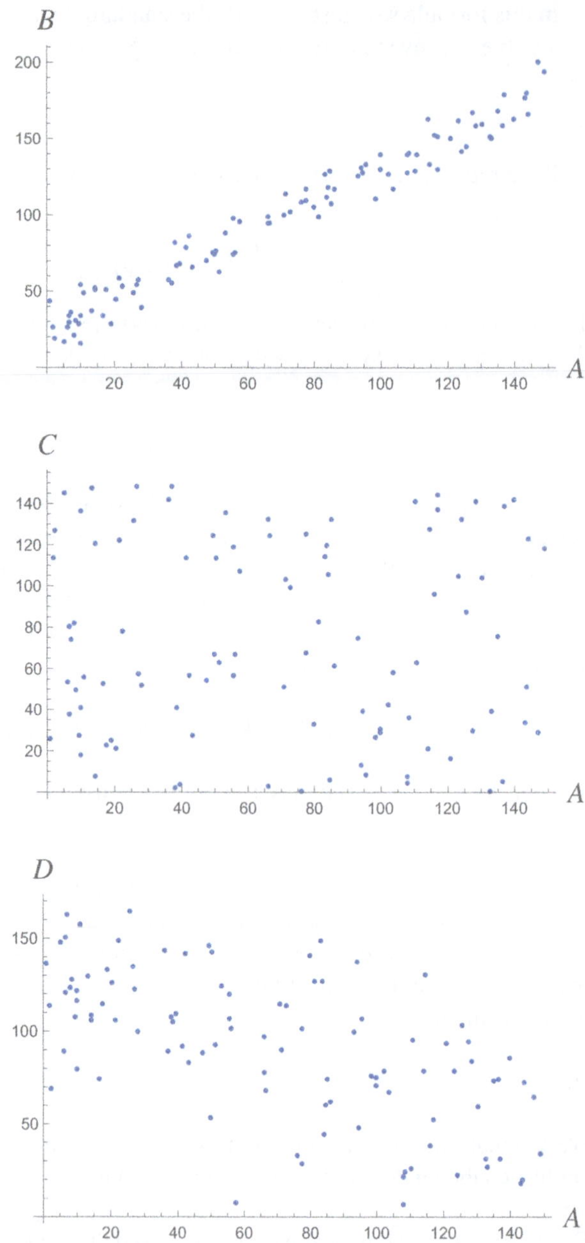

Fig. 1.6 Corresponding stock prices

From Fig. 1.6 we see that there is clearly positive covariation between A and B; when the price on A is low, so is the price on B, and a high price on A typically is seen together with a high price on B. The coefficient of variation confirms this, $R_{AB} = 0.98$. We can't see much connection between A and C. For the numbers reported in the figure we have $R_{AC} = -0.01$. There seems to be a clear connection between A and D. The tendency is that the stock price of D is high when the stock price of A is low and the reverse is also true. This is negative covariation and for the numbers reported in the figure $R_{AD} = -0.62$.

1.8 Using Excel

At a first glance it may seem as if there are lots of work involved when we compute mean, variance, and covariance. This is not so. Such computations are almost exclusively carried out via computer software which makes computation fast and simple. There are several programs we could use. In this book we will use Excel since this is a program most people have access to. Computations are hardly different in other programs.

We return to the computations in Example 1.9, but this time we will use Excel to carry out the calculations. We start typing $X_1 = 242, X_2 = 266, X_3 = 218, X_4 = 234$ and $Y_1 = 363, Y_2 = 399, Y_3 = 327, Y_4 = 351$ in columns A and B in the worksheet. We then click in C1 and write "=Average(A1:A4)." If we push return, we get the result shown in Fig. 1.7. The mean of B1 through B4 is computed similarly, see Fig. 1.8.

Fig. 1.7 Average of column A

C1 =AVERAGE(A1:A4)

	A	B	C
1	242	363	240
2	266	399	
3	218	327	
4	234	351	

Fig. 1.8 Average of column B

C2 =AVERAGE(B1:B4)

	A	B	C
1	242	363	240
2	266	399	360
3	218	327	
4	234	351	

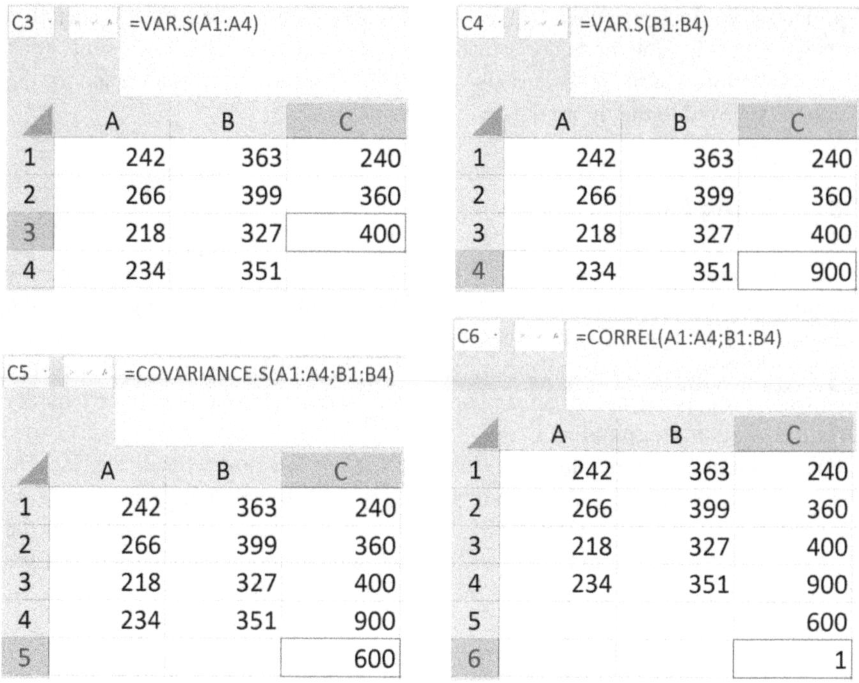

C3 =VAR.S(A1:A4)

	A	B	C
1	242	363	240
2	266	399	360
3	218	327	400
4	234	351	

C4 =VAR.S(B1:B4)

	A	B	C
1	242	363	240
2	266	399	360
3	218	327	400
4	234	351	900

C5 =COVARIANCE.S(A1:A4;B1:B4)

	A	B	C
1	242	363	240
2	266	399	360
3	218	327	400
4	234	351	900
5			600

C6 =CORREL(A1:A4;B1:B4)

	A	B	C
1	242	363	240
2	266	399	360
3	218	327	400
4	234	351	900
5			600
6			1

Fig. 1.9 The sample variance of column A and B, the sample covariance of A and B, and the coefficient of variation

The sample variances, covariance, and coefficient of variation are computed in the same way, see Fig. 1.9. To compute the sample standard deviation we may use the command STDEV.S. Instead of writing the commands in full it is possible to click and drag the corresponding menus. This is simple, but is not something we will discuss here.

1.9 Summary of Chap. 1

- The median of n observations in ascending order

$$\text{Median} = \text{Observation number } \frac{n+1}{2}.$$

Interpretation: Roughly one half of the observations are below the median, and the other half above.

- The first and third quartiles of n observations in ascending order

$$\text{First quartile} = \text{Observation number } \frac{n+1}{4},$$

$$\text{First quartile} = \text{Observation number } \frac{3(n+1)}{4}.$$

Interpretation: Roughly half of the observations are found between the 1. and 3. quartiles.

- The mode of a set of observations: The most frequent observation.
- The mean of a set of observations

$$\overline{X} = \frac{1}{n}(X_1 + X_2 + \cdots + X_n) = \frac{1}{n}\sum_{i=1}^{n} X_i.$$

- The sample variance of a set of observations

$$S_X^2 = \frac{1}{n-1}\left((X_1 - \overline{X})^2 + \cdots + (X_n - \overline{X})^2\right) = \frac{1}{n-1}\sum_{i=1}^{n}(X_i - \overline{X})^2.$$

Interpretation: A large value means that the observations are far apart.

- The sample standard deviation of a set of observations

$$S_x = \sqrt{S_X^2}.$$

Interpretation: The typical deviation from the mean.

- The sample covariance

$$\begin{aligned} S_{XY} &= \frac{1}{n-1}\left((X_1 - \overline{X})(Y_1 - \overline{Y}) + \cdots + (X_n - \overline{X})(Y_n - \overline{Y})\right) \\ &= \frac{1}{n-1}\sum_{i=1}^{n}(X_i - \overline{X})(X_i - \overline{X}). \end{aligned}$$

Interpretation: When $S_{XY} > 0$, the quantities pull in the same direction. When $S_{XY} < 0$, the quantities pull in opposite directions.

- Coefficient of variation

$$R_{XY} = \frac{S_{XY}}{S_X \cdot S_Y}.$$

Interpretation: Strong positive covariation when R_{XY} is close to 1, strong negative covariation when R_{XY} is close to -1, uncorrelated when R_{XY} is close to zero.

- Excel commands
  Mean: AVERAGE(A1:AN)
  Sample variance: VAR.S(A1:AN)
  Sample standard deviation STDEV.S(A1:AN)

Sample covariance: COVAR.S(A1:AN;B1:BN)
Coefficient of variation: CORREL(A1:AN;B1:BN).

1.10 Problems for Chap. 1

1.1 Table 1.7 gives a survey of the willingness to pay for $n = 675$ customers. The customers were asked about the maximum price they would be willing to pay for a specific good. Find the mode, median, and 1. and 3. quartiles for the numbers in the table.

1.2 Table 1.8 shows how frequent people visit their local food store. We have access to $n = 1275$ observations in total.

(a) Find the mode, median, and 1. and 3. quartiles for the numbers in the table.
(b) Find the mean of the observations.

1.3 Table 1.9 shows the stock price for 5 different companies.

(a) Find the mean of the 5 prices in the table.
(b) Company A has a total of 140,000 stocks, company B 50,000 stocks, company C 20,000 stocks, company D 10,000 stocks, and company E 30,000 stocks. Find the total market value of the five companies. How many stocks are there in total? What is the mean value of each stock in total? Compare with the result in (a).

1.4 (a) Find the mean of the numbers
i) $1, 3, 4, 2, 7, 9, 2$
ii) $2, 6, 8, 4, 14, 18, 4$
iii) $10, 30, 40, 20, 70, 90, 20$.
(b) How do the results in (a) connect?

Table 1.7 Data for Problem 1.1

Price in USD	100	110	120	130	140	150
Frequency	90	115	121	162	109	78

Table 1.8 Data for Problem 1.2

Number of days per week	0	1	2	3	4	5	6	7
Frequency	257	241	459	103	84	62	47	22

Table 1.9 Data for Problem 1.3

Company	A	B	C	D	E
Stock price in USD	100	200	400	300	500

Table 1.10 Data for Problem 1.8

Day	1	2	3	4	5
Stock price in USD	99	101	97	101	102

1.5 (a) Find the mean of the numbers
i) $1, 2, 3, 4, 5, 6, -21$
ii) $-2, 4, \frac{3}{2}, -4, \frac{1}{2}$.
(b) Do you see any connections between the numbers in (a)?

1.6 (a) Find the sample variance for the numbers
i) $8, 3, 7, 1, 11$
ii) $2, -3, 1, -5, 5$.
(b) Are there any connection between the numbers in (a)?

1.7 Let $X_1 = 12, X_2 = 1, X_3 = 7, X_4 = 5, X_5 = 5$. Find the mean, sample variance, and sample standard deviation.

1.8 Table 1.10 shows the stock price of a company through 5 consecutive days. Find the mean, sample variance, and sample standard deviation for these stock prices.

1.9 Let $X_1 = 1, X_2 = 4, X_3 = 5, X_4 = 7, X_5 = 13$.

(a) Use the formula

$$S^2 = \frac{1}{5}\left((X_1 - \overline{X})^2 + (X_2 - \overline{X})^2 + (X_3 - \overline{X})^2 + (X_4 - \overline{X})^2 + (X_5 - \overline{X})^2\right),$$

to compute S^2 and S.
(b) Use the formula

$$S^2 = \frac{1}{4}\left((X_1 - \overline{X})^2 + (X_2 - \overline{X})^2 + (X_3 - \overline{X})^2 + (X_4 - \overline{X})^2 + (X_5 - \overline{X})^2\right),$$

to compute S_X^2 and S_X.
(c) Use your calculator to compute the standard deviation. Does the answer coincide with (a) or (b)?

1.10 Assume that

$$S^2 = \frac{1}{n}\sum_{i=1}^{n}(X_i - \overline{X})^2 \quad \text{and that} \quad S_X^2 = \frac{1}{n-1}\sum_{i=1}^{n}(X_i - \overline{X})^2.$$

Table 1.11 Data for Problem 1.13

Price	$X_1 = 71$	$X_2 = 47$	$X_3 = 23$	$X_4 = 27$
Demand	$Y_1 = 58$	$Y_2 = 106$	$Y_3 = 154$	$Y_4 = 146$

Table 1.12 Data for Problem 1.14

Portfolio 1	$X_1 = 18$	$X_2 = 22$	$X_3 = 14$	$X_4 = 10$	$X_5 = 11$
Portfolio 2	$Y_1 = 36$	$Y_2 = 44$	$Y_3 = 28$	$Y_4 = 20$	$Y_5 = 22$

Show that

$$S = \sqrt{\frac{n-1}{n}}.$$

Is S greater or smaller than S_X?

1.11 Let $(X_1, \ldots X_5) = (140, 126, 133, 144, 152)$ and $(Y_1, \ldots, Y_5) = (248, 252, 254, 244)$. Find S_{XY}.

1.12 Let $(X_1, \ldots X_5) = (140, 126, 133, 144, 152)$ and $(Y_1, \ldots, Y_5) = (253, 221, 239, 229, 233)$. Find S_X, S_Y, S_{XY} and R_{XY}.

1.13 Table 1.11 shows 4 matching values of price (in USD) and demand (in units) of a good.

Find S_X, S_Y, S_{XY} and R_{XY}. What is the relation between demand and price?

1.14 Table 1.12 shows 5 matching values of the returns (in % per year) of two portfolios of stocks.

Find S_X, S_Y, S_{XY} and R_{XY}. What is the relation between Y_i and X_i? How can you put together two portfolios that behave like this?

1.15 This Exercise Provides the Rigorous Definitions of Quartiles: If n is the number of observations, we find the position of the quartiles computing $k_1 = \frac{n+1}{4}$ and $k_3 = \frac{3(n+1)}{4}$. Depending on n we get two reminders which are $0, \frac{1}{4}, \frac{1}{2}$, or $\frac{3}{4}$.

i) If the remainder is zero, we use observation k.
ii) If the reminder is $\frac{1}{4}$ we start at observation $k - \frac{1}{4}$ (an integer) and increase this value by 25% of the distance to the next observation.
iii) If the reminder is $\frac{1}{2}$ we start at observation $k - \frac{1}{2}$ (an integer) and increase this value by 50% of the distance to the next observation.
iv) If the reminder is $\frac{3}{4}$ we start at observation $k - \frac{3}{4}$ (an integer) and increase this value by 75% of the distance to the next observation.

Find the 1. and 3. quartiles for the observations

(a) $2, 6, 10, 14, 18, 22$
(b) $2, 6, 10, 12, 14, 18, 22$
(c) $2, 6, 10, 11, 13, 14, 18, 22$
(d) $2, 6, 10, 11, 12, 13, 14, 18, 22$.

1.16 You have made 25 observations of the price of a good. The results are shown below.

123	156	132	141	127	136	129	144	136	142	126	133	141
154	143	121	138	125	137	123	133	141	127	126	149	

Type these observations in Excel, and use Excel commands to answer the questions.

(a) Find the mean of the observations.
(b) Find the sample variance and the sample standard deviation.
(c) Use the command $QUARTILE(A1 : A25; 1)$ to find the 1. quartile, and figure out how you can modify the command to find the 2. and the 3. quartiles. What is a different name for the 2. quartile?

1.17 Portfolio Optimization: Table 1.13 shows the development of the stocks in the two companies ALPHA and BETA. The price on the stocks (in USD) has been observed monthly over a period of 20 consecutive months. The stock prices on ALPHA are quoted by $a_1, \ldots, a_{20}$ and the stock prices for BETA are quoted by $b_1, \ldots, b_{20}$.

(a) Compute the mean stock price for the stocks in ALPHA and BETA (separately).
(b) Make a plot of the time development of the two stock prices in the same figure. Which stock do you consider to be the most unsure?

Table 1.13 Stock prices for company ALPHA and BETA

a_1	a_2	a_3	a_4	a_5	a_6	a_7	a_8	a_9	a_{10}
92	86	90	86	95	92	96	102	106	96
a_{11}	a_{12}	a_{13}	a_{14}	a_{15}	a_{16}	a_{17}	a_{18}	a_{19}	a_{20}
95	102	101	107	106	110	103	107	116	112
b_1	b_2	b_3	b_4	b_5	b_6	b_7	b_8	b_9	b_{10}
127	114	141	113	128	115	84	101	96	119
b_{11}	b_{12}	b_{13}	b_{14}	b_{15}	b_{16}	b_{17}	b_{18}	b_{19}	b_{20}
93	88	79	103	63	60	116	82	82	96

(c) Compute the sample variances S_a^2 and S_b^2, you might prefer to use Excel to do this. Do the values on S_a^2 and S_b^2 coincide with the conclusions you could draw in (b)?
(d) Can a large sample variation be an advantage? Which of the stocks ALPHA and BETA do you consider the best?
(e) Compute the covariance S_{ab}, you may prefer to use Excel.
(f) You want to invest 1,000,000 USD in these stocks. We assume that you buy each stock at their mean value, and that you invest $x\%$ of the money in ALPHA and $y\% = 100\% - x\%$ in BETA. Let a_n and b_n denote the price on the stocks at any time n. Show that the value c_n of your investment is given by

$$c_n = 100xa_n + 100yb_n.$$

(g) We cannot say anything for sure about the future, but it may sometimes be reasonable to assume that the mean and the sample variance will remain constant. What would the mean value of c_n be based on the data above?
(h) Show that $S_c^2 = 10{,}000(x^2S_a^2 + 2xyS_{ab} + y^2S_b^2$, and use this to find a value for x such that S_c^2 is as small as possible. How much must you buy of each stock if you prefer low risk?

1.18 Market Segments and Profit Optimization: You have carried out a market survey to identify travel habits of young and old people. The results are shown in Table 1.14. We wish to identify if there are notable differences between different groups of customers. We will divide the customers by two criteria.

- Young, 30 years or younger/Old, 31 years or more.
- Low season (fall and winter)/high season (spring and summer).

We divide the customers into four categories:

1: Young in low season	1: Young in high season
3: Old in low season	4: Old in high season

(a) Compute the mean expense $\overline{p}$ for all the observations in the table.
(b) Find the sample variance S_p^2 for all the observations in the table.
(c) Now divide the data into 4 groups as indicated above and compute the mean expense and sample variance within each group. Compare the sample variances with S_p^2. Give a short comment/tentative explanation to the differences. How do people behave in a group where the sample variance is zero? Is there a connection between the sample variance and a uniform behavior within a group?

A travel agency wants to survey possible profits from the sales in low season. They reserve 5000 first class tickets. In addition they plan to sell x low price tickets to young people and y low price tickets to old people. On average it takes

Table 1.14 Survey on total expenditure (USD) for travelers

Number	Season	Age	Expense	Number	Season	Age	Expense
1	Winter	22	3018	21	Summer	23	1687
2	Winter	66	4086	22	Summer	45	7011
3	Winter	19	3034	23	Summer	75	6643
4	Winter	51	3730	24	Summer	15	1915
5	Winter	17	2623	25	Summer	16	2006
6	Winter	15	2757	26	Summer	36	7678
7	Winter	29	2927	26	Summer	17	1796
8	Winter	50	3844	28	Summer	71	7159
9	Winter	15	3569	29	Summer	49	7403
10	Winter	76	4102	30	Summer	65	7325
11	Spring	64	6949	31	Fall	22	3029
12	Spring	38	6885	32	Fall	72	4240
13	Spring	76	6839	33	Fall	27	3242
14	Spring	16	1577	34	Fall	16	3390
15	Spring	34	6746	35	Fall	24	3204
16	Spring	24	1965	36	Fall	58	4146
17	Spring	57	7387	37	Fall	50	3854
18	Spring	21	2077	38	Fall	71	4089
19	Spring	18	2091	39	Fall	15	2959
20	Spring	68	6985	40	Fall	37	3817

20 min to process a low price ticket for young people, while the corresponding number for old people is 35 min. To process the tickets the company has 3 people each of whom works 37.5 hours per week. The managers have decided that low price tickets for young people should not exceed 20% of the total number of tickets.

(e) The price per ticket for first class is 7500 USD. To calculate the price on the other tickets, we use that mean values we computed above. The price for young people should be 10% lower than the average expense reported from the data, while the price for old people should be 5% below the reported mean for this category. How many tickets should you sell to each customer group to maximize total profit? Note: This is a linear programming problem and requires knowledge on how to solve such problems. If you don't have this knowledge, proceed to (g).

(f) Assume that the price on tickets for young people is fixed. How much must you raise the price on tickets for old people so that it is most profitable to sell all low price tickets to old people?

(g) The young people can be subdivided into two new categories A and B. We have carried out a supplementary survey indicating that the two subgroups have a similar mean expenditure over time. The two subgroups have different sample variances $S_A^2 = 20{,}000$ and $S_B^2 = 40{,}000$. In addition we have computed that the sample covariance is $S_{AB} = -20{,}000$. We will sell $\alpha\%$ to group A and

$\beta\% = 100\% - \alpha\%$ to group B. This gives a combined sample variance

$$S^2_{\alpha\beta} = \frac{1}{10{,}000}(\alpha^2 S^2_A + 2\alpha\beta S_{AB} + \beta^2 S^2_B).$$

(you may take this for granted). Compute values for α and β to minimize the sample variance for the combination.

Probability

2

Abstract

In this short chapter we will go through the basic definitions of probability. To ease the exposition, we will only discuss very simple examples. It is important to notice that the concepts we develop in this chapter are central to all thinking about statistics. Regardless of level and purpose these concepts provide tools that can be used to describe statistical methods. From this point of view the theory provides us with a framework that can be used to study any statistical phenomenon.

2.1 Sample Space

When we carry out an experiment, we get a result. This result is called the outcome. If we test 10 goods and find 3 defective items, the outcome is 3 defective items. An experiment can have several possible outcomes, and the collection of all of these is called the sample space. If we test 10 goods if they are defective or not, the outcome can be anything from 0 to 10 defectives. The sample space is the set of all the individual outcomes, i.e.

$$\{0 \text{ defective}, 1 \text{ defective}, \ldots, 10 \text{ defectives}\}.$$

We usually use the letter Ω to denote a sample space. If an experiment can have the outcomes $\omega_1, \omega_2, \ldots, \omega_m$, the sample space is the set $\Omega = \{\omega_1, \omega_2, \ldots, \omega_m\}$. We use the following definition:

J. Ubøe, *Introductory Statistics for Business and Economics*, Springer Texts in Business and Economics, https://doi.org/10.1007/978-3-319-70936-9_2

Definition 2.1 A sample space is a list of the outcomes of an experiment.

- The list must cover any possible outcome.
- The outcomes must be mutually exclusive.

When these two conditions are satisfied, we say that the sample space is complete and distinguishing.

Example 2.1 Assume that we toss a dice once and look at the result. The sample space is $\Omega = \{1, 2, 3, 4, 5, 6\}$.

Example 2.2 Assume that we watch a soccer match and consider the number of points for the home team. The sample space is $\Omega = \{0, 1, 3\}$.

Example 2.3 Assume that we watch a soccer match and consider the goals made by both teams separately. The sample space is

$$\Omega = \{(0,0), (0,1), (1,0), (2,0), (1,1), (0,2), (3,0), \ldots\}.$$

By the notation $|\Omega|$ we mean the number of elements in the sample space. In Examples 2.1 and 2.2 we have $|\Omega| = 6$ and $|\Omega| = 3$, respectively. In Example 2.3, however, there is no limit to how many goals can be scored. In practice it might be difficult to imagine cases with millions of goals, but no matter how many goals are scored, it is in theory possible to score once more. In this case it is natural to define $|\Omega| = \infty$.

Example 2.4 We measure the temperature in a room in $°C$. In that case $\Omega = [-273, \infty)$, i.e., an interval. In this case, too, $|\Omega| = \infty$.

Even though $|\Omega| = \infty$ in Example 2.3 and in Example 2.4, there is an important difference between the two cases. In Example 2.3 it is possible to sort all outcomes in a sequence where each outcome is given a specific number, while no such enumeration is possible in Example 2.4.

A sample space Ω where all outcomes can be enumerated in a sequence is called discrete. In this case we may write $\Omega = \{\omega_1, \omega_2, \ldots, \omega_n\}$, where $n = \infty$ signifies a case with infinitely many outcomes.

2.2 Probability

One of the most important concepts in statistics is the probability for the different outcomes in the sample space. Somewhat simplified these numbers express how often we can expect to observe the different outcomes.

The probability for an outcome is an idealized quantity which defines the relative frequency we will observe in the long run, i.e., in the course of infinitely many trials. It is of course impossible to carry out an experiment infinitely many times, but the idea is that the more repetitions we make, the closer will the relative frequency be to the probability of the outcome. Imagine that we have repeated an experiment a large number of times, and observed that the relative frequency of one of the outcomes is 10%. We then have a clear impression that this outcome will occur in 10% of the cases no matter how many times we repeat the experiment. We then say that the probability of the outcome is 10%.

Definition 2.2 By a probability on a discrete sample space Ω, we mean a set of real numbers

$$p_1, p_2, \ldots, p_n$$

with the properties

- $0 \leq p_i \leq 1$, for all $i = 1, 2, \ldots, n$.
- $p_1 + p_2 + \cdots + p_n = 1$.

Here p_1 is the probability of outcome ω_1, p_2 is the probability of outcome ω_2, and so on, so we write

$$p_i = p(\omega_i), \qquad i = 1, \ldots, n.$$

The last expression makes it clear that a probability is a function defined on the sample space. Verbally we can express the conditions as follows: A probability is a number between 0 and 1, and the probability of all the outcomes must sum to 1. In some cases we speak about subjective probabilities, which are more or less well-founded suggestions of how often an outcome will occur. We will return to subjective probabilities in Chap. 4.

2.2.1 Events

By an event in statistics we mean a subset of the sample space. The use of the word may seem strange at a first glance, but quickly makes more sense if we consider an example.

Example 2.5 We toss a dice twice. The sample space is $\Omega = \{(1,1),(1,2),\ldots,(6,6)\}$. Consider the subset $A = \{(1,6),(2,6),(3,6),(4,6),(5,6),(6,6)\}$. Since A is a subset of the sample space, it is an event. Verbally we can see that A expresses that something very explicit has happened: "The second toss was a 6."

The probability $P(A)$ of an event A is defined as the sum of the probabilities of all outcomes which are elements in A, i.e.

$$P(A) = \sum_{\omega \in A} p(\omega).$$

Example 2.6 We toss a fair dice twice. The sample space is

$$\Omega = \{(1,1),(1,2),\ldots,(6,6)\}.$$

The dice is fair when all these outcomes are equally probable, i.e., when $p(\omega) = \frac{1}{36}$. The probability of the event

$$A = \{(1,6),(2,6),(3,6),(4,6),(5,6),(6,6)\}$$

is hence

$$P(A) = \frac{1}{36} + \frac{1}{36} + \frac{1}{36} + \frac{1}{36} + \frac{1}{36} + \frac{1}{36} = \frac{1}{6}.$$

2.2.2 Uniform Probability

We will often study cases where all outcomes are equally probable. If there are n different outcomes, the probability of each outcome is hence $\frac{1}{n}$. We call this a uniform probability. When the probabilities are uniform, it is particularly easy to figure out the probability of an event. We can simply count the number of elements in the subset. If A has a elements, then

$$P(A) = \frac{a}{n}.$$

Example 2.7 In a market segment of 1000 persons we know that 862 persons are worthy of credit. What is the probability that a randomly selected person is worthy of credit?

Solution: When we choose a randomly selected person, we are tacitly assuming a uniform probability. The subset of persons worthy of credit has 862 elements, while there are 1000 outcomes in total. The probability p that a randomly selected person is worthy of credit is hence $p = \frac{862}{1000} = 82.6\%$.

Example 2.8 We toss a dice once. A uniform probability on the sample space is

$$p(1) = p(2) = p(3) = p(4) = p(5) = p(6) = \frac{1}{6}.$$

2.2.3 Set Theory

Since sample spaces are formulated as sets and events as subsets, set theory is a natural tool in this context. The classical set operations have very specific interpretations in statistics, and we will now briefly consider how this is done. When we carry out an experiment and get an outcome ω which is an element of a subset A, we say that the event A has occurred. Each set operation has a similar interpretation (Figs. 2.1, 2.2, 2.3, 2.4, 2.5, and 2.6).

- Intersection

$$A \cap B = \text{The event that } A \text{ and } B \text{ both occurs.}$$

- Union

$$A \cup B = \text{The event that either } A \text{ or } B \text{ or both occurs.}$$

- Complement

$$A^c = \text{The event that } A \text{ does not occur.}$$

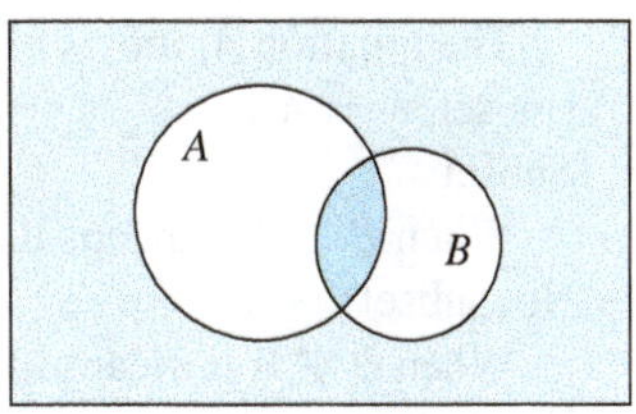

Fig. 2.1 $A \cap B$

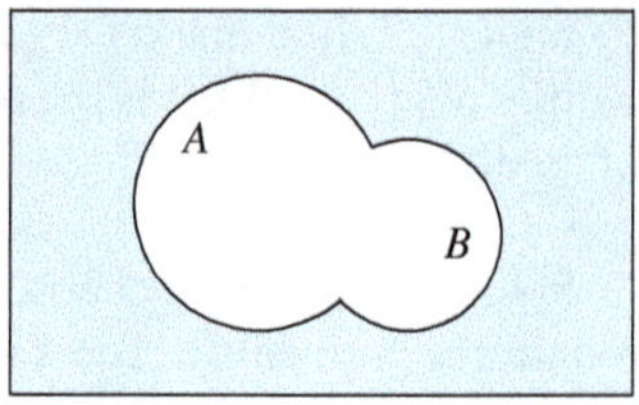

Fig. 2.2 $A \cup B$

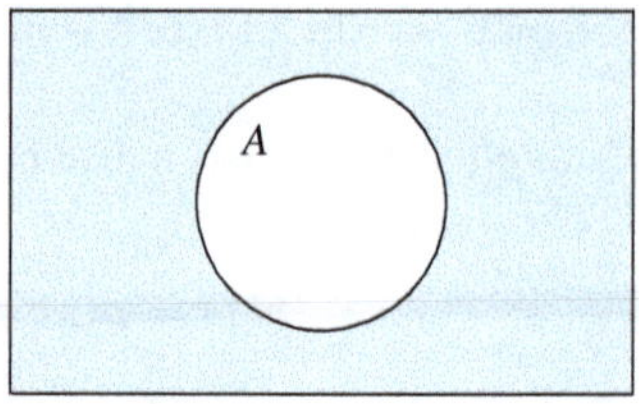

Fig. 2.3 A^c is here the blue shaded area

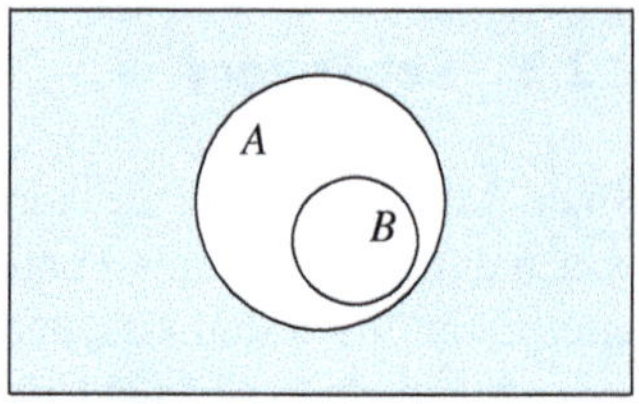

Fig. 2.4 $B \subset A$

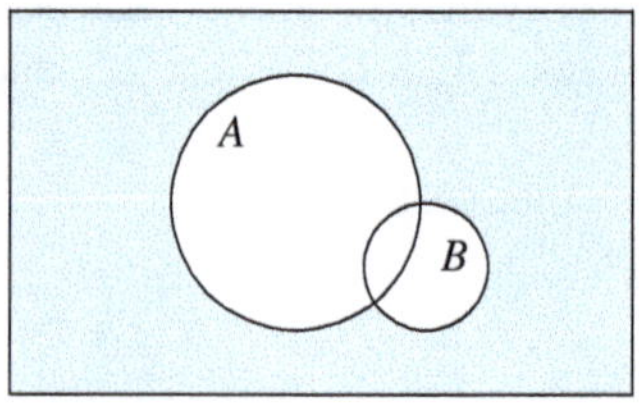

Fig. 2.5 $B \not\subset A$

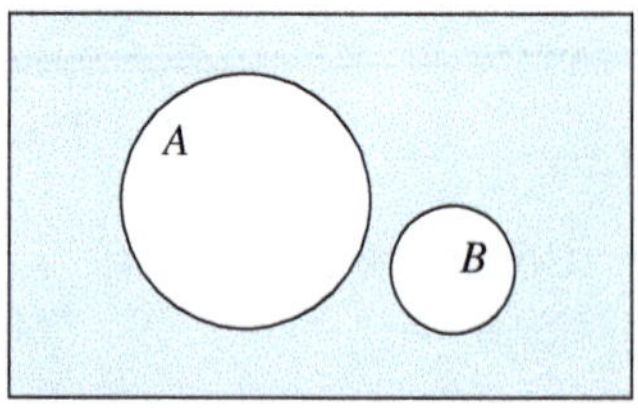

Fig. 2.6 $A \cap B = \emptyset$

The notation $\overline{A}$, too, is often used with exactly the same meaning, i.e., when A is a set, $\overline{A} = A^c$.

- Subset

  When $B \subset A$ it means that when B occurs, A will always occur.
- Not subset

  When $B \not\subset A$ it means that when B occurs, A will not always occur.
- Empty intersection

$$A \cap B = \emptyset, \text{ when } A \text{ and } B \text{ never occurs simultaneously.}$$

Example 2.9 We toss a dice once, and define the following subsets.

$$A: \text{ I tossed 1, 3, or 4.} \quad B: \text{ I tossed 3, 4, or 5.} \quad C: \text{ I did not toss 5.}$$

Then

$$\begin{aligned}
&A \cap B = \{3,4\}, A \cap C = \{1,3,4\}, B \cap C = \{3,4\},\\
&A \cup B = \{1,3,4,5\}, A \cup C = \{1,2,3,4,6\}, B \cup C = \{1,2,3,4,5,6\},\\
&A^c = \{2,5,6\}, B^c = \{1,2,6\}, C^c = \{5\}.
\end{aligned}$$

Here $A \subset C$, while $C \not\subset A, C \not\subset B, B \not\subset C, B \not\subset A, A \not\subset B$. Notice that the list does not provide all subsets we can find combining A, B, and C using set operations.

2.2.4 Computing Probabilities

The special addition principle is useful when we want to compute the probability of a union. If the two sets do not intersect, we can simply sum the probability of each subset, i.e.

$$\text{If } A \cap B = \emptyset, \text{ then } P(A \cup B) = P(A) + P(B).$$

Example 2.10 We toss a dice once. $A = \{1,2,3\}, B = \{5,6\}, C = \{2,3,4,5,6\}$. Here $A \cap B = \emptyset$, and we get

$$P(A \cup B) = P(\{1,2,3,5,6\}) = \frac{5}{6} = \frac{3}{6} + \frac{2}{6} = P(A) + P(B).$$

If we add $P(A) + P(C)$, however, we find

$$P(A) + P(C) = \frac{3}{6} + \frac{5}{6} = \frac{4}{3}.$$

There is nothing wrong with this, but the sum is *not* the probability of an event. The problem is that the two subsets intersect, and we need to take this into account. To carry out the calculation correctly, we need to apply the general addition principle, which can be stated as follows:

$$P(A \cup B) = P(A) + P(B) - P(A \cap B).$$

If we use this rule, we find

$$P(A \cup C) = P(\{1,2,3,4,5,6\}) = 1 = \frac{3}{6} + \frac{5}{6} - \frac{2}{6} = P(A) + P(C) - P(A \cap C).$$

The general addition principle can be extended to cover unions of more than two subsets. If we have three subsets A, B, and C, the result can be stated as follows:

$$\begin{aligned} P(A \cup B \cup C) = &P(A) + P(B) + P(C) \\ &-P(A \cap B) - P(A \cap C) - P(B \cap C) \\ &+P(A \cap B \cap C). \end{aligned}$$

Example 2.11 In a customer survey all the people who participated used at least one of the three products A, B, or C. All three products were used by 60% of the customers. 95% of the customers used at least one of the products A and B, 85% used at least one of the products B and C, and 30% used both A and C. How big share of the customers used all the three products?

Solution: In this example there are lots of information, and we need to find a systematic way of dealing with this. Since all the customers used at least one of the products A, B or C, we know that

$$P(A \cup B \cup C) = 1 = 100\%.$$

Since all three products were used by 60% of the customers, we know that

$$P(A) = P(B) = P(C) = 60\%.$$

From the text we have

$$P(A \cup B) = 95\%, \qquad P(B \cup C) = 85\%, \qquad P(A \cap C) = 30\%.$$

If we use the general addition principle for two subsets, we get

$$95\% = 60\% + 60\% - P(A \cap B) \;\Rightarrow\; P(A \cap B) = 25\%.$$

$$85\% = 60\% + 60\% - P(B \cap C) \;\Rightarrow\; P(B \cap C) = 35\%.$$

If we plug all the above into the general addition formula for 3 subsets, we get the equation

$$100\% = 60\% + 60\% + 60\% - 25\% - 30\% - 35\% + P(A \cap B \cap C).$$

Solving this equation, we get $P(A \cap B \cap C) = 10\%$. It is hence 10% of the customers who use all the three products.

2.2.5 The Negation Principle

Since A and A^c never intersect and $A \cup A^c = \Omega$, it follows from the special addition principle that

$$P(A) + P(A^c) = P(A \cup A^c) = P(\Omega) = 1.$$

If we view this as an equation, we can solve for $P(A)$ or $P(A^c)$ to see that

$$P(A) = 1 - P(A^c) \qquad P(A^c) = 1 - P(A).$$

Hence to find the probability that A occurs, we can instead find the probability that A does not occur. At a first glance this not appear to be very useful, but we will throughout this book see many cases where this angle of approach simplifies calculations.

2.3 Summary of Chap. 2

- Sample space:

$$\Omega = \text{The set of all outcomes.}$$

- Event: A subset of a sample space.
- General addition principles:

$$P(A \cup B) = P(A) + P(B) - P(A \cap B).$$

$$\begin{aligned} P(A \cup B \cup C) = \; & P(A) + P(B) + P(C) \\ & -P(A \cap B) - P(A \cap C) - P(B \cap C) \\ & +P(A \cap B \cap C). \end{aligned}$$

- The negation principle:

$$P(A) + P(A^c) = 1.$$

2.4 Problems for Chap. 2

2.1 A bank serves three customers in succession. The customers are either worthy of credit or not worthy of credit. Suggest a suitable sample space for this situation. Write down the events:

A: At least one customer is worthy of credit.
B: Customer number 2 is worthy of credit.
C: All the customers have the same credit rating.

2.2 We observe the Dow Jones Index over two consecutive days and will consider a sample space with four different outcomes:

ω_1: The index rises both days.
ω_2: The index rises the first day and does not rise the second day.
ω_3: The index does not rise the first day and rises the second day.
ω_4: The index does not rise the first day and does not rise the second day.

Define two events A and B by:

A: The Dow Jones rises the first day.
B: The Dow Jones rises the second day.

(a) Find the events $A \cup B$, $A \cap B$, A^c, and B^c.
(b) Show that $(A \cap B) \cup (A^c \cap B) = B$.
(c) Show that $A \cup (A^c \cap B) = A \cup B$.

2.3 An auditing firm regularly inspects the accounting done by a large company. In many such inspections the firm reveals one or more errors, see Table 2.1.

Let A denote the event "There is at least one error," and let B denote the event "There are less than 10 errors."

(a) Find the probabilities for A and A^c.
(b) Find the probabilities for B and B^c.
(c) Find the probability for $A \cup B$.
(d) Find the probability for $A \cap B$. How would you express this event in words?

Table 2.1 Data for Problem 2.3

Number or errors	0	1 to 3	4 to 6	7 to 9	10 to 12	More than 12
Probability in %	10	30	25	20	10	5

Table 2.2 Data for Problem 2.4

Processing time in days	1	2	3	4	5	6 or more
Probability in %	10	40	30	10	5	5

Table 2.3 Data for Problem 2.5

Warehouse/Type	Regular	Superior	Superior extra
Warehouse 1	12	9	10
Warehouse 2	25	16	5
Warehouse 3	9	9	3

2.4 A company uses at least one day to process a particular type of order. A survey of the processing time is shown in Table 2.2.

(a) Define a suitable sample space for this situation and explain why the numbers in the table define a probability on this sample space.
(b) Find the probability of the events:

A: Processing time shorter than 3 days.
B: Processing time at least 3 days.

(c) What is the connection between A and B?

2.5 A company produces a good in three different types: Regular, Superior, and Superior Extra. The goods are stored in three different warehouses. The distribution of the production is shown in Table 2.3.

(a) We choose a good randomly. How many outcomes are there in the sample space? Explain why the table defines a probability.
(b) We choose a good randomly, and let A, B, and C denote the events

$$A: \text{The good is of type Regular}$$

$$B: \text{The good is of type Superior}$$

$$C: \text{The good is stored at warehouse 3}$$

Express the following events in words, and find the probability for each event.

(i) $A \cap C$
(ii) $A \cup C$
(iii) $A \cap B$
(iv) $A \cup B$

2.6 In a customer survey 70% of the customers used at least one of the products A and B. 60% used product A and 40% used product B. 50% used product B. How many % of the customers used both products?

2.7 In a customer survey 70% of the customers used at least one of the products A and B, while 40% used both products. 50% used product B. How many % of the customers used product A?

2.8 In a customer survey 30% of the customers used both products A and B. 60% used product A and 40% used product B. 50% used product B. How many % of the customers used none of the products?

2.9 In this exercise we will consider the stocks in 5 companies. Company A has 140,000 stocks, company B has 50,000 stocks, company C has 20,000 stocks, company D has 10,000, and company E has 30,000 stocks. In total there are 250,000 stocks. We choose a stock randomly among the 250,000 stocks. Suggest a suitable sample space, and define a probability which describes this situation.

2.10 Unions of 3 Subsets: In a customer survey 89% of the customers used at least one of the products A, B, and C. 60% used product A, 50% used product B and 45% used product C. 82% of the customers used at least one of the products A and B, 73% used at least one of the products A and C, and 74% used at least one of the products B and C.

(a) How big share of the customers used
(i) Both A and B?
(ii) Both A and C?
(iii) Both B and C?
(b) How big share of the customers used all the three products?

2.11 A Practical Illustration: In a customer survey we asked 80 customers if they liked the products A or B. The customers liking product A were numbers

$$1, 2, 3, 4, 5, 7, 8, 9, 10, 11, 13, 15, 16, 17, 18, 19, 20, 22, 23, 24, 27, 28, 30, 31, 33, 34,$$
$$35, 36, 37, 39, 40, 42, 43, 47, 48, 49, 50, 51, 52, 53, 56, 57, 58, 59, 60, 61, 62, 65, 67,$$
$$70, 71, 72, 73, 74, 75, 76, 77, 78, 79, 80.$$

while the customers liking product B were numbers

$$3, 6, 7, 11, 12, 18, 19, 20, 25, 27, 32, 33, 34, 38, 39, 41, 42, 43, 44, 45, 49, 53, 54, 55,$$
$$56, 57, 60, 61, 62, 65, 67, 68, 69, 71, 72, 73, 74, 76, 78, 80.$$

(a) Which customers liked both A and B?
(b) Which customers liked at least one of the two products?
(c) How big share of the customers liked
(i) Product A?
(ii) Product B?
(iii) Both A and B?
(iv) At least one of the two products?
(d) How do the numbers in (c) connect?

3 Combinatorics

Abstract

In this chapter we will study certain types of random selection within a uniform model. Such samples can occur when we select a representative from an audience, when we sample for errors, play lotteries, or generally when we choose between alternatives which are equally probable. The main problem is then to figure out how many combinations there are of a particular type. When we know the number of combinations, it is easy to figure out the probabilities, since in a uniform model all alternatives are equally probable. We then find the probability as the fraction between the number of combinations of the type we are looking for and the number of combinations in total.

3.1 Counting Combinations

The simplest basic principle in combinatorics takes its starting point in a sequence of choices where there are no connections between each choice. When choices are connected, certain outcomes may influence the other choices. When there are no connections, we find the total number of combinations when we multiply the number of possible outcomes of each choice.

Example 3.1 We want to select one girl and one boy from a class consisting of 15 girls and 12 boys. Since there are no connections, we have a total of $15 \cdot 12 = 180$ different combinations.

This principle applies in general: If we have c_1 possibilities in choice number 1, c_2 possibilities in choice number 2,..., c_m possibilities in choice number m, and the choices do not connect, there is a total of $c_1 \cdot c_2 \cdots c_m$ different combinations.

In combinatorics it is hence crucial to identify if there are connections or not. When the choices connect, the situation quickly becomes rather complex. In the following we will consider some standard connections which are not too complex,

J. Ubøe, *Introductory Statistics for Business and Economics*, Springer Texts in Business and Economics, https://doi.org/10.1007/978-3-319-70936-9_3

and in these cases we can compute the number of different combinations by explicit formulas.

3.1.1 Ordered Selections

In some selections the order of choices may be crucial. If we select a team, the first one selected may be the leader, while the next few members may take on predefined positions. Each sequence will then define a unique outcome. Sometimes the same person can be selected multiple times, and that may influence the number of different combinations. If no object can be selected more than once, we say that the choice is without replacement. When the same object can be selected again every time we make a new choice, we say that the choices are with replacement.

Example 3.2 We want to elect CEO and board leader for a company. There are 4 candidates, and all candidates are eligible for both positions. We first elect the CEO, and there are 4 possible outcomes. Next we should select the board leader, and then the situation is not clear. We have two different options:

- If the CEO can become board leader, the selection is with replacement, and we have a total of $4 \times 4 = 16$ different outcomes.
- If the CEO cannot become board leader, the selection is without replacement, and we have a total of $4 \times 3 = 12$ different outcomes (Fig. 3.1).

These simple principles apply in general:

> If we have n different elements in our choice set, and want to choose s of these elements with replacement, there are $n \cdot n \cdot n = n^s$ different ordered combinations.

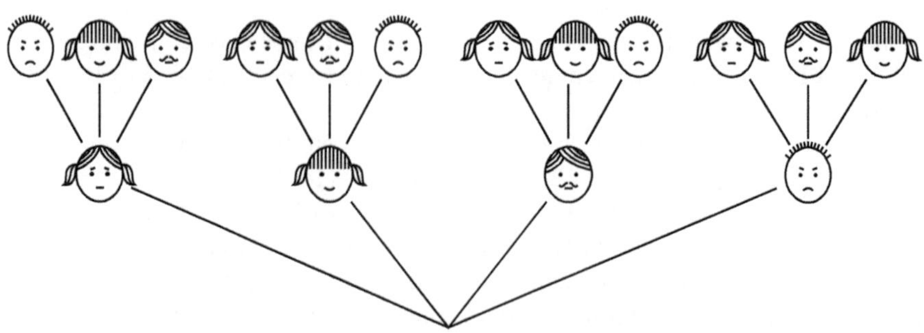

Fig. 3.1 12 different outcomes

If we have n different elements in our choice set, and want to choose s of these elements without replacement, there are

$$n(n-1)\cdots(n-s+1)$$

different ordered combinations.

Example 3.3 In how many ways can we make an ordered selection of 5 persons from a group of 20 people?

Solution: If the choice is with replacement, there are

$$20 \cdot 20 \cdot 20 \cdot 20 \cdot 20 = 3{,}200{,}000$$

different ordered combinations.

If the choice is without replacement, there are

$$20 \cdot 19 \cdot 18 \cdot 17 \cdot 16 = 1{,}860{,}480$$

different ordered combinations.

Since we often need to compute the number of ordered combinations in a sequence of choices without replacements, there is a special symbol for this:

$$(n)_s = n(n-1)\cdots(n-s+1).$$

The symbol $(n)_s$ can be expressed in terms of the factorial function. This function is defined as follows:

$$n! = n(n-1)\cdots 3 \cdot 2 \cdot 1,$$

where we in addition define

$$1! = 1 \qquad 0! = 1.$$

Example 3.4 $5! = 5 \cdot 4 \cdot 3 \cdot 2 \cdot 1 = 120$.

We hence compute the factorial of a positive integer n multiplying all the integers from 1 up to n. The definition $0! = 1$ is an exception and may appear a bit strange at a first glance, but several relevant formulas simplify with this convention. If we look at Example 3.3 again, we see that

$$\begin{aligned} 20 \cdot 19 \cdot 18 \cdot 17 \cdot 16 &= 20 \cdot 19 \cdot 18 \cdot 17 \cdot 16 \cdot \frac{15 \cdot 14 \cdots 3 \cdot 2 \cdot 1}{15 \cdot 14 \cdots 3 \cdot 2 \cdot 1} \\ &= \frac{20 \cdot 19 \cdot 18 \cdots 3 \cdot 2 \cdot 1}{15 \cdot 14 \cdots 3 \cdot 2 \cdot 1} = \frac{20!}{15!} \end{aligned} \tag{3.1}$$

This principle applies in general and

$$(n)_s = n(n-1)\cdots(n-s+1) = \frac{n!}{(n-s)!}$$

In the example above, we used $n = 20$ and $s = 5$. Then the calculation ended with the factor $(n-s+1) = 16$, and the nominator was $(n-s)! = 15!$. Notice that when we use a calculator to carry out the computations, it is often better to use the original definition as the factorials may become so large that the calculator cannot handle them. Using the definition we see that

$$(1000)_3 = 100 \cdot 999 \cdot 998 = 997{,}002{,}000$$

while

$$\frac{1000!}{997!}$$

may lead to trouble as $1000! \approx 4.0 \cdot 10^{2567}$, which is a number that is too large for most calculators to handle.

3.1.2 Unordered Choices Without Replacement

In some types of choices the order does not matter. If we are to select two board members instead of CEO and board leader, the order makes no difference. If Smith and Johnson are selected, it does not matter who is selected first. The ordered choices {Smith, Johnson} and {Johnson, Smith} both lead to the same result. When the order does not count, we will in general end up with fewer combinations. To figure out how many unordered combinations that are genuinely different, we need to be able to compute how many ordered combinations lead to the same unordered result (Fig. 3.2).

It is easy to understand that n different objects can be sorted in $n!$ different ways. In the first position we have n different options, in the second position $(n-1)$ options remains, and we may continue like this until we reach the last position where there is only one object left.

Fig. 3.2 Outcomes come in two versions

Example 3.5 In the Lotto lottery (England) the players select 6 out of 59 numbers without replacement. 6 out of 59 numbers are then drawn randomly without replacement, and any player who selected the same 6 numbers wins the Jackpot. What is the probability of winning the Jackpot?

Solution: The number of unique ordered outcomes is $(59)_6 = 32{,}441{,}381{,}280$, but each time we select 6 numbers they can be sorted in $6! = 720$ different ways that all lead to the same result. This means that the number of unordered outcomes is reduced by a factor 720, and the number of unique unordered outcomes is

$$\frac{32{,}441{,}381{,}280}{720} = 45{,}057{,}474.$$

As each such combination has the same probability of winning, the probability of winning the Jackpot is hence

$$\frac{1}{45{,}057{,}474}.$$

The same line of reasoning can be used in general. Whenever we pick s elements from n unique objects, there are $(n)_s$ different ordered combinations. Each such combination can be sorted into $s!$ different ordered combinations, all of which are leading to the same unordered outcome. The number of ordered combinations is reduced by a factor $s!$, and the number of unique unordered combinations is hence

$$\frac{(n)_s}{s!} = \frac{n!}{s!(n-s)!}.$$

The number of unique unordered combinations coincides with the binomial coefficient $\binom{n}{s}$ used in mathematics, and we use the same notation, i.e.

$$\binom{n}{s} = \frac{(n)_s}{s!} = \frac{n!}{s!(n-s)!}.$$

Example 3.6

$$\binom{10}{3} = \frac{10 \cdot 9 \cdot 8}{1 \cdot 2 \cdot 3} = 120.$$

Note that $s = 3$ and there are three terms both in the nominator and the denominator.

The principles above can be summarized as follows: When we select s elements from a set with n unique elements, we get the following number of unique combinations

Ordered with replacement:

$$n^s = \underbrace{n \cdot n \cdot n \cdots n}_{s \text{ terms}}.$$

Ordered without replacement:

$$(n)_s = n(n-1)\cdots(n-s+1) = \frac{n!}{(n-s)!}.$$

Unordered without replacement:

$$\binom{n}{s} = \frac{(n)_s}{s!} = \frac{n!}{s!(n-s)!}.$$

If we make efficient use of these principles we are able to solve many different problems related to combinatorics. One question remains, however: What about unordered selections with replacement? Curiously, this case becomes much more complex than any of the others. We will illustrate the problem with an example.

Example 3.7 How many unique unordered combinations exist when we select 3 elements out of 5 with replacement?

Solutions: Obviously there are $5 \cdot 5 \cdot 5 = 125$ ordered combinations. In the case without replacement, any ordered combination could be sorted into $s!$ different variants, but this is no longer true. The ordered combination $(1, 1, 1)$ only exists once, the ordered combination $(1, 1, 2)$ can be sorted in 3 different versions, and the ordered combination $(1, 2, 3)$ can be sorted in 6 different versions. We hence have to treat all such cases separately. There are 5 different ordered cases where all the elements are equal, and they are also different as unordered combinations. If we count carefully, we can figure out 60 ordered combinations where two elements are equal while the third is different. All such combinations can be sorted in 3 different ordered combinations which all lead to the same unordered outcome. This gives $60/3 = 20$ different unordered combinations. Finally there are 60 ordered combinations where all the three elements are different. These cases can be sorted in 6 different ordered versions, all leading to the same unordered outcome. This leads to $60/6 = 10$ unique unordered combinations. To summarize we end up with $5 + 20 + 10 = 35$ unique unordered combinations.

As we can see from the example, computation of the number of such unordered combinations is possible but quite cumbersome. It is possible to make a systematic treatment of this topic, but since we rarely will encounter such cases in practice, we will not enter more deeply into this.

3.1.3 Combinatorial Probabilities

In many connections it is reasonable to assume that all the different combinations are equally probable. This corresponds to a uniform probability as defined in Chap. 2. In particular it applies to situations where you guess possible outcomes without any prior information. In such cases we can compute probabilities simply by counting the number of cases with a specified outcome.

Example 3.8 A group of 300 students were given a list of 10 imaginary companies and asked to pick 4 different companies from the list. After all the students had made their choice, the stock price was simulated on a computer and the values of certain call options were calculated from this. The worth of 10,000 such call options are displayed in Table 3.1.

It turned out that 1 student had picked all the four best, i.e., NoWonder, DataFriends, UnitedMath, and SlowFix. 8 students had picked all the 3 best, 42 students had picked the two best, and 120 students had picked the best. The question is now if this was a good or bad achievement.

Since the students had no prior information about the companies, it may be reasonable to assume that the choices are purely random. Since the order makes no difference, the choices are unordered. The students should pick different companies, which means that the selection is without replacement. There is hence $\binom{10}{4} = 210$

Table 3.1 Values of 10,000 options

Groggy	USD	6700
Phrazebook	USD	0
Externet	USD	9500
NoWonder	USD	191, 700
McHeaven	USD	0
DataFriends	USD	241, 900
UnitedMath	USD	17, 100
AllStats	USD	0
LowTech	USD	0
SlowFix	USD	147, 000

unique outcomes, all of which are equally probable. We can then ask the following questions:

- What is the probability of picking all the four best?
- What is the probability of picking the three best?
- What is the probability of picking the two best?
- What is the probability of picking the best?

Solution: What is the probability of picking all the four best? As there is just one such combination, the probability is $\frac{1}{210}$.

What is the probability of picking the three best? If we are to pick the three best, the last company can be picked arbitrarily among the 7 companies that are left, and this can be done in $\binom{7}{1} = 7$ different ways. The probability is hence $\frac{7}{210} = \frac{1}{30}$.

What is the probability of picking the two best? If we are to pick the two best, the last two companies can be picked arbitrarily among the 8 companies that are left, and this can be done in $\binom{8}{2} = 28$ different ways. The probability is hence $\frac{28}{210} = \frac{2}{15}$.

What is the probability of picking the best company? If we are to pick the best company, the last three companies can be picked arbitrarily among the 9 companies that are left, and this can be done in $\binom{9}{3} = 84$ different ways. The probability is hence $\frac{84}{210} = \frac{2}{5}$.

If 300 students pick 4 out of 10 companies at random, we expect that about $\frac{300}{210} \approx 1$ pick all the four best, that about $300 \cdot \frac{1}{30} = 10$ pick the three best, that about $300 \cdot \frac{2}{15} = 40$ pick the two best, while $300 \cdot \frac{2}{5}$ pick the best. We see that the reported numbers do not differ much from what we would expect.

Example 3.9 We now consider a modified version of Example 3.8. Assume that the list contains 6 technology companies and 4 other, and assume that the students must pick exactly two technology companies and two other. How many combinations are there now, and what is the probability that the students pick the best company from both groups?

Solution: We can view this as two independent choices, where both are unordered without replacement. Since the choices do not connect, we can use the principle in the start of this chapter to compute the number of combinations within each choice, and then simply multiply them. This gives

$$\binom{6}{2}\binom{4}{2} = 15 \cdot 6 = 90$$

different combinations. The best technology company can be realized in 5 different ways, and the best other company in 3 different ways. The probability is hence

$$\frac{5 \cdot 3}{90} = \frac{1}{6}.$$

Proceeding as in Example 3.9, we can break down many problems in combinatorics into unconnected parts. The number of combinations within each part can often be found from the simple formulas we have been through, and when there are no connections we can just multiply the number of combinations within each part to find the total number of unique combinations.

3.2 Summary of Chap. 3

When we select s elements from a set with n unique elements, the number of unique combinations can be found as follows:

- Ordered with replacement:

$$n^s = \underbrace{n \cdot n \cdot n \cdots n}_{s \text{ terms}}.$$

- Ordered without replacement:

$$(n)_s = n(n-1)\cdots(n-s+1) = \frac{n!}{(n-s)!}.$$

- Unordered without replacement:

$$\binom{n}{s} = \frac{(n)_s}{s!} = \frac{n!}{s!(n-s)!}.$$

- If the choices are unordered with replacement, the problem can be broken down into separate cases as in Example 3.7.

3.3 Problems for Chap. 3

3.1 You should put together a portfolio consisting of one mutual fund, one bond fund, and one money market fund. There is in all 103 different mutual funds, 43 bond funds, and 39 money market funds. In how many different ways can you put together your portfolio?

3.2 You are to invest in 3 different out of 10 different mutual funds. In the first fund you should invest 10%, in the second 30%, and in the third 60%. In how many ways can this be done?

3.3 You want to rank 5 out of 20 different products. In how many ways can this be done?

3.4 You are to invest in 4 different out of 10 different mutual funds. In all the funds you should invest 25%. In how many different ways can this be done?

3.5 You should choose 4 different out of 15 different products. In how many ways can this be done?

3.6 You should answer 5 different questions. Every question has the alternatives Yes and No, and only one of these answers is correct. How many combinations end up with exactly 3 correct answers?

3.7 You should answer 20 different questions. Every question has the alternatives Yes and No, and only one of these answers is correct. How many combinations end up with exactly 5 correct answers?

3.8 You invest in 6 out of 30 different mutual funds, and do not have any prior information about the funds. We hence assume that they are selected randomly.

(a) How many different combinations of funds are there?
(b) At the end of the year you examine your investment. Compute the probability that you have
(i) the best fund.
(ii) the two best funds.

3.9 In the area where you live, there are 10,000 different households. A company sends a questionnaire to 1000 randomly selected households.

(a) What is the probability that you receive the questionnaire?
(b) What is the probability that you and your nearest neighbor receive the questionnaire?

3.10 In the area where you live there are N households. A company sends a questionnaire to n randomly selected households. What is the probability that you receive the questionnaire?

3.11 In a collection of 8 companies, all companies have a cooperation agreement with each of the other companies.

(a) How many cooperation documents are there?
(b) In each company there is an executive officer who has the responsibility of each cooperation document. We assume that no one has the responsibility of more than one document. How many executive officers are there?

3.12 A warehouse contains 105 crates. 14 of these crates contains goods with errors. We pick 2 crates randomly from the warehouse.

(a) What is the probability that none of the two crates contains errors?
(b) What is the probability that at least one of the crates contains errors?

3.13 A warehouse contains 13 crates with the product Regular, 7 crates with the product Superior, and 6 crates with the product Superior Extra. All the goods are stored in equally looking crates. We pick three crates at random.

(a) What is the probability that all the three crates contain the product Regular?
(b) What is the probability that all the crates contain different products?

3.14 8 persons buy one of the three products A, B, and C.

(a) How many different outcomes are there?
(b) How many different outcomes are there where exactly one person buys product A?
(c) How many cases are there where exactly 5 persons buy product A?
(d) How many cases are there where exactly 2 persons buy A, 3 persons buy B, and 3 persons buy C?
(e) How many cases are there where product A is bought by more persons than the number sold of products B and C in total?

3.15 A fund company offers investments in 30 different mutual funds. 18 of these invest in the USA, while 12 invest in China. A customer wants to invest in 4 funds from the USA and 3 funds from China.

(a) How many different combination of funds can the customer choose between?
(b) Assume that two of the US funds will give bad returns the next few years. What is the probability that the customer has these two funds in her portfolio?
(c) Assume that the customer evaluates her investment after one year. What is the probability that she has invested in the two best US funds and in the best China fund?

3.16 Nonuniform Combinations: In a customer survey the customers may select products from 4 different product groups. They must select 2 products, but can only select at most one product from each group.

(a) A customer selects two products, and we register which products have been selected. How many different combinations of 2 product groups are there?
Group 1 has 4 different products.
Group 2 has 2 different products.
Group 3 has 3 different products.
Group 4 has 6 different products.

All the products in the survey are considered to be different, hence there are 15 different products that can be selected.

A customer selected products from groups 1 and 4. In how many ways can this be done?

(b) How many different combinations of products can the customer end up with?
(c) Assume that the first product is selected randomly among the 15 products, and that the second product is selected among the remaining products the customer can select. Explain why not all the different combinations are equally probable.
(d) What is the probability that the customer selects products from groups 1 and 4?

3.17 Passing a Multiple Choice Test: You participate in a test where there are 20 questions, and each question has 3 alternatives. Each question has one and only one correct answer.

(a) How many different answer combinations are there in all? How many of these have 19 correct answers and 1 wrong answer?
(b) Assume that you are guessing (picking the answers randomly) on all the questions. What is the probability that you get exactly 14 correct answers?
(c) Assume that you know the answers to 10 of the questions, but have to guess the rest. What is the probability that you get at least 13 correct answers?

3.18 Random Investments: A finance company plans to focus a portfolio of 10 different mutual funds. In the market that that company wishes to focus, there are in all 75 different mutual funds.

(a) Assume that the company picks all the 10 funds randomly. How many different combinations of funds are possible?

The 75 funds have different historical performance. Table 3.2 shows how many funds performed, very bad, bad, average, good, and very good in relation to the reference index.

What is the probability that the company has focused 4 average, 3 good, and 3 very good funds?

(b) What is the probability that all the 10 funds performed average or worse? What is the probability that the company has focused at least one of the very good funds?

3.19 Finding the Most Probable Outcome in Terms of Entropy: In a market with only one good we assume there are 10 potential buyers and 5 potential sellers. We assume for simplicity that each buyer can buy 0 or 1 unit of the good, and that

Table 3.2 Data for Problem 3.18

Very bad	Bad	Average	Good	Very good
25	20	15	10	5

each seller can sell 0 or one unit. In this market we can hence have $0, 1, 2, 3, 4, 5$ transactions.

By a sales outcome we mean a list which specifies which persons have bought one unit and which persons have sold one unit. Two lists give the same outcome if the same persons are on both lists.

(a) How many different sales outcomes are there with 5 transactions?
(b) Make a complete table which specifies how many sales outcomes there are with $0, 1, 2, 3, 4, 5$ transactions. Assume for simplicity that any such outcome is equally probable. Use this to find the probabilities of each number of transactions. How many transactions are most probable?
(c) Alternatively we can make lists which specify which persons have bought one unit and who they bought the unit from. Two such lists are assumed equal if they consist of the same pairs. Make a complete table showing how many different lists have pairs of buyers/sellers leading to $0, 1, 2, 3, 4, 5$ transactions.

3.20 Multinomial Outcomes: 10 customers can buy 3 different goods. We call the goods A, B, and C. We imagine that the customers come in succession, choose a good, and leave the place in the cue for the next customer. The shop has more than 10 goods of each type, so it can always satisfy demand.

(a) Assume that x customers buy A, y customers buy B, and z customers buy C. Let $K(x, y, z)$ be the number of sequences leading to the outcome (x, y, z). Explain why

$$K(x, y, z) = \binom{10}{x} \cdot \binom{10-x}{y} \cdot \binom{10-x-y}{z},$$

and use this to show that

$$K(x, y, z) = \frac{10!}{x!y!z!}.$$

(b) Assume that all trades are unrelated, and the probabilities are
- 30% for buying A,
- 20% for buying B,
- 50% for buying C.

Assume that 3 customers bought A, 2 customers bought B, and 5 customers bought C. How probable is this outcome?
(c) Assume that all trades are unrelated and that the probabilities are as in (b). Find the probability that at least 8 customers bought A.

Conditional Probability

4

Abstract

In most cases where we study probabilities, we have some additional information about what has happened. Information of this sort will often pose a restriction on the sample space. In this chapter we will show how to compute probabilities under such restrictions.

4.1 Conditional Probability

Before we consider the definition of conditional probability, we take a look at a simple example.

Example 4.1 During the years 2016 and 2017 a total of 100 students participated in the exam for the course STAT000. The results are depicted in Fig. 4.1. Each square represents the result of one student.

From Fig. 4.1 we see that 20% of the students received the grad A, 30% got B, 30% got C, and 20% got D. Half of the students took the exam in 2017. The results of these students are indicated by the shaded squares in Fig. 4.2.

We see that 18 students got the grade A in 2017. This corresponds to 18% of the total number of students in 2016 and 2017. If we want to find the fraction of the students that got A in 2017, we must take into account that 50 students took the exam that year. The fraction is hence 36%.

Example 4.1 shows the underlying principle behind conditional probabilities; when we condition the probabilities, we must take into account that we change the outcomes under consideration.

J. Ubøe, *Introductory Statistics for Business and Economics*, Springer Texts in Business and Economics, https://doi.org/10.1007/978-3-319-70936-9_4

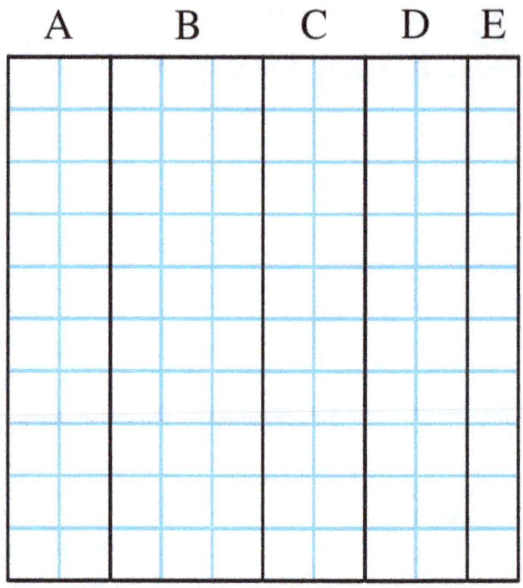

Fig. 4.1 Exam results from 2016 and 2017, each square corresponds to one student

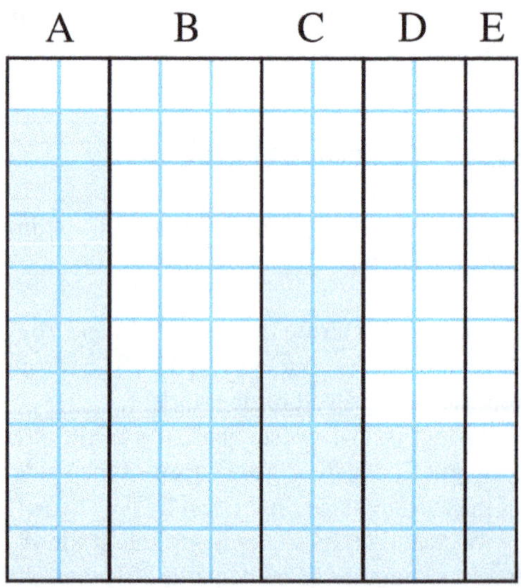

Fig. 4.2 Exam results from 2017, each shaded square corresponds to one student

Definition 4.1 If B is an event with $P(B) \neq 0$ and A is any event, we define the conditional probability $P(A|B)$ as follows:

$$P(A|B) = \frac{P(A \cap B)}{P(B)}.$$

We say that $P(A|B)$ is the probability for A given B.

If we use this definition in Example 4.1, the computation is as follows:

$$P(A|2017) = \frac{P(A \cap 2017)}{P(2017)} = \frac{0.18}{0.5} = 0.36 = 36\%.$$

We see that this is exactly what we want to know when we restrict attention to only those who took the exam in 2017. Note that the order of the events is important. If we change the order, we get

$$P(2017|A) = \frac{P(2017 \cap A)}{P(A)} = \frac{0.18}{0.20} = 0.90 = 90\%.$$

This number tells us that 90% of the students who obtained an A took the exam in 2017.

Example 4.2 In a customer survey we found that 60% of the customers used the brand Favorite, while 30% used the brand Super. 15% of the customers used both brands. How many percent of the Favorite users use Super, and how many percent of the Super users use Favorite?

Solution: We use the formulas for conditional probabilities to see that

$$P(S|F) = \frac{P(S \cap F)}{P(F)} = \frac{15\%}{60\%} = 25\%.$$

$$P(F|S) = \frac{P(F \cap S)}{P(S)} = \frac{15\%}{30\%} = 50\%.$$

This means that 25% of the Favorite users use Super, and that 50% of the Super users use Favorite.

4.1.1 Computing Conditional Probabilities

When we compute conditional probabilities, we can work with complements just as before. This can be seen as follows:

$$P(A|B) + P(A^c|B) = \frac{P(A \cap B) + P(A^c \cap B)}{P(B)} = \frac{P(B)}{P(B)} = 1.$$

From this we see that

$$P(A^c|B) = 1 - P(A|B).$$

The formula for conditional probability also provides us with some useful rearrangements which help in special situations. If we multiply the definition of $P(A|B)$ with $P(B)$ on both sides, we get

$$P(A \cap B) = P(A|B) \cdot P(B).$$

Correspondingly

$$P(B \cap A) = P(B|A) \cdot P(A)$$

Since $P(A \cap B) = P(B \cap A)$, we get

$$P(A|B) \cdot P(B) = P(B|A) \cdot P(A).$$

If we divide by $P(A)$ on both sides, we have proved Bayes' rule which is an important tool in statistics.

Bayes' rule:

$$P(B|A) = P(A|B) \cdot \frac{P(B)}{P(A)}.$$

Returning to Example 4.2, we now have an alternative way of finding the second answer:

$$P(F|S) = P(S|F) \cdot \frac{P(F)}{P(S)} = 25\% \cdot \frac{60\%}{15\%} = 50\%$$

This way of rearranging the probabilities turns out to be useful in many connections. We will return to this later in this chapter.

Example 4.3 A car dealer wanted to try some new incentives to increase sales. All visitors would be offered a scratch card if they were willing to participate in a meeting with a customer advisor. The new incentives were examined after one year. 10% of the visitors ended up buying a car. 30% of the visitors who bought a car received a scratch card, and 10% of the customers who did not buy a car received a scratch card.

The car dealer wanted to find the answer to the following question: Have customers receiving scratch cards, a higher probability of buying a car?

Solution: We define the events B : The customer bought a car, S : The customer received a scratch card. From the information in the text, we know that

$$P(B) = 0.1, \qquad P(B^c) = 0.9, \qquad P(S|B) = 0.3, \qquad P(S|B^c) = 0.1.$$

Since $\Omega = B \cup B^c$, we can split the sample space in two disjoint pieces. This can be used as follows:

$$\begin{aligned} P(S) &= P(S \cap B) + P(S \cap B^c) \\ &= P(S|B) \cdot P(B) + P(S|B^c) \cdot P(B^c) \\ &= 0.3 \cdot 0.1 + 0.1 \cdot 0.9 = 0.12. \end{aligned}$$

Hence

$$P(B|S) = P(S|B) \cdot \frac{P(B)}{P(S)} = 0.3 \cdot \frac{0.1}{0.12} = 0.25 = 25\%.$$

We conclude that customers receiving scratch cards have a higher probability of buying a car.

4.1.2 Splitting the Sample Space

The technique used in Example 4.3 can be formulated as a general principle. Assume that the sample space

$$\Omega = B_1 \cup B_2 \cup \cdots \cup B_n$$

where $B_1, B_2, \ldots, B_n$ are disjoint. For any subset A we have, see Fig. 4.3, that

$$P(A) = P(A \cap B_1) + P(A \cap B_2) + \cdots P(A \cap B_n).$$

If we use the formulas for conditional probabilities, this can be rewritten as follows:

$$P(A) = P(A|B_1) \cdot P(B_1) + P(A|B_2) \cdot P(B_2) + \cdots P(A|B_n) \cdot P(B_n).$$

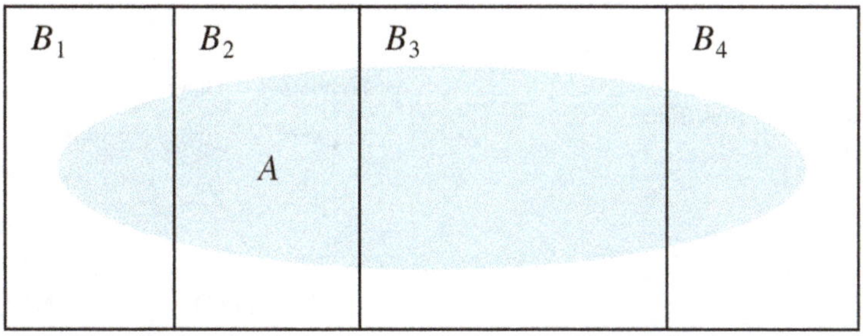

Fig. 4.3 Splitting the probability space into disjoint parts

The case where we split Ω into two pieces B and B^c is particularly important. The formula then reads as:

$$P(A) = P(A|B) \cdot P(B) + P(A|B^c) \cdot P(B^c).$$

At a first glance this may not appear very useful. Quite the contrary in fact, as the expression for A seems more complicated than where we started. Our notation, however, is playing us a trick here; A may be a complicated set, while the intersections may be more simple to handle. When this happens, the splitting principle is very useful, and that is just what we could see happen in Example 4.3.

4.1.3 Probability Trees

In many cases complex situations with several conditional probabilities can be made more manageable if we draw a tree showing the different cases.

Example 4.4 We want to study the investments made by a mutual fund. The fund invests in the USA, and the investments have been placed with 75% on NASDAQ (National Association of Securities Dealers Automated Quotations System) and 25% on NYSE (New York Stock Exchange). Of the funds invested on NASDAQ 100% are invested in technology, while 40% of the money invested on NYSE are invested in tech firms.

The text is relatively complex, and the information becomes more transparent if we draw a tree as in Fig. 4.4.

To illustrate how to use the figure, we try to answer an explicit question: How many percent of the US stocks are invested in technology?

Solution: The problem can be solved in several different ways. We define Ω = USA, A = Technology, B_1 = NASDAQ and B_2 = NYSE. Then B_1 and B_2 are disjoint and $\Omega = B_1 \cup B_2$. The splitting principle gives

$$\begin{aligned} P(A) &= P(A|B_1) \cdot P(B_1) + P(A|B_2) \cdot P(B_2) \\ &= 1 \cdot 0.75 + 0.4 \cdot 0.25 = 0.85 = 85\%. \end{aligned} \tag{4.1}$$

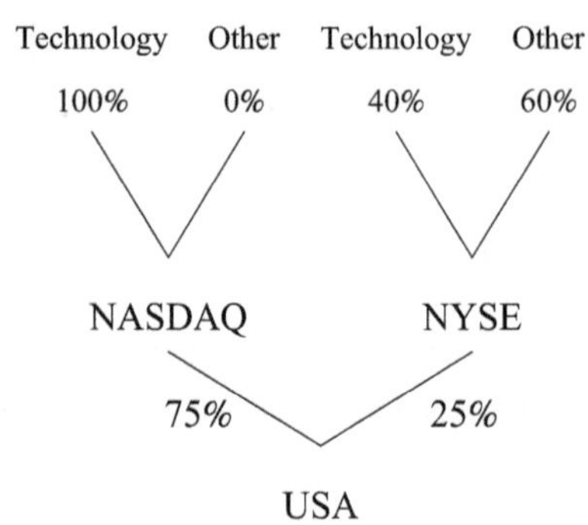

Fig. 4.4 The tree of conditional probabilities from Example 4.4

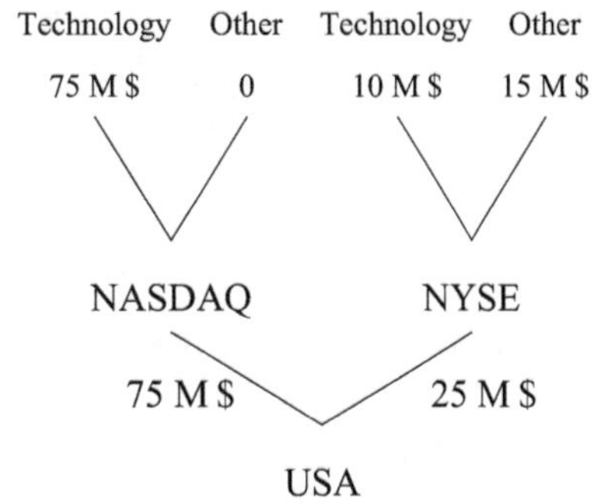

Fig. 4.5 Total investments using the rules from Example 4.4

There is, however, an alternative approach which most people find to be simpler. Let us imagine that we invest 100 M USD in the fund. It is then very simple to write down a tree displaying how much money we are investing, see Fig. 4.5.

From the information in Fig. 4.5, the question above has an almost trivial answer. We have invested 100 M USD and 85 M USD have been invested in technology. Hence the share of investments in technology is

$$\frac{85}{100} = 0.85 = 85\%.$$

Example 4.5 We consider a new question based on the same information as in Example 4.4: How many percent of the technology funds are invested on NYSE?

Solution: Again the solution is straightforward from Fig. 4.5. 85 M USD have been invested in technology, and 10 M USD of these have been invested on NYSE. The share is hence

$$\frac{10}{85} \approx 11.76\%.$$

Strictly speaking we have until now looked at shares and not probabilities. The point is now that we can reason with probabilities in exactly the same way.

Example 4.6 A firm has two main machines, Machine 1 and Machine 2. 60% of the goods are produced using machine 1, while the rest is produced on machine 2. The goods that are produced on machine 1 is in the next step finished on machine 3 or machine 4. 75% of these goods continue to machine 3, while the rest continue to machine 4. The goods that have been produced on machine 3 is in the next step finished on machine 5 or 6. 50% of these goods continue to machine 5, while the rest is treated on machine 6. All the goods produced on machine 3 are without errors. Of the goods produced on machine 4, 40% are OK. Of the goods treated by machine 5, 60% are OK, while only 10% of the goods treated on machine 6 are OK. A tree depicting all this information is shown in Fig. 4.6.

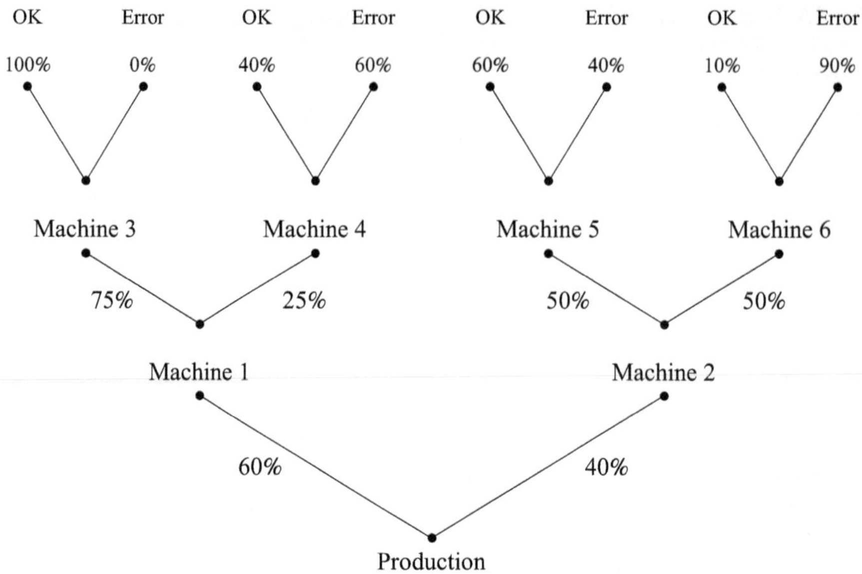

Fig. 4.6 Conditional probabilities

Just as in the examples above, it will in most cases help if we convert the conditional probabilities in Fig. 4.6 to absolute probabilities. When 60% of the goods are produced on machine 1 and 75% of these are fished on machine 3, there is in total $0.6 \cdot 0.75 = 0.45 = 45\%$ of the total that are produced on machines 1 and 3. If we translate all the numbers in this way, we end up with the tree in Fig. 4.7.

From the tree in Fig. 4.7 it is easy to answer several relevant questions.

Example 4.7 What is $P(\text{OK}|\text{Produced on machines 1 and 3})$?

Solution:

$$P(\text{OK}|\text{Produced on machines 1 and 3}) = \frac{P(\text{OK} \cap \text{machine 1} \cap \text{machine 3})}{P(\text{machine 1} \cap \text{machine 3})} \tag{4.2}$$

$$= \frac{45\%}{45\%} = 1 = 100\%.$$

What is $P(\text{Produced on machines 1 and 3}|\text{OK})$?

Solution:

$$P(\text{Produced on machines 1 and 3}|\text{OK}) = \frac{P(\text{OK} \cap \text{machine 1} \cap \text{machine 3})}{P(\text{OK})} \tag{4.3}$$

$$= \frac{45\%}{45\% + 6\% + 12\% + 2\%} \approx 69.23\%.$$

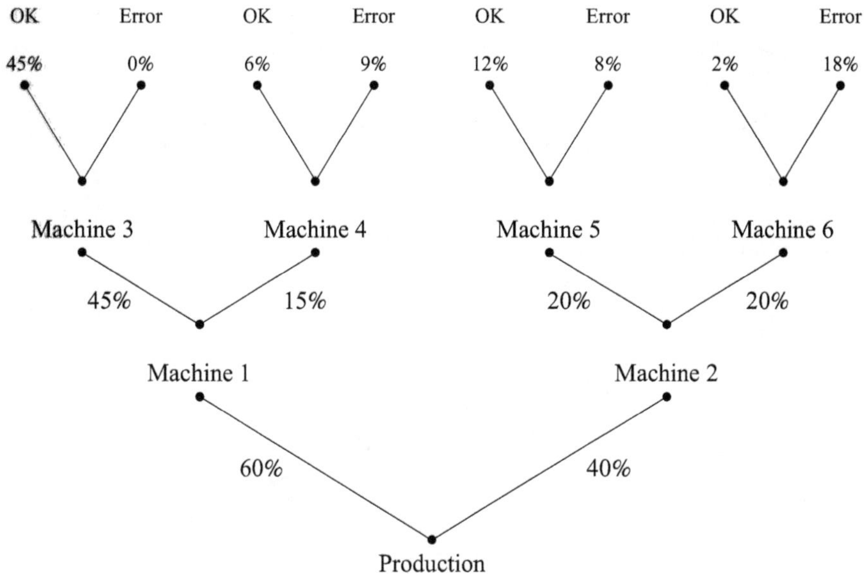

Fig. 4.7 Absolute probabilities

We can also find the answer to the last question using Bayes' rule:

$$
\begin{aligned}
& P(\text{Produced on machines 1 and 3}|\text{OK}) \\
= \; & P(\text{OK}|\text{machine 1} \cap \text{machine 3}) \cdot \frac{P(\text{machine 1} \cap \text{machine 3})}{P(\text{OK})} \\
= \; & 100\% \cdot \frac{45\%}{45\% + 6\% + 12\% + 2\%} \approx 69.23\%.
\end{aligned}
$$

From the examples above, we see that it is often a good idea to convert a tree with conditional probabilities to a tree of absolute probabilities. We now look at how we can do this quickly.

Example 4.8 To the left in Fig. 4.8 we show a part of a tree with conditional probabilities. We wish to compute the absolute probability of reaching the nodes shown to the right.

The node in the bottom of the tree represents 100%, and since 20% of this is transferred to A, $P(A) = 20\%$. The probability of reaching node B is

$$P(A \cap B) = P(B|A) \cdot P(A) = 50\% \cdot 20\% = 10\%.$$

Furthermore

$$
\begin{aligned}
P(A \cap B \cap C) = \; & P(C|A \cap B) \cdot P(A \cap B) = P(C|A \cap B) \cdot P(B|A) \cdot P(A) \quad (4.4) \\
= \; & 50\% \cdot 50\% \cdot 20\% = 5\%.
\end{aligned}
$$

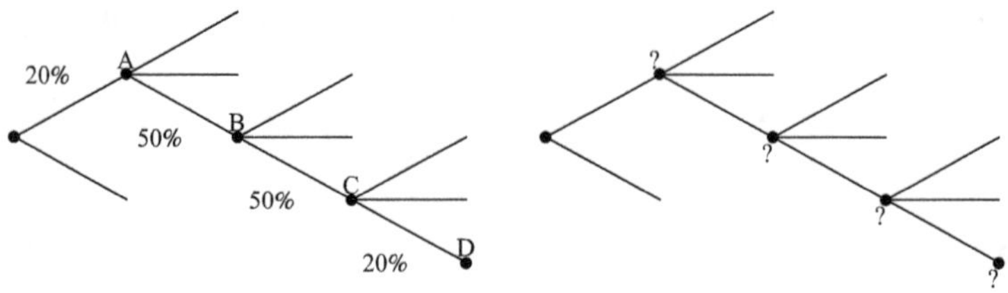

Fig. 4.8 A part of a probability tree

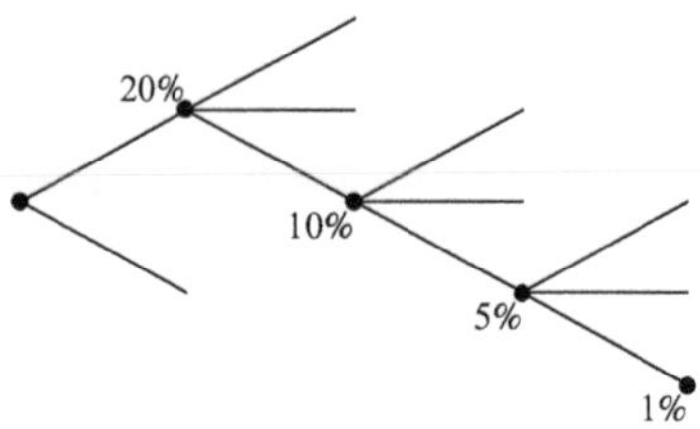

Fig. 4.9 Multiplying probabilities along branches

We can continue like this until we reach the end of the branch. Even though the derivation is somewhat complicated, we end up with a simple and transparent principle:

> We find the absolute probabilities multiplying the conditional probabilities in succession along each branch.

The end result is hence as shown in Fig. 4.9.

4.2 Subjective Probabilities

We often hear people make more of less wild guesses on the probabilities of something happening. Such probabilities are often based on wishful thinking; the person feels that a probability is large, or claims to have reason to believe that a probability is small. When a person speaks in public on such matters, it is easy to make contradictory statements.

Example 4.9 Two teams A and B are playing the final, and a supporter of team A claims that the chance of A winning the final is $P(A) = 80\%$. One of the best players on team B is injured however, and it is not clear that he will recover to play in the final. The supporter believes that the chance of recovery is $P(B) = 0.1$. If he recovers, the supporter claims that the chance of winning falls to 60%, while the chance of team A winning is 90% if he does not recover.

We let B denote the event that the best player on team B recovers, and the supporter has made the statements

$$P(A) = 0.8, P(B) = 0.1, P(A|B) = 0.6, P(A|B^c) = 0.9.$$

What are the consequences of these subjective statements?

We know that

$$P(A|B) = \frac{P(A \cap B)}{P(B)} = 0.6 \Rightarrow P(A \cap B) = 0.6\, P(B) = 0.06.$$

$$P(A|B^c) = \frac{P(A \cap B^c)}{P(B^c)} = 0.9 \Rightarrow P(A \cap B^c) = 0.9\, P(B^c) = 0.81.$$

Hence

$$P(A) = P(A \cap B) + P(A \cap B^c) = 0.06 + 0.81 = 0.87,$$

which is quite disturbing as the supporter already claimed that $P(A) = 0.8$. The numbers do not add up, and there must be something wrong with the subjective assessments. The reader is encouraged to check that only the value $P(B) = 1/3$ is consistent with the three other values.

4.3 Independence

Independence is one of the most central concepts in statistics. Broadly speaking we can say that two events are independent when there are no connections between them. Independence is particularly important when we conduct scientific experiments. It is important to carry out the experiments in a way such that the outcome of a new experiment does not depend on what has happened in the previous cases. Technically the definition of independence is surprisingly simple:

Two events A and B are independent if and only if $P(A \cap B) = P(A) \cdot P(B)$.

Independence is intimately related to conditional probability. If $P(B) \neq 0$, and A and B are independent events, then

$$P(A|B) = \frac{P(A \cap B)}{P(B)} = \frac{P(A) \cdot P(B)}{P(B)} = P(A).$$

Hence if A and B are independent the probability of A does not change when we condition on B. The multiplicative rule makes it simple to compute independent events, and the definition is easily extended to cases with more than two events.

A collection of events are mutually independent if and only if the probability of any intersection is equal to the product of the probabilities of the events included in the intersection.

Example 4.10 Assume that the events A, B, C, D are mutually independent. Then, e.g.

$$P(A \cap B \cap C \cap D) = P(A) \cdot P(B) \cdot P(C) \cdot P(D)$$

and

$$P(B \cap D) = P(B) \cdot P(D).$$

Example 4.11 Assume that an experiment has the outcome r with probability 0.2, s with probability 0.5, and t with probability 0.3. Assume that we repeat the experiment 4 times, and that the outcomes of each repetition are independent. What is the probability of the sequence $rrts$?

Solution: Since each repetition is independent from the rest, we get

$$P(rrts) = P(r) \cdot P(r) \cdot P(t) \cdot P(s) = 0.2 \cdot 0.2 \cdot 0.3 \cdot 0.5 = 0.006.$$

We notice that independence leads to the same simplicity we exploit in combinatorics when the choices are unconnected.

4.4 Summary of Chap. 4

- Definition of conditional probability

$$P(A|B) = \frac{P(A \cap B)}{P(B)}.$$

- Bayes' rule:

$$P(B|A) = P(A|B) \cdot \frac{P(B)}{P(A)}.$$

- The splitting principle

$$P(A) = P(A|B_1) \cdot P(B_1) + P(A|B_2) \cdot P(B_2) + \cdots + P(A|B_n) \cdot P(B_n).$$

- Two events are independent when $P(A \cap B) = P(A) \cdot P(B)$.

4.5 Problems for Chap. 4

4.1 In a customer survey we have found that 35% of the customers use the brand Favorite, while 56% use Super. 14% of the customers use both brands. How many percent of the Favorite users use Super, and how many percent of the Super users use Favorite?

4.2 In a customer survey we have found that 50% of the Favorite users use Super, while 25% of the Super users use Favorite. 20% of the customers use both brands. How many percent of the customers use Favorite, and how many percent of the customers use Super?

4.3 In a survey 160 men and 240 women were asked if they liked a particular product. 40% of the men and 20% of the women liked the product. How many percent of the participants liked the product?

4.4 You want to invest some money. 60% should be invested in mutual funds and 40% in money market funds. Of the money invested in mutual funds, 30% should be invested in China and 70% in other countries. Of the money invested in money market funds, 80% should be invested in Chinese funds and 20% in other countries.

(a) Make a tree displaying the information.
(b) How many percent of the money is invested in China?
(c) How many percent of the money invested in China are in mutual funds?

4.5 A company has 3 departments. 20% of the reports are from department A, 45% from department B, and 35% from department C. An examination revealed that 3% of the reports for A contained errors, 6% of the reports from B contained errors, and 2% of the reports from C contained errors.

(a) Make a tree displaying the information.
(b) How many percent of the reports contained errors?
(c) A report contained errors. What is the probability that the report came from department A?

4.6 We look at the stock price in two companies, and define the following events:

A: The stock price in company 1 increases.
B: The stock price in company 2 increases.
C: The stock price in company 2 does not increase.

We assume that there is 60% probability of an increase in the stock price of company 1, 40% probability of an increase in the stock price of company 2, and 24% probability of an increase in the stock price of both companies?

(a) Are A and B independent?
(b) Are A and C independent?
(c) Are B and C independent?

4.7 Show that if A and B are independent, then A and $C = B^c$ are independent.

4.8 We consider two events:

A: The stock price in company 1 increases.
B: The interest rate falls.

Assume that there is 60% probability for an increase in stock price, and that this probability does not change if the interest rate falls.

(a) Show that A and B are independent events.
(b) Try to formulate a general version of this result.

4.9 A shop has three goods on offer, A, B, and C. Each customer buys at most one of these goods. If a customer buys one of the goods on offer, then there is

- 50% probability for buying A.
- 20% probability for buying B.
- 30% probability for buying C.

4 customers buy goods on offer, and we assume that buys are independent.

(a) What is the probability that customer 1 buys A, customer 2 buys A, customer 3 buys B, and customer 4 buys C?
(b) What is the probability that at least 3 customers buy A?
(c) What is the probability that 2 customers buy C?

4.10 A company has two departments, department A with 60 employees and department B with 90 employees. Each department is divided into groups of 30 people, A_1 and A_2 at department A and B_1, B_2, B_3 at department B. During the last

Table 4.1 Performance at departments A and B in Problem 4.10

Group	Good	Average	Bad
A_1	50%	25%	25%
A_2	10%	70%	20%
B_1	40%	50%	10%
B_2	20%	60%	20%
B_3	30%	60%	10%

Table 4.2 Fractions liking the product in Problem 4.11

Fractions liking the product			
Women	Younger than 25 years	25–40 years	Older than 40 years
	60%	30%	80%
Fractions liking the product			
Men	Younger than 25 years	25–40 years	Older than 40 years
	20%	40%	60%
Fractions of the participants			
Women	Younger than 25 years	25–40 years	Older than 40 years
	15%	30%	15%
Fractions of the participants			
Men	Younger than 25 years	25–40 years	Older than 40 years
	20%	10%	10%

year the performance of each group has been examined, and the results are shown in Table 4.1.

We assume that the observed fractions represent the probabilities for the respective performances, and the probability that a project is carried out at a department is proportional to the number of workers at the department.

(a) Make a tree displaying the information.
(b) What is the probability that a project done at department A is good?
(c) A project is good. What is the probability that it has been done at department B?
(d) Is the probability of good performance independent of department?

4.11 Structuring Complex Information: In a customer survey a large number of people were asked if they liked a product. The question was posed to 6 different groups of the population. The fractions liking the product are shown in Table 4.2. The table also shows how large fractions of the participants belonged to each group.

(a) How large fraction of the participants liked the product?
(b) How large fraction of the women were in the group Younger than 25 years old?
(c) How large fraction of the women and how large fraction of the men liked the product?

Table 4.3 Investing strategies in Problem 4.12

Fund	USA	Europe	China
Global A	50%	30%	20%
Global B	20%	70%	10%
Aggressive C	30%	50%	20%

4.12 Extracting Information from Trees: A broker sells shares from three different global funds: Global A, Global B, and Aggressive C. 30% of the investments are placed in Global A, 60% in Global B, and 10% in Aggressive C. The funds diversify their investments and invest in the USA, Europe, and China. The fractions invested in these markets are shown in Table 4.3.

(a) Draw a tree displaying the information given above.
(b) How large share of the two funds Global A and B in total is invested in the USA?
(c) How large fraction of the US investments is invested in Global A?
(d) From the information provided above, is it possible to determine how many percent of the customers who invest more than 40% of their investments in the USA?

4.13 Untangling Conditional Information: In surveys focusing private/sensitive information it is important that the participants feel they are anonymous. A simple strategy taking this into account can be outlined as follows:

Split the participants into two categories:

- Category 1: Persons with date of birth from January 1 to August 31.
- Category 2: Persons with date of birth from September 1 to December 31.

The participants in Category 1 answer Yes/No to the question: Is your year of birth an even number?

The participants in Category 2 answer Yes/No to the question: Have you ever used illegal drugs?

The participants should not reveal their category, and the people conducting the survey hence do not know which question has been answered.

(a) We assume that all relevant dates/year of birth are equally probable, and we ignore leap years. How large fraction does each category make up? What is the probability of answering Yes, given that the person is in Category 1?
(b) We ask the questions to a large number of people, and find that in total 60% of the participants answered Yes. Assume that the answers were honest. How large fraction of Category 2 admitted using illegal drugs?
(c) Alternatively we could swap the questions for Category 1 and 2. Discuss if there can be advantages/disadvantages in swapping.

4.14 True/False Positives: A medical test gives a true positive in 77% of the cases where the patient has the illness, and a false positive in 2% of the cases where the patient does not have the illness. We assume that at any given time 2% of the population has the illness.

(a) The test is used on a randomly chosen patient. In how many percent of the cases will the test return a positive result? Given that the test returns a positive value, how large is the probability that the person has the illness?
(b) A person is tested and the test returns a positive value. Discuss circumstances that can influence the probability that the person has the illness.
(c) Can there exist circumstances where a positive value implies more than 77% chance that the person has the illness?

4.15 The Chance of True Positives Can Be Strongly Misleading: An auditing firm has developed a diagnostic tool to predict which firms will go bankrupt the next year. The model has been tested on old data and returned the following results:

- Of the companies that went bankrupt, 80% were flagged by the tool.
- Of the companies that did not go bankrupt, 95% were not flagged by the tool.

We assume that 10% of the firms will go bankrupt the next year, and that the performance of the diagnostic tool will stay in line with the performance on the old data.

(a) What is the probability that the firm is flagged given that it will not go bankrupt? How large percent of bankruptcies will the model predict?
(b) A firm has been flagged by the tool. What is the probability that the firm will in fact go bankrupt?

4.16 Markov Chains: A bank has some good and some bad customers.

- The probability that a good customer is downgraded to a bad customer during one time period is 30%.
- The probability that a bad customer is upgraded to a good customer during one time period is 20%.

We assume for simplicity that the development during any time period is independent of what has happened in the previous time periods, and that the time development of different customers is independent.

(a) A customer is rated as good. How probable is it that:
(i) The customer is rated as good in the next two time periods?
(ii) The customer is rated as good two time periods from now?
(b) A customer is rated as good. How probable is it that the customer is rated as good in exactly 9 of the 10 next time periods?

(c) Point to circumstances that can make the assumptions of independence questionable.

4.17 Simpson's Paradox: During the first six months of the year auditing firm A inspected 2000 documents and detected 120 errors. In the next 6 months they inspected 8000 documents and detected 240 errors. In the first six months auditing firm B inspected 4000 documents and detected 200 errors. In the next six months they inspected 1000 documents and detected 20 errors. We assume that the numbers are representative in that they reflect the probabilities of finding errors in the two periods.

(a) Which firm had the largest probability of finding errors in the first six months? Which firm had the largest probability of finding errors in the next six months? Which firm had the largest probability of finding errors during the whole year?
(b) Try to explain the connection between the results in (a).

4.18 Combining Splitting and Bayes' Rule: We classify firms into three different groups: Gr 1: Solvent, Gr 2: Worrisome, Gr 3: Bankrupt.

A bank gives the firms rating A, B, or C (A is the best rating.) Figures from previous years:

- 2.5% of the firms that went bankrupt had rating A.
- 15% that ended up as worrisome had rating A.
- 30% that ended up as solvent had rating A.

We assume that these numbers are stable from year to year. The numbers for rating B and C are omitted since they are not needed to answer the questions.

(a) How many percent of the firms get rating A?
(b) A firm has rating A. How large is the probability that it will go bankrupt?

4.19 Few False Positives Might Still Be Bad: An auditing firm has developed a tool to predict bankruptcy. The tool is very conservative. Among companies that do not go bankrupt, 5% are flagged for bankruptcy. We assume in this problem that a randomly selected firm has 0.1% probability of bankruptcy.

(a) Explain why

$$P(\text{The firm is flagged for bankruptcy}) \leq 1 \cdot 0.001 + 0.05 \cdot 0.999$$

(b) A firm has been flagged for bankruptcy with this tool. Show that the probability that the firm does not go bankrupt is larger than 98%.

4.20 Polls May Be Misleading: Assume that 60% of the viewers of TV program think that the level of taxation should be decreased, while 40% would like to see an increase. Assume further that 2% of those in favor of a reduction participate in a poll, while 7% of the viewers in favor of a tax raise participate in the poll.

(a) How large fraction of the viewers participate in the poll?
(b) How large fraction of the participants in the poll would like to see an increase in the tax level? Comment the result.

4.21 Combining Splitting and Bayes' Rule: There is often a connection between economic growth in a country and a strengthening of the currency. Assume that the probabilities for economic growth are as follows:

$P(\text{High growth}) = 0.3 \qquad P(\text{Medium growth}) = 0.5 \qquad P(\text{Low growth}) = 0.2.$

- When growth is high, there is a 70% chance of strengthening the currency.
- When growth is medium, there is a 50% chance of strengthening the currency.
- When growth is low, there is a 20% chance of strengthening the currency.

(a) How large is the probability that the currency will strengthen?
(b) The currency is strengthening. What is the probability of high economic growth?
(c) Are the events "High economic growth" and "The currency is strengthening" independent in this case. Justify the answer.

4.22 Spam Filtering: The frequency of special words is very different in e-mail spam than in ordinary e-mail. In e-mail spam the frequency of the word "debt" is 30.9%, while the frequency of the word is 0.447% in ordinary e-mail. In this problem we will assume that e-mail spam make up 50% of the e-mail that you receive.

(a) How large is the frequency of the word "debt" in all e-mail?
(b) An e-mail contains the word "debt." What is the probability that the e-mail is spam?

4.23 Untangling Conditional Probabilities: Assume that a special group of workers makes up 5% of the tax payers within a city. The taxation authorities have estimated that about 10% of the workers commit tax fraud. Previous data suggest that 1% of the workers who do not commit tax fraud belong to the special group.

(a) Use the information in the text to suggest how big share the special group makes up of those committing tax fraud.
(b) Use the answer in (a) to find the probability that a person in the special group commits tax fraud.

4.24 A Simpson's Paradox from Real Life: In a statistical survey from the period 1972–1974, 1316 women were interviewed regarding their smoking habits. The

Table 4.4 Mortality rates in age groups

Age	18–24	25–34	35–44	45–54	55–64	65–74	75+
Mortality in % smokers	3.6	2.4	12.8	20.8	44.3	80.6	100
Mortality in % nonsmokers	1.6	3.2	5.7	15.4	33.1	78.3	100

Table 4.5 Number of participants in each age group

Age	18–24	25–34	35–44	45–54	55–64	65–74	75+
Number of participants smokers	55	124	109	130	115	36	13
Number of participants nonsmokers	62	157	123	78	121	129	64

sample was drawn randomly and there were 582 smokers and 734 nonsmokers in the sample. 20 years later, the scientists recorded how many of the participants that were still alive. The results are shown in Tables 4.4 and 4.5. Age refers to the age at the start of the survey.

(a) What was (according to the tables) the probability of death given that the participant was a smoker in the age group 18–24? How big share of the smokers did this group make up? Use the splitting principle to compute the probability for death among smokers.
(b) What was (according to the tables) the probability of death given that the participant was a nonsmoker in the age group 18–24? How big share of the smokers did this group make up? Use the splitting principle to compute the probability for death among nonsmokers.
(c) The survey shows that the probability for death was considerably lower for smokers than for nonsmokers. Explain, using the tables above, that this does *not* show that smoking is healthy.

Random Variables, Mean, and Variance

5

Abstract

In this chapter we will introduce a general framework we will use to study statistical distributions. A statistical distribution specifies the probability of the different outcomes that can occur. We can, e.g., ask about the probability for exactly x defective items in a sample of 10 items. We let x run from 0 to 10, and compute 11 probabilities. The set of these probabilities we call the distribution. When the distribution is known, we are usually able to compute all the probabilities we may need. The distribution is hence the key to our calculations.

5.1 Random Variables

In many cases we wish to study a number which comes as a result of a random outcome. We call any such number a random variable. We first consider a few examples.

Example 5.1 Let Ω be the set of outcomes from one roll of a dice, and define a function X by

$$X(\omega) = \begin{cases} 1 & \text{if } \omega = 1, 3, 5 \\ -1 & \text{if } \omega = 2, 4, 6 \end{cases}.$$

Hence if the outcome is odd, the result is 1, and the result is -1 when the outcome is even. In any case X will be a real number.

J. Ubøe, *Introductory Statistics for Business and Economics*, Springer Texts in Business and Economics, https://doi.org/10.1007/978-3-319-70936-9_5

Example 5.2 Let Ω be the set of outcomes from two rolls of a dice, and define a function

$$X(\omega_1, \omega_2) = \omega_1 + \omega_2,$$

where ω_1 is the result of the first roll and ω_2 is the result of the second roll. Any outcome of the two tosses leads to a real number.

Example 5.3 Let v_1, v_2, v_3 denote the stock price for three different companies, and let the sample space Ω be all possible combinations of values that the stock prices can have tomorrow. We can then define a function

$$X(v_1, v_2, v_3) = \frac{1}{3}(v_1 + v_2 + v_3).$$

Whatever stock prices will occur tomorrow, the resulting value of X will be a real number.

All the three examples above have that in common that they define a function on the sample space leading to a real number. We call any such function a random variable.

Definition 5.1 By a random variable we mean a function defined on the sample space which returns a well-defined real number from any outcome.

In this chapter we will only consider random variables defined on a discrete sample space. When the sample space is discrete, we can define a random variable specifying the values $X(\omega_1), X(\omega_2), \ldots$. The same value can occur multiple times, and this is something we need to take into account.

Definition 5.2 The probability distribution of a random variable X is defined by

$$P(x) = P(X = x),$$

where x is any value that X can have.

The probability distribution hence specifies the probability of the different values that X can have. The probability distribution $P(x)$ is also called the point probabilities of X. In statistics it is common to use capital letters to define random variables, and use lowercase letters about constants. In the definition above X is a random variable, while x is used about all the constant values that X can have.

Example 5.4 Let $\Omega = \{\omega_1, \omega_2, \omega_3\}$ with uniform probabilities, and define a random variable by

$$X(\omega_1)1, \qquad X(\omega_2) = -2, \qquad X(\omega_3) = 1.$$

Then $P(X = -2) = \frac{1}{3}$ and $P(X = 1) = \frac{2}{3}$. For any other values of x, $P(X = x) = 0$.

Example 5.5 Let X be the number of heads in two tosses of a fair coin. There are three possible values for X: $0, 1, 2$. The value 1 can be realized in two different ways, and the probability distribution is hence:

$$P(X = 0) = \frac{1}{4}, \qquad P(X = 1) = \frac{1}{2}, \qquad P(X = 2) = \frac{1}{4}.$$

For any other values of x, $P(X = x) = 0$.

To get an overview of the distribution, we can display these values as bars in a histogram. The histogram in Fig. 5.1 shows the relative frequencies we would expect to find if we did a large number (ideally infinitely many) of independent tosses.

Example 5.6 Assume that $\Omega = \{\omega_1, \omega_2, \omega_3, \omega_4, \omega_5\}$,

$$p(\omega_1) = 0.2, \qquad p(\omega_2) = 0.3, \qquad p(\omega_3) = 0.1, \qquad p(\omega_4) = 0.1, \qquad p(\omega_5) = 0.3,$$

and that

$$X(\omega_1) = 1, \qquad X(\omega_2) = 2, \qquad X(\omega_3) = 1, \qquad X(\omega_4) = 2, \qquad X(\omega_5) = 3.$$

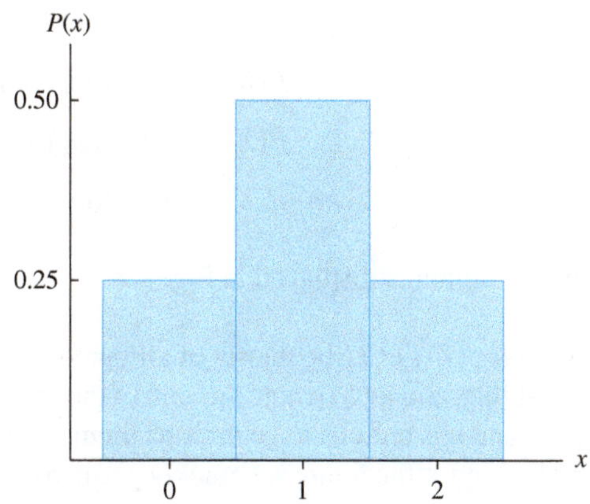

Fig. 5.1 The distribution in Example 5.5

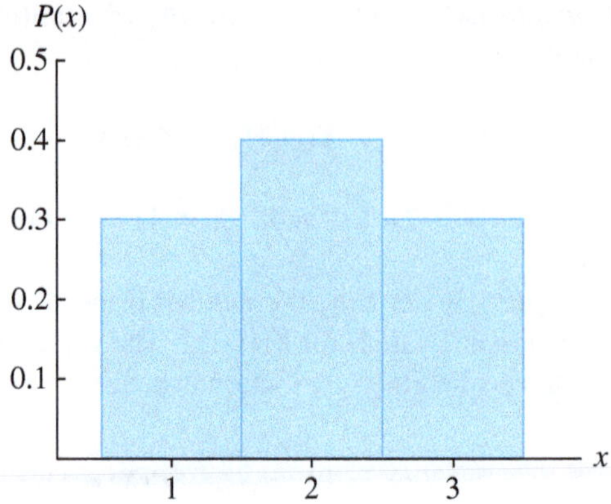

Fig. 5.2 The distribution in Example 5.6

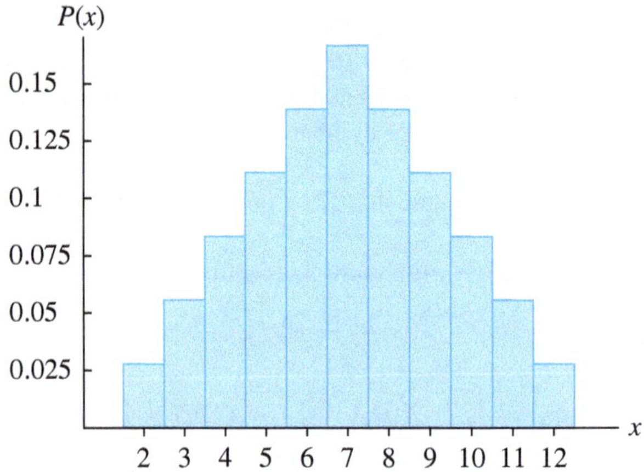

Fig. 5.3 The distribution of the sum of two dice tosses

Then

$$P(X = 1) = p(\omega_1) + p(\omega_3) = 0.3,$$

$$P(X = 2) = p(\omega_2) + p(\omega_4) = 0.4,$$

$$P(X = 3) = p(\omega_5) = 0.3.$$

The histogram is displayed in Fig. 5.2.

Example 5.7 Let Ω be the set of all outcomes of two tosses of a dice with uniform probability, and let S denote the sum of the two tosses. Here there are lots of different cases, and it is tedious to go through them all. The end result is displayed in Fig. 5.3, and looking at the figure we quickly get an overview of the distribution. We can, e.g., see that the result $S = 7$ is the most probable, and that the value is about 0.17.

Sometimes it may be convenient to organize the information a bit differently. Instead of giving the probability for each possible value of X, we might give the probability that X is below a threshold x. The probability that the random variable is less than or equal to a constant x, we call the cumulative distribution.

Definition 5.3 The cumulative distribution of a random variable X is defined by

$$F(x) = P(X \leq x),$$

which is defined for any real number x.

When the distribution of X is known, we see that

$$F(x) = \sum_{x_i \leq x} P(X = x_i).$$

That means that we find the value of the cumulative distribution adding the probability of all cases where $x_i \leq x$. Figure 5.4 shows the principle behind the function. It is piecewise constant and increases in jumps at $x_1, x_2, x_3 \ldots$. The sizes of the jumps are equal to the corresponding values of $P(X = x_i)$.

Example 5.8 Assume that $\Omega = \{\omega_1, \ldots, \omega_5\}$, and

$$p(\omega_1) = 0.2, \quad p(\omega_2) = 0.3, \quad p(\omega_4) = 0.1, \quad p(\omega_4) = 0.1, \quad p(\omega_5) = 0.3,$$

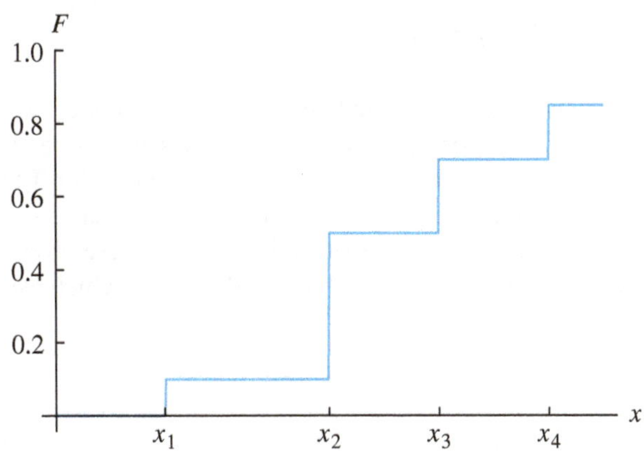

Fig. 5.4 A cumulative distribution

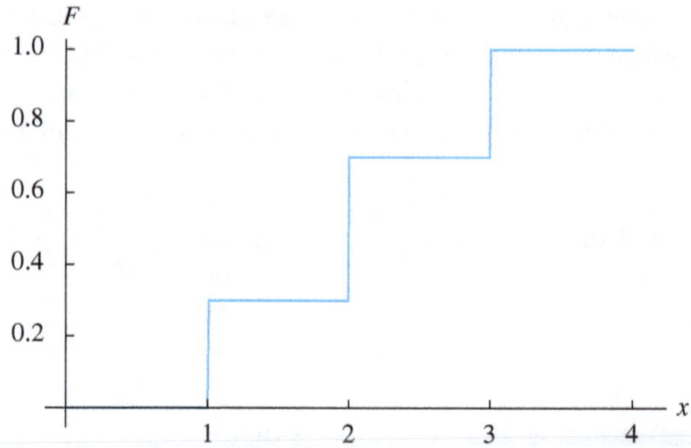

Fig. 5.5 The cumulative distribution of Example 5.8

and that

$$X(\omega_1) = 1, \quad X(\omega_2) = 2, \quad X(\omega_3) = 1, \quad X(\omega_4) = 2, \quad X(\omega_1) = 3.$$

Find the cumulative distribution.

Solution: If $x < 1$, then $F(x) = P(X \leq x) = 0$.

If $1 \leq x < 2$, then $F(x) = P(X \leq x) = p(\omega_1) + p(\omega_3) = 0.3$.
If $2 \leq x < 3$, then $F(x) = P(X \leq x) = p(\omega_1) + p(\omega_2) + p(\omega_3) + p(\omega_4) = 0.7$.
If $3 \leq x$, then $F(x) = P(X \leq x) = p(\omega_1) + p(\omega_2) + p(\omega_3) + p(\omega_4) + p(\omega_5) = 1$.

We see that the function is piecewise constant, and that it increases everywhere. The graph is shown in Fig. 5.5.

5.2 Expectation

In Chap. 1 we computed the mean of a sequence of numbers. The mean is one of the major practical concepts in statistics, and we will now look at the corresponding theoretical concept. The expectation E[X] of a random variable X is a theoretical quantity with the following property: If we make a large number of independent observations of X, the mean of these observations will approach E[X]. The expectation is hence an idealized quantity which we intuitively may think of as the mean of infinitely many observations. The rigorous definition reads as follows:

Definition 5.4 If X is a random variable with possible values $x_1, x_2, \ldots, x_m$, then

$$\mathrm{E}[X] = x_1 \cdot P(X = x_1) + x_2 \cdot P(X = x_2) + \cdots + x_m \cdot P(X = x_m).$$

We call E[X] the expectation of X, or the expected value when it is clear form context which random variable we are considering.

It is sometimes cumbersome to write the terms like this, and as an alternative we may use the summing symbol instead. Then the expression is

$$\mathrm{E}[X] = \sum_{i=1}^{m} x_i \cdot P(X = x_i).$$

Verbally we may express this as follows: We consider all the values that X can achieve, and multiply each such value by the probability that X has this particular value. The expected value is the sum of all such terms.

Example 5.9 Let X be the result from one toss of a dice. Find E[X].

Solution: Using the formula above, we find

$$\mathrm{E}[X] = 1 \cdot \frac{1}{6} + 2 \cdot \frac{1}{6} + 3 \cdot \frac{1}{6} + 4 \cdot \frac{1}{6} + 5 \cdot \frac{1}{6} + 6 \cdot \frac{1}{6} = 3.5.$$

Example 5.10 X is the number of items that a randomly selected customer buys in a special shop. We assume the following distribution:

$$P(X = 0) = 0.3, \quad P(X = 1) = 0.2, \quad P(X = 0) = 0.4, \quad P(X = 0) = 0.1.$$

Find E[X].

Solution:

$$\begin{aligned}
\mathrm{E}[X] &= 0 \cdot P(X = 0) + 1 \cdot P(X = 1) + 2 \cdot P(X = 2) + 3 \cdot P(X = 3) \\
&= 0 \cdot 0.3 + 1 \cdot 0.2 + 2 \cdot 0.4 + 3 \cdot 0.1 = 1.3.
\end{aligned}$$

Example 5.11 Let Ω be the outcome of two tosses of a fair dice, and let S be the sum of the two rolls. S has the values $2, 3, 4, 5, 6, 7, 8, 9, 10, 11, 12$, and

$$p(2) = \frac{1}{36}, p(3) = \frac{2}{36}, p(4) = \frac{3}{36}, p(5) = \frac{4}{36}, p(6) = \frac{5}{36}, p(7) = \frac{6}{36}, \quad (5.1)$$
$$p(8) = \frac{5}{36}, p(9) = \frac{4}{36}, p(10) = \frac{3}{36}, p(11) = \frac{2}{36}, p(12) = \frac{1}{36}.$$

Using the definition, we find

$$\mathrm{E}[S] = 2 \cdot \frac{1}{36} + 3 \cdot \frac{2}{36} + 4 \cdot \frac{3}{36} + \cdots + 12 \cdot \frac{1}{36} = 7.$$

We will, however, soon see that this was not an efficient way of computing the expectation. Using some general principles, we can avoid most of the work.

5.2.1 Computing Expectations

If X and Y are two random variables, and a and b are two constants, then the following rules may be used:

$$\mathrm{E}[X + Y] = \mathrm{E}[X] + \mathrm{E}[Y], \qquad \mathrm{E}[a] = a, \qquad \mathrm{E}[b \cdot X] = b \cdot \mathrm{E}[X].$$

The proofs of these rules are straightforward and we omit them. We see that the expectation of a sum is the sum of the expectations, and that the expectation of a constant is equal to the constant itself. The last rule says that constants may be moved outside the expectation. To see how to apply these rules, we return to Example 5.11. This time we define

$$X = \text{Result of the first toss}, \qquad Y = \text{Result of the second toss}.$$

It is easy to see (Example 5.9), that

$$\mathrm{E}[X] = \mathrm{E}[Y] = 3.5.$$

Since $S = X + Y$, we get

$$\mathrm{E}[S] = \mathrm{E}[X + Y] = \mathrm{E}[X] + \mathrm{E}[Y] = 3.5 + 3.5 = 7.$$

Comparing the two methods, we see that the second method is much simpler.

5.2.2 General Expectations and Variance

Sometimes we need to compute the expectation of a function of a random variable. We may, e.g., consider the quantity Q we could sell of a certain good. From microeconomic theory it is well known that the price P is a function $P(Q)$. If Q is a random variable, we would like to find the expected price; $\mathrm{E}[P(Q)]$.

If X is a random variable and h is a function, then $Y = h(X)$ is a new random variable. The expectation of Y can be found as follows:

$$\mathrm{E}[h(X)] = h(x_1) \cdot P(X = x_1) + h(x_2) \cdot P(X = x_2) + \cdots + h(x_m) \cdot P(X = x_m).$$

This can be expressed as follows: We find the expectation of a function of a random variable when we compute the function value for any value that X can have and multiply the function value by the probability that X has this particular value. The expectation is the sum of all such terms.

Example 5.12 Let X be the result of one toss of a dice, and let $h(x) = x^2$. Then

$$\mathrm{E}[X^2] = 1^2 \cdot \frac{1}{6} + 2^2 \cdot \frac{1}{6} + 3^2 \cdot \frac{1}{6} + 4^2 \cdot \frac{1}{6} + 5^2 \cdot \frac{1}{6} + 6^2 \cdot \frac{1}{6} = \frac{91}{6}.$$

In Chap. 1 we introduced the sample variance, which is very useful in practical applications. We will now consider its theoretical analogue. Intuitively the theoretical variance is the sample variance we would have obtained if we could do infinitely many independent observations. The rigorous definition reads as follows:

Definition 5.5 The variance $\mathrm{Var}[X]$ of a random variable is defined via

$$\mathrm{Var}[X] = \mathrm{E}[(X - \mathrm{E}[X])^2].$$

We see that the variance is a measure of the deviation from the expected value; if all the values of the random variable are close to $\mathrm{E}[X]$, then all the values $(X - \mathrm{E}[X])^2$ are small positive numbers, and the variance will be small. Once the variance is defined, we can define the standard deviation just as in Chap. 1.

Definition 5.6 The standard deviation $\sigma[X]$ of a random variable is defined via

$$\sigma[X] = \sqrt{\text{Var}[X]}.$$

Example 5.13 We assume that X is a random variable with the values $2, 4, 6, 8$ and that the distribution is $p(2) = p(4) = p(6) = p(8) = \frac{1}{4}$. Then

$$\text{E}[X] = 2 \cdot \frac{1}{4} + 4 \cdot \frac{1}{4} + 6 \cdot \frac{1}{4} + 8 \cdot \frac{1}{4} = 5.$$

If we define $Y = X - \text{E}[X] = X - 5$, Y becomes a new random variable with the values $-3, -1, 1, 3$. We find the variance of X by

$$\text{Var}[X] = \text{E}[Y^2] = (-3)^2 \cdot \frac{1}{4} + (-1)^2 \cdot \frac{1}{4} + 1^2 \cdot \frac{1}{4} + 3^2 \cdot \frac{1}{4} = 5.$$

When we want to compute the variance, it may be convenient to rearrange the terms. If we do that properly, we can find the relation

$$\text{Var}[X] = \text{E}[X^2] - (\text{E}[X])^2$$

We are generally not very concerned with proofs, but this time we make an exception. The reason is that the proof makes use of some central techniques, and it is valuable to see how they are applied. The proof goes as follows:

$$\begin{aligned}
\text{Var}[X] &= \text{E}[(X - \text{E}[X])^2] = \text{E}[X^2 - 2X \cdot \text{E}[X] + (\text{E}[X])^2] \\
&= \text{E}[X^2] - 2\text{E}[X \cdot \text{E}[X]] + \text{E}[(\text{E}[X])^2] \\
&= \text{E}[X^2] - 2\text{E}[X] \cdot \text{E}|X] - (\text{E}[X])^2\, \text{E}[1] \\
&= \text{E}[X^2] - 2(\text{E}[X])^2 - (\text{E}[X])^2 = \text{E}[X^2] - (\text{E}[X])^2 .
\end{aligned}$$

In the first line we used that $(a-b)^2 = a^2 - 2ab + b^2$, in the second line we used $\text{E}[U + V + W] = \text{E}[U] + \text{E}[V] + \text{E}[W]$, and in the third line $k = \text{E}[X]$ is a constant, which gives $\text{E}[k \cdot U] = k \cdot \text{E}[U]$. In addition we used $\text{E}[1] = 1$.

We return to Example 5.13 to see how the computation looks like when we use this new technique. We have

$$\text{E}[X^2] = 2^2 \cdot \frac{1}{4} + 4^2 \cdot \frac{1}{4} + 6^2 \cdot \frac{1}{4} + 8^2 \cdot \frac{1}{4} = 30.$$

This gives

$$\text{Var}[X] = \text{E}[X^2] - (\text{E}[X])^2 = 30 - 5^2 = 5.$$

We see that the computation becomes a bit simpler since we need not consider the $Y - s$.

The variance has some basic properties which we list below:

- If $X = k$ is a constant, then $\text{Var}[X] = 0$.
- If $Y = X + k$ where k is a constant, then $\text{Var}[Y] = \text{Var}[X]$.
- If k is a constant, then $\text{Var}[k \cdot X] = k^2\text{Var}[X]$.
- $\text{Var}[X] \geq 0$.
- $\text{Var}[X] = \text{Var}[-X]$.

We omit the proofs of the first two properties, but take a brief look at the third. The reason why we want to highlight this is that students often make errors when they apply this principle. It is possible to move constants outside the variance, but then the constant needs to be squared.

$$\begin{aligned} \text{Var}[k \cdot X] &= \text{E}[(k \cdot X - \text{E}[k \cdot X])^2] = \text{E}[(k \cdot X - k \cdot \text{E}[X])^2] \\ &= \text{E}[(k \cdot (X - \text{E}[X]))^2] = \text{E}[k^2 \cdot (X - \text{E}[X])^2] \\ &= k^2 \cdot \text{E}[(X - \text{E}[X])^2] = k^2 \cdot \text{Var}[X]. \end{aligned} \tag{5.2}$$

Example 5.14

$$\text{Var}[10X] = 10^2\text{Var}[X] = 100\text{Var}[X].$$

5.3 Some Simple Facts About Option Pricing

Most people have heard about options, but some definitions may be appropriate. There are many different kinds of options, and we will only discuss a special case: a European call option. A European call option gives the right but not the obligation to buy a stock for a certain price at some specific point in time.

Example 5.15 Assume that we own a European call option which gives us the right to buy a stock for 100 USD one year from now. If the stock price is above 100 USD one year from now, we use the option to buy the stock. Afterwards we can sell the stock and make a profit. If the stock price is less than 100 USD, the option is worthless and we do not buy the stock.

Clearly it is possible to profit from an option, so a right of this sort can't be free. We consider a strongly simplified example.

Example 5.16 A stock costs today 100 USD. Tomorrow only two cases can occur. Either the stock rises to 140 USD or it will fall to 90 USD. The probability that the price rises is $p = 0.6$ and the probability that it falls is $q = 0.4$. A customer comes to a bank and wants to purchase 100 call options which gives the right to buy 100 stocks for 100 USD each tomorrow. The bank demands 800 USD for the options.

Initially we disregard transaction costs, and wish to answer the following questions:

- The customer buys 8 stocks for 800 USD. What is the expected value of the stock tomorrow?
- The customer uses 800 USD to buy 100 call options. What is the expected value of the call options tomorrow?

Solution: We let X be the stock price. The expected value of 8 stocks tomorrow is

$$\mathrm{E}[8X] = 8 \cdot \mathrm{E}[X] = 8 \cdot (140 \cdot 0.6 + 90 \cdot 0.4) = 960.$$

We see that the expected value of the stock increases from 800 USD to 960 USD, which is an increase of 20%.

We let Z denote the value of the options. If the stock price rises to 140 USD, we use the options to buy the stock for 100 USD each. This leaves us with a profit of 40 USD for each option. If the stock price falls, the options are worthless. The expected value of the options is

$$\mathrm{E}[Z] = 40 \cdot 100 \cdot 0.6 + 0 \cdot 100 \cdot 0.4 = 2400.$$

We see that the expected value of the investment increases from 800 USD to 2400 USD, which is an increase of 200%.

5.3.1 Hedging Portfolios

At a first glance the example above might appear speculative, and one could question if banks should be involved in such businesses. Is the bank gambling with our savings? The rather surprising answer is no, the bank has no risk writing this contract. The reason is that the bank can eliminate all risk if it make special investments. The strategy the bank applies is the following: Receive 800 USD from the customer, take up a loan of 7200 USD from a bank account, and use the 8000 USD to buy 80 stocks. What happens if the bank employs this strategy?

If the stock rises to 140 USD, the bank owns 80 stock with a total worth of 11,200 USD. It has a debt of 7200 USD and need to pay the customer 4000 USD for the 100 options the customer redeems. When all is settled, the bank breaks even. If the stock falls to 90 USD, the bank owns 80 stocks with a total worth of 7200 USD which just matches the debt. The options are worthless in this case, so the bank do not need to pay anything to the customer. We see that the bank breaks even in this case as well.

Note that p and q have no influence on the strategy, and the bank will break even no matter what values p and q have. To set up a strategy of this kind is called hedging, where the idea is that the bank protects (hedges) itself from risk.

The numbers above may appear as pure magic, but there is a simple mathematical explanation: The strategy has three unknowns, the price x that the customer need to pay for the option, then number y of stock the bank should buy, and z the amount of money the bank should lend from the bank account. To decide these three unknowns, we need three equations:

$$\begin{aligned} y \cdot 100 &= x + z \\ y \cdot 140 - z - (140 - 100) \cdot 100 &= 0 \\ y \cdot 90 - z &= 0. \end{aligned}$$

The first equation says that we use $x + z$ USD to buy y stocks, and the other two equations say that the bank breaks even when the contract is settled. In this case the solution of the system of equations is $x = 800, y = 80, z = 7200$. In the example we ignored interests on the bank account, but it poses no problem to take this into account. If the per day interest rate is $r\%$, we can modify the equations as follows:

$$\begin{aligned} y \cdot 100 &= x + z \\ y \cdot 140 - z \cdot (1 + r/100) - (140 - 100) \cdot 100 &= 0 \\ y \cdot 90 - z \cdot (1 + r/100) &= 0. \end{aligned}$$

Regardless of the value we put on r, it is straightforward to solve these equations.

Example 5.17 Here is a slightly more advanced example: A customer wants to buy 60 call options which gives the right to buy a stock for 100 USD two days from now. The time development of the stock is shown in Fig. 5.6. The following strategy turns out to solve the problem: The price of the options is 840 USD. The bank initially buys 54 stocks and lends 4560 USD on a bank account. If the stock price rises to 140 USD, the bank sells 4 stocks. If the stock price falls to 90 USD, the bank sells 39 stocks. If you take the time to check all the outcomes, you will see that the bank breaks even in all the four cases. We omit the computations, but the main point is that the system is described by 5 unknowns which are settled from 5 equations, see Problem 5.19.

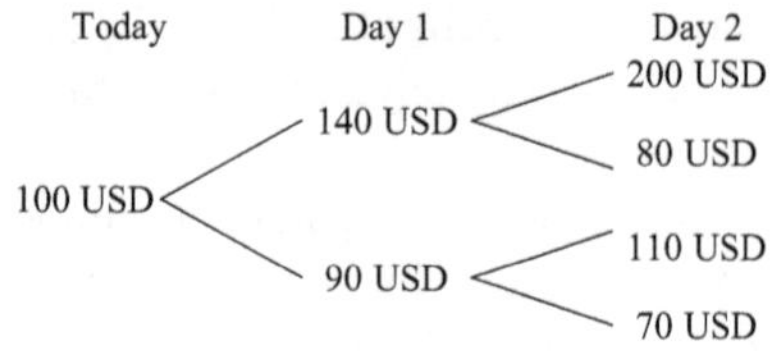

Fig. 5.6 Price evolution

Even though the examples above are simplified to the extreme, they still capture the main essence of the theory. In a real world stock market there is an unlimited number of possibilities for the stock price. Nevertheless it is often possible to construct trading strategies that eliminate all risk. R. C. Merton and M. S. Scholes were in 1997 awarded The Sveriges Riksbank Prize in Economic Sciences in Memory of Alfred Nobel (often wrongly referred to as the Nobel Prize in Economics) for the development of such models. Even though this theory is complicated beyond our imagination, what comes out of the theory is a quite simple procedure we will study closely in Chap. 7.

5.4 Summary of Chap. 5

- Random variable: Any function defined on the sample space which to each possible outcome defines a unique real number.
- The probability distribution of a random variable X:

$$P(x) = P(X = x).$$

- The cumulative distribution of a random variable X:

$$F(x) = P(X \leq x) = \sum_{x_i \leq x} P(X = x_i).$$

- The expectation of a discrete random variable X:

$$\mathrm{E}[X] = \sum_{x} x \cdot P(X = x).$$

- The expectation of a function of a discrete random variable X:

$$\mathrm{E}[h(X)] = \sum_{x} h(x) \cdot P(X = x).$$

- The variance of a discrete random variable X:

$$\mathrm{Var}[X] = \mathrm{E}[(X - \mathrm{E}[X])^2] = \mathrm{E}[X^2] - \mathrm{E}[X]^2.$$

- Computational rules for expectation and variance (a and b are constants):

$$\mathrm{E}[X+Y] = \mathrm{E}[X] + \mathrm{E}[Y], \qquad \mathrm{E}[a] = a, \qquad \mathrm{E}[b \cdot X] = b \cdot \mathrm{E}[X].$$

$$\mathrm{Var}[b \cdot X] = b^2 \mathrm{Var}[X].$$

5.5 Problems for Chap. 5

5.1 Which of the following quantities are random variables?

(i) The price of a stock in USD.
(ii) The number of units sold of a good.
(iii) The fraction of "Yes" in a poll.
(iv) The result of a soccer match.
(v) The fraction of stocks rising.
(vi) The number of defective items.

5.2 Assume that the stock price X in USD is a random variable with probability distribution

$$P(X = 95) = 20\%, \qquad P(X = 100) = 70\%, \qquad P(X = 110) = 10\%.$$

(a) Which values can the stock price have?
(b) We let $F(x)$ denote the cumulative distribution of X. Compute the following values:

$$F(90), \quad F(95), \quad F(100), \quad F(105), \quad F(110), \quad F(115).$$

5.3 The stock prices in the companies A, B, and C were all 100 USD. We used 200 USD to buy 2 stocks. The stocks were selected randomly.

(a) How many different outcomes are there? Find the probability of each such outcome.
(b) After we bought the stocks, the stock price of A was unchanged, the stock price on B rose to 104 USD, and the stock price of C rose to 102 USD. Let X denote the total value of our two stocks. Which values can X have? Find the probability distribution of X.
(c) Find the cumulative function $F(x)$ of X. How can we interpret $F(x)$ in this case?

5.4 A company has at most 6 days of delivery of a good. The fastest delivery time is 1 day, and the probabilities for the different delivery times are shown in Table 5.1. Let X be the number of days of delivery.

Table 5.1 Delivery times

Delivery time in days	1	2	3	4	5	6
Probability in %	55	20	10	5	5	5

Table 5.2 Stock prices

Company	A	B	C	D	E
Stock price in USD	100	200	400	300	500

Table 5.3 Number of units sold

Number of units sold	0	1	2	3
Probability	2.5%	5%	82.5%	10%

(a) Explain why X is a random variable.
(b) Find the cumulative distribution $F(x)$ of X. How can we interpret $F(x)$ in this case?
(c) Find the expected days of delivery $\mathrm{E}[X]$.

5.5 The number of defective items X in a random shipment of 100 items has the following distribution:

$$P(X = 0) = 65\%, \quad P(X = 1) = 25\%, \quad P(X = 1) = 5\%, \quad P(X = 3) = 5\%.$$

(a) What is the probability of 4 or more defective items?
(b) Find the expected number of defectives $\mathrm{E}[X]$.

5.6 Table 5.2 shows the stock price in 5 different companies. Company A has in all 140,000 stocks, company B has 50,000 stocks, company C has 20,000 stocks, company D has 10,000, and company E has 30,000. We pick a stock randomly from the 250,000 stocks, and let X be the price of the stock. Find the probability distribution of X and use it to compute the expected value $\mathrm{E}[X]$.

5.7 A customer comes to a shop, and we let X denote the number of items the customer buys of a certain good. The distribution of X is as follows:

$$P(X = 0) = 0.2, \quad P(X = 0) = 0.2, \quad P(X = 0) = 0.6.$$

Find the expected value $\mathrm{E}[X]$, the variance $\mathrm{Var}[X]$, and the standard deviation $\sigma[X]$.

5.8 Table 5.3 shows the number of units sold at a warehouse during a randomly selected week. Find the expected value $\mathrm{E}[X]$, the variance $\mathrm{Var}[X]$, and the standard deviation $\sigma[X]$.

5.9 Table 5.4 shows the number of days for delivery of an order.

Find the expected value $\mathrm{E}[X]$, the variance $\mathrm{Var}[X]$, and the standard deviation $\sigma[X]$.

Table 5.4 Delivery times

Number of days for delivery	1	2	3	4	5
Probability	10%	10%	60%	10%	10%

5.10 Let X_1, X_2, X_3 be random variable with $\mathrm{E}[X_1] = \mathrm{E}[X_2] = \mathrm{E}[X_2] = 25$.

(a) What is

$$\mathrm{E}[X_1 + X_2 + X_3]?$$

(b) Assume that p, q, r are constants such that $p + q + r = 1$. What is $\mathrm{E}[pX_1 + qX_2 + rX_3]$?

5.11 X is a random variable with $\mathrm{E}[X] = 100$ and $\mathrm{Var}[X] = 100$. Assume that p and q are constants such that $p + q = 1$. Define a new random variable Y by

$$Y = pX + q \cdot 100.$$

Find $\mathrm{E}[Y]$ and $\mathrm{Var}[Y]$. How should you choose p and q if you want that $\mathrm{Var}[Y]$ is as small as possible?

5.12 A stock cost today 100 USD. The company negotiates a new contract. If the contract is accepted, the stock price tomorrow will rise to 130 USD, if it fails the price tomorrow will fall to 90 USD. The probability that the contract is accepted is p.

(a) Assume that $p = 60\%$. What is the expected stock price tomorrow?
(b) How large must p be if the expected stock price tomorrow is at least 120 USD?

5.13 Queueing Theory: You wait in line outside an office that has just opened, and there are three people before you in the queue. Let X denote the processing time of a randomly selected client (in minutes), and assume that X has the distribution

$$P(X = 1) = 0.5, \quad P(X = 2) = 0.3, \quad P(X = 3) = 0.2.$$

We assume for simplicity that the processing time is an entire number of minutes and that the officials do not take breaks between clients. Let X_1, X_2, X_3 denote the processing time of the three first clients, and assume that these processing times are all independent.

(a) We first assume that the office only has one counter, and that you must wait until the three people before you have finished their business. The time you need to wait before you reach the counter Z is hence given by

$$Z = X_1 + X_2 + X_3.$$

Find the expected waiting time E[Z].

(b) Assume that the office only has one counter. What is the probability that the waiting time is less than or equal to 7 min.

(c) Assume instead the office has two counters, and that the clients draw queue tickets. Find the expected waiting time until you reach a counter.

5.14 Conditional Expectation: A bank make credit ratings of their customers. Previous data show that the bank has 75% good customers and 25% customers with payment difficulties. In a survey of the good customers it turned out that 10% of those were unmarried men with low income, while it was 50% unmarried men with low income among the customers with payment difficulties. We will assume that these numbers apply for new customers.

(a) How large percentage of the customer group were unmarried men with low income? What is the probability that an unmarried man with low income will have payment difficulties?

(b) Assume that the bank makes a profit of 6000 USD on good customers, but makes a 4000 USD loss on customers with payment difficulties. Is it profitable to offer new loans to young men with low income? Compute the expected profit on loans to this group.

5.15 Option Pricing: A stock cost today 100 USD. Tomorrow the price either rises to 120 USD or falls to 80 USD. A customer wants to buy 100 call options which gives the right to buy the stock for 100 USD tomorrow.

(a) What is the price for these call options, and how can the bank hedge against losses? We ignore interests and transaction costs.

(b) Let p denote the probability that the stock price rises. How large must p be such that the expected value of the options is as least as big as the price for them?

5.16 Option Pricing: A stock cost today 100 USD. Tomorrow the price either rises to 110 USD or falls to 70 USD. A customer wants to buy 100 call options which gives the right to buy the stock for 100 USD tomorrow.

(a) What is the price for these call options, and how can the bank hedge against losses? We ignore interests and transaction costs.

(b) Let p denote the probability that the stock price rises. How large must p be such that the expected value of the options is as least as big as the price for them?

5.17 Option Pricing: A stock costs today 300 USD. In a year the price can either rise to 330 USD or fall to 280 USD. A customer wants to buy 100 call options which gives the right to buy the stock for 100 USD one year from now. The bank interest rate is 5%. What must the customer pay for the options, and how can the bank hedge against losses? We ignore transaction costs.

5.18 Conditional Expectation: A stock has today the value $X_0 = 100$ (USD). Tomorrow it is 50% probable that the stock rises to $X_1 = 110$ (USD), while it is 50% probable that it falls to $X_1 = 95$ (USD). If $X_1 = 110$ (USD), there is 60% probability that $X_2 = 120$ (USD), and 40% probability that $X_2 = 100$ (USD). If $X_1 = 95$, there is 20% probability that $X_2 = 100$ (USD), and 80% probability that $X_2 = 80$ (USD). X_2 is the price the day after tomorrow.

(a) Draw a tree showing the price development for the stock, and use the results to compute $\mathrm{E}[X_2]$. Is this stock a good investment?
(b) A stock holder which has all his wealth in this stock owns 1000 stocks at time $t = 0$. She has decided to use the following trading strategy:
   - If the stock rises to 110 USD at time $t = 1$, she keeps all the stocks.
   - If the stock falls to 95 USD at time $t = 1$, she will sell half of the stocks and put the money in a bank account.

Let V denote the total wealth of the stock holder at $t = 2$, i.e., the value of the stocks plus any bank deposits. Since money is only deposited one day in the bank, we ignore interests. Find the expected wealth $\mathrm{E}[V]$. Can you find an alternative trading strategy which provides even larger expected wealth? Justify our answer.

5.19 Option Pricing, Two Time Periods: The time development of a stock is displayed in Fig. 5.7. A customer wants to buy 60 call options which gives the right to buy the stock for 100 USD in two days. We ignore interests and transactions costs. We let x denote the price the customer needs to pay for the 60 options, y the number of stocks the bank needs to purchase to set up a perfect hedge, and z the amount of money the bank needs to lend from a bank account to set up the hedge. Furthermore, u is the number of stocks the bank sells at day 1 if the stock rises the first day, and v is the number of stocks the bank sells if the stock falls the first day.

(a) Explain that x, y, z, u, v satisfy the equations

$$100y = x + z$$

$$200(y - u) + 140u - z - 6000 = 0$$

$$80(y - u) + 140u - z = 0$$

$$110(y - v) + 90v - z - 600 = 0$$

$$70(y - v) + 90v - z = 0.$$

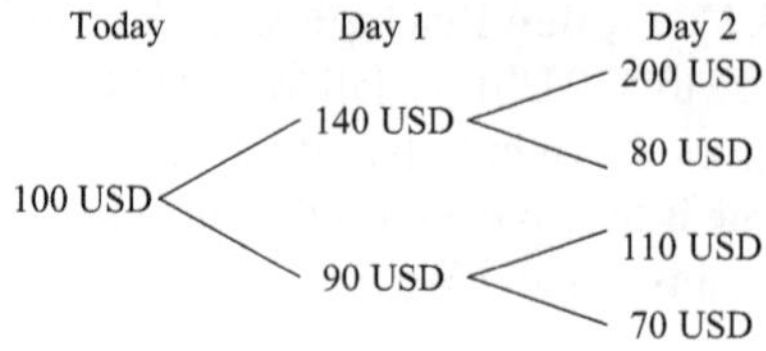

Fig. 5.7 Price evolution

(b) Solve the system in (a).
(c) Assume that there is 60% probability that the stock rises the first day, 50% probability that the stock rises on day 2 if it rose on day 1, and that there is 25% probability that the price rises on day 2 if it fell on day 1. Find the expected value of the 60 options.

5.20 Bounded Rationality: A buyer with limited information about the market can choose between 5 different, but equally useful objects. That they are equally useful means that the buyer has the same utility of any of the objects. Assume that the costs of buying the objects are

$$c_1 = 20, \quad c_2 = 25, \quad c_3 = 22, \quad c_4 = 18, \quad c_5 = 30.$$

A fully rational buyer will of course always buy object number 4, but our buyer is not fully informed about the costs. A commonly used model for limited information is the multinomial logit model. This model can be formulated as follows:

$$\text{The probability of buying object } i = \frac{e^{-\beta c_i}}{\sum_{j=1}^{5} e^{-\beta c_j}}.$$

Here $\beta \geq 0$ is a parameter measuring the amount of information about the market.

(a) Assume that $\beta = 0$. What kind of distribution does this lead to? What is the expected cost in this case?
(b) Assume that $\beta = 0.5$, and compute the probabilities for buying the different goods. What is the expected cost? Assume that 4 buyers are trading independently. What is the probability that at least one of them does not buy the cheapest good? What happens to this probability when β increases?
(c) Assume that $\beta \to +\infty$. What kind of distribution do we get in the limit? What is the expected cost if we use this distribution?

5.21 Bounded Rationality/Discrete Choice: We want to study a group of n agents where each agent can make four different choices. Assume that the four choices have utility values $u_1 = 3$, $u_2 = 8$, $u_3 = 2$, and $u_4 = 4$. The agents are not fully informed and do not always choose the best alternative (number 2). Let p_1, p_2, p_3, p_4 be the probabilities for the four different choices.

(a) Assume that $n = 5$, that

$$p_1 = 0.1, \qquad p_2 = 0.4, \qquad p_3 = 0.2, \qquad p_4 = 0.3,$$

and that each agent makes his or her choice independent of the rest. Find the probability that agent 1 chooses alternative 1, agent 2 chooses 3, agent 3 chooses 2, agent 4 chooses 1, and agent 5 chooses 2. We call a specification of this sort a specific outcome.

When the n agents have made their choices, we can count the frequencies of each different outcome. Let f_1 be how many chose alternative 1, f_2 how many chose alternative 2, and so on. Explain that we, regardless of the value of n, can find the probability P of a specific outcome by

$$P = p_1^{f_1} \cdot p_2^{f_2} \cdot p_3^{f_3} \cdot p_4^{f_4}.$$

(b) We find the total utility U of a specific outcome from $U = f_1u_1 + f_2u_2 + f_3u_3 + f_4u_4$. A group of agents are called boundedly rational if the probability of a specific outcome with lower total utility is always smaller than the probability of a specific outcome with higher total utility. Find a counterexample proving that the agents in (a) are *not* boundedly rational.

5.22 Bounded Rationality/Discrete Choice: We want to study a group of n agents where each agent can make four different choices. Assume that the four choices have utility values $u_1 = -1$, $u_2 = 1$, $u_3 = 1$, and $u_4 = -1$. The agents are not fully informed and do not always choose the best alternatives (number 2 and 3). Let p_1, p_2, p_3, p_4 be the probabilities for the four different choices.

(a) Assume that $n = 5$, and that

$$p_1 = 0.1, \qquad p_2 = 0.4, \qquad p_3 = 0.4, \qquad p_4 = 0.1.$$

Show that for $i = 1, \ldots, 4$, then $p_i = \frac{2^{u_i}}{5}$.

(b) When the n agents have made their choices, we can count the frequencies of each different outcome. Let f_1 be how many chose alternative 1, f_2 how many chose alternative 2, and so on. Regardless of the value of n, we can find the probability P of a specific outcome by

$$P = p_1^{f_1} \cdot p_2^{f_2} \cdot p_3^{f_3} \cdot p_4^{f_4}.$$

Show that

$$P = \frac{2^{f_1u_1 + f_2u_2 + f_3u_3 + f_4u_4}}{5^n}.$$

(c) We find the total utility U of a specific outcome from $U = f_1u_1 + f_2u_2 + f_3u_3 + f_4u_4$. A group of agents are called boundedly rational if the probability of a specific outcome with lower total utility is always smaller than the probability of a specific outcome with higher total utility. Use the result in (b) to prove that the agents in (a) are boundedly rational.

5.23 Adjusting Independent Orders Is a Bad Idea: You want to sell a good, and the demand for the good is a random variable D. We assume that D can have the values $10, 20, 30, 40, 50$, and that the distribution is uniform. If you order X units, while the customers demand D units, you have a deviation

$$\Delta = |D - X|.$$

If, e.g., you have ordered 10 units too much or 10 units too little, the deviation $\Delta = 10$ in both cases.

(a) Show that the expected deviation is 20 if you order $X = 10$ units of the good.
(b) Repeat the calculation in (a) for the cases where you order $20, 30, 40, 50$ units. Which order minimizes the expected deviation?
(c) You are about to sell the goods in two periods, and adjust the orders for the second period from the observed demand in the first period. If, e.g., the demand in the first period turned out to be $D_1 = 20$, you order $X_2 = 20$ units for period number two. Assume that D_1 and D_2 are independent. Use the splitting principle to compute $P(\Delta_2 = 10)$.
(d) Use similar expressions to compute the probability distribution of Δ_2, and use this to find the expected deviation in period 2. Is this a strategy reducing the deviation? What assumption must be changed for this to be a good idea?

6 Joint Distributions

Abstract
In this chapter we will look at situations that occur when we study two discrete random variables at the same time. One example of that sort could be that X is the price of a stock, while Y is the number of that stock that is sold each day. In many cases there can be more or less strong relations between the two variables, and it is important to be able to decide to what extent such relations are present. The theory has much in common with the theory in Chap. 1. In this case we need to take into account that different outcomes are not in general equally probable.

6.1 Simultaneous Distributions

When we study two random variables X and Y, we first make a list of all the possible values X and Y can have. The next step is to consider all the possible combinations that can occur, and to figure out the probability of each such combination.

Example 6.1 Let X be the price in USD on a good and let Y be the number of units we sell of the good. We assume that the price is 10 USD, 11 USD, and 12 USD, and that we can sell between 0 and 10 units of the good. Here there are in all 33 possible combinations. To make an overview of the interaction between the two variables, we have to make a table defining the probability of all these 33 different combinations.

J. Ubøe, *Introductory Statistics for Business and Economics*, Springer Texts in Business and Economics, https://doi.org/10.1007/978-3-319-70936-9_6

A table providing explicit values for each of the 33 combinations in Example 6.1, we call a joint distribution. The mathematical definition reads as follows:

Definition 6.1 By the joint distribution of two random variables X and Y, we mean the function

$$P(x, y) = P(X = x, Y = y).$$

The only thing this means is that we need to specify the possibility of all possible pairs of x and y. In Example 6.1 it would be possible to get arbitrary many different tables depending on the situation we want to model. We can, e.g., assume that all combinations are equally probable, i.e., a uniform distribution. In the real world it is usually reasonable to assume that the distribution of demand will change when we change the price, and a uniform distribution is not realistic in this case.

Example 6.2 In a town there are two different firms with about the same number of customers. We refer to these firms as Firm 1 and Firm 2. We let X denote which firm is chosen by a randomly selected customer, and let Y denote the number of days it takes to process an order. Based on a large number of previously recorded observations, the joint distribution is provided in Table 6.1.

From the numbers in Table 6.1 we can easily find the distribution of X and Y separately. For any value of x, we must have

$$P(X = x) = P(X = x, Y = 1) + P(X = x, Y = 2) + P(X = x, Y = 3).$$

The different values are hence found adding the numbers in each row. The end result is:

$$P_X(1) = 50\%, \qquad P_X(2) = 50\%.$$

Here we add X as a subscript to emphasize that it is the probability distribution of X we talk about. If we instead add the numbers in each column, we get the distribution of Y, i.e.:

$$P_Y(1) = 30\%, \quad P_Y(2) = 20\%, \quad P_Y(3) = 50\%.$$

Table 6.1 Number of days for delivery

Firm/Number of days for delivery	$Y = 1$	$Y = 2$	$Y = 3$
$X = 1$	10%	10%	30%
$X = 2$	20%	10%	20%

Table 6.2 Marginal distributions

Firm/Number of days for delivery	$Y = 1$	$Y = 2$	$Y = 3$	$P(X = x)$
$X = 1$	10%	10%	30%	50%
$X = 2$	20%	10%	20%	50%
$P(Y = y)$	30%	20%	50%	

We often call these distributions the marginal distributions of X and Y, respectively. It is often convenient to include the marginals in the table of the joint distribution, see Table 6.2.

When we discussed combinatorics in Chap. 3, it was crucial to identify if the choices were connected or not. Equally central in the theory of joint distributions is the independence of random variables. For each value of x, the statement $X = x$ defines an event, namely

$$\{\omega | X(\omega) = x\}.$$

Correspondingly the statement $Y = y$ defines an event for each value of y.

Definition 6.2 We say that two random variables X and Y are independent if and only if the events implied by $X = x$ and $Y = y$ are independent for any x and y. When this happens

$$P(X = x, Y = y) = P(X = x) \cdot P(Y = y).$$

If the probability distributions of X and Y are known, the joint distribution is given by the product, i.e.

$$P(x, y) = P_X(x) \cdot P_Y(y),$$

when X and Y are independent.

Looking at the marginal distributions of X and Y in Example 6.2, we easily see that these random variables are not independent. For example, we see that

$$P(1, 1) = 0.1 \neq 0.15 = 0.5 \cdot 0.3 = P_X(1) \cdot P_Y(1).$$

In general we find the marginal distributions as follows: When X has the different values $x_1, \ldots, x_L$ and Y has the different values $y_1, \ldots, y_M$, then

$$p_X(x) = p(x, y_1) + p(x, y_2) + \cdots + p(x, y_M),$$

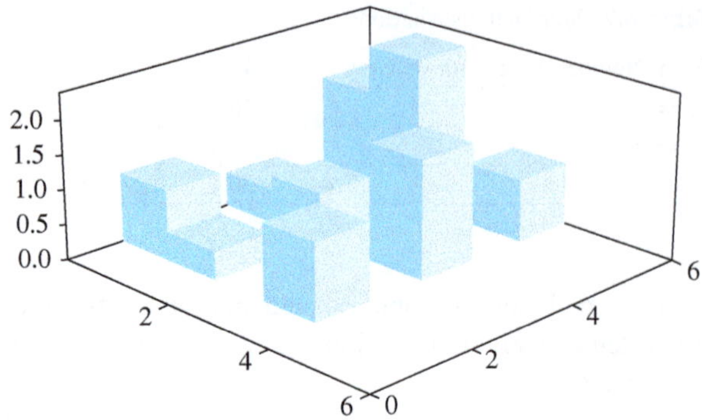

Fig. 6.1 The joint distribution in Example 6.2

Table 6.3 The joint distribution in Example 6.3

X/Y	$Y = 2$	$Y = 4$	$Y = 6$	$P(X = x)$
$X = 1$	10%	5%	15%	30%
$X = 2$	4%	7%	22%	33%
$X = 4$	11%	17%	9%	37%
$P(Y = y)$	25%	29%	46%	

and

$$p_Y(y) = p(x_1, y) + p(x_2, y) + \cdots + p(x_L, y).$$

This may seem complicated, but the content is simple; we find the marginal distributions when we sum the rows or the columns in the joint distribution (Fig. 6.1).

Example 6.3 We have two random variables X and Y where X can have the values $1, 2, 4$, while Y can have the values $2, 4, 6$. Assume that the joint distribution is as in Table 6.3.

The marginal distribution of X we find when we add the numbers in the rows, i.e.

$$P_X(1) = 30\%, P_X(2) = 33\%, P_X(4) = 37\%.$$

The marginal distribution of Y we find when we add the numbers in the columns, i.e.

$$P_Y(1) = 25\%, P_Y(2) = 29\%, P_Y(4) = 46\%.$$

When the joint distribution is known, we can in principle compute the expectation of any function of the two random variables. The expression below may seem very complicated, but the main principle is no different from what we have been using before. We compute all the values that can occur and multiply these values by the probability that they occur.

Definition 6.3 The expectation of a function of two random variables X and Y we find by

$$\begin{aligned}
&\mathrm{E}[h(X,Y)]\\
=\ & h(x_1,y_1)P(x_1,y_1)+h(x_1,y_2)P(x_1,y_2)+\cdots+h(x_1,y_M)P(x_1,y_M)\\
+\ & h(x_2,y_1)P(x_2,y_1)+h(x_2,y_2)P(x_2,y_2)+\cdots+h(x_2,y_M)P(x_1,y_M)\\
&\vdots\\
+\ & h(x_L,y_1)P(x_L,y_1)+h(x_L,y_2)P(x_L,y_2)+\cdots+h(x_L,y_M)P(x_L,y_M).
\end{aligned}$$

Example 6.4 Assume that X can have the values 0 and 1, that Y can have the values 1 and 2, and that the joint distribution is

$$P(0,1)=0.3, \qquad P(0,2)=0.1,$$
$$P(1,1)=0.2, \qquad P(1,2)=0.4.$$

Compute $\mathrm{E}[h(X,Y)]$ when $h(x,y)=(x+1)(y+5y^2)$.

Solution: We compute the four different values that can occur to get

$$\begin{aligned}
\mathrm{E}[h(X,Y)] &= (0+1)(1+5\cdot1^2)\cdot0.3+(0+1)(2+5\cdot2^2)\cdot0.1 \\
&\quad +(1+1)(1+5\cdot1^2)\cdot0.2+(1+1)(2+5\cdot2^2)\cdot0.4\\
&= 24.
\end{aligned} \tag{6.1}$$

An important case occurs when X and Y are independent. In that case

$$\mathrm{E}[X\cdot Y]=\mathrm{E}[X]\cdot\mathrm{E}[Y].$$

The proof for this is not terribly important, but is sufficiently short to be included:

$$\begin{aligned}
&\mathrm{E}[X\cdot Y]\\
=\ &\sum_{i=1}^{L}\sum_{j=1}^{M}x_i\cdot y_j\cdot P(x_i,y_j)=\sum_{i=1}^{L}\sum_{j=1}^{M}x_i\cdot y_j\cdot P_X(x_i)\cdot P_Y(y_j)\\
=\ &\sum_{i=1}^{L}x_i\cdot P_X(x_i)\cdot\sum_{j=1}^{M}y_j\cdot P_Y(y_j)=\mathrm{E}[X]\cdot\mathrm{E}[Y].
\end{aligned}$$

As these definitions are hard to digest for most people, we will look at a transparent example to see how they are used in practice.

Example 6.5 We let

$$X = \text{The number of stocks in a firm traded during a day,}$$
$$Y = \text{The stock price in USD.}$$

The daily trading volume we find when we multiply X and Y. If, e.g., one day we have $X = 80{,}000$ and $Y = 100$, the daily trading volume is 8,000,000 (USD). The daily trading volume is simply the total value of the stocks traded during a day. If X and Y are independent with $\mathrm{E}[X] = 100{,}000$, $\mathrm{E}[Y] = 100$, then the expected trading volume is

$$\mathrm{E}[X \cdot Y] = \mathrm{E}[X] \cdot \mathrm{E}[Y] = 10{,}000{,}000.$$

In most cases, however, it is not reasonable to assume that these quantities are independent. We will consider an example of this sort, and assume that the joint distribution is as in Table 6.4.

We first compute the marginal distributions of X and Y, and find

$$P(X = 80{,}000) = \frac{1}{12} + \frac{1}{6} + \frac{3}{12} = \frac{1}{2},$$
$$P(X = 120{,}000) = \frac{3}{12} + \frac{1}{6} + \frac{1}{12} = \frac{1}{2},$$
$$P(Y = 70) = \frac{1}{12} + \frac{3}{12} = \frac{1}{3},$$
$$P(Y = 100) = \frac{1}{6} + \frac{1}{6} = \frac{1}{3},$$
$$P(Y = 130) = \frac{3}{12} + \frac{1}{12} = \frac{1}{3}.$$

From these we find

$$\mathrm{E}[X] = 80{,}000 \cdot \tfrac{1}{2} + 120{,}000 \cdot \tfrac{1}{2} = 100{,}000.$$
$$\mathrm{E}[Y] = 70 \cdot \tfrac{1}{3} + 100 \cdot \tfrac{1}{3} + 130{,}000 \cdot \tfrac{1}{3} = 100.$$

Table 6.4 A joint distribution of trades and prices

Number of stocks traded/Stock price in USD	70	100	130
80,000	$\frac{1}{12}$	$\frac{1}{6}$	$\frac{3}{12}$
120,000	$\frac{3}{12}$	$\frac{1}{6}$	$\frac{1}{12}$

If we want to compute the expected trading volume, however, we need to take all the six cases into account.

$$\begin{aligned} E[X \cdot Y] = &\ 80{,}000 \cdot 70 \cdot \frac{1}{12} + 80{,}000 \cdot 100 \cdot \frac{1}{6} + 80{,}000 \cdot 130 \cdot \frac{3}{12} \\ &+ 100{,}000 \cdot 70 \cdot \frac{3}{12} + 100{,}000 \cdot 100 \cdot \frac{1}{6} + 100{,}000 \cdot 130 \cdot \frac{1}{12} \\ &= 9{,}800{,}000. \end{aligned}$$

We see that $E[X \cdot Y] = 9{,}800{,}000 \neq 10{,}000{,}000 = E[X] \cdot E[Y]$. We are hence able to conclude that X and Y are *not* independent. Where did the 200,000 USD "disappear"? Of course nothing has disappeared here, but it is nevertheless possible to explain the difference in more detail, see the next section.

6.2 Covariance

To measure the amount of covariation, we need a new definition:

By the covariance between two random variables X and Y we mean

$$\mathrm{Cov}[X, Y] = E[(X - E[X])(Y - E[Y])].$$

The purpose of the covariance is to provide a measure of the tendency that X and Y move in the same direction. To compute the covariance we need to compute all the values that $(X-E[X])(Y-E[Y])$ can have, multiply with the respective probabilities, and add all those values. Using the values from Example 6.5, we get

$$\begin{aligned} &E[(X - E[X]) \cdot (Y - E[Y])] \\ &= (-20{,}000) \cdot (-30) \cdot \frac{1}{12} + (-20{,}000) \cdot 0 \cdot \frac{1}{6} + (-20{,}000) \cdot 30 \cdot \frac{3}{12} \\ &+ 20{,}000 \cdot (-30) \cdot \frac{3}{12} + 20{,}000 \cdot 0 \cdot \frac{1}{6} + 20{,}000 \cdot 30 \cdot \frac{1}{12} \\ &= -200{,}000. \end{aligned}$$

The covariance between two random variables is interpreted in the same way as the covariance between two samples. If the covariance is positive, it is mostly the case that small values of X are found together with small values of Y, and when X is large, Y is usually large as well. Broadly speaking, the two variables pull in the same directions. The opposite happens when the covariance is negative, then the variables pull in the opposite direction. To getter a better understanding of the degree of covariation, we use the coefficient of variation, which is defined as follows:

Definition 6.4 The coefficient of variation $\rho[X, Y]$ between two random variables X and Y is defined by

$$\rho[X, Y] = \frac{\mathrm{Cov}[X, Y]}{\sqrt{\mathrm{Var}[X]} \cdot \sqrt{\mathrm{Var}[Y]}}.$$

The coefficient of variation is always a real number between -1 and 1, and the extremes define the maximum amount of negative and positive covariation. If $\mathrm{Cov}[X, Y] = 0$, we say that X and Y are uncorrelated.

If we compute the coefficient of variation using the values in Example 6.5, we get $\mathrm{Cov}[X, Y] \approx -0.41$. In this case we have a clear, but not extreme amount of negative covariation.

6.2.1 An Alternative Formula for the Covariance

When we worked with the variance, we showed that terms could be rearranged to simplify computations. In fact, the same argument can be used to rewrite the expression for the covariance. We omit the details, but the end result reads as follows:

$$\mathrm{Cov}[X, Y] = \mathrm{E}[X \cdot Y] - \mathrm{E}[X] \cdot \mathrm{E}[Y].$$

Using the formula above, we can see in detail how the results in Example 6.5 are related. In that example we found $\mathrm{E}[X \cdot Y] = 9{,}800{,}000$, and $\mathrm{E}[X] \cdot \mathrm{E}[Y] = 10{,}000{,}000$. The difference between the two quantities is precisely the covariance, which is $-200{,}000$.

When X and Y are independent, we know that $\mathrm{E}[X \cdot Y] = \mathrm{E}[X] \cdot \mathrm{E}[Y]$. From the formula above, we see that such random variables are uncorrelated, i.e., $\mathrm{Cov}[X, Y] = 0$. It is of some importance to notice that two random variables can be uncorrelated even in cases where they are *not* independent. Students often tend to think that $\mathrm{Cov}[X, Y] = 0$ implies independence, but this is not true in general.

6.2.2 Sums of Random Variables

The principles we just discussed are also useful when we want to consider sums of random variables. When we add such variables, the covariance pops up in the formula for the variance:

$$\mathrm{Var}[X+Y] = \mathrm{Var}[X] + \mathrm{Var}[Y] + 2\mathrm{Cov}[X,Y].$$

A quick look at the proof is of some value here, since it makes it easier to remember why we need to add the covariance in the formula.

$$\begin{aligned}
\mathrm{Var}[X+Y] &= \mathrm{E}[(X+Y-\mathrm{E}[X+Y])^2] \\
&= \mathrm{E}[(X-\mathrm{E}[X]+Y-\mathrm{E}[Y])^2] \\
&= \mathrm{E}[(X-\mathrm{E}[X])^2 + 2(X-\mathrm{E}[X])(Y-\mathrm{E}[Y]) + (Y-\mathrm{E}[Y])^2] \\
&= \mathrm{Var}[X] + 2\mathrm{Cov}[X,Y] + \mathrm{Var}[Y].
\end{aligned}$$

From the proof we see that this principle follows directly from the common rules we use to square binomials. A particular feature of this addition rule is that it can be generalized to sums of more than two variables. We omit the proof, but the final result reads as follows:

$$\mathrm{Var}[\sum_{i=1}^{n} X_i] = \sum_{i=1}^{n} \mathrm{Var}[X_i] + \sum_{\substack{i\neq j\\ i,j=1}}^{n} \mathrm{Cov}[X_i, X_j].$$

Of particular importance is the case where $X_1, X_2, \ldots, X_n$ are all independent. Then all the covariances equal zero, and we get the following result:

When $X_1, X_2, \ldots, X_n$ are all independent, then

$$\mathrm{Var}[\sum_{i=1}^{n} X_i] = \sum_{i=1}^{n} \mathrm{Var}[X_i].$$

When the variables are independent, it is hence the case that the variance of the sum equals the sum of the variances. This is a central result in statistics which we will use repeatedly throughout the book.

6.3 Summary of Chap. 6

- The joint distribution of two random variables

$$P(x, y) = P(X = x, Y = y).$$

- The marginal distribution of X: $P_X(x) = P(X = x) = \sum_y P(x, y)$.
- The marginal distribution of Y: $P_Y(y) = P(Y = y) = \sum_x P(x, y)$.
- The expectation of a function of two random variables

$$\mathrm{E}[h(X, Y)] = \sum_{x,y} h(x, y)P(x, y).$$

- The covariance of X and Y:

$$\mathrm{Cov}[X, Y] = \mathrm{E}[(X - \mathrm{E}[X])(Y - \mathrm{E}[Y])] = \mathrm{E}[X \cdot Y] - \mathrm{E}[X] \cdot \mathrm{E}[Y].$$

- When X and Y are independent, then

$$P(x, y) = P_X(x) \cdot P_Y(y), \qquad \mathrm{Cov}[X, Y] = 0, \qquad \mathrm{Var}[X + Y] = \mathrm{Var}[X] + \mathrm{Var}[Y].$$

- For all random variables X and Y

$$\mathrm{Var}[X + Y] = \mathrm{Var}[X] + \mathrm{Var}[Y] + 2\mathrm{Cov}[X, Y].$$

- The coefficient of variation

$$\rho[X, Y] = \frac{\mathrm{Cov}[X, Y]}{\sqrt{\mathrm{Var}[X]} \cdot \sqrt{\mathrm{Var}[Y]}} \in [-1, 1].$$

6.4 Problems for Chap. 6

6.1 Table 6.5 shows the probability that a randomly selected person has a given number of credit cards, and use the cards a given number of times per week.

We let X denote the number of credits cards (1–3) and Y the number of uses per week (0–4).

Table 6.5 Joint distribution of uses and number of credit cards

Number of credit cards/Number of uses per week	0	1	2	3	4
1	3%	7%	6%	9%	3%
2	2%	6%	5%	15%	9%
3	2%	3%	8%	10%	12%

(a) Find the marginal distributions of X and Y.
(b) What is the probability that a randomly selected person has more than one credit card?
(c) What is the probability that a randomly selected person uses her cards at least twice per week?

6.2 Table 6.6 shows how often two stores sell a good for the prices 9.0 USD, 9.1 USD, or 9.2 USD.

We let X denote the price at store A, and Y denote the price at store B.

(a) Find the marginal distributions of X and Y.
(b) What is the probability that the stores sell the goods for the same price?
(c) Find E[X] and E[Y].

6.3 We consider the stock price for two different companies A and B, and let X denote the stock price for company A and Y the stock price for company B. The joint distribution is shown in Table 6.7.

(a) Find the marginal distributions of X and Y.
(b) Are X and Y independent?
(c) Find E[X] and E[Y].

6.4 A shop sells a good. We let X denote the number of units bought by a randomly selected customer, and let Y denote the price of the good. The joint distribution is shown in Table 6.8.

Table 6.6 The joint distribution in Problem 6.2

Store A/Store B	9 USD	9.1 USD	9.2 USD
9.0 USD	27%	4%	2%
9.1 USD	5%	22%	6%
9.2 USD	3%	8%	23%

Table 6.7 The joint distribution in Problem 6.3

Stock prices for company B	Stock prices for company A	
	80 USD	120 USD
80 USD	10%	20%
120 USD	30%	40%

Table 6.8 The joint distribution in Problem 6.4

Number of units bought/Price	100 USD	240 USD
0	5%	35%
1	10%	20%
2	20%	10%

Table 6.9 The joint distribution in Problem 6.5

Price for A	Price for B	
	34 USD	24 USD
20 USD	25%	15%
30 USD	45%	15%

Table 6.10 The joint distribution in Problem 6.6

Price/Number of units bought	100	80	50
20 USD	20%	0%	0%
24 USD	0%	50%	0%
30 USD	0%	0%	30%

(a) Find the marginal distributions of X and Y.
(b) Find $\mathrm{E}[X]$ and $\mathrm{E}[Y]$.
(c) Find $\mathrm{E}[X \cdot Y]$ and $\mathrm{Cov}[X, Y]$.

6.5 We consider the price of two goods, let X denote the price of good A, and let Y denote the price of good B. The joint distribution is shown in Table 6.9.

(a) Find the marginal distributions of X and Y.
(b) Find $\mathrm{E}[X], \mathrm{Var}[X], \mathrm{E}[Y], \mathrm{Var}[Y]$.
(c) Find $\mathrm{E}[X \cdot Y], \mathrm{Cov}[X, Y]$, and $\rho[X, Y]$.

6.6 Table 6.10 shows the relationship between price X and demand Y for a good.

(a) Find the marginal distributions of X and Y.
(b) Find $\mathrm{E}[X]$ and $\mathrm{E}[Y]$.
(c) Find $\mathrm{E}[X \cdot Y]$ and $\mathrm{Cov}[X, Y]$.
(d) Find the coefficient of variation $\rho[X, Y]$. How are X and Y related?

6.7 Let X_1, X_2, X_3, and X_4 be independent, random variables with

$$\mathrm{E}[X_1] = 100, \quad \mathrm{E}[X_2] = 120, \quad \mathrm{E}[X_3] = 90, \quad \mathrm{E}[X_4] = 115.$$

$$\mathrm{Var}[X_1] = 230, \quad \mathrm{Var}[X_2] = 170, \quad \mathrm{Var}[X_3] = 260, \quad \mathrm{Var}[X_4] = 240.$$

We define $Y = X_1 + X_2 + X_3 + X_4$.

(a) Find $\mathrm{E}[Y], \mathrm{Var}[Y]$ and $\sigma[Y]$.
(b) Compute $\mathrm{E}[X_1 \cdot Y]$ and $\mathrm{Cov}[X_1, Y]$. Are X_1 and Y independent?

6.8 Conditional Expectations: We let X denote the number of units we sell of a good, and Y the price of the good. The joint distribution is shown in Table 6.11.

Table 6.11 The joint distribution in Problem 6.8

Number of units bought/Price	10 USD	15 USD	20 USD
90	5%	10%	15%
150	10%	20%	10%
210	15%	10%	5%

Table 6.12 The joint distribution in Problem 6.9

Number of units bought/Price	$Y = 100$	$Y = 120$	$Y = 140$
$X = 110{,}000$	10%	25%	15%
$X = 150{,}000$	15%	25%	10%

(a) Find the marginal distributions of X and Y and use these to compute $\mathrm{E}[X]$ and $\mathrm{E}[Y]$.
(b) Find the expected trading volume $\mathrm{E}[X \cdot Y]$. Are X and Y independent random variables?
(c) The price is fixed at $Y = 10$ (USD). What is the expected trading volume conditional on this fixation? Also find the expected trading volumes conditional on $Y = 15$ and $Y = 20$. Is it possible to change the values in the joint distribution such that the expected trading volume conditional on $Y = 20$ is smaller than the corresponding value conditional on $Y = 15$?

6.9 Conditional Expectations: In this problem X denotes the number of stocks that is traded per day in a particular company, and Y is the price of the stock. We assume that X only can have the values 110,000 (low turnover) or 150,000 (high turnover), and that the stock price only can have the values 100 (low), 120 (medium), and 140 (high). In a particular market X and Y have the joint distribution given in Table 6.12.

(a) Find the marginal distributions of X and Y, and compute the values $\mathrm{E}[X]$ and $\mathrm{E}[Y]$.
(b) Compute the conditional probabilities $P(X = x|Y = y)$ and $P(Y = y|X = x)$ for all possible pairs of (x, y).
(c) The condition expectation $\mathrm{E}[U|V = v]$ of a random variable U given the value of another random variable V is found from the expression

$$\mathrm{E}[U|V = v] = \sum_u u \cdot P(U = u|V = v).$$

Find the three conditional expectations $\mathrm{E}[X|Y = 100], \mathrm{E}[X|Y = 120]$, $\mathrm{E}[X|Y = 140]$, and the conditional expectations $\mathrm{E}[Y|X = 110{,}000], \mathrm{E}[Y|X = 150{,}000]$.
(d) Are X and Y independent random variables? Try to offer a short verbal interpretation of this market based on the results from (c).

6.10 Dummy Variables: A company has three types of workers, A, B, and C. 30% are of type A, 40% are of type B, and 30% are of type C. A worker is selected randomly, and we define three random variables as follows:

$$X = \begin{cases} 1 & \text{if the worker is of type A} \\ 0 & \text{otherwise} \end{cases}$$

$$Y = \begin{cases} 1 & \text{if the worker is of type B} \\ 0 & \text{otherwise} \end{cases}$$

$$Z = \begin{cases} 1 & \text{if the worker is of type C} \\ 0 & \text{otherwise} \end{cases}.$$

(a) Find $\mathrm{E}[X], \mathrm{E}[Y], \mathrm{E}[Z], \mathrm{Var}[X], \mathrm{Var}[Y], \mathrm{Var}[Z]$.
(b) Find $\mathrm{E}[X \cdot Y]$, and use this value to compute $\mathrm{Cov}[X, Y]$. Are X and Y independent? Justify your answer. Find the joint distribution of X and Y.

6.11 Portfolio Management: The stocks in companies A and B both cost 100 USD today. We let X and Y denote the stock price in the two companies one year from now. We assume that X and Y are independent random variables with

$$\mathrm{E}[X] = 110, \mathrm{E}[Y] = 110, \mathrm{Var}[X] = 100, \mathrm{Var}[Y] = 400.$$

We want to invest 10 million USD in the two stocks. Let p denote the fraction invested in company A.

(a) Show that the total value Z of the stocks one year from now is

$$Z = 10^5 \cdot p \cdot X + 10^5 \cdot (1 - p) \cdot Y.$$

(b) Find $\mathrm{E}[Z]$ and $\mathrm{Var}[Z]$. How should you choose p if you want as little variation as possible in your investment?

6.12 Portfolio Management: We want to invest 10 million USD in three different companies, A, B, and C. All the stocks cost 100 USD each today. The stock price (in USD) one year from now is X in company A, Y in company B, and Z in company C. All the stocks have an expected price of 120 USD each one year from now. Assume that we invest $x\%$ in company A, $y\%$ in company B, and $z\%$ in company C. Short-selling is not allowed, hence $x \geq 0, y \geq 0, z \geq 0$.

(a) Explain why the total value V of the stocks one year from now is given by the expression

$$V = 1000x \cdot X + 1000y \cdot Y + 1000z \cdot Z.$$

and use this to find the expected total value of the stocks one year from now.

(b) Assume $\mathrm{Var}[X] = 100$, $\mathrm{Var}[Y] = 200$, and $\mathrm{Var}[Z] = 600$. In which stock should you place most of your funds if you want that the variance in the total value is as small as possible?

(c) Assume that the variances are as in (b) and that the stock prices are independent. Compute how much you should invest in each of the stocks if you want that the variance in the total value is as small as possible. Compare the final result with (b).

(d) Assume that the stock prices are dependent, and that

$$X = 120 + 10\epsilon, \qquad Y = 120 + 10\sqrt{2} \cdot \epsilon, \qquad Z = 120 + 10\sqrt{6} \cdot \epsilon,$$

where ϵ is a distribution with $\mathrm{E}[\epsilon] = 0$, $\mathrm{Var}[\epsilon] = 1$. Find $\mathrm{E}[X], \mathrm{E}[Y], \mathrm{E}[Z]$, and $\mathrm{Var}[X], \mathrm{Var}[Y], \mathrm{Var}[Z]$.

(e) Assume that stock prices are as in (d). Show that

$$V = 12{,}000{,}000 + 10{,}000(x + \sqrt{2}y + \sqrt{6}z)\epsilon.$$

Compute how much you should invest in each of the stocks if you want that the variance in the total value is as small as possible. Compare the result with the answers from (b) and (c).

Basic Probability Distributions

7

Abstract
In this chapter we will discuss some of the most commonly used probability distributions. We will discuss basic properties of these distributions; in particular, we will provide explicit formulas for the mean and variance. We focus the binomial distribution, the hyper geometric distribution, the Poisson distribution, and the normal distribution. The literature making use of these distributions is really huge. The normal distribution alone is applied in thousands of scientific papers yearly. A full treatment is hence impossible, so we limit our ambitions to a basic survival kit.

7.1 The Indicator Distribution

To be able to discuss properties of the other distributions, we start out with a description of the indicator distribution. This distribution is defined as follows:

$$I = \begin{cases} 1 & \text{with probability } p \\ 0 & \text{with probability } 1 - p. \end{cases}$$

All computer programming rely on series of 0 and 1, so we should not underestimate the usefulness of this simple distribution. As there are only two outcomes, we see that

$$\mathrm{E}[I] = 0 \cdot (1 - p) + 1 \cdot p = p,$$

and

$$\mathrm{Var}[I] = \mathrm{E}[I^2] - \mathrm{E}[I]^2 = 0^2 \cdot (1 - p) + 1^2 \cdot p - p^2 = p(1 - p).$$

J. Ubøe, *Introductory Statistics for Business and Economics*, Springer Texts in Business and Economics, https://doi.org/10.1007/978-3-319-70936-9_7

In applications it is sometimes useful to think about the outcome 1 as "YES" and 0 as "NO." The indicator is typically triggered by an event. i.e., the set of outcomes where the value is 1.

7.2 The Binomial Distribution

As we could see in Chap. 4, it is easy to compute probabilities when we have independent trials. These computations are particularly simple if there are only two possible outcomes. Such situations arise in several different contexts. We can check if an item is defective or not, we can check if a computation is correct or not, or if a student passed an exam or not. The possibilities are endless. In all these cases there are only two possible outcomes.

An experiment where a trial with 2 possible outcomes is repeated a certain number of times, where the trials are independent and the probability of the each outcome is constant, is called binomial trials. The criteria for binomial trials can be emphasized as follows:

- Each trial has two outcomes, s (success) or f (failure).
- The probability of success is a constant p in all trials.
- All trials are independent.
- The number of trials is a constant n.

Since the trials are independent, it is easy to compute the probability of any sequence of outcomes. Using the principles from Chap. 4, we see that, e.g.

$$P(ssfsff) = p \cdot p \cdot (1-p) \cdot p \cdot (1-p) \cdot (1-p) = p^3(1-p)^3.$$

A central question is the following: What is the probability of exactly x successes in n trials? To answer this, we must first figure out how many sequences there are with x successes. We first consider a simple example.

Example 7.1 We do 5 trials. How many outcomes have exactly 3 successes?

Solution: In this case the situation is so simple that we can write down all 10 possibilities:

$$sssff, ssfsf, ssffs, sfssf, sfsfs, sffss, fsssf, fssfs, fsfss, ffsss$$

To understand it better, we think about this as a combinatorial problem where we select the positions of each success. Each position can only be selected once, so the selection is without replacement. We choose 3 of the 5 positions. The selection of the positions is unordered. If we choose the numbers 4, 3, and 2, we have s in position 2, 3, and 4, i.e., the outcome $fsssf$. The order of the numbers 2, 3, and 4 does not matter. The number of different combinations is hence equal to the number of different outcomes when we select 3 out of 5 different elements, unordered without replacement. From the theory in Chap. 3, we know that there are $\binom{5}{3} = 10$ different outcomes. We see that this coincides with the number of combinations we wrote down.

The advantage with the combinatorial reasoning above is that it applies in general. The number of different sequences with x successes in n trials is $\binom{n}{x}$. Each of these specific sequences has the same probability: $p^x(1-p)^{n-x}$. Since the outcomes are disjoint, we can simply add the probabilities (we are using the addition principle from Chap. 2), and adding $\binom{n}{x}$ equal numbers with value $p^x(1-p)^{n-x}$ gives the result $\binom{n}{x}p^x(1-p)^{n-x}$. The argument can be summarized as follows:

$$P(x \text{ successes in } n \text{ independent trials}) = \binom{n}{x} p^x(1-p)^{n-x}.$$

The expression above is often called a binomial probability.

Example 7.2 We want to produce 100 watches. The probability that a watch is defective is 5%. We assume that the outcomes of the production are independent. What is the probability of exactly 5 defective watches?

Solution: This is a binomial trial, where "success" means that a watch is defective. The probability P of exactly 5 defectives is hence:

$$P = \binom{100}{5} \cdot 0.05^5 \cdot 0.95^{95} \approx 18\%.$$

If we move one step further, we may ask about the probability of at most 5 defective watches. The calculation is more elaborate, but the principle is simple; we compute the probabilities for exactly 0, 1, 2, 3, 4, and 5 defective watches separately. If we let X denote the number of defective watches, we get:

$$\begin{aligned}
P(X \leq 5) &= P(X=0) + P(X=1) + P(X=2) \\
&\quad + P(X=3) + P(X=4) + P(X=5) \\
&= \binom{100}{0} 0.05^0 \cdot 0.95^{100} + \binom{100}{1} 0.05^1 \cdot 0.95^{99} \\
&\quad + \binom{100}{2} 0.05^2 \cdot 0.95^{98} + \binom{100}{3} 0.05^3 \cdot 0.95^{97} \\
&\quad + \binom{100}{5} 0.05^5 \cdot 0.95^{95} \\
&\approx 61.6\%.
\end{aligned}$$

Binomial trials are applied in just about every possible connection where we count the number of successes in a series of independent trials. Here are some examples:

- The number of successes in n independent trials.
- The number of Yes in a poll.
- The number of defect items in a consignment.
- The number of students attending a lecture.

With a binomial distribution we mean a random variable X defined by

$$X = \text{The number of outcomes } s \text{ in } n \text{ binomial trials.}$$

It is usual to think about the outcome s as success and the outcome f as failure, X is then simply counting the number of successes in n trials. A distribution of this kind is also called binomial $(n.p)$, and we sometimes write

$$X = \text{Bin}[n, p].$$

The probability distribution is given by

$$P(X = x) = \binom{n}{x} p^x (1 - p)^{n-x}.$$

We now wish to compute the expectation and variance for the binomial distributions. Using the definition, we see that

$$\text{E}[X] = \sum_{x=0}^{n} x \cdot P(X = x) = \sum_{x=0}^{n} x \cdot \binom{n}{x} p^x (1 - p)^{n-x}.$$

This expression can be simplified by brute force using recursive formulas for the binomial coefficients. It is quite a challenge to get through along this route, but it is not necessary to resort to such excesses. We can instead proceed as follows: If we add n independent indicator distributions, the sum provides us with the total number of 1-s in n trials using the indicator distribution. If we interpret 1 as a success, the sum equals the number of successes. Hence if X is a binomial distribution:

$$X = I_1 + I_2 + \cdots + I_n,$$

where $I_1, I_2, \ldots, I_n$ are independent indicator distributions. From Chap. 6 we know that the expected value of a sum is the sum of the expected values of each term. Hence

$$\text{E}[X] = \text{E}[I_1] + \text{E}[I_2] + \cdots + \text{E}[I_n] = p + p + \cdots + p = n \cdot p.$$

Moreover, the theory from Chap. 6 says that the variance of a sum of independent distributions equals the sum of the variances of each term. This can be applied here to see that

$$\begin{aligned}\mathrm{Var}[X] &= \mathrm{Var}[I_1] + \mathrm{Var}[I_2] + \cdots + \mathrm{Var}[I_n] \\ &= p(1-p) + p(1-p) + \cdots + p(1-p) = n \cdot p(1-p). \qquad (7.1)\end{aligned}$$

The results can be summarized as follows:

If X is $\mathrm{Bin}[n, p]$, then

$$\mathrm{E}[X] = n \cdot p, \qquad \mathrm{Var}[X] = n \cdot p(1-p).$$

See Fig. 7.1 for a display of a binomial distribution with $n = 6, p = 0.4$.

Example 7.3 Let X denote the number of defective items in a shipment of 7600 items, and assume that the probability of an item being defective is $p = 5\%$. What is the distribution of X, and what is the expectation, variance, and standard deviation for this distribution?

Solution: If we interpret the outcome "defective" as a success s, this is a binomial distribution with $n = 7600, p = 0.05$. The formulas above give

$$\mathrm{E}[X] = n \cdot p = 7600 \cdot 0.05 = 380,$$
$$\mathrm{Var}[X] = n \cdot p(1-p) = 7600 \cdot 0.05 \cdot 0.95 = 361,$$

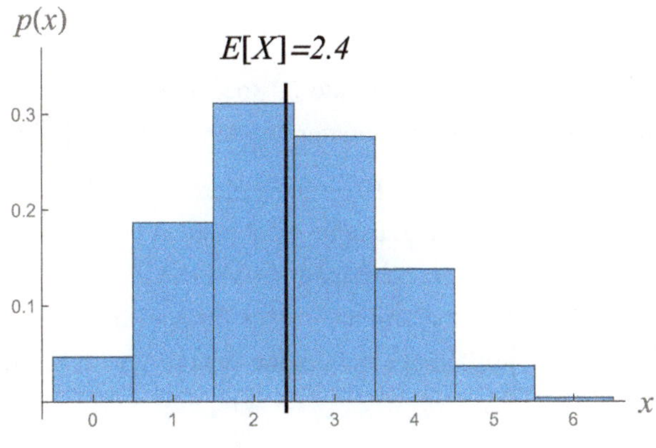

Fig. 7.1 Binomial distribution with $n = 6$ and $p = 0.4$

and

$$\sigma[X] = \sqrt{\text{Var}[X]} = \sqrt{361} = 19.$$

7.3 The Hypergeometric Distribution

Assume that we have 25 items and that 10 of these items are defective. If we randomly select an item, the probability of the item being defective is $\frac{10}{25}$. If, however, we select two items, the outcomes of the two selections are not independent. The probability of a defective second item depends on the first item we selected. If the first item was defective, the probability of the second item being defective is $\frac{9}{24}$, while this probability is $\frac{10}{24}$ if the first item was not defective. The conditions for binomial trials are not satisfied in this case.

Strictly speaking, the dilemma above arises in many different contexts. In general we can describe the context as follows: Assume that we have N elements in the population and that M of these elements is special, while the rest, i.e., $N-S$ elements are ordinary. From the population we randomly select a sample with n objects. The selection is unordered without replacement. We define a random variable X by

$$X = \text{The number of special elements in the sample.}$$

This random variable is called hypergeometric, and we will now derive its probability distribution. The foundations for this theory were established in Chap. 3, and the argument goes as follows: There is in total $\binom{N}{n}$ different unordered outcomes. A random selection means these outcomes are equally probable. The probability of each different outcome is hence $\frac{1}{\binom{N}{n}}$. How many of these outcomes gives $X = x$? To clarify this we consider a simple example.

Example 7.4 How many different combinations end up with $X = 3$ if $N = 30, M = 20$, and $n = 10$?

Solution: In total there are 20 special elements and we must select 3 of these. Since the order does not matter, we can do this in $\binom{20}{3}$ different ways. In addition we need to pick 7 of the 10 ordinary elements, and this can be done in $\binom{10}{7}$ different ways. All these choices can be combined with each other, and hence there are in all $\binom{20}{3} \cdot \binom{10}{7}$ different combinations where $X = 3$.

Exactly the same argument goes through in general. Hence there is a total of $\binom{M}{x} \cdot \binom{N-M}{n-x}$ different combinations where $X = x$. Since all these combinations are equally probable with probability $\frac{1}{\binom{N}{n}}$, the distribution of X is as follows:

$$P(X = x) = \frac{\binom{M}{x} \cdot \binom{N-M}{n-x}}{\binom{N}{n}}.$$

Any random variable with this probability distribution is called hypergeometric (N, M, n). For the example above we get

$$P(X = 3) = \frac{\binom{20}{3} \cdot \binom{10}{7}}{\binom{30}{10}}.$$

Example 7.5 We receive a shipment of 25 items where 10 items are defective. We sample 10 of the items, and let

$$X = \text{Number of defective items in the sample.}$$

Then X is hypergeometric $(25, 10, 10)$, and the distribution is

$$P(X = x) = \frac{\binom{10}{x} \cdot \binom{15}{10-x}}{\binom{25}{10}}.$$

For example we have

$$P(X = 1) = \frac{\binom{10}{1} \cdot \binom{15}{9}}{\binom{25}{10}} \approx 1.5\%,$$

and

$$P(X = 3) = \frac{\binom{10}{3} \cdot \binom{15}{7}}{\binom{25}{10}} \approx 23.6\%.$$

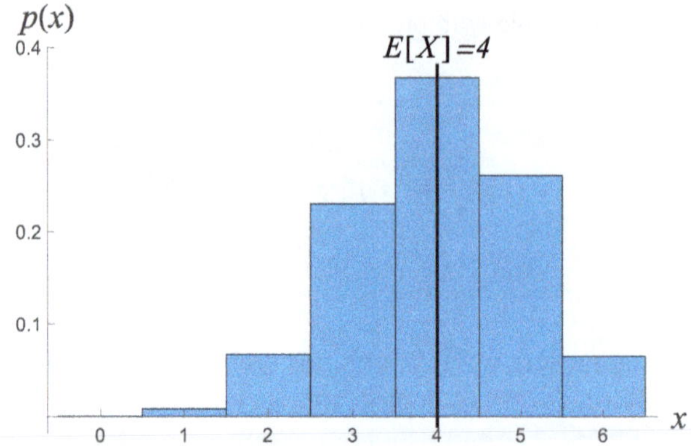

Fig. 7.2 A hypergeometric distribution with $N = 30, M = 20, n = 6$

We now know the formula for the hypergeometric distribution. An example of a hypergeometric distribution is shown in Fig. 7.2. From this formula it is possible to derive the formulas for the expected value and variance for this distribution. Since the details are tedious, we state the final results without proof:

If X is hypergeometric (N, M, n), then

$$\mathrm{E}[X] = n \cdot \frac{M}{N}, \qquad \mathrm{Var}[X] = \left(\frac{N-n}{N-1}\right) \cdot n \cdot \frac{M}{N} \cdot \left(1 - \frac{M}{N}\right).$$

When we conduct a survey where the answers are Yes/No, we do not ask the same person multiple times. The distribution is then hypergeometric. The population is all the people in the town/country, and the special elements are the people who will answer Yes to the question. In total we sample n observations. The selection is without replacement since we only ask each person once. In most such cases the sample is only a tiny fraction of the total population, and it is hence of interest to see what happens to the distribution when n is relatively small and N very big.

We define $p = \frac{M}{N}$ equal to the probability of selecting a special element the first time we select an element. If, e.g., $N = 100{,}000, M = 5000$, and $n = 10$, we find

$$\mathrm{E}[X] = n \cdot p,$$

$$\mathrm{Var}[X] = \left(\frac{100{,}000 - 10}{100{,}000 - 1}\right) \cdot n \cdot p \cdot (1-p) = 0.9999 \cdot n \cdot p \cdot (1-p)\,.$$

We see that these values are almost exactly the same as we get in a binomial distribution with the same n and p. This makes good sense. When N is very big, the odds of choosing a special element hardly change if we remove a moderate number of elements. In such cases we can use the binomial distribution, even if, strictly speaking, the true distribution is hypergeometric. The binomial distribution is simpler to handle, and we only use the hypergeometric distribution when n and N have the same order of magnitude. In general approximating a hypergeometric distribution by a binomial distribution is acceptable if $N \geq 20n$. Another advantage of using the binomial approximation is that we need not know the values on N and M. We only need to know the fraction between them.

Example 7.6 We receive a shipment of 100,000 items where a fraction p is defective. We inspect 10 items and have decided to accept the shipment if the number of defective items is less than or equal to two. What is the probability that we accept the shipment?

Solution: There are two issues of interest here. First, the answer will depend on the actual value of p, second, strictly speaking we are dealing with a hypergeometric distribution. Since we only inspect 10 items, the probability of choosing a defective item does not change much. A binomial approximation is legitimate in this case. To get an overview of the situation, we try out a few different values for p.

- $p = 0.05$. We put $X = \text{Bin}[10, 0.05]$, and wish to find

$$P(X \leq 2) = P(X = 0) + P(X = 1) + P(X = 2).$$

  Here we can of course use the binomial distribution function to compute these values, but it is more efficient to use a table. Tables for the binomial distribution can be found at the end of the book. If we use the table (Table A (continued)), we find

$$P(X \leq 2) = 0.5987 + 0.3151 + 0.0746 = 98.8\%.$$

- $p = 0.2$. We put $X = \text{Bin}[10, 0.2]$ and use the table to get

$$P(X \leq 2) = 0.1074 + 0.2684 + 0.3020 = 67.8\%.$$

We have provided a survey which can be used to make an opinion of the usefulness of our inspection. The next question is if the inspection is sufficient for our purposes. Questions of this type are intimately related to hypothesis testing that is something we study in detail later on.

The use of tables for the binomial distribution is not important for applications. Quite soon, however, we will enter situations where statistical tables are crucial for computation. Some practice using tables for the binomial distribution serves as a gentle introduction to the more advanced tables, and they hardly have any use beyond that.

7.4 The Poisson Distribution

Example 7.7 We receive a shipment of 1,000,000 items where 0.1% are defective. We inspect 1000 items and have decided to accept the shipment if the number of defective items is less than or equal to 4. What is the probability that we accept the shipment?

Solution: This is clearly an approximate binomial distribution with $n = 1000$ and $p = 0.001$, where

$$P(X = x) = \binom{1000}{x} p^x (1-p)^{1000-x}.$$

There are no tables that can be used here, and it may also happen that calculators have trouble with the large factorials involved here. There is, however, another distribution, the Poisson distribution, which is well suited to deal with this situation. The Poisson distribution arise as the limit of a sequence of binomial distributions when $p \to 0^+, n \to \infty$ in such a way that $n \cdot p = \lambda$ is constant.

A Poisson distribution X with parameter λ has the distribution

$$P(X = x) = \frac{\lambda^x}{x!} e^{-\lambda}.$$

To see how this works, let us compare the values of the Poisson distribution with the binomial distribution in Example 7.7. If we use the formulas for the binomial distribution, we see that

$$P(X = 0) = 0.3677 \qquad P(X = 1) = 0.3681$$

$$P(X = 2) = 0.1840 \qquad P(X = 3) = 0.0.0613.$$

If we instead compute the values from the Poisson distribution using $\lambda = n \cdot p = 1000 \cdot 0.001 = 1$, we get

$$P(X = 0) = 0.3679 \qquad P(X = 1) = 0.3679$$

$$P(X = 2) = 0.1839 \qquad P(X = 3) = 0.0.0613.$$

We see that there is a difference, but the difference is so small that it is of no practical consequence. The numbers we found for the Poisson distribution can be computed directly from the definition, but it is also possible to find these values in the tables at the end of the book (Table B).

The conditions $p \to 0^+, n \to \infty$ can be interpreted as follows: In practice it means that p is very small while n is very large. A small p means that success is a rare event. Roughly speaking the Poisson distribution arises when we try to achieve a rare outcome a large number of times. The Poisson distribution is sometimes called the law of rare events.

Approximating a $\text{Bin}[n, p]$ distribution with a Poisson distribution with parameter $\lambda = n \cdot p$ is passable when $n \geq 50$ and $p \leq 0.05$. The approximation improves if we increase n or decrease p.

The Poisson distribution admits explicit formulas for expectation and variance. We state the final results without proofs:

If X is a Poisson distribution with parameter λ, then

$$\text{E}[X] = \lambda, \qquad \text{Var}[X] = \lambda.$$

An example of a Poisson distribution with $\lambda = 2.5$ is shown in Fig. 7.3. In this book we will only consider cases where the Poisson distribution is related to the binomial distribution. The Poisson distribution may, however, also arise in contexts that have nothing to do with the binomial distribution. It is hence a distribution of independent interest.

Example 7.8 Every day a large and relatively constant number of customers visit a shopping center. In the center there is a shop that sells a very special product. Few customers buy this product, but since many people are visiting, the shop sells one such product per day on average. What is the probability that the shop sells 2 or more such products during a day?

Solution: This is clearly a situation where we can apply the law of rare events. If X is the number of items sold of the special product, it is reasonable to assume that X has Poisson distribution. Since the shop sells one such product per day on average, we assume $\text{E}[X] = 1$. As the expectation equals the parameter λ in this case, we use $\lambda = 1$. Hence

$$P(X = x) = \frac{1^x}{x!}\text{e}^{-1} = \frac{1}{x!}\text{e}^{-1}.$$

Moreover

$$P(X \geq 2) = 1 - P(X \leq 1) = 1 - P(X = 0) - P(X = 0).$$

Using the table for the Poisson distribution at the end of the book (Table B), we get

$$P(X \geq 2) = 1 - 0.3678 - 0.3679 = 26.42\%.$$

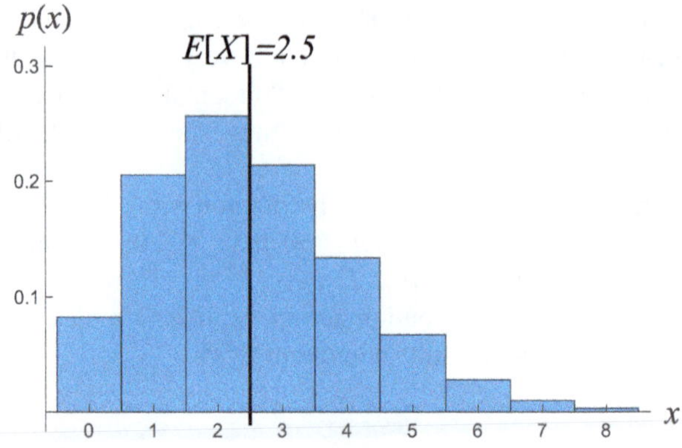

Fig. 7.3 A Poisson distribution with $\lambda = 2.5$

If we return to Example 7.7, we can solve this problem in exactly the same way. The distribution is an approximate Poisson distribution. Since $n \cdot p = 1000 \cdot 0.001 = 1$, we use the parameter $\lambda = 1$. Hence

$$\begin{aligned} P(X \leq 4) &= P(X = 0) + P(X = 1) + P(X = 2) + P(X = 3) + P(X = 4) \\ &= 0.3679 + 0.3679 + 0.1839 + 0.0613 + 0.0153 = 0.9963 = 99.63\%. \end{aligned}$$

The probability of accepting the shipment is as high as 99.63%.

7.5 The Normal Distribution

All the random variables we have considered so far had a discrete distribution. The next distribution is different in that it can attain any value on the interval $(-\infty, \infty)$, i.e., any real number. We will consider continuous distributions and need a different line of approach. We first introduce the density of a continuous random variable. The basic idea is that the area under the density function between a and b defines the probability that a continuous random variable has values in the interval $[a, b]$.

Definition 7.1 The density function $g(x)$ of a standard normal distribution is defined by

$$g(x) = \frac{1}{\sqrt{2\pi}} e^{-\frac{x^2}{2}}.$$

This function is defined for any real number x, and the graph is shown in Fig. 7.4. At a first glance the formula looks a bit odd, but it turns out that this density function is one of the most important tools we have available in statistics.

Fig. 7.4 The density function of a standard normal distribution

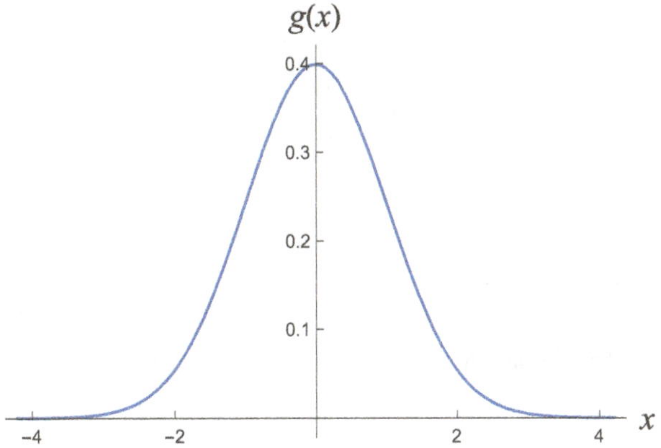

When the density function $f_X(x)$ of a random variable X is known, we define

$$P(a \leq X \leq b) = \int_a^b f_X(x)\mathrm{d}x.$$

The probability that X is between a and b is hence equal to the area under the density function between a and b. For this to be a sensible definition, we need to require that the area under the full graph is 1, i.e., that

$$\lim_{a \to -\infty, b \to \infty} P(a \leq X \leq b) = \int_{-\infty}^{\infty} f_X(x)\mathrm{d}x = 1.$$

It may seem cumbersome that we need integration to compute probabilities, but this is not much of a complication. The reason is that all the values we will need are available through statistical tables. The table for the standard normal distribution is available at the end of the book (Tables C and D). The table shows the values of the integral

$$G(z) = \int_{-\infty}^{z} \frac{1}{\sqrt{2\pi}} \mathrm{e}^{-\frac{x^2}{2}} \mathrm{d}x.$$

$G(z)$ is hence the area under the graph of the density function to the left of z, see Fig. 7.5. The table only contains the values for $G(z)$ when $z \geq 0$. The reason is that when z is negative, the value can be found by a simple symmetry argument. The density function is symmetric about zero, and hence the area to the right of z must

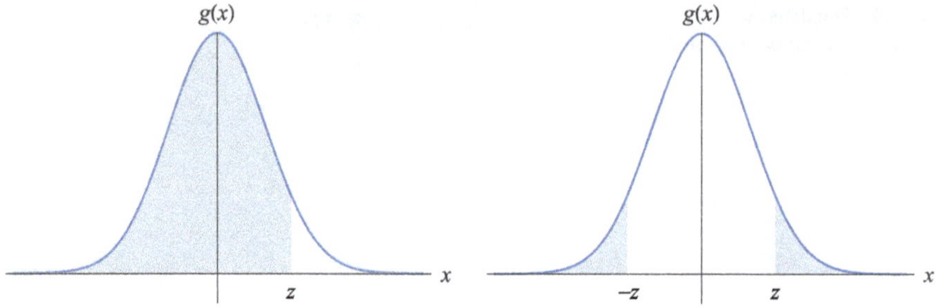

Fig. 7.5 The area to the left of z. The area to the left of $-z$ equals the area to the right of z

be equal to $G(-z)$, see Fig. 7.5. Hence

$$G(z) + G(-z) = \text{Area under the full graph} = 1.$$

and from this relation it follows that

$$G(-z) = 1 - G(z).$$

Example 7.9 How do we find $G(-1)$ from the table?

Solution: We use the formula $G(-1) = 1 - G(1)$. From the table we find $G(1) = 0.8413$. Hence

$$G(-1) = 1 - 0.8413 = 0.1587.$$

Example 7.10 Find the probability that a standard normal distribution has values between -2 and 1.

Solution: It follows from the definitions that

$$P(-2 \leq X \leq 1) = G(1) - G(-2).$$

From the table we get $G(1) = 0.8413$. To find the value of $G(-2)$, we use the relation $G(-2) = 1 - G(2)$. From the table we get $G(2) = 0.9772$, which gives

$$P(-2 \leq X \leq 1) = 0.8413 - (1 - 0.9772) = 0.8185.$$

7.5.1 The General Normal Distribution

The expectation of a continuous random variable X with density $f_X(x)$ is defined by

$$\mathrm{E}[X] = \int_{-\infty}^{\infty} x \cdot f_X(x)\mathrm{d}x,$$

and the variance is defined by

$$\mathrm{Var}[X] = \int_{-\infty}^{\infty} (x - \mathrm{E}[X])^2 \cdot f_X(x)\mathrm{d}x.$$

From these definitions it is possible to prove that a standard normal distribution X has

$$\mathrm{E}[X] = 0, \qquad \mathrm{Var}[X] = 1.$$

This, however, is a special case, and the general normal distribution X has a density function

$$f_X(x) = \frac{1}{\sqrt{2\pi\sigma^2}} \mathrm{e}^{-\frac{(x-\mu)^2}{2\sigma^2}}.$$

With this density it is possible to show that

$$\mathrm{E}[X] = \mu, \qquad \mathrm{Var}[X] = \sigma^2,$$

and we say that X is an $N(\mu, \sigma^2)$ random variable (Figs. 7.6 and 7.7).

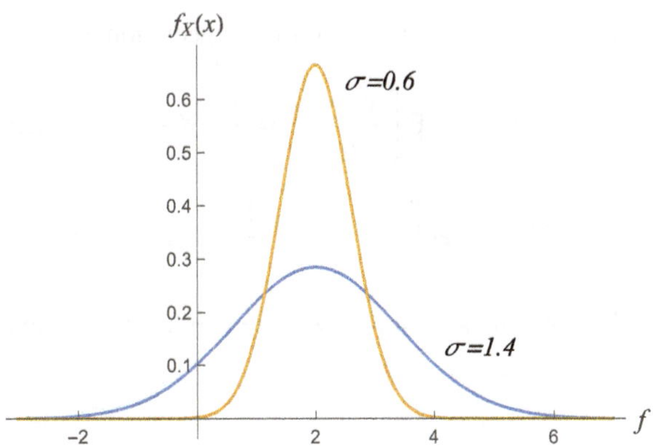

Fig. 7.6 Density functions of normal distributions with $\mu = 2, \sigma = 0.6$ and $\sigma = 1.4$

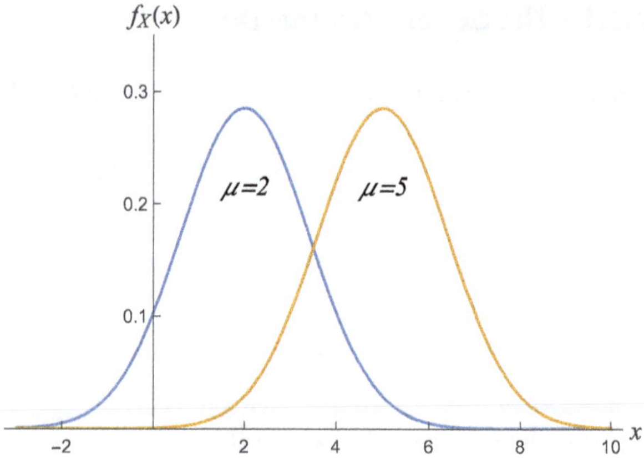

Fig. 7.7 Density functions of normal distributions with $\sigma = 0.6$, $\mu = 2$ and $\mu = 5$

7.5.2 Standardizing Random Variables

It turns out that we do not need new tables to compute probabilities related to the general normal distributions. A useful technical procedure solves the problem. If X is any random variable with

$$\mathrm{E}[X] = \mu \qquad \mathrm{Var}[X] = \sigma^2,$$

we can define a new random variable Z by

$$Z = \frac{X - \mu}{\sigma}.$$

Then $\mathrm{E}[Z] = 0$, $\mathrm{Var}[Z] = 1$.

Proof We use the general rules for expectation and variance to see that

$$\mathrm{E}[Z] = \mathrm{E}\left[\frac{X - \mu}{\sigma}\right] = \frac{1}{\sigma}\mathrm{E}[X - \mu] = \frac{1}{\sigma}(\mathrm{E}[X] - \mathrm{E}[\mu]) = 0,$$

$$\mathrm{Var}[Z] = \mathrm{Var}\left[\frac{X - \mu}{\sigma}\right] = \frac{1}{\sigma^2}\mathrm{Var}[X - \mu] = \frac{1}{\sigma^2}\mathrm{Var}[X] = \frac{1}{\sigma^2} \cdot \sigma^2 = 1.$$

The usefulness of this procedure will be clear from the following example.

Example 7.11 Assume that X is a normal distribution with $E[X] = 20$ and $\sigma^2 = 16$. Find $P(X \leq 28)$ and $P(24 \leq X \leq 28)$.

Solution: $Z = \frac{X-20}{4}$ is a standard normal distribution. Hence

$$P(X \leq 28) = P\left(\frac{X-20}{4} \leq \frac{28-20}{4}\right) = P(Z \leq 2) = G(2) = 0.9972.$$

Correspondingly (Note that $P(X = 24) = 0$ since X is a continuous distribution)

$$\begin{aligned} P(24 \leq X \leq 28) &= P(X \leq 28) - P(X \leq 24) \\ &= P\left(\frac{X-20}{4} \leq \frac{28-20}{4}\right) - P\left(\frac{X-20}{4} \leq \frac{24-20}{4}\right) \\ &= P(Z \leq 2) - P(Z \leq 1) = G(2) - G(1) \\ &= 0.9772 - 0.8413 = 0.1359. \end{aligned}$$

The method we used in the previous example is very useful in applications. It can also be used in cases where X is approximately normal, meaning that the distribution is very close to a normal distribution. The final result can be stated as follows:

If X is approximately normal with $E[X] = \mu$ and $\text{Var}[X] = \sigma^2$, then

$$P(X \leq z) \approx G\left(\frac{z-\mu}{\sigma}\right).$$

If X is a normal distribution, we get the same result but with equality instead of approximation.

7.5.3 The Central Limit Theorem

We will now consider one of the most important results in statistics. The results explain clearly why a standard normal distribution has such a prominent place. A rigorous proof is too difficult, so we omit the details. We will instead focus the meaning of the statement and explain how it can be applied in practical cases.

Example 7.12 Assume that we toss a coin 10 times. If we do this only once the result will be quite random. If we repeat this multiple times, it might happen that we see a pattern. The table below shows the result of a computer simulation where we have repeated the 10 coin tosses 1000 times.

$$\begin{aligned}
10 \text{ tails} &: \text{once} \\
9 \text{ tails, } 1 \text{ heads} &: 8 \text{ times} \\
8 \text{ tails, } 2 \text{ heads} &: 56 \text{ times} \\
7 \text{ tails, } 3 \text{ heads} &: 115 \text{ times} \\
6 \text{ tails, } 4 \text{ heads} &: 206 \text{ times} \\
5 \text{ tails, } 5 \text{ heads} &: 247 \text{ times} \\
4 \text{ tails, } 6 \text{ heads} &: 190 \text{ times} \\
3 \text{ tails, } 7 \text{ heads} &: 117 \text{ times} \\
2 \text{ tails, } 8 \text{ heads} &: 51 \text{ times} \\
1 \text{ tails, } 9 \text{ heads} &: 8 \text{ times} \\
10 \text{ heads} &: \text{once}
\end{aligned}$$

The frequencies have been plotted to the left in Fig. 7.8. We see that the plot forms a curve resembling the density of a normal distribution. The effect is even more pronounced in the graph to the right in Fig. 7.8. Here the results are based on 100 coin tosses in 100,000 repeated experiments.

The results in Fig. 7.8 are typical when we add the results from several repeated experiments. Regardless of what distribution we start out with, the sum of the results from many independent experiments will be close to a normal distribution. More precisely the following theorem holds:

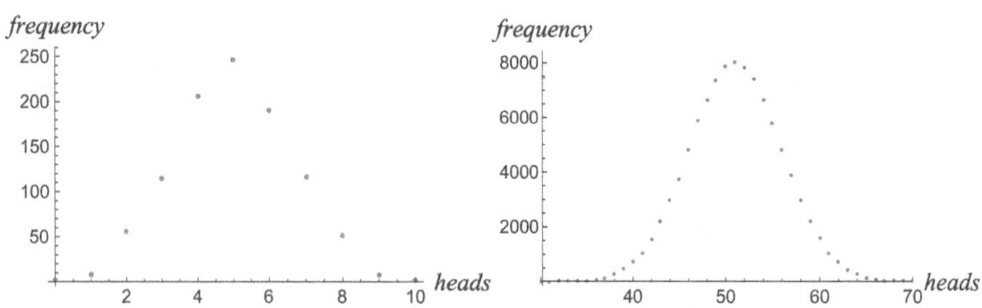

Fig. 7.8 Frequencies of heads in repeated coin tosses

Theorem 7.1 *Let $X_1, \ldots, X_n$ be independent random variables with the same distribution, and assume that* $\mathrm{E}[X_i] = \mu, \mathrm{Var}[X_i] = \sigma^2$ *for all* $i = 1, \ldots, n$. *Put*

$$S_n = X_1 + X_2 + \cdots + X_n.$$

Then for all z

$$P\left(\frac{S_n - \mathrm{E}[S_n]}{\sigma[S_n]} \leq z\right) \approx G(z), \qquad \text{when } n \text{ is sufficiently big.}$$

Theorem 7.1 is often called the central limit theorem and is one of the most important results in statistics. How big n needs to be depends on the distribution, but a crude rule of thumb says $n > 30$. In some special cases we can give a more precise answer. The proof of the central limit theorem is too difficult to be included here, so we will focus on applications.

Example 7.13 Assume that we know that $S = X_1 + X_2 + \cdots + X_n$, where $X_1, \ldots, X_n$ all are independent with the same distribution. We don't know the precise value of n, but we know that the value is large. Find an approximate value for $P(S \leq 8)$ when $\mathrm{E}[S] = 2, \mathrm{Var}[S] = 9$.

Solution: We want to use the central limit theorem. First we find

$$\sigma[S] = \sqrt{\mathrm{Var}[S]} = 3.$$

Next we subtract $\mathrm{E}[S]$ and then divide by $\sigma[S]$ on both sides of the inequality to see that

$$P(S \leq 8) = P\left(\frac{S - \mathrm{E}[S]}{\sigma[S]} \leq \frac{8-2}{3}\right) \approx G(2) = 0.9772.$$

The principle we used in this example is useful, and we formulate a general version of it:

Assume that n is big, and that $S = X_1 + X_2 + \cdots + X_n$, where $X_1, \ldots, X_n$ all are independent with the same distribution. Then

$$P(S \leq s) \approx G\left(\frac{s - \mathrm{E}[S]}{\sigma[S]}\right)$$

The central limit theorem also applies to the mean and can be stated as follows:

Theorem 7.2 *Let $X_1, \ldots, X_n$ be independent random variables with the same distribution, and assume that* $\mathrm{E}[X_i] = \mu, \mathrm{Var}[X_i] = \sigma^2$ *for all $i = 1, \ldots, n$. If n is big and we put*

$$S = X_1 + X_2 + \cdots + X_n$$

$$\overline{X} = \frac{1}{n}(X_1 + X_2 + \cdots + X_n),$$

then

$$S \approx N[n\mu, n\sigma^2] \qquad \textit{and} \qquad \overline{X} \approx N\left[\mu, \frac{\sigma^2}{n}\right].$$

When the conditions in Theorem 7.2 hold, we can show that

$$\mathrm{E}[S] = n\mu, \qquad \mathrm{Var}[S] = n\sigma^2,$$

and

$$\mathrm{E}[\overline{X}] = n\mu, \qquad \mathrm{Var}[\overline{X}] = \frac{\sigma^2}{n}.$$

The last relation is particularly useful in applications.

Example 7.14 Assume that 400 customers come to a shop every day and that their purchases are independent. They often buy milk, and we assume that the number of liters bought by each customer is a random variable X with distribution

$$P(X = 0) = 0.3, \qquad P(X = 1) = 0.5, \qquad P(X = 2) = 0.2.$$

Find an approximate value for the probability that the shop sells between 341 and 390 liters.

Solution: We call the total number of liters sold S, and have

$$S = X_1 + X_2 + \cdots + X_{400}.$$

To solve the problem, we need to compute

$$P(341 \leq S \leq 390) = P(S \leq 390) - P(S \leq 340).$$

We can find approximate values for these probabilities from the central limit theorem, but we need to know E[S] and Var[S]. To find these values we first need to compute E[X] and Var[X]. We get

$$\begin{aligned}
\mathrm{E}[X] &= 0 \cdot 0.3 + 1 \cdot 0.5 + 2 \cdot 0.2 = 0.9 \\
\mathrm{E}[X^2] &= 0^2 \cdot 0.3 + 1^2 \cdot 0.5 + 2^2 \cdot 0.2 = 1.3 \\
\mathrm{Var}[X] &= \mathrm{E}[X^2] - \mathrm{E}[X]^2 = 1.3 - 0.9^2 = 0.49.
\end{aligned}$$

We use these values to see that

$$\begin{aligned}
\mathrm{E}[S] &= \mathrm{E}[X_1] + \mathrm{E}[X_2] + \cdots + \mathrm{E}[X_{400}] \\
&= 0.9 + 0.9 + \cdots + 0.9 = 400 \cdot 0.9 = 360.
\end{aligned}$$

Since $X_1, X_2, \ldots, X_{400}$ all are independent

$$\begin{aligned}
\mathrm{Var}[S] &= \mathrm{Var}[X_1] + \mathrm{Var}[X_2] + \cdots + \mathrm{Var}[X_{400}] \\
&= 0.49 + 0.49 + \cdots + 0.49 = 400 \cdot 0.49 = 196.
\end{aligned}$$

Hence

$$\sigma[S] = \sqrt{\mathrm{Var}[S]} = \sqrt{196} = 14.$$

Now we have all the information we need to use the central limit theorem, and we get

$$\begin{aligned}
P(341 \leq S \leq 390) &= P(S \leq 390) - P(S \leq 340) \\
&\approx G\left(\frac{390 - 360}{14}\right) - G\left(\frac{340 - 360}{14}\right) \\
&\approx G(2.14) - G(-1.43) = G(2.14) - (1 - G(1.43)) \\
&= 0.9838 - (1 - 0.9236) = 0.9074.
\end{aligned}$$

The probability that the customers buy between 341 and 390 liters of milk is hence about 90%.

In the previous calculation we tacitly assumed that $n = 400$ is sufficient to apply the central limit theorem. A general problem in applications of the central limit theorem is the following: How many terms are sufficient? There is no simple answer to this question. In many cases our random variables come from a binomial distribution, and in that particular case it is possible to give a fairly precise rule for how many terms are needed. Note that a binomial distribution can always be viewed

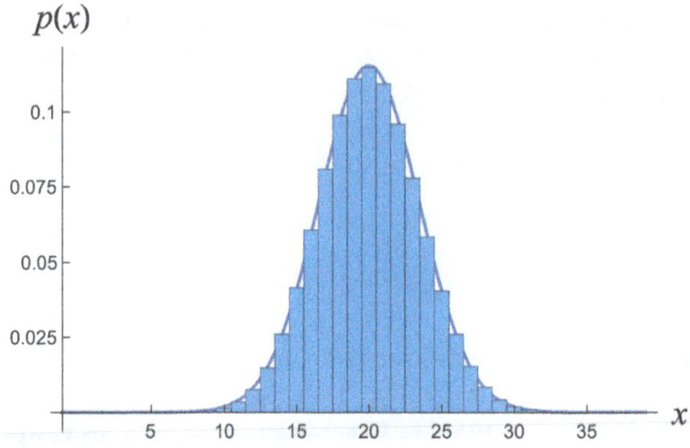

Fig. 7.9 Approximating a binomial distribution where $n = 50, p = 0.4$ by a normal distribution

as a sum of n independent indicator distributions, and the central limit theorem can hence be applied directly to the distribution. The following result holds:

If X is binomial (n, p), then

$$P(X \leq x) \approx G\left(\frac{x - n \cdot p}{\sqrt{n \cdot p(1-p)}}\right).$$

The approximation can be used if $n \cdot p(1-p) \geq 5$ and is good if $n \cdot p(1-p) \geq 10$. When these conditions fail, we should not approximate X by a normal distribution.

An example where a binomial distribution is approximated by a normal distribution is shown in Fig. 7.9. Note that $\mathrm{E}[X] = n \cdot p$ and $\mathrm{Var}[X] = n \cdot p(1-p)$ if X is binomial (n, p).

Example 7.15 400 customers drop by a shop during a day. The probability that a customer makes a buy is $p = 0.1$. Find the probability that at least 30 customers make a buy during the day.

Solution: Let X be the number of customers who make a buy during a day. Then $X = \mathrm{Bin}[400, 0.1]$. In this case $n \cdot p(1-p) = 400 \cdot 0.1 \cdot 0.9 = 36$. Since this number is bigger than 10, we can expect that the normal approximation works well. Hence

$$\begin{aligned} P(X \geq 30) &= 1 - P(X \leq 29) \approx 1 - G\left(\frac{29 - 40}{\sqrt{36}}\right) \\ &= 1 - G(-1.83) = G(1.83) = 0.9664. \end{aligned}$$

7.5.4 Integer Correction

When a random variable has a continuous distribution, the probability for any specific value is zero. The probability that $X = 2$, e.g., is smaller than the probability that $1.9999 \leq X \leq 2.0001$. The last probability is given by

$$\int_{1.9999}^{2.0001} f_X(x)\mathrm{d}x \approx 0,$$

since in all but exceptional cases the area under the graph is small. When we use the normal distribution to approximate a random variable with integer values, we sometimes need to handle inequalities with care. If X only has integer values, then

$$P(X \geq 30) = 1 - P(X \leq 29)$$

while

$$P(X \geq 30) = 1 - P(X \leq 30)$$

if X has a continuous distribution. If X is integer valued, then

$$P(X \leq 10) = P(X \leq 10.9999)$$

but the normal approximation will give different answers for left- and the right-hand side. We can hope that the difference is small, but in general it is difficult to judge which of the approximations provides the best approximation to the exact probability. In some cases the approximation

$$P(X \leq 10) \approx G\left(\frac{10 - \mathrm{E}[X]}{\sigma[X]}\right)$$

is best, while it may also happen that

$$P(X \leq 10) \approx G\left(\frac{10.9999 - \mathrm{E}[X]}{\sigma[X]}\right)$$

is closer to the exact answer. It is sometimes seen that a good option is to meet halfway, i.e.

$$P(X \leq 10) \approx G\left(\frac{10.5 - \mathrm{E}[X]}{\sigma[X]}\right)$$

This method is called integer correction. Integer correction must be handled with care, and it frequently happens that the "correction" provides a worse result.

Definition 7.2 If X is integer valued with an approximate normal distribution, the integer correction is defined via

$$P(X \leq x) \approx G\left(\frac{x + \frac{1}{2} - \mathrm{E}[X]}{\sigma[X]}\right).$$

If X is binomial (n, p) where $20 \leq n \leq 50$, then integer correction always improves the result in comparison with the standard approximation. In other cases it happens frequently that the "correction" leads to a larger error. Integer correction is somewhat obsolete. The reason why we still include some material on this topic is that it focuses an important difference between continuous and discrete variables. This difference can also be illustrated as follows: Assume that we quote stock prices and that the smallest unit is 1 USD. Then

$$P(X \geq 10) = 1 - P(X \leq 9).$$

If, however, the smallest unit is 1 cent, then

$$P(X \geq 10) = 1 - P(X \leq 9.99).$$

We see that the resolution matters. A continuous distribution has a resolution which is arbitrarily fine. Then

$$P(X \geq 10) = 1 - P(X \leq 10).$$

In computations we often need to reverse inequalities as above. In doing so we need to focus on the resolution of the variable.

7.5.5 Normal Approximation of Hypergeometric and Poisson Distributions

We mentioned above that a hypergeometric distribution is approximately binomial when $N \geq 20n$. Moreover a binomial distribution is approximately Poisson when $n \geq 50$ and $p \leq 0.05$. If we in addition assume that $np(1 - p) \geq 10$, we know that the binomial distribution is approximately normal (Figs. 7.10 and 7.11). This means that there cannot be much difference between the normal distribution and the hypergeometric distribution or between the normal distribution and the Poisson distribution in such cases. The final results can be summarized as follows:

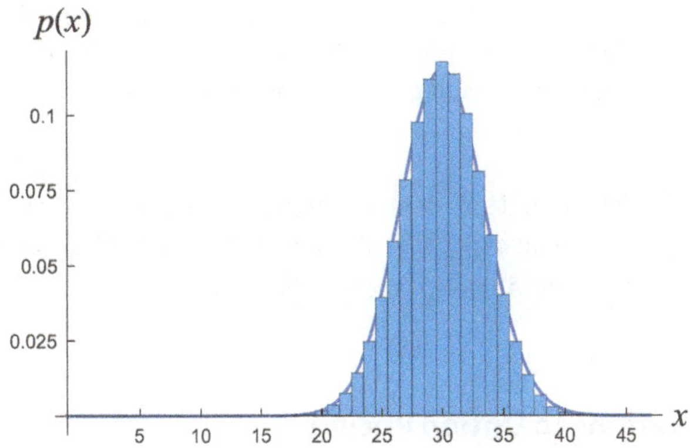

Fig. 7.10 Approximating a hypergeometric distribution where $N = 1000, M = 600, n = 50$ with a normal distribution

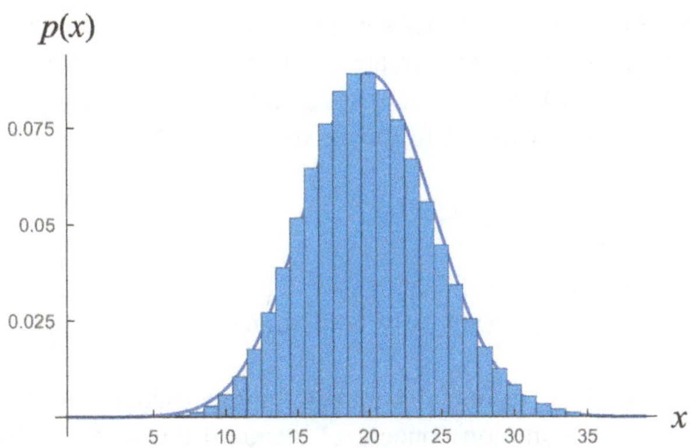

Fig. 7.11 Approximating a Poisson distribution where $\lambda = 20$ with a normal distribution

A hypergeometric distribution is approximatively normal if

$$N \geq 20n, \qquad n \cdot \frac{M}{N}\left(1 - \frac{M}{N}\right) \geq 10.$$

A Poisson distribution is approximatively normal if $\lambda \geq 10$.

7.5.6 Summing Normal Distributions

As we have seen in Chap. 6, the sum of two random variables X and Y can be quite complicated. If X and Y are normally distributed, it is possible to prove that the sum $Z = X + Y$ also has normal distribution. The situation is particularly simple if X and Y are independent. In that case Z is normally distributed with expectation $E[X] + E[Y]$ and variance $Var[X] + Var[Y]$. The result can be generalized to sums of arbitrary length, and the main result can be formulated as follows:

> If $X_1, X_2, \ldots, X_n$ all are independent and normally distributed, then the sum is a normal distribution with expected value equal to the sum of the expectations and variance equal to the sum of the variances.

7.5.7 Applications to Option Pricing

As we mentioned in Chap. 5, there are explicit formulas to price options in real world markets. We now have tools to take a brief look at this. To avoid too high levels of abstraction we will consider some special cases where most numbers are given. The principles we use, however, are true in general, and it is not very difficult to figure out what to do when we change some of these numbers.

Let us consider a stock with the following technical data:

- Stock price today: $K_0 = 100$ (USD).
- Volatility: $\beta = 10\%$.
- Expected annual return: $\alpha = 5\%$.
- Bank interest rate: $r = 5\%$ (annually, continuously compounded).

The volatility, β, is a technical parameter often used in finance. It can be translated to the more common concept of standard deviation by the following formula

$$\text{Standard deviation of the stock price } K_t \text{ at time } t = K_0 e^{\alpha t} \sqrt{e^{\beta^2 t} - 1}$$

We see that the standard deviation changes with time t. That makes good sense. We know the stock price at time $t = 0$. If we put $t = 0$ in the formula we get:

$$K_0 e^{\alpha \cdot 0} \sqrt{e^{\beta^2 \cdot 0} - 1} = K_0 e^0 \sqrt{e^0 - 1} = 0.$$

As time passes, the standard deviation increases. At time $t = 1$ (years), we get

$$100 e^{0.1 \cdot 0} \sqrt{e^{0.1^2 \cdot 0} - 1} = 11.08 \text{ (USD)}.$$

The standard deviation in the stock price one year into the future is hence 11.08 USD.

A commonly used model for the time development of stock prices can be formulated as follows:

$$K_t = K_0 e^{(\alpha - \frac{1}{2}\beta^2)t + \beta X_t},$$

where X_t is normally distributed with $E[X_t] = 0$ and $Var[X_t] = t$.

Now assume that we want to consider the distribution of possible stock prices one year into the future. We put $t = 1$ and get

$$K_1 = e^{0.095 + 0.1 X_1},$$

where X_1 is $N[0, 1]$. This is an example of a lognormal distribution. The distribution of K_1 follows easily from the distribution of X_1 if we use logarithms.

$$\begin{aligned} P(K_1 \leq k) &= P(100\, e^{0.095+0,1X_1} \leq k) \\ &= P(e^{0.095+0,1X_1} \leq k/100) \\ &= P(0.095 + 0,1X_1 \leq \ln[k/100]) \\ &= P(X_1 \leq 10 \cdot \ln[k/100] - 0.95). \end{aligned} \tag{7.2}$$

Since X_1 is a standard normal distribution, we get

$$P(K_1 \leq k) = G(10 \cdot \ln[k/100] - 0.95).$$

Instead of buying the stock, we could buy a call option to be redeemed one year from the start. If the strike of the option is, e.g., 110 USD, we have the right to buy the stock for 110 USD at time $t = 1$. Hence if the stock price raises by more than 10 USD, the option will pay out money. The price of a call option can be computed by the procedure below, which is often referred to as the Black and Scholes pricing formula.

The price V of a call option with strike K at time T is calculated as follows:

1. Compute $R = \ln\left[\dfrac{K}{K_0}\right] + (\dfrac{1}{2}\beta^2 - r)T$. 2. Compute $S = \beta\sqrt{T}$.

3. $V = K_0 \cdot (1 - G(R/S - S)) - K \cdot e^{-rT}(1 - G(R/S))$.

We now want to use the Black and Scholes formula to compute the price of 10,000 call options with strike $K = 110$ (USD) at time $T = 1$. When we insert the given quantities into the formulas, we get

$$R = \ln[110/100] + 0.005 - 0.05 = 0.0503, \qquad S = 0.1.$$

The price on one call option is

$$\begin{aligned} V &= 100 \cdot (1 - G(0.0503/0.1 - 0.1)) - 110 \cdot e^{-0.05}(1 - G(0.0503/0.1)) \\ &= 100 \cdot (1 - G(0.40)) - 110 \cdot e^{-0.05}(1 - G(0.50)) \\ &= 100 \cdot (1 - 0.6554) - 110 \cdot e^{-0,05}(1 - 0.6915) \\ &= 2.18. \end{aligned}$$

The price on 10,000 call options is hence 21,800 USD.

A question of interest is to figure out the probability that the investment is profitable. We make a profit when the value of the options exceeds 21,800 USD. The limiting stock price K_1 is determined by the equation

$$10{,}000 \cdot (K_1 - 110) = 21{,}800,$$

and we see that the stock price must be at least 112.18 USD before we begin to make a profit. The probability that we make a profit is

$$\begin{aligned} P(K_1 \geq 112.18) &= 1 - P(K_1 \leq 112.18) \\ &= 1 - G(10 \cdot \ln[112.18/100] - 0.95) = 1 - G(0.20) \\ &= 42.1\%. \end{aligned}$$

Note that the calculations critically depend on the given parameters. If the economy enters a recession, the parameters will most certainly change and this in turn will change the stock prices. Questions of this type will be discussed in the exercises.

7.6 Summary of Chap. 7

- $X = \text{Binomial}(n, p)$: Total number of successes in n independent trials when the probability of success is p.

$$P(X = x) = \binom{n}{x} p^x (1-p)^{n-x}, \qquad \mathrm{E}[X] = np, \qquad \mathrm{Var}[X] = np(1-p).$$

- X = Hypergeometric(N, M, n): Total number of special elements when we sample n elements from a population of N elements, where M elements are special.

$$P(X = x) = \frac{\binom{M}{x}\binom{N-M}{n-x}}{\binom{N}{n}}, \qquad \mathrm{E}[X] = n \cdot \frac{M}{N}.$$

$$\mathrm{Var}[X] = \frac{N-n}{n-1} \cdot n \cdot \frac{M}{N} \cdot \left(1 - \frac{M}{N}\right).$$

- X = Poisson λ: Total number of successes when an experiment where success is a rare outcome is repeated many times.

$$P(X = x) = \frac{\lambda^x}{x!}\mathrm{e}^{-\lambda}, \qquad \mathrm{E}[X] = \lambda, \qquad \mathrm{Var}[X] = \lambda.$$

- $X = N[0, 1]$ = Standard normaldistribution: A continuous distribution where

$$P(X \in [a, b]) = \int_a^b \frac{1}{\sqrt{2\pi}}\mathrm{e}^{-x^2/2}\mathrm{d}x, \qquad \mathrm{E}[X] = 0, \qquad \mathrm{Var}[X] = 1.$$

The cumulative distribution for the standard normal distribution is listed in tables and is defined by

$$G(z) = \int_{-\infty}^{z} \frac{1}{\sqrt{2\pi}}\mathrm{e}^{-x^2/2}\mathrm{d}x.$$

The following relations are useful in applications:

$$G(-z) = 1 - G(z), \qquad P(a \leq X \leq b) = G(b) - G(a)$$

- *The central limit theorem*: Let $S_n = X_1 + \cdots + X_n$, where $X_1, \ldots, X_n$ are independent variables with the same distribution. Then

$$\lim_{n\to\infty} P\left(\frac{S_n - \mathrm{E}[S_n]}{\sigma[S_n]}\right) = G(z).$$

- Any random variable S which (roughly speaking) appears as a sum of many independent effects will according to the central limit theorem lead to an approximate normal distribution. How many terms are needed for a satisfactory approximation depend on the situation. Some guidelines are provided in Table 7.1.

Table 7.1 Criteria for normal approximation

Binomial	$np(1-p) \geq 5$	OK
Binomial	$np(1-p) \geq 10$	Good
Hypergeometric	$N \geq 20n$ and $n \cdot \frac{M}{N} \cdot (1-\frac{M}{N}) \geq 5$	OK
Hypergeometric	$N \geq 20n$ and $n \cdot \frac{M}{N} \cdot (1-\frac{M}{N}) \geq 10$	Good
Poisson	$\lambda \geq 5$	OK
Poisson	$\lambda \geq 10$	Good

- When S is approximately normal, then

$$P(S \leq s) \approx G\left(\frac{s - \mathrm{E}[S]}{\sigma[S]}\right).$$

with equality if S is a normal distribution.
- Integer correction (somewhat obsolete): Is S and s are integer valued, and S is approximately normal, then

$$P(S \leq s) \approx G\left(\frac{s + \frac{1}{2} - \mathrm{E}[S]}{\sigma[S]}\right).$$

The values improve (in comparison with the usual approximation) when S is binomial with $20 \leq n \leq 50$ and $np(1-p) \geq 10$. The method is otherwise unreliable, in particular at the tails of the distribution.

7.7 Problems for Chap. 7

7.1 We have a shipment with 9 items and the probability that an item is defective is 10%. Let X be the number of defective items in the shipment.

(a) Find the probability that at most 3 items are defective.
(b) Find the probability that at least 2 items are defective.
(c) Find $\mathrm{E}[X]$, $\mathrm{Var}[X]$, and $\sigma[X]$.

7.2 We have randomly selected 25 documents during an audit of a company. Assume that the probability that a document contains errors is 2%, and let X be the number of documents containing errors.

(a) Find the probability that there are less than 2 documents with errors.
(b) Find the probability that there is at least one document with errors.
(c) Find $\mathrm{E}[X]$, $\mathrm{Var}[X]$, and $\sigma[X]$.

7.3 We ask a sample of 16 persons if they like a good. The probability that a randomly selected person likes the good is 20%. X is the number of people in the sample that like the good.

(a) Find the probability that 3 persons like the good.
(b) Find $\mathrm{E}[X]$, $\mathrm{Var}[X]$, and $\sigma[X]$.

7.4 We have a shipment with 26 items and know that half of the items, i.e., 13 items are defective. We randomly select 8 items from the shipment. X is the number of defective items in the sample.

(a) Find the probability that 4 items are defective.
(b) Find $\mathrm{E}[X]$, $\mathrm{Var}[X]$, and $\sigma[X]$.

7.5 A political party has 65 representatives, and we know that 20% of the representatives are negative to a proposal. We select 20 people randomly, and let X denote the number of representatives that are negative to the proposal.

(a) Find the probability that at least 2 representatives in the sample are negative to the proposal.
(b) Find $\mathrm{E}[X]$, $\mathrm{Var}[X]$, and $\sigma[X]$.

7.6 A company handles every day a large and relatively constant number of orders. On average the company receives 4 complaints per day. X is the number of complaints the company receives a randomly selected day.

(a) Find the probability that the company receives at most 3 complaints.
(b) Find $\mathrm{E}[X]$, $\mathrm{Var}[X]$, and $\sigma[X]$.

7.7 We receive a consignment of 2,000,000 items where the probability of an item being defective is 0.05%. We sample 500 items, and accept the consignment if the number of defective items in the sample is at most one.

(a) What is the probability that we accept the consignment?
(b) Find $\mathrm{E}[X]$, $\mathrm{Var}[X]$, and $\sigma[X]$.

7.8 Assume that X is a standard normal distribution.

(a) Find the probability that $X \leq 1.64$.
(b) Find the probability that $X = 1.64$.
(c) Find the probability that $X < 1.64$.

7.9 Assume that X is a standard normal distribution.

(a) Find the probability that $0 \leq X \leq 0.44$.
(b) Find the probability that $-1.96 \leq X \leq 1.96$.
(c) Find the probability that $X > -2.33$.

7.10 Assume that X is a random variable with $\mathrm{E}[X] = 5$ and $\mathrm{Var}[X] = 16$. Define a new random variable $Y = \frac{X-5}{4}$. Prove that

$$\mathrm{E}[Y] = 0, \qquad \mathrm{Var}[Y] = 1.$$

7.11 Assume that $S = X_1 + X_2 + \cdots + X_n$ where $X_1, \ldots, X_n$ are independent with the same distribution and n is very large. $\mathrm{E}[S] = 3$ and $\mathrm{Var}[S] = 16$.

(a) Find the probability that $S \leq 7$.
(b) Find the probability that $-1 \leq S \leq 11$.
(c) Find the probability that $S \geq 5$.
(d) Is there a good reason to use integer correction in this problem?

7.12 Assume that S is normally distributed with $\mathrm{E}[S] = 10$ and $\mathrm{Var}[S] = 25$. How large must z be if

$$P(S \leq z) = 95\%?$$

7.13 We have a consignment with 225 items and the probability that an item is defective is 20%. Let X be the number of defective items in the consignment.

(a) Find $\mathrm{E}[X]$, $\mathrm{Var}[X]$, and $\sigma[X]$.
(b) Find the probability that at most 50 items are defective.
(c) Find the probability that at least 35 items are defective.

7.14 We ask a sample of 48 persons if they like a good. Assume that the probability that a randomly selected person likes the good is 25%. X is the number of people in the sample who like the good.

(a) Find $\mathrm{E}[X]$, $\mathrm{Var}[X]$, and $\sigma[X]$.
(b) Why could integer correction be a good idea in this problem?
(c) Use integer correction to find the probability that at least 15 persons like the good.
(d) Find the probability that at least 15 persons likes the good using a normal approximation without integer correction. The exact answer is $P(X \leq 15) = 87.68\%$. Comment the answers in (c) and (d).

7.15 Assume that X_1, X_2, X_3, X_4 are independent and normally distributed with

$$\mathrm{E}[X_1] = 100 \quad \mathrm{E}[X_2] = 90 \quad \mathrm{E}[X_3] = 95 \quad \mathrm{E}[X_4] = 105$$

$$\mathrm{Var}[X_1] = 30 \quad \mathrm{Var}[X_2] = 20 \quad \mathrm{Var}[X_3] = 25 \quad \mathrm{Var}[X_4] = 15.$$

(a) What is the distribution of $S = X_1 + X - 2 + X_3 + X_4$? Can we use the central limit theorem in this case?
(b) Find $\mathrm{E}[S]$, $\mathrm{Var}[S]$, and $\sigma[S]$.
(c) Compute $P(S \leq 390)$. Is the answer different from $P(S < 390)$?

7.16 Option Pricing Theory: A stock has today a price $K_0 = 100$ USD, and it has an expected annual return $\alpha = 15\%$ and a volatility $\beta = 20\%$. The bank interest rate is $r = 5\%$.

(a) Find the standard deviation in the stock price 6 months from now.
(b) What is the price of a call option that gives the right to buy the stock for 112 USD 6 months from now?

7.17 Option Pricing Theory: A stock has today a price $K_0 = 200$ USD, it has an expected annual return $\alpha = 9\%$ and a volatility $\beta = 2\%$. The bank interest rate is $r = 5\%$.

(a) What is the price of a call option that gives the right to buy the stock for 205 USD 3 months from now?
(b) What is the probability that the option will be worthless?
(c) A short time after the option was bought, the company met serious problems. The stock price fell instantly to 198 USD and the expected annual return went down to 5%. What is the probability that the option will be worthless?

7.18 Option Pricing Theory: A stock has today a price $K_0 = 98$ USD, and it has an expected annual return $\alpha = 12\%$ and a volatility $\beta = 12\%$. The bank interest rate is $r = 5\%$.

(a) What is the price of a call option that gives the right to buy the stock for 109 USD 1 year from now?
(b) You spend 10,000 USD to buy options like in (a). Instead of buying the options you could have made a safe investment putting your money in the bank. What must the stock be worth one year from now so that you get at least as much profit as you would have gotten from a bank deposit?
(c) What is the probability that the options give at least as much profit from the options as you would get from a bank deposit?

7.19 Option Pricing Theory: The price of a stock at time t (in years) is given by the formula

$$K_t = 100e^{0.08t+0.2X_t},$$

where X_t is normally distributed with expected value zero and standard deviation $\sqrt{t}$.

(a) Find the probability that the stock price is above 115 USD when $t = 4$.
(b) What is the volatility of the stock? Assume that the bank interest rate is $r = 3\%$. Use the Black and Scholes pricing formula to find the price on a call option that gives the right to buy the stock for 115 USD 4 years from now.

7.20 Applications of the Central Limit Theorem: Every day about 10,000 people walk past an ice cream store. We let $X_1, X_2, \ldots, X_{10,000}$ denote the number of ice cream bought by each person. Assume that $X_1, X_2, \ldots, X_{10,000}$ are independent with the same distribution, and that the distribution is given by

$$P(X = 0) = 86\% \quad P(X = 1) = 8\% \quad P(X = 2) = 2\% \quad P(X = 3) = 4\%$$

(a) Find E[X] and Var[X].
(b) Put $S = X_1 + X_2 + \cdots + X_{10,000}$. Find E[$S$], Var[$S$], and $\sigma[S]$.
(c) Find the probability that the store sells more than 2450 ice cream.
(d) How many ice cream must the store have in stock to be 99% sure that they can meet the demand?

7.21 Applications of the Central Limit Theorem: A building plot area is planned for 900 houses. Let X be the number of cars per household, and assume that

$$P(X = 0) = 0.1 \qquad P(X = 1) = 0.6 \qquad P(X = 2) = 0.3.$$

(a) Find E[X] and Var[X].
(b) Is it reasonable to assume that the number of cars in each household are independent random variables? Point (shortly) to issues for and against this assumption.
(c) Assume that the number of cars in each household are independent random variables, and define $Y = \sum_{i=1}^{900}$. Find E[Y] and Var[Y]. How many parking lots are needed if we require 90% probability that all the cars can park simultaneously? Approximate Y by a normal distribution in your calculations.

7.22 Applications of the Central Limit Theorem: The probability that a randomly selected customer in a bookstore buys a textbook in statistics is $p = 0.001$. During a day the store has about 10,000 customers. We assume that the customers shop independently and let X denote the number of textbooks in statistics bought during a day.

(a) What is the exact distribution of X? Find $E[X]$ and $Var[X]$.
(b) Use a normal approximation with and without integer correction to compute an approximate value for $P(X \leq 3)$.
(c) The exact answer in (b) is $P(X \leq 3) = 0.0103$. Let Y be a Poisson random variable with $\lambda = 10$. Compute the probability $P(Y \leq 3)$ and compare the results in (b) and (c).

7.23 Portfolio Computations: You want to invest 400,000 USD in two stocks, A and B. The two stocks cost today

$$A : 100 \text{ USD per stock} \qquad B : 200 \text{ USD per stock}$$

(a) Let a be the number of A stocks and b be the number of b stocks. Find a and b when you want to invest the same total amount in the two stocks.
(b) We assume that the prices on the two stocks one year from now are independent random variables X_A and X_B. The total value V of your portfolio one year from now is given by

$$V = a X_A + b X_B,$$

where a and b are the values you found in (a). Find $E[V]$ and $Var[V]$ if we assume that $E[X_A] = 200, E[X_B] = 300, Var[X_A] = 1500$, and $Var[X_B] = 400$. Also find the standard deviation $\sigma[V]$.
(c) Assume that X_A and X_B are normally distributed. What is the probability that the value of the portfolio exceeds 800,000 USD after one year?

7.24 Poisson Versus Normal Approximation: A shop sells a good. We let X be a random variable showing how many units each customer buys of the good. The probability distribution of X is given by

$$P(X = 0) = 0.905 \qquad P(X = 1) = 0.090 \qquad P(X = 2) = 0.005.$$

(a) Find $E[X]$ and $Var[X]$.
(b) During one day 100 customers visit the shop. We can compute the total number of units the customers buy of the good, and denote this number by Y. We assume that the customers shop independently. Find $E[Y]$ and $Var[Y]$ and use normal approximation to compute the probability that the shop sells at most 5 units of the good during a day.
(c) Since the distribution of X is special, we don't have any simple criteria to decide if the normal approximation is good or not. The distribution of X is, however, quite close to a Poisson random variable Z with parameter λ. Suggest a value for λ and compute $P(Z \geq 3)$.
(d) A sum of 100 independent Poisson random variables, all with parameter λ, is a Poisson random variable with parameter 100λ. Use this result to compute the probability that the shop sells at most 5 units of the good during a day, without

the use of normal approximation. Compare with the exact answer $P(Y \leq 5) = 6.72\%$ and give a comment.

7.25 Extreme Values: A company has 5 relatively equal production units, and each unit produces 10 items. We assume that the probability that an item is defective is 10% and that the number of defective items at each unit are independent random variables.

(a) We assume that outcomes (defective/not defective) of each item are independent random variables, and let X denote the number of defective items at randomly selected unit. What is the distribution of X? What is $P(X \geq 4)$?
(b) Let Y be the number of defective items at the unit with the worst result, i.e., the unit with the most defective items. What is $P(Y \geq 4)$?

7.26 Stochastic Game Theory:

(a) Assume that X is a normal distribution with expectation μ and variance σ^2, and that C is a constant. What is $P(X \leq \mu)$ and $P(X = C)$?

A simplified model for a wage negotiation can be formulated as follows: The employer presents an offer o and the workers (simultaneously) present a demand d. The outcome is decided by a mediator who thinks that a fair outcome of the negotiations is X. The value of X is a random variable which is unknown to the parties. The party which comes closest to X gets full acceptance for their claim. If the parties are equally close to X, X will be the outcome of the negotiations. The expected result E[R] from the negotiations is given by the formula

$$\mathrm{E}[R] = o \cdot P\left(X < \frac{o+d}{2}\right) + d \cdot P\left(X > \frac{o+d}{2}\right) + \frac{1}{2}(o+d) \cdot P\left(X = \frac{o+d}{2}\right).$$

(b) Explain the terms in the formula for E[R] (o and d are constants). How can you simplify this expression if you know that X is a normal distribution with expected value μ and variance σ^2?
(c) If the employer wishes to minimize the expected result while the workers want to maximize it, it is possible to prove that equilibrium is obtained if and only if

$$(d - o) \cdot f_X\left(\frac{o+d}{2}\right) = 2 \cdot P\left(X \leq \frac{o+d}{2}\right),$$

$$(d - o) \cdot f_X\left(\frac{o+d}{2}\right) = 2 \cdot P\left(X > \frac{o+d}{2}\right).$$

where f_X is the density of X. Explain why this leads to $P(X \leq \frac{o+d}{2}) = \frac{1}{2}$. How would you interpret this result?

(d) If X is normally distributed with expected value μ and variance σ^2, the density is given by

$$f_X(x) = \frac{1}{\sqrt{2\pi\sigma^2}} e^{-\frac{(x-\mu)^2}{2\sigma^2}}.$$

Show that the solution to the system of equations in (c) is

$$o = \mu - \sqrt{\frac{\pi}{2}} \cdot \sigma, \qquad d = \mu + \sqrt{\frac{\pi}{2}} \cdot \sigma.$$

What happens to the distance between the parties when σ increases?

7.27 Stochastic Game Theory: A simplified model for a wage negotiation can be formulated as follows: The employer presents an offer o and the workers (simultaneously) present a demand d. The outcome is decided by a mediator who thinks that a fair outcome of the negotiations is X. The value of X is a random variable which is unknown to the parties. The party which comes more close to X gets full acceptance for their view. If the parties are equally close to X, X will be the outcome of the negotiations. The expected result $\mathrm{E}[R]$ from the negotiations is given by the formula

$$\mathrm{E}[R] = o \cdot P\left(X < \frac{o+d}{2}\right) + d \cdot P\left(X > \frac{o+d}{2}\right) + \frac{1}{2}(o+d) \cdot P\left(X = \frac{o+d}{2}\right).$$

(a) Assume that the employer offers $o = 3\%$ while the workers demand $d = 6\%$. Compute the expected outcome of the negotiations when X is a normal distribution with $\mu = 5\%$ and standard deviation $\sigma = 0.5\%$.
(b) Assume that the employer offers $o = 3\%$ while the workers demand $d = 6\%$. Compute the expected outcome of the negotiations when X is a normal distribution with $\mu = 5\%$ and standard deviation $\sigma = 2\%$. Compare the answer with (a) and comment the results.

7.28 Poisson Versus Normal Distribution: In this problem X denotes the total quantity of a good that is sold during a day.

(a) We first assume that X is a normal distribution with expected value $\mu = 1$ and standard deviation $\sigma = 1$. What is the probability that $X \geq 3$?
(b) We now assume that the good is sold at a shopping center where there are a huge number of customers every day. The customers either buy one unit or nothing of the good, and all customers have the same probability of buying one unit. What distribution do you assume for X in this case? We assume as above that expected value is $\mu = 1$ and standard deviation $\sigma = 1$. Find $P(X \geq 3)$ under these new assumptions.

(c) Compare the results from (a) and (b) and try to explain the difference. Why do we in (b) need to assume that all customers have the same probability of buying one unit?

7.29 Stocks That Fail in the Long Run: In a standard model for stock prices the stock price K_t (in USD) at time t (in years) is given by

$$K_t = K_0 e^{(\alpha - \frac{1}{2}\beta^2)t + \beta X_t},$$

where X_t is normally distributed with $E[X_t] = 0$, $Var[X_t] = t$, and $X_0 = 0$. K_0 is the stock price at $t = 0$ and α, β are constants. We will in this problem assume that $K_0 = 100, \alpha = 0.03, \beta = 0.5$. In addition we will assume that the bank interest rate is $r = 2.5\%$ annually. We disregard transaction costs.

(a) Find the price of a call option that gives the right to buy a stock of this sort for 100 USD after 9 years.
(b) Find the probability that the stock price exceeds 1 USD after 100 years.
(c) It is possible to prove that

$$E[e^{\beta X_t}] = e^{\frac{1}{2}\beta^2}.$$

Use this to compute the expected stock price after 100 years. This result is in sharp contrast to the result in (b). Try to explain how this is possible.

7.30 Expected Utility: A game has 6 different outcomes all of which are equally probable. The first 5 outcomes give a reward equal to one unit, while the last outcome results in a loss of 4 units.

(a) Compute the expected result of the game.
(b) The players participating in the game have a utility function

$$u(x) = \sqrt{x + a^2} - a.$$

We interpret $u(x)$ as the utility of winning x units (a negative x is a loss), and $2 \leq a \leq 4$ is a constant that can differ from player to player. Compute the expected utility of the game in the two cases (i) $a = 2$ and (ii) $a = 4$. Also find the expected utility of not playing for arbitrary a (this we may interpret as a game that pays 0 units on all the 6 outcomes).
(c) It is possible to prove (you can take that for granted) that expected utility is an increasing function of a. Assume that a player participates in the game only if he or she has greater expected utility from playing than for not playing. Explain that there exists a constant a_0 such that a player participates in the game if and only if $a > a_0$. Compare the result with (a) and try to explain this from a behavioral point of view.

7.31 Life Insurance: When insurance companies price life insurances, they use a death rate function

$$\mu_x = \alpha + \beta c^x.$$

Here μ_x is the probability that a man of age x dies in the course of one year given that he is x years today, α, β, and c are constants. Commonly used values are

$$\alpha = 9.0 \cdot 10^{-4}, \qquad \beta = 4.4 \cdot 10^{-5}, \qquad c = 1.10154.$$

(a) Explain that the death rate increases with x. Compute the value μ_{50}.
(b) Let T_x be the remaining lifetime of a man with age x (this is a random variable which varies between individuals). It is possible to show that T_x has a cumulative distribution F_x given by

$$F_x(t) = P(T_x \leq t) = 1 - \mathrm{e}^{-\int_0^t \mu_{x+s} ds}.$$

You can take this for granted. Use the result to compute the value

$$P(T_{40} > 10).$$

(c) Compute the conditional probability

$$P(10 < T_{40} \leq 11 | T_{40} > 10).$$

Compare the result with (a), and try to interpret these results.

7.32 Binomial Distribution Conditional on Events: A company has 6 main collaborating companies. The probability that a collaborating company takes contact during one week is 70%. We assume that the collaborating companies act independently.

(a) Let X be the number of collaborating companies that takes contact during one week. What is the distribution of X? Find the probability that $X = 4$.
(b) The probability that a collaborating company taking contact writes a contract is 60%. Find the probability that the company writes 4 contracts with collaborators during one week.

7.33 The Distribution of a Sum: 10 men and 10 women apply for admission to a study. The admission is divided into two rounds. In the first round 4 men and 6 women apply, while the rest apply in the second round. In the first round 3 students will be admitted, while 7 will be admitted in the second round. We assume that all applicants have the same chance to be admitted in each round.

(a) Find the probability that 2 men are admitted in the first round. Find the probability that at least 5 men are admitted in the second round.
(b) Find the probability that at least 5 men are admitted in total. Is this procedure discriminating with regards to gender? Explain your answer and try to suggest what causes the difference.

7.34 Put Options: A stock has today a price $K_0 = 400$ USD, it has an expected annual return $\alpha = 15\%$ and a volatility $\beta = 12\%$. The bank interest rate is $r = 5\%$ (continuously compounded).

(a) Find the price of a call option that gives the right to buy the stock for 390 USD one year from now.
A (European) put option is a right (but not a duty) to sell a stock for a certain price (strike) after a time T. An option of this sort makes it possible to profit when prices are falling.
(b) We will compare two contracts. Contract A consists of one put option and one stock. Contract B consists of one call option and a bank deposit B. Both options have strike 390 USD and the size of the bank deposit B is given by

$$B = \text{strike} \cdot e^{-rT}.$$

Disregard any transaction costs and explain why the two contracts pay out the same amount regardless of the stock price K_T at time T. Take into account that you get interest on the bank deposit.
(c) Since the two contracts in (b) pays out the same amount of money, they must have the same price at $t = 0$. Use this to find the price of a put option with strike 390 USD at time $T = 1$.
(d) Expected annual return is adjusted down to $\alpha = -5\%$. What happens to the price of the options after the adjustment? Find the probability that the value of the put option is at least 8 USD.

7.35 Basic Properties of Brownian Motion: Most models for financial markets use a Brownian motion B_t where $0 \leq t < \infty$. At each point in time Brownian motion is a random variable with the properties

- For every $t \in [0, \infty)$, B_t is a normal distribution.
- $B_0 = 0, \mathrm{E}[B_t] = 0$ and $\mathrm{Var}[B_t] = t$.
- If $t_1 \leq t_2 \leq t_3 \leq t_4$, then the two differences $B_{t_2} - B_{t_1}$ and $B_{t_4} - B_{t_3}$ are independent random variables.

(a) Explain why $\mathrm{Var}[B_t] = \mathrm{E}[B_t^2]$ for all values of t.
(b) Let $t = 100$ and find $P(B_{100} \leq 10)$.
(c) Assume $t \geq s$. Use the two last bullet points above to compute $\mathrm{E}[B_s(B_t - B_s)]$. Hint: Put $t_1 = 0, t_2 = s, t_3 = s, t_4 = t$.

(d) Assume $t \geq s$. Show that $\mathrm{E}[B_t B_s] = s$, and use this expression to find an expression for $\mathrm{E}[(B_t - B_s)^2]$.

7.36 Basic Properties of Brownian Motion: Most models for financial markets use a Brownian motion B_t where $0 \leq t < \infty$. At each point in time Brownian motion is a random variable with the properties

- For every $t \in [0, \infty)$, B_t is a normal distribution.
- $B_0 = 0, \mathrm{E}[B_t] = 0$ and $\mathrm{Var}[B_t] = t$.
- If $t \geq s$, then $\mathrm{E}[(B_t - B_s)^2 = t - s$.
- If $t_1 \leq t_2 \leq t_3 \leq t_4$, then the two differences $B_{t_2} - B_{t_1}$ and $B_{t_4} - B_{t_3}$ are independent random variables.

(a) Let $X_t = 2B_t + 6$. Find $\mathrm{E}[X_t]$, and explain why $\mathrm{Var}[X_t] = 4t$ for any t.
(b) Let $X_t = 2B_t + 6$. Find $P(X_{25} \leq 16)$.
(c) Assume $t \geq s$. Use the last 3 bullet points above to compute

$$\mathrm{E}[B_s^2 B_t^2 - 2B_t B_s^3 + B_s^4].$$

7.37 Basic Properties of Brownian Motion: Most models for financial markets use a Brownian motion B_t where $0 \leq t < \infty$. At each point in time Brownian motion is a random variable with the properties

- For every $t \in [0, \infty)$, B_t is a normal distribution.
- $B_0 = 0, \mathrm{E}[B_t] = 0$ and $\mathrm{Var}[B_t] = t$.
- If $t \geq s$, then $\mathrm{E}[(B_t - B_s)^2 = t - s$.
- If $t_1 \leq t_2 \leq t_3 \leq t_4$, then the two differences $B_{t_2} - B_{t_1}$ and $B_{t_4} - B_{t_3}$ are independent random variables.

(a) Find the probability $P(100e^{B_9} \leq 2000)$.
(b) Assume $t \geq s$, and find an expression for $\mathrm{E}[B_s^2(B_t - B_s)^2]$.
(c) Assume $0 = t_0 < t_1 < \cdots < t_{n+1} = T$. Find the value for

$$\mathrm{E}[B_{t_i} B_{t_j} (B_{t_{i+1}} - B_{t_i})(B_{t_{j+1}} - B_{t_j})]$$

for each of the cases (i) $i < j$, (ii) $i = j$, and (iii) $i > j$. The answers must be justified in detail.

7.38 Bayesian Priors: In this problem X is a binomial (n, p) variable.

(a) We first assume that $p = \frac{1}{3}$ and that $n = 6$. Compute $P(X = 2)$.
(b) We now assume that p is unknown, but we know that p can only have the values $0, \frac{1}{3}, \frac{2}{3}, 1$. We assume a priori that these four values are equally probable.

Assume $n > 2$ and prove that

$$P(X = 2) = \binom{n}{2}\left(\left(\frac{1}{3}\right)^2\left(\frac{2}{3}\right)^{n-2} \cdot \frac{1}{4} + \left(\frac{2}{3}\right)^2\left(\frac{1}{3}\right)^{n-2} \cdot \frac{1}{4}\right).$$

Explain why this formula is wrong if $n = 2$.

(c) Now assume that $n = 6$. We observe $X = 2$. Compute the conditional probability

$$P\left(p = \frac{1}{3}\middle|X = 2\right).$$

7.39 Lognormal Distribution and Expected Stock Prices: A random variable Y is called *lognormal* if it can be written on the form

$$Y = \mathrm{e}^X,$$

where X is a normal distribution $N(\mu, \sigma^2)$.

(a) Assume that $Y = \mathrm{e}^X$, where X is $N(2, 2^2)$, i.e., $\mu = 4$ and $\sigma = 2$. Compute the probability

$$P(Y \leq 403.43).$$

(b) If Y is lognormal, it is possible to prove that

$$\mathrm{E}[Y] = \mathrm{e}^{\mu+\frac{1}{2}\sigma^2}.$$

You can take this formula for granted. Use the formula to find the expected value of $Y = \mathrm{e}^X$, where X is $N(2, 2^2)$. Compare the answer with (a) and give a comment.

(c) Assume that K_t is given by

$$K_t = K_0\mathrm{e}^{(\alpha-\frac{1}{2}\beta^2)t+\beta Z_t}.$$

where Z_t is $N(0, t)$, and where α and β are two constants. Explain why K_t has a lognormal distribution for each t, and find $\mathrm{E}[K_t]$.

7.40 Distributions Conditional on Events: A newspaper has two types of buyers, regular buyers and special buyers. We assume throughout this exercise that the newspaper is printed in more than 16,000 copies. The regular buyers have a total demand D_1 which is normally distributed with expectation μ_1 and variance σ_1^2 where

$$\mu_1 = 10{,}000, \qquad \sigma_1^2 = 3000^2.$$

(a) Find the probability that at most 16,000 regular buyers buy the newspaper.
(b) The special buyers only buy the newspaper if a special event S occurs. If S occurs, the special buyers have a total demand D_2 which is normally distributed with expected value μ_2 and variance σ_2^2, where

$$\mu_2 = 16{,}000, \qquad \sigma_2^2 = 4000^2.$$

We assume that D_1 and D_2 are independent, and that D_1 is independent of S.

Assume that S occurs and find expectation and variance for the total demand $D = D_1 + D_2$. What is the probability of selling at most 16,000 newspapers under this condition?
(c) Assume that $P(S) = 0.2$. Find the probability of selling at most 16,000 newspapers. Hint: When D_1 is independent of S it is also independent of S^c.

7.41 About the Newsvendor Problem: A retailer wants to order a number of items from a manufacturer. The demand D is a random variable. We first assume that D only can have the values

$$1, 2, 3, 4, 5, 6, 7, 8, 9, 10.$$

all with probability 0.1 (i.e., a uniform distribution).

(a) Assume that the retailer has ordered q items. Then he can sell

$$S = \min[D, q]$$

items. If for example $q = 5$, the sales get the distribution

$$1, 2, 3, 4, 5, 5, 5, 5, 5, 5.$$

with uniform probability. Find the expected sale E[S] when $q = 5$. It is possible to prove that if $q = x$, then

$$\mathrm{E}[S] = \frac{1}{20}(21x - x^2).$$

You can take this formula for granted. Use the formula to check the answer when $q = 5$.
(b) The items are sold for a retail price R per item and are bought from the manufacturer for a wholesale price W per item. The profit Π is given by the expression

$$\Pi = R \cdot \min[D, q] - Wq.$$

Find an expression for the expected profit when the retailer orders $q = x$ items. Assume that $R = 20$ and $W = 5$, and find x such that the profit is maximal. Hint: R, W, q are constants with respect to the expectation.

(c) It is possible to prove that if D has a continuous distribution with cumulative distribution F_D, then maximal expected profit is obtained when

$$F_D(x) = 1 - \frac{W}{R}.$$

You can take this for granted. Assume that D is a normal distribution with expected value $\mu = 5.5$ and variance $\sigma^2 = 1$, and that $R = 20, W = 5$. Find x such that expected profit is maximal. Why is the optimal order less than in (b)?

7.42 Hinting at Significance: You want to sell a good and assume that a randomly selected person demands D units of the good, where D is normally distributed with expectation $\mu = 10$ and variance $\sigma^2 = 10$.

(a) In all there are 1000 people demanding the good. We assume that the demands are all independent with the distribution above. Let Z denote the total demand from 1000 people. Compute E[Z] and Var[Z].

(b) First assume that the market is as in (a). How many units do you need to order if you want at least 95% probability of satisfying the total demand? Now assume that a large number of people demand the good, and that the market is otherwise as above. How many units do you need to order if you want at least 95% probability of satisfying the demand?

7.43 Adjusting Random Fluctuations Is a Bad Idea: Assume that the weekly surplus from a branch of a company is a random variable. Let X_i denote the surplus in week i, where $i = 1, 2, \ldots$. We assume that $X_1, X_2, \ldots$ are independent random variables all with the same expectation μ and variance σ^2.

(a) Assume that X_i is normally distributed with $\mu = 45, \sigma^2 = 900$. Find the probability that $X_i \leq 0$.

(b) The managers of the company want to reduce bad results for this particular branch and suggest the following strategy: If the result is below the expected value, the management injects extra amounts of cash the next week. If the result is above the expected value, the management withdraws a corresponding amount of cash. We assume that the injections/withdrawals are proportional to the deviation from the expected result, i.e.

$$\text{Adjusted surplus in the next period} = Y_{i+1} = X_{i+1} - \alpha(\mu - X_i),$$

where α is the constant of proportionality.

Assume that X_i and X_{i+1} are normally distributed with $\mu = 45, \sigma^2 = 900$, and that $\alpha = 0.75$. Find the probability that $Y_{i+1} \leq 0$.

(c) Assume that μ, σ, and α are arbitrary numbers. Is it possible to find a combination of these numbers such that the branch gets higher adjusted surplus after adjustment? What value on α should the company use if they want to minimize the probability of deficit?

7.44 Adjusting Random Fluctuations Can Be Very Costly: A producer of machine parts has a lathe. The lathe produces sleeves with diameter 100 mm. Since the material may vary, the sleeves differ slightly in diameter. We assume that the diameter is a random variable which is normally distributed with expected value $\mu = 100$ and standard deviation $\sigma = 0.1$, measured in mm.

(a) The sleeves are discarded if the deviation is more than 0.2 mm. Find the probability that a sleeve is discarded. Hint: $P(|X - 100| \geq 0.2) = 2 \cdot P(X \geq 100.2)$.

(b) The management wants to improve quality by letting the worker adjust the machine after every sleeve they produce. Assume that the first sleeve has a diameter X_1, where

$$X_1 = \mu_1 + \epsilon_1,$$

$\mu_1 = 100$ and ϵ_1 is normally distributed with expected value zero and standard deviation $\sigma_1 = 0.1$. The value after the first adjustment is

$$X_2 = \mu_2 + \epsilon_2,$$

where ϵ_2 is normally distributed with expected value zero and standard deviation $\sigma_1 = 0.1$ and independent of ϵ_1. The adjusted expectation is

$$\mu_2 = \mu_1 - (X_1 - \mu_1).$$

Show that $X_2 = \mu_1 - \epsilon_1 + \epsilon_2$, and use this to find expectation and variance for X_2. How probable is it that X_2 must be discarded? Comment the result.

(c) Correspondingly

$$X_3 = \mu_3 + \epsilon_3,$$

with adjusted expectation $\mu_3 = \mu_2 - (X_2 - \mu_1)$. Find a simple expression for X_3 and use it to show that X_3 has the same distribution as X_2.

Estimation

8

Abstract

In this chapter we will try to find the values of unknown parameters in our models from observations. We know for example that there is a probability p of errors in a shipment of goods, but we do not know the exact value. This requires a line of approach which is different from what we have been using so far. In the previous chapters the distribution was known, and the purpose of the distribution was to compute the probabilities of special events. Now we will assume that only parts of the distribution are known, and we need to develop strategies to fill the gaps.

8.1 Estimation

Imagine that we toss a coin 10 times and get 7 heads and 3 tails. Is this a fair coin? Obviously we cannot be sure about this. The observation is slightly skewed, but that might be a coincidence. If the coin is fair, then the probability of coins is $p = 1/2$. From the information we have so far, we cannot decide if the coin is fair or not. We hence hold the opportunity open that p might have another value.

Since we got 70% coins in our 10 tosses, we have estimated p to have the value $\hat{p} = 0.7$. This does not mean that we know that $p = 0.7$, it only means that the value 0.7 is our best shot given the information we have available. To examine our coin in more detail we carried out several series of n coin tosses, each series with an increasing value on n. Assume that we see the results below:

$$n = 100 \qquad \hat{p} = 0.53$$

$$n = 1000 \qquad \hat{p} = 0.507$$

$$n = 10{,}000 \qquad \hat{p} = 0.4915$$

J. Ubøe, *Introductory Statistics for Business and Economics*, Springer Texts in Business and Economics, https://doi.org/10.1007/978-3-319-70936-9_8

$$n = 100{,}000 \qquad \hat{p} = 0.50104$$

$$n = 1{,}000{,}000 \qquad \hat{p} = 0.499127.$$

For each new series we get a new suggestion $\hat{p}$, and since each new series is based on more tosses, we imagine that our suggestions improve. With one million coin tosses we get $\hat{p} = 0.499127$. Note that we still do not know for sure that the coin is fair, but it now seems likely that the true value for p is very close to $1/2$.

When we make observations to find the value of one or more unknown constants, we say that we estimate the unknowns. Typically our estimates will improve when we make more observations. Nonetheless there will always be room for errors, we usually never obtain certainly about the value.

8.1.1 Estimators

Expected values and variances are examples of numbers that we often would like to know. Constants in our models are usually called parameters. If the constants $\mu = \text{E}[X]$ and $\sigma^2 = \text{Var}[X]$ are unknowns, we wish to estimate their values from observations. An estimator $\hat{\theta}$ is a random variable we use to estimate the value of an unknown constant θ. In this chapter we will use the symbols θ and $\hat{\theta}$ when we discuss general properties of estimators, while symbols like $\hat{\mu}$ and $\hat{\sigma}^2$ are used in specific contexts.

Example 8.1 The most widely used estimator is the mean

$$\overline{X} = \frac{1}{n}(X_1 + X_2 + \cdots + X_n).$$

The mean is used to estimate the expected value $\mu = \text{E}[X]$, and we write $\hat{\mu} = \overline{X}$ when we use the mean to estimate the expected value. If we assume that $X_1, X_2, \ldots, X_n$ are random variables which all have the same expected value $\mu = \text{E}[X_i]$, then

$$\begin{aligned} \text{E}[\hat{\mu}] &= \text{E}\Big[\frac{1}{n}(X_1 + X_2 + \cdots + X_n)\Big] \\ &= \frac{1}{n}(\text{E}[X_1] + \cdots + \text{E}[X_n]) = \frac{1}{n}(\mu + \cdots + \mu) = \mu. \end{aligned}$$

If the expectation of an estimator equals the unknown constant under consideration, we say that the estimator is unbiased. We have hence seen that the mean is often an unbiased estimator for the expected value.

Definition 8.1 An estimator $\hat{\theta}$ for a constant θ is called unbiased if $\mathrm{E}[\hat{\theta}] = \theta$. A biased estimator is an estimator where $\mathrm{E}[\hat{\theta}] \neq \theta$.

When we want to estimate a constant, we can often choose between several unbiased estimators. If $X_1, X_2, \ldots, X_n$ are independent random variables which all have the same expected value $\mu = \mathrm{E}[X_i]$ and variance $\sigma^2 = \mathrm{Var}[X_i]$, then

$$\begin{aligned}
\mathrm{Var}[\overline{X}] &= \mathrm{Var}\left[\frac{1}{n}(X_1 + X_2 + \cdots + X_n)\right] \\
&= \frac{1}{n^2}\mathrm{Var}[X_1 + X_2 + \cdots + X_n] \\
&= \frac{1}{n^2}(\mathrm{Var}[X_1] + \cdots \mathrm{Var}[X_n]) \\
&= \frac{1}{n^2}(\sigma^2 + \cdots + \sigma^2) = \frac{1}{n^2} \cdot n\sigma^2 = \frac{\sigma^2}{n}.
\end{aligned}$$

In this case the mean is an unbiased estimator for the expected value regardless of the value of n, but larger n leads to smaller variance. This makes perfect sense from a practical point of view; the more observations we have, the better is the performance of the estimator.

If we are to choose between two unbiased estimators, we will usually prefer the one with the smallest variance. In some special cases we might even prefer a biased estimator over an unbiased one. This might happen when the variance of the biased estimator is much smaller than the variance of the unbiased one.

Example 8.2 Assume that X and Y are two random variables with $\mathrm{E}[X] = \mu$ and $\mathrm{E}[Y] = 2\mu$, and that a is a constant. Show that for any value of a, then

$$Z = (1 - 2a)X + aY,$$

is an unbiased estimator of μ. We further assume that X and Y are independent and that $\mathrm{Var}[X] = 1, \mathrm{Var}[Y] = 4$. Find a value for a such that the variance of Z is as small as possible.

Solution:

$$\mathrm{E}[Z] = \mathrm{E}[(1 - 2a)X + aY] = (1 - 2a)\mu + a \cdot 2\mu = \mu.$$

Hence Z is an unbiased estimator for μ. Since X and Y are independent, we get

$$\begin{aligned}\mathrm{Var}[Z] &= \mathrm{Var}[(1-2a)X + aY] = \mathrm{Var}[(1-2a)X] + \mathrm{Var}[aY] \\ &= (1-2a)^2\mathrm{Var}[X] + a^2\mathrm{Var}[Y] = (1-2a)^2 + 4a^2 \\ &= 1 - 4a + 4a^2 + 4a^2 = 1 - 4a + 8a^2.\end{aligned}$$

We have to find minimum for the function $f(a) = 1 - 4a + 8a^2$. The derivative is zero when $a = \frac{1}{4}$, and since $f''(a) = 16 > 0$, this is a global minimum for the function. The preferred estimator is hence $Z = \frac{1}{2}X + \frac{1}{4}Y$.

8.1.2 Reporting Estimates

The standard deviation of an estimator is important to discuss the amount of uncertainty related to an estimate. In a scientific survey the authors often report

$$\text{estimated value} \pm \text{standard deviation of the estimator.}$$

It is important to notice that this does *not* mean that the true value is between these extremes. The notation focuses the estimated value, and the last term just quotes the standard deviation. We will later in this chapter be able to form an opinion on where we expect to find the true value we have estimated.

8.1.3 The Measurement Model

We have already seen that the mean is usually an unbiased estimator for the expected value. In most cases we also face an unknown variance, and we might need to estimate this quantity as well. The sample variance S_X^2 which we studied in Chap. 1 is a natural candidate. We recall

$$S_X^2 = \frac{1}{n-1}\left((X_1 - \overline{X})^2 + (X_s - \overline{X})^2 + \cdots + (X_n - \overline{X})^2\right).$$

By tedious verification, we omit the details, and it is possible to prove the following result:

> If $X_1, X_2, \ldots, X_n$ are independent random variables which all have the same expected value $\mu = \mathrm{E}[X_i]$ and variance $\sigma^2 = \mathrm{Var}[X_i]$, then
>
> $$\mathrm{E}[S_X^2] = \sigma^2.$$

The conclusion of the above result is hence that the sample variance is an unbiased estimator of the (theoretical) variance σ^2. We sometimes write $\hat{\sigma}^2 = S_X^2$ to emphasize that S_X^2 is an estimator of σ^2. The results above can be summarized as follows:

Assume that $X_1, \ldots, X_n$ are independent random variables with $\mathrm{E}[X_i] = \mu$ and $\mathrm{Var}[X_i] = \sigma^2$ for all $i = 1, \ldots, n$. When we carry out a survey where μ and σ^2 are unknowns, we make n independent observations/measurements and compute

$$\hat{\mu} = \overline{X} = \frac{1}{n}(X_1 + X_2 + \cdots + X_n),$$

and

$$\hat{\sigma}^2 = S_X^2 = \frac{1}{n-1}\left((X_1 - \overline{X})^2 + (X_s - \overline{X})^2 + \cdots + (X_n - \overline{X})^2\right).$$

These estimators are unbiased estimators for μ and σ^2.

In many scientific surveys we want to compute $\hat{\mu}$ and $\hat{\sigma}^2$. To estimate the standard deviation σ we use

$$\hat{\sigma} = S_X = \sqrt{\hat{\sigma}}.$$

Curiously, $\hat{\sigma}$ is not in general an unbiased estimator for σ, and that is one reason why we prefer to work with the variance instead.

Example 8.3 Let X be the production at a department a randomly selected day. We observe

$$X_1 = 210, \quad X_2 = 220, \quad X_3 = 210, \quad X_4 = 225, \quad X_5 = 220, \quad X_6 = 217.$$

Find unbiased estimates for $\mu = \mathrm{E}[X]$ and $\mathrm{Var}[X] = \sigma^2$.

Solution: We know that $\overline{X}$ and S_X^2 are unbiased estimates for $\mu = \mathrm{E}[X]$ and $\mathrm{Var}[X] = \sigma^2$. Inserting the observations into the formulas we get $\hat{\mu} = 217$ and $\hat{\sigma}^2 = 36$.

8.2 Confidence Intervals

For obvious reasons, any given interval either contains an unknown parameter or it does not. A confidence interval is an interval where the limits are random variables, and prior to the observations there is a certain probability that the interval covers the unknown parameter. Once observations have been made, the interval either covers the unknown parameter, or it does not.

A 95% confidence interval hence has 95% chance of covering the unknown parameter, prior to the observations. When observations have been made, the limits of the confidence interval can be computed, and we are quite confident that a 95% confidence interval does indeed contain the unknown parameter. In most cases we have no way of finding the true value for the unknown parameter, and a confidence interval is then our best shot of where the parameter is likely to be.

Correspondingly, a $(1-\alpha)100\%$ confidence interval has $(1-\alpha)100\%$ chance of covering the unknown parameter, prior to the observations. The smaller the value of α, the better is the chance that the confidence interval does indeed cover the unknown parameter. Hence when we decrease α we get more confidence, since it rarely happens that the interval does not cover the unknown value.

8.2.1 Constructing Confidence Intervals

Assume that $\hat{\theta}$ is an estimator for an unknown parameter θ. Even though intervals need not be symmetric about the estimated value, symmetry is our preferred choice. To find a $(1-\alpha)100\%$ confidence interval we hence seek a number d such that

$$P(|\hat{\theta} - \theta| \leq d) = (1 - \alpha).$$

If such a value of d can be found, the interval $[\hat{\theta} - d, \hat{\theta} + d]$ has probability $1-\alpha$ of covering θ. Here α is the probability that the interval does not contain θ, and we want that this probability is rather small. Most commonly used is the case where $\alpha = 0.05$, which yields a 95% confidence interval.

Example 8.4 Assume for the sake of discussion that we know that $\theta = 0$ and that a 95% confidence interval has limits $\hat{\theta} \pm 0.1$. If we observe $\hat{\theta} = 0.12$, a common misconception is that we are 95% sure that θ is in the interval $[0.01, 0.22]$. This makes no sense since we know for sure that θ is *not* in this interval. Occasionally it might even happen that another researcher carries out the same experiment and find $\hat{\theta} = -0.12$, leading to a 95% confidence interval from $[-0.22, -0.02]$. Clearly they cannot both be 95% sure that the unknown value is covered by their intervals. The randomness of confidence intervals makes such cases possible. A good way of thinking about this case is that each repetition of the experiment will lead to a new confidence interval, and that 5% of these intervals will not contain zero.

To construct formulas for confidence intervals we will now assume that the estimator $\hat{\theta}$ is unbiased, with known standard deviation $\sigma[\hat{\theta}]$ and that $\hat{\theta}$ is approximately normal. If we put $d = z \cdot \sigma[\hat{\theta}]$, we get

$$\begin{aligned} P(|\hat{\theta} - \theta| \leq d) &= P\left(\left|\frac{\hat{\theta} - \theta}{\sigma[\hat{\theta}]}\right| \leq z\right) \approx G(z) - G(-z) \\ &= G(z) - (1 - G(z)) = 2G(z) - 1. \end{aligned}$$

To find a $(1 - \alpha)100\%$ confidence interval, we need to solve the equation

$$2G(z) - 1 = 1 - \alpha.$$

We find a 95% confidence interval as follows:

$$2G(z) - 1 = 0.95 \;\Leftrightarrow\; G(z) = 0.975 \;\Leftrightarrow\; z = 1.96.$$

Figure 8.1 illustrates this result and also shows the corresponding result for a 99% confidence interval. We conclude that the interval with limits $\hat{\theta} \pm 1.96 \cdot \sigma[\hat{\theta}]$ has a 95% chance of covering θ, prior to observations.

Example 8.5 Assume that $\hat{\theta}$ is unbiased, approximately normal, and that $\sigma[\hat{\theta}] = 25$. Find a 95% confidence interval for θ when we have observed $\hat{\theta} = 210$.

Solution: From the discussion above, we know that the limits are $\hat{\theta} \pm 1.96 \cdot \sigma[\hat{\theta}]$. If we insert the given values, we get

$$\hat{\theta} - 1.96 \cdot \sigma[\hat{\theta}] = 210 - 1.96 \cdot 25 = 161,$$

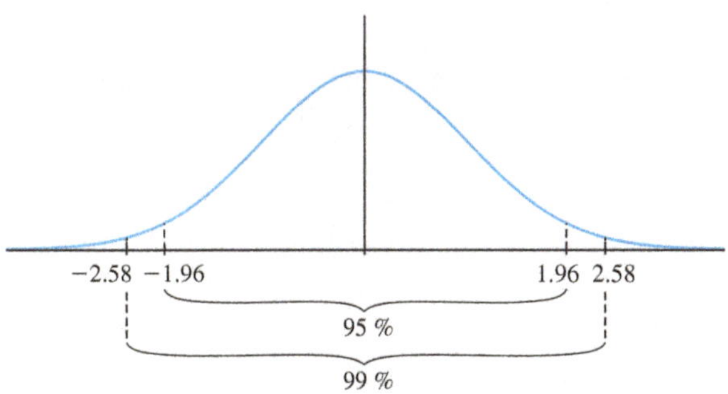

Fig. 8.1 Standard normal distribution with confidence limits

and

$$\hat{\theta} + 1.96 \cdot \sigma[\hat{\theta}] = 210 + 1.96 \cdot 25 = 259.$$

A 95% confidence interval is hence [161, 259].

The argumentation above requires that $\sigma[\hat{\theta}]$ is known and that approximation by a normal distribution can be used. In cases where we have a large number of independent observations, it follows from the central limit theorem that the mean $\overline{X}$ satisfies these conditions. Strictly speaking the standard deviation is not known, but when we have a large number of observations, then $\sigma[\overline{X}] \approx \frac{S_X}{\sqrt{n}}$. The following result is very useful in applications:

Assume that $X_1, \ldots, X_n$ are independent random variables with $\mathrm{E}[X_i] = \mu$ and $\mathrm{Var}[X_i] = \sigma^2$ for all $i = 1, \ldots, n$, and that μ and σ are both unknown. If n is large, an approximate 95% confidence interval is given by the limits

$$\overline{X} \pm 1.96 \cdot \frac{S_X}{\sqrt{n}}.$$

In cases with many observations, we estimate σ by S_X and assume that the approximation is sufficiently good to treat S_X as a constant. Often, however, we will encounter cases with relatively few observations, and then the formulas above do not apply. Since this is a common situation in statistical surveys, statisticians have developed methods to deal with this. Surprisingly, cases with few observations can be dealt with using more or less the same line of approach. The solution is to replace the normal distribution with a new distribution which is called the t-distribution.

8.2.2 The *t*-Distribution

To find confidence intervals for the expected value in cases with few observations, we consider a new random variable T defined by

$$T = \frac{\overline{X} - \mu}{S[\overline{X}]},$$

where

$$S[\overline{X}] = \frac{S_X}{\sqrt{n}}.$$

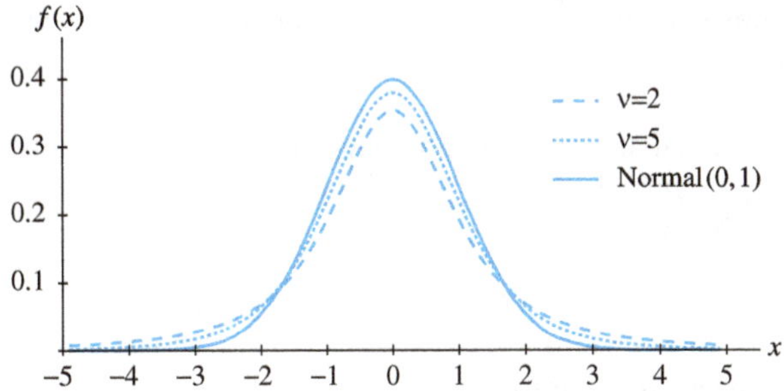

Fig. 8.2 *t*-distributions

In these expressions, $\overline{X}$ is the mean and S_X is the sample standard deviation. In cases with many observations, we could appeal to the central limit theorem and treat S_X as a constant, but these principles no longer apply. To deal with this case, we need to assume that each $X_i, i = 1, \ldots, n$ is approximately normal. The reader should notice that this is a much stronger restriction than what we have been using so far. Since linear combinations of normal distributions are normal, it follows that $\overline{X} - \mu$ is approximately normal, but that does not make T approximately normal. When n is small, the nominator $S[\overline{X}]$ can change considerably if we repeat the experiment, and hence T is a fraction between two random variables. These fractions are well behaved, however, and their statistical distributions can be found directly from tables for the *t*-distribution.

The *t*-distribution is a statistical distribution with a parameter ν. The parameter really means that we are talking about a family of distributions, one for each value of the parameter. Once the parameter is known, we can look up the distribution in a statistical table. The shape of *t*-distributions are all quite similar to the standard normal distribution, see Fig. 8.2. In fact as $\nu \to \infty$, the *t*-distributions converge to the standard normal distribution. The convergence is quite fast, and the difference from the standard normal distribution is hardly noticeable when $\nu \geq 100$. It is also useful to note that the *t*- distributions are always symmetric about zero, since this is something we need to make confidence intervals.

The *t*-distributions have several uses in statistics, and they are hence an object of independent interest. They let us deal with confidence intervals via the following result:

> Assume that $X_1, \ldots, X_n$ are independent, approximately normal, with expectation $\mathrm{E}[X_i] = \mu$ and variance $\mathrm{Var}[X] = \sigma^2$. Then $T = \frac{\overline{X}-\mu}{S[\overline{X}]}$ is *t*-distributed with parameter $\nu = n - 1$.

To see how this can be used to construct confidence intervals, we consider the following example.

Example 8.6 Assume that $X_1, \ldots, X_n$ are independent, approximately normal, with expectation $E[X_i] = \mu$ and variance $\text{Var}[X] = \sigma^2$. We make $n = 9$ independent experiments and observe

$$43, 11, 16, 34, 40, 25, 35, 22, 44.$$

Find a 95% confidence interval for μ.

Solution: From the result above we know that T is t-distributed with parameter $\nu = 9-1 = 8$, and write $T_{(8)}$ to emphasize that we are talking about a t-distribution with this parameter. We look up the 2.5% level in this table to find

$$P(T_{(8)} \geq 2.306) = 2.5\%.$$

Hence by symmetry, with 95% probability $|T_{(8)}| \leq 2.306$ (prior to observations). Now

$$\begin{aligned}\left|\frac{\overline{X}-\mu}{S[\overline{X}]}\right| \leq 2.306 \quad &\Leftrightarrow \; -2.306 \leq \frac{\overline{X}-\mu}{S[\overline{X}]} \leq 2.306 \\ &\Leftrightarrow \; -2.306\, S[\overline{X}] \leq \overline{X}-\mu \leq 2.306\, S[\overline{X}] \\ &\Leftrightarrow \; \overline{X} - 2.306\, S[\overline{X}] \leq \mu \leq \overline{X} + 2.306\, S[\overline{X}]. \end{aligned} \tag{8.1}$$

We conclude that the limits in a 95% confidence interval is

$$\overline{X} \pm 2.306\, S[\overline{X}].$$

Using Excel or a direct approach, we find $\overline{X} = 30$ and $S_X = 12$. Using this information in the formulas above, we get

$$S[\overline{X}] = \frac{S_X}{\sqrt{n}} = \frac{12}{\sqrt{9}} = 4.$$

The limits in a 95% confidence interval are hence $30 \pm 2.306 \cdot 4$ which gives the interval $[20.8, 39.2]$.

The line of approach used in Example 8.6 can of course be used in general:

To construct a $(1-\alpha)100\%$ confidence interval, we first look up a number $t_{\alpha/2}^{(n-1)}$ such that

$$P(T_{(n-1)} \geq t_{\alpha/2}^{(n-1)}) = \alpha/2.$$

(continued)

The limits in a $(1-\alpha)100\%$ confidence interval are then

$$\overline{X} \pm t_{\alpha/2}^{(n-1)} \cdot S[\overline{X}] = \overline{X} \pm t_{\alpha/2}^{(n-1)} \cdot \frac{S_X}{\sqrt{n}}.$$

Example 8.7 Assume that $X_1, \ldots, X_n$ are independent, approximately normal, with expectation $E[X_i] = \mu$ and variance $\mathrm{Var}[X] = \sigma^2$. We make $n = 100$ independent experiments and observe $\overline{X} = 30$ and $S_X = 12$. Find a 95% confidence interval for μ.

Solution: Here the parameter in the t-distribution is 99. We don't have a table for this case, but see that there is hardly any difference between the numbers for $\nu = 90$ and $\nu = 100$. We hence use the table for $\nu = 100$ to see that $t_{0.025}^{(99)} = 1.984$. From the observations we find

$$S[\overline{X}] = \frac{12}{\sqrt{100}} = 1.2.$$

The limits in a 95% confidence interval is $30 \pm 1.984 \cdot 1.2$, which gives the interval $[27.6, 32.4]$.

For the sake of comparison let us assume that we know that $\sigma = 12$ in the previous example. If we use the corresponding framework for cases with many observations, the limits in a 95% confidence interval are $30 \pm 1.96 \cdot 1.2$, which (rounded to one decimal) gives the interval $[27.6, 32.4]$, i.e., the same as in Example 8.7. The reason is that 100 observations is enough to invoke the central limit theorem, and t-tables are no different from the standard normal distribution in this case.

8.3 The Lottery Model

So far in this chapter we have assumed independent observations. In some cases this assumption may not be appropriate. In particular this happens when the population is small. Sampling without replacement may then put new restrictions on the next outcomes. An extreme case happens when we sample the entire population, in that case there is no randomness left. The effect originates from the same core that leads to hyper-geometric distributions in Chap. 7. This context is typical for a lottery where each ticket can be drawn only once. The word lottery model is a collective name for such kind of models, though we should note that applications go beyond pure lotteries.

In general the lottery model can be described as follows: Assume that we have a population with N elements, $v_1, \ldots, v_N$. Here N is a constant. The population has an (unknown) mean

$$\mu = \overline{v} = \frac{1}{N}(v_1 + \cdots + v_N),$$

and an (unknown) variance

$$\sigma^2 = \frac{1}{N}((v_1 - \overline{v})^2 + \cdots (v_N - \overline{v})^2).$$

From the population we draw (without replacement) random elements $Y_1, \ldots, Y_n$. A natural estimator for μ is then

$$\hat{\mu} = \overline{Y} = \frac{1}{n}(Y_1 + \cdots + Y_n).$$

It is then possible to prove (we omit the details) that

$$\mathrm{E}[\hat{\mu}] = \mu, \qquad \mathrm{Var}[\hat{\mu}] = \frac{N-n}{N-1} \cdot \frac{\sigma^2}{n}.$$

We see that the sample mean is an unbiased estimator for the population mean. Since the factor $\frac{N-n}{N-1} < 1$ when $n > 1$, the variance is smaller than what we would get when we sample random elements with replacement. As already noted above, all randomness disappear when $N = n$, and we see that $\mathrm{Var}[\hat{\mu}] = 0$ in that case.

Example 8.8 A company has 50 production units of the same type and wants to check 10 of these units. As it would be quite unnatural to check the same unit twice, the 10 units are drawn randomly without replacement. Previous work with these units suggested $\sigma = 0.4$. The results are shown in Table 8.1.

This is a lottery model, and we find $\overline{Y} = 2.067$. If we use the formulas above with $\sigma = 0.4$, we find

$$\mathrm{Var}[\overline{Y}] = \frac{40}{49} \cdot \frac{0.4^2}{10} = 0.013,$$

which gives $\sigma[\overline{Y}] = 0.11$. In comparison an assumption of independence would have given $\mathrm{Var}[\overline{Y}] = \sqrt{\frac{\sigma^2}{n}} = 0.13$. We see that the effect of dependence is moderate, but the direction is clear; we get less variance when we take into account that the population is small.

Table 8.1 Data for Example 8.8

Y_1	Y_2	Y_3	Y_4	Y_5	Y_6	Y_7	Y_8	Y_9	Y_{10}
2.11	1.99	2.35	1.64	1.32	2.84	2.21	2.28	1.92	2.01

In most cases the population variance σ^2 will be unknown, and it is possible to prove that

$$S^2 = \frac{N}{N-1} \cdot \frac{1}{n-1}((Y_1 - \overline{Y})^2 + \cdots + (Y_n - \overline{Y})^2),$$

is an unbiased estimator for σ^2. We see that when N is large, there is hardly any difference from the expression

$$\frac{1}{n-1}((Y_1 - \overline{Y})^2 + \cdots + (Y_n - \overline{Y})^2),$$

which we use to estimate the variance when observations are independent. If we use the unbiased estimator in the example above, we get

$$S = \sqrt{\frac{50}{49} \cdot \frac{1}{9}((Y_1 - \overline{Y})^2 + \cdots + (Y_{10} - \overline{Y})^2)} = 0.41.$$

In other words there is no reason to believe that the variance has changed.

8.4 Summary of Chap. 8

- An unbiased estimator for a number θ: A random variable $\hat{\theta}$ with $\mathrm{E}[\hat{\theta}] = \theta$. When we choose between several unbiased estimators we usually prefer the one with the smallest variance.
- A biased estimator for a number θ: A random variable $\hat{\theta}$ with $\mathrm{E}[\hat{\theta}] \neq \theta$.
- A $(1-\alpha)100\%$ confidence interval for θ: A random interval that with probability $(1-\alpha)100\%$ covers θ prior to observations.
- When we have a large number of independent variables with the same distribution, the limits of a 95% confidence interval for the mean μ is given by

$$\overline{X} \pm 1.96 \frac{S_X}{\sqrt{n}}.$$

- If we have a small or moderate number of independent variables with the same distribution, and that distribution is approximately normal, we find confidence intervals from the t-distribution: First we find $t_{\alpha/2}^{(n-1)}$ such that

$$P(T_{(n-1)} \geq t_{\alpha/2}^{(n-1)}) = \frac{\alpha}{2}.$$

A $(1-\alpha)100\%$ confidence interval for the mean μ is given by

$$\overline{X} \pm t_{\alpha/2}^{(n-1)} \frac{S_X}{\sqrt{n}}.$$

8.5 Problems for Chap. 8

8.1 Let X denote the income (in USD) of a randomly selected person. We observe

$$X_1 = 30{,}000, \quad X_1 = 40{,}000, \quad X_1 = 28{,}000, \quad X_1 = 20{,}000, \quad X_1 = 60{,}000.$$

Find unbiased estimates for $\text{E}[X] = \mu$ and $\text{Var}[X] = \sigma^2$ based on these observations.

8.2 Let X denote the income (in USD) of a randomly selected person. We have made 10,000 independent observations and found

$$\overline{X} = 35{,}600, \qquad S_X^2 = 441{,}000{,}000.$$

Find a 95% confidence interval for $\text{E}[X] = \mu$.

8.3 Let X denote the wealth (in USD) of a randomly selected person. We have made 2500 independent observations and found the values

$$\overline{X} = 120{,}000, \qquad S_X^2 = 90{,}000{,}000{,}000.$$

Find a 95% confidence interval for $\text{E}[X] = \mu$.

8.4 Let p be the probability that a randomly selected person wants to buy a specific good.

(a) Let X be the number of people in a random selection of 40,000 persons who want to buy the good. What is the distribution of X?
(b) Define

$$\hat{\theta} = \frac{X}{40{,}000}.$$

Show that $\text{E}[\hat{\theta}] = p$ and $\text{Var}[\hat{\theta}] = \frac{p(1-p)}{40{,}000}$.
(c) We asked 40,000 people, and 14,400 of them wanted to buy the good. Find a 99% confidence interval for p. Hint: Assume that $\sigma[\hat{\theta}]$ is constant.
(d) What values will $\sigma[\hat{\theta}]$ get if p is at the endpoint of the confidence interval. Can this affect the answers in this problem?

8.5 The probability that a certain document has errors is p. 5 consecutive days we check 10 randomly selected documents per day, and note how many documents have errors.

(a) Let

$$\overline{X} = \frac{1}{5}(X_1 + X_2 + X_3 + X_4 + X_5)$$

$$S_X^2 = \frac{1}{4}((X_1 - \overline{X})^2 + (X_2 - \overline{X}])^2 + (X_3 - \overline{X}])^2 + (X_4 - \overline{X})^2 + (X_5 - \overline{X})^2).$$

What is E[X] and Var[S_X^2] in this case?

(b) We observe

$$X_1 = 2, \quad X_2 = 1, \quad X_3 = 2, \quad X_4 = 2, \quad X_5 = 3.$$

Compute $\overline{X}$ and S_X^2. Are these values in conflict with the results from (a)?

(c) Define $\hat{\theta} = \frac{\overline{X}}{10}$. Show that $\hat{\theta}$ is an unbiased estimator for p. What is Var[$\hat{\theta}$]?

8.6 Assume that X_1, X_2, X_3, X_4 are independent variables, all with the same distribution. Let E[X_i] $= \mu$ and Var[X_i] $= \sigma^2$. Define

$$V = X_1 + X_2 + X_3 + X_4.$$

(a) Compute E[V] and Var[V]. Can V be used as an estimator for μ?

(b) Define $W = V - 3\mu$. Show that W is an unbiased estimator for μ. What is the problem using W as an estimator?

8.7 Let X denote the income (in USD) of a randomly selected person. We have made 25 independent observations and found

$$\overline{X} = 35{,}600, \qquad S_X^2 = 441{,}000{,}000.$$

Assume that X is approximately normal and find a 95% confidence interval for E[X] $= \mu$.

8.8 Let X denote the wealth (in USD) of a randomly selected person. We have made 9 independent observations and found the values

$$\overline{X} = 120{,}000, \qquad S_X^2 = 90{,}000{,}000{,}000.$$

Assume that X is approximately normal and find a 90% confidence interval for E[X] $= \mu$.

8.9 A producer of a good claims that the net contents of a pack is more than 100 gram in average. Let X be the net contents of a randomly drawn pack. We bought 4 such packs and weighed the net contents. The results were as follows:

$$X_1 = 96, X_2 = 93, X_3 = 96, X_4 = 94.$$

Assume that X is approximately normal. Find a 99% confidence interval for $\mathrm{E}[X]$. Comment the result.

8.10 In a special group of workers there are 1014 persons in total. We make calls to gather information about their income, and manage to get replies from 312 people. We assume that our sample is representative in that it is purely random whether a person can be reached on the phone or not. Computations show that

$$\overline{Y} = \frac{1}{312}\sum_{i=1}^{312} Y_i = 678{,}995,$$

$$S^2 = \frac{1014}{1013} \cdot \frac{1}{311}\sum_{i=1}^{312}(Y_i - \overline{Y})^2 = 1.04814 \cdot 10^{10}.$$

Assume that $\overline{Y}$ has normal distribution, and find a 95% confidence interval for the mean income of this group of workers. Hint: Regard S as a constant and put

$$\mathrm{Var}[\overline{Y}] = \frac{N-n}{N-1} \cdot \frac{S^2}{n}.$$

8.11 In a special industry a total of 522 firms are registered. We manage to get information about the net return after tax from 478 firms. We assume that our sample is representative in that it is purely random if results are missing or not. Our computations show that

$$\overline{Y} = \frac{1}{478}\sum_{i=1}^{478} Y_i = 2{,}133{,}190,$$

$$S^2 = \frac{522}{521} \cdot \frac{1}{477}\sum_{i=1}^{478}(Y_i - \overline{Y})^2 = 6.7123 \cdot 10^{11}.$$

(a) Assume that $\overline{Y}$ is approximatively normal, and find a 95% confidence interval for the mean net return after tax for these firms. Hint: Regard S as a constant and put

$$\mathrm{Var}[\overline{Y}] = \frac{N-n}{N-1} \cdot \frac{S^2}{n}.$$

(b) Assume that $\overline{Y} = 2{,}133{,}190$ and that $S_Y^2 = 6.7123 \cdot 10^{11}$. What would the confidence interval be if the 478 firms instead were a random sample from a large number of firms?

8.12 Merging Two Observation Sets: Two researchers make independent observations of a random variable X with mean $\mathrm{E}[X] = \mu$ and $\mathrm{Var}[X] = \sigma^2$. The first researcher makes 100 independent observations, while the second researcher makes 400 new and independent observations. They use

$$\hat{\theta}_1 = \frac{1}{100}\sum_{i=1}^{100} X_i,$$

$$\hat{\theta}_2 = \frac{1}{400}\sum_{i=1}^{400} X_i'.$$

as estimators for the mean.

(a) What are $\mathrm{E}[\hat{\theta}_1], \mathrm{E}[\hat{\theta}_2], \mathrm{Var}[\hat{\theta}_1]$ and $\mathrm{Var}[\hat{\theta}_2]$ in this case?
(b) To extract as much information as possible from the observations, we would like to use a combination of the two estimators. We let c be any constant and define

$$\hat{\theta}_c = c\hat{\theta}_1 + (1-c)\hat{\theta}_2.$$

Show that $\hat{\theta}_c$ is an unbiased estimator for μ regardless of the value on c, and show that

$$\mathrm{Var}[\hat{\theta}_c] = (4c^2 + (1-c)^2)\cdot\frac{\sigma^2}{400}.$$

(c) Find a value $c = c^*$ such that $\mathrm{Var}[\hat{\theta}_{c*}]$ is as small as possible. Give a verbal description of the optimal estimator $\hat{\theta}_{c*}$ and comment the result.

Hypothesis Testing

9

Abstract

In this chapter we will study statistical testing of a hypothesis. Hypothesis testing has found widespread applications in many different fields. We can, e.g., ask if a poll confirms that voters have changed their opinion, or if a manager of mutual funds is performing systematically better than another. To test different hypotheses against each after, we need to make observations. From observations we can determine which hypothesis is more likely, but we can seldom draw a certain conclusion. The best we can achieve is to say that a hypothesis is most likely false. We sometimes have to settle with a conclusion stating that the observed difference is too small to decide which hypothesis is the better, i.e., we can't say anything for sure.

9.1 Basic Ideas

Hypothesis testing is often viewed as technically demanding, but the theory rests on very simple ideas which we can understand without the use of mathematical formulas. In many cases it may be difficult, or simply not possible, to offer a direct proof that a hypothesis is true. To prove that a hypothesis is wrong, however, all we need to do is to come up with a convincing counter example. In statistical hypothesis testing the basic line of approach is to provide strong evidence against a hypothesis.

All hypothesis testing originates from a null hypothesis and an alternative hypothesis. The two hypotheses should be mutually exclusive; if one of them is wrong the other should be true. We aim to find strong evidence against the null hypothesis. If we succeed, we can claim that the alternative hypothesis probably is true. The direction is crucial and should be taken into account when we design a hypothesis test. Designing a test of this sort, we usually take the alternative hypothesis as our starting point, it is this hypothesis we hope to prove.

J. Ubøe, *Introductory Statistics for Business and Economics*, Springer Texts in Business and Economics, https://doi.org/10.1007/978-3-319-70936-9_9

When we execute a test of this sort, the test sometimes succeeds, sometimes not. If we fail to find strong evidence against the null hypothesis, this does not mean that the null hypothesis is true. It does not exclude the possibility that we later may find such evidence. From that point of view, failure to reject a null hypothesis makes us unable to progress. Our alternative hypothesis may still be true, but we have not found sufficient evidence to support it. It is only when we are able to reject the null hypothesis that we have something interesting to say, i.e., the alternative hypothesis is then probably true.

All hypothesis tests have a test static and a rejection region. The test static is a random variable we can evaluate from empirical data. If the value of the test static falls in the rejection region, it means that we believe we have found sufficient evidence to reject the null hypothesis. In all but exceptional cases we are unable to be 100% certain about the conclusion. No matter how we organize the test, there is always a chance that we reject a true null hypothesis. This type of mistake is called a false positive or type 1 error.

The probability of a false positive is called the significance level and should, for obvious reasons, be small. In practice statisticians very often use a significance level of 5%. While there is little or no scientific support for this convention, it is a fruitful rule of thumb. If the significance level is too low, it leads to paralysis. If it is too high, conclusions are drawn from weak evidence. A significance level of 5% provides a proper balance between the two effects. It is a guideline supporting the correct result in 19 out of 20 cases, and most decision makers will be comfortable with that level of precision. It is certainly not sufficient to convict a person for a serious offense, in such cases the significance level should be much, much smaller.

A false negative or type 2 error occurs when the test fails to reject a false null hypothesis. No matter how we organize a test, errors of this kind cannot completely be avoided. The probability of a type 2 error should of course be small, but contrary to the type 1 errors, there are no simple guidelines on how to proceed. The alternative hypothesis is usually a collection of many different outcomes, and to be able to compute the probability of a type 2 error, we usually need to specify a proper subset of those outcomes. If we specify an alternative too close (measured in terms of the test static) to the null hypothesis, the test will often fail to detect the difference. The probability of a type 2 error is then large. If we specify an alternative far from the null hypothesis, however, we can expect that the probability of a type 2 error is very small. Hence the probability of a type 2 error will usually depend on which alternative we believe to be true.

The strength of a statistical test is the complement of the probability of a type 2 error. The strength hence depends on which alternative we believe is true. The strength is high when the probability of a type 2 error is low. Conversely, high strength means low probability of a type 2 error.

When we execute a statistical test, we use the test static to measure how much the observed value deviates from the null hypothesis. We reject the null hypothesis when the deviation is too large. In this connection it may be valuable to know how probable the deviation is. We measure this probability in terms of P-value. The P-value is the probability of a deviation which is larger than or equal to the observed deviation, given that the null hypothesis is true. We should reject the null hypothesis when the P-value is less than or equal to the significance level, but the P-value offers information beyond rejection/non-rejection. The lower the P-value, the less likely it seems that the null hypothesis can be true. Hence if the P-value is very small we are quite confident that the null hypothesis is false. The reader should note the resemblance in logic with confidence intervals. The P-value is *not* the probability that the null hypothesis is true; this probability is either 0 or 1.

Some of the material in this chapter is quite technical. If you are to use hypothesis testing in practice, it is of some importance to notice that computations of this sort are often fully automated in statistical software. Hence in applications the hardship of mathematical computation can often be avoided. The reader should hence focus the rather nonmathematical concepts we have just been through.

9.2 Motivation

To motivate the discussion later in this chapter, we consider an example. The example is not a hypothesis test. Nevertheless it contains much of the logic behind such tests.

Example 9.1 Assume that the stock price K of a stock in a collection of some particular companies is a random variable which is normally distributed with mean zero and variance σ^2. The mean and variance are both unknown.

We start to assume that $\mu = 100$ and $\sigma^2 = 100$. We pick a random stock and observe $K = 131$. Since this value is rather high, we wonder if we can really believe our assumptions. We hence ask the following question: If our assumptions are true, what is the probability of observing $K \geq 131$? As K is normally distributed

$$P(K \geq 131) = 1 - P(K \leq 131) = 1 - G\left(\frac{131 - 100}{\sqrt{100}}\right) = 0.001.$$

Since an observation as large as 131 or more only occurs in 1 out of 1000 cases, it is difficult to believe in our assumptions. We hence reject these assumptions. Reading through some old surveys of these stocks, we find some results suggesting that $\mu = 127$ and $\sigma^2 = 85$ might be reasonable. Assuming that these new assumptions are true, what is then the probability of observing 131 or more? Here we get

$$P(K \geq 131) = 1 - P(K \leq 131) = 1 - G\left(\frac{131 - 127}{\sqrt{85}}\right) = 0.332.$$

With these new parameters we then expect to observe 131 or more in 1 out of 3 cases. As this is very common, we no longer have a just cause for rejection. A frequent misconception is to interpret $P(K \geq 131)$ as the probability that our assumptions (our hypothesis) are true. That interpretation is wrong. The basic idea in hypothesis testing is to reject when our observation would be rare if the assumptions were true. Something that happens in 1 out of 3 cases is not rare in any meaningful sense.

Believing that $\mu = 127$ and $\sigma^2 = 85$ might be sensible values, we make 100 independent observations. We call these $K_1, \ldots, K_{100}$. As mentioned in Chap. 7, a sum of normally distributed variables is normally distributed. $\overline{K}$ hence has normal distribution. If our assumptions are true, then

$$\mathrm{E}[\overline{K}] = \mu = 127,$$

and

$$\mathrm{Var}[\overline{K}] = \frac{\sigma^2}{n} = \frac{85}{100} = 0.85.$$

We carry out the observations, and find, e.g., $\overline{K} = 128.6$. How should we interpret that? Ideally the mean and the expected value should match, and we should ask if it is common to see a difference of 1.6 when our assumptions are true. We compute the probability

$$P(\overline{K} \geq 128.6) = 1 - P(\overline{K} \leq 128.6) = 1 - G\left(\frac{128.6 - 127}{\sqrt{0.85}}\right) = 0.04.$$

This case is more awkward to interpret. A deviation of this magnitude is slightly uncommon, but not very rare. In statistics it is common to draw a line at probabilities less than 5%, and the rule of thumb is to reject our assumptions in such cases. Even though rejection appears to be the right decision, we should proceed with care. Rejection is the correct decision in 19 out of 20 cases, but we keep in mind that in 1 out of 20 cases rejection would be wrong.

Since the basis for rejection was slightly fragile, we decide to make a closer examination. This time we make 10,000 observations. Assume that we, e.g., observe $\overline{K} = 127.05$. This time too, the mean deviates somewhat from the expected value. We should examine how common the deviation could be. The computations are similar to the previous case, the only difference is that the variance is reduced to

$$\mathrm{Var}[\overline{K}] = \frac{\sigma^2}{n} = \frac{85}{10{,}000} = 0.0085.$$

Hence

$$P(\overline{K} \geq 127.05) = 1 - P(\overline{K} \leq 127.05) = 1 - G\left(\frac{127.05 - 127}{\sqrt{0.0085}}\right) = 0.293.$$

Assuming that we make 10,000 observations and that our assumptions are true, we would expect a deviation of $+0.05$ or more in about 1 out of 3 cases. By symmetry we would expect a deviation of -0.05 or more in roughly 1 out of 3 cases.

A deviation of this magnitude is hence very common, and we have no reason to expect that something is wrong. We have not proved that our assumptions are true, but taking into account that we now have 10,000 observations and that our assumptions are supported by old surveys, we seem to be on the right track.

Seemingly we have two surveys that are logically inconstant, the first survey with 100 observations says reject, and the second with 10,000 observations says not reject. Since the latter survey is based on much more data, it is our preferred choice. The deviation we observed in the first survey would appear in 1 out of 20 cases, and it seems reasonable to assume that by coincidence we encountered one of those cases. The inconsistency is resolved if we interpret the first observation as a false positive, i.e., that we rejected a true assumption. The reader should note that rejection is nevertheless the right decision after the first survey. Based on the information we had at that point, the deviation was too large to be accepted. That does not exclude the possibility that we later may find information supporting the opposite view. The dilemma does not disappear if probabilities are much smaller. Even if we observe a deviation that only occurs in 1 out of 1000 cases, it is nevertheless possible that we are rejecting a true assumption.

The simple discussion above focuses a clear distinction between mathematics and statistics. Mathematicians make a calculation, and, assuming that no mistake is done, they can be 100% sure about the result. Statisticians, however, can seldom draw certain conclusions. There is always a risk that a decision will turn out to be wrong, but we should strive to make that risk as small as possible.

9.3 General Principles for Hypothesis Testing

A statistical hypothesis test consists of the following elements:

- A null hypothesis, which we signify by the symbol H_0.
- An alternative hypothesis, which we signify by the symbol H_A.
- A random variable T, which we call the test statistic.
- A rejection region. When the value of the test statistic falls in the rejection region, we reject the null hypothesis.

When we formulate hypotheses, it is often natural to state H_A first, and then H_0. When H_A is decided, H_0 should include all outcomes that are not covered by H_A. The leading idea is that we hope to prove that H_A is true, and we achieve that if we are able to demonstrate that H_0 probably is false.

From a statistician's point of view it is more interesting if we can reject the null hypothesis, it is only in this case we have something interesting to say. If our observations do not support rejection, this does not prove that the null hypothesis is true. It only means that from the data we have collected so far, we have no sufficient evidence to support H_A. That does not exclude the possibility that such evidence can turn up later.

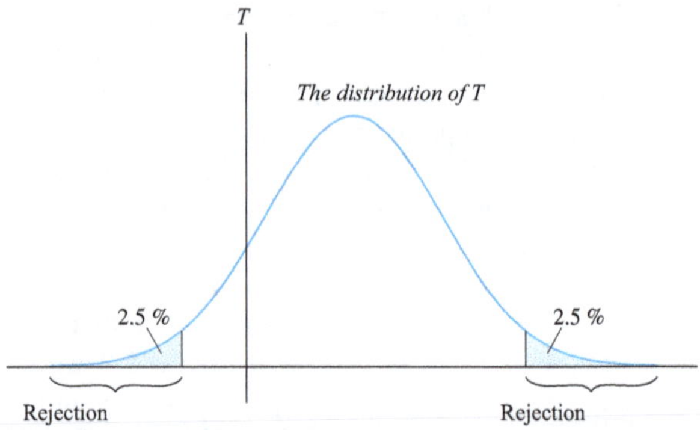

Fig. 9.1 A typical rejection region

The example we discussed in the motivation section has much in common with a hypothesis test. The context there could have been formulated as follows:

- H_0: The parameters in the normal distribution are $\mu = 100$ and $\sigma^2 = 100$.
- H_A: $\mu \neq 100$ or $\sigma^2 \neq 100$.
- $T = K$.
- Reject H_0 if $T \leq 80.3$ or $T \geq 119.7$.

If we formulate a test as above, what is then the probability of a false positive? To answer that, we should assume that H_0 is true, and find the probability that the test static T falls in the rejection region see Fig. 9.1, i.e.

$$\begin{aligned} P(T \leq 80.2) + P(T \geq 119.7) &= G\left(\frac{80.3 - 100}{\sqrt{100}}\right) + 1 - G\left(\frac{80.3 - 100}{\sqrt{100}}\right) \\ &= G(-1.97) + 1 - G(1.97) \\ &= 1 - G(1.97) + 1 - G(1.97) \\ &= 2.5\% + 2.5\% = 5\%. \end{aligned}$$

From this computation we see that the rejection region was designed in such a way that the probability of a false positive is 5%. The probability of a false positive, given that the null hypothesis is true, is called the significance level. The significance level is here 5%, which, as we have already remarked, is a typical choice.

The probability of a false negative will depend on which alternative that is true. In this context we could, e.g., ask about the probability of a false negative if $\mu = 127$ and $\sigma^2 = 85$, i.e., the values we decided to use after rejecting our initial choice. We do not reject the null hypothesis when $80.3 < T < 119.7$, and, conditional on our specific alternative, the probability is computed as follows:

$$\begin{aligned} P(80.3 < T \leq 119.7) &= P(T < 119.7) - P(T \leq 80.3) \\ &= G\left(\frac{119.7 - 127}{\sqrt{85}}\right) - G\left(\frac{80.3 - 127}{\sqrt{85}}\right) \\ &= G(-0.79) - G(-5.07) \\ &= 1 - G(0.79) - (1 - G(5.07)) \\ &= G(5.07) - G(0.79) = 1.000 - 0.7852 = 21.48\%. \end{aligned}$$

We see that the probability of making a false negative is more than 20% in this case. The strength is the complement of this quantity, and we conclude that the strength is 78.52% when we consider this particular alternative.

The significance level of a hypothesis test is α when the maximum probability for a false positive is α. The strength of a specific alternative is the probability that we reject the null hypothesis when the alternative is true.

9.4 Designing Statistical Tests

When we are in the process of designing a test to analyze a given set of observations, there are several pitfalls we could walk into. The conditions for most statistical test are violated if we inspect the data first and then decide which test to use. While seemingly innocent, this sequence of events is actually a serious mistake. To explain why this is a mistake, we consider an example.

Example 9.2 Assume that we have collected data from 10 different departments. We inspect the data and observe, e.g., that department number 3 performed quite badly. It could then be tempting to try to test if department 3 is performing worse than average. A reasonable null hypothesis is that all departments are equally good. When H_0 is true, any department will be the worst in 1 out of 10 cases. Inspecting the data and selecting the worst department, we have tacitly increased the probability of testing the worst department to 100%. If H_0 is true, the probability of a bad result will be much higher than for a randomly selected department, and most statistical tests do not take this into account.

Unusual events will always pop up randomly when we inspect sufficiently many cases, and, moreover, unusual events will become common when we do so. Rarity must always be seen in comparison with how many cases we have inspected, and most statistical tests are tacitly assuming that we are inspecting only one case. A legitimate line of action in Example 9.2 would be to state an alternative hypothesis that department 3 is performing worse than average. To examine this hypothesis,

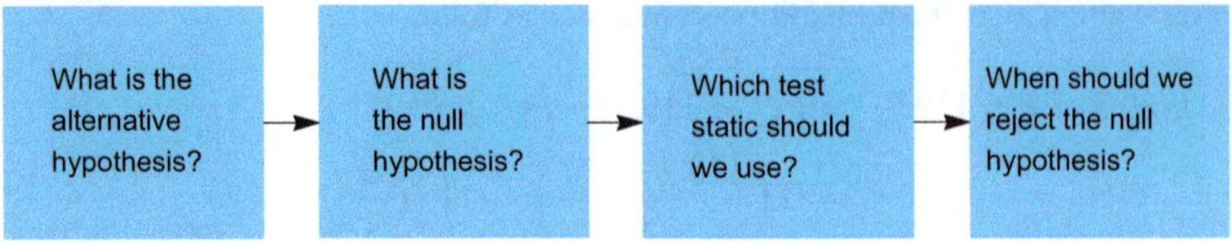

Fig. 9.2 The line of events in hypothesis testing

however, we then need to collect an entirely new set of observations, and use this new set to determine the performance. If the performance of department 3 continues to be bad, we then have legitimate evidence in favor of the alternative.

When we design statistical tests, it is important to find a proper balance between high strength and a sufficiently low level of significance. In most cases good strength comes at the expense of unsatisfactory significance levels, and vice versa. The only way we can increase both is by collecting more observations, but that option is frequently too costly or time consuming. As mentioned above all such considerations should be done prior to the collection of data.

The proper line of events in hypothesis testing is outlined in Fig. 9.2.

Only when all of these questions have been answered, should we begin to collect data. In practice we often need to analyze data that already has been collected. That is perfectly OK as long as we do not inspect the data before we decide which tests to use.

Example 9.3 We are flipping coins with a friend, and after loosing 50 times in a row, we get a sneaking feeling that something is wrong. To examine this in detail we formulate our problem in terms of a hypothesis test. The test is made as follows:

$$H_0 : \text{ The probability of heads is } p = 1/2.$$
$$H_A : \text{ The probability of heads is } p > 1/2.$$

The test is executed by flipping the coin 1000 times, and we let

$$X_i = \begin{cases} 1 & \text{if the result is heads in flip number } i \\ 0 & \text{if the result is tails in flip number } i \end{cases}.$$

Each X_i is hence an indicator distribution with $\mathrm{E}[X_i] = p$ and $\mathrm{Var}[X_i] = p(1-p)$ where p is unknown. As test static we use the mean

$$\hat{p} = \frac{1}{1000}(X_1 + X_2 + \cdots + X_{1000}).$$

Here:

$$\mathrm{E}[\hat{p}] = p, \qquad \mathrm{Var}[\hat{p}] = \frac{p(1-p)}{1000}.$$

We should reject the null hypothesis if we observe too many heads, but where should we draw the line? The rejection region should be an interval $[p_{\text{limit}}, \infty)$, where p_{limit} is the exact place where we draw the line.

With a 5% significance level, we should design the test such that the probability of a false positive is 5%. Hence when H_0 is true, i.e., $p = 1/2$, the probability of ending up in the rejection region should be 5%. We are then in the fortunate situation that p is known, and we can consider the statement

$$P(\hat{p} \geq \theta_{\text{limit}}) = 0.05.$$

From the central limit theorem we know that $\hat{p}$ is approximately normal. Hence

$$P(\hat{p} \geq p_{\text{limit}}) = 1 - P(\hat{p} < p_{\text{limit}}) \approx 1 - G\left(\frac{p_{\text{limit}} - p}{\sqrt{\frac{p(1-p)}{1000}}}\right) = 0.05.$$

Since we know that $p = 0.5$, we can view this as an equation with a single unknown, p_{limit}. From the table for the standard normal distribution, we see that $G(z) = 0.95$ if and only if $z = 1.6449$. Hence

$$\frac{p_{\text{limit}} - 0.5}{\sqrt{\frac{0.5(1-0.5)}{1000}}} = 1.6449 \Leftrightarrow p_{\text{limit}} = 0.5 + 1.6449 \cdot \sqrt{\frac{0.5(1-0.5)}{1000}} = 0.526.$$

In other words, we reject the null hypothesis if we carry out the test and observe at least 526 heads.

Example 9.4 In Example 9.3 we were fortunate that H_0 identified a single value for p. This will not always be the case. To examine this in detail, we modify the example as follows:

$$H_0: \text{ The probability of heads is } p \leq 1/2.$$

$$H_A: \text{ The probability of heads is } p > 1/2.$$

We use the same test static $\hat{p}$ and the same rejection region as before. What is the significance level of the new test?

Solution: We assume that H_0 is true, and want to compute $P(\hat{p} \geq 0.526)$. The problem now is that p is unknown. The only information we have is that $p \leq 1/2$. The smaller the true value of p, the smaller is the probability $P(\hat{p} \geq 0.526)$. Hence for any $p < 1/2$, then

$$P(\hat{p} \geq 0.526) \leq P_{p=1/2}(\hat{p} \geq 0.526) = 5\%.$$

We see that $p = 1/2$ is an extreme case, and that all other cases lead to lower risk of type 1 error. The maximum probability of a false positive is hence 5%. In accordance with the general definition of significance level, the significance level remains at 5% in this extended case.

Example 9.4 demonstrates why we need to consider the maximum probability of false positives in the general definition of significance level, and also explains how we might compute the significance level in such extended cases. The basic idea is to consider the most extreme case, and, with luck, that makes the computation sufficiently explicit to be carried out.

To proceed, we continue to consider the test in Example 9.4, but now we want to figure out the strength of alternatives. As we remarked above, the strength will depend on which alternative that is true. We hence look at some explicit cases.

Case 1 Assume that the true value of $p = 0.58$. What is the probability of a false negative?

Solution: A false negative occurs when the outcome of the test leads to non-rejection of the null hypothesis. In our case we do not reject when $\hat{p} < 0.526$. If $p = 0.58$, then

$$P(\hat{p} < 0.526) \approx G\left(\frac{0.526 - 0.58}{\sqrt{\frac{0.58 \cdot 0.42}{1000}}}\right) = G(-3.46) = 1 - G(3.46) = 0.03\%.$$

We see that test is really strong in that case, i.e., we will nearly always reject H_0 if the true value of p is 0.58.

Case 2 Assume that the true value of $p = 0.51$. What is the probability of a false negative?

Solution: We still do not reject when $\hat{p} < 0.526$. If $p = 0.51$, then

$$P(\hat{p} < 0.526) \approx G\left(\frac{0.526 - 0.51}{\sqrt{\frac{0.51 \cdot 0.49}{1000}}}\right) = G(1.01) = 84\%.$$

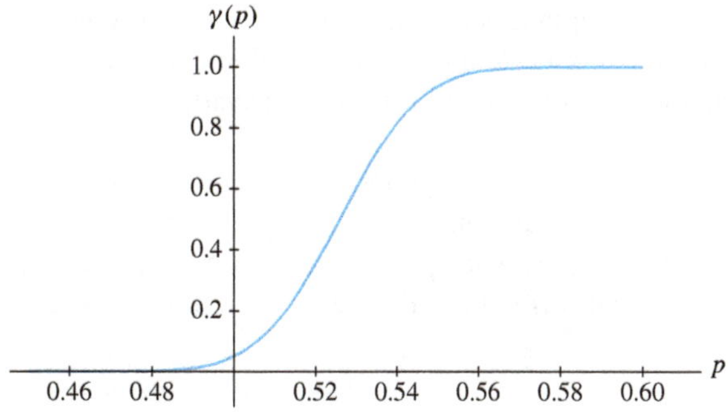

Fig. 9.3 The strength function of Example 9.4

We see that test is not at all strong when the true value of p is 0.51. In a majority of outcomes, we will not detect the difference.

Note that as long as we keep the number of observations fixed at 1000, we reduce the probability of false positives if we increase p_{limit}. This, however, will come at the expense of less strength of any alternative. The only way of improving both strength and significance level is to increase the number of observations.

In a test with one unknown parameter θ, the strength function γ is defined as follows:

$$\gamma(\theta) = \text{Probability of a false negative given that the true value is } \theta.$$

The graph of the strength function for the test in Example 9.4 is shown in Fig. 9.3.

From Fig. 9.3 we see that the strength is nearly zero when p is less than 0.47 and nearly 100% when p is larger than 0.6.

9.4.1 One-Sided and Two-Sided Tests

A test involving one unknown parameter θ is called one-sided if the hypotheses are on one of the forms

$$H_0 : \theta \leq \theta_0, \; H_A : \theta > \theta_0,$$
$$H_0 : \theta = \theta_0, \; H_A : \theta > \theta_0,$$
$$H_0 : \theta \geq \theta_0, \; H_A : \theta < \theta_0,$$
$$H_0 : \theta = \theta_0, \; H_A : \theta < \theta_0.$$

In theory other versions are possible, but are generally avoided.

The test is called two-sided when it is on the form

$$H_0 : \theta = \theta_0, \; H_A : \theta \neq \theta_0.$$

For computational simplicity we have only considered one-sided tests so far. One-sided tests should, however, only be used in special situations. Typically there should be some kind of information available that excludes certain outcomes.

Example 9.5 Imagine you wish to examine if some special form of training leads to improved production. We measure production in terms of an unknown parameter θ, which increases when production improves. It may be unreasonable to assume that this special form of training can lead to lower production. Hence the alternative

$$\theta_{\text{after training}} < \theta_{\text{before training}}$$

is excluded by common sense. In that case it is legitimate to consider

$$H_0 : \theta_{\text{after training}} = \theta_{\text{before training}}, \qquad H_A : \theta_{\text{after training}} > \theta_{\text{before training}}.$$

Example 9.6 Imagine that you wish to examine if some form of new security measure affects production. In this case there is nothing to exclude that production can go up or down, and hence a two-sided test is then appropriate.

9.4.2 Confidence Intervals and Hypothesis Testing

We should notice that symmetric confidence intervals are closely connected to two-sided tests. To see how this works, we consider the following example.

Example 9.7 Assume that we have made several independent observations of a random variable with unknown μ and variance σ^2. The observations are approximately normal, and we have used the t-distribution to find a 95% confidence interval for the unknown expectation. The resulting interval was $[6.2 - 1.4, 6.2 + 1.4]$. Next assume that we want to test the null hypothesis $H_0 : \mu = 4$ against the two-sided alternative $H_A : \mu \neq 4$. What conclusion can we draw from this if we use 5% significance level?

Solution: From the confidence interval we can see that $\overline{X} = 6.2$. We don't know $n, t_{0.025}^{(n-1)}$ or $S[\overline{X}]$, but we know that $t_{0.025}^{(n-1)} \cdot S[\overline{X}] = 1.4$. In a two-sided test we use the test static $\overline{X}$ and should reject H_0 if $\overline{X} > 4 + 1.4$ or if $\overline{X} < 4 - 1.4$. In conclusion we reject H_0.

If we look more closely on the previous example, we see that we keep H_0 if and only if the expected value defined by H_0 is an element of the confidence interval. If the expectation defined by H_0 is outside the confidence interval, it always leads to rejection.

9.4.3 *P*-Value

The single most important concept in applications of hypothesis testing is the *P*-value. The reason for this is that most statistical software reports the outcomes of statistical tests in terms of *P*-values. The definition reads as follows:

Definition 9.1 Assuming that the null hypothesis is true, the *P*-value is the probability of a deviation (from the null hypothesis) which is greater than or equal to the observed deviation.

The somewhat awkward part of this definition is to understand what we mean by a deviation from the null hypothesis. To examine this more closely, we first consider a one-sided test where we reject when $T \geq T_{\text{limit}}$. The larger the value of T, the larger is the deviation from the null hypothesis. This means that the *P*-value is defined by

$$P\text{-value} = P_{H_0}(T \geq T_{\text{observed}}).$$

The notation P_{H_0} means that when we compute the probability, we assume that H_0 is true.

If the level of significance is α and the *P*-value is less than α, this combination of values can only occur if $T_{\text{observed}} \geq T_{\text{limit}}$, which means that the observed value leads to rejection. One advantage of this approach is that we need not find an explicit value for T_{limit}, it suffices to see that the *P*-value is less than the confidence level. Another advantage of *P*-values is that they offer information about the quality of rejection. The smaller the *P*-value, the less we believe in the null hypothesis.

When the *P*-value is smaller than the confidence level, but rather close to this level, the rejection is weak. We are much more confident if the test returns a very small *P*-value. In that case the rejection is strong.

Example 9.8 Assume that the test static is $T = 131$, and that the conditions in the null hypothesis imply that $P_{H_0}(T \geq 131) = 0.001$. This means that our observation is very rare given that the null hypothesis is true. The *P*-value is 0.001, and we will reject the null hypothesis at any reasonable significance level. See Fig. 9.4.

Example 9.9 Assume that the test static is $T = 131$, and that the conditions in the null hypothesis imply that $P_{H_0}(T \geq 131) = 0.332$. This means that our observation is very common given that the null hypothesis is true. This gives no reason to reject, and we keep the null hypothesis at any reasonable significance level. See Fig. 9.5.

If we instead consider one-sided tests where we reject when $T \leq T_{\text{limit}}$, we proceed in the same way. The only difference is that smaller observed values are interpreted as larger deviations. The *P*-value is hence defined via

$$P\text{-value} = P_{H_0}(T \leq T_{\text{observed}}).$$

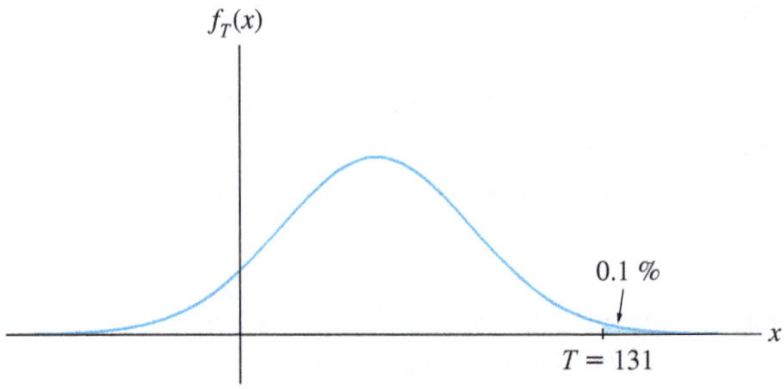

Fig. 9.4 P-value equal to 0.001

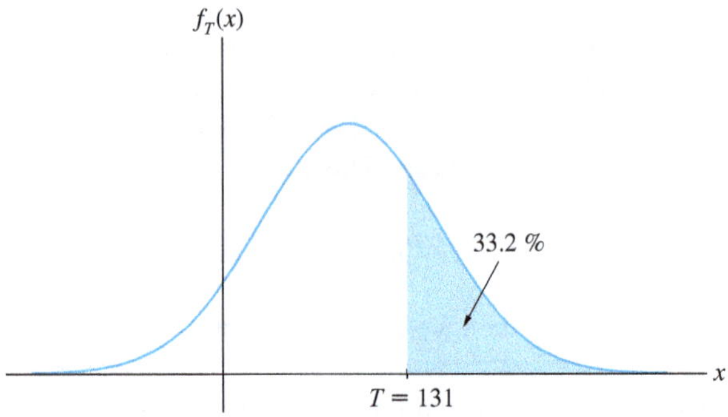

Fig. 9.5 P-value equal to 0.332

Considering two-sided tests with symmetric distribution, deviation can work in two directions. We reject if the value is too large, but also when it is too small. Under symmetry, we reject when $T \geq T_{\text{limit}}$ and also when $T \leq -T_{\text{limit}}$. When that happens, we need to modify the computation of P-value accordingly, i.e.

$$P\text{-value} = P_{H_0}(T \geq |T_{\text{observed}}|) + P_{H_0}(T \leq -|T_{\text{observed}}|).$$

Example 9.10 We want to test if the expected value is 4, and use a two-sided test with test static

$$T = \frac{1}{1000}(X_1 + X_2 + \cdots + X_{1000}) - 4.$$

We observe the value $T = -0.1$. The P-value we then find as

$$P\text{-value} = P_{H_0}(T \leq -0.1) + P_{H_0}(T \geq 0.1).$$

We should reject the null hypothesis when the P-value is less than or equal to the significance level. The smaller the P-value, the more confident we are that rejection is the right thing to do. Conversely, we keep the null hypothesis when the P-value is greater than the significance level. The greater the P-value, the less reason we have for rejection.

Example 9.11 We carry out a survey, and find that the P-value is 0.1%. This means that if H_0 is true, then we would only expect to see a deviation as large as the one we have observed in 1 out of 1000 cases. This makes it hard to believe in H_0, and we will almost always reject it.

Example 9.12 We carry out a survey and find that the P-value is 40%. This means that if H_0 is true, then we would expect to see a deviation as large as the one we have observed in 4 out of 10 cases. As this is very common, there is no indication that something is wrong with the null hypothesis, and we will never reject H_0 based on this information.

Example 9.13 We carry out a survey and find that the P-value is 4%. This means that if H_0 is true, then we would expect to see a deviation as large as the one we have observed in 1 out of 20 cases. This is quite rare, but there is a nonzero chance that we observed a large deviation by coincidence. We will reject H_0 if the significance level is 5%, but will not reject H_0 if the significance level is 1%.

Example 9.14 A firm with many customers considers to introduce a new product. The firm think they will be able to make a profit if more than 20% of their customers will buy the product. The firm asks 40 randomly selected customers, and 10 of those confirm that they want to buy the product.

Question: Based on this survey, is it likely that more than 20% of the customers will buy the product?

Solution: We let p be the fraction of the customers who want to buy the product, and formulate our question as a hypothesis test. The null hypothesis is that $p \leq 20\%$, and the alternative is $p > 20\%$. We ask 40 randomly selected customers, and let X be the number of these customers who want to buy the product. Since the firm has many customers, it is reasonable to assume that X has binomial distribution with $n = 40$. With this information we can compute the P-value of the observation $X = 10$.

$$P\text{-value} = P_{p=0.2}(X \geq 10) = \sum_{i=10}^{40} \binom{40}{i} 0.2^i 0.8^{40-i} = 26.82\%.$$

Since the P-value is quite large, we keep the null hypothesis. There is a considerable risk that the project will not make a profit.

If, for the sake of argument, we instead had observed, e.g., $X = 17$, the conclusion would be different. Then

$$P\text{-value} = P_{p=0.2}(X \geq 17) = \sum_{i=17}^{40} \binom{40}{i} 0.2^i 0.8^{40-i} = 0.01\%.$$

Here the P-value is so small that it seems very unlikely that the null hypothesis can be true, and we are hence confident that the project will profit.

9.5 Summary of Chap. 9

- A hypothesis test has the following elements:
  (i) A null hypothesis H_0.
  (ii) An alternative hypothesis H_A.
  (iii) A test static T.
  (iv) A rejection region.
  The test is executed by an observation of $\hat{T}$. If $\hat{T}$ falls in the rejection region, we reject H_0 and claim that H_A is probably true. If $\hat{T}$ is outside the rejection region, we keep H_0, but that does not mean that we have found proof that H_0 is true.
- A false positive or type 1 error occurs when we reject a true null hypothesis.
- A test has significance level α if the probability of a false positive is at most α.
- A false negative or type 2 error occurs if we keep a false null hypothesis. The probability will depend on which alternative is true.
- The strength of an alternative is the probability of not getting a false negative when the alternative that is true.
- The P-value is the probability of a deviation (from the null hypothesis) that is at least as large as the observed value, given that the null hypothesis is true.
- We reject the null hypothesis if the P-value is at least as small as that of the significance level, and are more confident about rejection the smaller the P-value is.
- We keep the null hypothesis when the P-value is larger than the significance level, and are more confident about keeping it the larger the P-value is.

9.6 Problems for Chap. 9

9.1 In this problem we want to study the power consumption in a small city. We assume that the power consumption X (in kWh) of a randomly selected consumer in the first quarter of the year has expectation μ and variance $\sigma^2 = 4{,}000{,}000$. Last year the average power consumption was 8000 kWh. To test if the expected power consumption has decreased, we checked the power consumption for 100 randomly selected customers.

(a) What is the natural null hypothesis and alternative hypothesis?
(b) As test static we use

$$T = \overline{X} = \frac{1}{100}(X_1 + X_2 + \cdots + X_{100}).$$

What is E[T] and $\sigma[T]$?
(c) What is the rejection region if we use a significance level of 5%?
(d) We observe $T = 7800$ (kWh). Which conclusion can we draw from this?

9.2 In this problem we study the fee usage in a bank. We assume that the total fee X (in USD) of a randomly selected customer has expectation μ and variance $\sigma^2 = 1600$. Last year the average fee was 120 USD. To test if the fees have increased, we checked 400 randomly selected customers.

(a) What is the natural null hypothesis and alternative hypothesis?
(b) As test static we use

$$T = \overline{X} = \frac{1}{400}(X_1 + X_2 + \cdots + X_{400}).$$

What is E[T] and $\sigma[T]$?
(c) What is the rejection region if we use a significance level of 5%?
(d) We observe $T = 130$ (USD). Which conclusion can we draw from this?

9.3 A company claims that firms buying their new Internet package improve their sales by 10% on average. We doubt that this can be true, and check the sales at 25 randomly selected firms. Let X be the sales improvement (in percent of previous sales volumes) of a randomly selected customer that bought the new Internet package. Assume that X is normally distributed with expectation μ and variance σ^2. We assume that trade volumes at different firms are roughly equal.

(a) What is the natural null hypothesis and alternative hypothesis?
(b) As test static we use

$$T = \frac{\overline{X} - 0.1}{S[\overline{X}]}.$$

What is the distribution of T when H_0 is true?
(c) What is the rejection region if we use a significance level of 5%?
(d) We observe $\overline{X} = 0.09$ and $S_X = 0.05$. Which conclusion can we draw from this?

9.4 A small company has introduced flextime as a means to reduce absence due to illness. Before the introduction of flextime, the average absence due to illness was 11 days per year. Let X be the total number of days a randomly selected worker is absent due to illness during a whole year. Assume that X is normally distributed with expectation μ and variance σ^2. The company has 36 workers.

(a) What is the natural null hypothesis and alternative hypothesis?
(b) As test static we use

$$T = \frac{\overline{X} - 11}{S[\overline{X}]}.$$

What is the distribution of T when H_0 is true?
(c) What is the rejection region if we use a significance level of 5%?
(d) We observe $\overline{X} = 10$ and $S_X = 3$. Which conclusion can we draw from this?

9.5 A firm claims that more than 50% of the population prefer their new product. We ask 5 randomly selected people if they prefer the new product. Let X be the number of people in the sample who answer yes.

(a) We believe that the company may be right, and wish to execute a test where it will be possible to conclude that the firm probably is right. What is the natural null hypothesis and alternative hypothesis in this test?
(b) We use X as a test static. What is the distribution of X when H_0 is true?
(c) 5 out of 5 people say that they prefer the new product. Which conclusion can we draw from this? Use 5% significance level.

9.6 A firm claims that at most 10% of the customers are dissatisfied with the items they have bought from the firm. We ask 400 randomly selected customers if they are dissatisfied. Let X be the number of customers who are dissatisfied.

(a) We believe the firm is mistaken and want to execute a test where it is possible to conclude that the firm probably is mistaken. What is the natural null hypothesis and alternative hypothesis in this test?
(b) We use X as a test static. What is the distribution of X when H_0 is true?
(c) 53 persons answer that they are dissatisfied. Find the P-value of this observation by normal approximation. What is the conclusion if the significance level is 5%?

9.7 An accountant checks 400 randomly selected documents from a firm. The accounting is approved if at most 3 documents contain errors. Let X be the number of documents with errors, and let p be the true fraction of documents with errors.

(a) Find the strength of the alternative $p = 1\%$ by
(i) The Poisson distribution. (ii) The binomial distribution.

(b) What result would normal approximation give in this case? Try with and without integer correction.

9.8 A finance institution offers a special type of contracts. It takes very long time to find the exact price for a contract of this type, but the company has developed a system for approximate prices, and offer to sell the contracts at the approximate price. We assume that the error has expectation μ and variance $\sigma^2 = 100{,}000{,}000$, and wish to examine the hypothesis $H_0 : \mu = 0$ against $H_A : \mu \neq 0$.

(a) The company tests their method on 400 randomly chosen contracts, and compute $\overline{X}$. Find the rejection region. Use 5% significance level.
(b) What is the strength of the alternative $\mu = 2000$?

9.9 Simultaneous Strength and Significance: A company believes that less than 2.5% of the items they produce contain errors. We want to design a test where we test n items. Let p be the fraction of the tested items that contain errors. The test should have 5% significance level, and the produce is approved if there is no reason to reject the null hypothesis $H_0 : p \leq 2.5\%$.

How large must n be if we want that the strength of the alternative $p = 5\%$ is at least 95%? Hint: Use normal approximation. Formulate two equations that n and T_{limit} must satisfy, and eliminate T_{limit} from these equations.

9.10 Logarithmic Transformation: Table 9.1 shows daily observations of the stock price in a company.

(a) Discuss shortly if it is reasonable to assume that X_i are independent?
(b) We define new data

$$Y_i = \ln\left[\frac{X_i}{X_{i-1}}\right], \qquad i = 1, \ldots, 10,$$

and the values of these transformed data are shown in Table 9.2.

Assume that all Y_i have the same distribution with expectation μ. Use the values in the table to find an estimate for μ.

Table 9.1 Data for Problem 9.10

X_0	X_1	X_2	X_3	X_4	X_5	X_6	X_7	X_8	X_9	X_{10}
100	92	96	117	120	126	149	152	176	196	184

Table 9.2 Logarithmic transformed data

Y_1	Y_2	Y_3	Y_4	Y_5	Y_6	Y_7	Y_8	Y_9	Y_{10}
−0.083	0.043	0.198	0.025	0.049	0.168	0.020	0.147	0.108	−0.063

(b) The company claims that the numbers clearly demonstrate considerable potential for growth. Technically this is equivalent to the claim $\mu > 0$. Assume that all Y_i are independent, normally distributed with expectation μ and variance $\sigma^2 = 0.01$. We want to test $H_0 : \mu \leq 0$ against $H_A : \mu > 0$. Execute this test.
(c) Find the P-value for the test in (b).

9.11 Strength and t-Distribution: A mutual fund has invested in 10 different stocks. The fund achieved a return of 20.3% last year. The fund is compared with a reference index showing that stocks of this type had a mean return of 15%. The fund manager claims that this clearly demonstrates outstanding abilities in finding good investment opportunities.

For simplicity we assume that the fund has invested equally much in each stock. The return is hence decided from $\overline{X} = \frac{1}{10}\sum_{i=1}^{10} X_i$, where $X_1, \ldots, X_{10}$ is the return of each of the individual stocks.

(a) Assume that $X_1, \ldots, X_{10}$ are independent random variables with expectation μ and variance σ^2. Find $\mathrm{E}[\overline{X}]$ and $\mathrm{Var}[\overline{X}]$.
(b) Assume that $X_1, \ldots, X_{10}$ are independent, normally distributed with expectation μ and variance σ^2. Let S_X^2 be the sample variance. What is the distribution of $Y = \frac{\overline{X}-\mu}{S_X/\sqrt{10}}$?
(c) We want to formulate a hypothesis test which is able to support the managers point of view, i.e., where rejection of the null hypothesis implies that the manager probably performs above average. We let $H_0 : \mu \leq 15\%,\ H_A : \mu > 15\%$. Find the rejection region using a 5% significance level.
(d) We execute the test and observe the results in Table 9.3.

If we process these observations, we find

$$\overline{X} = 0.203, \qquad S_X = 0.099.$$

Use the results to compute the test static Y. What can you conclude from this?
(e) If we want to consider the strength of the alternative $A : \mu = 0.023$, we need to compute

$$P_A(Y \geq Y_{\text{limit}}) = P_A\left(\frac{\overline{X}-\mu}{S_X/\sqrt{10}} > Y_{\text{limit}} - \frac{0.053}{S_X/\sqrt{10}}\right).$$

When A is true, we know that $\frac{\overline{X}-\mu}{S_X/\sqrt{10}}$ is t-distributed. Why can't we use the t-table to compute this probability?

Table 9.3 Data for Problem 9.11

X_1	X_2	X_3	X_4	X_5	X_6	X_7	X_8	X_9	X_{10}
17.8	4.3	13.9	21.7	25.7	38.9	12.2	14.3	28.2	26.2

9.12 Using Poisson Distribution in Accounting: An auditing firm checks samples from the accounting of a large company. There are 100,000 documents, and 1000 randomly selected documents are inspected. We assume that a share p of the documents contains errors, and the accountant approves the accounting, if there is no valid reason to reject the claim $p \leq 1$ at 5% significance level.

(a) Let X be the total number of checked documents containing errors. What is the exact distribution of X? What distributions can be used as approximations to the exact distribution?
(b) Formulate a hypothesis test where you specify the null hypothesis, alternative hypothesis, test static, and rejection region. Use normal approximation to compute the rejection region.
(c) The auditing firm finds 11 documents with errors. Find the P-value for this observation. What is your conclusion?
(d) In reality 2% of the 100,000 documents contained errors. Find the probability that the auditing firm approves the accounting.
(e) In auditing it is usual to work with Poisson approximations. Use this to find the rejection region. Comment the finding.

9.13 Variable "Constants": We want to test if the transaction volumes for a stock are different on Mondays than on Wednesdays. We have data for the 10 last years, and select randomly 16 Mondays and 16 Fridays. We let $X_1, \ldots, X_{16}$ denote the transaction volumes on Mondays, and $Y_1, \ldots, Y_{16}$ denote the transaction volumes on Wednesdays. We estimate mean and variance for these data, and find

$$\overline{X} = 1200, \qquad \overline{Y} = 1020,$$

and

$$S_X^2 = 75{,}000, \qquad S_Y^2 = 85{,}000.$$

(a) Assume that $X_1, \ldots, X_{16}, Y_1, \ldots, Y_{16}$ are independent, normally distributed and define new variables S^2, T, and U by

$$S^2 = \frac{S_X^2 + S_Y^2}{2}, \qquad T = \frac{\overline{X} - \overline{Y}}{\sqrt{S^2/8}}, \qquad U = \frac{\overline{X} - \overline{Y}}{\sqrt{80{,}000/8}}.$$

What kind of distribution has U? Are T and U different random variables? Justify the answer.
(b) We want to test the hypotheses

H_0 : Trade volumes on Mondays and Wednesdays have the same expectation,

H_A : Trade volumes on Mondays and Wednesdays have different expectations.

Table 9.4 Data for Problem 9.14

1	2	3	4	5	6	7	8
149	150	134	155	104	147	147	123

You can take for granted that when H_0 is true, then T is t-distributed with parameter $\nu = 30$. Find the rejection region. What conclusion can you draw? Use 5% significance level.

(c) What is the problem using U as a test static?

9.14 One-Sided Test Versus Two-Sided Confidence Interval: The production at a department was observed 8 consecutive working days. The results are shown in Table 9.4.

Processing these numbers we get

$$\overline{X} = 138.625, \qquad S_X = 17.3612.$$

(a) Assume that the observations are approximately normal and find a 95% confidence interval for expected production.
(b) A few years before, the company carried out an extensive survey at the same department. This survey found a mean production 125 (units/day). Use a one-sided test. Can we claim that production has increased? Compare with the result from (a) and comment the answer.

9.15 Testing Extremes: In this problem we will study a food chain with 100 branches. We assume that the branches are equally large. Previous surveys concluded that yields were approximately normal with expectation 5% and standard deviation 2%.

(a) Let X denote the yield of a randomly selected branch. Compute the probabilities i) $P(X < 2\%)$ ii) $P(X < -1\%)$.
(b) The management decided at the start of the year to follow a certain department. At the end of the year the department had a yield equal to 2%. From this information, can you reject a null hypothesis saying that the branch had the same expected yield as the others? Use a two-sided test and find the P-value. Use 5% significance level.
(c) The management collected numbers from all the branches, and it turned out the worst department had a yield of -1%. From this number can you reject a hypothesis claiming that all the departments have the same expected yield as before? Use a two-sided test with 5% significance level. Use a two-sided test and find the P-value. Use 5% significance level.
(d) The branch with the worst result in (c) reported a yield of -1% also the following year. From this number can you reject a hypothesis claiming that all the departments have the same expected yield as before?

9.16 Testing Extremes: A company has 10 different production units. When the production equipment functions properly, all the units have an expected production of 100 items per day. The standard deviation is 5 items. All produced units are checked, and only approved items are included in the production numbers. We let $X_1, \ldots, X_{10}$ denote the number of produced items at the 10 different units, and we assume that these values are approximately normal. Throughout the problem we will use 5% level of significance.

(a) Unusual production numbers indicate that the equipment does not function properly. Why is it natural to use one-sided tests to examine this?
(b) Assume that Z is a normal distribution with expectation μ and standard deviation σ. Explain why

$$P(Z \leq z) = 0.05 \Leftrightarrow z = \mu - 1.645\,\sigma.$$

(c) How low must the value of X_1 be before you would reject the null hypothesis $\mu_1 = 100$ against $\mu < 100$?
(d) Assume that the production equipment functions properly, and that all units have an expected production of 100 items with a standard deviation of 5 items. What is the probability that at least one of the units produces less than 92 items?
(e) Let $X_{\min}$ be the number of items produced at the worst unit. How low must the value of $X_{\min}$ be before you would reject the null hypothesis

$$H_0 : \mu_1 = \mu_2 = \cdots = \mu_{10} = 100,$$

against the alternative that at least one of the expectations is less than 100?

9.17 Misinterpreting Randomness: In this problem we will assume that the probability of bankruptcy (during one year) for a certain type of company is 5%. We also assume that bankruptcy or not are independent events among the different companies.

(a) Assume that there are in total 120 companies of this type, and that X is the number of companies going bankrupt during one year. What is the distribution of X?
(b) i) Find the probability that exactly 2 of 120 companies go bankrupt. ii) Find the probability that at most 2 of such companies go bankrupt.
(c) Assume that 2 of the 120 companies went bankrupt the last year. A journalist points out that only 1.7% of the companies went bankrupt, and this shows that the probability of bankruptcy is not 5%. Comment this claim.
(d) Point at circumstances that would make the assumption of independence among companies unreasonable. How would that affect the distribution of X?

9.18 *P*-Values in Repeated Samples: You want to examine if a new training has effect, and carry out a statistical test of the effect. The null hypothesis is that the training has no effect, and the alternative hypothesis is that it has effect. We use 5% significance level.

(a) A randomly selected school has completed this training, and after completion the statistical test returns a *P*-value equal to 25%. How would you interpret this result, and what conclusion would you draw?
(b) 25 different schools have completed this training. At one of the schools the test returned a *P*-value of 4%. How would you interpret that result, and what conclusion would you draw?

10 Commonly Used Tests

Abstract

In this chapter we will look at some special hypothesis tests. These tests have found widespread applications and are used by almost everyone that need to process statistical data. The tests we consider are: A test for binomial variables, the t-test for expected value, the t-test for comparison of two populations, Wilcoxons' distribution free tests, the U test, and the chi-square tests. The tests are presented in terms of recipes, i.e., step by step explanations on how to execute the test and how to interpret the outcomes. As we focus applications, we make no attempt to explain in detail why these tests work. They are based on quite lengthy mathematical derivations, but these details are omitted.

10.1 Testing Binomial Distributions

In many cases we need to test the probability for success in a binomial distribution. This can be carried out if we make n independent trials and observe the total number of successes X. To test $H_0 : p = p_0$ against $H_A : p \neq p_0$, we compute the standardized test static

$$Z = \frac{X - np_0}{\sqrt{np_0(1 - p_0)}}.$$

If we have reasonably many observations, then Z is an approximate standard normal distribution. The test can be summarized as follows:

J. Ubøe, *Introductory Statistics for Business and Economics*, Springer Texts in Business and Economics, https://doi.org/10.1007/978-3-319-70936-9_10

Two-sided test for binomial trials where $np_0(1-p_0)$ is at least 5.

$$H_0: p = p_0 \qquad \text{against} \qquad H_A: p \neq p_0.$$

Significance level α.

1. Compute
$$Z = \frac{X - np_0}{\sqrt{np_0(1-p_0)}}.$$
2. Find $z_{\alpha/2}$ from the table of the standard normal distribution such that
$$P(Z \geq z_{\alpha/2}) = z_{\alpha/2}.$$
3. Reject H_0 if $Z \geq z_{\alpha/2}$ or if $Z \leq -z_{\alpha/2}$.

If we can use one-sided tests instead, we proceed similarly.

One-sided test for binomial trials where $np_0(1-p_0)$ is at least 5.

$$H_0: p \leq p_0 \qquad \text{against} \qquad H_A: p > p_0.$$

Significance level α.

1. Compute
$$Z = \frac{X - np_0}{\sqrt{np_0(1-p_0)}}.$$
2. Find z_α from the table of the standard normal distribution such that
$$P(Z \geq z_\alpha) = z_\alpha.$$
3. Reject H_0 if $Z \geq z_\alpha$.

One-sided test for binomial trials where $np_0(1 - p_0)$ is at least 5.

$$H_0 : p \geq p_0 \qquad \text{against} \qquad H_A : p < p_0.$$

Significance level α.

1. Compute
$$Z = \frac{X - np_0}{\sqrt{np_0(1 - p_0)}}.$$
2. Find z_α from the table of the standard normal distribution such that
$$P(Z \geq z_\alpha) = z_\alpha.$$
3. Reject H_0 if $Z \leq -z_\alpha$.

Example 10.1 We have carried out 100 binomial trials and observed a total of 56 successes. We want to test $H_0 : p = 0.5$ against $H_A : p \neq 0.5$. What is the conclusion from the test?

Solution: We use the recipe above:

$$Z = \frac{56 - 100 \cdot 0.5}{\sqrt{100 \cdot 0.5(1 - 0.5)}} = 1.2.$$

When no significance level is stated, we tacitly assume that the significance level is 5%, i.e., $\alpha = 5\%$. Since the test is two-sided, we need to look up the 2.5% level. We find $z_{0.025} = 1.96$. Since the observed test static is smaller than the rejection limit, we keep H_0. There is no sufficient evidence to claim that p is different from 0.5.

10.2 *t*-Test for Expected Value

It happens frequently that we want to test an unknown expected value, and the most common situation is that the variance, too, is unknown. If we assume that we have n independent and approximately normal observations, we know that

$$T = \frac{\overline{X} - \mu}{S[\overline{X}]}$$

is t-distributed with parameter $\nu = n-1$. A test for $H_0 : \mu = \mu_0$ against $H_A : \mu \neq \mu_0$ can then be executed as follows:

Two-sided t-test for expected value. Independent and approximately normal observations with unknown expectation and variance.

$$H_0 : \mu = \mu_0 \qquad \text{against} \qquad H_A : \mu \neq \mu_0.$$

Significance level α.

1. Find $\overline{X}$.
2. Find S_X.
3. Compute $S[\overline{X}] = S_X/\sqrt{n}$.
4. Compute $T = \frac{\overline{X}-\mu_0}{S[\overline{X}]}$.
5. Use the t-table with parameter $\nu = n-1$ to find $t_{\alpha/2}^{(n-1)}$ such that

$$P(T_{(n-1)} \geq t_{\alpha/2}^{(n-1)}) = \alpha/2.$$

6. Reject H_0 if $T \geq t_{\alpha/2}^{(n-1)}$ or if $T \leq -t_{\alpha/2}^{(n-1)}$.

The one-sided versions read as follows:

One-sided t-test for expected value. Independent and approximately normal observations with unknown expectation and variance.

$$H_0 : \mu \leq \mu_0 \qquad \text{against} \qquad H_A : \mu > \mu_0.$$

Significance level α.

1. Find $\overline{X}$.
2. Find S_X.
3. Compute $S[\overline{X}] = S_X/\sqrt{n}$.
4. Compute $T = \frac{\overline{X}-\mu_0}{S[\overline{X}]}$.
5. Use the t-table with parameter $\nu = n-1$ to find $t_{\alpha}^{(n-1)}$ such that

$$P(T_{(n-1)} \geq t_{\alpha}^{(n-1)}) = \alpha.$$

6. Reject H_0 if $T \geq t_{\alpha}^{(n-1)}$.

One-sided t-test for expected value. Independent and approximately normal observations with unknown expectation and variance.

$$H_0 : \mu \geq \mu_0 \qquad \text{against} \qquad H_A : \mu < \mu_0.$$

Significance level α.

1. Find $\overline{X}$.
2. Find S_X.
3. Compute $S[\overline{X}] = S_X/\sqrt{n}$.
4. Compute $T = \frac{\overline{X}-\mu_0}{S[\overline{X}]}$.
5. Use the t-table with parameter $\nu = n-1$ to find $t_\alpha^{(n-1)}$ such that

$$P(T_{(n-1)} \geq t_\alpha^{(n-1)}) = \alpha.$$

6. Reject H_0 if $T \leq -t_\alpha^{(n-1)}$.

Example 10.2 We have 9 independent observations and have found $\overline{X} = -11.2$ and $S_X = 9.6$. We assume that observations are approximately normal and want to test $H_0 : \mu \geq 0$ against $H_A : \mu < 0$. What is the conclusion from the test?

Solution: We follow the recipe above. The first two steps follow from the text, so we proceed to step 3.

$$S[\overline{X}] = \frac{9.6}{\sqrt{9}} = 3.2.$$

Since $\mu_0 = 0$, we get

$$T = \frac{-11.2 - 0}{3.2} = -3.5.$$

The rejection limit we find from a t-table with parameter 8. If we use 5% significance, we must find the 5% level in this table. This gives $t_{0.05}^{(8)} = 1.86$. We should hence reject H_0 if $T < -1.86$. As this is certainly true, we reject H_0 and claim that the expected value is probably negative.

10.3 Comparing Two Groups

In statistics we often need to compare properties of two different groups. We will now consider some special techniques that can be used to decide if the groups are different.

10.3.1 *t*-Test for Comparison of Expectation in Two Groups

Assume that we have two groups. In the first group we observe X and in the second group we observe Y. Expectations and variances are unknown, and we want to test if $\mathrm{E}[X] = \mathrm{E}[Y]$ or not. As in the previous t-test we need to assume that observations are approximately normal.

We let $X_1, \ldots, X_{n_1}$ denote the observations from the first group, while $Y_1, \ldots, Y_{n_2}$ denote observations from the second group. We assume that

$$\mathrm{E}[X_i] = \mu_X, \qquad \mathrm{Var}[X_i] = \sigma_X^2, \qquad i = 1, \ldots, n_1,$$

and

$$\mathrm{E}[Y_i] = \mu_Y, \qquad \mathrm{Var}[X_i] = \sigma_Y^2, \qquad i = 1, \ldots, n_2.$$

Two- and one-sided tests can then be executed as follows:

Two-sided test for comparison of expectations in two groups. Independent and approximately normal observations with unknown expectation and variance. Equal variances in the two groups.

$$H_0: \mu_X = \mu_Y \qquad \text{against} \qquad H_A: \mu_X \neq \mu_Y.$$

Significance level α.

1. Find $\overline{X}$ and $\overline{Y}$.
2. Find S defined via

$$S^2 = \frac{1}{n_1 + n_2 - 2}\left(\sum_{i=1}^{n_1}(X_i - \overline{X})^2 + \sum_{i=1}^{n_2}(Y_i - \overline{Y})^2\right).$$

(continued)

3. Compute

$$S[\hat{\delta}] = S \cdot \sqrt{\frac{1}{n_1} + \frac{1}{n_2}}.$$

4. Compute

$$T = \frac{\overline{X} - \overline{Y}}{S[\hat{\delta}]}.$$

5. Use the t-table with parameter $\nu = n_1 + n_2 - 2$ to find $t^{(\nu)}_{\alpha/2}$ such that

$$P(T_{(\nu)} \geq t^{(\nu)}_{\alpha/2}) = \alpha/2.$$

6. Reject H_0 if $T \geq t^{(\nu)}_{\alpha/2}$ or if $T \leq -t^{(\nu)}_{\alpha/2}$.

Extra: The limits for a $(1-\alpha)100\%$ confidence interval for the difference $\mu_X - \mu_Y$ are given by

$$\overline{X} - \overline{Y} \pm t^{(\nu)}_{\alpha/2} \cdot S[\hat{\delta}].$$

One-sided test for comparison of expectations in two groups. Independent and approximately normal observations with unknown expectation and variance. Equal variances in the two groups.

$$H_0 : \mu_X \leq \mu_Y \qquad \text{against} \qquad H_A : \mu_X > \mu_Y.$$

Significance level α.

1. Find $\overline{X}$ and $\overline{Y}$.
2. Find S defined via

$$S^2 = \frac{1}{n_1 + n_2 - 2}\left(\sum_{i=1}^{n_1}(X_i - \overline{X})^2 + \sum_{i=1}^{n_2}(Y_i - \overline{Y})^2\right).$$

(continued)

3. Compute

$$S[\hat{\delta}] = S \cdot \sqrt{\frac{1}{n_1} + \frac{1}{n_2}}.$$

4. Compute

$$T = \frac{\overline{X} - \overline{Y}}{S[\hat{\delta}]}.$$

5. Use the t-table with parameter $\nu = n_1 + n_2 - 2$ to find $t_\alpha^{(\nu)}$ such that

$$P(T_{(\nu)} \geq t_\alpha^{(\nu)}) = \alpha.$$

6. Reject H_0 if $T \geq t_\alpha^{(\nu)}$.

One-sided test for comparison of expectations in two groups. Independent and approximately normal observations with unknown expectation and variance. Equal variances in the two groups.

$$H_0 : \mu_X \geq \mu_Y \qquad \text{against} \qquad H_A : \mu_X < \mu_Y.$$

Significance level α.

1. Find $\overline{X}$ and $\overline{Y}$.
2. Find S defined via

$$S^2 = \frac{1}{n_1 + n_2 - 2}\left(\sum_{i=1}^{n_1}(X_i - \overline{X})^2 + \sum_{i=1}^{n_2}(Y_i - \overline{Y})^2\right).$$

3. Compute

$$S[\hat{\delta}] = S \cdot \sqrt{\frac{1}{n_1} + \frac{1}{n_2}}.$$

(continued)

4. Compute

$$T = \frac{\overline{X} - \overline{Y}}{S[\hat{\delta}]}.$$

5. Use the t-table with parameter $\nu = n_1 + n_2 - 2$ to find $t_\alpha^{(\nu)}$ such that

$$P(T_{(\nu)} \geq t_\alpha^{(\nu)}) = \alpha.$$

6. Reject H_0 if $T \leq -t_\alpha^{(\nu)}$.

Remark In these tests we had to assume that the variances are equal in the two groups. Modern statistical software can easily handle situations where the variances are different.

Example 10.3 Assume that a factory can use two different methods in production. We make 10 independent observations of the production, 5 using method 1 and 5 using method 2. Method 1 gave the results:

$$4.7, 3.5, 3.3, 4.2, 3.6,$$

while the corresponding numbers for method 2 was

$$3.2, 4.2, 3.3, 3.9, 3.0.$$

Assuming that we have normally distributed observations with equal variances, we compute

$$\overline{X} = 3.86, \overline{Y} = 3.52, S = 0.543, S[\hat{\delta}] = 0.344.$$

We insert these quantities into the formula, and get

$$T = \frac{\overline{X} - \overline{Y}}{S[\hat{\delta}]} = \frac{0.34}{0.344} = 0.99.$$

In this case we should refer to a t-table with parameter

$$\nu = n_1 + n_2 - 2 = 5 + 5 - 2 = 8.$$

From this table we find $t_{0.025}^{(8)} = 2.306$. Since the observed T value is well within the non-rejection region, there is no reason to reject H_0. We hence keep the null

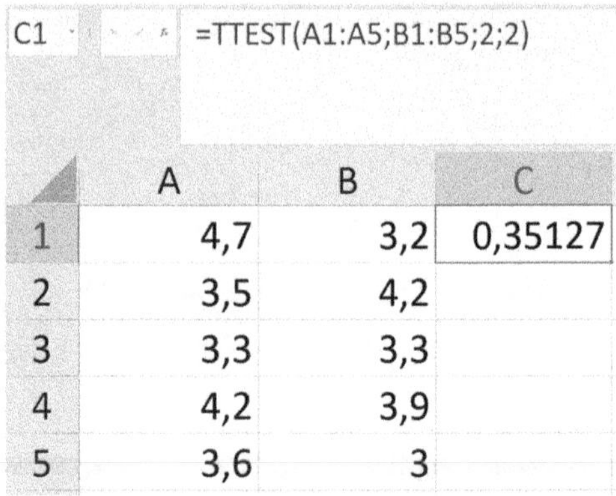

C1 =TTEST(A1:A5;B1:B5;2;2)

	A	B	C
1	4,7	3,2	0,35127
2	3,5	4,2	
3	3,3	3,3	
4	4,2	3,9	
5	3,6	3	

Fig. 10.1 t-test executed in Excel

hypothesis saying there is no difference in expectation. The limits for a 95% confidence interval for the difference $\mu_X - \mu_Y$ are given by

$$\overline{X} - \overline{Y} \pm t_{\alpha/2}^{(\nu)} \cdot S[\hat{\delta}] = 0.34 \pm 2.306 \cdot 0.344.$$

The confidence interval is hence $[-0.45, 1.13]$. We notice that the value zero is contained in this interval, which is consistent with our null hypothesis.

10.3.2 t-Test Executed in Excel

Using the Excel command $TTEST(A1 : An; B1 : Bn; 2, 2)$, we can easily execute the two-sided test we examined in Example 10.3. We write the observations from method 1 in the first column, and the corresponding results for method 2 in the second column. The final result is displayed in Fig. 10.1.

The result displayed in C1 is the P-value for this test, and we see that the P-value is as large as 35%. There is hence no reason to suspect that the null hypothesis is wrong, and we keep the hypothesis about equal expectations.

10.3.3 t-Test for Comparison of Expectation in Two Groups, Paired Observations

It sometimes happens that we want to compare observations from two different groups where the observations are paired in a natural way. Let $(X_1, Y_1), \ldots, (X_n, Y_n)$ denote the observed pairs. In the previous t-test we assumed that all observations were independent. In our new case X_1 and Y_1 may be dependent, and the same applies for any pair. The different pairs, however, are independent of each other. With a structure like this, we need to modify the procedure to take the pairing into account. This is done as follows:

Two-sided test for comparison of expectations in two groups, paired observations. Independent pairs and approximately normal observations with unknown expectation and variance.

$$H_0: \mu_X = \mu_Y \qquad \text{against} \qquad H_A: \mu_X \neq \mu_Y.$$

Significance level α.

1. Find $\overline{X}$ and $\overline{Y}$.
2. Find S defined via

$$S^2 = \frac{1}{n-1}\sum_{i=1}^{n_1}(X_i - Y_i - \overline{X} + \overline{Y})^2.$$

3. Compute

$$S[\hat{\delta}] = S/\sqrt{n}.$$

4. Compute

$$T = \frac{\overline{X} - \overline{Y}}{S[\hat{\delta}]}.$$

5. Use the t-table with parameter $\nu = n - 1$ to find $t^{(\nu)}_{\alpha/2}$ such that

$$P(T_{(\nu)} \geq t^{(\nu)}_{\alpha/2}) = \alpha/2.$$

6. Reject H_0 if $T \geq t^{(\nu)}_{\alpha/2}$ or if $T \leq -t^{(\nu)}_{\alpha/2}$.

Extra: The limits for a $(1-\alpha)100\%$ confidence interval for the difference $\mu_X - \mu_Y$ are given by

$$\overline{X} - \overline{Y} \pm t^{(\nu)}_{\alpha/2} \cdot S[\hat{\delta}].$$

Two-sided test for comparison of expectations in two groups, paired observations. Independent pairs and approximately normal observations with unknown expectation and variance.

$$H_0 : \mu_X \leq \mu_Y \qquad \text{against} \qquad H_A : \mu_X > \mu_Y.$$

Significance level α.

1. Find $\overline{X}$ and $\overline{Y}$.
2. Find S defined via

$$S^2 = \frac{1}{n-1}\sum_{i=1}^{n_1}(X_i - Y_i - \overline{X} + \overline{Y})^2.$$

3. Compute

$$S[\hat{\delta}] = S/\sqrt{n}.$$

4. Compute

$$T = \frac{\overline{X} - \overline{Y}}{S[\hat{\delta}]}.$$

5. Use the t-table with parameter $\nu = n - 1$ to find $t_\alpha^{(\nu)}$ such that

$$P(T_{(\nu)} \geq t_\alpha^{(\nu)}) = \alpha.$$

6. Reject H_0 if $T \geq t_\alpha^{(\nu)}$.

Two-sided test for comparison of expectations in two groups, paired observations. Independent pairs and approximately normal observations with unknown expectation and variance.

$$H_0 : \mu_X \geq \mu_Y \qquad \text{against} \qquad H_A : \mu_X < \mu_Y.$$

Significance level α.

1. Find $\overline{X}$ and $\overline{Y}$.

(continued)

2. Find S defined via

$$S^2 = \frac{1}{n-1}\sum_{i=1}^{n_1}(X_i - Y_i - \overline{X} + \overline{Y})^2.$$

3. Compute

$$S[\hat{\delta}] = S/\sqrt{n}.$$

4. Compute

$$T = \frac{\overline{X} - \overline{Y}}{S[\hat{\delta}]}.$$

5. Use the t-table with parameter $\nu = n - 1$ to find $t_\alpha^{(\nu)}$ such that

$$P(T_{(\nu)} \geq t_\alpha^{(\nu)}) = \alpha.$$

6. Reject H_0 if $T \leq -t_\alpha^{(\nu)}$.

Example 10.4 We now return to the numbers used in Example 10.3, but this time we assume that the same workers first used method 1 and then method 2. X_1 and Y_1 are hence the results of the same worker using two different methods. If we order the results in the same order as the workers, it turned out that the workers obtained the following results:

$$4.7, 3.5, 3.3, 4.2, 3.6$$

with method 1, and

$$4.2, 3.2, 3.0, 3.9, 3.3$$

with method 2. By inspection we notice that all the workers reported larger numbers by method 1 than by method 2. The unpaired test we used in the previous section did not take this into account. Our new test does, and it makes a lot of difference. If we carry out a two-sided test using the recipe above, we get

$$n = 5, \overline{X} = 3.86, \overline{Y} = 3.52, S = 0.089.$$

With

$$T = \frac{\overline{X} - \overline{Y}}{S/\sqrt{n}},$$

we get $T = 8.5$. Using a t-table with parameter $\nu = n - 1 = 4$, we see that $t_{0.025}^{(4)} = 2.775$ which is the rejection limit with 5% significance level. The observed T falls deep into the rejection region, and there is good reason to claim that the two methods lead to different expected production.

We should notice that this does not mean that the analysis from the unpaired test was wrong. The information regarding the pairs provides new evidence, and it is not surprising that more evidence can alter the conclusion. When we fail to reject a null hypothesis, it does not mean that we have proved that the null hypothesis is true. Furthermore it does not exclude the possibility that we later may come up with more convincing evidence. Statistical data can often be analyzed using different tests, and it is not uncommon that different tests provide different conclusions. In such situations we should put more weight on the test that best makes use of the available information.

10.3.4 *t*-Test with Paired Observations Executed in Excel

Using the Excel command $TTEST(A1:An; B1:Bn; 2, 1)$, we can easily execute the two-sided test we examined in Example 10.4. The only difference is that we change the last digit in the command from 2 to 1. This makes Excel understand that we want to use a paired test (Fig. 10.2).

We see that the P-value for the paired test is as small as 0.1% meaning that we are very confident in rejecting the null hypothesis. It seems very probable that the two methods lead to different expected production.

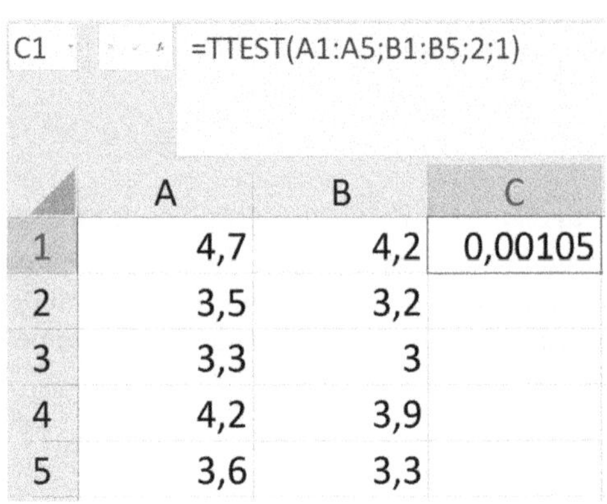

Fig. 10.2 Paired t-test executed in Excel

10.4 Wilcoxon's Distribution Free Tests

A general weakness with the t-tests we have discussed so far is that they assume approximately normal observations. This assumption may not be true, and we can then not trust the results. In cases where the assumption may be questionable, we can use what is called distribution free tests, i.e., tests that do not assume that the observations have a particular distribution. The price for doing so is that we withdraw invalid evidence, and with less evidence the chances of rejection are reduced.

We will now consider Wilcoxon's tests for the comparison of two different groups. The basis for these tests is exactly the same as for the t-test for comparison of expected values in two different groups. The only difference is that we no longer assume that observations are normally distributed.

The Wilcoxon rank-sum test takes its starting point in the so-called rank-sum of the observations. A simplistic procedure for finding the rank-sum can be described as follows: First write all the observations from the two groups in ascending order. The next step is to underline the observations from the first group. The rank-sum is defined as the sum of the positions of the underlined numbers. The basic idea is that W will be small if the numbers from group 1 are largely smaller than the numbers from group 2, and large if the differences go in the opposite direction.

Example 10.5 We have observed working times (measured in seconds) for workers in two different groups. In group 1 the working times were:

$$47, 59, 43, 50, 45, 45, 49, 41, 47, 95, 50,$$

while the working times for group 2 were

$$45, 48, 61, 52, 48, 63, 52, 54, 50, 58.$$

To compute the rank-sum of these observations, we sort all the observations in ascending order and underline the observations from group 1:

$$\underline{41}, \underline{43}, \underline{45}, 45, \underline{45}, \underline{47}, \underline{47}, 48, 48, \underline{49}, \underline{50}, 50, \underline{50}, 52, 52, 54, 58, \underline{59}, 61, 63, \underline{95}.$$

The rank-sum W is found from the sum of the positions of the underlined numbers, i.e.

$$W = 1 + 2 + 3 + 5 + 6 + 7 + 10 + 11 + 13 + 18 + 21 = 97.$$

Remark When we write the observations in ascending order, it may happen that some observations are equal. It is then not clear which one to write first. It is common practice to swap the order every second time, i.e., the first time we have equality, we write down the value from group 1 first, and the next time we have equality, we write down the observation from group 2 first. Modern computer software uses a more refined version where the program computes the rank-sum for any possible permutation of equal numbers, and takes the mean over all these rank-sums. The difference is often negligible.

The Wilcoxon rank-sum two-sided test for comparison of expectations in two groups. Independent observations with any distribution.

$$H_0: \mu_X = \mu_Y \qquad \text{against} \qquad H_A: \mu_X \neq \mu_Y.$$

Significance level α.

1. Compute $\mathrm{E}[W] = \frac{1}{2}n_1(n_1 + n_2 + 1)$.
2. Compute $\mathrm{Var}[W] = \frac{1}{12}n_1 n_2(n_1 + n_2 + 1)$.
3. Compute

$$Z = \frac{W - \mathrm{E}[W]}{\sqrt{\mathrm{Var}[W]}}.$$

4. Find $z_{\alpha/2}$ from the table of the standard normal distribution such that

$$P(Z \geq z_{\alpha/2}) = \alpha/2.$$

5. Reject H_0 if $Z \geq z_{\alpha/2}$ or if $Z \leq -z_{\alpha/2}$.

The Wilcoxon rank-sum one-sided test for comparison of expectations in two groups. Independent observations with any distribution.

$$H_0: \mu_X \leq \mu_Y \qquad \text{against} \qquad H_A: \mu_X > \mu_Y.$$

Significance level α.

1. Compute $\mathrm{E}[W] = \frac{1}{2}n_1(n_1 + n_2 + 1)$.
2. Compute $\mathrm{Var}[W] = \frac{1}{12}n_1 n_2(n_1 + n_2 + 1)$.
3. Compute

$$Z = \frac{W - \mathrm{E}[W]}{\sqrt{\mathrm{Var}[W]}}.$$

(continued)

4. Find z_α from the table of the standard normal distribution such that

$$P(Z \geq z_\alpha) = \alpha.$$

5. Reject H_0 if $Z \geq z_\alpha$.

The Wilcoxon rank-sum one-sided test for comparison of expectations in two groups. Independent observations with any distribution.

$$H_0: \mu_X \geq \mu_Y \qquad \text{against} \qquad H_A: \mu_X < \mu_Y.$$

Significance level α.

1. Compute $\mathrm{E}[W] = \frac{1}{2}n_1(n_1 + n_2 + 1)$.
2. Compute $\mathrm{Var}[W] = \frac{1}{12}n_1 n_2(n_1 + n_2 + 1)$.
3. Compute

$$Z = \frac{W - \mathrm{E}[W]}{\sqrt{\mathrm{Var}[W]}}.$$

4. Find z_α from the table of the standard normal distribution such that

$$P(Z \geq z_\alpha) = \alpha.$$

5. Reject H_0 if $Z \leq -z_\alpha$.

Remark Even though these tests rest on the central limit theorem, the number of observations need not be very large. As stated above, there should be at least 8–10 observations in each group. Modern statistical software, however, can handle cases with fewer observations.

Example 10.6 We want to carry out a two-sided test for the observations in Example 10.5. We use the values $n_1 = 11$ and $n_2 = 10$ to get:

1. $\mathrm{E}[W] = \frac{1}{2} \cdot 11 \cdot 22 = 121$.
2. $\mathrm{Var}[W] = \frac{1}{12} \cdot 11 \cdot 10 \cdot 22 = 201.667$.
3. $Z = \frac{97-121}{\sqrt{201.667}} = -1.69$.

Using 5% significance level, we get $z_{0.025} = 1.96$, and we conclude that we have to keep our null hypothesis of no difference in expected values.

10.4.1 The Wilcoxon Signed-Rank Test

When we studied *t*-test previously in this chapter, we could see that it made a lot of difference if the observations were paired. There is a Wilcoxon test dealing with this situation, and it is called the Wilcoxon signed-rank test. A simplistic version of the procedure can be described as follows:

Compute the differences between each pair of number, i.e.

$$\text{difference} = \text{value from group } 2 - \text{value from group } 1,$$

and write all these differences in ascending order with respect to absolute value. The rank V is the sum of the positions of the negative terms. The idea behind the test is that V is small if the numbers from group 1 is largely smaller than the numbers from group 2, and V will be large if the effect goes in the opposite direction.

Example 10.7 10 workers performed the same working operation twice, the first time without training and the second time after training. The required working times were as follows:

Without training:

$$48, 53, 52, 57, 43, 83.59, 71, 40, 61,$$

while the working times after training were

$$45, 42, 58, 50, 41, 47, 53, 66, 45, 53.$$

If we compute the differences between each such pair, we get:

$$-3, -11, 6, -7, -2, -36, -6, -5, 5, -8.$$

We sort these numbers in ascending order with respect to absolute value and underline the negative numbers. We get:

$$\underline{-2}, \underline{-3}, \underline{-5}, 5, 6, \underline{-6}, \underline{-7}, \underline{-8}, \underline{-11}, \underline{-36}.$$

We find the rank V when we compute the sum of the positions of the underlined numbers, i.e.

$$V = 1 + 2 + 3 + 6 + 7 + 8 + 9 + 10 = 46.$$

Once the rank is computed, the tests are carried out using the recipes below:

The Wilcoxon signed-rank two-sided test for comparison of expectations in two groups, paired observations. Independent pairs with any distribution.

$$H_0 : \mu_X = \mu_Y \qquad \text{against} \qquad H_A : \mu_X \neq \mu_Y.$$

Significance level α.

1. Compute $\mathrm{E}[V] = \frac{1}{4}n(n+1)$.
2. Compute $\mathrm{Var}[V] = \frac{1}{24}n(n+1)(2n+1)$.
3. Compute

$$Z = \frac{V - \mathrm{E}[V]}{\sqrt{\mathrm{Var}[V]}}.$$

4. Find $z_{\alpha/2}$ from the table of the standard normal distribution such that

$$P(Z \geq z_{\alpha/2}) = \alpha/2.$$

5. Reject H_0 if $Z \geq z_{\alpha/2}$ or if $Z \leq -z_{\alpha/2}$.

The Wilcoxon signed-rank one-sided test for comparison of expectations in two groups, paired observations. Independent pairs with any distribution.

$$H_0 : \mu_X \leq \mu_Y \qquad \text{against} \qquad H_A : \mu_X > \mu_Y.$$

Significance level α.

1. Compute $\mathrm{E}[V] = \frac{1}{4}n(n+1)$.
2. Compute $\mathrm{Var}[V] = \frac{1}{24}n(n+1)(2n+1)$.
3. Compute

$$Z = \frac{V - \mathrm{E}[V]}{\sqrt{\mathrm{Var}[V]}}.$$

4. Find z_{α} from the table of the standard normal distribution such that

$$P(Z \geq z_{\alpha}) = \alpha.$$

5. Reject H_0 if $Z \geq z_{\alpha}$.

The Wilcoxon signed-rank one-sided test for comparison of expectations in two groups, paired observations. Independent pairs with any distribution.

$$H_0 : \mu_X \geq \mu_Y \qquad \text{against} \qquad H_A : \mu_X < \mu_Y.$$

Significance level α.

1. Compute $\mathrm{E}[V] = \frac{1}{4}n(n + 1)$.
2. Compute $\mathrm{Var}[V] = \frac{1}{24}n(n + 1)(2n + 1)$.
3. Compute

$$Z = \frac{V - \mathrm{E}[V]}{\sqrt{\mathrm{Var}[V]}}.$$

4. Find z_α from the table of the standard normal distribution such that

$$P(Z \geq z_\alpha) = \alpha.$$

5. Reject H_0 if $Z \leq -z_\alpha$.

Remark The number of observations need not be very large, but is recommended to have at least 20 observations of each pair. Modern statistical software, can, however, handle cases with fewer observations.

Example 10.8 If we want to test if the training in Example 10.7 had effect, we can make use of a one-sided test. This is natural since it seems unlikely that training can have a negative impact. Here we have $n = 10$ pairs of observations, and we get:

1. $\mathrm{E}[V] = \frac{1}{4} \cdot 10 \cdot 11 = 27.5$.
2. $\mathrm{Var}[V] = \frac{1}{24} \cdot 10 \cdot 11 \cdot 21 = 96.25$.
3. $Z = \frac{46-27.5}{\sqrt{96.25}} = 1.88$.

If we use 5% significance level, then $z_{0.05} = 1.64$. In this one-sided test we should reject H_0 if $Z \geq 1.64$. Since this is the case, we are confident that training reduced expected working time. Strictly speaking, we have too few observations to use the simple version of the Wilcoxon signed-rank test. If we run the same data using modern statistical software, however, we get the same conclusion.

10.4.2 Comparison of t-Tests and Wilcoxon Test

In cases where the observations are approximately normal, we can use both t-tests and the Wilcoxon tests. In such cases it might happen that the tests lead to opposite conclusions. When this occurs, we put more weight on the results from the t-tests. In general the Wilcoxon tests are weaker, i.e., the deviation from the null hypothesis needs to be larger before we can confidently reject it. In other words, the deviation from the null hypothesis needs to be stronger before the Wilcoxon tests lead to rejection.

It might happen that we have run both tests, and only later understand that the assumption of normally distributed observations may be questionable. In such cases we should disregard the results from the t-tests and only rely on the results from the Wilcoxon tests.

10.5 The U-Test for Comparison of Success Probabilities

Instead of comparing expected values, we might want to compare success probabilities in two groups. To study this in detail, we proceed as follows:

- We make n_1 binomial trials in the first group, and n_2 in the second group.
- We let p_1 denote the probability of success in the first group, and p_2 the probability of success in the second group.
- X_1 is the total number of successes in the first group, and X_2 is the total number of successes in the second group.

We want to test if the success probabilities are different, and can use the following test:

Two-sided U-test for comparison of success probabilities. Binomial trials.

$$H_0: p_1 = p_2 \qquad \text{against} \qquad H_A: p_1 \neq p_2.$$

Significance level α.

1. Find

$$\hat{p_1} = \frac{X_1}{n_1}, \qquad \hat{p_2} = \frac{X_2}{n_2}.$$

(continued)

2. Find $\hat{p}$ defined by

$$\hat{p} = \frac{X_1 + X_2}{n_1 + n_2}.$$

3. Compute

$$U = \frac{\hat{p_1} - \hat{p_2}}{\sqrt{\left(\frac{1}{n_1} + \frac{1}{n_2}\right)\hat{p}(1-\hat{p})}}.$$

4. When the numbers of observations are sufficiently large, see note below, U is approximately normal. Use the table for the standard normal distribution to find $z_{\alpha/2}$ such that

$$P(Z \geq z_{\alpha/2}) = \alpha/2.$$

5. Reject H_0 if $U \geq z_{\alpha/2}$ or if $U \leq -z_{\alpha/2}$.

Extra: The limits for a $(1-\alpha)100\%$ significance interval for $p_1 - p_2$ are

$$\hat{p_1} - \hat{p_2} \pm z_{\alpha/2}\sqrt{\frac{\hat{p_1}(1-\hat{p_1}}{n_1} + \frac{\hat{p_2}(1-\hat{p_2})}{n_2}}.$$

One-sided U-test for comparison of success probabilities. Binomial trials.

$$H_0: p_1 \leq p_2 \qquad \text{against} \qquad H_A: p_1 > p_2.$$

Significance level α.

1. Find

$$\hat{p_1} = \frac{X_1}{n_1}, \qquad \hat{p_2} = \frac{X_2}{n_2}.$$

2. Find $\hat{p}$ defined by

$$\hat{p} = \frac{X_1 + X_2}{n_1 + n_2}.$$

(continued)

3. Compute

$$U = \frac{\hat{p_1} - \hat{p_2}}{\sqrt{\left(\frac{1}{n_1} + \frac{1}{n_2}\right)\hat{p}(1-\hat{p})}}.$$

4. When the numbers of observations are sufficiently large, see note below, U is approximately normal. Use the table for the standard normal distribution to find z_α such that

$$P(Z \geq z_\alpha) = \alpha.$$

5. Reject H_0 if $U \geq z_\alpha$.

One-sided U-test for comparison of success probabilities. Binomial trials.

$$H_0 : p_1 \geq p_2 \qquad \text{against} \qquad H_A : p_1 < p_2.$$

Significance level α.

1. Find

$$\hat{p_1} = \frac{X_1}{n_1}, \qquad \hat{p_2} = \frac{X_2}{n_2}.$$

2. Find $\hat{p}$ defined by

$$\hat{p} = \frac{X_1 + X_2}{n_1 + n_2}.$$

3. Compute

$$U = \frac{\hat{p_1} - \hat{p_2}}{\sqrt{\left(\frac{1}{n_1} + \frac{1}{n_2}\right)\hat{p}(1-\hat{p})}}.$$

4. When the numbers of observations are sufficiently large, see note below, U is approximately normal. Use the table for the standard normal distribution

(continued)

to find z_α such that

$$P(Z \geq z_\alpha) = \alpha.$$

5. Reject H_0 if $U \leq -z_\alpha$.

Note: These tests all require that the numbers of observations are sufficiently large. More precisely it is usual to require that $n_1\hat{p}_1, n_1(1-\hat{p}_1), n_2\hat{p}_2, n_2(1-\hat{p}_2)$ are all greater than 5.

Example 10.9 40 men and 60 women have been asked if they think statistics is an interesting subject. 11 men and 14 women answered No, the rest Yes. What conclusion can we draw from this?

Solution: We use a two-sided U-test to answer this. We have

$$\hat{p_1} = \frac{11}{40}, \qquad \hat{p_2} = \frac{14}{60}.$$

$$\hat{p_1} = \frac{11+14}{40+60} = \frac{25}{100}.$$

We insert these quantities in the formula below and get

$$U = \frac{\hat{p_1} - \hat{p_2}}{\sqrt{\left(\frac{1}{n_1} + \frac{1}{n_2}\right)\hat{p}(1-\hat{p})}} = 0.47.$$

At 5% significance level, $z_{0.025} = 1.96$. The observed U is well within the non-rejection region. We keep the null hypothesis saying there is no difference in opinion between men and women.

10.6 Chi-Square Test for Goodness-of-Fit

The chi-square test for probabilities is a useful test when we want to examine a given set of probabilities. The starting point is a sample space with m different outcomes. We want to test if the different outcomes occur with frequencies that are compatible with a given set of probabilities. To settle this, we make n independent observations and record how many times we got each outcome. Here

$$X_i = \text{Number of times we observed outcome } i, \qquad i = 1, \ldots, m.$$

The test is executed as follows:

Chi-square test for a given set of probabilities $p_1, p_2, \ldots, p_m$ (goodness-of-fit).

H_0 : The probability distribution of the outcomes equals $p_1, p_2, \ldots, p_m$.

H_A : The probability of at least one outcome differs from the given distribution.

Requires n independent observations where $np_i > 5$ for $i = 1, \ldots, m$.
Significance level α.

1. Compute

$$Q = \frac{(X_1 - np_1)^2}{np_1} + \frac{(X_2 - np_2)^2}{np_2} + \cdots + \frac{(X_m - np_m)^2}{np_m}.$$

2. Use a chi-square table with parameter $\nu = m - 1$ to find $q_\alpha^{(\nu)}$ such that

$$P(Q_{(\nu)} \geq q_\alpha^{(\nu)}) = \alpha.$$

3. Reject H_0 if $Q \geq q_\alpha^{(\nu)}$.

Notice that this test does not have a two-sided version. The chi-square distribution is always positive, and a two-sided test makes no sense. We should also notice that the distribution is not approximately normal, so we cannot use the standard normal distribution in this case.

Example 10.10 A country has 5 political parties, A,B,C,D,E. In the previous election votes were distributed as follows:

$$A : 20\%, \quad B : 30\%, \quad C : 20\%, \quad D : 2\%, \quad E : 28\%.$$

In our model we hence have $p_1 = 0.2, p_2 = 0.3, p_3 = 0.2, p_4 = 0.02, p_5 = 0.28$. To see if the distribution has changed, we asked $n = 1000$ randomly selected persons. The results of the poll were:

$$X_1 = 220, \quad X_2 = 280, \quad X_3 = 225, \quad X_1 = 25, \quad X_1 = 250.$$

Has the distribution of votes changed?

Solution: We compute

$$
\begin{aligned}
Q &= \frac{(220-200)^2}{200} + \frac{(280-300)^2}{300} + \frac{(225-200)^2}{200} + \frac{(25-20)^2}{20} + \frac{(250-280)^2}{280} \\
&= 10.92.
\end{aligned}
$$

Since we have $m = 5$ different outcomes, we should use a chi-square table with parameter $\nu = m - 1 = 4$. Using 5% significance level we find $q_{0.05}^{(4)} = 9.49$. Since the observed $Q > 9.49$, we reject the null hypothesis. We are confident that the distribution of votes has changed (Fig. 10.3).

10.6.1 The Chi-Square Test Executed in Excel

Using the Excel command CHITEST, we can easily carry out the test in Example 10.10. We write the observed frequencies in the first column. In the second column we write the corresponding probabilities multiplied by n, i.e., we multiply the given probabilities with the total number of observations (Fig. 10.4).

The test reports the P-value 2.7448%. Since the P-value is less than 5%, we reject the null hypothesis at 5% significance level. In Example 10.10 we computed

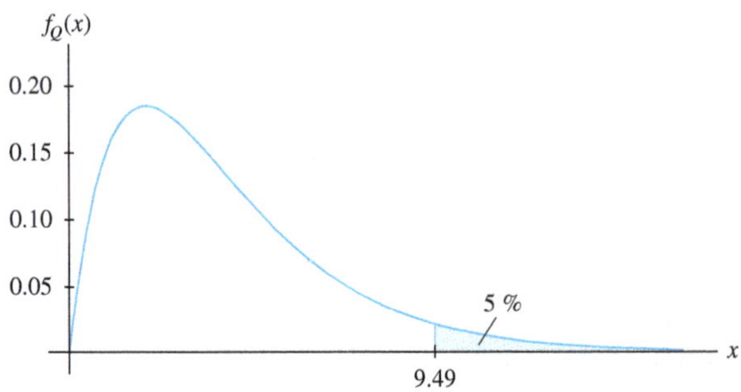

Fig. 10.3 Chi-square distribution with parameter $\nu = 4$

C1 =CHISQ.TEST(A1:A5;B1:B5)

	A	B	C
1	220	200	0,02745
2	280	300	
3	225	200	
4	25	20	
5	250	280	

Fig. 10.4 Chi-square test executed in Excel

$Q = 10.92$. The P-value is then

$$P(Q_{(4)} \geq 10.92) \approx P(Q_{(4)} \geq 11.0) = 0.027.$$

where we could find the last probability in the chi-square table. We see that our calculations coincide with those made by Excel.

10.7 The Chi-Square Test for Independence

Assume that you have a population of 10,000 persons, half of which are men and the other half women. Furthermore, assume that 20% of those people have problems paying their bills. If the distribution of people with payment problem is independent of gender, we would expect the distribution displayed in Table 10.1.

If the observed distribution is very different from this, we would think that gender makes a difference. This simple idea is the basis for the chi-square test for independence. In general we proceed as follows:

Assume that we have a sample with a total of n objects, and where each object has two factors. The first factor has I different versions, while the second factor has J different versions. We can then write a table with elements X_{ij} where

$$X_{ij} = \text{Number of objects where the first factor is version } i\text{, and the second } j.$$

To assess these numbers, we need all the marginals, i.e.

$$A_i = \sum_{j=1}^{J} X_{ij},\ i = 1, \ldots, I, \qquad B_j = \sum_{i=1}^{I} X_{ij},\ j = 1, \ldots, J.$$

Here A_i is the total number of object where the first factor is version i, and B_j is the total number of objects where the second factor is version j. To see what this means in practice, we consider an explicit example.

Example 10.11 A traveling agency has asked $n = 10{,}000$ customers if they were satisfied with their holiday. The holidays took place in 4 different towns, and the customers could choose the alternatives: Satisfied, Not satisfied, Don't know. The results are shown in Table 10.2 which also shows the marginals.

In this example factor 1 is the town the customer stayed in, and factor 2 is the reply to the question. Is there a connection between these factors?

Table 10.1 Distribution of customer under independence

	Payment problems	No payment problems	Total
Women	1000	4000	5000
Men	1000	4000	5000
Total	2000	5000	10,000

Table 10.2 Observed satisfaction levels

	Town 1	Town 2	Town 3	Town 4	Total
Satisfied	1100	800	400	1400	3700
Not satisfied	1700	1000	800	2100	5600
Don't know	200	100	100	300	700
Total	3000	1900	1300	3800	10,000

Table 10.3 Expected satisfaction levels under independence

	Town 1	Town 2	Town 3	Town 4	Total
Satisfied	1110	703	481	1406	3700
Not satisfied	1680	1064	728	2128	5600
Don't know	210	133	91	266	700
Total	3000	1900	1300	3800	10,000

Solution: From the table we see that the choice of town has the distribution:

$$\text{Town 1:}30\%, \quad \text{Town 2:}19\%, \quad \text{Town 3:}13\%, \quad \text{Town 4:}38\%,$$

while the answers had the distribution:

$$\text{Satisfied:}37\%, \quad \text{Not satisfied:}56\%, \quad \text{Don't know:}7\%.$$

If the distribution of replies is independent of the locations, it would have been possible to calculate the expected number in each entry multiplying the total number of observations by the corresponding probabilities, e.g., in the first entry we would expect:

$$10{,}000 \cdot 0.3 \cdot 0.37 = 1110.$$

If we carry out similar computations for all the other entries, we end up with the expected values shown in Table 10.3.

We see that the numbers in Tables 10.2 and 10.3 are somewhat different, but is the difference significant in the sense that we can reject a null hypothesis of independence? We can answer this question by a chi-square test for independence, and the recipe for this test reads as follows:

Chi-squared test for independence of two factors. We have n independent observations, and the test requires that all expected values are at least 5. Significance level α.

$$H_0: \text{The factors are independent},$$

(continued)

against

$$H_A: \text{The factors are dependent.}$$

$$I = \text{Number of different versions of factor 1.}$$

$$J = \text{Number of different versions of factor 2.}$$

$$X_{ij} = \text{Number of observations with } i\text{th version of factor 1, } j\text{th of factor 2.}$$

1. Find all marginals

$$A_i = \sum_{j=1}^{J} X_{ij},\ i = 1, \ldots, I, \qquad B_j = \sum_{i=1}^{I} X_{ij},\ j = 1, \ldots, J.$$

2. Compute the table of expectations:

$$E_{ij} = \frac{A_i B_j}{n}, \qquad i = 1, \ldots, I, j = 1, \ldots, J.$$

3. Compute Q by

$$Q = \sum_{i=1}^{I} \sum_{j=1}^{J} \frac{(X_{ij} - E_{ij})^2}{E_{ij}}.$$

4. Use a chi-square table with parameter $\nu = (I-1)(J-1)$ to find $q_\alpha^{(\nu)}$ such that

$$P(Q_{(\nu)} \geq q_\alpha^{(\nu)}) = \alpha.$$

5. Reject H_0 if $Q \geq q_\alpha^{(\nu)}$.

If we use this test in Example 10.11, we see that we already did most of the work. The observations X_{ij} are shown in Table 10.2 and the expected values E_{ij} are shown in Table 10.3. We see that the smallest expected value is 100, so we meet the requirements for the test. All what remains is to use these numbers to compute Q.

$$Q = \frac{(1100 - 1110)^2}{1110} + \frac{(800 - 703)^2}{703} + \cdots + \frac{(300 - 266)^2}{266} = 52.62.$$

In this case we should refer to a chi-square table with parameter $\nu = 3 \cdot 2 = 6$. Using 5% significance level, we see that $q_{0.05}^{(6)} = 12.6$. The observed value $Q = 52.62$ is

E1 =CHISQ.TEST(A1:D3;A4:D6)

	A	B	C	D	E
1	1100	800	400	1400	1,40107E-09
2	1700	1000	800	2100	
3	200	100	100	300	
4	1110	703	481	1406	
5	1680	1064	728	2128	
6	210	133	91	266	

Fig. 10.5 Chi-square test for independence

much larger than the rejection limit. We should hence reject the null hypothesis, and we are confident that there is a connection between the towns and the answers that have been given. If we look a bit closer on the numbers, we see, e.g., that there are far more satisfied customers than we expected in town 2, and far less satisfied customers than we expected in town 3. The differences are so huge that they are probably not due to chance. The value

$$\frac{(800 - 703)^2}{703} = 13.38,$$

is alone sufficient to bring Q above the rejection limit.

10.7.1 The Chi-Square Test for Independence Executed in Excel

Using the Excel command CHISQ.TEST, we can easily carry out the test in Example 10.11. We write the observed values from Table 10.2 in the first 4 columns, and the expected values from Table 10.3 below.

The test reports the P-value $1.4 \cdot 10^{-9}$ (Fig. 10.5), which is very small indeed. It is hence clear that we should reject the null hypothesis of independence.

10.8 Summary of Chap. 10

- Test for probability in binomial trials.
  - Keywords: Is the probability of success different from before?
  - Model assumptions: $H_0 : p = p_0$ or $p \leq p_0$ or $p \geq p_0$.
  - Alternatives: $H_A : p \neq p_0$ or $p > p_0$ or $p < p_0$.

- t-test for expected value.
  - Keywords: Is the expectation different from before?
  - Approximately normal observations.
  - Model assumptions: $H_0: \mu = \mu_0$ or $\mu \leq \mu_0$ or $\mu \geq \mu_0$.
  - Alternatives: $H_A: \mu \neq \mu_0$ or $\mu > \mu_0$ or $\mu < \mu_0$.
- t-test for comparison of expectations in two groups.
  - Keywords: Are the expectations in two groups equal?
  - Approximately normal observations.
  - Model assumptions: $H_0: \mu_X = \mu_Y$ or $\mu_X \leq \mu_Y$ or $\mu_X \geq \mu_Y$.
  - Alternatives: $H_A: \mu_X \neq \mu_Y$ or $\mu_X > \mu_Y$ or $\mu_X < \mu_Y$.
- The Wilcoxon tests for comparison of expectations in two groups.
  - Keywords: Are the expectations in two groups equal?
  - Observations may have any distribution.
  - Model assumptions: $H_0: \mu_X = \mu_Y$ or $\mu_X \leq \mu_Y$ or $\mu_X \geq \mu_Y$.
  - Alternatives: $H_A: \mu_X \neq \mu_Y$ or $\mu_X > \mu_Y$ or $\mu_X < \mu_Y$.
- The U test for comparison of probabilities.
  - Keywords: Are the probabilities in two groups equal?
  - Model assumptions: $H_0: p_1 = p_2$ or $p_1 \leq p_2$ or $p_1 \geq p_2$.
  - Alternatives: $H_A: p_1 \neq p_2$ or $p_1 > p_2$ or $p_1 < p_2$.
- The chi-square test for goodness-of-fit.
  - Keywords: Are the probabilities the same as before?
  - Model assumption: $H_0:$ The outcomes have the given probabilities.
  - Alternative: $H_A:$ The outcomes do not have the given probabilities.
- The chi-square test for independence.
  - Keywords: Are two factors independent?
  - Model assumption: $H_0:$ The factors are independent.
  - Alternative: $H_A:$ The factors are dependent.

10.9 Problems for Chap. 10

10.1 We have made 200 independent binomial trials and have observed 132 successes. We want to test $H_0: p = 0.5$ against $H_A: p \neq 0.5$. What conclusion can we draw?

10.2 We have made 50 independent binomial trials and have observed 25 successes. We want to test $H_0: p = 0.6$ against $H_A: p \neq 0.6$. What conclusion can we draw?

10.3 We have made 120 independent binomial trials and have observed 70 successes. We want to test $H_0: p = 0.5$ against $H_A: p \geq 0.5$. What conclusion can we draw?

Table 10.4 Data for Problem 10.7

Women	200	210	185	290	225	
Men	205	190	180	220	195	160

Table 10.5 Data for Problem 10.8

Department 1	Department 2
123	113
129	124
125	132
126	128
133	127
139	131
143	119
130	118

10.4 We have made 12 independent observations and have found the values $\overline{X} = 106.3$ and $S_X = 13.6$. We assume that observations are approximately normal and want to test $H_0 : \mu = 100$ against $H_A : \mu \neq 100$. What conclusion can we draw?

10.5 We have made 20 independent observations and have found the values $\overline{X} = 16.9$ and $S_X = 22.1$. We assume that observations are approximately normal and want to test $H_0 : \mu = 0$ against $H_A : \mu \neq 0$. What conclusion can we draw?

10.6 We have made 11 independent observations and have found the values $\overline{X} = 12.96$ and $S_X = 3.22$. We assume that observations are approximately normal and want to test $H_0 : \mu = 10$ against $H_A : \mu < 10$. What conclusion can we draw?

10.7 In a small survey in a shop we have asked 6 men and 5 women how much money they have spent on food the last week. The answers (in USD) are shown in Table 10.4.

Use a *t*-test for comparison of expected values to decide if gender makes a significant difference. Use 5% significance level, and assume that variances in the two groups are equal.

10.8 A company wants to compare the production at two departments. The company has observed how many units were produced during one hour at some randomly selected points in time. They have made 8 observations for each department, and the results are reported in Table 10.5.

Department 1 has gotten some new production equipment, and hence the company wants to test if department 1 is doing significantly better than department 2. Assume that observations are approximately normal and use Excel to execute a one-sided *t*-test to see if the effect is significant.

Hint: A one-sided test can either be executed by TTEST(A1:A8;B1:B8;1,2) or you can divide the *P*-value for TTEST(A1:A8;B1:B8;2,2) by 2. Excel do not take

Table 10.6 Data for Problem 10.9

Month	Department 1	Department 2
January	125	126
February	122	128
March	131	129
April	142	145
May	139	135
June	145	151
July	152	160
August	147	145
September	142	148
October	138	137
November	129	130
December	130	134

into account which mean is the largest, so to reject the null hypothesis you need to verify that the mean for department 1 is greater than the mean for department 2.

10.9 A company has two sales departments. We have observed the sales from each department every month during one year. The results are shown in Table 10.6.

(a) A two-sided t-test for two groups reported a P-value of 60%, while a two-sided t-test for paired observations reported a P-value of 8%. Which of the two tests do you trust? What conclusion could you draw from the test?
(b) Data from previous years indicate that the departments has had the same expected sales volumes for a number of years. Prior to the survey above, department 2 ran a comprehensive advertising campaign for their products. May this information be of importance here?

10.10 In a survey the participants were asked if they believed that the annual inflation would surpass 2.5%. 250 people in group 1 were asked this question, while 225 people in group 2 got the same question. In group 1, 60 people answered YES, while 78 of the people in group 2 gave the same answer. Examine if the two groups are different using the U-test. What is the P-value?

10.11 In a survey people in two different working groups were asked if the wage level was decisive for their choice of profession. The question was posed to 120 persons in group 1 and to 140 persons in group 2. In group 1 there were 68 people answering YES, while 65 people answered YES in group 2. Examine if the two groups are different using the U-test. What is the P-value?

10.12 In a market survey 500 people should choose which out of 4 different products they liked the best. The distribution of answers was as follows:

$$A : 129 \qquad B : 140 \qquad C : 113 \qquad D : 118.$$

Use a chi-square test to determine if all the 4 products had the same probability of being chosen. Hint: When the null hypothesis is true, then $p_1 = p_2 = p_3 = p_4 = 0.25$.

10.13 In a market survey 300 people should choose which out of three products they liked the best. The distribution of answers was as follows:

$$A : 98 \qquad B : 120 \qquad C : 92.$$

Use a chi-square test to determine if all the three products had the same probability of being chosen.

10.14 1000 persons chose which out of 10 products they liked the best. The distribution of answers was as follows:

$$115 \quad 112 \quad 44 \quad 72 \quad 320 \quad 9 \quad 42 \quad 152 \quad 61 \quad 73.$$

In a previous survey, the distribution of preferences was as follows:

$$12\% \quad 11\% \quad 5\% \quad 7\% \quad 30\% \quad 1\% \quad 4\% \quad 14\% \quad 7\% \quad 9\%.$$

Use Excel to execute a chi-square test to determine if preferences have changed.

10.15 In a market survey 800 people were asked about their view on their bank. The answers were distributed as follows:

$$\text{Dissatisfied} : 345 \quad \text{Neither satisfied nor dissatisfied} : 238 \quad \text{Satisfied} : 217.$$

A previous survey reported the following distribution:

$$\text{Dissatisfied} : 40\% \quad \text{Neither satisfied nor dissatisfied} : 30\% \quad \text{Satisfied} : 30\%.$$

Use a chi-square test to determine if preferences have changed.

10.16 In an election the votes were distributed as follows:

$$\text{Party A} : 24.3\% \quad \text{Party B} : 21.3\% \quad \text{Party C} : 14.6\%$$
$$\text{Party D} : 12.5\% \quad \text{Party E} : 12.4\% \quad \text{Party F} : 14.9\%.$$

A survey with 400 participants reported the following distribution:

$$\text{Party A} : 23\% \quad \text{Party B} : 18\% \quad \text{Party C} : 17\%$$

$$\text{Party D} : 16\% \quad \text{Party E} : 10\% \quad \text{Party F} : 16\%.$$

Use a chi-square test to determine if the distribution in the survey differs significantly from the election. Hint: Find how many people in the survey would have voted for the respective parties.

10.17 To check for quality in production, we regularly check 3 consecutive units. The distribution of errors in 1000 checks was as follows:

No errors : 829 One error : 163 Two errors : 6 Three errors : 2.

Use a chi-square test to determine if errors are independent and occur randomly with probability 6%. Hint: Under the null hypothesis we have a binomial distribution.

10.18 The customers in a bank are classified using two characteristics: marital status and credit rating. Marital status is 1 (unmarried) or 2 (married). Credit rating is A, B, or C. Classifying 1000 customers, we found results in Table 10.7.

Use a chi-square test for independence to determine if there is a connection between marital status and credit rating.

10.19 A travel agency has carried out a customer survey. A total of 1000 customers did not want to return to the hotel they had visited. The customers who did not want to return, was asked to point out a primary reason for this. The replies are shown in Table 10.8.

Use a chi-square test for independence to determine if there is a connection between which hotel the customers visited and the reason why they did not want to return.

Table 10.7 Data for Problem 10.18

Credit rating	Unmarried	Married
A	200	300
B	140	260
C	40	60

Table 10.8 Data for Problem 10.19

Reason	Hotel A	Hotel B	Hotel C
Too expensive	50	100	150
Bad attractions	100	200	100
Poor cleaning	150	100	50

10.20 Merging Observations: A travel agency has changed their primary collaborator. A survey carried out before the change reported the following distribution:

$$\text{Very satisfied} : 20\% \quad \text{Quite satisfied} : 10\% \quad \text{Somewhat satisfied} : 50\%$$
$$\text{Somewhat dissatisfied} : 15\% \quad \text{Very dissatisfied} : 5\%.$$

After the change they carried out a similar survey with $n = 740$ customers. The answers were as follows:

$$\text{Very satisfied} : 188 \quad \text{Quite satisfied} : 80 \quad \text{Somewhat satisfied} : 330$$
$$\text{Somewhat dissatisfied} : 92 \quad \text{Very dissatisfied} : 50.$$

(a) Use a chi-square test with 5% significance level to determine if the customers have changed opinions.
(b) Carried out a similar test using the merged data, i.e.

$$\text{Satisfied} : 80\% \qquad \text{Dissatisfied} : 20\%.$$
$$\text{Satisfied} : 598 \qquad \text{Dissatisfied} : 142.$$

How would you interpret this?
(c) Let X_5 denote the number of very dissatisfied customers in a survey with n participants where the probability of being very dissatisfied is p_5. What approximative distribution has

$$\frac{X_5 - n p_5}{\sqrt{n p_5(1 - p_5)}},$$

if n is large? Use this to approximate $P(X_5 \geq 50)$ under the condition that the customers have the same opinions as before the change. Comment the answer.

10.21 Testing Binomial Distribution: A questionnaire has 6 questions. Each question has two alternatives, and only one alternative is correct.

(a) Let R be the number of correct answers from a person guessing the answer on all questions. What is the distribution of R? Write a table showing the probability for each possible value of R.
(b) 300 persons answered the questionnaire. The number of correct answers were distributed as shown in Table 10.9. We assume that the answers were independent, and want to test if the observed distribution is consistent with pure guessing. Find a test suitable for this purpose, and execute the test on these observations. Use 5% significance level. What do you conclude?

Table 10.9 Data for Problem 10.21

Number of correct answers	Number of persons
0	7
1	34
2	54
3	85
4	79
5	34
6	7

Table 10.10 Data for Problem 10.23

Product	1	2	3	4	5	6
Number of people choosing the product	28	42	25	52	25	28

Table 10.11 Previous observations

Product	1	2	3	4	5	6
Percentages choosing the product	10	20	15	30	10	15

10.22 Is One Manager Significantly Better Than Another? Two finance companies sell mutual funds. Company A offers a total of $n_1 = 100$ different funds, while company B offers $n_2 = 110$ different funds. We assume that all funds within the same company have a constant probability of beating the reference index during a given year. We call these probabilities p_A and p_B. Let X_A be the number of funds from company A that beat the reference index, and X_B be the corresponding number at company B.

(a) Assume that the results for each fund are different random variables. What is the distribution of X_A and X_B?
(b) Last year 30 of the funds in A and 23 of the funds in B beat their reference index. Find a suitable test for this situation, execute the test and find the P-value. What is your conclusion? Use 5% significance level.
(c) The analysis above assumes that the results for each fund are independent. Point at circumstances where this assumption may be unrealistic.

10.23 Did Preferences Change? 200 persons should choose which product they liked the best among 6 different products. Each person could only choose one product. The answers were distributed as shown in Table 10.10.

In a previous survey the distribution was as in Table 10.11.

(a) We want to examine if the customers have changed their opinion. Find a suitable test for this. State the null hypothesis, alternative hypothesis, test static, and rejection region. Use 5% significance level.
(b) Execute the test in (a). How large (approximately) is the P-value? What is your conclusion?

10.24 Checking Normality: We have observed the production at two different departments. At department 1 the production numbers were:

101, 103, 105, 102, 101, 100, 117, 100, 102, 104.

At department 2 we recorded:

107, 106, 108, 125, 112, 108, 107, 106, 104, 105.

In the tests below we will use 5% significance level.

(a) We have used a two-sided t-test to compare the two sets of observations. With data as above, the P-value for this test is 4.8% (you can take this for granted). What is the null hypothesis and the alternative hypothesis in this test? What conclusion can you draw from the test?
(b) If we join the two observation sets, the mean value is 106.15 and the sample variance is $S_X^2 = 36.87$. Imagine that we make 20 independent draws from a normally distributed random variable with expectation $\mu = 106.15$ and variance $\sigma^2 = 36.87$. What is the probability that the largest value is greater than or equal to 125?
(c) A Shapiro test can be used to determine if data are normally distributed. The hypotheses in this test are:

$$H_0: \text{ Data are normally distributed}$$

$$H_A: \text{ Data are not normally distributed.}$$

A Shapiro test based on the numbers from department 1 and 2 returns the P-value 0.14%. What conclusion can you draw from this? Does this conclusion have any consequences for the analysis in (a)?

10.25 Can Different Tests Lead to Different Conclusions? We have observed production before and after training at a department. The observation was not paired. Before training the production numbers were:

113, 124, 132, 128, 127, 131, 119, 118.

After training the results were as follows:

123, 129, 125, 126, 133, 139, 140, 130.

(a) Use a one-sided t-test with 5% significance level to determine if the training affected expected production. You can make use of the results $\overline{X} = 124, \overline{Y} = 130.63$, and $S^2 = 42.71$.

(b) Use a one-sided Wilcoxon test with 5% significance level to determine if the training affected expected production. You can make use of the result $W = 53$.
(c) Compare the results from the two tests above. Assume that you have information indicating that production numbers are not normally distributed. What conclusion would you draw?

10.26 Unpaired/Paired Observations: We have examined working times (in seconds) before and after training at a department. Before training we got the results:

$$239,\ 237,\ 235,\ 224,\ 259,\ 227,\ 220,\ 268,\ 228,\ 252,$$
$$238,\ 288,\ 283,\ 248,\ 285,\ 279,\ 245,\ 210,\ 251,\ 286.$$

After training the results were as follows:

$$218,\ 240,\ 241,\ 206,\ 247,\ 211,\ 212,\ 263,\ 214,\ 253,$$
$$219,\ 264,\ 276,\ 246,\ 260,\ 275,\ 232,\ 195,\ 229,\ 296.$$

(a) Use a one-sided Wilcoxon test with 5% significance level to determine if training has had effect.
(b) Used a one-sided Wilcoxon test for paired observations with 5% significance level to determine if training has had effect.
(c) The observations were done in pairs. The order of the results corresponds to the same workers in both observation sets. What conclusion can you draw from this?

10.27 When Can We Use One-Sided Tests? The workers at a factory have gotten training with the intention of reducing the number of defective items. To examine the effect of training, we observed the number of defective units before and after training. The results before training were:

Among 100 items, we found 10 defective items.

After training the results were as follows:

Among 120 items, we found 8 defective items.

(a) Use a one-sided U-test to examine the effect of training. Why can we use a one-sided test in this situation? What is the P-value for the test. What conclusion can you draw from the results? Use 5% significance level.
(b) Alternatively we can imagine a different scenario where the workers have received training to improve the security at the department. What kind of test is appropriate in this situation?

10.28 Outliers: We have examined the effect of training, and observed the production of each worker before and after training. X is the results before training, while Y is the result after training. The results are listed such that the production of worker 1 is listed first, then the result for worker 2, and so on.

$$X: 12, 11, 15, 17, 12, 14, 15, 11, 12, 14, 11, 11, 15, 12, 56$$

$$Y: 20, 21, 20, 19, 18, 22, 20, 18, 18, 17, 19, 22, 17, 19, 19.$$

To examine if training has had effect, we first executed a one-sided t-test for paired observations, then a one-sided Wilcoxon test for paired observations.

(a) Why can we use one-sided test in this situation? What is the null hypothesis and the alternative hypothesis for these tests?
(b) The P-value for the t-test was 13.53% and the P-value for the Wilcoxon test was 0.57%. What conclusion can you draw from the two tests? Use 5% significance level.
(c) The two tests give conflicting conclusions. What conclusion would you draw in total? Hint: Inspect the observed pairs. Do you notice a pattern?

10.29 Sorting Paired Observations: You want to consider production numbers before and after training, and have collected 50 production numbers from 50 workers before and after training. The observations are paired, i.e., production numbers from the same worker occur in the same position in the two sequences.

(a) We have no information indicating that data has normal distribution, and we will first use a Wilcoxon rank-sum test with rank-sum W to examine the data. We let μ_X be the expected production before training, and μ_Y the expected production after training. What is the null hypothesis and the alternative hypothesis in this case? Find the values for $\mathrm{E}[W]$ and $\mathrm{Var}[W]$ under the null hypothesis.
(b) We observe $W = 2455$ in the test from (a). What is your conclusion? Use 5% significance level.
(c) Since the observations are paired, we will also use a one-sided Wilcoxon signed-rank test with rank V. Find $\mathrm{E}[V]$ and $\mathrm{Var}[V]$ under the null hypothesis.
(d) We observe $V = 604$ in the test from (c). What is your conclusion? Use 5% significance level.
(e) It is suggested that you alternatively might proceed as follows:
  - Sort the data prior to training in ascending order.
  - Sort the data after training in ascending order.
  - Compute the signed-rank for the sorted data.

  After sorting we observed $V = 364$. What conclusion do you draw from this?
(f) The tests in (d) and (e) give conflicting answers. Which answer is the right one?

10.30 Equivalence Testing: We have examined average wages in two different regions, and have collected data from 5000 persons in region 1 and 7000 persons in region 2. In region 1 we found $\overline{X} = 31{,}200$ (USD), while $\overline{Y} = 31{,}000$ (USD) in region 2. Estimated standard deviation was $S = 4300$ (USD), where

$$S = \frac{1}{n_1 + n_2 - 2} \left(\sum_{i=1}^{n_1} (X_i - \overline{X})^2 + \sum_{i=1}^{n_2} (Y_i - \overline{Y})^2 \right).$$

(a) Use a two-sided t-test with 5% significance level to determine if there is a significant difference between the regions.

(b) Equivalence tests have been suggested in situations where we want to compare the expectations of two random variables X and Y, and where we want to examine if the difference is so small that it is of no practical relevance. In this test we define $\mu_X = \mathrm{E}[X]$ and $\mu_Y = \mathrm{E}[Y]$, and define

$$\delta = \mu_X - \mu_Y.$$

In a test of this kind we need to specify how small δ need to be before we can say the difference is of no practical relevance. We call this quantity Δ, and we say that the two expected values are equivalent when

$$-\Delta < \delta < \Delta.$$

An equivalence test can then be formulated as follows:

$$H_0 : \delta \leq -\Delta \text{ or } \delta \geq \Delta, \qquad H_A : -\Delta < \delta < \Delta.$$

The test is executed via

$$T_1 = \frac{\hat{\delta} + \Delta}{S[\hat{\delta}]}, \qquad T_2 = \frac{\Delta - \hat{\delta}}{S[\hat{\delta}]}.$$

where $\hat{\delta}$ and $S[\hat{\delta}]$ are computed in exactly the same way as we do in a t-test for the comparison of two expectations. We reject H_0 at significance level α if

$$\min(T_1, T_2) \geq t_\alpha^{(n_1+n_2-2)}.$$

Choose $\Delta = 500$ (USD) and carry out an equivalence test for the two regions. Compare the results from (a) and (b).

10.31 Strength Considerations:

(a) Assume that Q is chi-square distributed with parameter 20. Find q such that $P(Q \geq q) = 5\%$.

Let X denote the time it takes to serve one randomly selected customer. We will assume that X is exponentially distributed with expectation $\theta > 0$, i.e., it is a continuous distribution with density

$$f_X(x) = \frac{1}{\theta}e^{-\frac{x}{\theta}}.$$

To estimate θ we will make 10 independent observations and observe $\overline{X}$.

(b) We want to test if expected service time θ is larger than 10 (minutes), and formulate the hypotheses

$$H_0 : \theta = 10 \qquad H_A : \theta > 10.$$

For simplicity we assume that a one-sided test can be used here. It is possible to show (you can take this for granted) that if we make n observations, then

$$Q = \frac{2n\overline{X}}{\theta}$$

is chi-square distributed with parameter $2n$. How large must X be before we can reject H_0? Use 5% significance level and $n = 10$. We observe $\overline{X} = 15$. What conclusion can we draw from this?

(c) What do we mean by the strength of the alternative $\theta = 20$? What (approximately) is the strength of this alternative when $n = 10$? How large must n be if the strength of the alternative $\theta = 12.5$ is at least 50%? Hint: Examine different values of n using trial and error.

10.32 Confidence Intervals Provides More Information: We have collected data for wages from two different regions. In region 1 we collected $n_1 = 15{,}000$ observations and found $\overline{X} = 32{,}378$ (USD). In region 2 we collected $n_2 = 10{,}000$ observations and found $\overline{Y} = 32{,}209$ (USD). For the spread (as defined in the t-test) we computed $S = 2900$ (USD).

(a) We want to test if expected wages are significantly different in the two regions. Execute a two-sided t-test with 5% significance level. What is your conclusion?

(b) Find a 95% confidence interval for the difference in expected wages. Comment the result.

10.33 Misinterpreting Unscaled Variables: A travel agency has collected data on the level of satisfaction among their customers. The answered were ranked 1 to 5:

$$\text{Very dissatisfied} = 1$$

$$\text{Somewhat dissatisfied} = 2$$

$$\text{Neither satisfied nor dissatisfied} = 3$$

Table 10.12 Data for Problem 10.33

Answer	1	2	3	4	5	Number of respondents
Before	160	240	160	240	160	960
After	264	310	230	115	460	1379

$$\text{Somewhat satisfied} = 4$$

$$\text{Very satisfied} = 5.$$

The agency has carried out a new arrangement where the customers have received more support than before, and wants to examine the effect of the new arrangement. They collected the data shown in Table 10.12.

(a) Let X denote the reply from a customer. We want to use data to compute the average value before and after the new arrangement. Compute $\overline{X}$ = Average before, and $\overline{Y}$ = Average after.
(b) Use a one-sided t-test to examine if the expected answer has increased significantly under the new arrangement.
(c) Point to problems related to the test in (b).
(d) As an alternative to the test in (b) we can use one-sided U-tests. Use U-tests with 5% significance level to answer the following:
- Is the fraction of very satisfied customers significantly higher than before?
- Is the fraction of satisfied customers significantly higher than before?
- Is the fraction of very dissatisfied customers significantly higher than before?

(e) Are the tests in (d) more credible than the test in (b)?

10.34 Extreme Values: 100 randomly selected pupils participate in a standardized test at a school. We assume that the skill of a randomly selected pupil is normally distributed with mean 489 and standard deviation 90, and that the skill of different pupils are independent random variables.

(a) Let $\overline{X}$ be the average score at the school. Explain why $E[\overline{X}] = 489$ and $\text{Var}[\overline{X}] = 81$.
(b) How probable is it that the average score for the school is 463 or below?
(c) The test is executed at 500 different schools. Assume that the pupils at all these schools have skills with the distribution above. How probable is it that the average score at all schools are 463 or better?
(d) How probable is it that the worst of the 500 schools have a score that is 463 or below? Compare with (b) and comment the answer.

10.35 Interpreting Random Fluctuation: A large industrial company has 100 relatively similar production units.

(a) A t-test of the production numbers from the worst department against the production numbers from all the other departments leads to a P-value of 4%. Is that normal? What should the management do?
(b) A t-test of the production numbers from the worst department against the production numbers from all the other departments leads to a P-value of 0.01%. Is that normal? What should the management do?
(c) Assume that the production numbers $Z_i, i = 1, \ldots, 100$, all are independent and log normally distributed with

$$Z_i = e^{X_i}, \qquad \text{where } \mathrm{E}[X_i] = 10, \mathrm{Var}[X_i] = 9,\ X_i \text{ are normally distributed.}$$

How probable is it that the result at the worst department is less than or equal to 10?

10.36 Strength Is a Strong Issue: In this problem we will use t-tests for the comparison of expected values in two groups. We assume for simplicity that the issue is such that we can ignore the case $\mu_X < \mu_Y$, i.e., that we are allowed to use one-sided tests. We assume that data are normally distributed and use 5% significance level.

(a) A researcher has collected data from two different groups. There were 40 observations from each group, but the observations were not paired. For group 1 she found $\overline{X} = 101.75$ and for group 2 $\overline{Y} = 112.12$. The S-value was $S = 23.23$. Use a one-sided t-test to determine if we have significant support for the claim $\mu_X < \mu_Y$. Suggest an approximate P-value for the test. What conclusion would you draw from this?
(b) To confirm the finding, the researcher was advised to repeat the study with 10 observations in each group. The observed values turned out as follows:

$$\overline{X} = 103.62, \qquad \overline{Y} = 110.88, \qquad S = 19.91.$$

What conclusion would you draw if you see these results in isolation from the first study?
(c) It is possible to show that if the true values equal the observed values in (a), i.e.

$$\mu_X = 101.75, \qquad \mu_Y = 112.12, \qquad \sigma_X = 23.23, \qquad \sigma_Y = 23.23,$$

then the strength of the test in (b) is about 25%. What does that mean in practice? Is it a good idea to try to confirm the finding in this way?
(d) If we see the two studies in conjunction, i.e., we merge the datasets into two datasets with 50 observations in each, we get

$$\overline{X} = 102.12, \qquad \overline{Y} = 111.88, \qquad S = 22.42.$$

What conclusion can you draw from the two studies seen in conjunction? Compare the result with (a) and (b).

Linear Regression

11

Abstract

When we make observations, we often encounter cases where the size of observations appears to change in some systematic way. One possible cause for this is that we have done the observations over a period of time, and as time passes the distribution of values may change. To determine if such changes are random or systematic, we can use linear regression. Linear regression is a widely used technique that has a lot to offer, in particular since we are often able to quantify systematic changes.

11.1 Linear Correspondence

In this section we take a new look on the relation between two variables. Previously we used the covariance or the coefficient of variation to determine a relationship. We now proceed a step further; we want to see if there is a linear relationship between the two variables. Before we try to write down any expressions, we take a look at some figures.

In Fig. 11.1 we have observed the values of two different stocks at 100 different points in time. We let X be the stock price of company A and Y the stock price of company B. From the figure we see there is strong covariation between the two stock prices. The coefficient of variation confirms this. We have $\rho[X, Y] = 0.98$. If we look at the numbers, we see that Y is largely twice as big as X. That we can express mathematically by

$$Y = 2 \cdot X.$$

This function is a straight line through the origin with slope 2. In Fig. 11.2 we have included this line.

J. Ubøe, *Introductory Statistics for Business and Economics*, Springer Texts in Business and Economics, https://doi.org/10.1007/978-3-319-70936-9_11

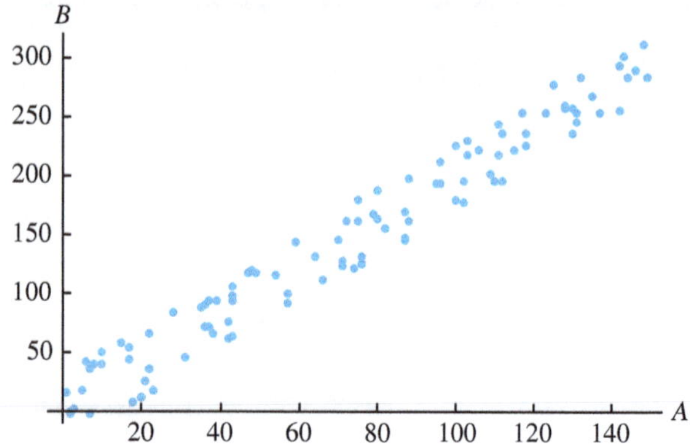

Fig. 11.1 Pairs of stock prices

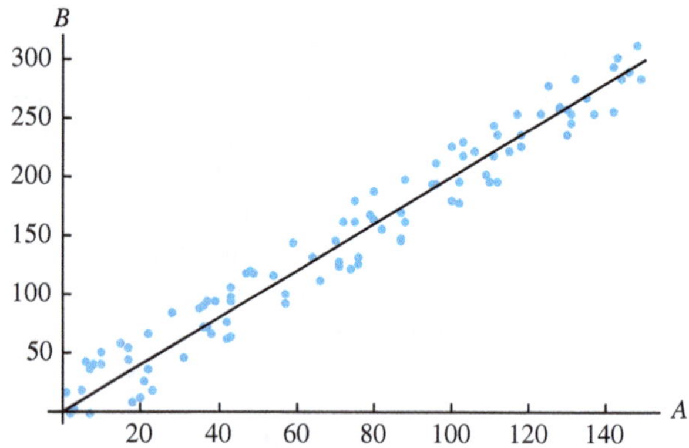

Fig. 11.2 A regression line through the data

The figure confirms that the expression $Y = 2 \cdot X$ provides a good assessment, but it is not 100% correct. We hence write

$$Y = 2 \cdot X + \text{“error”},$$

where the term “error” is a random variable which explains the deviations from the straight line. This example is particularly simple, but it tells us what we are after. When we have data which are distributed as a band around a straight line, we want the formula for the line, and we want to use the formula to study the connection between the two quantities.

Example 11.1 In Fig. 11.3 we have again studied the values of two stocks at 100 different points in time. We see that the observations are located in a band around a straight line, and this line is included in Fig. 11.4.

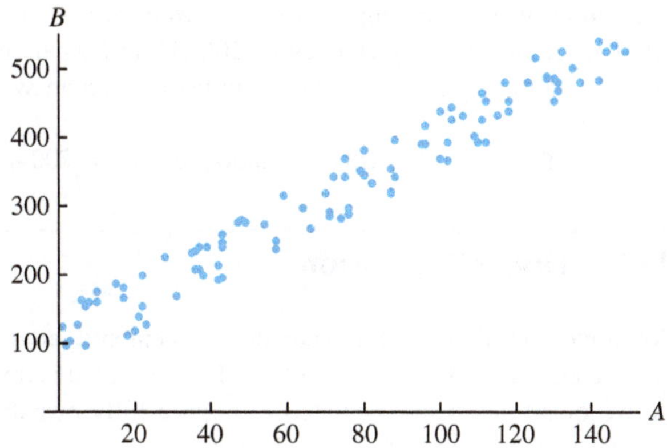

Fig. 11.3 Pairs of stock prices

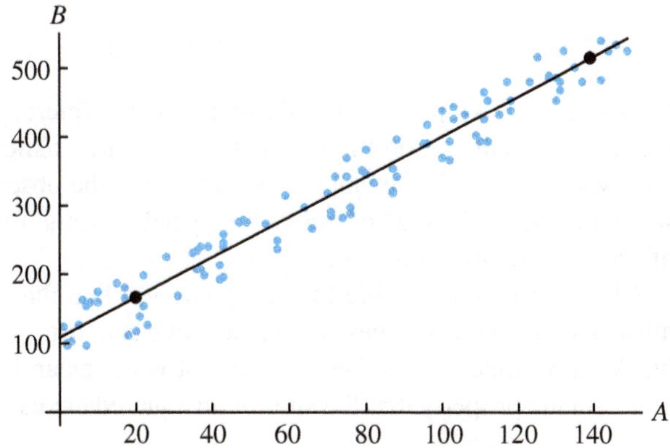

Fig. 11.4 A regression line through the data

Since we need to find a formula for the straight line, we read the values at two different points on the line. We choose $X = 20$ and read $Y = 160$, and when $X = 140$ we read $Y = 520$. We can now use a two-point formula for a straight line, i.e.

$$y = \frac{y_1 - y_0}{x_1 - x_0}(x - x_0) + y_0.$$

If we insert the values into the formula, we get

$$Y = \frac{520 - 160}{140 - 20}(X - 20) + 160 = 3 \cdot (X - 20) + 160 = 3 \cdot X + 100.$$

We conclude that

$$Y = 3 \cdot X + 100 + \text{"random errors"}.$$

A relation of that sort might be useful when we want to make predictions. If the stock price of company A rises to 200 (USD), what can we expect the price for stocks in company B to be? The formula offers an answer to this question.

$$Y = 3 \cdot 200 + 100 + \text{“random error”} = 700 + \text{“random error”}.$$

11.2 Linear Regression

An important field within statistics is centered around phenomena which are connected via a systematic coupling. The key word is trend. The typical framework is two quantities x and y related through a fully or partially known function, i.e., $y = f(x)$. Here we will focus the linear case

$$y = \alpha + \beta x.$$

In this case the graph is a straight line, α is the intercept with the y-axis and β is the slope. A common problem is that α and β are unknowns, and we need to make observations to settle the values. In many cases the observations are not prefect but subject to errors. Instead of points on a perfect straight line, we might have a band of observations as in Fig. 11.5.

Clearly it is not possible to draw a straight line through all these points, so we must settle for less. The best we can achieve is to draw a line with the best possible fit. What we mean by the best possible fit is not clear, but it is usual to construct a line with the property that the sum of all squared errors is as small as possible. The

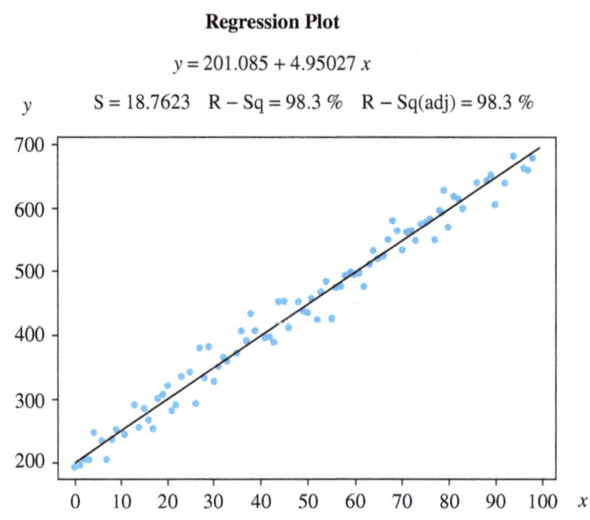

Fig. 11.5 Corresponding values of x and y

method is commonly called the ordinary least squares method or OLS for short. Since our primary concern is to study properties of the optimal line, we will not explain in detail why the construction below works. Some details are provided in Exercises 11.23 and 11.18.

Construction of the OLS line:
Assume we have n observation pairs $(X_1, Y_1), \ldots, (X_n, Y_n)$.

1. Compute

$$\overline{X} = \frac{1}{n}(X_1 + \cdots + X_n).$$

2. Compute

$$\overline{Y} = \frac{1}{n}(Y_1 + \cdots + Y_n).$$

3. Compute the sum of squares

$$M = (X_1 - \overline{X})^2 + \cdots + (X_n - \overline{X})^2.$$

4. Compute

$$\hat{\beta} = \frac{1}{M}\left((X_1 - \overline{X})(Y_1 - \overline{Y}) + \cdots + (X_n - \overline{X})(Y_n - \overline{Y})\right).$$

5. Compute

$$\hat{\alpha} = \overline{Y} - \hat{\beta}\overline{X}.$$

6. The OLS line is

$$\hat{Y} = \hat{\alpha} + \hat{\beta} \cdot X.$$

Technically we assume that all X and Y are related through

$$Y = \alpha + \beta \cdot X + \epsilon$$

where ϵ are independent random variables (one variable for every X) with $\mathrm{E}[\epsilon] = 0$ and $\mathrm{Var}[\epsilon] = \sigma^2$ (the same variance regardless of X). Under these assumptions it is possible to prove that $\hat{\alpha}$ is an unbiased estimator for the (unknown) constant α, and that $\hat{\beta}$ is an unbiased estimator for the (unknown) constant β. We will often need to estimate the unknown constant σ^2, and the following expression is useful:

An unbiased estimator for σ^2 is

$$S^2 = \frac{1}{n-2}\left((Y_1 - \hat{Y}_1)^2 + \cdots + (Y_1 - \hat{Y}_1)^2\right).$$

where $\hat{Y}_i = \hat{\alpha} + \hat{\beta} \cdot X_i, i = 1, \ldots, n$.

In this context X is often called an explanatory variable, and Y a dependent variable. The idea is that when we know X, we can suggest a reasonable value for Y. We say that X explains Y since the value of Y depends on X.

The formulas above require considerably manual labor to compute, but we will hardly ever need to carry them out. Computations of this sort are fully automated in statistical software, and we only need a broad view of how the expressions work.

Example 11.2 Find the OLS line when we have the observations (1,1), (2,3), (3.3).

Solution: Here $n = 3$ and $X_1 = 1, X_2 = 2, X_3 = 3$ and $Y_1 = 1, Y_2 = 3, Y_3 = 3$. If we use these numbers in the formulas above, we find

$$\begin{aligned}
\overline{X} &= 2, \\
\overline{Y} &= \frac{7}{3} \\
M &= (1-2)^2 + (2-2)^2 + (3-2)^2 = 2, \\
\hat{\beta} &= \frac{1}{2}\left((1-2)(1-\frac{7}{3}) + (2-2)(3-\frac{7}{3}) + (3-2)(3-\frac{7}{3})\right) = 1, \\
\hat{\alpha} &= \frac{7}{3} - 1 \cdot 2 = \frac{1}{3}.
\end{aligned}$$

The regression line is hence $\hat{Y} = \frac{1}{3} + X$; see the straight line in Fig. 11.6.

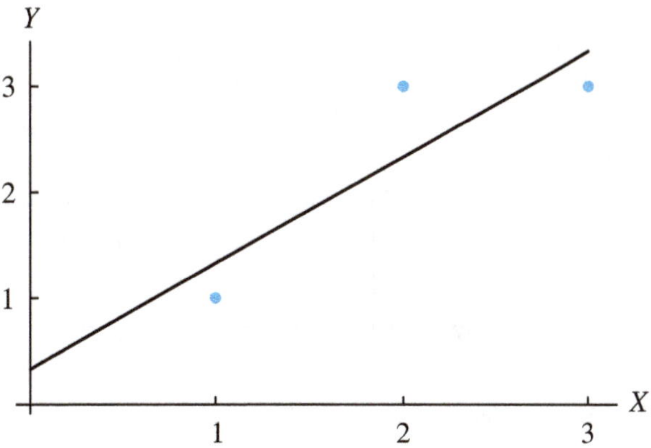

Fig. 11.6 The regression line in Example 11.2

11.3 Residuals and Explanatory Power

The regression line will usually not go through all the points. For each X_i we will usually see a difference between the observed value Y_i and the point on the regression line $\hat{Y}_i = \hat{\alpha} + \hat{\beta} \cdot X_i$. This difference we call the i-th residual, and we use the symbol R_i. That is,

$$R_i = Y_i - \hat{Y}_i, \qquad i = 1, \ldots, n.$$

The residuals hence measure the errors we make when we replace the observed values by the corresponding values on the regression line. To quantify the overall error, statisticians use the quantity SSE (sum squared errors) which is the sum of the squares of all residuals, i.e.

$$\text{SSE} = \sum_{i=1}^{n} (Y_i - \hat{Y}_i)^2.$$

A measure for the total variation in Y is the SST (sum squares total) which is defined by

$$\text{SST} = \sum_{i=1}^{n} (Y_i - \overline{Y})^2,$$

see Fig. 11.7.

The idea is now that if the total squared error is much smaller than the total squared variation, then the regression line captures most of the variation in Y. Phrased differently, we can say that the explanatory variable X explains most of

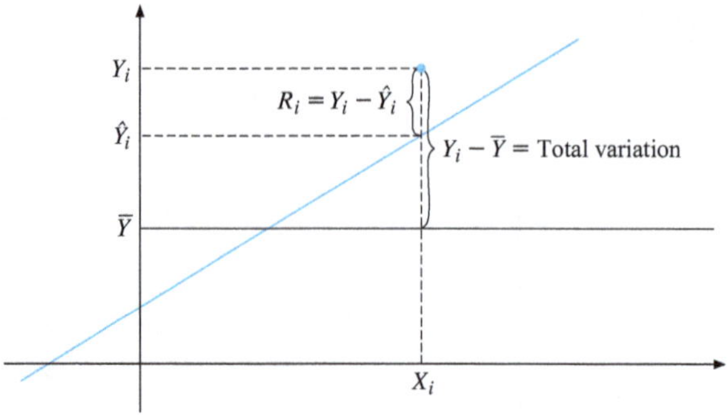

Fig. 11.7 Residuals and total variation

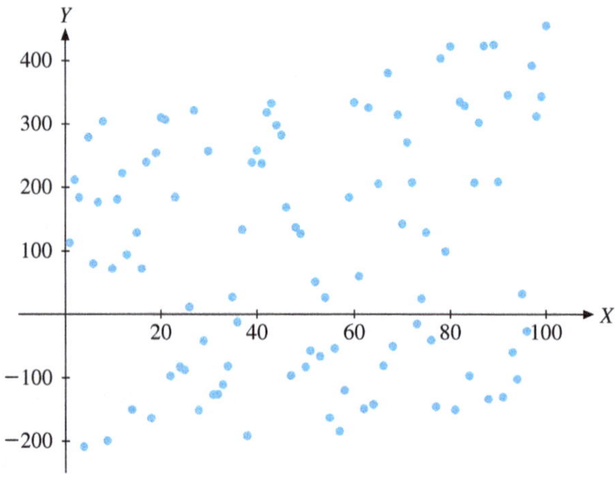

Fig. 11.8 Small explanatory power

the variation in Y. We define the explanatory power R^2 of the model as follows:

$$R^2 = 1 - \frac{\text{SSE}}{\text{SST}}.$$

It is possible to show mathematically that $R^2 = 100\%$ if and only if all the observed points lie on the regression line. In practice that means that if the explanatory power is nearly 100%, then nearly all the observation points must be very close to the regression line. The explanatory power R^2 is relatively easy to interpret, and the value gives a good impression of how close the observations are to a linear relationship. Consider the plots in Figs. 11.8, 11.9, and 11.10.

In Fig. 11.8 there hardly seems to be a relationship between X and Y. The explanatory power $R^2 = 2.3\%$ for this dataset. In Fig. 11.9 there seems to be a relation between the variables, and an explanatory power $R^2 = 30.7\%$ confirms

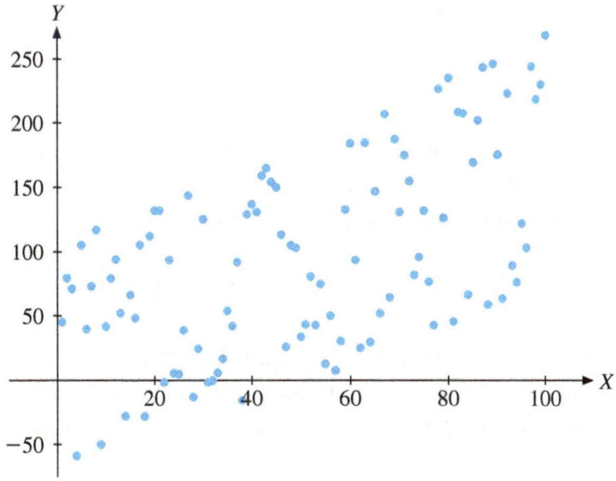

Fig. 11.9 Some explanatory power

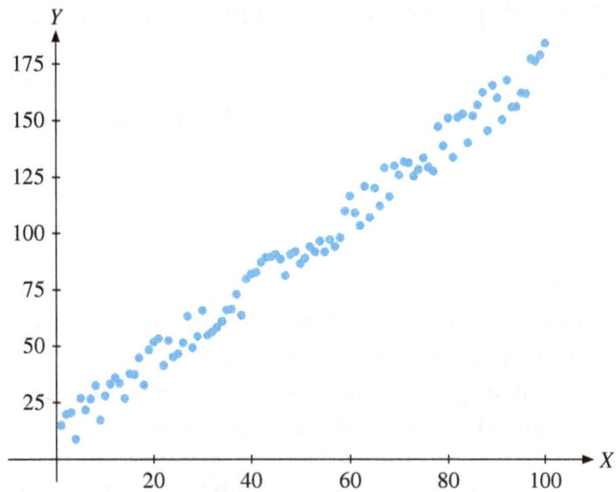

Fig. 11.10 Large explanatory power

that there is some relationship. In Fig. 11.10 the relationship is quite strong, here $R^2 = 98.3\%$.

11.3.1 Naming Variables

In the general exposition of the theory we have used the notation X for the explanatory variable and Y for the dependent variable. In practical cases it is useful to equip the variables with more descriptive names. Some examples:

- If we want to examine if there is a linear relationship between a stock price and time, then S (short for stock) and t are natural names, i.e., we consider the regression line

$$\hat{S} = \hat{\alpha} + \hat{\beta} \cdot t.$$

- Sometimes it may be appropriate to write some variable names in full. If we want to examine a relation between quantity Q and price, P is not a good variable name, since it can be confused with probability. In such cases we might write

$$\hat{Q} = \hat{\alpha} + \hat{\beta} \cdot \text{price}.$$

Full names on variables are quite common when we use statistical software. Later in this chapter we will use convenient variable names when we study regressions, and that does not affect the mathematical formulas we will use.

11.4 Hypothesis Testing in the Regression Model

One of the most important questions in statistics is the following: Does X affect Y? If the answer is yes, the distribution of Y changes when we change X. When X and Y have a linear relation

$$Y = \alpha + \beta \cdot X + \epsilon,$$

we want to know if $\beta = 0$ or not. If $\beta = 0$, then Y never changes when we change X. In most cases α and β are unknown constants, and we make observations to estimate those constants. Even in cases where $\beta = 0$, we will usually find $\hat{\beta} \neq 0$. If $\hat{\beta}$ is small, it appears quite likely that the true value for β may be zero. This problem is well suited for hypothesis testing, where

$$H_0 : \beta = 0, \qquad H_A : \beta \neq 0.$$

If we can reject H_0, we are able to conclude that β is probably not zero, which in turn means that X probably affects Y.

Formally the test is executed as follows:

Two-sided hypothesis test for the slope β in a linear regression:

$$H_0 : \text{The explanatory variable has no impact, i.e., } \beta = 0.$$
$$H_A : \text{The explanatory variable has impact, i.e., } \beta \neq 0.$$

(continued)

The test requires either many independent observations or that the residuals are independent and normally distributed. Significance level γ.

1. Find the values for $\hat{\beta}, S,$ and M using the formulas from the OLS regression.
2. Compute

$$S[\hat{\beta}] = S/\sqrt{M}.$$

3. The test static is

$$T = \hat{\beta}/S[\hat{\beta}].$$

4. Use the t-table with parameter $\nu = n - 2$, and find $t^{(\nu)}_{\gamma/2}$ such that

$$P\left(T_{(\nu)} \geq t^{(\nu)}_{\gamma/2}\right) = \gamma/2.$$

5. Reject H_0 if $T \geq t^{(\nu)}_{\gamma/2}$ or if $T \leq -t^{(\nu)}_{\gamma}$.

Extra: The limits for a $(1 - \gamma)100\%$ confidence interval for β are given by

$$\hat{\beta} \pm t^{(\nu)}_{\gamma/2} \cdot S[\hat{\beta}].$$

Note that we here use γ to denote the significance level. This is to avoid confusion with the intercept α in the OLS regression.

One-sided hypothesis test for the slope β in a linear regression:

$$H_0 : \text{The explanatory variable has no impact, i.e., } \beta \leq 0.$$

$$H_A : \text{The explanatory variable has impact, i.e., } \beta > 0.$$

The test requires either many independent observations or that the residuals are independent and normally distributed. Significance level γ.

1. Find the values for $\hat{\beta}, S,$ and M using the formulas from the OLS regression.

(continued)

2. Compute

$$S[\hat{\beta}] = S/\sqrt{M}.$$

3. The test static is

$$T = \hat{\beta}/S[\hat{\beta}].$$

4. Use the t-table with parameter $\nu = n-2$, and find $t_\alpha^{(\nu)}$ such that

$$P\left(T_{(\nu)} \geq t_\gamma^{(\nu)}\right) = \gamma.$$

5. Reject H_0 if $T \geq t_\gamma^{(\nu)}$.

One-sided hypothesis test for the slope β in a linear regression:

$$H_0 : \text{The explanatory variable has no impact, i.e., } \beta \geq 0.$$
$$H_A : \text{The explanatory variable has impact, i.e., } \beta < 0.$$

The test requires either many independent observations or that the residuals are independent and normally distributed. Significance level γ.

1. Find the values for $\hat{\beta}, S$, and M using the formulas from the OLS regression.
2. Compute

$$S[\hat{\beta}] = S/\sqrt{M}.$$

3. The test static is

$$T = \hat{\beta}/S[\hat{\beta}].$$

4. Use the t-table with parameter $\nu = n-2$, and find $t_\gamma^{(\nu)}$ such that

$$P\left(T_{(\nu)} \geq t_\gamma^{(\nu)}\right) = \gamma.$$

5. Reject H_0 if $T \leq -t_\gamma^{(\nu)}$.

If H_0 can be rejected at 5% significance level, we say that the explanatory variable is significant. If the explanatory variable can be rejected at any sensible significance level, we say that the explanatory variable is strongly significant. The wording is commonly used when the P-value is less than 0.1%, but values other than 0.1% are used sometimes. We should note that statistical software reports the P-values of such tests.

The value of M is usually not reported in printouts. As we sometimes need this value to do calculations, it may help to note that:

- $M = (n-1)\text{Var}[X]$.
- $M = \frac{S^2}{S[\hat{\beta}]}$. The values of S and $S[\hat{\beta}]$ are often reported.

Example 11.3 In a regression with $n = 10$ independent and normally distributed observations we have found the regression line

$$\hat{Y} = 104.28 + 4.409 \cdot X.$$

Furthermore we have computed $S = 25.53$ and $M = 110$. What is the conclusion of a two-sided test for zero slope? We use 5% significance level.

Solution: We compute

$$S[\hat{\beta}] = \frac{25.53}{\sqrt{110}} = 2.43.$$

From the regression line we see that $\hat{\beta} = 4.409$. That gives

$$T = \frac{4.409}{2.43} = 1.81.$$

Using a t-table with parameter $\nu = 10 - 2 = 8$, we find $t_{0.025}^{(8)} = 2.306$ (the test is two-sided). The test static is well within the non-rejection region. The effect of X is not significant, and we keep the null hypothesis saying that X has no impact on Y.

11.5 Prediction/Estimation

An important application of linear regression is to suggest the value of the dependent variable Y when we know the value of the explanatory variable X. We have, e.g., observed the time development over the last 12 months, and want to predict the value at some specific point in the future. We should note that there are two somewhat different angles of approach:

- We can predict the value of Y itself when $X = x$.
- We can estimate the expectation $\mathrm{E}[Y]$ when $X = x$.

The reader should notice the exact wording here. Statisticians use the word predict when they talk about random variables, and the word estimate when they talk about constants. The two versions have much in common, but there is a principal difference. The uncertainty in Y itself is larger than the uncertainty in the expectation $\mathrm{E}[Y]$. Confidence intervals are hence smaller in the latter case.

By definition we have

$$Y = \alpha + \beta \cdot x + \epsilon,$$

and hence

$$\mathrm{E}[Y] = \mathrm{E}[\alpha + \beta \cdot x + \epsilon] = \alpha + \beta \cdot x,$$

since we always assume $\mathrm{E}[\epsilon] = 0$. The principal difference is that Y contains the term ϵ causing it to vary a lot more. In both cases our best shot is the value on the regression line, i.e., $\hat{Y} = \hat{\alpha} + \hat{\beta} \cdot x$. There is some uncertainty in $\mathrm{E}[Y]$ as well. This uncertainty is caused by a finite number of observations. If we repeat the experiment with a similar number of observations, we will probably end up with a slightly different regression line. The uncertainty in the regression line is depicted in Fig. 11.11.

If we want to predict the value of Y itself, we should imagine what would happen if we made several new observations of Y when $X = x$. In Fig. 11.12, we see that Y varies with a certain bandwidth in the interval $[0, 10]$ (it is here we have our observations). There is no reason to expect that Y will vary less at $X = 20$. Hence if changing X from 10 to 20 does not change the behavior of Y, we would expect

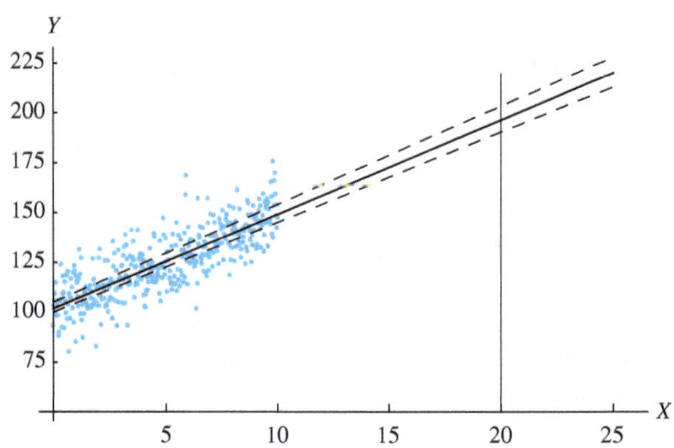

Fig. 11.11 Uncertainty in the line of regression

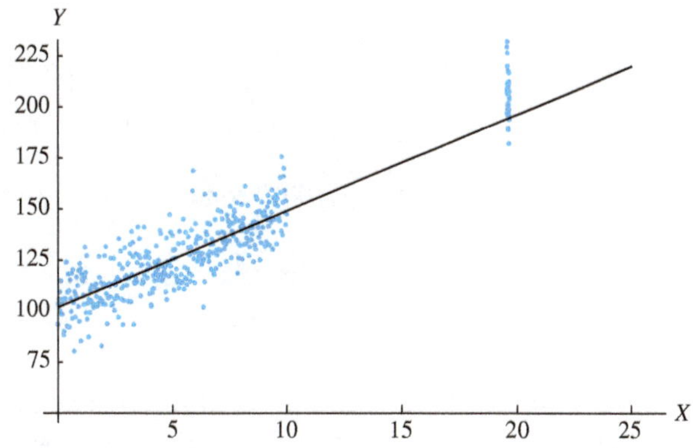

Fig. 11.12 Uncertainty in the line of regression plus the natural variation

to see a variation in Y like in Fig. 11.12. The uncertainty in Fig. 11.12 is caused by two effects, uncertainty in the regression line plus the fluctuations in Y.

If we assume that we have independent observations with normal distribution, it is possible to show that the uncertainty follows a t-distribution with parameter $\nu = n - 2$. Explicit formulas for the confidence intervals can then be found as follows:

Estimated value E[Y] when $X = x$, we find by

$$\hat{Y} = \hat{\alpha} + \beta \cdot x.$$

We compute

$$S[\hat{Y}] = S \cdot \sqrt{\frac{1}{n} + \frac{(x - \overline{X})^2}{M}},$$

and the limits for a $(1 - \gamma)100\%$ confidence interval is found from

$$\hat{Y} \pm t_{\gamma/2}^{(n-2)} \cdot S[\hat{Y}].$$

Predicted value of Y when $X = x$, we find by

$$\hat{Y} = \hat{\alpha} + \beta \cdot x.$$

We compute

(continued)

$$S[Y-\hat{Y}] = S\cdot\sqrt{1+\frac{1}{n}+\frac{(x-\overline{X})^2}{M}},$$

and the limits for a $(1-\gamma)100\%$ confidence interval is found from

$$\hat{Y} \pm t_{\gamma/2}^{(n-2)} \cdot S[Y-\hat{Y}].$$

Example 11.4 We have made $n = 401$ observations of the price of a good at different times t, and notice that the prices grow over time. The regression equation is

$$\hat{\text{price}} = 101.773 + 4.733\cdot t.$$

Furthermore we have computed

$$S = 25.85, \qquad \bar{t} = 5, \qquad M = 3358.38.$$

Use this information to predict the price at time $t = 20$, and find a 95% confidence interval for the price. Then estimate the expected price at time $t = 20$, and find a 95% confidence interval for the expected price.

Solution: When $t = 20$, then

$$\widehat{\text{price}} = 101.773 + 4.733\cdot 20 = 196.43.$$

We have

$$S[\text{price}-\widehat{\text{price}}] = 25.85\cdot\sqrt{1+\frac{1}{20}+\frac{(20-5)^2}{3358.58}} = 26.73,$$

and

$$S[\widehat{\text{price}}] = 25.85\cdot\sqrt{\frac{1}{20}+\frac{(20-5)^2}{3358.58}} = 6.81.$$

To find the confidence intervals we should use tables for a t-distribution with parameter $\nu = 399$, but with so many observations we can just as well use the table for the standard normal distribution. We get $t_{0.025}^{(399)} = z_{0.025} = 1.96$. The limits for the confidence intervals are

$$196.43 \pm 1.96\cdot 26.73,$$

and

$$196.43 \pm 1.96 \cdot 6.81.$$

A 95% confidence interval for the price itself at $t = 20$ is then $[144, 249]$, and a 95% confidence interval for the expected price at $t = 20$ becomes $[183, 210]$. We notice that the latter interval is much smaller.

11.6 Regression Using Excel

As we already mentioned, calculation of the regression line is fully automated in statistical software. If we use Excel, we first enter the x-coordinates in column A and the y-coordinates in column B. Using the values from Example 11.2, we get the display in Fig. 11.13.

We then click *Data* and choose *Data Analysis*. If you don't see this option, you must load the Data Analysis package, see *Options* in the *File* tab. In the Data Analysis package choose *Regression* and a dialog box will open. Mark the input Y-range and the input X-range, and click OK. We then get a detailed summary of the results as shown in Figs. 11.14 and 11.15

There are lots of details in the output, and we only comment the most relevant information.

- *R Square*: The value is 0.75, which means that the explanatory power $R^2 = 75\%$.
- Standard Error. This is the value of S in the regression model, and $S = 0.81645$.
- The numbers under *Coefficients* are the regression coefficients, i.e., $\hat{\alpha} = 0.3333$ and $\hat{\beta} = 1$.
- The numbers to the right of *X variable* offer important information about $\hat{\beta}$. Under *Standard Error* we find $S[\hat{\beta}] = 0.57735$. The value under t Stat is the test static for a hypothesis test of $\beta = 0$, i.e., $T = 1.732051$, and the two following numbers are the limits for a 95% confidence interval for β, i.e., the interval $[-6.33593, 8.335931]$.

Fig. 11.13 Input data for linear regression

	A	B
1	1	1
2	2	3
3	3	3

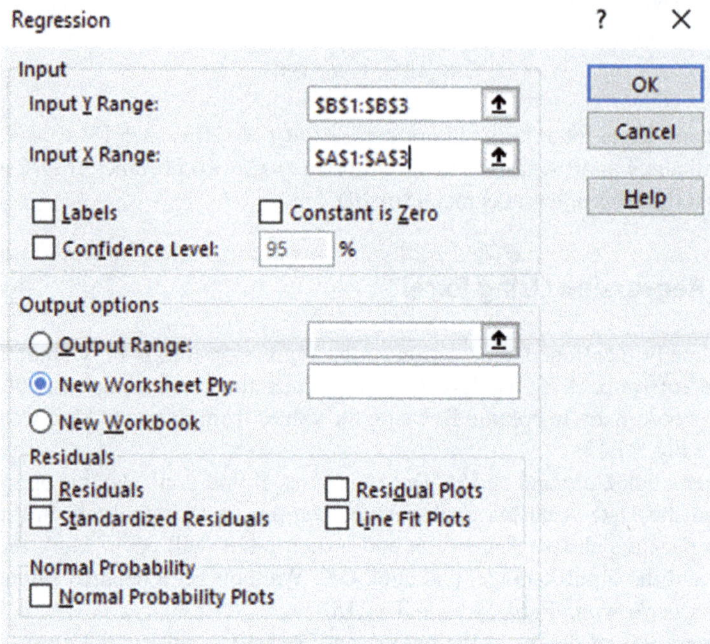

Fig. 11.14 Dialogue box in Excel

	A	B	C	D	E	F	G	H	I
1	SUMMARY OUTPUT								
2									
3	*Regression Statistics*								
4	Multiple R	0,866025							
5	R Square	0,75							
6	Adjusted F	0,5							
7	Standard E	0,816497							
8	Observatic	3							
9									
10	ANOVA								
11		*df*	*SS*	*MS*	*F*	*gnificance F*			
12	Regressior	1	2	2	3	0,333333			
13	Residual	1	0,666667	0,666667					
14	Total	2	2,666667						
15									
16		*Coefficients*	*andard Err*	*t Stat*	*P-value*	*Lower 95%*	*Upper 95%*	*ower 95,0%*	*pper 95,0%*
17	Intercept	0,333333	1,247219	0,267261	0,833742	-15,5141	16,18075	-15,5141	16,18075
18	X Variable	1	0,57735	1,732051	0,333333	-6,33593	8,335931	-6,33593	8,335931

Fig. 11.15 Final results reported by Excel

11.7 Multiple Regression

In the linear regression model above we used one explanatory variable X to explain the development of a dependent variable Y. In many situations it makes good sense to use more than one explanatory variable. We then get a model on the form

$$Y = \alpha + \beta_1 X_1 + \beta_2 X_2 + \cdots + \beta_r X_r + \epsilon.$$

Here α is the intercept, $X_1, \ldots, X_r$ are called explanatory variables, and $\beta_1, \ldots, \beta_r$ called regression coefficients. The major part of the theory works just as before. We need to collect n observations of $(X_1, X_2, \ldots, X_r, Y)$ and find the coefficients such that the total squared error is as small as possible. The construction is more or less the same as we used in the case with one explanatory variable. In practice we will always use statistical software to compute the coefficients, and we omit the details of the construction.

11.7.1 Explanatory Power

The explanatory power R^2 works just as before and shows the fraction of the variation in Y that can be explained by the explanatory variables. We illustrate this by a few examples.

Example 11.5 During 9 consecutive days we sold

$$1\ 3\ 2\ 4\ 2\ 2\ 3\ 5\ 2,$$

units of a good, respectively. The total prices we obtained were

$$12\ 39\ 31\ 55\ 34\ 38\ 50\ 76\ 45.$$

How big fraction of the variation in total prices can be explained by changes in sold quantities and time?

Solution: We let Q denote the quantities we sold each day. A regression with Q as explanatory variable gives

$$\widehat{\text{total price}} = 6.296 + 13.472 \cdot Q,$$

with explanatory power $R^2 = 86.9\%$. The P-value from a test of $\beta = 0$ is 0.025%. This shows, not surprisingly, that Q explains much of the variation in total prices. To see if time also matters, we carry out a new regression using time as explanatory variable. This gives

$$\widehat{\text{total price}} = 20.22 + 4.40 \cdot \text{time},$$

Table 11.1 Data for Example 11.6

Crop size in kg per area unit	70	60	80	80	90	60	70	50
Rainfall in centimeters	10	20	25	20	18	15	30	25
Mean temperature in degrees Celsius	25	18	22	22	25	18	16	16

with explanatory power $R^2 = 46.3\%$. The P-value from a test of $\beta = 0$ is 4.36%. We conclude that time probably matters and that the variation in time explains a large portion of the variation in total prices. Even though the two models above provide some relevant information, it is better to use a joint model which makes use of both explanatory variables. We then get the following

$$\widehat{\text{total price}} = -0.6541 + 11.3871\, Q + 2.5022 \cdot \text{time}.$$

The explanatory power is now $R^2 = 99.8\%$. The P-value from a test of $\beta_1 = 0$ is as small as $2.9 \cdot 10^{-8}$, and P-value from a test of $\beta_2 = 0$ is only $2.0 \cdot 10^{-6}$. The conclusion is that both variables are strongly significant and that they together explain almost all the variation in total prices.

Example 11.6 We want to see if there is a connection between the size of crops, rainfall, and temperature. We have observations from 8 different years, and the numbers are shown in Table 11.1.

We first want to see if there is a connection between crop size and rainfall. A regression gives the result

$$\widehat{\text{crop size}} = 72.93 - 0.1439 \cdot \text{rainfall}.$$

The explanatory power $R^2 = 0.5\%$, and the P-value for $\beta = 0$ is 87%. We notice that the regression coefficient is negative, but it is strongly insignificant and the model explains nothing. That seems rather strange. A regression against temperature works better. In that case

$$\widehat{\text{crop size}} = 16.00 + 2.667 \cdot \text{temperature},$$

with explanatory power $R^2 = 57\%$. The P-value for $\beta = 0$ is 2.86%. Temperature hence seems to explain a good deal of the crop size. A multiple regression using both variables yields a surprising result

$$\widehat{\text{crop size}} = -38.35 + 1.3159 \cdot \text{rainfall} + 4.0265 \cdot \text{temperature}.$$

Here the explanatory power increases to $R^2 = 82.8\%$. The P-value for the coefficient $\beta_1 = 0$ is 4.2%, and the P-value for $\beta_2 = 0$ is 0.44%. In conclusion both variables are significant, and together they explain a lot more than a model only using temperature.

At first sight the result above may seem surprising, but there is a simple explanation. Temperature is the primary cause here. If we compare years with the same amount of rainfall, crops are larger when there is more rainfall. A lot of rain is hence good for crops, but lots of rain lead to lower temperature, which is bad. Seen in isolation the effect of rainfall is negligible since the benefit of more water balances the loss due to lower temperature.

11.8 Causality

From the examples above we have seen that regression can be used to measure the extent that one variable explains another. High explanatory power, however, does not in general imply causality. There exist lots of cases where one can find a systematic relation between two variables and where changes in one of the variables do not cause changes in the other.

Example 11.7 In a survey of several small towns it turned out that there were more newborn children in towns with many storks. The explanatory power was nearly 100%. Does that mean that the number of storks causes more newborn children?

Solution: For obvious reasons the answer is no. A more likely explanation is the number of houses in each town. When a town has more houses, there are more families living there and hence more children are born. Storks build their nests on roofs, and with more houses there are more places to nest. Hence in larger towns there are more storks. Both variables increase more or less in proportion to the size of the towns. When a town is twice as big as another, we expect twice as many newborns and twice as many storks. If planners want more newborns, they should not try to increase the number of storks!

Example 11.8 In a survey of car ownership we found that older people had more sport cars. Does that mean that the interest for sport cars increases with age?

Solution: The answer is probably no. A more reasonable explanation is that older people tend to have more wealth. As wages/wealth often increases with age, the opportunities for owning sport cars increases with age. If we compare car owners with the same wages/wealth, it may happen that the covariation changes direction, i.e., that the interest for owning sport cars decreases with age.

The examples above show that we must not jump to conclusions when we have demonstrated significant covariation between variables. To prove that changes in one variables causes variation in another variable, we must be able to argue that there are no other relationships that can explain the connection. A statistical regression is never sufficient evidence of causality.

11.9 Multicollinearity

In a regression with several explanatory variables it is undesirable if some of the variables have the same cause. When this happens, numerical results are unstable, and sometimes the coefficients may have signs that appear to make no sense.

Example 11.9 We have made observations in a group of people between 6 and 18 years old. Our explanatory variables are X_1 = age and X_2 = months of education. Assuming that holidays are counted as education, we largely have

$$X_2 = 12(X_1 - 6).$$

Is it possible to see a difference between the regressions

$$Y = 100 + 10X_1 + X_2 \qquad \text{and} \qquad Y = 28 + 22X_1?$$

Solution: If $X_2 = 12(X_1 - 6)$, then

$$100 + 10X_1 + X_2 = 100 + 10X_1 + 12X_1 - 72 = 28 + 22X_1.$$

Due to rounding and a small number of people dropping out from school, the relation $X_2 = 12(X_1 - 6)$ is only approximatively true. For some data the best fit may be $Y = 100 + 10X_1 + X_2$. If we change one single observation in that dataset, it may happen that $Y = 28 + 22X_1$ provides the best fit.

Ideally all explanatory variables should be independent. Deviations from this requirement is called multicollinearity. If we suspect that one of the explanatory variables, e.g., X_j, may be expressed by the others, we can check the explanatory power R^2 of the regression

$$X_j = \alpha + \beta_1 X_1 + \cdots + \beta_{j-1} X_{j-1} + \beta_{j+1} X_{j+1} + \cdots + \beta_r X_r.$$

If R^2 of this regression exceeds 90%, it means that problems with multicollinearity probably are so severe that it may be better to remove the variable X_j from the regression.

If the primary use of the regression is prediction, multicollinearity need not be a problem. Admittedly marginally different datasets may lead to very different coefficients, but if we use these to predict a new value for the dependent variable, we will get approximately the same answer. The predicted value is only slightly affected by those differences.

Example 11.10 We have made 10 observations of monthly allowances (USD), age and months of education. The results are shown in Table 11.2.

Table 11.2 Monthly allowances

Pocket money	50	70	75	55	60	75	35	50	60	65
Age in years	12	17	18	13	15	18	8	12	15	16
Months of education	72	120	144	84	108	144	24	72	108	120

A regression of this dataset gave the result

$$\widehat{\text{pocket money}} = 1.032 + 4.222 \cdot \text{age} - 0.235 \cdot \text{education},$$

with explanatory power $R^2 = 99.1\%$. The P-value for $\beta_1 = 0$ was 2.2%, and the P-value for $\beta_2 = 0$ was 85.4%. We conclude that months of education appear to have no impact. To check for multicollinearity, we regress education against age. The result of this regression is

$$\widehat{\text{education}} = -86.23 + 11.655 \cdot \text{age},$$

with explanatory power $R^2 = 99.0\%$. Since the explanatory power of this regression exceeds 90%, we conclude, as expected, that there are multicollinearity between age and months of education. If we remove education as explanatory variable, we get

$$\widehat{\text{pocket money}} = 2.6327 + 3.9491 \cdot \text{age},$$

with explanatory power $R^2 = 99.1\%$. The P-value for a test of $\beta = 0$ is $1.71 \cdot 10^{-9}$. We see that explanatory power remains at the same level when we use less parameters. Less parameters imply a simpler explanation, which is something we usually prefer. The reduced model is hence better than the first one.

11.10 Dummy Variables

In a regression explanatory variables should be quantities that can be measured on a scale in a meaningful way. We call such variables as scale variables. Variables that do not possess a clear size and direction should not be used.

Example 11.11 We want to study if there is a connection between wages Y and country X. We have coded X such that $X = 0$ means a person living in Norway, $X = 1$ means a person from Denmark, while $X = 2$ denotes a person from Sweden. We have 12 observations, shown in Table 11.3.

Notice that country is not a scale variable. It makes no sense to say that Swedes are twice as good as Danes. As mentioned above, such variables cannot be used in regressions, at least not directly. What happens if we try this anyway? With data as above, we get

$$\widehat{\text{wages}} = 33{,}2727 + 181.8 \cdot \text{country},$$

Table 11.3 Observation for Example 11.11

Salary in USD	Country	Salary in USD	Country
30,000	0	32,000	2
31,000	0	32,500	2
29,000	0	31,500	2
40,500	1	32,000	2
40,000	1	32,500	2
39,500	1	31,500	2

with explanatory power $R^2 = 0.15\%$. P-value for a test of $\beta = 0$ is 90.5%. The conclusion is that country does not matter, and that country does not explain any of the variation. Mathematically that is correct, but nevertheless entirely wrong. The reason is that such explanatory variables cannot be used in regressions.

What happens if we try to change the coding? We may instead use the coding $X = 0$ is Norwegian, $X = 1$ is Swedish, and $X = 2$ is Danish. Then

$$\widehat{\text{wages}} = 28{,}500 + 5000 \cdot \text{country},$$

with explanatory power $R^2 = 83.1\%$. P-value for a test of $\beta = 0$ is $3.7 \cdot 10^{-5}$. Now country appears to be significant and country seems to explain the major part of the variation. This analysis is just as bad as the first one. There is, however, a legitimate way of coding this using dummy variables. We proceed as follows:

$$X_1 = \begin{cases} 1 & \text{if Norwegian} \\ 0 & \text{otherwise} \end{cases}, \quad X_2 = \begin{cases} 1 & \text{if Danish} \\ 0 & \text{otherwise} \end{cases}, \quad X_3 = \begin{cases} 1 & \text{if Swedish} \\ 0 & \text{otherwise} \end{cases}.$$

Such variables may be used in regressions, but some care must be taken. Notice that the three variables exhibit multicollinearity, e.g.

$$X_3 = 1 - X_1 - X_2.$$

To avoid this problem, we have to delete one of these variables, e.g., we can delete X_3. Using X_1 and X_2 as explanatory variables, a multiple regression returns

$$\widehat{\text{wages}} = 32{,}000 - 2000\,X_1 + 8000\,X_2,$$

with explanatory power $R^2 = 98\%$. P-value for a test of $\beta_1 = 0$ is 0.14%, and P-value for a test of $\beta_2 = 0$ is $2.14 \cdot 10^{-8}$. The correct conclusion is that country is significant and explains almost everything. If we take a closer look at our data, we see that the new model makes good sense. In our dataset all Norwegians earn around 30,000 USD, all the Danes around 40,000 USD, and all the Swedes around 32,000 USD. If a person is Norwegian, then $X_1 = 0, X_2 = 0$ and our model predicts

$$\widehat{\text{wages}} = 32{,}000 - 2000 \cdot 1 + 8000 \cdot 0 = 30{,}000.$$

If the person is Danish, then $X_1 = 0, X_2 = 1$ and our model predicts

$$\widehat{\text{wages}} = 32{,}000 - 2000 \cdot 0 + 8000 \cdot 1 = 40{,}000.$$

The person is Swedish if and only if $X_1 = 0, X_2 = 0$, and then we get the value

$$\widehat{\text{wages}} = 32{,}000 - 2000 \cdot 0 + 8000 \cdot 0 = 32{,}000.$$

We see that the model returns values that make sense in all cases, and that will always be the case when we make use of dummy variables for such cases.

11.11 Analyzing Residuals

Regression analysis using t-tests takes for granted that the residuals are

- Independent.
- Normally distributed with expectation zero.
- Same variance for all values of the explanatory variables.

We can use diagnostic plots of the residuals to examine these assumptions. We will inspect four different plots here; histogram, normal score, residuals in observed order, and residuals sorted with respect to the size of the dependent variable. We assess these plots by visual inspection. In practice it takes years of experience to analyze such plots with confidence, so we start out with some particularly easy cases.

11.11.1 Histogram

The histogram of the residuals should resemble the density of a normal distribution. Frequently we only have a relatively small number of observations, and cannot expect a perfect fit. We are content if we see a fairly symmetric distribution centered at zero. The plot in Fig. 11.16 is acceptable.

In Fig. 11.17, however, the distribution appears to be skewed, suggesting that the residuals are not normally distributed.

11.11.2 Normal Score Plot

The normal score plot also tests for normal distribution. Ideally, this plot should be a straight line. We are content with the shape we see in Fig. 11.18.

In Fig. 11.19, however, the plot has a profound banana shape, suggesting that the residuals are not normally distributed.

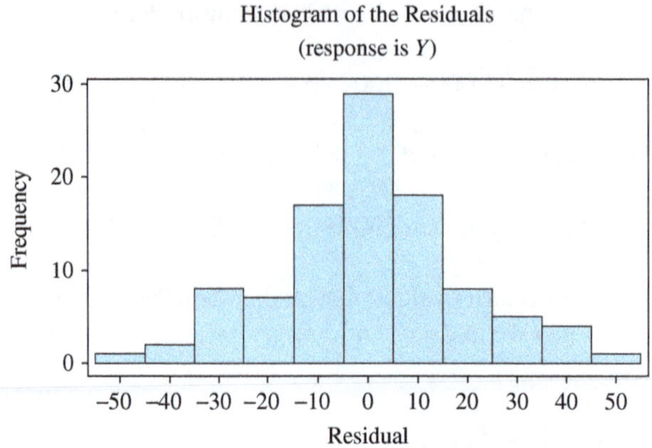

Fig. 11.16 Histogram of residuals

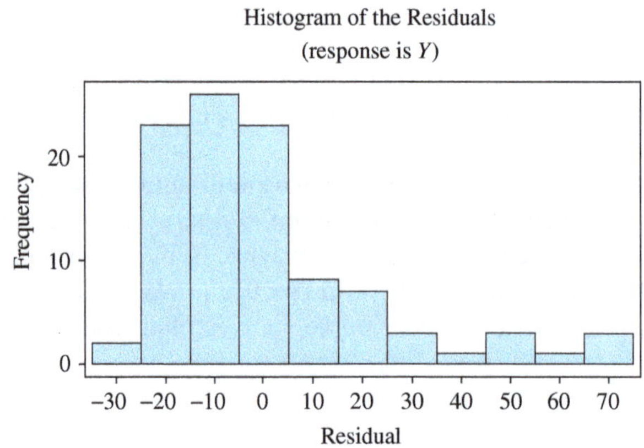

Fig. 11.17 Histogram of residuals

11.11.3 Residuals in Observed Order

The residuals should be evenly spread around zero and the spread should not change along the axis. The plot in Fig. 11.20 is satisfactory.

In Fig. 11.21, however, we see a clear trend where the shape changes along the axis. It does not appear that the residuals have expectation zero for all values of the explanatory variable.

11.11.4 Residuals Sorted with Respect to Size

Sometimes trends that we do not notice when the residuals are plotted in the same order as the observations may appear if we rearrange them. The standard approach

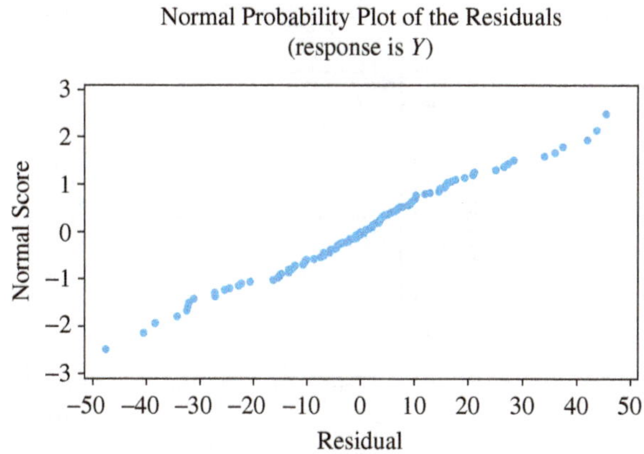

Fig. 11.18 Normal score plot of residuals

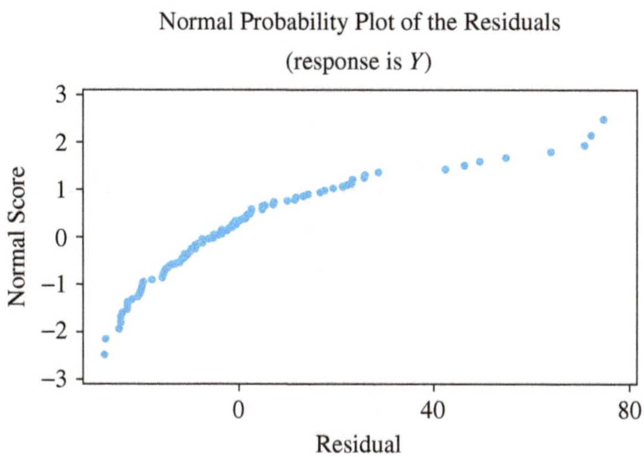

Fig. 11.19 Normal score plot of residuals

is to sort the residuals according to the size of the observed values. Again we hope to see an even spread around zero which do not change along the axis. The plot in Fig. 11.22 is satisfactory.

In Fig. 11.23, however, we see a clear trend where the shape changes along the axis. It does not appear that the residuals have expectation zero for all values of the explanatory variable.

11.12 Summary of Chap. 11

- Ordinary least squares (OLS) is a method to find the best line through a set of observation pairs.

Fig. 11.20 Residuals sorted in observed order

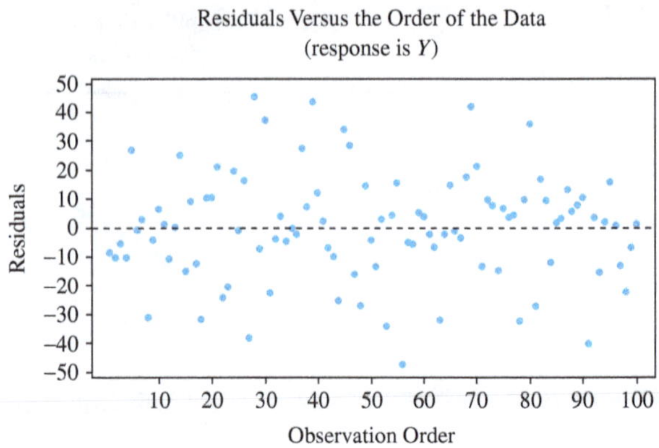

Fig. 11.21 Residuals sorted in observed order

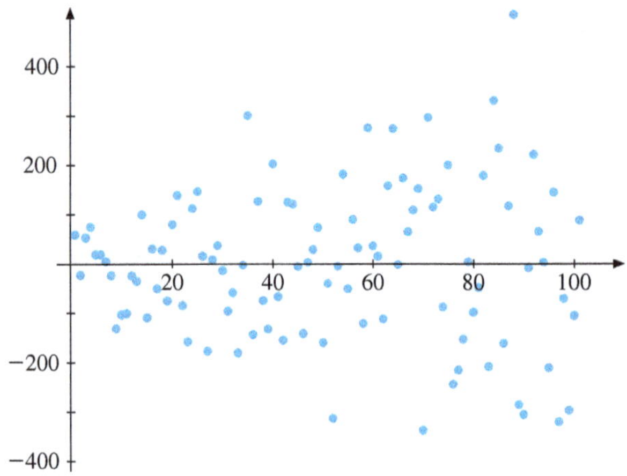

- The intercept $\hat{\alpha}$ and the slope $\hat{\beta}$ are unbiased estimators of a relationship

$$Y = \alpha + \beta \cdot X + \epsilon.$$

  Y is called the dependent variable and X the explanatory variable.
- The explanatory power R^2 is interpreted as the fraction of the variation of the dependent variable that can be explained by the explanatory variable.
- To check if an explanatory variable matters, we can perform a statistical test with null hypothesis $\beta = 0$. If this hypothesis is rejected, then the value of the explanatory variable matters.
- The regression line can be used to predict values for the dependent variable outside the observation set. Such predictions should in general be used close to the set where we have observations.

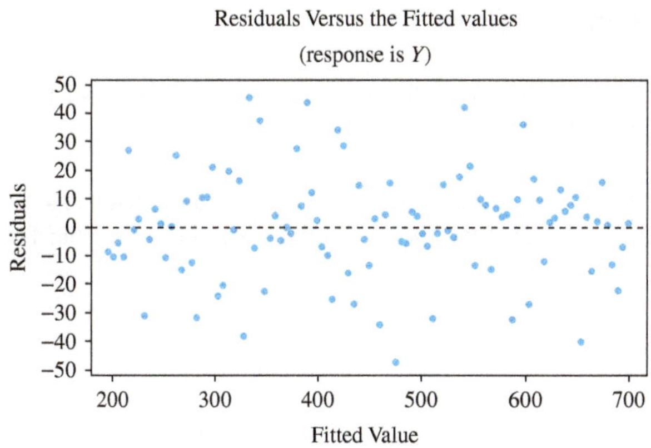

Fig. 11.22 Residuals sorted with respect to the size of the dependent variable

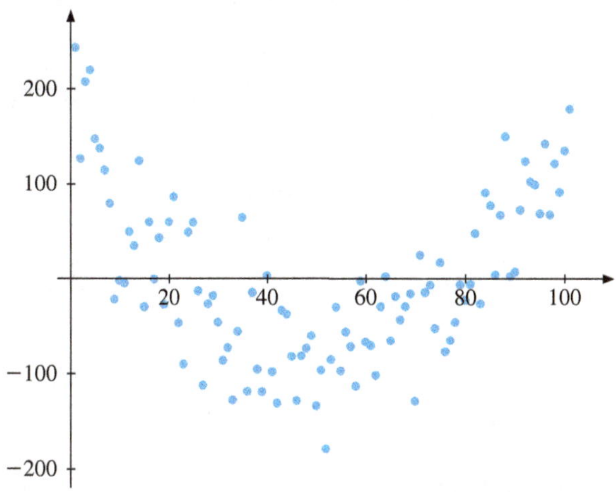

Fig. 11.23 Residuals sorted with respect to the size of the dependent variable

- In multiple regression we have more than one explanatory variables and use a model on the form

$$Y = \alpha + \beta_1 X_1 + \beta_{''} X_2 + \cdots + \beta_r X_r + \epsilon.$$

- A significant linear relationship does not in general prove that a change in an explanatory variable will cause a change in the dependent variable.
- Explanatory variables with a common cause may lead to collinearity and should be avoided.
- Explanatory should be scalable, but non-scale variables can sometimes be coded in terms of dummy variables.
- Diagnostic plots are tools for visual inspection. They can be used to assess the assumptions in the OLS model.

11.13 Problems for Chap. 11

11.1 Figure 11.24 displays four different sets of data. Which of these are suitable for linear regression?

11.2 Choose two points and draw a line that fits reasonably well with the observations in Fig. 11.25. Use the two-point formula to find the formula for this line.

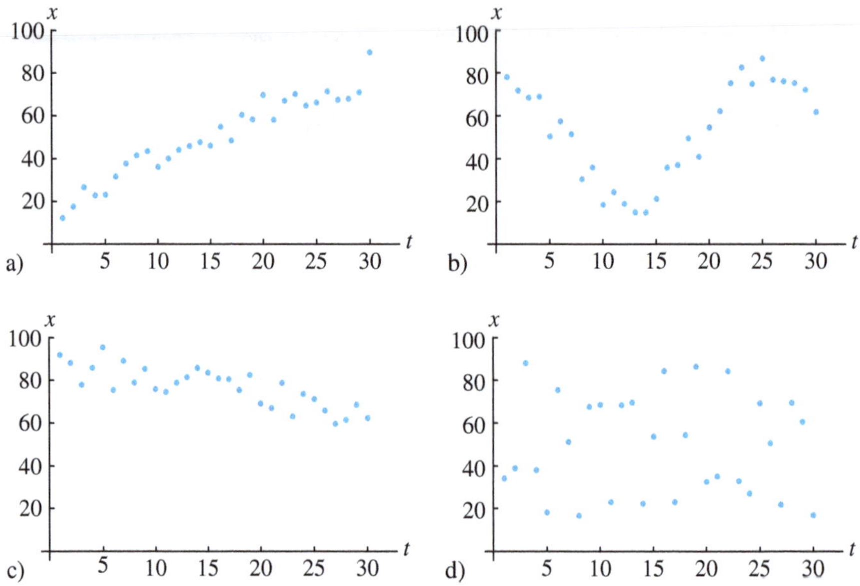

Fig. 11.24 Data sets for Problem 11.1

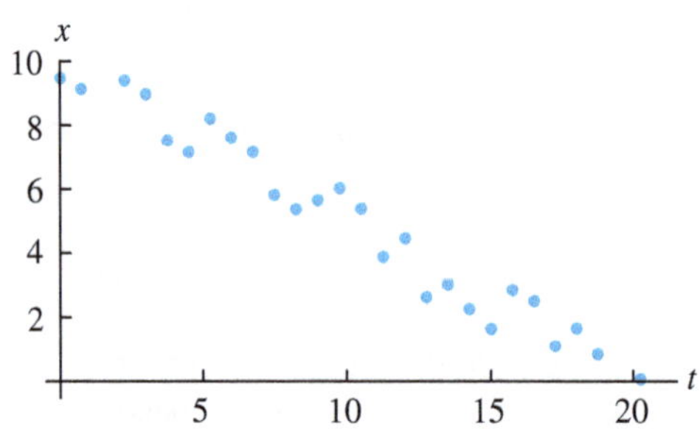

Fig. 11.25 Data set for Problem 11.2

11.3 Find the formula for the OLS regression line when we have the observations

$$(1,3),\ (3,7),\ (5,9),\ (7,9).$$

11.4 In a regression with $n = 21$ observations we have found the regression line

$$\hat{X} = 52.47 + 2.06\,t.$$

Furthermore

$$S = 5.70, \qquad M = \sum_{i=1}^{21}(t_i - \bar{t})^2 = 770.$$

We want to test the null hypothesis $\beta = 0$ against the alternative $\beta \neq 0$ using 5% significance level. What is the conclusion?

11.5 In a regression with $n = 16$ observations we have found the regression line

$$\hat{X} = 104.10 - 0.32\,t.$$

Furthermore

$$S = 5.37, \qquad M = \sum_{i=1}^{21}(t_i - \bar{t})^2 = 340.$$

We want to test the null hypothesis $\beta = 0$ against the alternative $\beta \neq 0$ using 5% significance level. What is the conclusion?

11.6 We have made $n = 12$ observations and the regression line is

$$\hat{X} = 78.32 - 3.01\,t.$$

Furthermore

$$S = 5.81, \qquad \bar{t} = 5.5, \qquad M = \sum_{i=1}^{21}(t_i - \bar{t})^2 = 143.$$

(a) Use this information to estimate the expected value E[X] at $t = 15$.
(b) Make a prediction of X at $t = 15$.
(c) Compute 95% confidence intervals for the quantities in (a) and (b).

11.7 We have made $n = 32$ observations and the regression line is

$$\hat{X} = 64.37 + 1.81\,t.$$

Furthermore

$$S = 5.76, \qquad \bar{t} = 15.5, \qquad M = \sum_{i=1}^{21}(t_i - \bar{t})^2 = 2728.$$

(a) Use this information to estimate the expected value E[X] at $t = 40$.
(b) Make a prediction of X at $t = 40$.
(c) Compute 95% confidence intervals for the quantities in (a) and (b).

11.8 Find the values for the residuals when the observations are

$$(1,3),\ (3,7),\ (5,9),\ (7.9),$$

with the regression line $\hat{X} = 3 + t$.

11.9 We have collected data from 1000 persons in four different professions. For each person we know

- Number of years in the occupation: *practice*.
- Gender: *gender* coded 0 (man) 1 (woman).
- Number of years with higher education: *education*.
- Profession: Coded as dummy variables: *prof1, prof2, prof 3, prof4*.
- Yearly wages in USD: *wages*.

Employment in profession 1 requires 4 years of formal education, profession 2 requires 5 years, profession 3 requires 6 years, while profession 4 does not require any formal higher education.

(a) A linear regression of *wages* against *education* gives

$$\widehat{\text{wages}} = 27{,}405 + 1896 \cdot \textit{education},$$

with explanatory power $R^2 = 22.7\%$. The P-value of a test for $\beta = 0$ is $2 \cdot 10^{-16}$. How will you interpret these results?
(b) Why should we not use all the four dummy variables *prof1, prof2, prof 3, prof4* in a linear regression?

(c) We have carried out a multiple regression of *wages* against *practice, gender, education, prof1, prof2, prof3*. The results read as follows

$$\widehat{\text{wages}} = 14{,}970 + 506 \cdot \textit{practice} + 5171 \cdot \textit{gender} - 98 \cdot \textit{education}$$
$$+2705 \cdot \textit{prof}1 + 15{,}380 \cdot \textit{prof}2 + 10{,}658 \cdot \textit{prof}3.$$

$R^2 = 95.7\%$, and the P-values for the explanatory variables were

$$\begin{aligned} \textit{practice} &: P\text{-value } 2 \cdot 10^{-16}, \\ \textit{gender} &: P\text{-value } 2 \cdot 10^{-16}, \\ \textit{education} &: P\text{-value } 43.5\%, \\ \textit{prof}1 &: P\text{-value } 4 \cdot 10^{-7}, \\ \textit{prof}2 &: P\text{-value } 2 \cdot 10^{-16}, \\ \textit{prof}3 &: P\text{-value } 2 \cdot 10^{-16}. \end{aligned}$$

How will you interpret these results? Compare the answers with the conclusion in (a) and try to explain the difference.

(d) To examine if there is collinearity between *education* and professions, we have made a new regression. The results read as follows:

$$\widehat{\text{education}} = 0.496 + 4.03 \cdot \textit{prof}1 + 5.04 \cdot \textit{prof}2 + 6.00 \cdot \textit{prof}3.$$

$R^2 = 95.6\%$, and the P-values for the explanatory variables were

$$\begin{aligned} \textit{prof}1 &: P\text{-value } 2 \cdot 10^{-16}, \\ \textit{prof}2 &: P\text{-value } 2 \cdot 10^{-16}, \\ \textit{prof}3 &: P\text{-value } 2 \cdot 10^{-16}. \end{aligned}$$

What conclusion can you draw from this analysis?

(e) We have made a new regression where we have deleted *education* as explanatory variable. The results read as follows

$$\widehat{\text{wages}} = 14{,}924 + 506 \cdot \textit{practice} + 5167 \cdot \textit{gender}$$
$$+2312 \cdot \textit{prof}1 + 14{,}889 \cdot \textit{prof}2 + 10{,}721 \cdot \textit{prof}3.$$

$R^2 = 95.7\%$, and the P-values for the explanatory variables were

$$\begin{aligned} \textit{practice} &: P\text{-value } 2 \cdot 10^{-16}, \\ \textit{gender} &: P\text{-value } 2 \cdot 10^{-16}, \end{aligned}$$

$$prof1 \;: P\text{-value } 2 \cdot 10^{-7},$$
$$prof2 \;: P\text{-value } 2 \cdot 10^{-16},$$
$$prof3 \;: P\text{-value } 2 \cdot 10^{-16}.$$

How will you interpret these results? Compare with the conclusions in (a) and (c).

(f) Use one of the regressions above to predict the salary of a woman with 12 years practice, 6 years of higher education, and working in profession 3.

11.10 We have used three different production methods, and the production (in units) was registered on nine consecutive days. The 27 results are shown in Table 11.4.

Table 11.4 Data for Problem 11.10

	Method	Day	Production
1	1	1	162
2	2	1	208
3	3	1	172
4	1	2	168
5	2	2	221
6	3	2	180
7	1	3	181
8	2	3	232
9	3	3	189
10	1	4	192
11	2	4	242
12	3	4	201
13	1	5	198
14	2	5	249
15	5	5	208
16	1	6	210
17	2	6	208
18	3	6	221
19	1	7	222
20	2	7	268
21	3	7	230
22	1	8	231
23	2	8	279
24	3	8	238
25	1	9	240
26	2	9	291
27	3	9	252

(a) To examine if there is a connection between production, method, and time, we carried out a linear regression. The results read as follows

$$\widehat{\text{production}} = 106.2 + 4.83 \cdot \textit{method} + 9.67 \cdot \textit{time}.$$

$R^2 = 59.9\%$. The P-value for $\beta_1 = 0$ was 35.9%, and the P-value for $\beta_2 = 0$ was $4.2 \cdot 10^{-6}$. Comment these results.

(b) We have introduced two new variables

$$X_1 = \begin{cases} 1 & \text{if we use method 1} \\ 0 & \text{otherwise} \end{cases}, \qquad X_2 = \begin{cases} 1 & \text{if we use method 3} \\ 0 & \text{otherwise} \end{cases}.$$

A regression of production against time, X_1, and X_2 gave the result

$$\widehat{\text{production}} = 195.9 + 9.67 \cdot \textit{time} - 43.77 \cdot X_1 - 34.11 \cdot X_2.$$

$R^2 = 91.5\%$, and P-values for all explanatory variables were less than 10^{-6}. Comment these results.

(c) Compare the results in (a) and (b). Which method is best?

11.11 Figure 11.26 displays diagnostic plots from a regression. To what extent are the assumptions on normality and independence satisfied in this case?

11.12 Figure 11.27 displays diagnostic plots from a regression. To what extent are the assumptions on normality and independence satisfied in this case?

11.13 Double Logarithmic Transformation: In this exercise we will study the connection between sold quantity Q and the price p for a good. We have observed $Q_3, Q_4, \ldots, Q_{100}$ for $p = 3, 4, \ldots, 100$, respectively. The results are shown below.

(a) We have carried out a regression of Q against p, and got the following results: Regression line

$$\hat{Q} = 775 - 8.55 \cdot p, \qquad S = 198.1, \qquad R^2 = 59.9\%.$$

Figure 11.28 displays diagnostic plots for the residuals. Comment to what extent you think the assumptions for the regression model are satisfied in this case.

(b) Alternatively we have carried out a new regression where we observe $\ln(Q)$ as a function of $\ln(p)$.

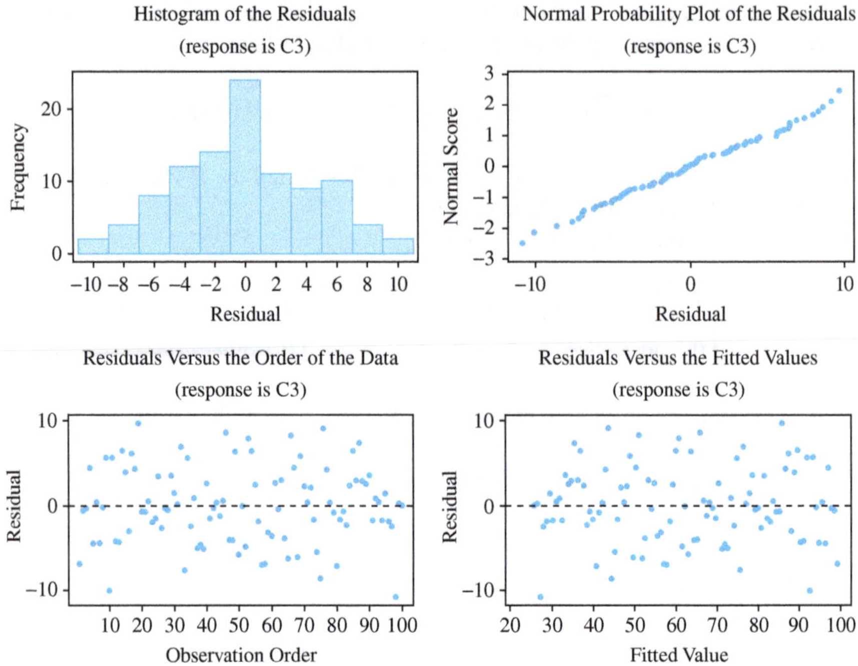

Fig. 11.26 Residual plots for Problem 11.11

Regression line

$$\widehat{\ln(Q)} = 8.91 - 0.914 \cdot \ln(p), \qquad S = 0.2162, \qquad R^2 = 91.3\%.$$

Diagnostic plots for the residuals are shown in Fig. 11.29. Comment to what extent you think the assumptions for the regression model is satisfied in this case.

(c) Use the results from (b) to suggest a value for $\hat{Q} = \mathrm{e}^{\widehat{\ln(Q)}}$ for the expected value of Q when $p = 110$. You need not consider the uncertainty in this value.

(d) Assume that $Q = K \cdot p^{\beta} \cdot U$, where K and β are (unknown) constants and $U > 0$ is a random variable. Show that $\ln(Q)$ can be written in the form

$$\ln(Q) = \gamma + \beta \cdot \ln(p) + \epsilon,$$

where γ is a constant and ϵ is a random variable with $\mathrm{E}[\epsilon] = 0$.

(e) If ϵ in (d) is normally distributed $N(0, \sigma^2)$, then $\mathrm{E}[\ln(U)] = \ln(\mathrm{E}[U]) - \frac{1}{2}\sigma^2$. You can take that relation for granted. Show that

$$\mathrm{E}[Q] = \mathrm{e}^{\gamma + \beta \ln(p) + \frac{1}{2}\sigma^2},$$

and use this to estimate $\mathrm{E}[Q]$ again when $p = 110$.

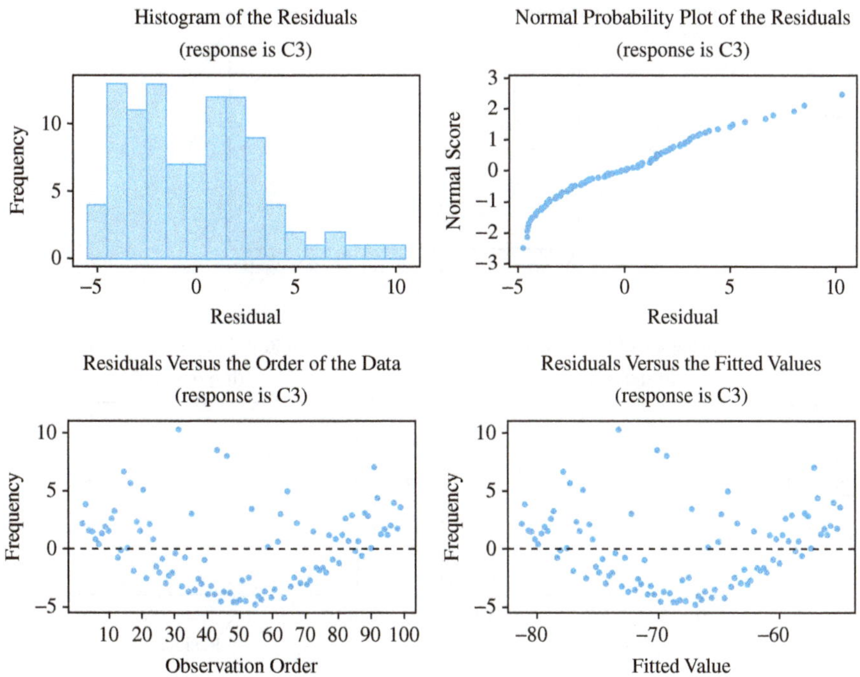

Fig. 11.27 Residual plots for Problem 11.12

11.14 Logarithmic Transformation: We have observed the price of a stock on 100 consecutive days. The price is increasing and there is a clear tendency of increasing growth. The plot has a convex profile.

(a) Why is it futile to use linear regression on these observations? Why is it reasonable to assume that the prices on stocks, bonds, and bank deposits grow exponentially?

(b) As an alternative to linear regression we have plotted $\ln(X)$ against t for $t = 0, 1, \ldots, 100$ and carried out a linear regression on the transformed data.

Regression line

$$\widehat{\ln(X)} = 4.23 + 0.0175 \cdot t, \qquad S = 0.3025, \qquad R^2 = 74.4\%.$$

Diagnostic plots for the regression are displayed in Fig. 11.30. To what extent are the assumptions on normality and independence satisfied in this case?

(c) Assume that $\ln(X) = \gamma + \beta \cdot t + \epsilon$ where γ and β are constants and ϵ is normally distributed with expectation zero and variance σ^2. It is possible to show that $\mathrm{E}[\mathrm{e}^{\epsilon}] = \mathrm{e}^{\frac{1}{2}\sigma^2}$ (you can take that for granted). Use this formula to find an expression for $\mathrm{E}[X]$, and write down a general estimator for the expected value. Estimate the expectation of X when $t = 110$.

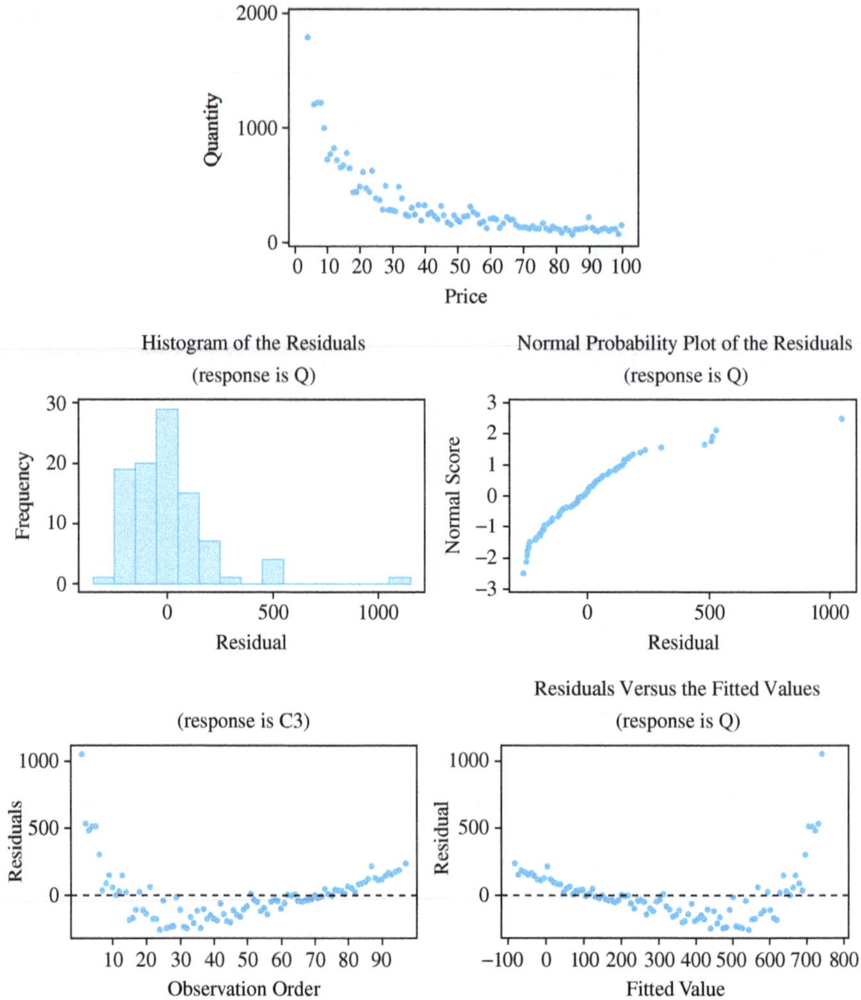

Fig. 11.28 Observation and residual plots for Problem 11.13

(d) Why is it reasonable to assume that the variance of a stock price changes when there is a considerable change in the price? How and in what direction can this influence a prediction of expected value into the future?

11.15 Cyclic Behavior: We have made weekly observations of the daily power consumption in a small city. Data were obtained each Monday starting in week 10 and ending in week 26. The results of the survey are displayed in Fig. 11.31.

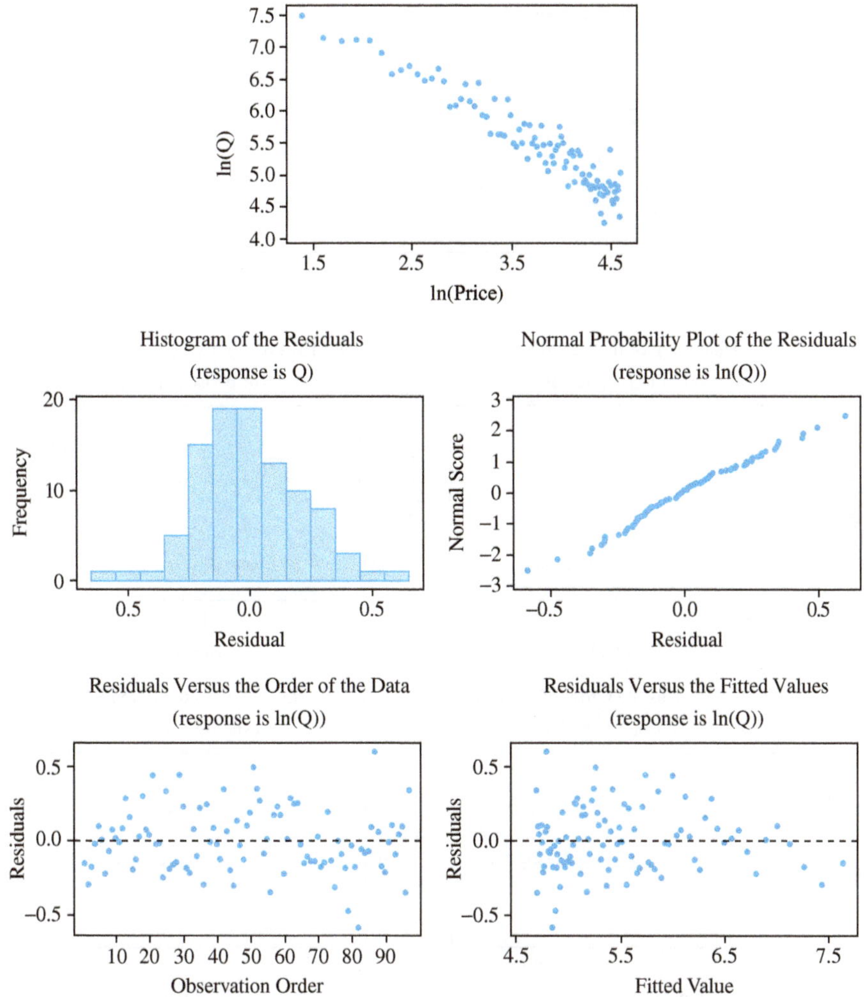

Fig. 11.29 Observation and residual plots for the transformed data in Problem 11.13

(a) Does it seem that the usual assumptions for the regression model are satisfied in this case? Justify your answer.
(b) Find a 95% prediction interval for the power consumption Tuesday in week 18.
(c) We supply the survey by collecting data from week 5 to 9 and week 27 to 31 in addition to our original data. We run a new regression, and the results are shown in Fig. 11.32. Comment the differences from the first printout and try to explain what happens here.
(d) How would you predict the daily power consumption Tuesday in week 18 the following year? Try to suggest effects that increase the uncertainty in this prediction.

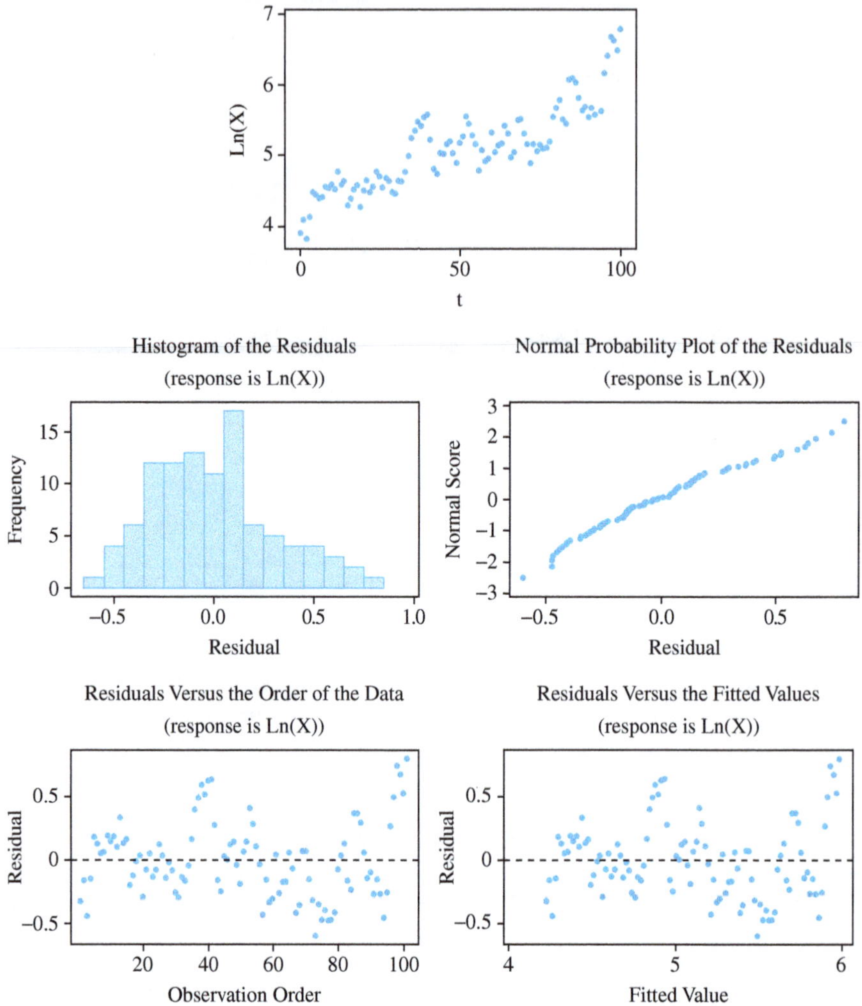

Fig. 11.30 Observation and residual plots for the transformed data in Problem 11.14

11.16 Autocorrelation: In an analysis of productivity we have made daily observations of the production over a period of 100 days. A regression of production against time gave the result:

Regression line

$$\widehat{\text{production}} = 1.07 + 2.09 \cdot t, \qquad S = 6.802, \qquad R^2 = 98.8\%.$$

Diagnostic plots are displayed in Fig. 11.33.

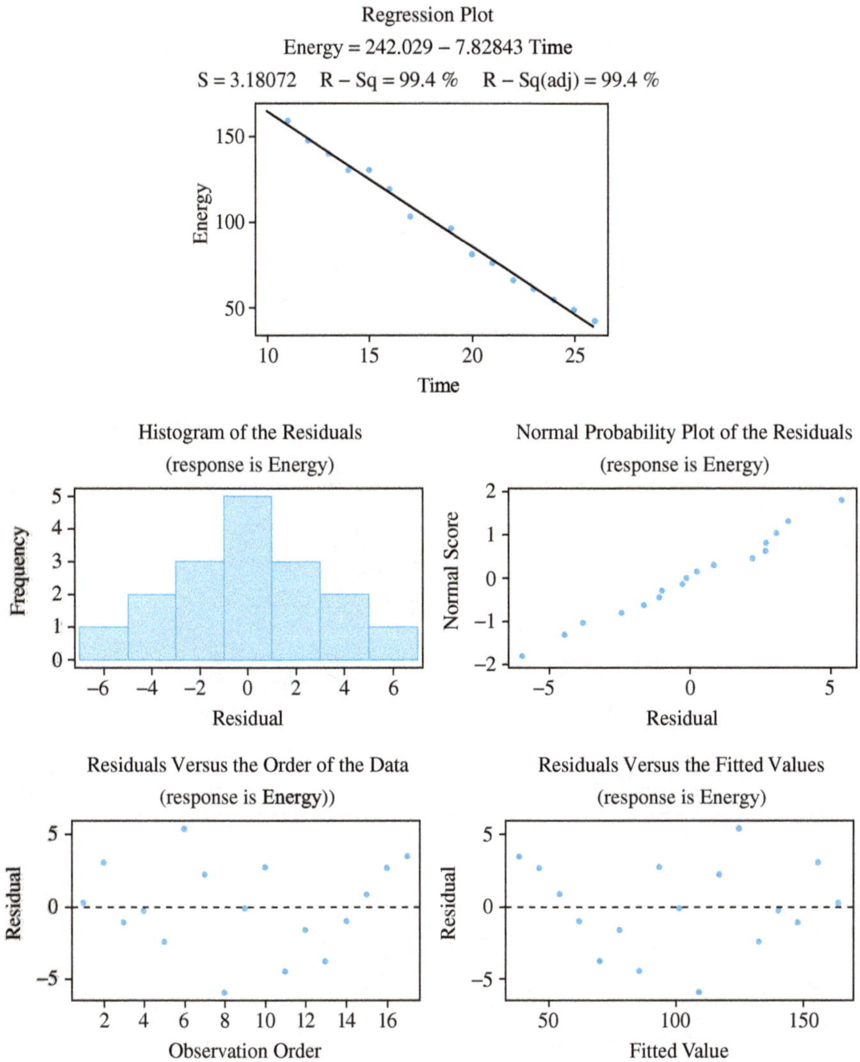

Fig. 11.31 Observation and residual plots for Problem 11.15

(a) Does it seem that the usual assumptions for the regression model are satisfied in this case? Justify your answer.
(b) Offer a prediction of the productivity at time $t = 110$ based on the linear regression of productivity as a function of time. What kinds of uncertainty do we have in this prediction? You need not quantify the uncertainty.
(c) A precise study of the residuals in the previous regression reveals that they are autocorrelated, i.e., dependent. In normal cases the degree of autocorrelation must be estimated. We will here, however, look at a simplified version where

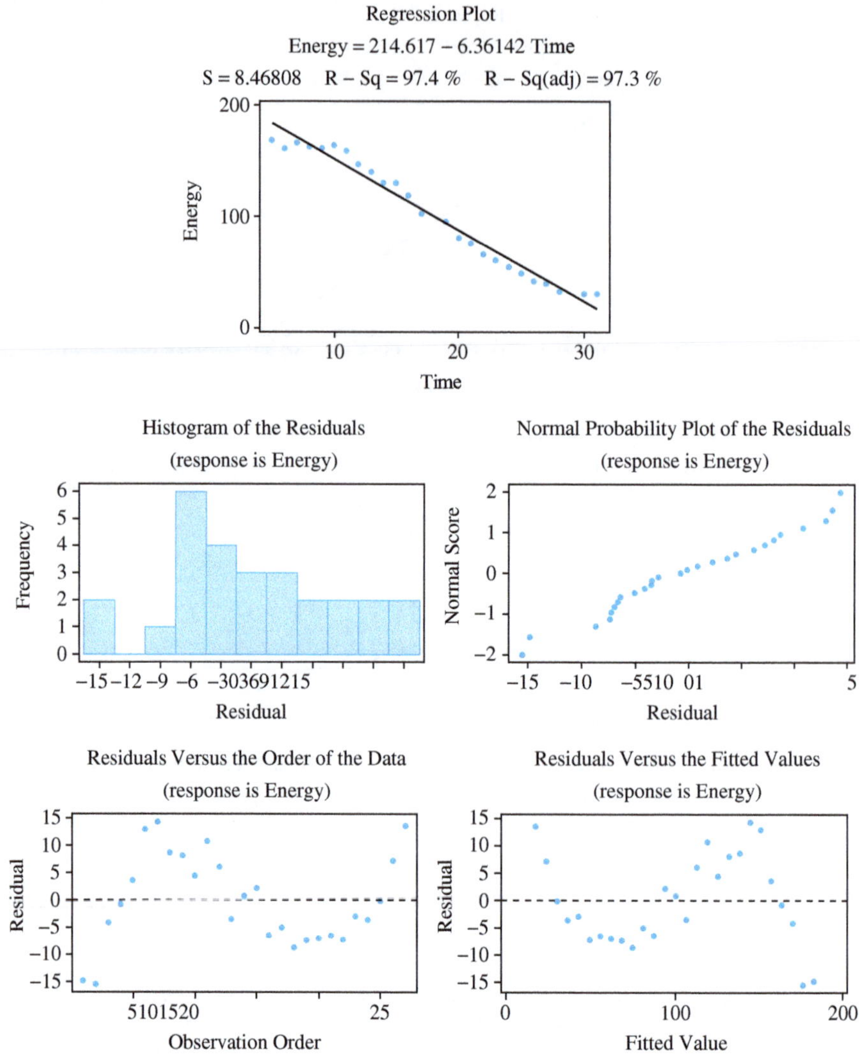

Fig. 11.32 Observation and residual plots for the extended data in Problem 11.15

the degree of autocorrelation is known. In a model of that kind we assume that

$$X_i = \gamma + \beta \cdot t + R_t,$$

where

$$R_t = \rho \cdot R_{t-1} + \epsilon_t,$$

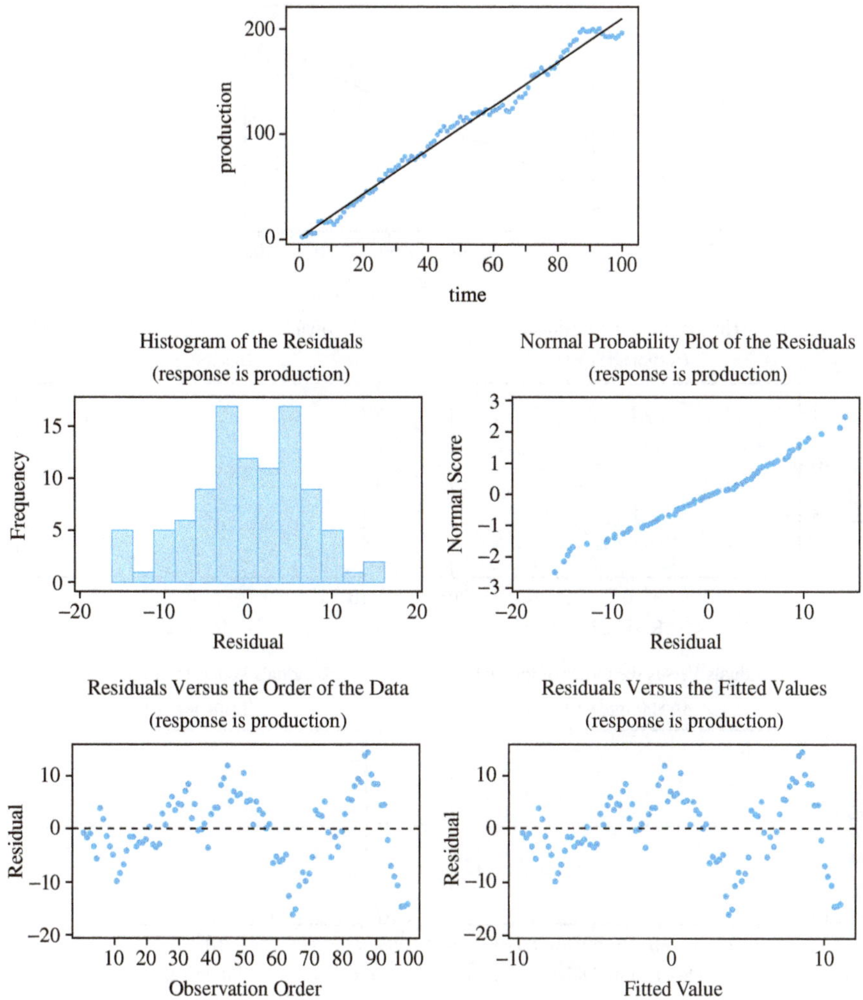

Fig. 11.33 Observation and residuals plots for Problem 11.16

where ρ is a known constant and where $\epsilon_1, \epsilon_2, \ldots$ are independent, normally distributed, with expectation zero and constant variance σ^2. We define a new set of observations $Y_1, Y_2, \ldots, Y_{100}$ by

$$Y_t = X_t - \rho \cdot X_{t-1}.$$

Show that

$$Y_t = \gamma(1 - \rho) + \rho \cdot \beta + (1 - \rho)\beta \cdot t + \epsilon_t.$$

Explain why Y_t satisfies the usual conditions in a linear regression model.

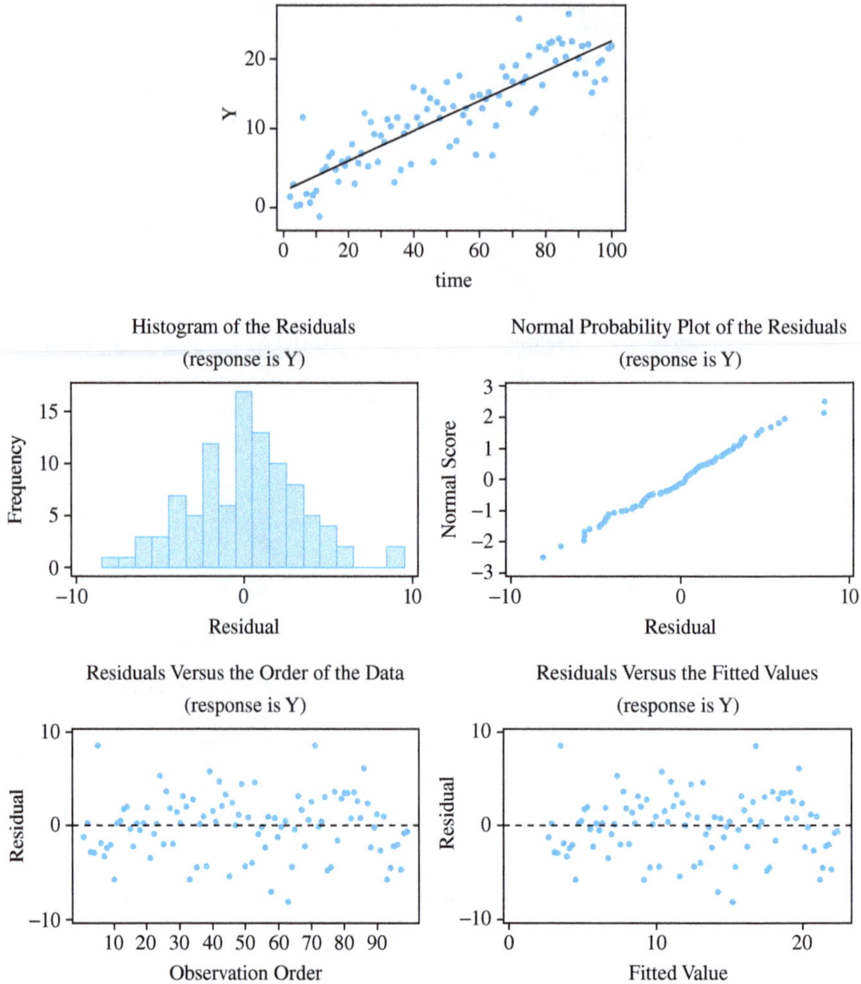

Fig. 11.34 Observation and residual plots for the transformed data in Problem 11.16

(d) The results from a linear regression of Y against t were:
Regression line

$$\hat{Y} = 2.30 + 0.201 \cdot t, \qquad S = 3.252, \qquad R^2 = 71.6\%.$$

Diagnostic plots are displayed in Fig. 11.34. Does it seem that the usual assumptions for the regression model are satisfied in this case? Justify your answer.

Table 11.5 Data for Problem 11.17

Location	Number of mobile phones sold	Number of cars sold
City 1	33,739	20, 664
City 2	28,646	17, 168
City 3	12,624	7890
City 4	17,885	11, 067
City 5	20,518	12, 349
City 6	14,035	8513
City 7	28,067	16, 990
City 8	16,697	9870
City 9	14,713	9197
City 10	27,202	16, 130

(e) In our calculations of $Y_1, Y_2, \ldots, Y_{100}$ we have used $\rho = 0.9$. Use the formula for Y_t in (c) together with the printout to estimate values for the constants γ and β. Use this to make a new prediction of the productivity X_{110} at time $t = 110$.

11.17 Causality: We want to see if there is a connection between sales of mobile phones and cars. We have collected data from 10 relatively small cities. The observations are shown in Table 11.5.

We have carried out a linear regression of car sales against sales of mobile phones, and the results were as follows:

$$\widehat{\text{carsales}} = 201.8 + 0.59694 \cdot \textit{mobilesales}, \qquad S = 231.0, \qquad R^2 = 99.8\%.$$

The P-value for a test of $\beta = 0$ was 0.000.

(a) Do the results give reason to claim that there is a connection between sales of cars and sale of mobile phones? Justify your answer.
(b) Diagnostic plots for the residuals are displayed in Fig. 11.35. Does it seem that the usual assumptions for the regression model are satisfied in this case? Justify your answer.
(c) How large share of the variation in car sales can be explained by the variation in sales of mobile phones?
(d) Predict the number of care sales in a city where sales of mobile phones are 150,000. What kind of uncertainties are attached to this prediction?
(e) A consultant for the car industry claims there is a clear connection between care sales and sales of mobile phones. He suggests to raise the car sales by giving away a large number of mobile phones. Is this a good idea?

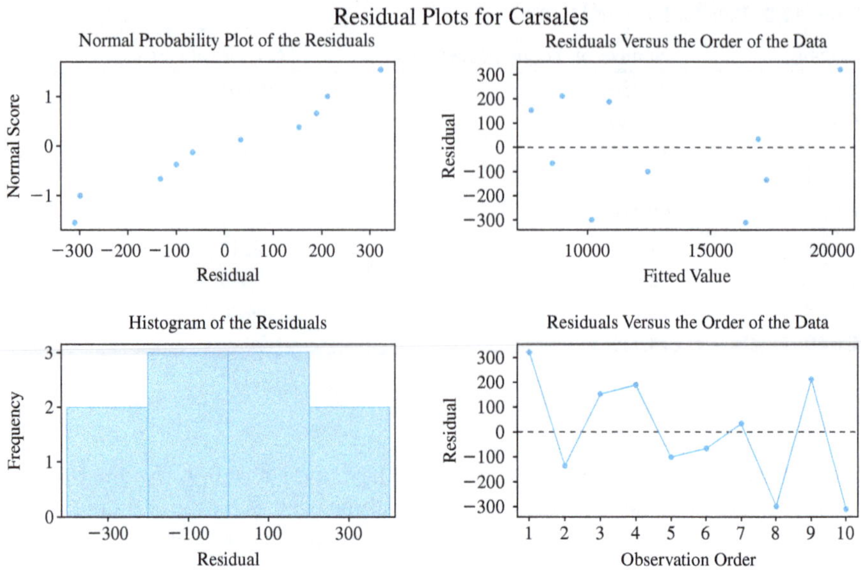

Fig. 11.35 Diagnostic plots of the residuals in Problem 11.17

11.18 Nonlinear Regression: A monopolist wishes to optimize his profit. The profit has a random fluctuation which may be due to, e.g., varying prices on raw materials. The profit is simulated selling 1 to 100 units of the good, and the result is shown in Fig. 11.36.

(a) Discuss statistical and economical issues which speak against using linear regression in this case.
(b) This case is well suited for quadric regression. In quadratic regression we use a model where the profit X and the production q is given by

$$X = a + b \cdot q + c \cdot q^2 + \epsilon,$$

and where ϵ denotes independent, normally distributed random variables with constant variance. Having observed $(X_1, q_1), \ldots, (X_n, Q_n)$, we want to fit a quadratic curve such that

$$\text{error}[a, b, c] = \sum_{i=1}^{n} (X_i - a - b \cdot q_i - c \cdot q_i^2)^2,$$

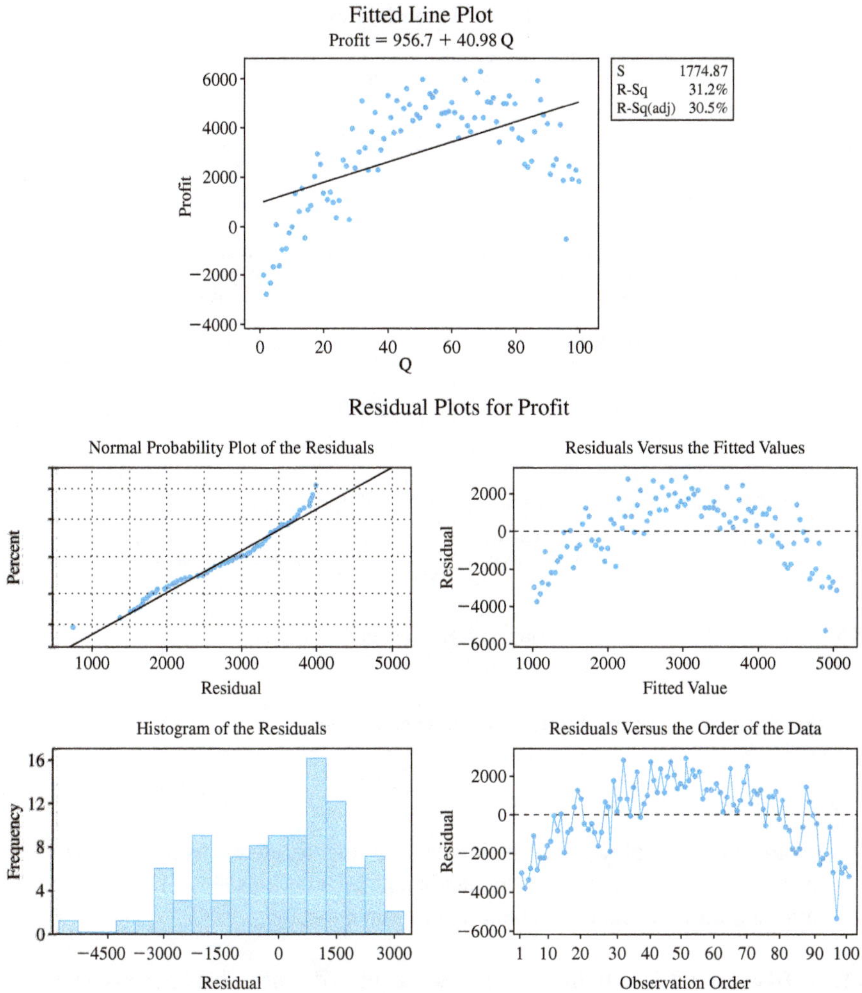

Fig. 11.36 Observation and residual plots for Problem 11.18

is as small as possible. Explain that we achieve optimal fit when a, b, c are solutions of the 3 linear equations

$$\sum_{i=1}^{n}(X_i - a - b \cdot q_i - c \cdot q_i^2) = 0$$

$$\sum_{i=1}^{n}(X_i - a - b \cdot q_i - c \cdot q_i^2)q_i = 0$$

$$\sum_{i=1}^{n}(X_i - a - b \cdot q_i - c \cdot q_i^2)q_i^2 = 0$$

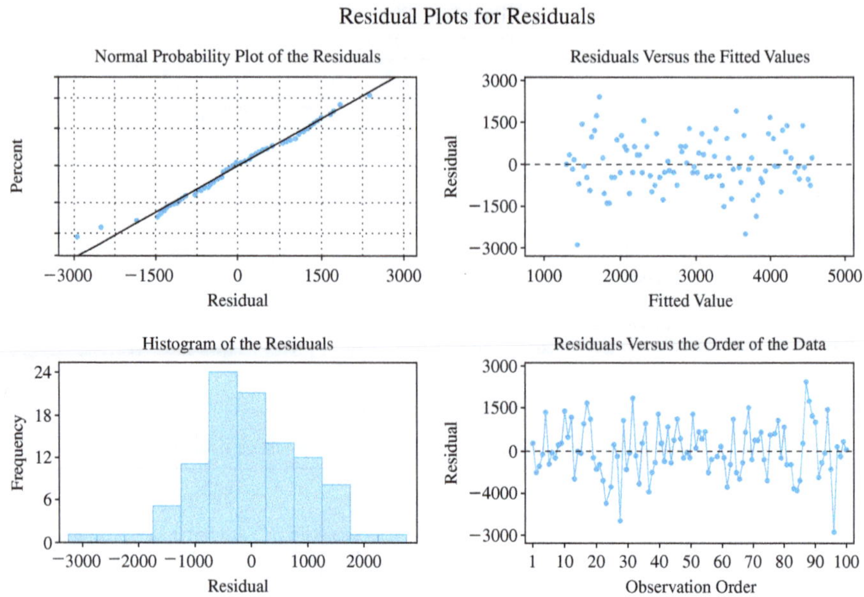

Fig. 11.37 Residual plots for the quadratic regression in Problem 11.18

(c) For the data above the solution of the system was

$$\hat{a} = -2482.2, \qquad \hat{b} = 243.275, \qquad \hat{c} = -2.003.$$

Figure 11.37 displays diagnostic plots of the residuals from the quadratic regression. Does it seem that the statistical assumptions are valid? How many units should we produce to obtain maximum expected profit?

11.19 Disaggregation: In this problem we want to discuss what happens when we disaggregate data into subgroups. Here *income* denotes annual wages in USD and *educ* denotes number of years of education. We have collected data from 700 women (W) and 1221 men (M). Aggregating the data for men and women, we get

$$\widehat{\text{income}} = 10{,}241 + 1114 \cdot educ,$$

with

$$S = 10{,}072, \qquad R^2 = 8.8\%, \qquad P\text{-value of } \beta = 0 = 0.000.$$

If we consider the data for men and women separately, we get

$$\widehat{\text{income}}_M = 9974 + 1371 \cdot educ_M,$$

with

$$S = 10{,}969, \qquad R^2 = 11.2\%, \qquad P\text{-value of } \beta = 0 = 0.000.$$

$$\widehat{\text{income}}_W = 11{,}223 + 621 \cdot educ_W,$$

with

$$S = 5368, \qquad R^2 = 9.3\%, \qquad P\text{-value of } \beta = 0 = 0.000.$$

(a) How do you interpret the *P*-values? Are there differences between men and women, and how does this turn out?
(b) The explanatory power is relatively low in all three cases. Is this something we would expect?
(c) Predict income for a woman with 17 years of education. Find a 95% confidence interval for this income. Here $\overline{educ_W} = 11.86361$ and $S[\hat{\beta}] = 73.26$. Hint: The formula $M = \frac{S^2}{S[\hat{\beta}]^2}$ will be useful.

11.20 Explains Everything—Predicts Nothing: In a survey we asked 500 hotel guests how satisfied they were with their stay. There were 6 alternatives as shown in Table 11.6.

The guests also answered the question "How likely is it that you will visit the same hotel again?" Alternatives: 0%,5%,10%,. . . ,95%,100%. As it appears there is a connection between the two questions, we have carried out a linear regression of the satisfaction level *SL* against the probability of returning *PR*.

$$\widehat{PR} = 14.4 + 14.8 \cdot SL,$$

with

$$S = 7.50500, \qquad R^2 = 91.5\%, \qquad P\text{-value (of } \beta = 0) = 0.000.$$

Table 11.6 Satisfaction levels n Problem 11.20

Very dissatisfied	0
Dissatisfied	1
Somewhat dissatisfied	2
Neutral	3
Somewhat satisfied	4
Satisfied	5

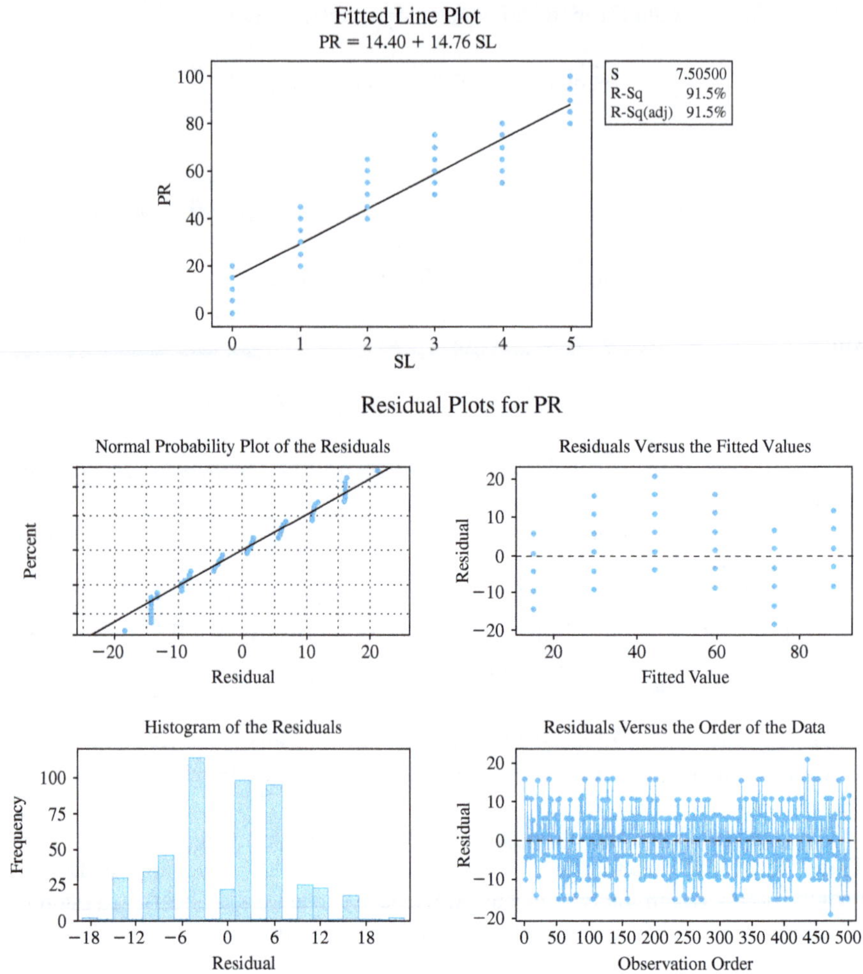

Fig. 11.38 Observation and residual plots for Problem 11.20

Diagnostic plots are displayed in Fig. 11.38.

(a) Does it seem that the usual assumptions for the regression model are satisfied in this case? Justify your answer.
(b) We can imagine that we introduced a new alternative: 6—very satisfied. Is it reasonable to use the regression model to predict the number of very satisfied guest?
(c) As an alternative we have used polynomial regression with a third degree polynomial:

$$\widehat{PR} = 5.710 + 40.06 \cdot SL - 11.66 \cdot SL^2 + 1.389 \cdot SL^3,$$

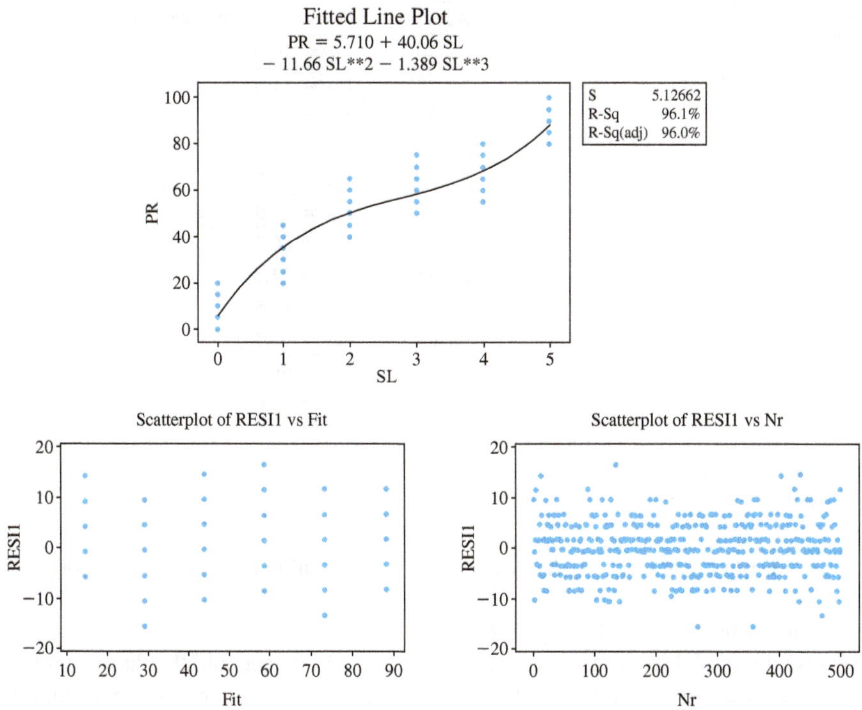

Fig. 11.39 Observation and residual plots for the cubic regression in Problem 11.20

with

$$S = 5.12662, \qquad R^2 = 96.1\%.$$

Some diagnostic plots are displayed in Fig. 11.39. Does this model appear to function better?

(d) Alternatively we could use the third degree polynomial from (c) to predict the outcome of the alternate $SL = 6$. Would that solve the problem in (b)?

11.21 Logistic Regression: A large number of people between 15 and 75 years old have been asked if they ever used a certain product. The answers were distributed as shown in Table 11.7.

(a) It seems reasonable to assume that the fraction that has ever used the product increases with age. To examine this further we have carried out a linear regression of fractions against age. Comment the results in this regression.

$$\widehat{\text{fraction}} = -8.12 + 1.78 \cdot age,$$

Table 11.7 Data for Problem 11.21

Age group	Fraction in % that has used the product
15–20	$Y_{15} = 10.0$
20–25	$Y_{20} = 11.0$
25–30	$Y_{25} = 31.2$
30–35	$Y_{30} = 52.2$
35–40	$Y_{35} = 61.3$
40–45	$Y_{40} = 77.0$
45–50	$Y_{45} = 86.7$
50–55	$Y_{50} = 92.2$
55–60	$Y_{55} = 93.5$
60–65	$Y_{60} = 97.3$
65–70	$Y_{65} = 98.7$
70–75	$Y_{70} = 99.6$

with

$$S = 11.7844, \qquad R^2 = 89.1\%, \qquad P\text{-value (of } \beta = 0) = 0.000.$$

Diagnostic plots are displayed in Fig. 11.40.

(b) Use the model from (a) to predict the fraction of 80 years old that has ever used the product. There are several problems connected to this prediction. Point out some of these problems.

(c) We define $f(x)$ as the expected fraction (in %) of persons of age x that has ever used the product. We assume that $f(x)$ can be written in the form

$$f(x) = \frac{100\,e^{\gamma+\beta x}}{1+e^{\gamma+\beta x}},$$

where γ and β are unknown constants. Use this expression to show that

$$\ln\left(\frac{f(x)}{100-f(x)}\right) = \gamma + \beta x.$$

(d) To estimate the values for γ and β, we have replaced $Y_{15}, \ldots, Y_{70}$ in the table above with the transformed values

$$Z_{15} = \ln\left(\frac{Y_{15}}{100-Y_{15}}\right), \ldots, Z_{70} = \ln\left(\frac{Y_{70}}{100-Y_{70}}\right).$$

We have then carried out a linear regression of Z_x against x. The results are shown below. Comment the results in this new regression.

$$\widehat{\text{values}} = -4.31 + 0.135 \cdot age,$$

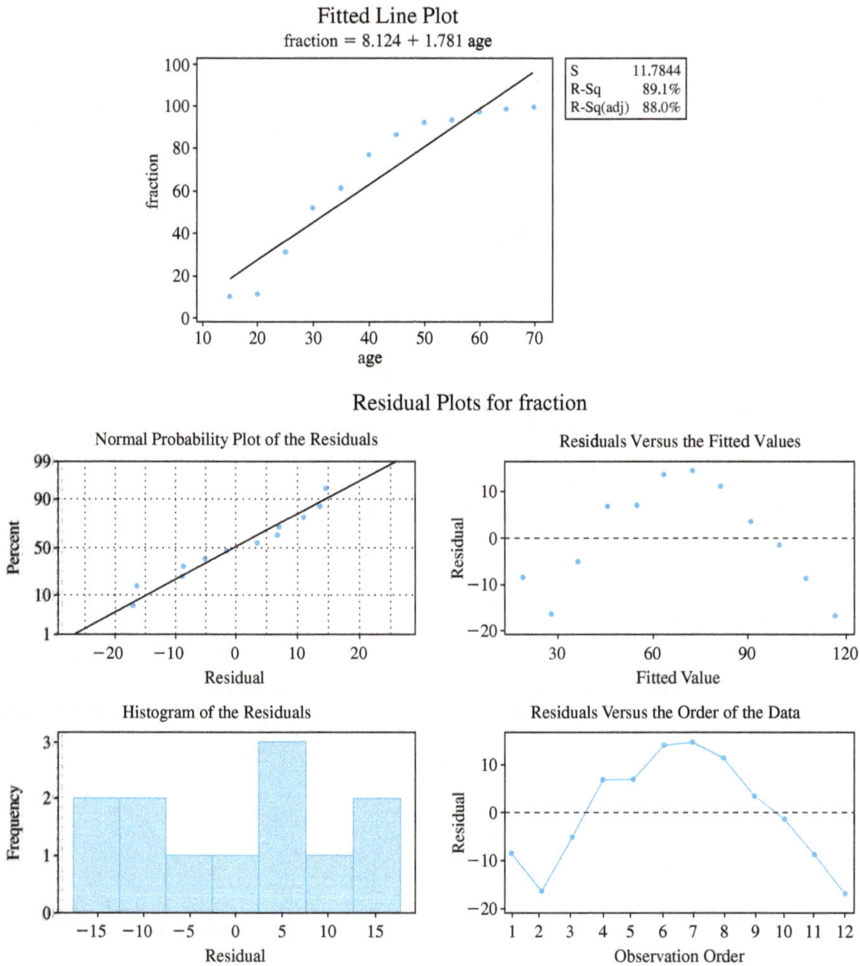

Fig. 11.40 Observation and residual plots for Problem 11.21

with

$$S = 0.2853, \qquad R^2 = 98.8\%, \qquad P\text{-value (of } \beta = 0) = 0.000.$$

Diagnostic plots are displayed in Fig. 11.41.

(e) Use the model from (c) and (d) to predict the fraction of 80 years old that has ever used the product. Comment the answer.

11.22 Outliers: We have collected data for the value of sales and sales costs. Data were observed on a weekly basis and we have data for 30 weeks. The observations are plotted in Fig. 11.42.

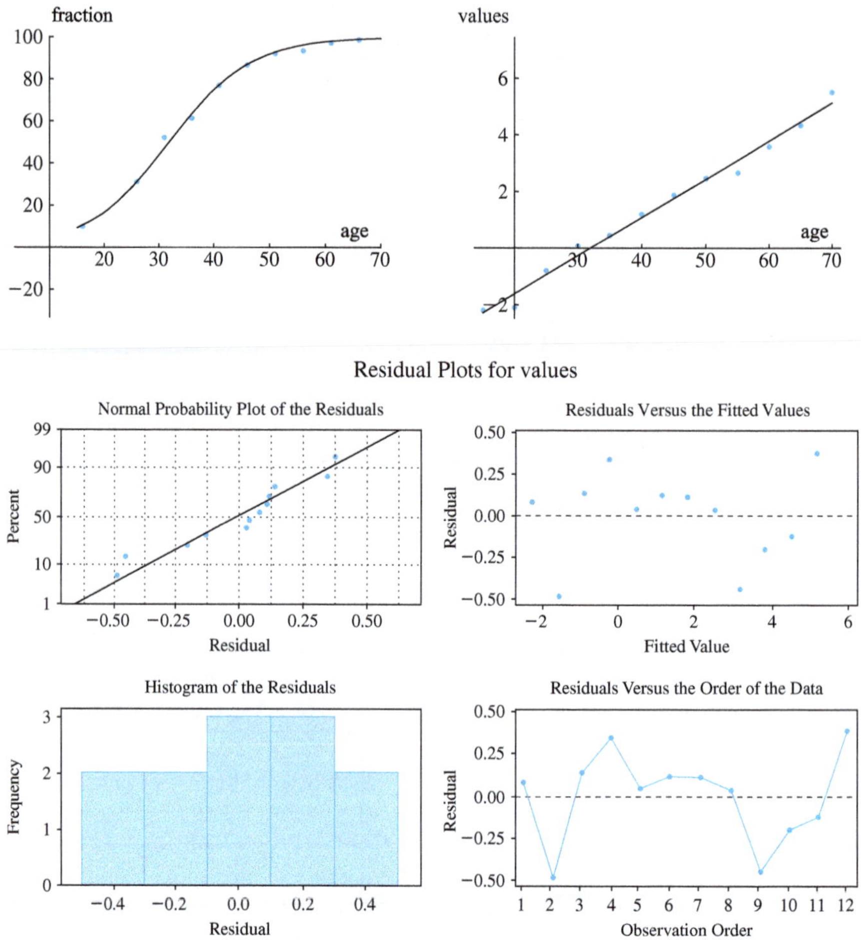

Fig. 11.41 Observation and residual plots for the logistic regression in Problem 11.21

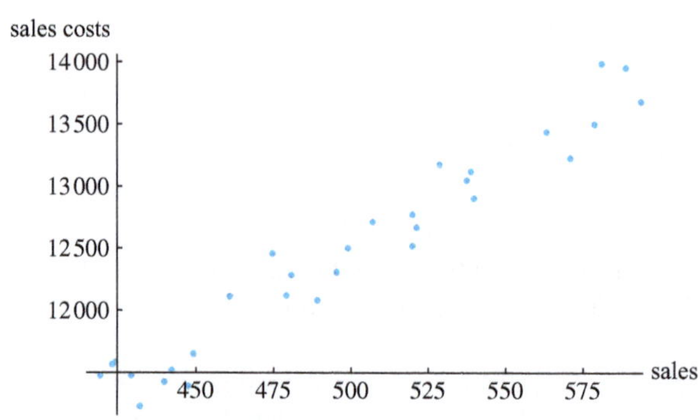

Fig. 11.42 Observations for Problem 11.22

(a) The figure indicates that there is a linear relationship between sales costs and the value of the sales. Is this something we could expect, and what could be the reason for that?

(b) We have carried out a linear regression, and the results were as follows:

$$\widehat{\text{sales costs}} = 5212.6 + 0.0145 \cdot \textit{sale},$$

with

$$S = 193.985, \qquad R^2 = 94.6\%, \qquad P\text{-value (of } \beta = 0) = 0.000.$$

Diagnostic plots are displayed in Fig. 11.43.

What kind of information can we draw from the printouts? Comment the results and the plots in detail.

(c) The week after the survey we observed a sales of 500,000 USD, while the reported sales costs were 14,500 USD. Find a 95% prediction interval for the sales costs, and discuss if the reported number seems reasonable. To compute the prediction interval you need to know that mean value of the sales were 499,110 USD and that $S[\hat{\beta}] = 0.0006543$. Use the formula $M = \frac{S^2}{S[\hat{\beta}]^2}$.

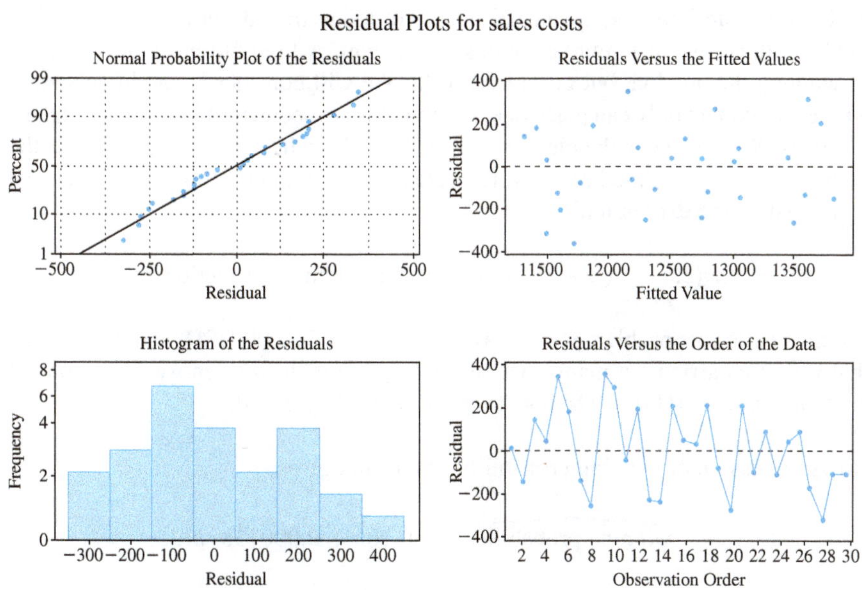

Fig. 11.43 Residual plots for Problem 11.22

11.23 Solving the OLS Equations: In this problem the aim is to find the best possible linear fit to the points $(1, 1), (2, 3), (3, 3)$. A straight line has the formula

$$x = \alpha + \beta \cdot t.$$

The errors we make at the three given values of t are

$$\begin{aligned}
\text{error}_1 &= \alpha + \beta \cdot 1 - 1, \\
\text{error}_2 &= \alpha + \beta \cdot 2 - 3, \\
\text{error}_3 &= \alpha + \beta \cdot 3 - 3.
\end{aligned}$$

(a) Show that

$$\text{error}_1^2 + \text{error}_2^2 + \text{error}_3^2 = 3\alpha^2 + 12\alpha\beta + 14\beta^2 - 14\alpha - 32\beta + 19.$$

(b) Find α and β such that

$$F(\alpha, \beta) = \text{error}_1^2 + \text{error}_2^2 + \text{error}_3^2,$$

is as small as possible. Hint: compute $\frac{\partial F}{\partial \alpha}$ and $\frac{\partial F}{\partial \beta}$, and solve the first order conditions $\frac{\partial F}{\partial \beta} = 0$, $\frac{\partial F}{\partial \beta} = 0$.

11.24 Bid Auctions: Many special items are today traded via bid auctions. The bidders often have different valuations of the item. A high bid has a good chance of winning the auction, but gives less profit. We will consider a simplified setting where the bidders only can place one bid (the bids are secret), and where the highest bid wins. We will let x denote the size of the bid, while y is the valuation of the item. The profit is defined as $y - x$. Expected profit $F(x, y)$ placing the bid x can be computed by the expression

$$F(x, y) = (y - x) \cdot \text{probability of winning the auction.}$$

For the rest of this problem we will assume that $y = 10{,}000$ USD, and we imagine that we have carried out many auctions and registered how often we have won the auction bidding x (USD). The results are shown in Fig. 11.44.

(a) A regression of winning probability against bid gives

$$\widehat{\text{winning probability}} = -0.164 + 0.000138 \cdot bid,$$

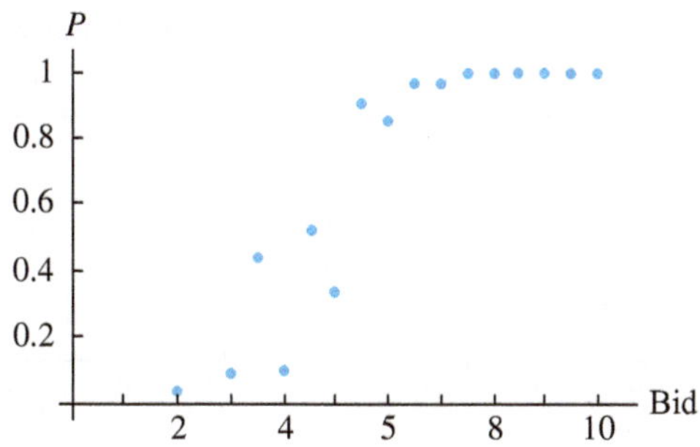

Fig. 11.44 Observed winning probability in Problem 11.24

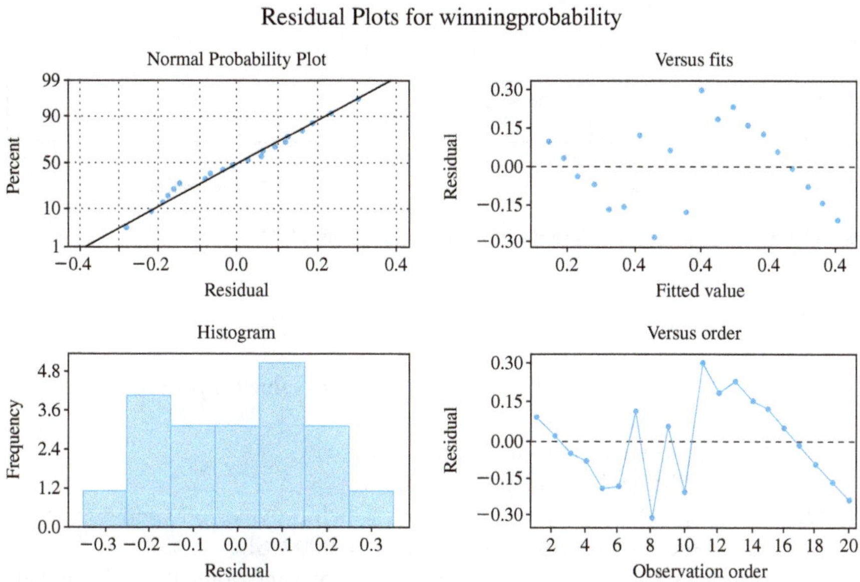

Fig. 11.45 Residual plots for Problem 11.24

with

$$S = 0.168797, \qquad R^2 = 86.1\%, \qquad P\text{-value (of } \beta = 0) = 0.000.$$

Diagnostic plots are displayed in Fig. 11.45.

Comment this information in detail.

(b) Alternatively we have carried out a new regression where we only consider bids in the interval [3000, 7000]. Why is that a good idea here?

$$\widehat{\text{winning probability}} = -0.164 + 0.000138 \cdot bid,$$

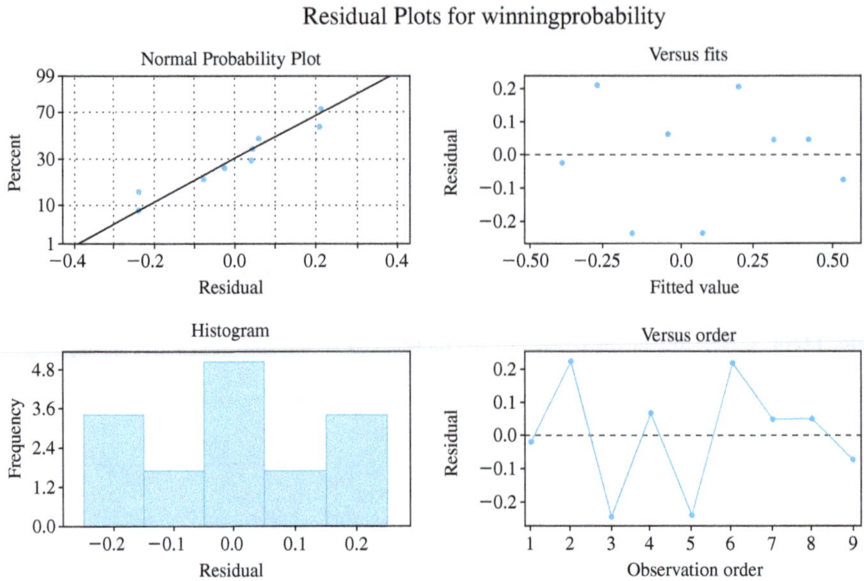

Fig. 11.46 Residual plots for the reduced data set in Problem 11.24

with

$$S = 0.0.175523, \qquad R^2 = 79.0\%, \qquad P\text{-value (of } \beta = 0) = 0.000.$$

Diagnostic plots are displayed in Fig. 11.46.

Comment the new information in detail.

(c) Use the results above to compute a bid x which provides maximum expected profit when the valuation of the item is $y = 10{,}000$ USD.

(d) Make crude estimates using the information above and argue that it is unlikely that maximum expected profit can be obtained in the intervals $[0, 3000]$ and $[7000, 10{,}000]$.

11.25 Faking Explanatory Power: You manage a stock of fish and need to estimate the growth potential. You make use of the following model

$$\Delta Z_t = \alpha + \beta \cdot Z_t - C_t + \epsilon.$$

In this model Z_t is the size of the stock at time t, $\Delta Z_t = Z_{t+1} - Z_t$, C_t is the amount caught in year t, α and β are constants, and ϵ are independent, normally distributed with expectation zero and constant variance.

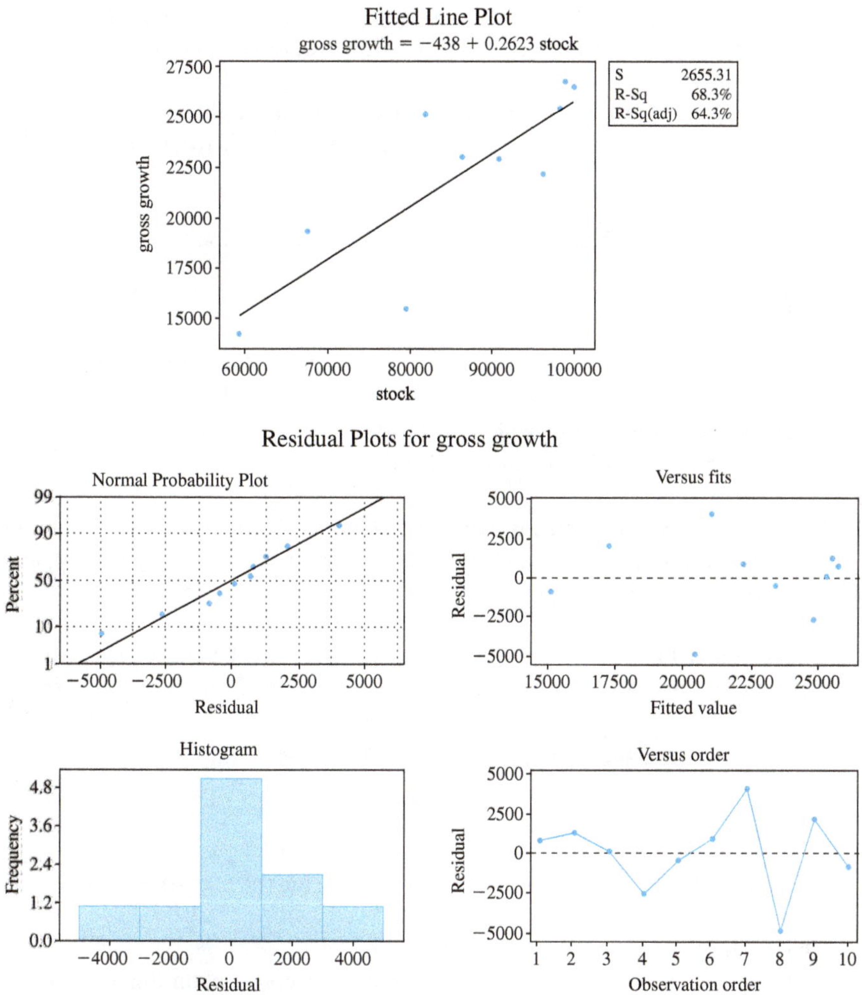

Fig. 11.47 Observation and residual plots for Problem 11.25

(a) We have carried out a linear regression of gross growth, i.e., $\Delta Z_t + C_t$ against stock, i.e., Z_t. The results read as follows:

$$\widehat{\text{gross growth}} = -438 + 0.262 \cdot \text{stock},$$

with

$$S = 2655.31, \qquad R^2 = 68.3\%, \qquad P\text{-value (of } \beta = 0) = 0.0032.$$

Diagnostic plots are displayed in Fig. 11.47.

Comment the information in detail.

(b) The P-value of a test of $H_0 : \alpha = 0$ against $H_A : \alpha \neq 0$ is 93.8%. Is this something we would expect in this case? How would you interpret the number 0.262?

(c) We have also made a regression where the dependent variable is $Z_{t+1} + C_t$, i.e., how large the stock would have been in the next period if we did not fish. The results read as follows:

$$\widehat{\text{catch adjusted stock}} = -437 + 1.262 \cdot \text{stock},$$

with

$$S = 2655.31, \qquad R^2 = 98\%, \qquad P\text{-value (of } \beta = 0) = 0.0032.$$

Diagnostic plots are displayed in Fig. 11.48.

Comment the new information in detail.

11.26 Price Versus Demand for Substitute Goods: A company sells a good in two different versions; Superior and Extra. The price for Superior is x_1 per unit, and the price for Extra is x_2 per unit.

(a) Suppose that the price for Extra is fixed at $x_2 = 50$ USD. We observe the demand for Superior for different values of x_1. The results were as follows:

$$\widehat{\text{Demand Superior}} = 155.1 + 2.102 \cdot \text{Price Superior},$$

with

$$S = 0.9956, \qquad R^2 = 99.4\%, \qquad P\text{-value (of } \beta = 0) = 0.0000.$$

Diagnostic plots are displayed in Fig. 11.49.

Comment the information in detail. How will you explain this connection from an economic point of view?

(b) Assume that the price for Superior is fixed at $x_1 = 40$ USD. We observed the demand Superior for different values of the price for Extra. The results were as follows:

$$\widehat{\text{Demand Superior}} = 66 + 0.1 \cdot \text{Price Superior},$$

with

$$S = 0.9090, \qquad R^2 = 30.0\%, \qquad P\text{-value (of } \beta = 0) = 0.0000.$$

Diagnostic plots are displayed in Fig. 11.50.

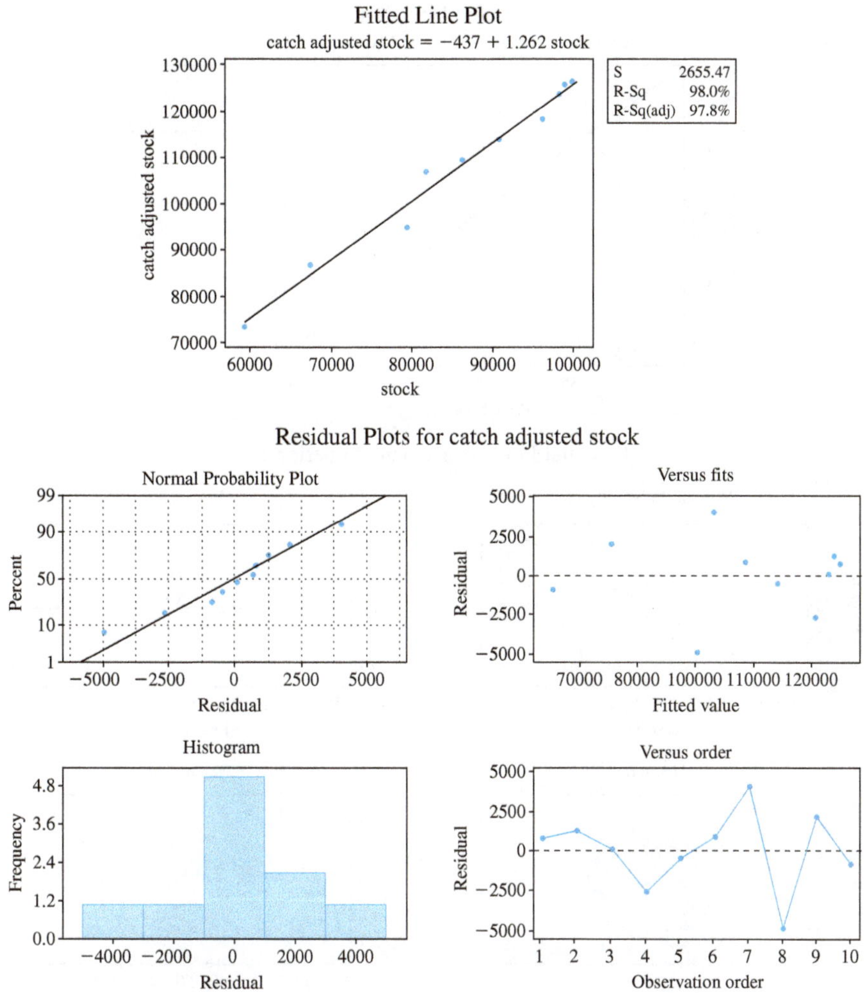

Fig. 11.48 Observation and residual plots for the adjusted data in Problem 11.25

Comment the information in detail. How will you explain this connection from an economic point of view?

(c) Assume that the connection is such that

$$\text{Expected demand Superior} = \alpha - 2.1x_1 + 0.1x_2.$$

What value must α have for this to be consistent with the results from (a) and (b)?

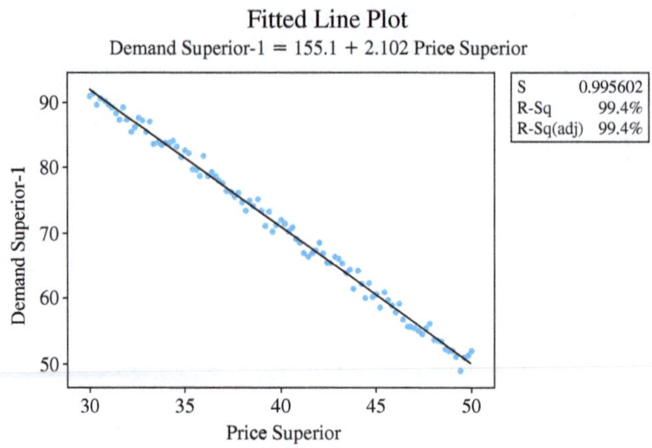

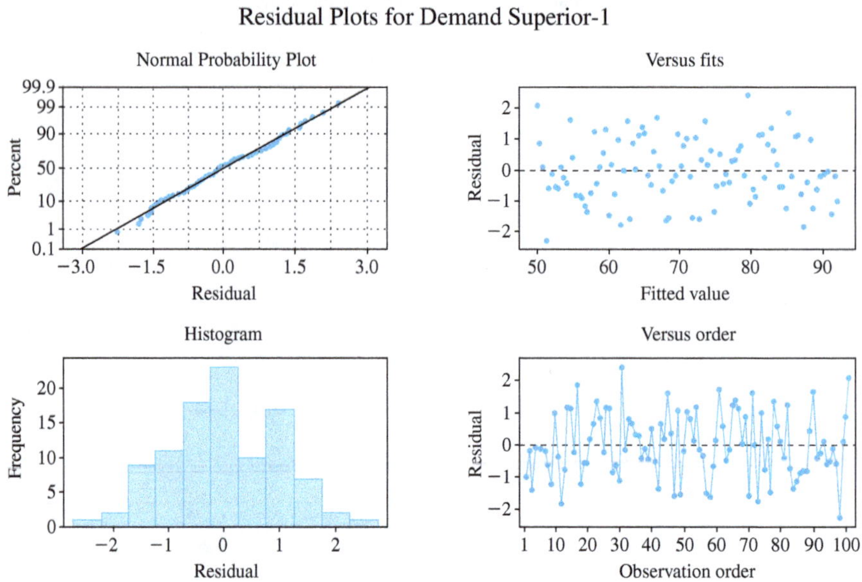

Fig. 11.49 Observation and residual plots for Problem 11.26

(d) The corresponding numbers for the demand of Extra is

$$\text{Expected demand Extra} = 216 + 0 - 2x_1 - 1.9x_2.$$

Find an expression for total expected sales value as a function of x_1 and x_2, and use this expression to determine values for x_1 and x_2 giving maximum expected sales value.

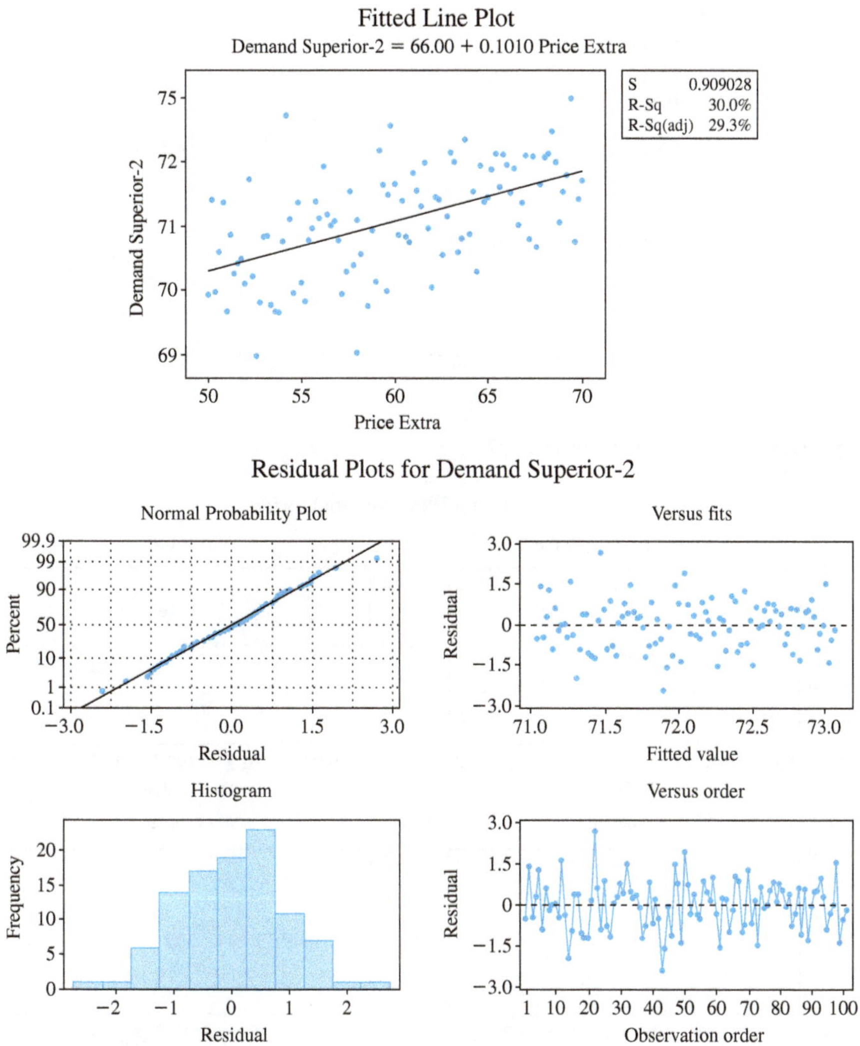

Fig. 11.50 Observation and residual plots for Problem 11.26

11.27 Non-existing Trends: Figure 11.51 shows the price of a stock over a period of 100 days.

In the period $t = 30$ to $t = 60$ there appears to be a linearly decreasing trend, and we have carried out a linear regression using data in that time span. The results were as follows:

$$\widehat{\text{Stock price}} = 121 - 0.37 \cdot \text{time},$$

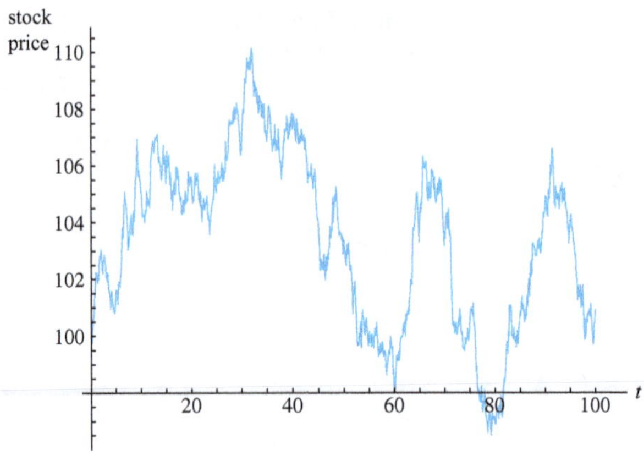

Fig. 11.51 Stock prices in Problem 11.27

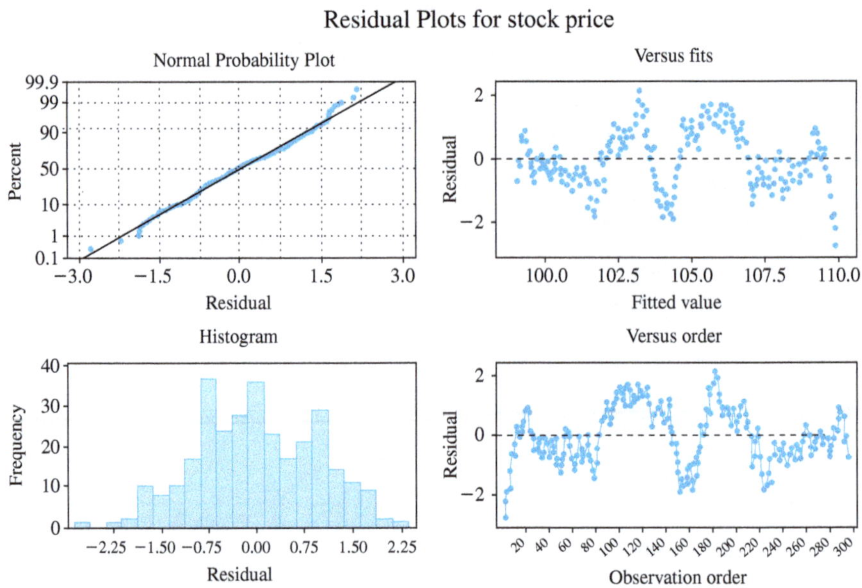

Fig. 11.52 Residual plots for Problem 11.27

with

$$S = 0.9302, \qquad R^2 = 92.3\%, \qquad P\text{-value (of } \beta = 0) = 0.0000.$$

Diagnostic plots are displayed in Fig. 11.52.

(a) Comment the information above in detail. Is this a model we can have confidence in?

(b) Use the regression model above to predict the stock price at time $t = 80$, and compare with the observed value. Is this a result we should trust?

11.28 Multiplicative Models: We have data for 100 different companies within a special industry and have observed

- Production Y (measured in million units).
- Capital K (measured in million USD).
- Labor L (measured in number of workers).

Data were analyzed by linear regression, and the results are shown below.

(a) Comment the following results in detail

$$\widehat{Y} = -1.63913 + 0.0197683 \cdot K + 0.0126971 \cdot L,$$

with

$$S = 0.119558, \qquad R^2 = 99.32\%, \qquad P\text{-value (of } \beta = 0) = 0.000.$$

Diagnostic plots are displayed in Fig. 11.53.

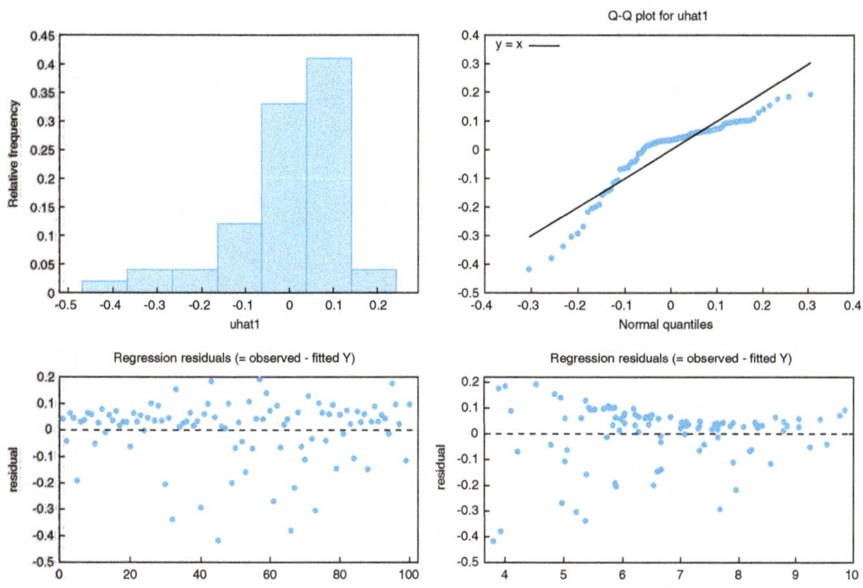

Fig. 11.53 Residual plots for Problem 11.28

(b) An alternative to the linear regression model is

$$Y = \alpha K^{\beta_1} L^{\beta_2} \cdot \epsilon,$$

where α, $\beta_!$, β_2 are constants and ϵ a random variable. Explain how we can use logarithms to transform this model into a model suitable for linear regression. What kind of distribution must ϵ have for this to work?

(c) We have used multiple regression to study the relation between the variables

- $\log Y = \ln(Y)$.
- $\log K = \ln(K)$.
- $\log L = \ln(L)$.

Comment the printout in detail and try to explain why the regression in (c) works better.

$$\widehat{\log Y} = -5.06822 + 0.299762 \cdot \log K + 0.900619 \cdot \log L,$$

with

$$S = 0.001023, \qquad R^2 = 99.99\%, \qquad P\text{-value (of } \beta = 0) = 0.000.$$

Diagnostic plots are displayed in Fig. 11.54.

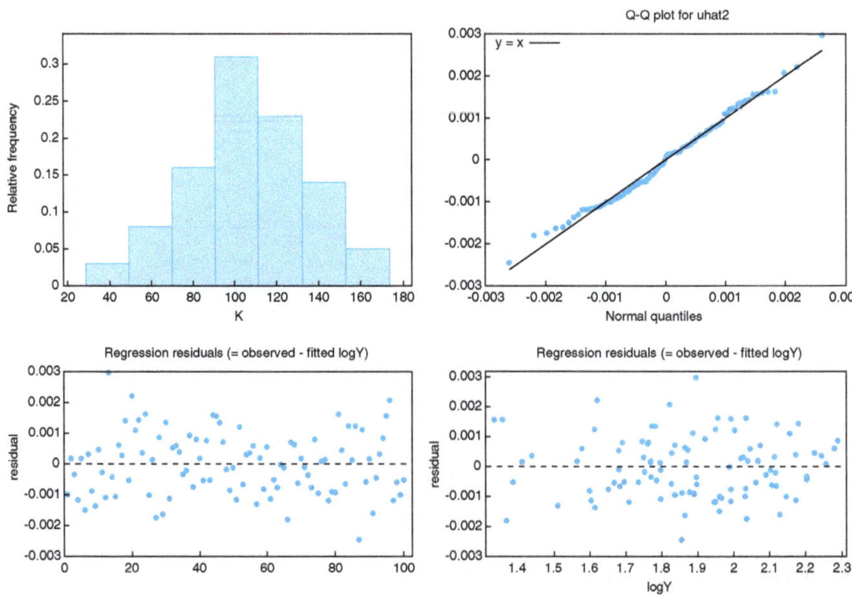

Fig. 11.54 Residual plots for the log-transformed model in Problem 11.28

(d) Use the printout in (c) to estimate the values for the constants α, β_1, β_2 in (b). Hint: When you compute α, you need to take into account that the numbers for K and Y are given in millions, as this affects the original value for α.

11.29 Multicollinearity: We have studied the relation between grades on a standardized test and the fraction of the population that has higher education. We have data from 19 different regions. In each region we know the fraction that has short higher education (EdSh, defined as ≤ 4 years) and long higher education (EdL, defined as > 4 years). The sum of these two fractions gives the fraction with either short or long higher education, Ed for short.

(a) We have used multiple regression to study the average result in each region as a function of EdSh and EdL (each measured in %). The results were as follows:

$$\widehat{\text{result}} = 1.65345 + 0.0650691 \cdot EdSh - 0.0150208 \cdot EdL,$$

with

$$S = 0.121993, \qquad R^2 = 52.97\%,$$

$$P\text{-value (of } \beta_1 = 0) = 13.47\%, \text{ and } P\text{-value (of } \beta_2 = 0) = 64.87\%.$$

We have also made a regression of EdSh as a function of EdL. The results were as follows:

$$\widehat{\text{EdSh}} = -16.3735 + 0.754853 \cdot EdL,$$

with

$$S = 2.604113, \qquad R^2 = 92.85\%, \qquad P\text{-value (of } \beta = 0) = 0.000.$$

Comment the two regressions in detail. What type of problem do we have here, and how can we deal with that problem?

(b) We merge the two variables EdSh and EdL into Ed. Using Ed as the only explanatory variable we get

$$\widehat{\text{result}} = 2.38286 + 0.0200711 \cdot Ed,$$

with

$$S = 0.121724, \qquad R^2 = 49.43\%,$$

$$P\text{-value (of } \beta = 0) = 0.000.$$

Diagnostic plots are displayed in Fig. 11.55.

Comment the new results in detail.

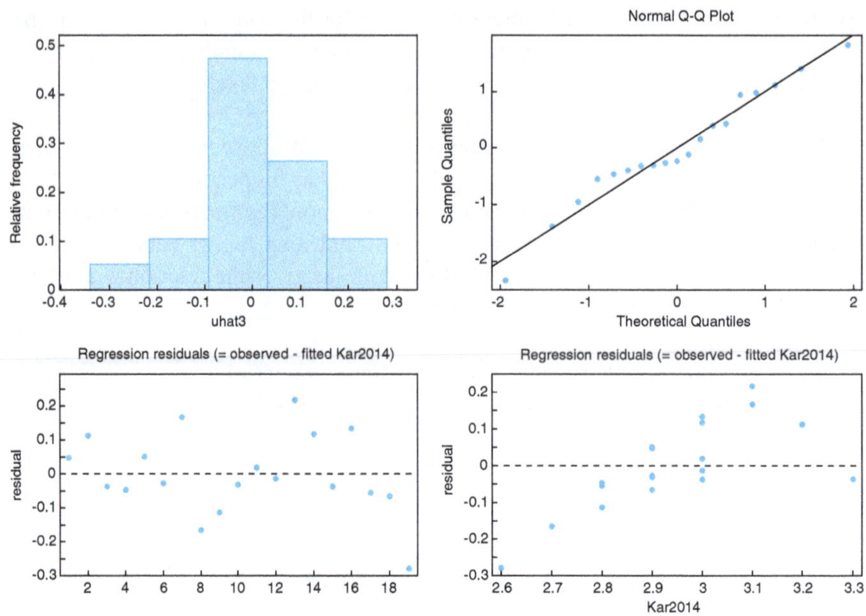

Fig. 11.55 Residual plots for Problem 11.29

(c) Use the model from (b) to predict the average result in a region where 47.5% of the population have higher education, and compute a 95% prediction interval for this value. To compute this interval we need the values $\overline{Ed} = 27.86$, $S[\hat{\beta}] = 0.00492369$. Use one decimal to specify the limits for the prediction interval. In the central region where 47.5% of the population had higher education, the result was 3.3. Do we have sufficient reason to claim that this result was weaker than expected?

11.30 Polynomial Regression: We want to study the relation between demand and price. Data are shown in Fig. 11.56 together with the best line fit.

(a) A linear regression of demand against price produced the results reported below. Comment these results in detail.

$$\widehat{\text{Demand}} = 911.713 - 112.057 \cdot Price,$$

with

$$S = 120.1707, \qquad R^2 = 85.73\%, \qquad P\text{-value (of } \beta = 0) = 0.000.$$

Diagnostic plots are displayed in Fig. 11.57.

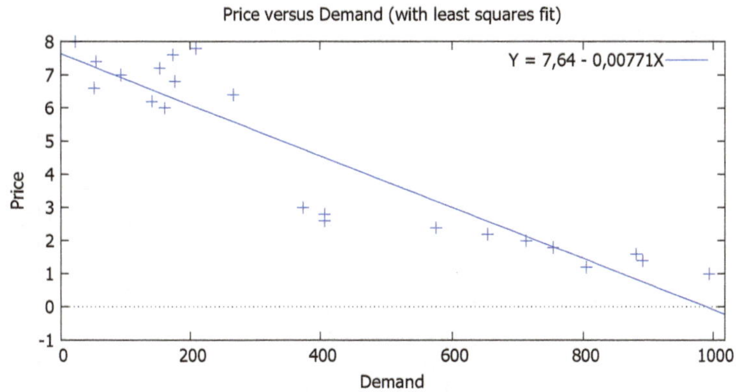

Fig. 11.56 Observed demand as a function of price in Problem 11.30

(b) We try to improve our model using polynomial regression, where we use second order and third order polynomials. The results were as follows:

$$\widehat{\text{Demand}} = 1281.78 - 356.953 \cdot Price + 27.2106 \cdot Price^2,$$

with

$$S = 80.752, \qquad R^2 = 94.17\%,$$

$$P\text{-value (of } \beta_1 = 0) = 0.000, \text{ and } P\text{-value (of } \beta_2 = 0) = 0.000.$$

and

$$\widehat{\text{Demand}} = 1513.62 - 581.236 \cdot Price + 84.7985 \cdot Price^2 - 4.26577 \cdot Price^3,$$

with

$$S = 74.295, \qquad R^2 = 95.33\%,$$

$$P\text{-value (of } \beta_1 = 0) = 0.000, P\text{-value (of } \beta_2 = 0) = 0.68\%, \text{ and}$$

$$P\text{-value (of } \beta_3 = 0) = 4.9\%.$$

Which of the three models is the best?

(c) Use the three models to estimate expected demand when $Price = 10$. Compare the estimated values with the plot above. Which of the three models is the best? What kind of problems do we face here, and what causes these problems?

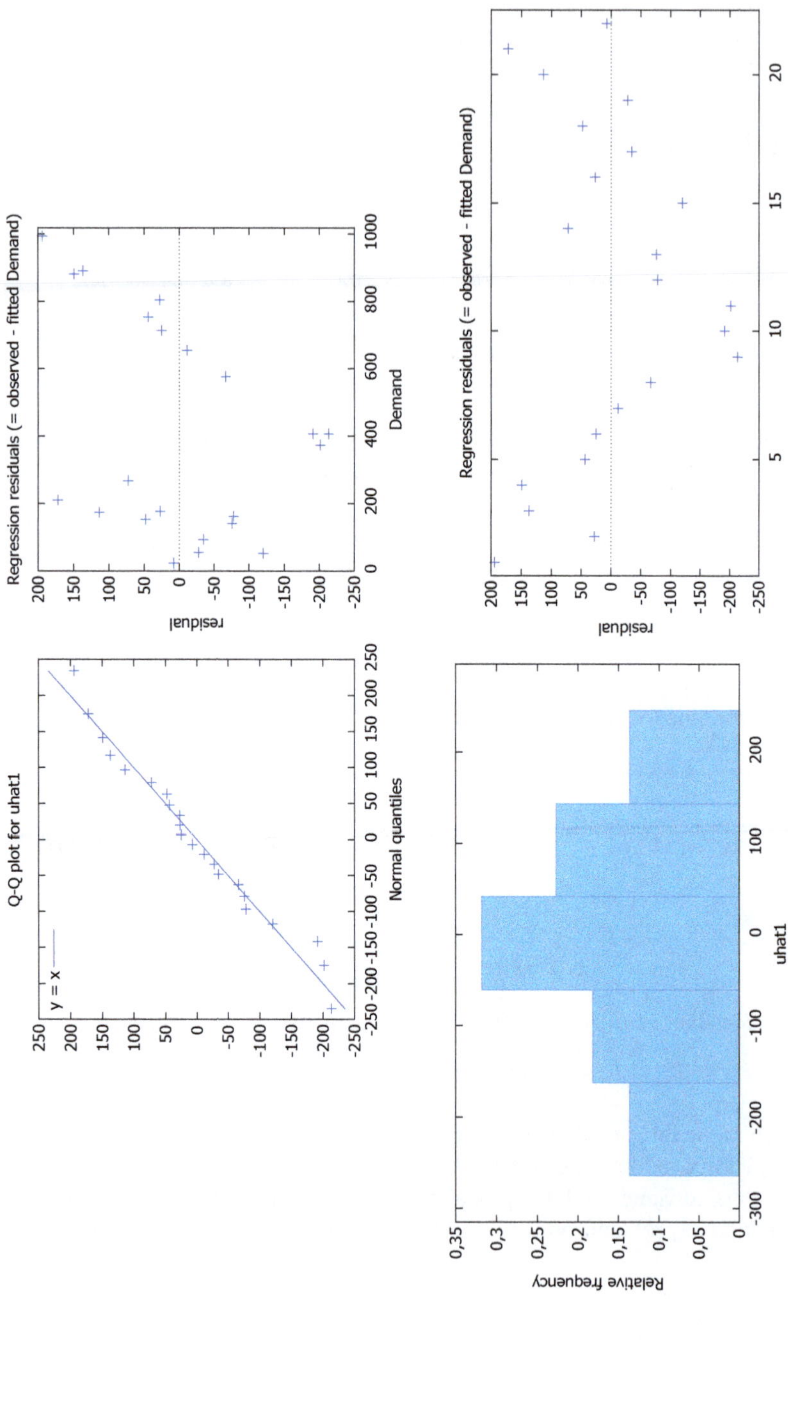

Fig. 11.57 Residual plots for Problem 11.30

Solutions

Problems of Chap. 1

1.1 The most frequent observation is 130, and the mode is hence 130 USD. The median is observation 338. By a little trial and error we see that $90 + 115 + 121 = 326$. Then observation 338 must belong to category number 4. The median is hence 130 USD. To find the 1. and 3. quartile we compute

$$\frac{675+1}{4} = 169, \qquad 169 \cdot 3 = 507.$$

We see that observation 169 must belong to category 2, i.e., the 1. quartile is 110 USD. Furthermore we see that $90 + 115 + 121 + 162 = 488$. This means that observation 507 must belong to category 5, i.e., the 3. quartile is 140 USD.

1.2

(a) The most frequent observation is 2, which we recorded 459 times. The median is observation 638. There is in total $257 + 241 = 498$ observations in the two first categories. Then observation 638 must be in category 3. The median is hence 2. To find the 1. and 3. quartile we compute

$$\frac{1275+1}{4} = 319, \qquad 319 \cdot 3 = 957.$$

We see that observation 319 must be in category 2, i.e., the 1. quartile is 1. Furthermore we see that in total $257 + 241 + 459 = 957$ observations are in categories 1,2,3. The 3. quartile must then be in category 3, and the 3. quartile is hence 2.

(b) To compute the mean, we have to remember that the same observation is listed multiple times.

$$\overline{X} = \frac{1}{1275}(0 + \cdots + 0 + 1 + \cdots + 1 + 2 + \cdots + 2$$

J. Ubøe, *Introductory Statistics for Business and Economics*, Springer Texts in Business and Economics, https://doi.org/10.1007/978-3-319-70936-9

$$+3+\cdots+3+4+\cdots+4+5+\cdots+5+6+\cdots+6+7+\cdots+7)$$

$$= \frac{1}{1275}(0\cdot 257+1\cdot 241+2\cdot 459$$

$$+3\cdot 103+4\cdot 84+5\cdot 62+6\cdot 47+7\cdot 22)=2.$$

1.3

(a) The mean value of the 5 stock prices is

$$\frac{1}{5}(100+200+400+300+500)=300.$$

(b) The total market value is

$$100\cdot 140{,}000+200\cdot 50{,}000+400\cdot 20{,}000+300\cdot 10{,}000+500\cdot 30{,}000=50{,}000{,}000.$$

(c) In total there are

$$140{,}000+50{,}000+20{,}000+10{,}000+30{,}000=250{,}000,$$

stocks in the companies. The mean value of a stock in these companies is hence

$$\frac{50{,}000{,}000}{250{,}000}=200.$$

The average in (a) is mathematically feasible, but does not make much sense economically as it does not reflect the total market value of the companies.

1.4

(a) i) $\overline{X}=4$ ii) $\overline{X}=8$ iii) $\overline{X}=40$.
(b) In case ii) all the numbers are twice as big as in case i), and the mean is also twice as big. In case iii) all the numbers are 10 times as big as in case i), and correspondingly the mean becomes 10 times as big.

1.5

(a) i) $\overline{X}=0$ ii) $\overline{X}=0$.
(b) The two sequences both have mean zero. Apart from that there are hardly any resemblances between them.

1.6

(a) i) $S_X^2 = 16$ ii) $S_X^2 = 16$.
(b) All the numbers in the second sequence are 6 less than the corresponding numbers in the first sequence. The two series have the same variance.

1.7 $\overline{X} = 6$, the sample variance is $S_X^2 = 16$, and the sample standard deviation $S_X = 4$.

1.8 $\overline{X} = 100$, the sample variance is $S_X^2 = 4$, and the sample standard deviation $S_X = 2$.

1.9

(a) $S^2 = 16$ and $S = 4$.
(b) $S_X^2 = 20$ and $S_X = \sqrt{20} \approx 4.47$.

1.10 We have $(n-1)S_X^2 = \sum_{i=1}^{n}(X_i - \overline{X})^2 = n \cdot S^2$. Hence

$$S = \sqrt{\frac{n-1}{n}} S_X.$$

Since $\sqrt{\frac{n-1}{n}} < 1$, then S will always be somewhat smaller than S_X. When n is large, the difference becomes negligible.

1.11 $S_{XY} = -45$.

1.12 $S_X = 10, S_Y = 12, S_{XY} = 30, R_{XY} = 0.25$.

1.13 $S_X = 22, S_Y = 44, S_{XY} = -968, R_{XY} = -1$. The points must be on a decreasing straight line. If we, e.g., use the two-point formula for a straight line, we find

$$Y_i = 200 - 2X_i.$$

1.14 $S_X = 5, S_Y = 10, S_{XY} = 50, R_{XY} = 1$. The points must be on an increasing straight line.

$$Y_i = 2X_i.$$

We can let the first portfolio be arbitrary. The relation will always be satisfied if we invest twice as much in all the stocks.

1.15

(a) $\frac{n+1}{4} = 1 + \frac{3}{4}$. The reminder is $\frac{3}{4}$. We then start at observation number 1, i.e., 2 and move 75% of the distance to 6. The 1. quartile is hence

$$2 + 0.75 \cdot (6 - 2) = 5.$$

Furthermore $\frac{3(n+1)}{4} = 5 + \frac{1}{4}$. and the reminder is $\frac{1}{4}$. We then start at observation number 5, i.e., 18 and move 25% of the distance to 22. The 3. quartile is hence

$$5 + 0.25 \cdot (22 - 18) = 19.$$

(b) Here $\frac{n+1}{4} = 2$ and $\frac{3(n+1)}{4} = 6$. Both reminders are zero and the 1. quartile is 6 and the 3.quartile is 18.

(c) Here $\frac{n+1}{4} = 2.25$ and $\frac{3(n+1)}{4} = 6.75$. The 1. quartile is hence

$$6 + 0.25 \cdot (10 - 6) = 7,$$

and the 3. quartile is

$$14 + 0.75 \cdot (18 - 14) = 17.$$

(d) Here $\frac{n+1}{4} = 2.5$ and $\frac{3(n+1)}{4} = 7.5$. The 1. quartile is hence

$$6 + 0.5 \cdot (10 - 6) = 8,$$

and the 3. quartile is

$$14 + 0.5 \cdot (18 - 14) = 16.$$

1.16

(a) $\overline{X} = 135.32$. Write the data in column A from A1 to A25. Click in any entry outside column A and write the command "=Average(A1:A25)" in the entry. Remember to write "=" in front of the command. If you press the return button, the answer 135.32 should be displayed in the entry.

(b) The sample variance is 93.31 and the sample standard deviation is 9.65971.

(c) The quartiles are 127, 136, and 141. The 2. quartile is called the median.

Remark Excel does not use the definitions in Problem 1.15 to compute the quartiles. Instead it, e.g., computes the 1. quartile as the median of the observations to the left of the median of the data. The difference is of no practical significance but is part of the reason why we never entered into details about quartiles in Chap. 1. As a rough thumb of rule a division by 4 will work fine to find the entry of the first quartile.

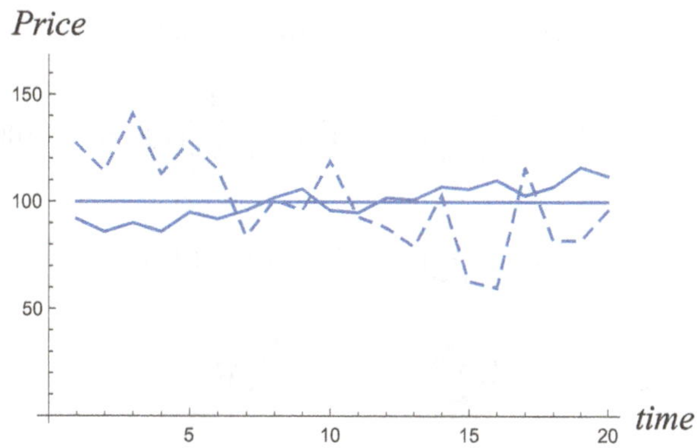

Fig. 1 Prices as functions of time

1.17

(a) $\bar{a} = 100, \bar{b} = 100$.
(b) The result is shown in Fig. 1. The solid line shows the stock prices for ALPHA, while the dashed line shows the stock prices for BETA. From the figure we see that the values of BETA vary considerably more than the values of ALPHA, and BETA is hence the most insecure stock.
(c) $S_a^2 = 73.16, S_b^2 = 471.05$. We see that S_b^2 is considerably bigger than S_a^2, reflecting the larger spread we see in the plot.
(d) A risk seeking investor will prefer a stock with a larger spread as it provides a bigger chance of high returns. A risk averse investor will prefer a low spread. Which of the stocks ALPHA or BETA that is better is hence a matter of opinion.
(e) $S_{ab} = -122.26$.
(f)

$$\begin{aligned}\text{Value of stocks} &= \text{Number of stocks in ALPHA} \cdot \text{Price per stock ALPHA}\\ &\quad + \text{Number of stocks in BETA} \cdot \text{Price per stock BETA}\\ &= \frac{\text{Money used to buy ALPHA}}{\text{Selling price ALPHA}} \cdot a_n + \frac{\text{Money used to buy BETA}}{\text{Selling price BETA}} \cdot b_n\\ &= \frac{1{,}000{,}000 \cdot \frac{x}{100}}{100} \cdot a_n + \frac{1{,}000{,}000 \cdot \frac{y}{100}}{100} \cdot b_n\\ &= 100x \cdot a_n + 100y \cdot b_n.\end{aligned}$$

(g) $\bar{c} = 1{,}000{,}000$.

(h) Note that $\overline{c} = 100x\overline{a} + 100y\overline{b}$ and that $y = 100 - x$.

$$
\begin{aligned}
S_c^2 &= \frac{1}{19}\sum_{n=1}^{20}(c_n - \overline{c})^2 = \frac{1}{19}\sum_{n=1}^{20}(100\,x\,a_n + 100\,y\,b_n - \overline{c})^2 \\
&= \frac{1}{19}\sum_{n=1}^{20}(100\,x\,(a_n - \overline{a}) + 100\,y\,(b_n - \overline{b}))^2 \\
&= \frac{1}{19}\sum_{n=1}^{20} 100^2\,x^2\,(a_n - \overline{a})^2 + 2\cdot 100^2\,x\,y\,(a_n - \overline{a})(b_n - \overline{b}) \\
&\quad +100^2\,y^2\,(b_n - \overline{b})^2 \\
&= 10^4\Big(x^2\frac{1}{19}\sum_{n=1}^{20}(a_n - \overline{a})^2 + 2\,x\,y\,\frac{1}{19}\sum_{n=1}^{20}(a_n - \overline{a})(b_n - \overline{b}) \\
&\quad +y^2\,\frac{1}{19}\sum_{n=1}^{20}(b_n - \overline{b})^2\Big) \\
&= 10^4(x^2\,S_a^2 + 2x\,y\,S_{ab} + y^2\,S_b^2) \\
&= 10{,}000(x^2 73.16 + 2x\,(100 - x)(-122.26) + (100 - x)^2 471.05) \\
&= 1{,}000{,}000(7.8873\,x^2 - 1186.62\,x + 47105).
\end{aligned}
$$

The minimum for this function is obtained at $x \approx 75$, i.e., if we want to minimize the variance of the investment we should buy 7500 stock in ALPHA and 2500 stocks in BETA.

1.18

(a) $\overline{p} = 4244.60$ (USD).
(b) $S_p^2 = 4{,}082{,}771.73$.
(c) Young people in low season: Mean category 1 = 3068.36 (USD), $S_1^2 = 74{,}256.62$.

Young people in high season: Mean category 2 = 1889.25 (USD), $S_2^2 = 33{,}761.88$.

Old people in low season: Mean category 3 = 3989.78 (USD), $S_3^2 = 31{,}572.53$.

Old people in high season: Mean category 4 = 7084.17 (USD), $S_4^2 = 97{,}390.52$.
(d) The variance within each category is considerably smaller than the variance for the whole sample. This means that the behavior within the categories is more uniform than for the group seen as a whole. If the variance within a subgroup is

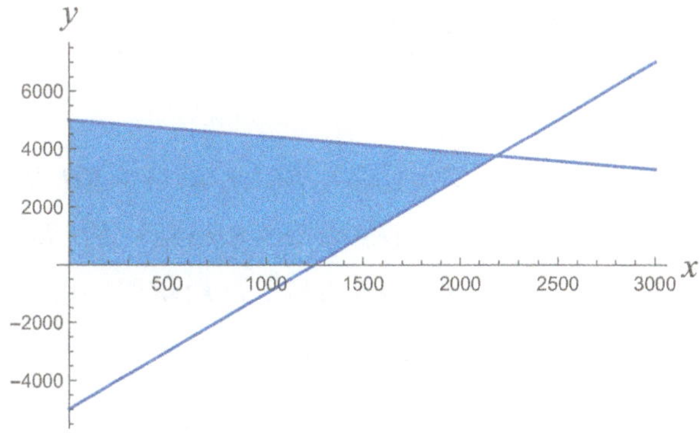

Fig. 2 Constrained linear optimization

zero, all people must spend the same amount. The variance is small only if all the members of a category spend approximately the same amount of money.

(e) Optimization constraints

$$x \geq 0 \qquad y \geq 0 \qquad 20x + 35y \leq 175{,}500$$
$$x \leq \frac{20}{100}(5000 + x + y) \Rightarrow 4x - y \leq 5000.$$

See Fig. 2. The prices: Young people 2761.52 USD, Old people 3790.29 USD. We should then find the maximum of the function

$$f(x, y) = 2761.52x + 3790.29,$$

under the constraints shown in the figure. LP-theory says that the maximum is obtained at the corners which are $(0, 0)$, $(1250, 0)$, $(2191, 3763)$, $(0, 5014)$. If we insert these points into $f(x, y)$, we see that the biggest value is obtained using $(2191, 3763)$. With these prices maximum profit is hence obtained selling 2191 tickets to young people and 3763 tickets to old.

(f) Call the unknown price for old people w, and find a value for w resulting in the same profit in the two last corners reported in (e).

$$2191 \cdot 2761.52 + 3763 \cdot w = 0 \cdot 2761.52 + 5014 \cdot w.$$

We hence obtain equal profit in the two corners if $w = 4836.52$ (USD). If the price on tickets to old people goes above this value, it will be more profitable to sell all the low price tickets to old people.

(g) Note that $\beta = 100-\alpha$. The variance is hence a function of α. Using the numbers given in the text we obtain $V(\alpha) = 2\alpha^2 - 4\alpha(100 - \alpha) + 4(100 - \alpha)^2$. Then $V'(\alpha) = 20\alpha - 1200$. If we solve $V'(\alpha) = 0$, we find $\alpha = 60, \beta = 40$. These values give the smallest possible variance.

Problems of Chap. 2

2.1

$$\begin{aligned} \Omega &= \{KKK, KKI, KIK, IKK, KII, IKI, IIK, III\} \\ A &= \{KKK, KKI, KIK, IKK, KII, IKI, IIK\} \\ B &= \{KKK, KKI, IKK, IKI\} \\ C &= \{KKK, III\}. \end{aligned}$$

2.2

(a) $A \cup B = \{\omega_1, \omega_2, \omega_3\}, A \cap B = \{\omega_1\}, A^c = \{\omega_3, \omega_4\}, B^c = \{\omega_2, \omega_4\}$.
(b) $(A \cap B) \cup (A^c \cap B) = \{\omega_1\} \cup \{\omega_3\} = \{\omega_1, \omega_3\} = B$.
(c) $A \cup (A^c \cap B) = \{\omega_1, \omega_2\} \cup \{\omega_3\} = \{\omega_1, \omega_2, \omega_3\} = A \cup B$.

2.3

(a) $P(A) = 90\%, P(A^c) = 10\%$.
(b) $P(B) = 85\%, P(B^c) = 15\%$.
(c) $P(A \cup B) = 1$.
(d) $P(A \cap B) = 75\%, A \cap B =$ "There are between 1 and 9 errors".

2.4

ω_1: Processing time is 1 day.
ω_2: Processing time is 2 days.
ω_3: Processing time is 3 days.
ω_4: Processing time is 4 days.
ω_5: Processing time is 5 days.
ω_6: Processing time is 6 or more days.

We have

$$p_1 = 0.1, \quad p_2 = 0.4, \quad p_3 = 0.3, \quad p_4 = 0.1, \quad p_5 = 0.05, \quad p_6 = 0.05.$$

These are all numbers between 0 and 1. In addition we see that

$$p_1 + p_2 + p_3 + p_4 + p_5 + p_6 = 0.1 + 0.4 + 0.3 + 0.1 + 0.05 + 0.05 = 1$$

This means that both conditions in the definition of a probability are satisfied.

(b)

$$P(A) = 0.1 + 0.4 = 0.5 = 50\%.$$
$$P(B) = 0.3 + 0.1 + 0.05 + 0.05 = 0.5 = 50\%$$

(c) $A = B^c$.

2.5

(a) We have a sample space with 9 possible outcomes. For this to define a probability p, we must have

$$0 \le p_i \le 1, \qquad i = 1, \ldots, 9$$

and

$$p_1 + p_2 + \cdots p_9 = 1 = 100\%.$$

The first requirement is clear. For the second we see that

$$\sum_{i=1}^{9} p_i = 12\% + 9\% + 10\% + 25\% + 16\% + 5\% + 11\% + 9\% + 3\% = 100\% = 1.$$

Since the probabilities sum to 1, both conditions are satisfied.

(b) (i) The good is of type Regular and is stored in warehouse 3.

$$P(A \cap C) = 11\%.$$

(ii) The good is either of type Regular or it is stored in warehouse 3 (or both).

$$P(A \cup C) = 12\% + 25\% + 11\% + 9\% + 3\% = 60\%.$$

(iii) The good is of type Regular and Superior. This is impossible.

$$P(A \cap B) = 0.$$

(iv) The good is of type Regular or Superior.

$$P(A \cup B) = 12\% + 25\% + 11\% + 9\% + 16\% + 9\% = 82\%.$$

Alternatively we use complements to see that

$$P(A \cup B) = 1 - 11\% - 9\% - 3\% = 82\%,$$

which is slightly more efficient.

2.6 We use the formula

$$P(A \cup B) = P(A) + P(B) - P(A \cap B),$$

to get the equation

$$70\% = 60\% + 40\% - P(A \cap B).$$

This gives $P(A \cap B) = 30\%$. 30% of the customers use both products.

2.7 We use the formula

$$P(A \cup B) = P(A) + P(B) - P(A \cap B),$$

to get the equation

$$70\% = P(A) + 50\% - 40\%.$$

This gives $P(A) = 60\%$. 60% of the customers use product A.

2.8 We use the formula

$$P(A \cup B) = P(A) + P(B) - P(A \cap B),$$

to get

$$70\% = 60\% + 40\% - 30\% = 70\%.$$

This means that 70% of the customers use at least one of the products. Hence 30% do not use any of the two products.

2.9 There are 5 possible outcomes

ω_1: The stock is in company A.
ω_2: The stock is in company B.
ω_3: The stock is in company C.
ω_4: The stock is in company D.
ω_5: The stock is in company E.

When we select a stock randomly, we are tacitly assuming that the probability is uniform. Hence

$$p_1 = \frac{140000}{250000} = 56\%, \qquad p_2 = \frac{50000}{250000} = 20\%,$$

$$p_3 = \frac{20000}{250000} = 8\%, \qquad p_4 = \frac{10000}{250000} = 4\%, \qquad p_5 = \frac{30000}{250000} = 12\%.$$

2.10

(a) (i)

$$P(A \cap B) = P(A) + P(B) - P(A \cup B) = 60\% + 50\% - 82\% = 28\%.$$

(ii)

$$P(A \cap C) = P(A) + P(C) - P(A \cup C) = 60\% + 45\% - 73\% = 32\%.$$

iii)

$$P(B \cap C) = P(B) + P(C) - P(B \cup C) = 50\% + 45\% - 74\% = 21\%.$$

(b)

$$\begin{aligned} & P(A \cap B \cap C) \\ = & P(A \cup B \cup C) \\ - & (P(A) + P(B) + P(C) - P(A \cap B) - P(A \cap C) - P(B \cap C)) \\ = & 89\% - 60\% - 50\% - 45\% + 28\% + 32\% + 21\% = 15\%. \end{aligned}$$

2.11

(a) The customers liking both A and B were numbers

$$3, 7, 11, 18, 19, 20, 27, 33, 34, 39, 42, 43, 49, 53, 56, 57, 60, 61, 62, 65, 67, 71, 72, 73, 74, 76, 78, 80.$$

(b) The customers liking at least one of the two products were

$$1, 2, 3, 4, 5, 6, 7, 8, 9, 10, 11, 12, 13, 15, 16, 17, 18, 19, 20, 22, 23, 24, 25, 27, 28, 30, 31, 32, 33, 34, 35, 36, 37, 38, 39, 40, 41, 42, 43, 44, 45, 47, 48, 49, 50, 51, 52, 53, 54, 55, 56, 57, 58, 59, 60, 61, 62, 65, 67, 68, 69, 70, 71, 72, 73, 74, 75, 76, 77, 78, 79, 80.$$

(c) (i) A total of 60 customers liked A, i.e., 60%.
(ii) A total of 40 customer liked B, i.e., 40%.
(iii) A total of 28 customers liked both A and B, i.e., 35%.
(iv) A total of 72 customers liked at least one of the two products, i.e., 90%.

(d)

$$90\% = 75\% + 50\% - 35\%,$$

which illustrates the general addition principle.

Problems of Chap. 3

3.1 As there are no connections between the choices, there are in all

$$103 \cdot 43 \cdot 39 = 172731,$$

different ways of making the portfolio.

3.2 The order makes a difference for how the money is invested, and since the funds must be different, the choices are without replacements. The number of different combinations is hence

$$(10)_3 = 10 \cdot 9 \cdot 8 = 720.$$

3.3 This is an ordered choice, since the order of the ranking makes a difference. For example will the ranking $7, 2, 11, 19, 15$ (where product 7 is best) be different from the ranking $2, 7, 11, 19, 15$ (where product 2 is best). A product can only be ranked once, and hence the choice is without replacement. The number of different combinations is

$$(20)_5 = 20 \cdot 19 \cdot 18 \cdot 17 \cdot 16 = 1{,}860{,}480.$$

3.4 In this problem the order makes no difference for how the money are invested, and the choices are without replacements. The number of different combinations is

$$\binom{10}{4} = 210.$$

3.5 This is an unordered choice, since the order makes no difference for the result. For example will the sequence $2, 5, 11, 12$ provide the same result as the sequence $5, 2, 11, 12$ since the same goods have been chosen in both cases. The number of different combinations is

$$\binom{15}{4} = 1365.$$

3.6 We choose 3 of the numbers 1–5, unordered without replacement. We interpret the 3 numbers as the position of our correct answers. The choices are unordered since the order makes no difference. For example will the sequence $1, 3, 5$ lead to the same result as the sequence $5, 1, 3$ since they both have the same interpretation: Answers 1, 3, and 5 are correct, while answers 2 and 4 are wrong. The choice is without replacements since the positions must be different. Any such choice corresponds to a combination of answers with exactly 3 correct answers. The number of different combinations is

$$\binom{5}{3} = 10.$$

3.7 We choose 5 of the numbers 1–20, unordered without replacement. These 5 numbers we interpret as the position of our correct answers. Any such choice corresponds to an answer combination with exactly 5 correct answers, hence the number of different combinations is

$$\binom{20}{5} = 15{,}504.$$

3.8 In this problem the order of the funds makes no difference, so we use the formulas for unordered choices without replacements.

(a) There is in all $\binom{30}{6} = 593{,}775$ different combinations of funds.

(b) (i) The probability that you have selected the best fund is

$$\frac{\binom{29}{5}}{\binom{60}{6}} = 20\%.$$

(ii) The probability that you have selected the two best funds is

$$\frac{\binom{28}{4}}{\binom{60}{6}} = \frac{1}{29} \approx 3.4\%.$$

3.9

(a) The probability that you receive the questionnaire is

$$\frac{\binom{1}{1}\binom{9999}{999}}{\binom{10000}{1000}} = \frac{1}{10}.$$

You hence have 10% probability of receiving the questionnaire.

(b) The probability that you and your nearest neighbor receive the questionnaire is

$$\frac{\binom{2}{2}\binom{9998}{998}}{\binom{10000}{1000}} = \frac{111}{11{,}110} \approx 0.009991.$$

Note that the answer is slightly different from the seemingly obvious (and wrong) answer $\frac{1}{100}$.

3.10 The probability that you do not receive the questionnaire is

$$\frac{\binom{N-1}{n}}{\binom{N}{n}} = \frac{\frac{(N-1)!}{n!(N-n-1)!}}{\frac{N!}{n!(N-n)!}} = \frac{n!(N-n)!(N-1)!}{n!(N-n-1)!N!} = \frac{N-n}{N} = 1 - \frac{n}{N}.$$

The probability that you receive the questionnaire is hence $\frac{n}{N}$.

3.11

(a) There are $\binom{8}{2} = 28$ different cooperation documents.
(b) There are $(8)_2 = 56$ different executive officers.

3.12

(a) The probability that none of the crates contain errors is

$$\frac{\binom{91}{2}}{\binom{105}{2}} = 75\%.$$

(b) The probability that at least one of the crates contain errors is

$$\frac{\binom{14}{1}\binom{91}{1}}{\binom{105}{2}} + \frac{\binom{14}{2}}{\binom{105}{2}} = 25\%.$$

Notice that a much simpler solution is to take the complement of the answer from (a).

3.13 There is in all $\binom{26}{3} = 2600$ ways of selecting 3 crates.

(a) There is in all $\binom{13}{3} = 286$ different choices leading to 3 crates containing Regular. The probability of this happening is

$$\frac{286}{2600} = 11\%.$$

(b) There is in all $13 \cdot 7 \cdot 6 = 546$ different choices leading to different products in all the three crates. The probability of this happening is

$$\frac{546}{2600} = 21\%.$$

3.14

(a) There is in all $3^8 = 6561$ different outcomes.
(b) There is in all $8 \cdot 2^7$ different outcomes where one person buys product A.
(c) There is in all $\binom{8}{5} \cdot 2^3 = 448$ different outcomes where 5 persons buy product A.
(d) There is in all $\binom{8}{2}\binom{6}{3}\binom{3}{3} = 560$ different outcomes where 2 persons buy A, 3 persons buy B, and 3 persons buy C.
(e) If it is sold more of product A than of product B and C in total, we must sell 5, 6, 7, or 8 of product A. This can happen in

$$\binom{8}{5} \cdot 2^3 + \binom{8}{6} \cdot 2^2 + \binom{8}{7} \cdot 2^1 + \binom{8}{8} \cdot 2^0 = 577$$

different ways.

3.15

(a) $\binom{18}{4} \cdot \binom{12}{3} = 673{,}200.$
(b) $\frac{\binom{2}{2}\binom{16}{2}}{\binom{18}{4}} = \frac{2}{51}.$
(c) $\frac{\binom{2}{2}\binom{16}{2} \cdot \binom{1}{1}\binom{11}{2}}{\binom{18}{4} \cdot \binom{12}{3}} = \frac{1}{102}.$

3.16

(a) There is $\binom{4}{2} = 6$ different combinations of two product groups. The customer can choose products from group 1 and 4 in $4 \cdot 6 = 24$ different ways.
(b)
- Group 1 and 2 can be selected in $4 \cdot 2 = 8$ ways.
- Group 1 and 3 can be selected in $4 \cdot 3 = 12$ ways.

- Group 1 and 4 can be selected in $4 \cdot 6 = 24$ ways.
- Group 2 and 3 can be selected in $2 \cdot 3 = 6$ ways.
- Group 2 and 4 can be selected in $2 \cdot 6 = 12$ ways.
- Group 3 and 4 can be selected in $3 \cdot 6 = 18$ ways.
  There is hence a total of 80 different combinations.

(c) When we choose the second product, the number of products we can choose between will depend on which group we selected first. If we order the products from number 1 to number 15, is, e.g., the probability of the combination $(1, 5)$ equal to $1/15 \cdot 1/11 + 1/15 \cdot 1/13$ and the probability of the combination $(5, 7)$ equal to $1/15 \cdot 1/13 + 1/15 \cdot 1/12$. Those probabilities are not equal.

(d) The probability of this is $4/15 \cdot 6/11 + 6/15 \cdot 4/9 = 32/99$.

3.17

(a) There are 3^{20} different combinations. $\binom{20}{19} \cdot 2 = \binom{20}{1} \cdot 2 = 40$ of these contain 19 correct and one wrong answer.

(b) $X = \text{Bin}[20, p]$ with $p = \frac{1}{3}$.

$$P(X = 14) = \binom{20}{14} p^{14}(1-p)^6 = \binom{20}{14} \frac{2^6}{3^{20}}.$$

(c)

$$P(X = 14) = \binom{10}{4} p^4(1-p)^6 = 22.8\%.$$

$$\begin{aligned} P(X \geq 13) &= 1 - P(X \leq 12) \\ &= 1 - P(X = 10) - P(X = 11) - P(X = 12) \\ &= 1 - \binom{10}{0} \frac{2^{10}}{3^{10}} - \binom{10}{1} \frac{2^9}{3^{10}} - \binom{10}{2} \frac{2^8}{3^{10}} = 70.1\%. \end{aligned}$$

3.18

(a) There are $\binom{75}{10} = 828931106355$ different portfolios. The probability that the company has 4 average, 3 good, and 3 very good funds is given by the expression:

$$\frac{\binom{15}{4}\binom{10}{3}\binom{5}{3}}{\binom{75}{10}} \approx 2.0 \cdot 10^{-6}.$$

(b) If none of the funds are good or very good, the selection must be made from the remaining 60 funds. The probability is hence

$$\frac{\binom{60}{10}}{\binom{75}{10}} \approx 9.1\%.$$

To find the probability of at least one very good fund, we first find the probability of none very good funds and consider the complement. Hence the probability is

$$1 - \frac{\binom{70}{10}}{\binom{75}{10}} \approx 52.1\%.$$

3.19

(a) If there are 5 transactions, the list needs to contain all the 5 sellers. In addition we need to select 5 buyers from the 10 potential buyers. The order makes no difference, hence the selection is unordered without replacement. There is

$$\binom{10}{5}\binom{5}{5} = 252.$$

different combinations with 5 transactions.

(b) With x transactions, the number of different combinations is given by

$$\binom{10}{x}\binom{5}{x}.$$

This leads to Table 1.

There are in all 3003 different combinations. If all of these are equally probable, we find the probabilities dividing the numbers in the previous table by 3003, Table 2.

The most probable number of transactions is hence 3 units.

Table 1 Number of combinations as a function of the number of transactions

Number of transactions	0	1	2	3	4	5
Number of combinations	1	50	450	1200	1050	252

Table 2 Probability as a function of the number of transactions

Number of transactions	0	1	2	3	4	5
Probability	0.0003	0.0167	0.1499	0.3996	0.3497	0.0839

Table 3 Number of different lists as a function of the number of transactions

Number of transactions	0	1	2	3	4	5
Number of different lists	1	50	900	7200	25,200	30,240

(c) When the number of transactions is x, any choice of x buyers can be combined with any choice of x sellers in $x!$ different ways. The number of unique lists is hence given by the expression

$$\binom{10}{x}\binom{5}{x}x!.$$

This leads to Table 3.

3.20

(a) We can, e.g., reason as follows: First we select which customers buy A. This can be done in $\binom{10}{x}$ different ways. After selection of these customers, there are $10 - x$ customers left. Among these we choose y customers buying B. This can be done in $\binom{10-x}{y}$ different ways. Finally we are left with $10 - x - y$ customers and z of these buy C. Note that $z = 10-x-y$, and the last factor is always equal to 1.

Using the definition of the binomial coefficients, we get

$$\begin{aligned}\binom{10}{x}\binom{10-x}{y}\binom{10-x-y}{z} &= \frac{10!}{x!(10-x)!}\frac{(10-x)!}{y!(10-x-y)!}\frac{(10-x-y)!}{z!(10-x-y-z)!} \\ &= \frac{10!}{x!y!z!0!} = \frac{10!}{x!y!z!}\end{aligned}$$

since $0! = 1$.

(b) The probability of each combination leading to 3 customers buying A, 2 customers buying B, and 5 customers buying C is $0.3^3 \cdot 0.2^2 \cdot 0.5^5$. There are $\frac{10!}{3!2!5!}$ different such combinations, and since these are all disjoint, the probability becomes

$$\frac{10!}{3!2!5!}0.3^3 \cdot 0.2^2 \cdot 0.5^5 = 8.5\%.$$

(c) There are 6 different outcomes leading to at least 8 customers buying A:

$$(8, 0, 2), (8, 1, 1), (8, 2, 0), (9, 0, 1), (9, 1, 0), (10, 0, 0).$$

The probability P for these outcomes is computed as follows:

$$\begin{aligned} P &= \frac{10!}{8!0!2!}0.3^8 \cdot 0.2^0 \cdot 0.5^2 + \frac{10!}{8!1!1!}0.3^8 \cdot 0.2^1 \cdot 0.5^1 \\ &+ \frac{10!}{8!2!0!}0.3^8 \cdot 0.2^2 \cdot 0.5^0 + \frac{10!}{9!0!1!}0.3^9 \cdot 0.2^0 \cdot 0.5^1 \\ &+ \frac{10!}{9!1!0!}0.3^9 \cdot 0.2^1 \cdot 0.5^0 + \frac{10!}{10!0!0!}0.3^{10} \cdot 0.2^0 \cdot 0.5^0 = 0.16\%. \end{aligned}$$

Problems of Chap. 4

4.1 We use the definition of conditional probability to get

$$P(S|\,F) = \frac{P(S \cap F)}{P(F)} = \frac{14\%}{35\%} = 40\%.$$

$$P(F|S) = \frac{P(F \cap S)}{P(S)} = \frac{14\%}{56\%} = 25\%.$$

Hence 40% of the Favorite users use Super, and 25% of the Super users use Favorite.

4.2 We use the definition of conditional probability to get

$$P(S|\,F) = \frac{P(S \cap F)}{P(F)} \Rightarrow 0.50 = \frac{0.20}{P(F)}.$$

$$P(F|S) = \frac{P(F \cap S)}{P(S)} \Rightarrow 0.25 = \frac{0.20}{P(S)}.$$

This gives $P(F) = 0.4$ and $P(S) = 0.8$. Hence 40% use Favorite and 80% use Super.

4.3 We use the formulas for splitting to see that

$$P(L) = P(L|M) \cdot P(M) + P(L|K) \cdot P(K) = 40\% \cdot \frac{160}{400} + 20\% \cdot \frac{240}{400} = 28\%.$$

Hence 28% like the product.

4.4

(a) The result is displayed in Fig. 3.
(b) The fraction invested in China is 18% + 32% = 50%.

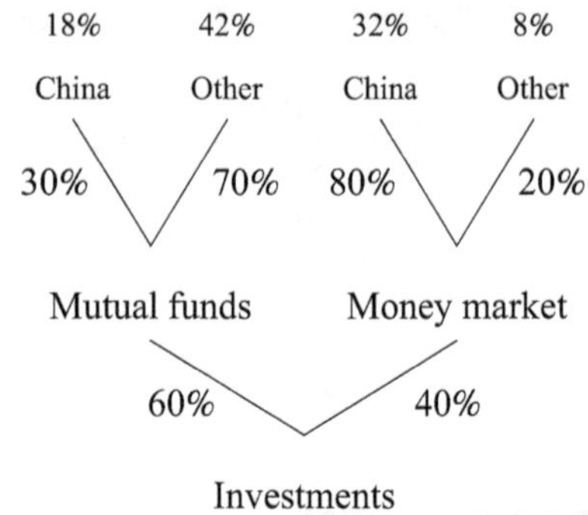

Fig. 3 Solution to Problem 4.4 (a)

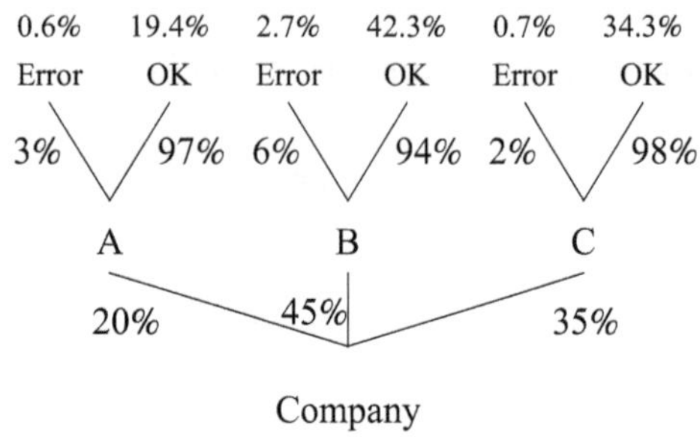

Fig. 4 Solution to Problem 4.5 (a)

(c) The fraction of mutual funds among the investments in China is

$$P(M|Ch) = \frac{P(M \cap Ch)}{P(Ch)} = \frac{0.18}{0.5} = 36\%.$$

4.5

(a) The result is displayed in Fig. 4.
(b) The fraction of reports with errors is

$$0.6\% + 2.7\% + 0.7\% = 4\%.$$

(c) The probability that a report with errors has been made at department A is

$$P(A|Err) = \frac{P(A \cap Err)}{P(Err)} = \frac{0.006}{0.04} = 15\%.$$

4.6

(a) Here we have

$$P(A) \cdot P(B) = 0.6 \cdot 0.4 = 0.24 = P(A \cap B),$$

which means that A and B are independent events.

(b) We have

$$P(A) = P(A \cap B) + P(A \cap B^c) = P(A \cap B) + P(A \cap C).$$

This gives

$$P(A \cap B) = P(A) - P(A \cap B) = 0.6 - 0.24 = 0.36.$$

Hence

$$P(A) \cdot P(C) = 0.6 \cdot 0.6 = 0.36 = P(A \cap C),$$

which means that A and B are independent events.

(c) Here

$$P(B) \cdot P(C) = 0.4 \cdot 0.6 \neq 0 = P(B \cap C).$$

This means that B and C are not independent events.

4.7 We have

$$P(A) = P(A \cap B) + P(A \cap B^c) = P(A \cap B) + P(A \cap C).$$

That gives

$$P(A \cap C) = P(A) - P(A \cap B).$$

Furthermore

$$\begin{aligned} P(A) \cdot P(C) &= P(A)(1 - P(B)) = P(A) - P(A) \cdot P(B) \\ &= P(A) - P(A \cap B) = P(A \cap C). \end{aligned}$$

Hence A and C are independent.

4.8

(a) We have

$$P(A|B) = 60\% = \frac{P(A \cap B)}{P(B)},$$

which gives

$$P(A \cap B) = 60\% \cdot P(B) = P(A) \cdot P(B).$$

This shows that A and B are independent.

(b) In general, when $P(B) \neq 0$, then A and B are independent if and only if $P(A) = P(A|B)$. This can be seen as follows:
  (i) Assume that A and B are independent, then

$$P(A|B) = \frac{P(A \cap B)}{P(B)} = \frac{P(A) \cdot P(B)}{P(B)} = P(A).$$

  (ii) Assume $P(A) = P(A|B)$, then

$$P(A) = P(A|B) = \frac{P(A \cap B)}{P(B)}.$$

If we multiply with $P(B)$ on both sides, we find

$$P(A) \cdot P(B) = P(A \cap B),$$

proving that A and B are independent.

4.9

(a)

$$P(AABC) = 0.5 \cdot 0.5 \cdot 0.2 \cdot 0.3 = 1.5\%.$$

(b) The following combinations provide the required result:

$$AAAA, AAAB, AABA, ABAA, BAAA, AAAC, AACA, ACAA, CAAA.$$

The probability is hence

$$\begin{aligned}P(\text{At least 4 customers buy } A) &= 0.5 \cdot 0.5 \cdot 0.5 \cdot 0.5\\ &+4 \cdot 0.5 \cdot 0.5 \cdot 0.5 \cdot 0.2 + 4 \cdot 0.5 \cdot 0.5 \cdot 0.5 \cdot 0.3 = 31.25\%.\end{aligned}$$

(c) The following combinations provide the required result:

$$\begin{aligned}&CCAA, CACA, CAAC, ACCA, ACAC, AACC,\\ &CCAB, CACB, CABC, ACCB, ACBC, ABCC,\\ &CCBA, CBCA, CBAC, BCCA, BCAC, BACC,\\ &CCBB, CBCB, CBBC, BCCB, BCBC, BBCC.\end{aligned}$$

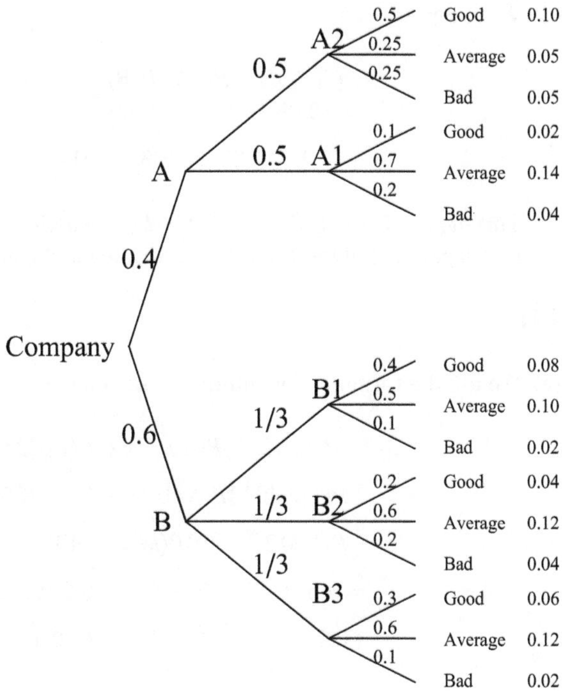

Fig. 5 Solution to Problem 4.10 (a)

The probability is hence

$$P(2 \text{ customers buy } C) = 6 \cdot 0.3 \cdot 0.3 \cdot 0.5 \cdot 0.5$$
$$+12 \cdot 0.3 \cdot 0.3 \cdot 0.5 \cdot 0.2 + 6 \cdot 0.3 \cdot 0.3 \cdot 0.2 \cdot 0.2 = 26.46\%.$$

4.10

(a) The result is displayed in Fig. 5.
(b)

$$P(G|B) = \frac{P(G \cap B)}{P(B)} = \frac{0.08 + 0.04 + 0.06}{0.6} = 0.3.$$

(c)

$$P(A|G) = \frac{P(A \cap G)}{P(G)} = \frac{0.1 + 0.02}{0.1 + 0.02 + 0.08 + 0.04 + 0.06} = 0.4.$$

(d) We compute

$$\begin{aligned}&P(G \cap B) - P(G) \cdot P(B)\\&= (0.08 + 0.04 + 0.06)\\&-(0.1 + 0.02 + 0.08 + 0.04 + 0.06) \cdot (0.6) = 0.\end{aligned}$$

This means that $P(G \cap B) = P(G) \cdot P(B)$ which means that the event G = Good is independent of the event B = Executed at department B.

4.11

(a) We use the formulas for splitting to see that

$$\begin{aligned}P(L) &= P(L|K25^-)P(K25^-) + P(L|K25-40)P(K25-40)\\&+P(L|K40^+)P(K40^+) + P(L|M25^-)P(M25^-)\\&+P(L|M25-40)P(M25-40) + P(L|M40^+)P(M40^+)\\&= 0.6 \cdot 0.15 + 0.3 \cdot 0.3 + 0.8 \cdot 0.15\\&+0.2 \cdot 0.2 + 0.4 \cdot 0.1 + 0.6 \cdot 0.1 = 44\%.\end{aligned}$$

(b) The women made up 60% of the participants, hence

$$P(K25^-|K) = \frac{P(K25^-)}{P(K)} = \frac{0.15}{0.60} = 25\%.$$

(c) The fraction of the women liking the product, we find from

$$\begin{aligned}P(L|K) &= P(L|K25^-)P(K25^-|K) + P(L|K25-40)P(K25-40|K)\\&+P(L|40^+)P(40^+|K)\\&= 0.6 \cdot \frac{0.15}{0.60} + 0.3 \cdot \frac{0.3}{0.60} + 0.8 \cdot \frac{0.15}{0.60} = 50\%.\end{aligned}$$

The fraction of the men liking the product, we find from

$$\begin{aligned}P(L|M) &= P(L|M25^-)P(M25^-|M) + P(L|M25-40)P(M25-40|M)\\&+P(L|40^+)P(40^+|M)\\&= 0.2 \cdot \frac{0.20}{0.40} + 0.4 \cdot \frac{0.1}{0.40} + 0.6 \cdot \frac{0.1}{0.40} = 35\%.\end{aligned}$$

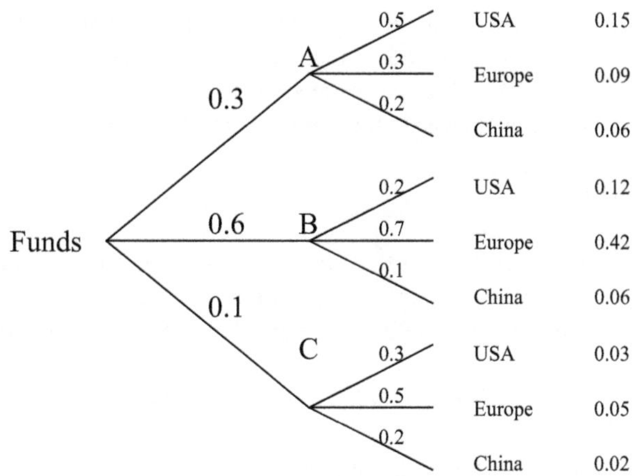

Fig. 6 Solution to Problem 4.12 (a)

4.12

(a) The result is displayed in Fig. 6.
(b) $P(\text{USA}|\text{Global}) = \frac{P(\text{USA}\cap\text{Global})}{P(\text{Global})} = \frac{0.15+0.12}{0.3+0.6} = 30\%$.
(c) $P(\text{Global A}|\text{USA}) = \frac{P(\text{USA}\cap\text{Global A})}{P(\text{USA})} = \frac{0.15}{0.15+0.12+0.03} = 50\%$.
(d) No. The customers may invest amounts of unequal size. If, e.g., 99 customers have invested a small amount in Global A, and one large investor the rest, the answer will be different from the case where everybody invested the same amount in all the different funds.

4.13

(a) Ignoring leap years, there are 243 possible days of birth from January 1 to August 31. This gives $P(\text{Category 1}) = \frac{243}{365} \approx 66.6\%$ and $P(\text{Category 2}) = \frac{122}{365} \approx 33.4\%$. (An answer based on months is sufficient). $P(\text{Yes}|\text{Category 1}) = 0.5$.
(b) We get the equation

$$\begin{aligned} P(\text{Yes}) &= P(\text{Yes}|\text{Category 1}) \cdot P(\text{Category 1}) \\ &\quad + P(\text{Yes}|\text{Category 2}) \cdot P(\text{Category 2}). \end{aligned}$$

Inserting the information provided in the text, we get

$$0.60 = 0.5 \cdot 0.666 + P(\text{Yes}|\text{Category 2}) \cdot 0.334$$

If we solve this equation, we find $P(\text{Yes}|\text{Category 2}) \approx 80\%$.

(c) The advantage of swapping is that twice as many will answer the relevant question. A disadvantage can be less feeling of anonymity. After swapping a majority will answer the sensitive question, and more might answer No hiding the true answer to the person who carries out the survey.

4.14

(a) We let I mean that the person has the illness, and $+$ denote that the test is positive. The information in the text says $P(+|I) = 0.77, P(+|I^c) = 0.02$ and that $P(I) = 0.02$. Hence $P(I^c) = 0.98$, and we find

$$P(+) = P(+|I) \cdot P(I) + P(+|I^c) \cdot P(I^c) = 0.77 \cdot 0.02 + 0.02 \cdot 0.98 = 3.5\%.$$

We use the result above to find

$$P(I|+) = \frac{P(+|I) \cdot P(I)}{P(+)} = \frac{0.77 \cdot 0.02}{0.035} = 44\%.$$

(b,c) If the person is not randomly selected, the analysis in (a) does not apply. If the person is tested because he or she has symptoms, the test is executed within a subpopulation where the probability of $P(I)$ can be much larger than 2%. In the most extreme case the symptoms can be so strong that we know for sure that the person has the illness, i.e., $P(I) = 1$, in which case $P(I|+) = 1$ as well. The probability that the person has the illness can hence be arbitrary large.

4.15 Let B denote the event "The company goes bankrupt," and let F denote the event "The company is flagged for bankruptcy." The information given in the text can be formulated as follows:

$$P(F|B) = 0.8, \qquad P(F^c|B^c) = 0.95.$$

(a) $P(F|B^c) = 1 - P(F^c|B^c) = 0.05 = 5\%$, i.e., 5% of the firms that do not go bankrupt are flagged for bankruptcy.

$$P(F) = P(F|B) \cdot P(B) + P(F|B^c) \cdot P(B^c) = 0.8 \cdot 0.1 + 0.05 \cdot 0.9 = 0.125 = 12.5\%.$$

The model will hence predict that 12.5% of the firms will go bankrupt.

(b) We use Bayes' formula to get

$$P(B|\,F) = \frac{P(B)}{P(F)} \cdot P(F|B) = \frac{0.1}{0.125} \cdot 0.8 = 0.64 = 64\%.$$

There is hence 64% probability a firm flagged for bankruptcy will in fact go bankrupt.

4.16

(a) (i) We have a time development Good-Good-Good. The probability of remaining good after one time step is 0.7, and the probability of this happening twice is $0.7 \cdot 0.7 = 49\%$.
  (ii) There are two possibilities: GGG with probability $0.7 \cdot 0.7 = 0.49$, and GBG with probability t $0.3 \cdot 0.2 = 0.06$. The total probability is 55%.

(b) There are 10 different variants. The first is *GGGGGGGGGD* with probability $0.7^9 \cdot 0.3$. All the 9 other variants have probability $0.7^8 \cdot 0.3 \cdot 0.2$. In total the probability becomes

$$0.7^9 \cdot 0.3 + 9 \cdot 0.7^8 \cdot 0.3 \cdot 0.2 = 4.32\%.$$

(c) Several different issues can be discussed here. Causes for things going bad are important for independence. If, e.g., the person has lost his or her job, it is likely that payments will continue to be bad. If the economy goes bad in general, it is likely that many customers will be affected, leading to dependence.

4.17

(a) In the first six months company A found 6% errors, while company B found 5% errors. Company A had hence the best results in the first six months. In the next six months company A found 3% errors, while company B found 2% errors. Company A had hence the largest probability of finding errors in the second half of the year.

  The year seen as a whole, company A found 3.6% errors, while company B found 4.4% errors. Company B hence have the best results for the year seen as a whole.

(b) The explanation is that there were a lot more errors in the first six months, and company B comes out as the overall winner since they focused their activity to the most important time period. Remark: The phenomenon is well known in statistics and is commonly referred to as the Yule-Simpson paradox.

4.18

(a) We use splitting to see that

$$\begin{aligned} P(A) &= P(A|B)P(B) + P(A|W)P(W) + P(A|S)P(S) \\ &= 0.025 \cdot 0.1 + 0.15 \cdot 0.15 + 0.30 \cdot 0.75 \\ &= 0.25 = 25\%. \end{aligned}$$

(b) Here we use Bayes' law

$$P(B|A) = P(A|B) \cdot \frac{P(B)}{P(A)} = 0.025 \cdot \frac{0.1}{0.25} = 0.01 = 1\%.$$

4.19 F = The company is flagged for bankruptcy. B = The company does in fact go bankrupt.

(a)

$$\begin{aligned} P(F) &= P(F|B)P(B) + P(F|B^c)P(B^c) = P(F|B) \cdot 0.001 + 0.05 \cdot 0.999 \\ &\leq 1 \cdot 0.001 + 0.05 \cdot 0.999 = 0.05095. \end{aligned}$$

(b)

$$P(B^c|\,F) = P(F|B^c) \cdot \frac{P(B^c)}{P(F)} = 0.05 \cdot \frac{0.999}{P(F)} \geq 0.05 \cdot \frac{0.999}{0.05095} = 0.9804.$$

This means that a huge majority of the firms that are flagged for bankruptcy will in fact not go bankrupt.

Remark The tool flags 5% of the companies that do not go bankrupt. As we can see from the calculations, this does not mean that 95% of the flags are correct. Quite the contrary, at least 98% of the flagged companies will not go bankrupt. Regrettably, this confusion of terms is a common misconception.

4.20

(a) Let p denote participation in the poll, and let up mean that the person would like to see an increase in taxes. Then

$$P(p) = P(p|up)P(up) + P(p|up^c)P(up^c) = 0.02 \cdot 0.6 + 0.07 \cdot 0.4 = 4\%.$$

(b) We use Bayes' law:

$$P(up|\,p) = P(p|up) \cdot \frac{P(up)}{P(p)} = 0.07 \cdot \frac{0.4}{0.04} = 70\%.$$

We see that 70% of the participants in the poll would like to see an increase in taxes, while a majority of the viewers do not want that.

4.21 We let S denote the event that the currency is strengthening, H denotes high economic growth, A denotes average economic growth, and L denotes low economic growth.

(a) From the splitting principle we get

$$\begin{aligned} P(S) &= P(S|H)P(H) + P(S|A)P(A) + P(S|L)P(L) \\ &= 0.7 \cdot 0.3 + 0.5 \cdot 0.5 + 0.2 \cdot 0.2 = 0.5 = 50\%. \end{aligned}$$

The probability of strengthening of the currency is hence 50%.

(b) We use Bayes' law and find

$$P(H|S) = P(S|H) \cdot \frac{P(H)}{P(S)} = 0.7 \cdot \frac{0.3}{0.5} = 0.42 = 42\%.$$

If the currency is strengthening, it is hence 42% probability of high economic growth.

(c) We have

$$\begin{aligned} &P(S \cap H) = P(S|H)P(H) = 0.7 \cdot 0.3 = 0.21 \\ &P(S) \cdot P(H) = 0.5 \cdot 0.3 = 0.15. \end{aligned}$$

Since the two values do not match, the events S and H are dependent.

4.22

(a)

$$\begin{aligned} P(debt) &= P(debt|spam)P(spam) + P(debt|spam^c)P(spam^c) \\ &= 0.309 \cdot 0.5 + 0.00447 \cdot 0.5 = 15.67\%. \end{aligned}$$

(b)

$$P(spam|debt) = P(debt|spam) \cdot \frac{P(spam)}{P(debt)} = 0.309 \cdot \frac{0.5}{0.1567} = 98.6\%.$$

4.23

(a) We define S: a tax payer is in the special group, F: the tax payer commits tax fraud. With this notation the information in the text can be stated as follows:

$$P(S) = 0.05, \qquad P(F) = 0.1, \qquad P(S|\, F^c) = 0.01.$$

(b)

$$P(S) = P(S|\, F)P(F) + P(S|\, F^c)P(S^c).$$

This leads us to the equation

$$0.05 = P(S|\, F) \cdot 0.1 + 0.01 \cdot 0.9.$$

Solving this equation, we find $P(S|\, F) = 0.41 = 41\%$.

(c) Bayes' rule gives

$$P(F|S) = P(S|\, F) \cdot \frac{P(F)}{P(S)} = 0.41 \cdot \frac{0.1}{0.05} = 82\%.$$

4.24

(a) $P(D|S18-24) = 3.6\%$, $P(S18-24) = 55/582 = 9.45\%$.

$$\begin{aligned} P(D|S) &= P(D|S18-24) \cdot P(S18-24) + P(D|S25-34) \cdot P(S25-34) \\ &+ P(D|S35-44) \cdot P(S35-44) + P(D|S45-54) \cdot P(S45-54) \\ &+ \cdots + P(D|S75+) \cdot P(S75+) \\ &= 0.036 \cdot \frac{55}{582} + 0.024 \cdot \frac{124}{582} + 0.128 \cdot \frac{109}{582} + 0.208 \cdot \frac{130}{582} \\ &+ 0.443 \cdot \frac{115}{582} + 0.806 \cdot \frac{36}{582} + 1.0 \cdot \frac{13}{582} = 23.87\%. \end{aligned}$$

(b) $P(D|NS18-24) = 1.6\%$, $P(NS18-24) = 62/734 = 8.45\%$.

$$\begin{aligned} P(D|NS) &= P(D|NS18-24) \cdot P(NS18-24) + P(D|NS25-34) \cdot P(NS25-34) \\ &+ P(D|NS35-44) \cdot P(NS35-44) + P(D|NS45-54) \cdot P(NS45-54) \\ &+ \cdots + P(D|NS75+) \cdot P(NS75+) \\ &= 0.16 \cdot \frac{62}{734} + 0.032 \cdot \frac{157}{734} + 0.057 \cdot \frac{123}{734} + 0.154 \cdot \frac{78}{734} \\ &+ 0.331 \cdot \frac{121}{734} + 0.783 \cdot \frac{129}{734} + 1.0 \cdot \frac{64}{734} = 31.35\%. \end{aligned}$$

(c) We see that the death rate for smokers (23.87%) is considerably lower than for nonsmokers (31.35%). If we compare the numbers in the tables, we see (with a marginal exception for the group 25–34) that the death rate for smokers is considerably higher than for nonsmokers. The reason why we come to the opposite conclusion for the groups seen as a whole is that there are relatively fewer elderly smokers among the participants. Regrettably, the elderly smokers were already dead when the sample was drawn.

Problems of Chap. 5

5.1 (i), (ii), (iii), (v), and (vi) all give out a real number as the result, and hence define random variables. The outcome of a soccer match, e.g., 2–2, is a pair of numbers and does not define a random variable (but the results for each team are random variables).

5.2

(a) The stock price can only have the values 95,100, and 110.
(b) The definition of the cumulative distribution is $F(x) = P(X \leq x)$. $F(90)$ is hence the probability that the stock price is at most 90 USD. Since the stock price is never less than 95 USD, $F(90) = 0$. Furthermore,

$$F(95) = 20\%, \quad F(100) = 20\% + 70\% = 90\%, \quad F(105) = 90\%,$$
$$F(110) = 20\% + 70\% + 10\% = 100\%, \quad F(115) = 100\%.$$

5.3

(a) There are 6 different outcomes: AA, BB, CC, AB, AC, BC. Note that AB and BA give the same outcome here. The probabilities of AA, BB, CC are all $\frac{1}{9}$, while the probabilities of AB, AC, BC are all $\frac{2}{9}$.
(b) AA gives $X = 200$, BB gives $X = 208$, CC gives $X = 204$, AB gives $X = 204$, AC gives $X = 202$, and BC gives $X = 206$. X can hence achieve 5 different values; $200, 202, 204, 206, 208$. The distribution of X is as follows:

$$P(X = 200) = \frac{1}{9}, \quad P(X = 202) = \frac{2}{9}, \quad P(X = 204) = \frac{3}{9},$$
$$P(X = 206) = \frac{2}{9}, \quad P(X = 208) = \frac{1}{9}.$$

(c) We find the cumulative distribution when we progressively add the values in the probability distribution, i.e.

$$F(200) = \frac{1}{9}, \quad F(202) = \frac{1}{9} + \frac{2}{9} = \frac{3}{9}, \quad F(204) = \frac{1}{9} + \frac{2}{9} + \frac{3}{9} = \frac{6}{9},$$
$$F(206) = \frac{1}{9} + \frac{2}{9} + \frac{3}{9} + \frac{2}{9} = \frac{8}{9}, \quad F(208) = \frac{1}{9} + \frac{2}{9} + \frac{3}{9} + \frac{2}{9} + \frac{1}{9} = 1.$$

The interpretation is that $F(x)$ is the probability that the value of the stocks is at most x USD.

5.4

(a) Regardless of outcome, X becomes an integer between 1 and 6 and is hence a random variable.
(b) We find the cumulative distribution when we progressively add the probabilities in the table, i.e.

$$\begin{aligned}
&F(1) = 55\%, \qquad F(2) = 55\% + 20\% = 75\%, \\
&F(3) = 55\% + 20\% + 10\% = 85\% \\
&F(4) = 55\% + 20\% + 10\% + 5\% = 90\%, \\
&F(5) = 55\% + 20\% + 10\% + 5\% + 5\% = 95\%, \\
&F(6) = 55\% + 20\% + 10\% + 5\% + 5\% + 5\% = 1.
\end{aligned}$$

When x is an integer, we can interpret $F(x)$ as the probability that the delivery time is at most x days.

$$\mathrm{E}[X] = 1 \cdot 0.55 + 2 \cdot 0.2 + 3 \cdot 0.1 + 4 \cdot 0.05 + 5 \cdot 0.05 + 6 \cdot 0.05 = 2.$$

The expected delivery time is hence 2 days.

5.5

(a) We have

$$\begin{aligned}
& P(4 \text{ or more errors}) \\
= \; & 1 - P(X = 0) - P(X = 1) - P(X = 2) - P(X = 3) \\
= \; & 1 - 0.65 - 0.25 - 0.05 - 0.05 = 0.
\end{aligned}$$

(b)

$$\mathrm{E}[X] = 0 \cdot 0.65 + 1 \cdot 0.25 + 2 \cdot 0.05 + 3 \cdot 0.05 = 0.5.$$

5.6

$$p(100) = \frac{140000}{400000} = 56\%, \qquad p(200) = \frac{50000}{400000} = 20\%,$$

$$p(300) = \frac{10000}{400000} = 4\%, \qquad p(400) = \frac{20000}{400000} = 8\%,$$

$$p(500) = \frac{30000}{400000} = 12\%.$$

$$\mathrm{E}[X] = 100 \cdot 0.56 + 200 \cdot 0.2 + 300 \cdot 0.04 + 400 \cdot 0.08 + 500 \cdot 0.12 = 200.$$

5.7

$$\mathrm{E}|X] = 0 \cdot 0.2 + 1 \cdot 0.2 + 2 \cdot 0.6 = 1.4.$$

$$\begin{aligned}\mathrm{Var}[X] &= \mathrm{E}[X^2] - \mathrm{E}[X]^2 \\ &= 0^2 \cdot 0.2 + 1^2 \cdot 0.2 + 2^2 \cdot 0.6 - 1.4^2 = 0.64.\end{aligned}$$

$$\sigma[X] = \sqrt{\mathrm{Var}[X]} = \sqrt{0.64} = 0.8.$$

5.8

$$\mathrm{E}|X] = 0 \cdot 0.025 + 1 \cdot 0.05 + 2 \cdot 0.825 + 3 \cdot 0.1 = 2.$$

$$\begin{aligned}\mathrm{Var}[X] &= \mathrm{E}[X^2] - \mathrm{E}[X]^2 \\ &= 0^2 \cdot 0.025 + 1^2 \cdot 0.05 + 2^2 \cdot 0.825 + 3^2 \cdot 0.1 - 2^2 = 0.25.\end{aligned}$$

$$\sigma[X] = \sqrt{\mathrm{Var}[X]} = \sqrt{0.25} = 0.5.$$

5.9

$$\mathrm{E}|X] = 1 \cdot 0.1 + 2 \cdot 0.1 + 3 \cdot 0.6 + 4 \cdot 0.1 + 5 \cdot 0.1 = 3.$$

$$\begin{aligned}\mathrm{Var}[X] &= \mathrm{E}[X^2] - \mathrm{E}[X]^2 \\ &= 1^2 \cdot 0.1 + 2^2 \cdot 0.1 + 3^2 \cdot 0.6 + 4^2 \cdot 0.1 + 5^2 \cdot 0.1 - 9^2 = 1.\end{aligned}$$

$$\sigma[X] = \sqrt{\mathrm{Var}[X]} = \sqrt{1} = 1.$$

5.10

(a)

$$\mathrm{E}[X_1 + X_2 + X_3] = \mathrm{E}[X_1] + \mathrm{E}[X_2] + \mathrm{E}[X_3] = 25 + 25 + 25 = 75.$$

(b)

$$\mathrm{E}[pX_1 + qX_2 + rX_3] = p\mathrm{E}[X_1] + q\mathrm{E}[X_2] + r\mathrm{E}[X_3] = 25(p + q + r) = 25.$$

5.11

$$\mathrm{E}[Y] = \mathrm{E}[pX + q \cdot 100] = p\mathrm{E}[X] + q \cdot 100 = p \cdot 100 + q \cdot 100 = 100(p+q) = 100.$$

$$\mathrm{Var}[Y] = \mathrm{Var}[pX + q \cdot 100] = \mathrm{Var}[pX] = p^2\mathrm{Var}[X] = 100p^2.$$

The variance becomes as small as possible when we choose $p = 0$ and $q = 1$.

5.12

(a)

$$\mathrm{E}[X] = 30 \cdot 0.6 + 90 \cdot 0.4 = 114.$$

(b) We need to solve

$$130 \cdot p + 90 \cdot (1 - p) = 120.$$

This implies

$$130p + 90 - 90p = 120 \Rightarrow 30p = 40,$$

which gives $p = 75\%$. The probability that the contract is accepted must be at least 75%.

5.13

(a) We first find $\mathrm{E}[X] = 1 \cdot 0.5 + 2 \cdot 0.3 + 3 \cdot 0.2 = 1.7$. That gives

$$\mathrm{E}[Z] = \mathrm{E}[X_1] + \mathrm{E}[X_2] + \mathrm{E}[X_3] = 1.7 + 1.7 + 1.7 = 5.1.$$

The expected waiting time is 5.1 min in this case.

(b)

$$P(Z \leq 7) = 1 - P(Z = 8) - P(Z = 9).$$

$Z = 8$ in the three cases $(X_1, X_2, X_3) = (3, 3, 2), (3, 2, 3), (2, 3, 3)$. That gives

$$P(Z = 8) = 0.2 \cdot 0.2 \cdot 0.3 + 0.2 \cdot 0.3 \cdot 0.2 + 0.3 \cdot 0.2 \cdot 0.2 = 0.036.$$

$Z = 9$ only in the case $(X_1, X_2, X_3) = (3, 3, 3)$, giving

$$P(Z = 9) = 0.2 \cdot 0.2 \cdot 0.2 = 0.008.$$

In total we get

$$P(Z \leq 7) = 1 - 0.036 - 0.008 = 95.6\%.$$

(c) Let W denote the new waiting time. $W = 1$ only occur if $X_1 = X_2 = 1$, and the probability for this is

$$P(W = 1) = 0.5 \cdot 0.5 = 0.25.$$

If $(X_1, X_2) = (1, 2), (2, 1), (2, 2)$, then $W = 2$. The probability for this is

$$0.5 \cdot 0.3 + 0.3 \cdot 0.5 + 0.3 \cdot 0.3 = 0.39.$$

In addition $W = 2$ if $(X_1, X_2, X_3) = (1, 3, 1), (3, 1, 1)$, and the probability for this is

$$0.5 \cdot 0.2 \cdot 0.5 + 0.2 \cdot 0.5 \cdot 0.5 = 0.1.$$

In total we get

$$P(W = 2) = 0.39 + 0.1 = 0.49.$$

$W = 3$ in all other cases. Hence

$$P(W = 3) = 1 - P(W = 1) - P(W = 2) = 1 - 0.25 - 0.49 = 0.26.$$

Hence

$$\mathrm{E}[W] = 1 \cdot 0.25 + 2 \cdot 0.49 + 3 \cdot 0.26 = 2.10.$$

5.14

(a) We use the following abbreviations U = unmarried, L = low income, G = good, B = payment difficulties.

$$P(UL) = P(UL|G)P(G) + P(UL|B)P(B) = 0.1 \cdot 0.75 + 0.50 \cdot 0.25 = 0.2.$$

Unmarried men with low income hence make up 20% of the customers.

$$P(B|UL) = P(UL|B) \cdot \frac{P(B)}{P(UL)} = 0.50 \cdot \frac{0.25}{0.2} = 0.625.$$

The probability that an unmarried man with low income has payment difficulties is hence 62.5%.

(b) First observe that $P(G|UL) = 1 - P(B|UL) = 0.375$. The expected profit by approving a loan is hence

$$\mathrm{E}[\text{profit}|UL] = 6000 \cdot 0.375 - 4000 \cdot 0.625 = -250.$$

It is hence not profitable to approve a loan. Remark: It is nevertheless not obvious that a decision to reject such customers is optimal. A policy of this kind can lead to a loss of goodwill that can be very costly, and such additional issues must be taken into account.

5.15

(a) We let x be the price for 100 options, y the number of stocks that the bank buys today, and z the number of USD that the bank lends from a bank account. We solve the system of equations:

$$\begin{aligned} y \cdot 100 &= x + z \\ y \cdot 120 - z - 20 \cdot 100 &= 0 \\ y \cdot 80 - z &= 0. \end{aligned}$$

This system of equations has the solution $x = 1000, y = 50, z = 4000$. The customer hence needs to pay 1000 USD, the bank buys 50 stocks and lends 4000 USD (free of charge) from a bank account. The bank then breaks even in both cases.

(b) We let Y be the value of the options tomorrow. The customer paid 1000 USD for the options, and the expected value for Y is

$$\mathrm{E}[Y] = p \cdot 2000 + q \cdot 0 = 2000p.$$

We solve the equation

$$2000p = 1000,$$

and find $p = 50\%$. The probability of a rise must then be at least 50% if the expected value of the stock is to exceed the price paid by the customer.

5.16

(a) We let x be the price for 100 options, y the number of stocks that the bank buys today, and z the number of USD that the bank lends from a bank account. We solve the system of equations:

$$\begin{aligned} y \cdot 100 &= x + z \\ y \cdot 110 - z - 10 \cdot 100 &= 0 \\ y \cdot 70 - z &= 0. \end{aligned}$$

This system of equations has the solution $x = 750, y = 25, z = 1750$. The customer hence needs to pay 750 USD, the bank buys 25 stocks and lends 1750

USD (free of charge) from a bank account. The bank then breaks even in both cases.

(b) We let Y be the value of the options tomorrow. The customer paid 750 USD for the options, and the expected value for Y is

$$E[Y] = p \cdot 1000 + q \cdot 0 = 1000p.$$

We solve the equation

$$1000p = 750,$$

and find $p = 75\%$. The probability of a rise must then be at least 75% if the expected value of the stock is to exceed the price paid by the customer.

5.17

(a) We let x be the price for 100 options, y the number of stocks that the bank buys today, and z the number of USD that the bank lends from a bank account. We solve the system of equations:

$$\begin{aligned} y \cdot 300 &= x + z \\ y \cdot 330 - z \cdot 1.05 - 30 \cdot 100 &= 0 \\ y \cdot 280 - z \cdot 1.05 &= 0. \end{aligned}$$

This system of equations has the solution $x = 2000, y = 60, z = 16{,}000$. The customer hence needs to pay 2000 USD, the bank buys 60 stocks and lends 16,000 USD (5% interest per day) from a bank account. The bank then breaks even in both cases.

5.18

(a) The result is displayed in Fig. 7.

$$E[X_2] = 120 \cdot 0.3 + 100 \cdot 0.2 + 100 \cdot 0.1 + 80 \cdot 0.4 = 98.$$

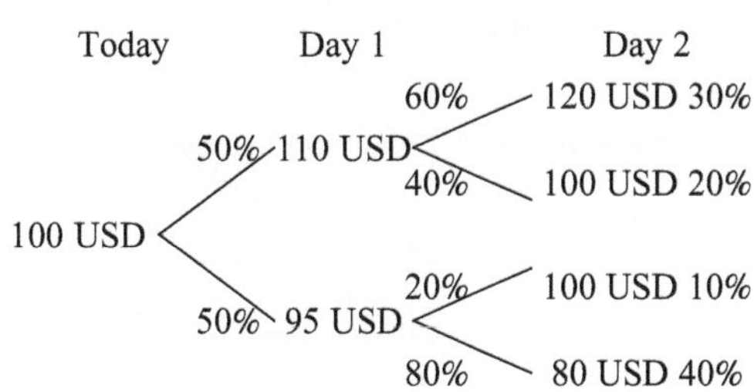

Fig. 7 Solution to Problem 5.18 (a)

Even though it might seem as if this is a bad investment, it will be clear from (b) that this is not the case. The investment is bad if the buyer stays inactive, but there is nothing preventing an active approach.

(b)

$$\begin{aligned} E[V] &= 1000 \cdot 120 \cdot 0.3 + 1000 \cdot 100 \cdot 0.2 \\ &+(500 \cdot 95 + 500 \cdot 100) \cdot 0.1 + (500 \cdot 95 + 500 \cdot 80) \cdot 0.4 \\ &= 100{,}750. \end{aligned}$$

An even better strategy is to sell all the stocks if they fall the first day. Then

$$\begin{aligned} E[V] &= 1000 \cdot 120 \cdot 0.3 + 1000 \cdot 100 \cdot 0.2 \\ &+1000 \cdot 95 \cdot 0.1 + 1000 \cdot 95 \cdot 0.4 \\ &= 103{,}500. \end{aligned}$$

5.19

(a) The equation $100y = x + z$ expresses that the bank uses $x + z$ USD to buy y stocks. The other four equations express that the bank must break even in all the four cases.
(b) The solution of the system is $x = 840, y = 54, z = 4560, u = 4, v = 39$.
(c) The probabilities for the four end states is

$$\begin{aligned} P(X_2 = 200) &= 0.6 \cdot 0.5 = 0.3, \\ P(X_2 = 80) &= 0.6 \cdot 0.5 = 0.3, \\ P(X_2 = 110) &= 0.4 \cdot 0.25 = 0.1, \\ P(X_2 = 70) &= 0.4 \cdot 0.75 = 0.3. \end{aligned}$$

The expected value of the 60 options is hence

$$60 \cdot 100 \cdot 0.3 + 60 \cdot 0 \cdot 0.3 + 60 \cdot 10 \cdot 0.1 + 60 \cdot 0 \cdot 0.3 = 1860.$$

5.20

(a) If $\beta = 0$, then

$$\text{Probability of buying object number } i = \frac{\exp[-\beta c_i]}{\sum_{j=1}^{5} \exp[-\beta c_j]} = \frac{1}{1+1+1+1+1} = \frac{1}{5},$$

which is a uniform distribution corresponding to the case where the buyer has no information. The expected cost is

$$20 \cdot \frac{1}{5} + 25 \cdot \frac{1}{5} + 22 \cdot \frac{1}{5} + 18 \cdot \frac{1}{5} + 30 \cdot \frac{1}{5} = 23.$$

(b) We insert $\beta = 0.5$ in the formula, and find

$$p_1 = 0.2395, \quad p_2 = 0.01966, \quad p_3 = 0.08812, \quad p_4 = 0.6511, \quad p_5 = 0.00161.$$

The expected cost becomes

$$20 \cdot 0.2395 + 25 \cdot 0.01966 + 22 \cdot 0.08812 + 18 \cdot 0.6511 + 30 \cdot 0.00161 = 18.99.$$

$$\begin{aligned} &\text{At least one buyer does not buy the cheapest item} \\ = &\ 1 - \text{Probability that they all buy the cheapest item} = 1 - 0.651088^4 \\ = &\ 82.03\%. \end{aligned}$$

When β increases (more information), the probability of buying the cheapest item increases, and the probability that at least one does not buy the cheapest item decreases.

(c) To find the limit we can multiply by $e^{18\beta}$ both in the nominator and the denominator:

$$\begin{aligned} &\text{The probability of buying item number 4} \\ = &\ \frac{\exp[-18\beta]}{\exp[-20\beta] + \exp[-25\beta] + \exp[-22\beta] + \exp[-18\beta]] + \exp[-30\beta]} \\ = &\ \frac{1}{\exp[-2\beta] + \exp[-7\beta] + \exp[-4\beta] + 1 + \exp[-12\beta]} \to 1. \end{aligned}$$

The same computation gives that the other probabilities approach zero. In the limit the buyer is fully informed and always buys the cheapest alternative. The expected cost is then 18.

5.21

(a)

$$P = 0.1 \cdot 0.2 \cdot 0.4 \cdot 0.1 \cdot 0.4 = 0.032\%.$$

Since the value of the product does not change when we rearrange the terms, we can (after completion of all choices) put the ones choosing 1 first, then the ones choosing 2, and so on, i.e.

$$P = \underbrace{0.1 \cdots 0.1}_{f_1} \cdot \underbrace{0.4 \cdots 0.4}_{f_2} \cdot \underbrace{0.2 \cdots 0.2}_{f_3} \cdot \underbrace{0.1 \cdots 0.1}_{f_4}.$$

The frequencies are just how many such terms we have of each type, and hence

$$P = 0.1^{f_1} 0.4^{f_2} 0.2^{f_3} 0.1^{f_4}.$$

If we change the choice probabilities, we can use the same argument to see that in general

$$P = p_1^{f_1} \cdot p_2^{f_2} \cdot p_3^{f_3} \cdot p_4^{f_4}.$$

(b) We notice that alternative number 3 has less utility than number 1, but larger probability. If $(f_1, f_2, f_3, f_4) = (5, 0, 0, 0)$, total utility is 15 while the probability is 0.1^5. If $(f_1, f_2, f_3, f_4) = (0, 0, 5, 0)$, total utility is 10 while the probability is 0.2^5. This contradicts our definition of bounded rationality. These agents are *not* boundedly rational, they are irrational.

5.22

(a)

$$p_1 = \frac{2^{-1}}{5} = 0.1, \qquad p_2 = \frac{2^1}{5} = 0.4, \qquad p_3 = \frac{2^1}{5} = 0.4, \qquad p_4 = \frac{2^{-1}}{5} = 0.1.$$

(b)

$$\begin{aligned} P &= p_1^{f_1} \cdot p_2^{f_2} \cdot p_3^{f_3} \cdot p_4^{f_4} \\ &= \left(\frac{2^{u_1}}{5}\right)^{f_1} \left(\frac{2^{u_2}}{5}\right)^{f_2} \left(\frac{2^{u_3}}{5}\right)^{f_3} \left(\frac{2^{u_4}}{5}\right)^{f_4} \\ &= \frac{2^{f_1 u_1 + f_2 u_2 + f_3 u_3 + f_4 u_4}}{5^{f_1 + f_2 + f_3 + f_4}} = \frac{2^{f_1 u_1 + f_2 u_2 + f_3 u_3 + f_4 u_4}}{5^n}. \end{aligned}$$

since $f_1 + f_2 + f_3 + f_4 = n$.

(c) Assume that $U_1 < U_2$ where

$$\begin{aligned} U_1 &= f_1^{(1)} u_1 + f_2^{(1)} u_2 + f_3^{(1)} u_3 + f_4^{(1)} u_4 \\ U_2 &= f_1^{(2)} u_1 + f_2^{(2)} u_2 + f_3^{(2)} u_3 + f_4^{(2)} u_4. \end{aligned}$$

Then

$$P^{(1)} = \frac{2^{U_1}}{5^n} < \frac{2^{U_2}}{5^n} = P^{(2)}.$$

This means that all outcomes with frequencies $(f_1^{(1)}, f_2^{(1)}, f_3^{(1)}, f_4^{(1)})$ are less probable that outcomes with frequencies $(f_1^{(2)}, f_2^{(2)}, f_3^{(2)}, f_4^{(2)})$. Smaller total utility implies smaller probability for those outcomes. The agents are hence boundedly rational according to our definition.

5.23

(a) If the order $B = 10$, the deviations become $0, 10, 20, 30, 40$, each with probability 1/5. This gives

$$\mathrm{E}[A|B = 10] = 0 \cdot \frac{1}{5} + 10 \cdot \frac{1}{5} + 20 \cdot \frac{1}{5} + 30 \cdot \frac{1}{5} + 40 \cdot \frac{1}{5} = 20.$$

(b) If $B = 20$, we get deviations $10, 0, 10, 20, 30$ in the 5 cases. This gives

$$\mathrm{E}[A|B = 20] = 10 \cdot \frac{1}{5} + 0 \cdot \frac{1}{5} + 10 \cdot \frac{1}{5} + 20 \cdot \frac{1}{5} + 30 \cdot \frac{1}{5} = 14.$$

If $B = 30$, we get deviations $20, 10, 0, 10, 20$ in the 5 cases. This gives

$$\mathrm{E}[A|B = 30] = 20 \cdot \frac{1}{5} + 10 \cdot \frac{1}{5} + 0 \cdot \frac{1}{5} + 10 \cdot \frac{1}{5} + 20 \cdot \frac{1}{5} = 12.$$

If $B = 40$, we get deviations $30, 20, 10, 0, 10$ in the 5 cases. This gives

$$\mathrm{E}[A|B = 40] = 30 \cdot \frac{1}{5} + 20 \cdot \frac{1}{5} + 10 \cdot \frac{1}{5} + 0 \cdot \frac{1}{5} + 10 \cdot \frac{1}{5} = 14.$$

If $B = 50$, we get deviations $40, 30, 20, 10, 0$ in the 5 cases. This gives

$$\mathrm{E}[A|B = 50] = 40 \cdot \frac{1}{5} + 30 \cdot \frac{1}{5} + 20 \cdot \frac{1}{5} + 10 \cdot \frac{1}{5} + 0 \cdot \frac{1}{5} = 20.$$

We see, not surprisingly, that we get the smallest expected deviation if we order 30 units of the good.

(c) Here we need to consider all the variants that can occur. The formula for splitting gives

$$\begin{aligned} P(A_2 = 10) &= P(A_2 = 10|D_1 = 10)P(D_1 = 10) + P(A_2 = 10|D_1 = 20)P(D_1 = 20) \\ &\quad + P(A_2 = 10|D_1 = 30)P(D_1 = 30) + P(A_2 = 10|D_1 = 40)P(D_1 = 40) \end{aligned}$$

$$+P(A_2 = 10|D_1 = 50)P(D_1 = 50)$$
$$= \frac{1}{5} \cdot \frac{1}{5} + \frac{2}{5} \cdot \frac{1}{5} + \frac{2}{5} \cdot \frac{1}{5} + \frac{2}{5} \cdot \frac{1}{5} + \frac{1}{5} \cdot \frac{1}{5} = \frac{8}{25}.$$

(d) The principle is the same as in (c), but requires more work. The answers become:

$$P(A_2 = 0) = \frac{1}{5} \cdot \frac{1}{5} + \frac{1}{5} \cdot \frac{1}{5} + \frac{1}{5} \cdot \frac{1}{5} + \frac{1}{5} \cdot \frac{1}{5} + \frac{1}{5} \cdot \frac{1}{5} = \frac{5}{25}.$$

$$P(A_2 = 20) = \frac{1}{5} \cdot \frac{1}{5} + \frac{1}{5} \cdot \frac{1}{5} + \frac{2}{5} \cdot \frac{1}{5} + \frac{1}{5} \cdot \frac{1}{5} + \frac{1}{5} \cdot \frac{1}{5} = \frac{6}{25}.$$

$$P(A_2 = 30) = \frac{1}{5} \cdot \frac{1}{5} + \frac{1}{5} \cdot \frac{1}{5} + \frac{0}{5} \cdot \frac{1}{5} + \frac{1}{5} \cdot \frac{1}{5} + \frac{1}{5} \cdot \frac{1}{5} = \frac{4}{25}.$$

$$P(A_2 = 40) = \frac{1}{5} \cdot \frac{1}{5} + \frac{0}{5} \cdot \frac{1}{5} + \frac{0}{5} \cdot \frac{1}{5} + \frac{0}{5} \cdot \frac{1}{5} + \frac{1}{5} \cdot \frac{1}{5} = \frac{2}{25}.$$

This gives

$$\mathrm{E}[A_2] = 0 \cdot \frac{5}{25} + 10 \cdot \frac{8}{25} + 20 \cdot \frac{6}{25} + 30 \cdot \frac{4}{25} + 40 \cdot \frac{2}{25} = 16.$$

We see that this strategy is relatively bad. It is not the worst strategy, but is inferior to the second best strategy in (b). A strategy of this kind can be a good idea if there is strong positive correlation between the demands in the two periods, but that is not the case here.

Problems of Chap. 6

6.1

(a)

$$P_X(1) = 3\% + 7\% + 6\% + 9\% + 3\% = 28\%,$$

$$P_X(2) = 2\% + 6\% + 5\% + 15\% + 9\% = 37\%,$$

$$P_X(3) = 2\% + 3\% + 8\% + 10\% + 12\% = 35\%,$$

$$P_Y(0) = 3\% + 2\% + 2\% = 7\%,$$

$$P_Y(1) = 7\% + 6\% + 3\% = 16\%,$$

$$P_Y(2) = 6\% + 5\% + 8\% = 19\%,$$

$$P_Y(3) = 9\% + 15\% + 10\% = 34\%,$$

$$P_Y(4) = 3\% + 9\% + 12\% = 24\%.$$

(b)

$$P(X \geq 1) = 1 - P_X(1) = 1 - 28\% = 72\%.$$

(c)

$$P(Y \geq 2) = P_Y(2) + P_Y(3) + P_Y(4) = 19\% + 34\% + 24\% = 77\%.$$

6.2

(a)

$$P_X(9,00) = 27\% + 4\% + 2\% = 33\%,$$

$$P_X(9,10) = 5\% + 22\% + 6\% = 33\%,$$

$$P_X(9,20) = 3\% + 8\% + 23\% = 34\%,$$

$$P_Y(9,00) = 27\% + 5\% + 3\% = 35\%,$$

$$P_Y(9,10) = 4\% + 22\% + 8\% = 34\%,$$

$$P_Y(9,20) = 2\% + 6\% + 23\% = 31\%.$$

(b)

$$P(X = Y) = 27\% + 22\% + 23\% = 72\%.$$

(c)

$$\mathrm{E}[X] = 9.00 \cdot 0.33 + 9.10 \cdot 0.33 + 9.20 \cdot 0.34 = 9.101.$$

$$\mathrm{E}[Y] = 9.00 \cdot 0.35 + 9.10 \cdot 0.34 + 9.20 \cdot 0.31 = 9.096.$$

6.3

(a)

$$P_X(80) = 10\% + 30\% = 40\%,$$

$$P_X(120) = 20\% + 40\% = 60\%,$$

$$P_Y(80) = 10\% + 20\% = 30\%,$$

$$P_Y(120) = 30\% + 40\% = 70\%.$$

(b) X and Y are not independent. For example

$$P_X(80) \cdot P_Y(80) = 0.4 \cdot 0.3 = 0.12 \neq 0.1 = P(80, 80).$$

(c)

$$\mathrm{E}[X] = 80 \cdot 0.4 + 120 \cdot 0.6 = 104.$$

$$\mathrm{E}[Y] = 80 \cdot 0.3 + 120 \cdot 0.7 = 108.$$

6.4

(a)

$$P_X(0) = 5\% + 35\% = 40\%,$$

$$P_X(1) = 10\% + 20\% = 30\%,$$

$$P_X(2) = 20\% + 10\% = 30\%,$$

$$P_Y(100) = 5\% + 10\% + 20\% = 35\%,$$

$$P_Y(240) = 35\% + 20\% + 10\% = 65\%.$$

(b)

$$\mathrm{E}[X] = 0 \cdot 0.4 + 1 \cdot 0.3 + 2 \cdot 0.3 = 0.9.$$

$$\mathrm{E}[Y] = 100 \cdot 0.35 + 240 \cdot 0.65 = 191.$$

(c)

$$\begin{aligned} \text{E}[X \cdot Y] &= 0 \cdot 100 \cdot 0.05 + 0 \cdot 240 \cdot 0.35 \\ &+1 \cdot 100 \cdot 0.10 + 1 \cdot 240 \cdot 0.20 \\ &+2 \cdot 100 \cdot 0.20 + 2 \cdot 240 \cdot 0.10 = 146. \end{aligned}$$

$$\text{Cov}[X, Y] = \text{E}[X \cdot Y] - \text{E}[X] \cdot \text{E}[Y] = 146 - 191 \cdot 0.9 = -25.9.$$

6.5

(a)

$$P_X(20) = 25\% + 15\% = 40\%,$$

$$P_X(30) = 45\% + 15\% = 60\%,$$

$$P_Y(34) = 25\% + 45\% = 70\%,$$

$$P_Y(24) = 15\% + 15\% = 30\%.$$

(b)

$$\text{E}[X] = 20 \cdot 0.4 + 30 \cdot 0.6 = 26.$$

$$\text{Var}[X] = 20^2 \cdot 0.4 + 30^2 \cdot 0.6 - 26^2 = 24.$$

$$\text{E}[Y] = 34 \cdot 0.7 + 24 \cdot 0.3 = 31.$$

$$\text{Var}[Y] = 34^2 \cdot 0.7 + 24^2 \cdot 0.3 - 31^2 = 21.$$

(c)

$$\begin{aligned} \text{E}[X \cdot Y] &= 20 \cdot 34 \cdot 0.25 + 20 \cdot 24 \cdot 0.15 \\ &+30 \cdot 34 \cdot 0.45 + 30 \cdot 24 \cdot 0.15 = 809. \end{aligned}$$

$$\text{Cov}[X, Y] = \text{E}[X \cdot Y] - \text{E}[X] \cdot \text{E}[Y] = 809 - 26 \cdot 31 = 3.$$

$$\rho[X, Y] = \frac{\text{Cov}[X, Y]}{\sqrt{\text{Var}[X] \cdot \text{Var}[Y]}} = \frac{3}{\sqrt{24 \cdot 21}} = 0.134.$$

6.6

(a)

$$P_X(10) = 20\%,$$

$$P_X(12) = 50\%,$$

$$P_X(15) = 30\%,$$

$$P_Y(50) = 20\%,$$

$$P_Y(40) = 50\%,$$

$$P_Y(25) = 30\%.$$

(b)

$$\mathrm{E}[X] = 20 \cdot 0.2 + 24 \cdot 0.5 + 30 \cdot 0.3 = 25.$$

$$\mathrm{E}[Y] = 100 \cdot 0.2 + 80 \cdot 0.5 + 50 \cdot 0.3 = 75.$$

(c)

$$\mathrm{E}[X \cdot Y] = 20 \cdot 100 \cdot 0.2 + 24 \cdot 80 \cdot 0.5 + 30 \cdot 50 \cdot 0.30 = 1810.$$

$$\mathrm{Cov}[X, Y] = \mathrm{E}[X \cdot Y] - \mathrm{E}[X] \cdot \mathrm{E}[Y] = 1810 - 25 \cdot 75 = -65.$$

(d)

$$\mathrm{Var}[X] = 20^2 \cdot 0.2 + 24^2 \cdot 0.5 + 30^2 \cdot 0.3 - 25^2 = 13$$

$$\mathrm{Var}[Y] = 100^2 \cdot 0.2 + 80^2 \cdot 0.5 + 50^2 \cdot 0.3 - 75^2 = 325.$$

$$\rho[X, Y] = \frac{\mathrm{Cov}[X, Y]}{\sqrt{\mathrm{Var}[X] \cdot \mathrm{Var}[Y]}} = \frac{-65}{\sqrt{13 \cdot 325}} = -1.$$

Y is a linear function of X. Using the two-point formula for a straight line, we find

$$Y = 200 - 10X.$$

6.7

(a)

$$E[Y] = 100 + 120 + 90 + 115 = 425.$$

Since X_1, X_2, X_3, X_4 all are independent, we get

$$\begin{aligned} \text{Var}[Y] &= \text{Var}[X_1 + X_2 + X_3 + X_4] \\ &= \text{Var}[X_1] + \text{Var}[X_2] + \text{Var}[X_3] + \text{Var}[X_4] \\ &= 230 + 170 + 260 + 240 = 900. \end{aligned}$$

(b) Note that $\text{Var}[X_1] = E[X_1^2] - E[X_1]^2$ gives

$$E[X_1^2] = \text{Var}[X_1] + E[X_1]^2 = 10{,}230.$$

$$\begin{aligned} E[X_1 \cdot Y] &= E[X_1^2 + X_1X_2 + X_1X_3 + X_1X_4] \\ &= E[X_1^2] + E[X_1] \cdot E[X_2] + E[X_1] \cdot E[X_3] + E[X_1] \cdot E[X_4] \\ &= 10230 + 100 \cdot 120 + 100 \cdot 90 + 100 \cdot 115 \\ &= 42{,}730. \end{aligned}$$

$$\text{Cov}[X_1, Y] = E[X_1 \cdot Y] - E[X_1] \cdot E[Y] = 42{,}730 - 100 \cdot 425 = 230.$$

Since $\text{Cov}[X_1, Y] \neq 0$, X_1 and Y are not independent.

6.8

(a)

$$\begin{aligned} &P(X = 90) = 0.3, \quad P(X = 150) = 0.4, \quad P(X = 210) = 0.3, \\ &P(Y = 10) = 0.3, \quad P(Y = 12) = 0.4, \quad P(Y = 20) = 0.3. \end{aligned}$$

This gives $E[X] = 150$ and $E[Y] = 15$.

(b) $E[X \cdot Y] = 2190$. Since $E[X] \cdot E[Y] = 150 \cdot 15 = 2250 \neq 2190 = E[X \cdot Y]$, X and Y cannot be independent.

(c) If $Y = 10$, the expected trade volume is 1700, $Y = 15$ gives expected trade volume 2250, and $Y = 20$ gives expected trade volume 2600. The largest expected trade volume occurs when $Y = 20$. It is not necessarily so that the highest price implies the largest trade volume. If, e.g., the joint distribution is as in Table 4, then expected trade volume is 1800 when $Y = 20$. As the other expected trade volumes do not change, maximum is obtained at $Y = 15$.

Table 4 Example of a joint distribution

Number of units bought/Price	10 USD	15 USD	20USD
90	5%	10%	30%
150	10%	20%	0%
210	15%	10%	0%

6.9

(a)

$$P(X = 110{,}000) = 10\% + 25\% + 15\% = 50\%,$$

$$P(X = 150{,}000) = 15\% + 25\% + 10\% = 50\%,$$

$$\mathrm{E}[X] = 110{,}000 \cdot 0.5 + 150{,}000 \cdot 0.5 = 130{,}000.$$

$$P(Y = 100) = 10\% + 15\% = 25\%,$$

$$P(Y = 120) = 25\% + 25\% = 50\%,$$

$$P(Y = 140) = 15\% + 10\% = 25\%,$$

$$\mathrm{E}[Y] = 100 \cdot 0.25 + 120 \cdot 0.5 + 140 \cdot 0.25 = 120.$$

(b)

$$P(X = 110{,}000 | Y = 100) = \frac{0.1}{0.25} = 0.4,$$

$$P(X = 150{,}000 | Y = 100) = \frac{0.15}{0.25} = 0.6,$$

$$P(X = 110{,}000 | Y = 120) = \frac{0.25}{0.5} = 0.5,$$

$$P(X = 150{,}000 | Y = 120) = \frac{0.25}{0.5} = 0.5,$$

$$P(X = 110{,}000 | Y = 140) = \frac{0.15}{0.25} = 0.6,$$

$$P(X = 150{,}000 | Y = 140) = \frac{0.10}{0.25} = 0.4,$$

$$P(Y = 100|X = 110{,}000) = \frac{0.10}{0.5} = 0.2,$$

$$P(Y = 120|X = 110{,}000) = \frac{0.25}{0.5} = 0.5,$$

$$P(Y = 140|X = 110{,}000) = \frac{0.15}{0.5} = 0.3,$$

$$P(Y = 100|X = 150{,}000) = \frac{0.15}{0.5} = 0.3,$$

$$P(Y = 120|X = 150{,}000) = \frac{0.25}{0.5} = 0.5,$$

$$P(Y = 140|X = 150{,}000) = \frac{0.10}{0.5} = 0.2.$$

(c)

$$E[X|\,Y = 100] = 110{,}000 \cdot 0.4 + 150{,}000 \cdot 0.6 = 134{,}000,$$

$$E[X|\,Y = 120] = 110{,}000 \cdot 0.5 + 150{,}000 \cdot 0.5 = 130{,}000,$$

$$E[X|\,Y = 140] = 110{,}000 \cdot 0.6 + 150{,}000 \cdot 0.4 = 126{,}000,$$

$$E[Y|X = 110{,}000] = 100 \cdot 0.2 + 120 \cdot 0.5 + 140 \cdot 0.3 = 122,$$

$$E[Y|X = 150{,}000] = 100 \cdot 0.3 + 120 \cdot 0.5 + 140 \cdot 0.2 = 118.$$

(d) No. If X and Y are independent, then, e.g., the conditional expectation $E[X|\,Y = y]$ will *not* change with y, and here we see that the value changes. In this market there is a clear tendency of high turnover when the price is low, and low turnover when the price is high.

6.10

(a)

$$E[X] = 1 \cdot 0.3 + 0 \cdot 0.4 + 0 \cdot 0.3 = 0.3,$$
$$E[Y] = 0 \cdot 0.3 + 1 \cdot 0.4 + 0 \cdot 0.3 = 0.4,$$
$$E[Z] = 0 \cdot 0.3 + 0 \cdot 0.4 + 1 \cdot 0.3 = 0.3.$$

$$E[X^2] = 1^2 \cdot 0.3 + 0^2 \cdot 0.4 + 0^2 \cdot 0.3 = 0.3,$$
$$E[Y^2] = 0^2 \cdot 0.3 + 1^2 \cdot 0.4 + 0^2 \cdot 0.3 = 0.4,$$
$$E[Z^2] = 0^2 \cdot 0.3 + 0^2 \cdot 0.4 + 1^2 \cdot 0.3 = 0.3.$$

That gives

$$\text{Var}[X] = E[X^2] - E[X]^2 = 0.21,$$
$$\text{Var}[Y] = E[Y^2] - E[Y]^2 = 0.24,$$
$$\text{Var}[Z] = E[Z^2] - E[Z]^2 = 0.21.$$

(b)

$$E[X \cdot Y] = 1 \cdot 0 \cdot 0.3 + 0 \cdot 1 \cdot 0.4 + 0 \cdot 0 \cdot 0.3 = 0.$$

$$\text{Cov}[X, Y] = E[X \cdot Y] - E[X] \cdot E[Y] = -0.12.$$

When two variables are independent, the covariance is always zero. Since this is not the case here, X and Y are *not* independent. The joint distribution is shown in Table 5.

6.11

(a) When we invest $p \cdot 10{,}000{,}000$ USD in company A, we get in all

$$\frac{p \cdot 10{,}000{,}000}{100} = 10^5 \cdot p$$

stocks in the company. The value of those stocks one year from now is

$$10^5 \cdot p \cdot X.$$

Correspondingly the values of the stocks in company B becomes

$$10^5 \cdot (1 - p) \cdot Y.$$

Table 5 The joint distribution in Problem 6.10

	$Y = 0$	$Y = 1$
$X = 0$	0.3	0.4
$X = 1$	0.3	0

(b)

$$\begin{aligned}E[Z] &= E[10^5 \cdot p \cdot X + 10^5 \cdot (1-p) \cdot Y] \\ &= 10^5 \cdot p \cdot E[X] + 10^5 \cdot (1-p) \cdot E[Y] \\ &= 10^7 p + 10^7(1-p) = 10^7.\end{aligned}$$

Since X and Y are independent, pX and $(1-p)Y$ are independent. Then

$$\begin{aligned}\text{Var}[Z] &= 10^{10}\text{Var}[p \cdot X + (1-p)Y] = 10^{10}(p^2\text{Var}[X] + (1-p)^2\text{Var}[Y]) \\ &= 10^{12}(p^2 + 4(1-p)^2).\end{aligned}$$

(c) We need to find the minimum of

$$f(p) = p^2 + 4(1-p)^2.$$

Since this function is a parabola, we find the minimum where $f'(p) = 0$.

$$f'(p) = 2p - 8(1-p) = 10p - 8 = 0.$$

This gives $p = 80\%$. We should invest 8 million in company A and 2 million in company B.

6.12

(a) Since each stock costs 100 USD, we are to buy 100,000 stocks. For each percent we invest, we get 1000 stocks. We hence buy $1000x$ stocks in company A, $1000y$ stocks in company B, and $1000z$ stocks in company C. The total value V becomes

$$\begin{aligned}V &= \text{number of stocks in A} \cdot \text{price per stock A} \\ &\quad + \text{number of stocks in B} \cdot \text{price per stock B} \\ &\quad + \text{number of stocks in C} \cdot \text{price per stock C} \\ &= 1000x \cdot X + 1000y \cdot Y + 1000z \cdot Z.\end{aligned}$$

$$\begin{aligned}E[V] &= E[1000x \cdot X + 1000y \cdot Y + 1000z \cdot Z] \\ &= 1000xE[X] + 1000yE[Y] + 1000zE[Z] \\ &= 1000 \cdot 120 \cdot (x + y + z) = 12{,}000{,}000.\end{aligned}$$

since $x + y + z = 100$.

(b) Since the stocks in A have the smallest variance, we should buy more of these stocks than the others.

(c) We first compute the variance of V:

$$\begin{aligned}\text{Var}[V] &= \text{Var}[1000x \cdot X + 1000y \cdot Y + 1000z \cdot Z] \\ &= 1{,}000{,}000x^2\text{Var}[X] + 1{,}000{,}000y^2\text{Var}[Y] + 1{,}000{,}000z^2\text{Var}[Z] \\ &= 100{,}000{,}000(x^2 + 2y^2 + 6z^2).\end{aligned}$$

We have to find x, y, z such that $x^2 + 2y^2 + 6z^2$ is as small as possible. Since $z = 100 - x - y$, we can find the minimum for the function

$$f(x, y) = x^2+2y^2+6(100-x-y)^2 = 60000-1200x+7x^2-1200y+12xy+8y^2.$$

We compute the partial derivatives to get the system

$$\begin{aligned}14x + 12y &= 1200 \\ 12x + 16y &= 1200.\end{aligned}$$

This system of equations has the solution $x = 60, y = 30$, which gives the minimum of the function. If we want that the variance is as small as possible, we should invest 60% in company A, 30% in company B, and 10% in company C. We see that we invest most of the money in A (as indicated by (b)), but we also need to invest some of the money in the other companies.

(d) Since $\text{E}[\epsilon] = 0$, then $\text{E}[X] = \text{E}[Y] = \text{E}[Z] = 120$ as before. If we use the rule

$$\text{Var}[a + b\epsilon] = b^2\text{Var}[\epsilon],$$

we get

$$\text{Var}[X] = 100, \text{Var}[Y] = 200, \text{Var}[Z] = 600,$$

as in (b) and (c).

(e) We insert the expressions for X, Y, and Z into the formula to get:

$$\begin{aligned}V &= 1000x \cdot X + 1000y \cdot Y + 1000z \cdot Z \\ &= 1000x(120 + 10\epsilon) + 1000y(120 + 10\sqrt{2}\epsilon) + 1000z(120 + 10\sqrt{6}\epsilon)) \\ &= 120{,}000(x + y + z) + 10{,}000(x + \sqrt{2} \cdot y + \sqrt{6} \cdot z)\epsilon \\ &= 12{,}000{,}000 + 10{,}000(x + \sqrt{2} \cdot y + \sqrt{6} \cdot z)\epsilon.\end{aligned}$$

In this case

$$\text{Var}[V] = 100{,}000{,}000(x + \sqrt{2} \cdot y + \sqrt{6} \cdot z)^2.$$

This function has its minimum in $x = 100, y = 0, z = 0$. In this particular case we get minimum variance when we invest all the money in A. This agrees with the result from (b). Here the stock prices are 100% correlated and there is nothing to gain by diversifying the investments as we did in (c).

Remark ϵ can be viewed as a market indicator. "Things are going well" when this indicator is positive, but correspondingly bad when it is negative. Company A is the company where the indicator has least influence, and we get minimum variance when we invest all the money there. If short-sale had been permitted, we could have eliminated almost all variation if we, e.g., bought about 169,000 stocks in company A, while at the same time shorting about 69,000 stocks in company C.

Problems of Chap. 7

7.1 This is a binomial distribution with $p = 10\%$ and $n = 9$.

(a) We use the table and find

$$\begin{aligned} P(X \leq 3) &= P(X = 0) + P(X = 1) + P(X = 2) + P(X = 3) \\ &= 0.3874 + 0.3874 + 0.1722 + 0.0446 = 99.16\%. \end{aligned}$$

(b) We use the table and find

$$P(X \geq 2) = 1 - P(X = 0) - P(X = 1) = 1 - 0.3874 - 0.3874 = 22.52\%.$$

(c)

$$\mathrm{E}[X] = n \cdot p = 9 \cdot 0.1 = 0.9,$$

$$\mathrm{Var}[X] = n \cdot p(1 - p) = 9 \cdot 0.1 \cdot 0.9 = 0.81,$$

$$\sigma[X] = \sqrt{\mathrm{Var}[X]} = \sqrt{0.81} = 0.9.$$

7.2 This is a binomial distribution with $p = 2\%$ and $n = 25$.

(a)

$$\begin{aligned} P(X \leq 1) &= P(X = 0) + P(X = 1) \\ &= \binom{25}{0} p^0 (1 - p)^{25} + \binom{25}{1} p^1 (1 - p)^{24} \\ &= 0.6035 + 0.3079 = 91.14\%. \end{aligned}$$

(b)

$$P(X \geq 1) = 1 - P(X = 0) = 1 - 0.6035 = 39.65\%.$$

(c)

$$\mathrm{E}[X] = n \cdot p = 25 \cdot 0.02 = 0.5,$$

$$\mathrm{Var}[X] = n \cdot p(1-p) = 25 \cdot 0.02 \cdot 0.98 = 0.49,$$

$$\sigma[X] = \sqrt{\mathrm{Var}[X]} = \sqrt{0.49} = 0.7.$$

7.3 This is a binomial distribution with $p = 20\%$ and $n = 16$.

(a)

$$P(X = 3) = \binom{16}{3} p^3 (1-p)^{13} = 24.63\%.$$

(b)

$$\mathrm{E}[X] = n \cdot p = 16 \cdot 0.2 = 3.2,$$

$$\mathrm{Var}[X] = n \cdot p(1-p) = 16 \cdot 0.2 \cdot 0.8 = 2.56,$$

$$\sigma[X] = \sqrt{\mathrm{Var}[X]} = \sqrt{2.56} = 1.6.$$

7.4 This is a hypergeometric distribution with $n = 8, M = 13$, and $N = 26$.

(a)

$$P(X = 4) = \frac{\binom{13}{4}\binom{26-13}{8-4}}{\binom{26}{8}} = 32.72\%.$$

(b)

$$\begin{aligned} P(X \geq 2) &= 1 - P(X = 0) - P(X = 1) \\ &= 1 - \frac{\binom{13}{0}\binom{26-13}{8-0}}{\binom{26}{8}} - \frac{\binom{13}{1}\binom{26-13}{8-1}}{\binom{26}{8}} = 98.49\%. \end{aligned}$$

(c)

$$\mathrm{E}[X] = n \cdot \frac{M}{N} = 8 \cdot \frac{13}{26} = 4,$$

$$\begin{aligned}\mathrm{Var}[X] &= \frac{N-n}{N-1} \cdot n \cdot \frac{M}{N} \cdot \left(1 - \frac{M}{N}\right) \\ &= \frac{26-8}{26-1} \cdot 8 \cdot \frac{13}{26} \cdot \left(1 - \frac{13}{26}\right) = 1.44, \\ \sigma[X] &= \sqrt{\mathrm{Var}[X]} = \sqrt{1.44} = 1.2.\end{aligned}$$

7.5 This is a hypergeometric distribution with $n = 20, M = 13$, and $N = 65$.

(a)

$$\begin{aligned}P(X \geq 2) &= 1 - P(X = 0) - P(X = 1) \\ &= 1 - \frac{\binom{13}{0}\binom{65-13}{20-0}}{\binom{65}{20}} - \frac{\binom{13}{1}\binom{65-13}{20-1}}{\binom{65}{20}} = 96.05\%.\end{aligned}$$

(b)

$$\mathrm{E}[X] = n \cdot \frac{M}{N} = 20 \cdot \frac{13}{65} = 4,$$

$$\begin{aligned}\mathrm{Var}[X] &= \frac{N-n}{N-1} \cdot n \cdot \frac{M}{N} \cdot \left(1 - \frac{M}{N}\right) \\ &= \frac{65-20}{65-1} \cdot 20 \cdot \frac{13}{65} \cdot \left(1 - \frac{13}{65}\right) = 2.25, \\ \sigma[X] &= \sqrt{\mathrm{Var}[X]} = \sqrt{2.25} = 1.5.\end{aligned}$$

7.6 This is a Poisson distribution with parameter $\lambda = 4$.

(a)

$$\begin{aligned}P(X \leq 3) &= P(X = 0) + P(X = 1) + P(X = 2) + P(X = 3) \\ &= \frac{4^0}{0!}\mathrm{e}^{-4} + \frac{4^1}{1!}\mathrm{e}^{-4} + \frac{4^2}{2!}\mathrm{e}^{-4} + \frac{4^3}{3!}\mathrm{e}^{-4} = 43.35\%.\end{aligned}$$

(b)

$$E[X] = \lambda = 4,$$

$$Var[X] = \lambda = 4,$$

$$\sigma[X] = \sqrt{Var[X]} = \sqrt{4} = 2.$$

7.7 This is a Poisson distribution with parameter $\lambda = 500 \cdot 0.0005 = 0.25$.

(a)

$$\begin{aligned} P(X \leq 1) &= P(X = 0) + P(X = 1) \\ &= \frac{0.25^0}{0!} e^{-0.25} + \frac{0.25^1}{1!} e^{-0.25} = 97.35\%. \end{aligned}$$

(b)

$$E[X] = \lambda = 0.25,$$

$$Var[X] = \lambda = 0.25,$$

$$\sigma[X] = \sqrt{Var[X]} = \sqrt{0.25} = 0.5.$$

7.8

(a) We find the answer from the table of the standard normal distribution.

$$P(X \leq 1.64) = \int_{-\infty}^{1.64} \frac{1}{\sqrt{2\pi}} e^{-x^2/2} dx = G(1.64) = 0.9495.$$

(b)

$$P(X = 1.64) = \int_{1.64}^{1.64} \frac{1}{\sqrt{2\pi}} e^{-x^2/2} dx = G(1.64) - G(1.64) = 0.$$

Remark For any continuous random variable the probability of a point value is zero.

(c)

$$P(X < 1.64) = P(X \leq 1.64) - P(X = 1.64) = 0.9495.$$

Remark For continuous random variables it does not matter if inequalities are strict or not.

7.9

(a)

$$P(0 \leq X \leq 0.44) = G(0.44) - G(0) = 0.6700 - 0.5000 = 17\%.$$

(b)

$$\begin{aligned} P(-1.96 \leq X \leq 1.96) &= G(1.96) - G(-1.96) \\ &= G(1.96) - (1 - G(1.96)) \\ &= 0.9750 - (1 - 0.9750) = 95\%. \end{aligned}$$

(c)

$$\begin{aligned} P(X > -2.33) &= 1 - P(X \leq -2.33) \\ &= 1 - (1 - G(2.33)) \\ &= 1 - (1 - 0.9901) = 99.01\%. \end{aligned}$$

7.10

$$\mathrm{E}[Y] = \mathrm{E}\left[\frac{X - \mu}{\sigma}\right] = \frac{1}{\sigma}\mathrm{E}[X - \mu] = \frac{1}{\sigma}(\mathrm{E}[X] - \mu) = \frac{1}{\sigma}(\mu - \mu) = 0,$$

$$\mathrm{Var}[Y] = \mathrm{Var}\left[\frac{X - \mu}{\sigma}\right] = \frac{1}{\sigma^2}\mathrm{Var}[X - \mu] = \frac{1}{\sigma^2}\mathrm{Var}[X] = \frac{1}{\sigma^2}\sigma^2 = 1.$$

7.11 Here we apply the central limit theorem.

(a)

$$P(S \leq 7) \approx G\left(\frac{7 - 3}{4}\right) = G(1) = 84.13\%.$$

(b)

$$\begin{aligned} P(-1 \leq S \leq 11) &= P(S \leq 11) - P(S < -1) \\ &\approx G\left(\frac{11 - 3}{4}\right) - G\left(\frac{-1 - 3}{4}\right) \\ &= G(2) - G(-1) = G(2) - (1 - G(1)) \\ &= 0.9772 - (1 - 0.8413) = 81.85\%. \end{aligned}$$

(c)

$$P(S \geq 5) = 1 - P(S < 5) \approx 1 - G\left(\frac{5-3}{4}\right)$$
$$= 1 - G(0.5) = 1 - 0.6915 = 30.85\%.$$

7.12 We have

$$P(S \leq z) \approx G\left(\frac{z-10}{5}\right) = 95\% = G(1.64).$$

Then

$$\frac{z-10}{5} = 1.64 \Rightarrow z = 10 + 1.64 \cdot 5 = 18.2.$$

7.13 This is a binomial distribution with $n = 225$ and $p = 0.2$. The problem is that we do not have tables for such cases. Moreover there are numerous values that need to be checked. Since $np(1-p) = 36 > 10$, a normal approximation works well.

(a)

$$\mathrm{E}[X] = np = 225 \cdot 0.2 = 45,$$
$$\mathrm{Var}[X] = np(1-p) = 225 \cdot 0,2 \cdot 0.8 = 36,$$
$$\sigma[X] = \sqrt{\mathrm{Var}[X]} = \sqrt{36} = 6.$$

(b)

$$P(S \leq 50) \approx G\left(\frac{50-45}{6}\right) = G(0,83) = 79.67\%.$$

(c) Notice that S is an integer. If $S < 35$, then $S \leq 34$.

$$P(S \geq 35) = 1 - P(S < 35) = 1 - P(S \leq 34)$$
$$= 1 - G\left(\frac{34-45}{6}\right) = 1 - G(-1.83)$$
$$= 1 - (1 - G(1.83)) = G(1.83) = 96.64\%.$$

(d) Since $n > 50$, we are outside the domain where we know for sure that the result improves. With modern software we can easily compute the exact values. It then turns out that integer correction improves the result in (b) while the error in (c) increases slightly if we use this method.

7.14 This is a binomial distribution with $n = 48$ and $p = 0.25$. The problem is that we do not have tables for such cases. Moreover there are numerous values that need to be checked. Since $np(1-p) = 9 > 5$, a normal approximation works well.

(a)

$$E[X] = np = 48 \cdot 0.25 = 12,$$

$$\text{Var}[X] = np(1-p) = 48 \cdot 0.25 \cdot 0.75 = 9,$$

$$\sigma[X] = \sqrt{\text{Var}[X]} = \sqrt{9} = 3.$$

(b) Since $20 \leq n \leq 50$, integer correction will improve the result.

(c)

$$P(S \leq 15) \approx G\left(\frac{15.5 - 12}{3}\right) = G(1.17) = 87.90\%,$$

(d)

$$P(S \leq 15) \approx G\left(\frac{15 - 12}{3}\right) = G(1) = 84.13\%.$$

Since the exact answer is 87.68%, we see that integer correction improves the result in this case.

7.15

(a) S is a normal distribution since it is a sum of normal distributions. The central limit theorem can't be used since the conditions fail.

(b)

$$E[S] = 100 + 90 + 95 + 105 = 400.$$

Since X_1, X_2, X_3, X_4 are independent, then

$$\begin{aligned}\text{Var}[S] &= \text{Var}[X_1 + X_2 + X_3 + X_4] \\ &= \text{Var}[X_1] + \text{Var}[X_2] + \text{Var}[X_3] + \text{Var}[X_4] \\ &= 30 + 20 + 25 + 15 = 100,\end{aligned}$$

$$\sigma[S] = \sqrt{100} = 10.$$

(c)

$$P(S \leq 390) = G\left(\frac{390-400}{10}\right) = G(-1)$$
$$= 1 - G(1) = 1 - 0.8413 = 15.87\%.$$

Since S is a normal distribution $P(S = 390) = 0$, and there is no difference between $P(S \leq 390)$ and $P(S < 390)$.

7.16

(a)

$$\sigma[K_{0,5}] = 100\mathrm{e}^{0.15\cdot 0.5}\sqrt{\mathrm{e}^{0.2^2\cdot 0.5}-1} = 15.32\ \text{(USD)}.$$

(b) We compute

$$R = \ln[112/100] + \left(\frac{1}{2}0.2^2 - 0.05\right)\cdot 0.5 = 0.0983,$$

$$S = 0.2\cdot\sqrt{0.5} = 0.1424.$$

The price of the option is then

$$\begin{aligned} V &= 100\cdot(1 - G(R/S - S)) - 112\cdot \mathrm{e}^{-0.05\cdot 0.5}(1 - G(R/S)) \\ &= 100\cdot(1 - G(0.55)) - 112\cdot \mathrm{e}^{-0.05\cdot 0.5}(1 - G(0.70)) \\ &= 100\cdot(1 - 0.7088) - 112\cdot \mathrm{e}^{-0.05\cdot 0.5}(1 - 0.7580) \\ &= 2.69. \end{aligned}$$

Remark The answer is somewhat inaccurate since 2 decimal accuracy is too little here.

7.17

(a) We compute

$$R = \ln[205/200] + \left(\frac{1}{2}0.02^2 - 0.05\right)\cdot 0.25 = 0.01224,$$

$$S = 0.02\cdot\sqrt{0.25} = 0.01.$$

The price of the option is

$$\begin{aligned} V &= 200 \cdot (1 - G(R/S - S)) - 205 \cdot \mathrm{e}^{-0.05 \cdot 0.25}(1 - G(R/S)) \\ &= 200 \cdot (1 - G(1,21)) - 205 \cdot \mathrm{e}^{-0,05 \cdot 0.25}(1 - G(1.22)) \\ &= 200 \cdot (1 - 0.8869) - 205 \cdot \mathrm{e}^{-0.05 \cdot 0.25}(1 - 0.8888) \\ &= 0.107. \end{aligned}$$

(b) The options are worthless when

$$K_{0.25} \leq 205.$$

This gives

$$200\mathrm{e}^{\left(0.09 - \frac{1}{2}0.02^2\right) \cdot 0.25 + 0.02X_{0.25}} \leq 205$$

$$(0.09 - \frac{1}{2}0.02^2) \cdot 0.25 + 0.02X_{0.25} \leq \ln[1.025]$$

$$0.02245 + 0.02X_{0.25} \leq 0.02469$$

$$X_{0.25} \leq \frac{0.02469 - 0.02245}{0.02} = 0.112.$$

We know that $\mathrm{E}[X_{0.25}] = 0$ and that $\mathrm{Var}[X_{0.25}] = 0.25$. This gives $\sigma[X_{0.25}] = 0.5$. Since $X_{0.25}$ is a normal distribution, we find

$$\begin{aligned} P(K_{0,25} \leq 205) = P(X_{0.25} \leq 0.112) &\approx G\left(\frac{0.112}{0.5}\right) \\ &= G(0.22) = 58.71\%. \end{aligned}$$

(c) The same computation as above gives

$$K_{0.25} \leq 205,$$

if and only if

$$198\mathrm{e}^{\left(0.05 - \frac{1}{2}0.02^2\right) \cdot 0.25 + 0.02X_{0.25}} \leq 205$$

$$(0.05 - \frac{1}{2}0.02^2) \cdot 0.25 + 0.02X_{0.25} \leq \ln[1.035]$$

$$0.01245 + 0.02X_{0.25} \leq 0.03440$$

$$X_{0.25} \leq \frac{0.03440 - 0.01245}{0.02} = 1.10.$$

$E[X_{0.25}] = 0$, $Var[X_{0.25}] = 0.25$ and $\sigma[X_{0.25}] = 0.5$. Since $X_{0.25}$ is a normal distribution, we find

$$P(K_{0.25} \leq 205) = P(X_{0.25} \leq 1.10) \approx G\left(\frac{1.10}{0.5}\right)$$
$$= G(2.20) = 98.61\%.$$

7.18

(a) We compute

$$R = \ln[109/98] + (\frac{1}{2}0.12^2 - 0.05) \cdot 1 = 0.06358.$$

$$S = 0.12 \cdot \sqrt{1} = 0.12.$$

The price of the option is then

$$\begin{aligned} V &= 98 \cdot (1 - G(R/S - S)) - 109 \cdot e^{-0.05 \cdot 1}(1 - G(R/S)) \\ &= 98 \cdot (1 - G(0.41)) - 109 \cdot e^{-0.05}(1 - G(0.53)) \\ &= 98 \cdot (1 - 0.6591) - 109 \cdot e^{-0.05}(1 - 0.7019) \\ &= 2.50. \end{aligned}$$

(b) We use 10,000 USD to buy 4000 options. If we put the money in the bank, we can withdraw 10,500 USD after one year. If the options are at least as profitable as putting the money in the bank, the stock price K_1 must fulfill the relation

$$10{,}500 \leq (K_1 - 109) \cdot 4000.$$

This gives $K_1 \geq 111.63$. The probability that this occurs is computed as follows

$$K_1 \geq 111.63,$$

if and only if

$$98e^{\left(0.12 - \frac{1}{2}0.12^2\right) \cdot 1 + 0.12X_1} \geq 111.63$$

$$\left(0.12 - \frac{1}{2}0.12^2\right) + 0.12X_1 \geq \ln[1.1391]$$

$$0.1128 + 0.12X_1 \geq 0.1302$$

$$X_1 \geq \frac{0.1302 - 0.1128}{0.12} = 0.15.$$

$E[X_1] = 0, Var[X_1] = 1$, and $\sigma[X_1] = 1$. Since X_1 is a standard normal distribution, we find

$$P(K_1 \geq 111.63) = P(X_1 \geq 0.15) = 1 - G(0.15)$$
$$= 1 - 0.5596 = 44.04\%.$$

7.19

(a)

$$P(K_4 \geq 115) = P(100\, e^{0.32+0.2X_4} \geq 115) = P\left(X_4 \geq \frac{\ln[1.15] - 0.32}{0.2}\right)$$
$$= P(X_4 \geq -0.90) = 1 - P(X_4 \leq -0.90)$$
$$= 1 - G\left[\frac{-0.90 - 0}{2}\right] = 1 - G[-0.45] = G[0.45] = 67.36\%.$$

(b) The volatility $\beta = 0.2$. We compute

$$R = \ln\left[\frac{115}{100}\right] + \left(\frac{1}{2}0.2^2 - 0.03\right) \cdot 4 = 0.1, \qquad S = 0.2 \cdot \sqrt{4} = 0.4.$$

The Black-Scholes pricing formula gives

$$V = 100 \cdot \left(1 - G\left[\frac{0.1}{0.4} - 0.4\right]\right) - 115 \cdot e^{-0.12} \cdot \left(1 - G\left[\frac{0.1}{0.4}\right]\right)$$
$$= 100 \cdot (1 - G[-0.15]) - 115 \cdot e^{-0.12} \cdot (1 - G[0.25])$$
$$= 100 \cdot G[0.15] - 115 \cdot e^{-0.12} \cdot (1 - G[0.25])$$
$$= 100 \cdot 0.5596 - 115 \cdot e^{-0.12} \cdot (1 - 0.5987) = 15.03.$$

The price of this option is hence 15.03 USD.

7.20

(a)

$$E[X] = 0 \cdot 0.86 + 1 \cdot 0.08 + 2 \cdot 0.02 + 3 \cdot 0.04 = 0.24,$$

$$Var[X] = 0^2 \cdot 0.86 + 1^2 \cdot 0.08 + 2^2 \cdot 0.02 + 3^2 \cdot 0.04 = -0, 24^2 = 0.4624.$$

(b)

$$\begin{aligned}E[S] &= E[X_1] + E[X_2] + \cdots + E[X_{10,000}] \\ &= 0.24 + 0.24 + \cdots + 0.24 = 10{,}000 \cdot 0.24 = 2400.\end{aligned}$$

Since $X_1, \ldots, X_{10,000}$ are independent, then

$$\begin{aligned}\text{Var}[S] &= \text{Var}[X_1] + \text{Var}[X_2] + \cdots + \text{Var}[X_{10,000}] \\ &= 0.4624 + 0.4624 + \cdots + 0.4624 = 10{,}000 \cdot 0.4624 = 4624.\end{aligned}$$

$$\sigma[S] = \sqrt{\text{Var}[S]} = \sqrt{4624} = 68.$$

(c)

$$\begin{aligned}P(S > 2450) &= 1 - P(S \leq 2450) \approx 1 - G\left(\tfrac{2450-2400}{68}\right) \\ &= 1 - G(0.74) = 1 - 0.7704 = 22.96\%.\end{aligned}$$

(d)

$$P(S \leq s_0) \approx G\left(\frac{s_0 - 2400}{68}\right) = 99\% = G(2,33).$$

Then

$$\frac{s_0 - 2400}{68} = 2.33 \Rightarrow s_0 = 2400 + 2.33 \cdot 68 = 2558.44.$$

The ice cream shop must order at least 2559 ice cream to be 99% sure that they satisfy the demand.

7.21

(a) $E[X] = 0 \cdot 0.1 + 1 \cdot 0.6 + 2 \cdot 0.3 = 1.2.$
$\text{Var}[X] = E[X^2] - E[X]^2 = 0^2 \cdot 0.1 + 1^2 \cdot 0.6 + 2^2 \cdot 0.3 - 1.2^2 = 0.36.$

(b) A condition that speaks against independence is that a household can be influenced by the actions of their neighbors. Here we are in the planning phase, so people moving in are hardly aware of any such circumstances. In any case it does not seem as if any particular choice will influence many other decisions.

(c) $E[Y] = 900 \cdot E[X] = 1080$. By independence $\text{Var}[Y] = 900 \cdot \text{Var}[X] = 324$. That gives $\sigma[Y] = 18$. We call the unknown capacity Z_0. We use the central limit theorem to see that

$$P(Y \leq Z_0) = P\left(\frac{Y - 1080}{18} \leq \frac{Z_0 - 1080}{18}\right) \approx G\left(\frac{Z_0 - 1080}{18}\right)$$
$$= 0.9 \approx G(1.28).$$

This gives the equation

$$\frac{Z_0 - 1080}{18} = 1.28 \Rightarrow Z_0 = 1080 + 1.28 \cdot 18 \approx 1103.$$

7.22

(a) $X = \text{Bin}[10{,}000, p]$. $\text{E}[X] = np = 10$, and $\text{Var}[X] = np(1-p) = 9.99$.

(b) Without integer correction

$$P(X \leq 3) \approx G\left(\frac{3 - 10}{\sqrt{9.99}}\right) = G(-2.21) = 1 - G(2.21) = 0.0136.$$

With integer correction

$$P(X \leq 3) \approx G\left(\frac{3.5 - 10}{\sqrt{9.99}}\right) = G(-2.06) = 1 - G(2.06) = 0.0197.$$

(c) We use the table for the Poisson distribution, and get

$$P(Y \leq 3) = P(Y = 0) + P(Y = 1) + P(Y = 2) + P(Y = 3)$$
$$= 0.0000 + 0.0005 + 0.0023 + 0.0076 = 0.0104.$$

We see that the Poisson distribution gives the best result, and that integer correction increases the error.

7.23

(a) $a = 2000$ and $b = 1000$.

(b)

$$\text{E}[V] = a\text{E}[X_1] + b\text{E}[X_2] = 2000 \cdot 200 + 1000 \cdot 300 = 700{,}000.$$

Since X_1 and X_2 are independent,

$$\text{Var}[V] = \text{Var}[aX_1] + \text{Var}[bX_2] = a^2\text{Var}[X_1] + b^2\text{Var}[X_2] = 6{,}400{,}000{,}000.$$

That gives $\sigma[V] = 80{,}000$.

(c) When X_1 and X_2 are normally distributed, then V has normal distribution. Hence

$$P(V > 800{,}000) = 1 - P(V \leq 800{,}000) = 1 - P\left(\frac{V - \mathrm{e}[V]}{\sigma[V]} \leq \frac{800{,}000 - 700{,}000}{80{,}000}\right)$$

$$= 1 - G\left(\frac{800{,}000 - 700{,}000}{80{,}000}\right) = 1 - G(1.25) \approx 10.56\%.$$

7.24

(a) $\mathrm{E}[X] = 0.1,\ \mathrm{Var}[X] = 0.1.$
(b) $\mathrm{E}[Y] = 10,\ \mathrm{Var}[Y] = 10.$

$$P(Y \leq 5) \approx G\left(\frac{5 - 10}{\sqrt{10}}\right) = G(-1.58) = 1 - G(1.58) = 5.71\%.$$

With integer correction we get the answer 7.78%, which can also be approved as an answer to the problem.
(c) $\lambda = 0.1$. That gives

$$P(Z \geq 3) = 1 - P(Z = 0) - P(Z = 1) - P(Z = 2)$$

$$= 1 - 0.9048 - 0.0905 - 0.0045 = 0.0002 = 0.02\%.$$

(d) The distribution of Y can be approximated by a Poisson distribution W with parameter $\lambda = 10$. That gives

$$P(Y \leq 5) \approx P(W \leq 5)$$

$$= P(W = 0) + P(W = 1) + P(W = 2) + P(W = 3) + P(W = 4)$$

$$+ P(W = 5)$$

$$= 0.000 + 0.0005 + 0.0023 + 0.0076 + 0.0189 + 0.0378 = 6.71\%.$$

We see that the approximation is very close to the exact answer, and considerably closer than the normal approximation. This is what we expect since the distribution of X is very close to a Poisson distribution with parameter $\lambda = 0.1$. It follows from (c) that outcomes where $Z \geq 3$ are very rare, and have little impact on the final results.

7.25

(a) X is binomial with $n = 10$ and $p = 0.1$. We use the table for the binomial distribution to find

$$P(X \geq 4) = 1 - P(X \leq 3) = 1 - 0.3487 - 0.3874 - 0.1937 - 0.0574$$

$$= 1 - 0.9872 = 1.28\%.$$

(b) We let X_i be the number of defective items produced at unit i. These variables are assumed to be independent with binomial distribution. We note that the result by the worst unit has at most 3 defective items if and only if all the all units have at most 3 defective items, and that

$$P(X_i \leq 3) = 0.9872.$$

This gives

$$\begin{aligned} P(Y \geq 4) &= 1 - P(Y \leq 3) \\ &= 1 - P(X_1 \leq 3) \cdot P(X_2 \leq 3) \cdot P(X_3 \leq 3) \cdot P(X_4 \leq 3) \cdot P(X_5 \leq 3) \\ &= 1 - 0.9872^5 = 6.24\%. \end{aligned}$$

7.26

(a) $P(X \leq \mu) = G\left(\frac{\mu-\mu}{\sigma}\right) = G(0) = 50\%$ and $P(X = C) = 0$ since X has a continuous distribution.

(b) The result R can have the values o, d, and $\frac{1}{2}(o + d)$. R gets the value o if and only if o is closer to X than d. This happens if and only if the midpoint between o and d is to the left of X, i.e., $X < \frac{o+d}{2}$. The first term is hence the value of R multiplied with the probability that this value occurs. This applies to all the terms, and the sum gives us the expected value. If X is a normal distribution, the last term vanishes. Then

$$\begin{aligned} \mathrm{E}[R] &= o \cdot G\left(\frac{\frac{o+d}{2} - \mu}{\sigma}\right) + d \cdot \left(1 - G\left(\frac{\frac{o+d}{2} - \mu}{\sigma}\right)\right) \\ &= o \cdot G\left(\frac{o + d - 2\mu}{2\sigma}\right) + d \cdot \left(1 - G\left(\frac{o + d - 2\mu}{2\sigma}\right)\right). \end{aligned}$$

Alternatively one can use the distribution of X. Then the expression is as follows:

$$\mathrm{E}[R] = o \cdot F_X\left(\frac{o + d}{2}\right) + d \cdot \left(1 - F_X\left(\frac{o + d}{2}\right)\right).$$

Remark The last expression can easily be used to derive the equations for equilibrium. Nash equilibrium is obtained if and only if

$$\frac{\partial \mathrm{E}[R]}{\partial o} = 0, \qquad \frac{\partial \mathrm{E}[R]}{\partial d} = 0.$$

If we use the product rule and the chain rule for the derivatives, we find

$$\frac{\partial \mathrm{E}[R]}{\partial o} = F_X\left(\frac{o+d}{2}\right) + o \cdot F_X'\left(\frac{o+d}{2}\right) \cdot \frac{1}{2} - d \cdot F_X'\left(\frac{o+d}{2}\right) \cdot \frac{1}{2}$$

Here we put $F_X\left(\frac{o+d}{2}\right) = P\left(X \leq \frac{o+d}{2}\right)$ and $F_X'(x) = f_X(x)$, and get

$$\frac{\partial \mathrm{E}[R]}{\partial o} = P\left(X \leq \frac{o+d}{2}\right) + \frac{o-d}{2} \cdot f_X\left(\frac{o+d}{2}\right).$$

A corresponding calculation gives

$$\frac{\partial \mathrm{E}[R]}{\partial d} = P\left(X > \frac{o+d}{2}\right) + \frac{o-d}{2} \cdot f_X\left(\frac{o+d}{2}\right),$$

and we find the system of equations if we simplify the equations

$$\frac{\partial \mathrm{E}[R]}{\partial o} = 0, \qquad \frac{\partial \mathrm{E}[R]}{\partial d} = 0.$$

(c) From the equation we see that we must have

$$P\left(X > \frac{o+d}{2}\right) = P\left(X \leq \frac{o+d}{2}\right).$$

That gives

$$1 - P\left(X \leq \frac{o+d}{2}\right) = P\left(X \leq \frac{o+d}{2}\right).$$

Hence

$$P\left(X \leq \frac{o+d}{2}\right) = \frac{1}{2}.$$

The result can be interpreted as follows: At equilibrium the parties will have the same distance to the expected view of the mediator. This principle serves to moderate the parties. An unreasonably low offer or unreasonably high demand will be punished since the opponent will usually get full support for a moderate claim.

(d) From (a) we know that $P\left(X \leq \frac{o+d}{2}\right) = \frac{1}{2}$ if and only if $\frac{o+d}{2} = \mu$. That provides us with the equation

$$(d-o) \cdot f_X(\mu) = 2 \cdot \frac{1}{2} = 1.$$

If we insert $x = \mu$ in the expression for $f_X(x)$, we find $f_X(\mu) = \frac{1}{\sqrt{2\pi\sigma^2}}$. We must hence solve the system

$$d - o = \sqrt{2\pi\sigma^2}d + t = 2\mu.$$

If we add the two equations, we get

$$2d = 2\mu + \sqrt{2\pi\sigma^2} \Rightarrow d = \mu + \sqrt{\frac{\pi}{2}} \cdot \sigma \Rightarrow o = \mu - \sqrt{\frac{\pi}{2}} \cdot \sigma.$$

When σ increases, the distance between the parties gets bigger. When the uncertainty in X is large, it will not pay to be close to the expected view. If the opponent is less moderate, he or she might still get full support in almost 50% of the cases, and profit from this strategy in the long run.

7.27

(a) We compute

$$\begin{aligned} P\left(X < \frac{o+d}{2}\right) &= P(X < 0.045) = G\left[\frac{0.045 - 0.05}{0.005}\right] \\ &= G[-1] = 1 - G[1] = 1 - 0.8413 = 0.1587. \end{aligned}$$

That gives $P\left(X > \frac{o+d}{2}\right) = 0.8413$. Since X is continuous, $P\left(X = \frac{o+d}{2}\right) = 0$. If we insert this in the given formula, then

$$\mathrm{E}[R] = 0.03 \cdot 0.1587 + 0.06 \cdot 0.8413 = 5.52\%.$$

(b) We compute

$$\begin{aligned} P\left(X < \frac{o+d}{2}\right) &= P(X < 0.045) = G\left[\frac{0.045 - 0.05}{0.02}\right] \\ &= G[-0.25] = 1 - G[0.25] = 1 - 0.5987 = 0.4013. \end{aligned}$$

This gives $P\left(X > \frac{o+d}{2}\right) = 0.5987$. If we insert this in the given formula, then

$$\mathrm{E}[R] = 0.03 \cdot 0.4013 + 0.06 \cdot 0.5987 = 4.80\%.$$

Remark We see that when the insecurity in the view of the mediator is low (0.5%), it pays to be close to the expected view. When the insecurity is high (2%), however, the probability increases to get full support for a bold claim. It then pays to present a claim further from the expected view of the mediator.

7.28

(a) If we assume that the good is sold in continuous quantities, we get

$$P(X \geq 3) = 1 - P(X < 3) \approx 1 - G\left(\frac{3-1}{1}\right) = 1 - 0.9772 = 0.0228.$$

The probability of selling at least 3 units during a randomly selected day is hence about 2.3%. If the good is only sold in integer units, then

$$P(X \geq 3) = 1 - P(X \leq 2) \approx 1 - G\left(\frac{2-1}{1}\right) = 1 - 0.8413 = 0.1587.$$

From the text we used to formulate the problem, it is natural to use the first interpretation, but the second interpretation, too, is considered a full solution to the problem.

(b) The distribution arise as a limit of a binomial (n, p) variable where n is large and p is small, and a distribution of this sort will be Poisson distributed. For the Poisson distribution we have $\mathrm{E}[X] = \lambda$ and $\sigma^2[X] = \lambda$, and from the numbers given in the problem we can conclude that $\lambda = 1$. This gives

$$\begin{aligned} P(\geq 3) &= 1 - P(X = 0) - P(X = 1) - P(X = 2) \\ &= 1 - 0.3679 - 0.3679 - 0.1839 = 0.0803. \end{aligned}$$

The probability of selling at least 3 units during a randomly selected day is about 8% in this case.

(c) The answers are quite different. The reason is that the Poisson distribution is approximately normal only when λ is sufficiently large, and this is not the case here. If the customers do not have the same probability of buying the good, the resulting distribution need not be of Poisson type. It might, e.g., happen that there is a small but devoted group of customers that buy the good relatively often, while that rest never buy it. In this case we cannot appeal to the law of rare events, and it may be more natural to use a binomial distribution where p is not small. The information $\mu = 1, \sigma = 1$, however, speak against an interpretation where p is not small.

7.29

(a) We use the Black and Scholes pricing formula. We compute

$$R = \ln(110/100) + \left(\frac{1}{2}0.5^2 - 0.025\right) \cdot 9 = 0.9, \qquad S = 0.5 \cdot \sqrt{9} = 1.5.$$

This gives $R/S = 0.6$. The price of the option is then

$$\begin{aligned} V &= 100(1 - G[-0.9]) - 100\mathrm{e}^{-0.225}(1 - G[0.6]) \\ &= 100G[0.9] - 100\mathrm{e}^{-0.025\cdot 9}(1 - G[0.6]) \\ &= 100 \cdot 0.8159 - 100\mathrm{e}^{-0.225}(1 - 0.7257) \\ &= 59.69 \text{ (USD)}. \end{aligned}$$

(b)

$$100\mathrm{e}^{\left(0.03-\frac{1}{2}0.5^2\right)100+0.5X_{100}} \geq 1$$

$$\Updownarrow$$

$$(0.03 - \frac{1}{2}0.5^2)100 + 0.5X_{100} \geq \ln[0.01]$$

$$\Updownarrow$$

$$X_{100} \geq 9.79.$$

This gives

$$\begin{aligned} P(K_{100} \geq 1) &= P(X \geq 9.79) = 1 - P(X_{100} \leq 9.79) \\ &= 1 - G\left[\frac{9.79 - 0}{\sqrt{100}}\right] = 1 - G[0.98] = 1 - 0.8365 \\ &= 16.35\%. \end{aligned}$$

It is hence only 16.35% probability that the stock price exceeds 1 USD after 100 years.

(c)

$$\begin{aligned} \mathrm{E}[K_t] &= \mathrm{E}[K_0\mathrm{e}^{(\alpha-\frac{1}{2}\beta^2)t+\beta X_t}] = K_0\mathrm{e}^{(\alpha-\frac{1}{2}\beta^2)t}\mathrm{E}[\mathrm{e}^{\beta X_t}] \\ &= K_0\mathrm{e}^{\left(\alpha-\frac{1}{2}\beta^2\right)t}\mathrm{e}^{\frac{1}{2}\beta^2 t} = K_0\mathrm{e}^{\alpha t}. \end{aligned}$$

This gives

$$\mathrm{E}[K_{100}] = 100\mathrm{e}^{0.03\cdot 100} = 2008.55 \text{ (USD)}.$$

From (b) we see that the stock price will usually be less than 1 USD after 100 years. This seems to contradict an expected value of 2000 USD. The reason why this is possible is that while most outcomes lead to small values this is balanced by some outcomes leading to extremely large values.

7.30 We call the outcome of the game X.

(a)

$$\mathrm{E}[X] = 5/6 \cdot 1 + 1/6 \cdot -4 = 1/6.$$

(b) $a = 2$

$$\mathrm{E}[U(X)] = 5/6\cdot(\sqrt{1+2^2}-2)+1/6\cdot(\sqrt{-4+2^2}-2) = 5\sqrt{5}/6-2 \approx -0.137.$$

$a = 4$

$$\mathrm{E}[U(X)] = 5/6\cdot(\sqrt{1+4^2}-4)+1/6\cdot(\sqrt{-4+4^2}-4) = 5\sqrt{17}/6+\sqrt{3}/3-5 \approx 0.013.$$

The expected utility of not playing, we find as

$$\mathrm{E}[U(X)] = 5/6 \cdot (\sqrt{a^2} - a) + 1/6 \cdot (\sqrt{a^2} - a) = 0.$$

(c) Since the expected utility of not playing is zero, a rational player chooses to participate if and only if he has strictly positive expected utility of playing. Expected utility is an increasing function of a. We call this function $e(a)$. From (b) we know that $e(2) < 0$ and that $e(4) > 0$. Since the function is increasing, it has exactly one point $a_0 \in (2, 4)$ where it is zero. When $a > a_0$, expected utility is strictly positive proving the claim. From (a) we know that the game has positive expected outcome. Players who are sufficiently risk averse will nevertheless choose not to play. We can divide the population into two parts: those with high risk aversion ($a \leq a_0$) do not play, and those with low risk aversion ($a > a_0$) choose to play.

7.31

(a) We see that the base $c = 1.10154$ in the exponential function is bigger than 1. Then the value increases with x. We put $x = 50$, and find

$$\mu_{50} = 9.0 \cdot 10^{-4} + 4.4 \cdot 10^{-5} \cdot 1.10154^{50} = 0.644\%.$$

(b)

$$\begin{aligned} P(T_{40} > 10) &= 1 - P(T_{40} \leq 10) = 1 - (1 - \mathrm{e}^{-\int_0^{10} \alpha+\beta c^{40+s} ds}) \\ &= \mathrm{e}^{-\int_0^{10} \alpha+\beta c^{40+s} ds} = \mathrm{e}^{-10\alpha - \frac{\beta}{\ln(c)}(c^{50}-c^{40})} = 95.65\%. \end{aligned}$$

(c)

$$\begin{aligned} P(T_{40} > 11) &= 1 - P(T_{40} \leq 11) = 1 - (1 - e^{-\int_0^{10} \alpha + \beta c^{40+s} ds}) \\ &= e^{-\int_0^{11} \alpha + \beta c^{40+s} ds} = e^{-10\alpha - \frac{\beta}{\ln(c)}(c^{51} - c^{40})} = 95.01\%. \end{aligned}$$

The conditional probability is computed as follows:

$$\begin{aligned} P(10 < T_{40} \leq 11 | T_{40} > 10) &= \frac{P(10 < T_{40} \leq 11 \cap T_{40} > 10)}{P(T_{40} > 10)} \\ &= \frac{P(10 < T_{40} \leq 11)}{P(T_{40} > 10)} \\ &= \frac{P(T_{40} > 10) - P(T_{40} > 11)}{P(T_{40} > 10)} \\ &= \frac{95.65\% - 95.01\%}{95.65\%} = 0.669\%. \end{aligned}$$

We can interpret this quantity as the probability that the man dies in the course of the year of insurance given that he was 50 years old and alive when the year of insurance started. This probability is approximately equal to the death rate in (a). There is a slight difference which is caused by the rate in (a) being an instant rate, while the rate in (c) is an average rate.

Remark Insurance companies do not always use the same tables for men and women. The death rates of women are lower than for men, and for some types of life insurance, women pay the same amount as a man who is 3 years younger.

7.32

(a) X er Bin[6,0.7].

$$P(N = 4) = \binom{6}{4} 0.7^4 0.3^2 = 32.41\%.$$

(b) Let Y be the number of contracts that are signed. The simplest way to solve the problem is to see that the probability for a collaborator writing a contract is $0.7 \cdot 0.6 = 0.42$. Y is hence Bin[6,0.42], and

$$P(Y = 4) = \binom{6}{4} 0.42^4 0.58^2 = 15.70\%.$$

Alternatively, the conditional probabilities can be computed as follows: If the collaborators sign 4 contracts, then $X = 4, 5$, or 6.

$$\begin{aligned} & P(Y = 4) \\ = \; & P(Y = 4|X = 4))P(X = 4) + P(Y = 4|X = 5)P(X = 5) \\ + \; & P(Y = 4|X = 6)P(X = 6) \\ = \; & \binom{4}{4} 0.6^4 0.4^0 \cdot \binom{6}{4} 0.7^4 0.3^2 \\ + \; & \binom{5}{4} 0.6^4 0.4^1 \cdot \binom{6}{5} 0.7^5 0.3^1 \\ + \; & \binom{6}{4} 0.6^4 0.4^2 \cdot \binom{6}{6} 0.7^6 0.3^0 = 15.70\%. \end{aligned}$$

7.33 We let X denote the number of men admitted in the first round and Y the number of men admitted in the second round. In general

$$P(X = x) = \frac{\binom{4}{x}\binom{6}{3-x}}{\binom{10}{3}}, \qquad P(Y = y) = \frac{\binom{6}{y}\binom{4}{7-y}}{\binom{10}{7}}.$$

(a)

$$P(X = 2) = \frac{\binom{4}{2}\binom{6}{1}}{\binom{10}{3}} = 0.3.$$

$$P(Y \geq 5) = P(Y = 5) + P(Y = 6) = 1/3.$$

(b) In the second round at least 3 men are admitted, hence $P(Y \geq 3) = P(Y \geq 2) = P(Y \geq 1) = 1$.

$$\begin{aligned} P(X + Y \geq 5) = \; & P(X = 0)P(Y \geq 5) + P(X = 1)P(Y \geq 4) \\ & + P(X = 2)P(Y \geq 3) + P(X = 3)P(Y \geq 2) \\ & + P(X = 4)P(Y \geq 1) = 80.56\%. \end{aligned}$$

The men have a larger chance of being admitted. This scheme is in favor of men. The majority of the men are allowed to apply in the second round where the chance of being admitted in higher than in the first round.

7.34

(a) We use the Black and Scholes formula and find

$$R = \ln[390/400] + (1/2 \cdot 0.12^2 - 0.05) \cdot 1 = -0.06812,$$

$$S = 0.12 \cdot \sqrt{1} = 0.12.$$

This gives

$$\begin{aligned} V &= 400(1 - G[-0.69]) - 390e^{-0.05} \cdot (1 - G[-0.57]) \\ &= 400 \cdot G[0.69] - 390e^{-0.05} \cdot G[0.57] \\ &= 400 \cdot 0.7549 - 390e^{-0.05} \cdot 0.7157 = 36.45. \end{aligned}$$

(b) After T years of continuous interest r, the value of a bank deposit of $390e^{-rT}$ USD is equal to 390 USD.

If $K_T \geq 390$, then the put option is worthless and the value of contract A is

$$0 + K_T = K_T.$$

The value of the call option is $K_T - 390$ in this case, and the total value of contract B is

$$(K_T - 390) + 390 = K_T.$$

If $K_T \leq 390$, the value of the put option is $390 - K_T$, and the total value of contract A is

$$(390 - K_T) + K_T = 390.$$

The call option is worthless in this case, and hence the value of contract B is

$$0 + 390 = 390.$$

We see that the values of contract A and B are equal no matter what happens.

(c) We call the price of the put option W. Since we can buy the stock for 400 USD, the price of contract A is $W + 400$. The call option costs 36.45 USD, and a bank deposit of $390e^{-0.05} = 370.98$ USD costs exactly this amount. Since the two contracts must have the same price, we get the equation

$$W + 400 = 36.45 + 370.98. \qquad (*)$$

If we solve this equation, we get $W = 7.43$ (USD).

Remark The equation (*) is referred to as put/call parity in the literature.

(d) The prices on the options do not depend on the expected return, so they do not change. If we are to profit at least 8 USD on the put options, the price of the stock must be at most 382 USD after one year. We must hence find which values of X_T lead to

$$400e^{(\alpha-1/2\beta^2)T+\beta X_T} \leq 382.$$

A standard rewriting of this expression gives

$$X_T \leq 0.09.$$

Since X_T is normally distributed with $\mu = 0$ and variance $\sigma^2 = T = 1$, then

$$P(K_T \leq 382) = P(X_T \leq 0.09) = G[0.09] = 53.59\%.$$

7.35

(a) In general

$$\text{Var}[X] = \text{E}[X^2] - \text{E}[X]^2.$$

but in this case $\text{E}[B_t] = 0$ and the second term is zero.

(b) B_{100} is a normal distribution with expectation zero and variance $\sigma^2 = 100$. Hence

$$P(B_{100} \leq 10) = G\left(\frac{10-0}{10}\right) = G(1) = 84.13\%.$$

(c) It follows from the third bullet point that B_s and $B_t - B_s$ are independent random variables. Hence

$$\text{E}[B_s(B_t - B_s)] = \text{E}[B_s] \cdot \text{E}[B_t - B_s] = 0 \cdot (0 - 0) = 0.$$

(d) From (c) we have

$$\text{E}[B_s(B_t - B_s)] = 0.$$

If we expand the left-hand side, we see that

$$\text{E}[B_sB_t] - \text{E}[B_s^2] = 0.$$

This gives

$$\text{E}[B_sB_t] = \text{E}[B_tB_s] = \text{E}[B_s^2] = s.$$

Furthermore

$$E[(B_t - B_s)^2] = E[B_t^2 - 2B_tB_s + B_s^2] = t - 2s + s = t - s.$$

7.36

(a) $E[X_t] = E[2B_t + 6] = 2E[B_t] + 6 = 6.$

$$\text{Var}[X_t] = \text{Var}[2B_t + 6] = \text{Var}[2B_t] = 2^2\text{Var}[B_t] = 4t.$$

(b) X_{25} is a normal distribution with $E[X_{25}] = 6$ and $\text{Var}[X_{25}] = 4 \cdot 25 = 100$. This gives

$$P(X_{25} \le 16) = G\left(\frac{16-6}{\sqrt{100}}\right) = G(1) = 84.13\%.$$

(c)

$$\begin{aligned} E[B_s^2B_t^2 - 2B_tB_s^3 + B_s^4] &= E[B_s^2(B_t^2 - 2B_tB_s + B_s^2)] = E[B_s^2(B_t - B_s)^2] \\ &= E[B_s^2] \cdot E[(B_t - B_s)^2] = s(t-s). \end{aligned}$$

7.37

(a)

$$P(100e^{B_9} \le 2000) = P(B_9 \le \ln[20]) = G\left[\frac{\ln[20] - 0}{\sqrt{9}}\right] = G[1.00] = 84.13\%.$$

(b) Here the terms B_s^2 and $(B_t - B_s)^2$ are independent, and we get

$$E[B_s^2(B_t - B_s)^2] = E[B_s^2] \cdot E[(B_t - B_s)^2] = s(t-s).$$

(c) i) Assume $i < j$. Then the term $(B_{t_{j+1}} - B_{t_j})$ is independent of the three other terms B_{t_i}, B_{t_j}, and $(B_{t_{i+1}} - B_{t_i})$. That gives

$$E[B_{t_i}B_{t_j}(B_{t_{i+1}} - B_{t_i})(B_{t_{j+1}} - B_{t_j})] = E[B_{t_i}B_{t_j}(B_{t_{i+1}} - B_{t_i})] \cdot E[(B_{t_{j+1}} - B_{t_j})] = 0.$$

ii) If $i = j$, we get

$$E[B_{t_i}B_{t_j}(B_{t_{i+1}} - B_{t_i})(B_{t_{j+1}} - B_{t_j})] = E[B_{t_i}^2(B_{t_{i+1}} - B_{t_i})^2] = t_i(t_{i+1} - t_i).$$

(the last equality follows from (b)).

iii) Assume $i > j$. Then the term $(B_{t_{i+1}} - B_{t_i})$ is independent of the three other terms B_{t_i}, B_{t_j} and $(B_{t_{j+1}} - B_{t_j})$. This gives

$$\mathrm{E}[B_{t_i}B_{t_j}(B_{t_{i+1}}-B_{t_i})(B_{t_{j+1}}-B_{t_j})] = \mathrm{E}[B_{t_i}B_{t_j}(B_{t_{j+1}}-B_{t_j})]\cdot\mathrm{E}[(B_{t_{i+1}}-B_{t_i})] = 0.$$

Remark The calculations above are central to the construction of *a stochastic integral* which plays an important part of mathematical finance.

7.38

(a)

$$P(X=2) = \binom{6}{2}\left(\frac{1}{3}\right)^2\left(\frac{2}{3}\right)^4 = 32.92\%.$$

(b)

$$\begin{aligned}P(X=2) &= P(X=2|p=0)P(p=0) + P(X=2|p=1/3)P(p=1/3)\\ &\quad + P(X=2|p=2/3)P(p=2/3) + P(X=2|p=1)P(p=1).\end{aligned}$$

If $n > 2$, the first and the last term are both zero. Then we get

$$P(X=2) = \binom{n}{2}\left(\frac{1}{3}\right)^2\left(\frac{2}{3}\right)^{n-2}\cdot\frac{1}{4} + \binom{n}{2}\left(\frac{2}{3}\right)^2\left(\frac{1}{3}\right)^{n-2}\cdot\frac{1}{4}.$$

If we put $\binom{n}{2}$ outside as a common factor, we have proved the claim. If $n = 2$, then $P(X = 2|p = 1) = 1$, and this term comes in addition.

(c) We use Bayes' formula to get

$$P\left(p = \frac{1}{3}\middle|X = 2\right) = P\left(X = 2\middle|p = \frac{1}{3}\right)\cdot\frac{P\left(p=\frac{1}{3}\right)}{P(X=2)}.$$

If we insert $n = 6$ in the formula from (b), we get $P(X = 2) = 10.29\%$. This together with the answer for (a) gives

$$P\left(p = \frac{1}{3}\middle|X = 2\right) = 0.3292\cdot\frac{\frac{1}{4}}{0.1029} = 0.800 = 80\%.$$

Remark This problem is a simple example of Bayesian statistics. Prior to the examination we have what we call an *a priori* distribution:

$$P(p=0) = 1/4 \quad P(p=1/3) = 1/4 \quad P(p=2/3) = 1/4 \quad P(p=1) = 1/4.$$

After we have done 6 trials and observed $X = 2$ successes, we modify the distribution to what we call an *a posteriori* distribution:

$$P(p = 0|X = 2) = 0 \quad P(p = 1/3|X = 2) = 80\%$$

$$P(p = 2/3|X = 2) = 20\% \quad P(p = 1|X = 2) = 0.$$

We now believe there is a large probability (80%) that $p = \frac{1}{3}$, but we still hold it possible (20%) that p can be $\frac{2}{3}$.

7.39

(a)

$$P(Y \leq 403.43) = P(\mathrm{e}^X \leq 403.43) = P(X \leq \ln[403.43])$$
$$= G\left[\frac{\ln[403.43]-4}{2}\right] = G[1] = 84.13\%.$$

(b) If we put $\mu = 4, \sigma = 2$ in the formula, we find

$$\mathrm{E}[Y] = \mathrm{e}^{4+\frac{1}{2}2^2} = \mathrm{e}^6 = 403.43.$$

We see that the answer is the same as in (a). The explanation is that the distribution is skewed, it is much more likely (84.13%) that the value of Y is below $\mathrm{E}[Y]$ than above the same value (15.87%).

(c) We can rewrite the expression as follows:

$$K_t = \mathrm{e}^{\ln[K_0]+(r-\frac{1}{2}\beta^2)t+\beta Z_t}.$$

If we put $X = \ln[K_0] + (r - \frac{1}{2}\beta^2)t + \beta Z_t$, then X is a normal distribution with $\mu = \ln[K_0] + (r - \frac{1}{2}\beta^2)t$ and $\sigma = \beta\sqrt{t}$. The formula from (b) gives

$$\mathrm{E}[K_t] = \mathrm{e}^{\mu+\frac{1}{2}\sigma^2} = \mathrm{e}^{\ln[K_0]+(r-\frac{1}{2}\beta^2)t+\frac{1}{2}\beta^2 t} = \mathrm{e}^{\ln[K_0]+rt} = K_0\mathrm{e}^{rt}.$$

7.40

(a)

$$P(D_1 \leq 16{,}000) = G\left[\frac{16{,}000 - 10{,}000}{3000}\right] = G[2] = 97.72\%.$$

(b)

$$\mathrm{E}[D] = \mathrm{E}[D_1] + \mathrm{E}[D_2] = 10{,}000 + 16{,}000 = 26{,}000.$$

Since D_1 and D_2 are independent, then

$$\text{Var}[D] = \text{Var}[D_1] + \text{Var}[D_2] = 3000^2 + 4000^2 = 25{,}000{,}000 = 5000^2.$$

which gives

$$P(D \le 16{,}000|S) = G\left[\frac{16{,}000 - 26{,}000}{5000}\right] = G[-2] = 1 - 0.9772\% = 2.28\%.$$

(c)

$$\begin{aligned} P(\text{Sell at most 16,000 newspapers}) &= P(D \le 16{,}000|S)P(S) \\ &\quad + P(D_1 \le 16{,}000|S^c)P(S^c) \\ &= 0.0228 \cdot 0.2 + 0.9772 \cdot 0.8 = 78.63\%. \end{aligned}$$

7.41

(a) The expected sale is given by

$$\text{E}[S] = 1 \cdot 0.1 + 2 \cdot 0.1 + 3 \cdot 0.1 + 4 \cdot 0.1 + 5 \cdot 0.6 = 4.$$

If we instead put $x = 5$ in the formula, we get

$$\text{E}[S] = \frac{1}{20}(21 \cdot 5 - 5^2) = 4.$$

The two answers are in agreement.

(b)

$$\text{E}[\Pi] = \text{E}[R \min[D, q] - W q] = R\,\text{E}[S] - W q = R \cdot \frac{1}{20}(21x - x^2) - Wx.$$

If $R = 20$, $W = 5$, then

$$\text{E}[\Pi] = (21x - x^2) - 5x = 16x - x^2.$$

If we compute the derivative of this function and set it equal to zero, we find that maximum is achieved when $x = 8$.

(c) Maximum is achieved when x is such that

$$F_D(x) = P(D \le x) = 1 - \frac{5}{20} = 0.75.$$

If D is normally distributed $N(\mu, \sigma^2)$, then

$$P(D \leq x) = G\left(\frac{x-\mu}{\sigma}\right).$$

From the table of the normal distribution we find

$$G\left(\frac{x-\mu}{\sigma}\right) = 0.75 \Leftrightarrow \frac{x-\mu}{\sigma} = 0.6745.$$

This gives

$$x = \mu + 0.6745\,\sigma = 5.5 + 0.6745 \cdot 1.0 = 6.1745.$$

When the sales distribution is normal, it is not probable (2.5%) that the value is larger than $5.5 + 1.96 \cdot 1.0 = 7.46$. In comparison this probability is more than 25% for the uniform distribution. We order less since high demand is less probable.

7.42

(a) We have

$$\mathrm{E}[Z] = \mathrm{E}\left[\sum_{i=1}^{1000} D_i\right] = \sum_{i=1}^{1000} \mathrm{E}[D_i] = 1000 \cdot 10 = 10{,}000.$$

Since the variance of a sum of independent variables is equal to the sum of the variances, we get

$$\mathrm{Var}[Z] = \mathrm{Var}\left[\sum_{i=1}^{1000} D_i\right] = \sum_{i=1}^{1000} \mathrm{Var}[D_i] = 1000 \cdot 10 = 10{,}000.$$

(b)

$$P(D \leq z) = 0.95 \Leftrightarrow G\left[\frac{z - 10{,}000}{100}\right] = 0.95 \Leftrightarrow \frac{z - 10{,}000}{100} = 1.6449.$$

If we order 10,165 units, we have at least 95% probability of satisfying the demand. If the number of people in the market is very large, we need to order more than 10 units for each person. The variance will in this case be very small in comparison to the expected value. Hence if we order just slightly more than expected, we can be quite sure to satisfy the demand.

7.43

(a)

$$P(X_i \leq 0) = G\left(\frac{0-45}{30}\right) = G(-1.5) = 1 - G(1.5) = 1 - 0.9332 = 6.68\%.$$

(b) We first need to find expectation and variance for Y_{i+1}. We have

$$\mathrm{E}[Y_{i+1}] = \mathrm{E}[X_{i+1}] + \alpha(\mu - \mathrm{E}[X_i]) = \mu + \alpha(\mu - \mu) = \mu = 45.$$

Since X_{i+1} and X_i are independent, we find

$$\begin{aligned}\mathrm{Var}[Y_{i+1}] &= \mathrm{Var}[X_{i+1}] + \mathrm{Var}[\alpha\mu - \alpha X_i] = \mathrm{Var}[X_{i+1}] + \mathrm{Var}[-\alpha X_i] \\ &= \mathrm{Var}[X_{i+1}] + (-\alpha)^2\mathrm{Var}[X_i] = (1+\alpha^2)\sigma^2 = 1406.25.\end{aligned}$$

That leads to a standard deviation

$$\sigma[Y_{i+1}] = \sqrt{1406.25} = 37.5.$$

A linear combination of normal distributions is normal, and hence

$$P(Y_{i+1} \leq 0) = G\left(\frac{0-45}{37.5}\right) = G(-1.2) = 1 - G(1.2) = 1 - 0.8849 = 11.51\%.$$

(c) No, all values of α give the same expected surplus. The larger the value of α, the larger will the standard deviation be. This in turn leads to a larger probability of deficit. Even though the intention is good, the best strategy is to do nothing, i.e., $\alpha = 0$. Any other strategy will be worse.

7.44

(a)

$$\begin{aligned}P(|X-100| \geq 0.2) &= 2 \cdot P(X \geq 100.2)) = 2(1 - P(X \leq 100.2)) \\ &= 2\left(1 - G\left(\frac{100.2-100}{0.1}\right)\right) = 2(1 - G(2)) = 2(1 - 0.9772) \\ &= 4.56\%.\end{aligned}$$

(b)

$$X_2 = \mu_2 + \epsilon_2 = \mu_1 - (X_1 - \mu_1) + \epsilon_2 = \mu_1 - \mu_1 - \epsilon_1 + \mu_1 + \epsilon_2 = \mu_1 - \epsilon_1 + \epsilon_2.$$

$$E[X_2] = E[\mu_1] - E[\epsilon_1] + E[\epsilon_2] = \mu_1 - 0 + 0 = 100.$$

Since ϵ_1 and ϵ_2 are independent, then

$$\begin{aligned}\text{Var}[X_2] &= \text{Var}[-\epsilon_1 + \epsilon_2] = \text{Var}[-\epsilon_1] + \text{Var}[\epsilon_2] = \text{Var}[\epsilon_1] + \text{Var}[\epsilon_2] = \sigma_1^2 \\ &\quad + \sigma_2^2 = 2 \cdot 0.1^2 = 0.02.\end{aligned}$$

$$\begin{aligned}P(|X_2 - 100| \geq 0.2) &= 2 \cdot P(X_2 \geq 100.2)) = 2(1 - P(X_2 \leq 100.2)) \\ &= 2\left(1 - G\left(\frac{100.2 - 100}{\sqrt{0.02}}\right)\right) \\ &= 2(1 - G(1.41)) = 2(1 - 0.9207) = 15.86\%.\end{aligned}$$

We see that this attempt to improve quality is a disaster as the parts that need to be discarded are more than tripled.

(c) Since $X_2 = \mu_2 + \epsilon_2$, we get

$$X_3 = \mu_3 + \epsilon_3 = \mu_2 - (X_2 - \mu_1) + \epsilon_3 = \mu_2 - \mu_2 - \epsilon_2 + \mu_1 + \epsilon_3 = \mu_1 - \epsilon_2 + \epsilon_3,$$

leading to the same distribution as before.

Remark By induction it is possible to prove that

$$X_n = \mu_1 - \epsilon_{n-1} + \epsilon_n,$$

which shows that the distribution does not change when we carry on with the procedure. Note that it is the adjustment, not the measurement that creates the problem. A basic idea in the control of processes is to measure continuously, but to adjust only if the deviation is statistically significant.

Problems of Chap. 8

8.1 We know that $\overline{X}$ and S^2 are unbiased estimators for μ and σ^2. If we compute the values, we find

$$\overline{X} = 35{,}600, \qquad S^2 = 236{,}800{,}000.$$

8.2 Since we have lots of observations, we can appeal to the central limit theorem. We can also assume that S_X^2 is a quite accurate estimate for σ^2. We can hence assume that $\overline{X}$ is approximately normal with $\mathrm{E}[\overline{X}] = \mu$ and $\mathrm{Var}[\overline{X}] = \frac{\sigma^2}{10{,}000}$. We have to find z such that

$$P\left(\frac{\overline{X} - \mu}{\sigma[\overline{X}]} \geq z\right) = 2.5\%.$$

That gives $z = 1.96$. A 95% confidence interval is then

$$\overline{X} \pm 1.96 \cdot \sigma[\overline{X}] = 35{,}600 \pm 1.96 \cdot 210.$$

This gives the interval [35,188, 36,012].

8.3 Since we have lots of observations, we can appeal to the central limit theorem. We can also assume that S_X^2 is a quite accurate estimate for σ^2. We can hence assume that $\overline{X}$ is approximately normal with $\mathrm{E}[\overline{X}] = \mu$ and $\mathrm{Var}[\overline{X}] = \frac{\sigma^2}{2500}$. We have to find z such that

$$P\left(\frac{\overline{X} - \mu}{\sigma[\overline{X}]} \geq z\right) = 2.5\%.$$

That gives $z = 1.96$. A 95% confidence interval is then

$$\overline{X} \pm 1.96 \cdot \sigma[\overline{X}] = 120{,}000 \pm 1.96 \cdot 6000.$$

This gives the interval [108,240, 131,760].

8.4

(a) X is a binomial distribution with $n = 40{,}000$ and $p = p$.
(b)

$$\mathrm{E}[\hat{\theta}] = \frac{1}{40{,}000}\mathrm{E}[X] = \frac{1}{40{,}000} \cdot 40{,}000 \cdot p = p.$$

$$\mathrm{Var}[\hat{\theta}] = \frac{1}{40{,}000^2}\mathrm{Var}[X] = \frac{1}{40{,}000^2} \cdot 40{,}000 \cdot p(1-p) = \frac{p(1-p)}{40{,}000}.$$

(c) We have observed $\hat{\theta} = 0.36$. Since we have lots of observations, we can assume that $\hat{\theta}$ is approximately normal and that

$$\sigma[\hat{\theta}] = \sqrt{\frac{p(1-p)}{40{,}000}} \approx \sqrt{\frac{0.36(1-0.36)}{40{,}000}} = 0.0024.$$

We must find z such that

$$P\left(\frac{\hat{\theta}-\mu}{\sigma[\hat{\theta}]} \geq z\right) = 0.5\%.$$

That gives $z = 2.5758$. A 99% confidence interval is then

$$\hat{\theta} \pm 2.5758 \cdot \sigma[\hat{\theta}] = 0.36 \pm 2.5758 \cdot 0.0024.$$

That gives the interval $[0.354, 0.366]$.

(d) If $p = 0.354$, then $\sigma[\hat{\theta}] = 0.00239$, and if $p = 0.366$, then $\sigma[\hat{\theta}] = 0.00241$. If we use these values instead, the confidence interval still becomes $[0.354, 0.366]$. The error we make when we use the constant $\sigma[\hat{\theta}] = 0.0024$ can hence be ignored.

8.5 In this problem X is a binomial distribution with $n = 10$ and $p = p$.

(a) We know that $\overline{X}$ and S^2 are unbiased estimators for $\mathrm{E}[X]$ and $\mathrm{Var}[X]$. Then

$$\mathrm{E}[\overline{X}] = \mathrm{E}[X] = n \cdot p = 10p.$$

$$\mathrm{E}[S^2] = \mathrm{Var}[X] = n \cdot p(1-p) = 10p(1-p).$$

(b) We insert the values to find

$$\overline{X} = \frac{1}{5}(2+1+2+2+3) = 2.$$

$$S^2 = \frac{1}{4}((2-2)^2 + (1-2)^2 + (2-2)^2 + (2-2)^2 + (3-2)^2) = \frac{1}{2}.$$

There is no conflict between these results. The result in (b) is the consequence of one single execution of the experiment, while the result in (a) tells us what to expect when we repeat it several times.

(c)

$$\mathrm{E}[\hat{\theta}] = \frac{1}{10}\mathrm{E}[\overline{X}] = \frac{1}{10} \cdot 10p = p.$$

$$\begin{aligned}\mathrm{Var}[\hat{\theta}] &= \frac{1}{10^2}\mathrm{Var}[\overline{X}] \\ &= \frac{1}{10^2} \cdot \frac{1}{5^2}\mathrm{Var}[X_1 + X_2 + X_3 + X_4 + X_5]\end{aligned}$$

$$= \frac{1}{10^2} \cdot \frac{1}{5^2}(\mathrm{Var}[X_1] + \mathrm{Var}[X_2] + \mathrm{Var}[X_3] + \mathrm{Var}[X_4] + \mathrm{Var}[X_5])$$

$$= \frac{1}{10^2} \cdot \frac{1}{5^2} \cdot 5 \cdot 10p(1-p) = \frac{p(1-p)}{50}.$$

Remark The results in this problem coincide with what we would have gotten from a single binomial variable with $n = 50$.

8.6

(a)

$$\begin{aligned} \mathrm{E}[V] &= \mathrm{E}[X_1 + X_2 + X_3 + X_4] \\ &= \mathrm{E}[X_1] + \mathrm{E}[X_2] + \mathrm{E}[X_3] + \mathrm{E}[X_4] \\ &= \mu + \mu + \mu + \mu = 4\mu. \end{aligned}$$

$$\begin{aligned} \mathrm{Var}[V] &= \mathrm{Var}[X_1 + X_2 + X_3 + X_4] \\ &= \mathrm{Var}[X_1] + \mathrm{Var}[X_2] + \mathrm{Var}[X_3] + \mathrm{Var}[X_4] \\ &= \sigma^2 + \sigma^2 + \sigma^2 + \sigma^2 = 4\sigma^2. \end{aligned}$$

From a formal point of view, V is an estimator, but there is no reason to expect that the value is close to μ.

(b) We have

$$\mathrm{E}[W] = \mathrm{E}[V - 3\mu] = \mathrm{E}[V] - 3\mu = 4\mu - 3\mu = \mu.$$

W is hence unbiased. The problem is that W contains the unknown number that we want to find. This is not useful, and in more advanced textbooks we can find definitions excluding constructions of this type.

8.7 Since we have few, but normally distributed observations, we can use the t-distribution. We know that

$$T = \frac{\overline{X} - \mu}{S[\overline{X}]}$$

is t-distributed with parameter $\nu = 24$. We must find z such that

$$P\left(T_{(24)} \geq z\right) = 2.5\%.$$

That gives $z = 2.064$. A 95% confidence interval is hence given by

$$\overline{X} \pm 2.064 \cdot S[\overline{X}] = 35{,}600 \pm 2.064 \cdot 4200$$

That gives the interval [26,931, 44,269].

8.8 Since we have few, but normally distributed observations, we can use the t-distribution. We know that

$$T = \frac{\overline{X} - \mu}{S[\overline{X}]}$$

is t-distributed with parameter $\nu = 8$. We must find z such that

$$P\left(T_{(8)} \geq z\right) = 5\%.$$

That gives $z = 1.86$. A 90% confidence interval is hence given by

$$\overline{X} \pm 1,86 \cdot S[\overline{X}] = 120{,}000 \pm 1,86 \cdot 100{,}000.$$

That gives the interval [−66,000, 306,000].

8.9 We compute

$$\overline{X} = 94.75, \qquad S^2 = \frac{1}{3}\sum_{i=1}^{4}(X_i - \overline{X})^2 = 2.25.$$

That gives

$$S[\overline{X}] = \sqrt{\frac{S^2}{4}} = 0.75.$$

We know that

$$T = \frac{\overline{X} - \mu}{S[\overline{X}]}$$

is t-distributed with parameter $\nu = 3$. We must find z such that

$$P\left(T_{(3)} \geq z\right) = 0.5\%.$$

That gives $z = 5.841$. A 99% confidence interval is hence given by

$$\overline{X} \pm 5.841 \cdot S[\overline{X}] = 94.75 \pm 5.841 \cdot 0.75.$$

That gives the interval [90.37, 99.13]. The value 100 is outside the confidence interval. If the claim was true, that would only happen in 1 out of 100 such experiments. It hence seems unlikely that the claim is true.

8.10 We use the formula and find

$$\mathrm{Var}[\overline{Y}] = \frac{N-n}{N-1} \cdot \frac{S^2}{n} = \frac{1014-312}{1014-1} \cdot \frac{1.04814 \cdot 10^{10}}{312} = 2.32805 \cdot 10^7.$$

That gives

$$\sigma[\overline{Y}] = 4825.$$

For the normal distribution a 95% confidence interval is given by

$$\overline{Y} \pm 1.96\sigma[\overline{Y}] = 678{,}995 \pm 1.96 \cdot 4825.$$

That gives the interval [669,498, 688,412].

8.11

(a) We use the formula and find

$$\mathrm{Var}[\overline{Y}] = \frac{N-n}{N-1} \cdot \frac{S^2}{n} = \frac{522-478}{522-1} \cdot \frac{6.7123 \cdot 10^{11}}{478} = 1.18593 \cdot 10^8.$$

That gives

$$\sigma[\overline{Y}] = 10{,}890.$$

For the normal distribution a 95% confidence interval is given by

$$\overline{Y} \pm 1.96\sigma[\overline{Y}] = 2{,}133{,}190 \pm 1.96 \cdot 10{,}890.$$

That gives the interval [2,111,846, 2,154,534].

(b) If N is very large, we can use the formula

$$\mathrm{Var}[\overline{Y}] = \frac{S^2}{n} = \frac{6.7123 \cdot 10^{11}}{478} = 1.40425 \cdot 10^9.$$

That gives

$$\sigma[\overline{Y}] = 37{,}473.$$

For the normal distribution a 95% confidence interval is then given by

$$\overline{Y} \pm 1.96\sigma[\overline{Y}] = 2{,}133{,}190 \pm 1.96 \cdot 37{,}473.$$

That gives the interval [2,059,743, 2,206,637]. We see that the confidence interval is much wider when we ignore the previous information.

8.12

(a) $\mathrm{E}[\hat{\theta}_1] = \mathrm{E}[\hat{\theta}_2] = \mu$, $\mathrm{Var}[\hat{\theta}_1] = \frac{\sigma^2}{100}$ and $\mathrm{Var}[\hat{\theta}_2] = \frac{\sigma^2}{400}$.

(b)

$$\mathrm{E}[\hat{\theta}_c] = \mathrm{E}[c\hat{\theta}_1 + (1-c)\hat{\theta}_2] = c\mathrm{E}[\hat{\theta}_1] + (1-c)\mathrm{E}[\hat{\theta}_2] = c\mu + (1-c)\mu = \mu.$$

$$\begin{aligned}\mathrm{Var}[\hat{\theta}_c] &= \mathrm{Var}[c\hat{\theta}_1 + (1-c)\hat{\theta}_2] = c^2\mathrm{Var}[\hat{\theta}_1] + (1-c)^2\mathrm{Var}[\hat{\theta}_2] \\ &= c^2 \cdot \frac{\sigma^2}{100} + (1-c)^2 \cdot \frac{\sigma^2}{400} = (4c^2 + (1-c)^2) \cdot \frac{\sigma^2}{400}.\end{aligned}$$

(c) We define

$$f(c) = (4c^2 + (1-c)^2) \cdot \frac{\sigma^2}{400}.$$

This is a parabola, and minimum is found where $f'(c) = 0$. That gives

$$f'(c) = (8c + 2(1-c) \cdot -1) \cdot \frac{\sigma^2}{400} = 0.$$

$$10c - 2 = 0 \Rightarrow c = \frac{1}{5}.$$

When $c^* = \frac{1}{5}$, then

$$\theta_{c^*} = \frac{1}{5} \cdot \frac{1}{100} \sum_{i=1}^{100} X_i + \frac{4}{5} \cdot \frac{1}{400} \sum_{i=1}^{400} X_i' = \frac{1}{500}\left(\sum_{i=1}^{100} X_i + \sum_{i=1}^{400} X_i'\right).$$

This is just the mean of all the 500 observations, and we see that it is not possible to improve the estimator by combining the observations in a particularly clever way.

Problems of Chap. 9

9.1

(a) We have $H_0 : \mu = 8000$ and $H_A : \mu < 8000$.
(b) $\mathrm{E}[\overline{X}] = \mu$ and $\mathrm{Var}[\overline{X}] = \frac{\sigma^2}{n} = \frac{4{,}000{,}000}{100} = 40{,}000$. That gives $\sigma[\overline{X}] = 200$.
(c) We reject H_0 when $\overline{X} \leq x_{\text{limit}}$ where

$$P_{H_0}(\overline{X} \leq x_{\text{limit}}) = 5\%.$$

Since we have many observations, we can use the central limit theorem. When H_0 is true, then

$$P_{H_0}(\overline{X} \leq x_{\text{limit}}) \approx G\left(\frac{x_{\text{limit}} - 8000}{200}\right) = G(-1.6449).$$

That gives

$$x_{\text{limit}} = 8000 - 1.6449 \cdot 200 = 7671.$$

The rejection region is hence the interval $(-\infty, 7671]$.
(d) Since the observed value of $\overline{X}$ is outside the rejection region, we must keep H_0. There is not sufficient evidence to conclude that the power consumption has decreased.

9.2

(a) We have $H_0 : \mu = 1200$ and $H_A : \mu > 1200$.
(b) $\mathrm{E}[\overline{X}] = \mu$ and $\mathrm{Var}[\overline{X}] = \frac{\sigma^2}{n} = \frac{160{,}000}{400} = 400$. That gives $\sigma[\overline{X}] = 20$.
(c) We reject H_0 when $\overline{X} \geq x_{\text{limit}}$ where

$$P_{H_0}(\overline{X} \geq x_{\text{limit}}) = 5\%.$$

Since we have many observations, we can use the central limit theorem. When H_0 is true, then

$$P_{H_0}(\overline{X} \geq x_{\text{limit}}) \approx 1 - G\left(\frac{x_{\text{limit}} - 1200}{20}\right) = 5\%.$$

Hence

$$G\left(\frac{x_{\text{limit}} - 1200}{20}\right) = 0.95 = G(1.6449).$$

That gives

$$x_{\text{limit}} = 1200 + 1.6449 \cdot 20 = 1232.90.$$

The rejection region is hence the interval $[1232.90, \infty)$.

(d) Since the observed value of $\overline{X}$ is inside the rejection region, we reject H_0. There is hence sufficient evidence to conclude that the fee usage probably has increased.

9.3

(a) We have $H_0: \mu = 0.1$ and $H_A: \mu \neq 0.1$.
(b) T is t-distributed with parameter $\nu = 24$.
(c) We reject H_0 when $|T_{(24)}| \geq t_{\text{limit}}$ where

$$P_{H_0}(|T_{(24)}| \geq t_{\text{limit}}) = 5\%.$$

Hence

$$P_{H_0}(T_{(24)} \geq t_{\text{limit}}) = 2.5\%.$$

That gives $t_{\text{limit}} = 2.064$. The rejection region is hence the interval $(-\infty, -2.064] \cup [2.064, \infty)$.

(d) Here we have

$$S^2[\overline{X}] = \frac{S^2}{n} = \frac{0.05^2}{25} = 0.0001.$$

That gives $S[\overline{X}] = 0.01$. If we insert this, we find that the observed value for T is

$$T = \frac{0.09 - 0.1}{0.1} = -1.$$

Since this value is outside the rejection region, we keep H_0. There is not sufficient evidence to claim that $\mu \neq 0.1$.

9.4

(a) We have $H_0: \mu = 11$ and $H_A: \mu < 11$.
(b) T is t-distributed with parameter $\nu = 35$.
(c) We reject H_0 when $T_{(35)} \leq t_{\text{limit}}$ where

$$P_{H_0}(T_{(35)} \leq t_{\text{limit}}) = 5\%.$$

That gives $t_{\text{limit}} = -1.69$. The rejection region is hence the interval $(-\infty, -1, 69]$.

(d) Here we have

$$S^2[\overline{X}] = \frac{S^2}{n} = \frac{3^2}{36} = 0.25.$$

That gives $S[\overline{X}] = 0.5$. If we insert this, we find that the observed value for T is

$$T = \frac{10 - 11}{0.5} = -2.$$

Since the observed value of $\overline{X}$ is inside the rejection region, we reject H_0. There is hence sufficient evidence to conclude that the absence due to illness probably has decreased.

9.5

(a) Let p denote the probability that a randomly selected person prefers the new product. We have $H_0 : p \leq 50\%$ and $H_A : p > 50\%$.
(b) X is a binomial distribution with parameters $n = 5$ and $p = p$.
(c) P-value of the observed result is

$$P_{H_0}(X \geq 5) = P_{H_0}(X = 5) = \binom{5}{5} p^5 \cdot (1-p)^0 \leq \binom{5}{5} 0.5^5 = 3.1\%.$$

Since the P-value is smaller than the significance level, we reject H_0. There is hence sufficient evidence to conclude that more than 50% of the population probably prefer the new product.

Remark When the tendency in the data is strong, it is sometimes possible to draw conclusions based on very few observations.

9.6

(a) Let p denote the probability that a randomly selected person is dissatisfied. We have $H_0 : p \leq 10\%$ and $H_A : p > 10\%$.
(b) X is a binomial distribution with parameters $n = 400$ and $p = p$.
(c) P-value for the observations is

$$\begin{aligned} P_{H_0}(X \geq 53) &\leq P_{p=10\%}(X \geq 53) = 1 - P_{p=10\%}(X \leq 52) \\ &\approx 1 - G\left(\frac{52-40}{6}\right) = 1 - G(2) = 1 - 0.997 \\ &= 2.28\%. \end{aligned}$$

Since the P-value is less than the significance level, we reject the null hypothesis. There is sufficient evidence to conclude that more than 10% of the customers probably are dissatisfied.

9.7

(a) We assume that $p = 1\%$, and find the probability that the accounting is not rejected, i.e.

$$P(X \leq 3) = P(X = 0) + P(X = 1) + P(X = 2) + P(X = 3).$$

i) Using the table for the Poisson distribution with parameter $\lambda = n \cdot p = 4$, we find

$$P(X \leq 4) = 0.0183 + 0.0733 + 0.1465 + 0.1954 = 43.35\%.$$

ii) Exact computation gives

$$\begin{aligned} P(X \leq 4) &= \binom{400}{0} 0.01^0 \cdot 0.99^{400} + \binom{400}{1} 0.01^1 \cdot 0.99^{399} \\ &+ \binom{400}{2} 0.01^2 \cdot 0.99^{398} + \binom{400}{3} 0.01^3 \cdot 0.99^{397} \\ &= 43.25\%. \end{aligned}$$

This is the probability that the accountant approves an accounting with too many errors. The strength of this alternative is the probability that the accounting is not approved, i.e.

$$\text{Strength} = 1 - 43.25\% = 56.75\%.$$

(b) Using normal approximation, we find $n \cdot p(1 - p) = 3.96$ and get

$$\begin{aligned} P(X \leq 3) &\approx G\left(\frac{3 - 4}{\sqrt{3.96}}\right) = G(-0.50) \\ &= 1 - G(0.50) = 1 - 0.6915 = 30.85\%. \end{aligned}$$

and

$$\begin{aligned} P(X \leq 3) &\approx G\left(\frac{3.5 - 4}{\sqrt{3.96}}\right) = G(-0.25) \\ &= 1 - G(0.25) = 1 - 0.5987 = 40.13\%. \end{aligned}$$

We see that integer correction gives a better result, but that both answers are somewhat wrong. The reason is that $n \cdot p(1 - p) = 3.96 < 5$, and we are hence considering a case where normal approximation is not recommended.

9.8

(a) We have $H_0 : \mu = 0$ and $H_A : \mu \neq 0$.
(b) We have $\mathrm{Var}[\overline{X}] = \frac{\sigma^2}{n} = \frac{100{,}000{,}000}{400} = 250{,}000$. Which gives $\sigma[\overline{X}] = 500$. We reject H_0 when $|\overline{X}| \geq x_{\text{limit}}$, where

$$P_{H_0}(\overline{X} \geq x_{\text{limit}}) = 2.5\%.$$

Since we have lots of observations, we can use the central limit theorem. When H_0 is true, then

$$P_{H_0}(\overline{X} \leq x_{\text{limit}}) \approx G\left(\frac{x_{\text{limit}}}{500}\right) = G(1.96).$$

That gives

$$x_{\text{limit}} = 1.96 \cdot 500 = 980.$$

(c) The strength of the alternative $\mu = 2000$, we find as follows:

$$\begin{aligned} P(X \leq 980) &\approx G\left(\frac{980 - 2000}{500}\right) = G(-2.04) \\ &= 1 - G(2.04) = 1 - 0.9793 = 2.07\%. \end{aligned}$$

This is the probability of a false negative. The strength is the complement, and hence the strength is 97.93%.

9.9 The following conditions must be satisfied

$$P_{p=2.5\%}(X \leq x_{\text{limit}}) = 95\%, \qquad P_{p=5\%}(X \leq x_{\text{limit}}) = 5\%.$$

X is a binomial distribution, and we have $\mathrm{E}[X] = n\cdot, \sigma[X] = \sqrt{n \cdot p(1-p)}$. If $p = 2.5\%$, then $\mathrm{E}[X] = n \cdot 0.025, \sigma[X] = \sqrt{n \cdot 0.025 \cdot 0.975}$. Using normal approximation, we find

$$P_{p=2.5\%}(X \leq x_{\text{limit}}) = 95\% = G\left(\frac{x_{\text{limit}} - \mathrm{E}[X]}{\sigma[X]}\right) = G(1.6449).$$

This gives

$$x_{\text{liimit}} = \mathrm{E}[X] + 1.6449 \cdot \sigma[X],$$

which gives rise to the equation

$$x_{\text{limit}} = n \cdot 0.025 + 1.6449 \cdot \sqrt{n \cdot 0,025 \cdot 0.975}.$$

Similarly we can use $p = 5\%$ to find a new equation

$$x_{\text{limit}} = n \cdot 0.05 - 1.6449 \cdot \sqrt{n \cdot 0.05 \cdot 0.95}.$$

If we equate the two expressions for x_{limit} and collect terms, we find

$$0.025n = 1.6449 \cdot (\sqrt{0.025 \cdot 0.975} + \sqrt{0.05 \cdot 0.95})\sqrt{n},$$

i.e.,

$$\sqrt{n} = \frac{1.6449 \cdot (\sqrt{0.025 \cdot 0.975} + \sqrt{0.05 \cdot 0.95})}{0.025} \approx 24.61,$$

which implies $n = 606$. Note: Since $606 \cdot 0.025 \cdot 0.975 = 14.77 > 10$, approximation with the normal distribution works fine.

9.10

(a) It is not reasonable to assume that X_i are independent. If, e.g., the stock price is 120 today, it is more likely that the price is 125 tomorrow than if the price had been 80 today. There is hence reason to believe that the stock price in the near future depends quite strongly on previous prices. The logarithmic transformation below removes this problem.
(b) $\hat{\mu} = \overline{Y} = \frac{1}{10}\sum_{i=1}^{10} Y_i = 0.0612$.
(c) $\text{Var}[\overline{Y}] = \frac{1}{100}\sum_{i=1}^{10} \text{Var}[Y_i] = 0.001 \Rightarrow \sigma[\overline{Y}] \approx 0.0316$.

$$0.05 = P(\overline{Y} \geq Y_{\text{limit}}) \Rightarrow P(\overline{Y} \leq Y_{\text{limit}}) = 0.95.$$

$$G(1.645) \approx 0.95 = P\left(\frac{\overline{Y} - \mu}{\sigma[\overline{Y}]} \leq \frac{Y_{\text{limit}} - \mu}{\sigma[\overline{Y}]}\right) = G\left(\frac{Y_{\text{limit}} - \mu}{\sigma[\overline{Y}]}\right).$$

Hence

$$Y_{\text{limit}} = \mu + 1.645\sigma[\overline{Y}] = 0.052.$$

Since $\hat{\mu} = 0.0612 > 0.052 = Y_{\text{limit}}$, we reject the null hypothesis at 5% significance level. There is hence reason to believe that the stock price increases.
(d) The P-value is found via $P(\overline{Y} \geq \hat{\mu})$ assuming that the null hypothesis is true. Here

$$
\begin{aligned}
&P(\overline{Y} \le \hat{\mu}) \\
&= P\left(\frac{\overline{Y}-\mu}{\sigma[\overline{Y}]} \le \frac{\hat{\mu}-\mu}{\sigma[\overline{Y}]}\right) = G\left(\frac{\hat{\mu}-\mu}{\sigma[\overline{Y}]}\right) = G(\frac{0.0612}{0.0316}) = G(1.94) \approx 0.974,
\end{aligned}
$$

i.e.

$$P\text{-value} = P(\overline{Y} \ge \hat{\mu}) = 1 - P(\overline{Y} \le \hat{\mu}) = 2.6\%.$$

In other words we would reject H_0 at 5% significance level, but we would not be able to reject at 1% significance level.

9.11

(a) $\mathrm{E}[\overline{X}] = \mu$ and $\mathrm{Var}[\overline{X}] = \frac{\sigma^2}{10}$.
(b) Y is t-distributed with parameter 9.
(c) $H_0 : \mu = 0.15,\ H_A : \mu > 0.15$. We reject H_0 when $Y \ge Y_{\text{limit}}$ where

$$P(Y \ge Y_{\text{limit}}) = 5\%,$$

which using the 5% level in the t-table gives $Y_{\text{limit}} = 1.833$.
(d) We compute the observed value for Y assuming that H_0 is true.

$$Y = \frac{0.203 - 0.15}{\frac{0.099}{\sqrt{10}}} = 1.19.$$

Since $Y < Y_{\text{limit}}$, we keep H_0 at 5% significance level. There is reason to assume that the result may be due to pure chance.
(e) The expression at the right side of the inequality, i.e., $Y_{\text{limit}} - \frac{0.053}{S_X/\sqrt{10}}$ is not a constant. If we repeat the experiment, the value of the right-hand side would probably change. This problem can be solved using theory of asymmetric t-distribution.

9.12

(a) X is hypergeometric with parameters $N = 100{,}000$, $M = 100{,}000 \cdot p$, and $n = 1000$. This distribution is very close to a binomial distribution with parameters $n = 1000$ and $p = p$. When p is relatively small, we can approximate by a normal distribution with parameters $\mu = 1000 \cdot p$, $\sigma^2 = \frac{100{,}000-1000}{100{,}000-1} \cdot 1000 \cdot p \cdot (1-p)$ (the first factor can be skipped). When p is relatively small, we can also approximate by a Poisson distribution with parameter $\lambda = 1000 \cdot p$.
(b) $H_0 : p \le 1\%,\ H_a : p > 1\%$. Rejection limit: Find x such that

$$P(X \ge x) = 5\%.$$

Put $p = 0.01, \sigma = 3.13$

$$P(X \geq x) \approx G\left(\frac{x-10}{3.13}\right) = 5\%,$$

i.e.

$$\frac{x-10}{3.13} = 1.645 \qquad \Rightarrow \qquad x = 10 + 3.13 \cdot 1.645 = 15.15.$$

Since the rejection limit must be an integer, we keep H_0 if $X \leq 15$ and reject if $X \geq 16$.

(c) To find the P-value we compute

$$P(X \geq 11) = 1 - P(X \leq 10) \approx 1 - G\left(\frac{10-10}{3.13}\right) = 50\%.$$

Since the P-value is very large, there is no reason to reject H_0.

(d) We need to compute $P(X \leq 15)$ assuming that $p = 0.02$. Then we get

$$P(X \leq 15) \approx G\left(\frac{15-20}{4.43}\right) = G(-1.13) = 1 - G(1.13) = 1 - 0.8708 = 12.9\%.$$

(e) When $p = 1\%$, we can use the Poisson distribution with parameter $\lambda = 10$. Then we get

$$P(X \leq 15) = 0.9513.$$

This corresponds well with 16 as rejection limit.

9.13

(a) Since $\overline{X}$ and $\overline{Y}$ both have normal distribution and the denominator is constant, then U has normal distribution. The variables T and U are different; if we repeat the experiment we will probably observe $S_X^2 \neq 80{,}000$.

(b) This is a two-sided test, and we use T as a test static. We reject if $T \leq -z$ and $T \geq z$, where $P(T \geq z) = 2.5\%$. Using the t-table with parameter 30, we find $z = 2.042$. The rejection region is hence $(-\infty, -2.042] \cup [2.042, \infty)$. When we compute T for our particular observation, we find $T = 1.8$. Since this value is outside the rejection region, we cannot reject H_0 at 5% significance level.

(c) U has normal distribution, but we have problems computing probabilities on the form

$$P\left(\frac{U - \mathrm{E}[U]}{\sigma[U]} \leq z\right).$$

When the null hypothesis is true, $\mathrm{E}[U] = 0$, but we do not know $\sigma[U]$. To circumvent this problem we might use an estimated variance, but then we revert to the original T static.

9.14

(a) We first compute $S[\overline{X}] = \frac{S_X}{\sqrt{8}} = 6.13811$. To find a 95% confidence interval, we use the t-table with parameter $\nu = 8 - 1 = 7$. The 2.5% level in that table is $t = 2.365$, and the limits for the confidence interval are

$$138.625 + \pm 2.365 \cdot 6.13811.$$

This provides us with the interval [124, 153].

(b) Here we can try a one-sided test of $H_0 : \mu \leq 125$ against $H_A : \mu > 125$. As test static we use $T = \frac{\overline{X}-125}{S[\overline{X}]}$. We insert the numbers from (a) and get $T = 2.22$. We know that if H_0 is true, then T is t-distributed with parameter 7. The rejection limit for a one-sided alternative in that table is 1.895. Since T is in the rejection region, we reject the null hypothesis.

If we compare with the confidence interval from (a), we see that the observed value falls inside a 95% confidence interval. There is hence not sufficient evidence to reject H_0 in a two-sided test. This may seem as a contradiction, but one-sided tests should only be used if we have additional information excluding alternatives in the opposite direction. The conclusion in (b) is only valid if we can argue that expected production cannot decline. If we have no such arguments, we should use a two-sided test and keep a null hypothesis of no change.

9.15

(a)

(i)

$$P(X < 2\%) = G\left(\frac{2\% - 5\%}{2\%}\right) = G(-1.5) = 1 - G(1.5) = 1 - 0.9332 = 6.68\%.$$

(ii)

$$\begin{aligned} P(X > -1\%) &= 1 - P(X < -1\%) = 1 - G\left(\frac{-1\% - 5\%}{2\%}\right) \\ &= 1 - G(-3) = G(3) = 0.9987. \end{aligned}$$

(b) We do not have reason to assume that this department are worse than the others, hence the alternative hypothesis is that department has an expected yield different from 5%. We let X denote the result for this department. From (a) we get

$$P(X < 2\%) = 6.68\%.$$

Since the test is two-sided, the P-value is twice as big, i.e., 13.36%. There is hence no reason to reject the null hypothesis.

(c) We let Y denote the result for the worst department and find

$$P(Y < -1\%) = 1 - P(Y > -1\%) = 1 - P(X > -1\%)^{100} = 1 - 0.9987^{100} = 12.20\%.$$

In a two-sided test, the P-value is twice as big, i.e., 24.40%. There is no reason to reject the null hypothesis.

(d) In this case we are in some sense back to the case in (b). We have

$$P(X < -1\%) = 1 - 0.9987 = 0.13\%.$$

The result the first year will further reduce the P-value, and hence the P-value for a two-sided test must be less than 0.26%. We hence reject the null hypothesis stating that this department was as good as all the others.

9.16

(a) Since we only include items of approved quality, it is hard to imagine that the equipment suddenly performs better than normal. We can hence disregard cases where expected production increases. If there is a change in expected production, the change must be negative, and there is hence good reason to use a one-sided test.

(b) Since Z has normal distribution

$$P(Z \leq z) = G\left(\frac{z-\mu}{\sigma}\right) = 0.05 = G(-1.645).$$

That gives

$$\frac{z-\mu}{\sigma} = -1.645 \Leftrightarrow z = \mu - 1.645\,\sigma.$$

(c) We must place the rejection limit such that

$$P(X_1 < x_{\text{grense}}) = 0.05.$$

Since X_1 is normally distributed, we have from (b) that

$$x_{\text{limit}} = 100 - 1.645 \cdot 5 = 91.78.$$

We reject H_0 if the production is less than 91.78 units.

(d) Let

$$Y = \min_{i=1,\dots,10} X_i.$$

Then

$$P(Y \leq 92) = 1 - P(Y \geq 92) = 1 - P(X \geq 92)^{10}.$$

We compute

$$P(X \geq 92) = 1 - P(X \leq 92) = 1 - G\left(\frac{92 - 100}{5}\right) = 1 - G(-1.6) = G(1.6) = 0.9452.$$

That gives $P(Y \leq 92) = 1 - 0.9452^{10} = 0.4308$. The probability of this happening is hence 43.08%.

(e) We should reject H_0 when

$$P(Y \leq y_{\text{grense}}) = 0.05.$$

That gives

$$P(X \geq y_{\text{limit}})^{10} = 0.95 \Rightarrow P(X \leq y_{\text{limit}}) = 1 - 0.95^{1/10} = 0.0051.$$

Which implies

$$\frac{y_{\text{limit}} - 100}{5} = -2.57 \Rightarrow y_{\text{limit}} = 87.15.$$

We reject H_0 when production is not more than 87.15 units.

9.17

(a) X is Bin[120,0.05].

(b)

$$P(X = 2) = \binom{120}{2} 0.05^2 0.95^{118} = 4.2\%.$$

$$\begin{aligned} P(X \leq 2) &= P(X = 0) + P(X = 1) + P(X = 2) \\ &= \binom{120}{0} 0.05^0 0.95^{120} + \binom{120}{1} 0.05^1 0.95^{119} \\ &\quad + \binom{120}{2} 0.05^2 0.95^{118} = 5.8\%. \end{aligned}$$

(c) We cannot say anything sure about the probability for bankruptcy from only one observation. A statistician would interpret this statement in terms of a hypothesis test. With a null hypothesis stating $p = 5\%$, we see that an observation where $X = 2$ is not very rare (occurs in 4.2% of the cases). From the computation in (b) we see that the P-value for a one-sided test is 5.8%. In normal cases we would keep a null hypothesis stating $p = 5\%$. We cannot claim that the journalist is wrong, but can point out that 2 or less bankruptcies will occur quite often even when p is as large as 5%.

(d) If the firms are relatively similar, the probability of bankruptcy will largely depend on the market for such firms. Even when firms are quite different, market prospects may depend on the general economic development. When the economy is growing, we will see less bankruptcies than when it falls. If the probability of bankruptcy depends on such external circumstances, we will see more extreme distributions. In some years very few, while in other years they may appear in large numbers. We cannot assume that X is binomial, and in any case it will be much harder to reject $p = 5\%$ since the distribution is not clear.

9.18

(a) Since the P-value is very large, we cannot reject the null hypothesis. There is no indication that the training has effect.

(b) If the school had been selected randomly, then a P-value of 4% would lead to rejection when it is seen in isolation. Here, however, we have repeated the experiment 25 times. If training has no effect, we expect to observe a P-value of 4% in 1 out of 25 cases. The result is hence not surprising, and there is no reason to assume that the training has effect when we see all the 25 cases in conjunction.

Problems of Chap. 10

10.1 This is a binomial test and we compute

$$Z = \frac{132 - 200 \cdot 0.5}{\sqrt{200 \cdot 0.5 \cdot (1 - 0.5)}} = 4.53.$$

Since the test is two-sided, we look up $z_{0.025} = 1.96$ in the table over the standard normal distribution. The observed value is greater than the rejection limit, and we reject the null hypothesis. The conclusion is that p is probably not equal to 0.5.

10.2 This is a binomial test and we compute

$$Z = \frac{25 - 50 \cdot 0.6}{\sqrt{50 \cdot 0.6 \cdot (1 - 0.6)}} = -1.44.$$

Since the test is two-sided, we look up $z_{0.025} = 1.96$ in the table over the standard normal distribution. The observed value is well within the non-rejection region, and we keep the null hypothesis that $p = 0.6$.

10.3 This is a binomial test and we compute

$$Z = \frac{70 - 120 \cdot 0.5}{\sqrt{120 \cdot 0.5 \cdot (1 - 0.5)}} = 1.83.$$

Since the test is one-sided, we look up $z_{0.05} = 1.65$ in the table over the standard normal distribution. The observed value is greater than the rejection limit, and we reject the null hypothesis. The conclusion is that p is probably greater than 0.5.

10.4 We compute

$$S[\overline{X}] = \frac{13.6}{\sqrt{12}} = 3.93.$$

Since $\mu_0 = 100$, we find

$$T = \frac{106.3 - 100}{3.93} = 1.6.$$

The rejection limits we find from the t-table with parameter 11. We have a two-sided test. Using 5% significance level, we look up the 2.5% level in the table. This gives $t_{0.025}^{(19)} = 2.201$. The non-rejection region is hence $(-2.201, 2.201)$. Since the observed value 1.6 is well within this region, we must keep the null hypothesis. There is not sufficient evidence to support a claim that the expected value is different from 100.

10.5 We compute

$$S[\overline{X}] = \frac{22.1}{\sqrt{20}} = 4.94.$$

Since $\mu_0 = 0$, we find

$$T = \frac{16.9 - 0}{4.94} = 3.42.$$

The rejection limits we find from the t-table with parameter 19. We have a two-sided test. Using 5% significance level, we look up the 2.5% level in the table. This gives $t_{0.025}^{(19)} = 2.093$. Since the observed value 1.6 is greater than the rejection limit, we reject the null hypothesis. We have sufficient evidence to claim that the expected value is probably different from zero.

10.6 We compute

$$S[\overline{X}] = \frac{3.22}{\sqrt{11}} = 0.97.$$

Since $\mu_0 = 10$, we find

$$T = \frac{12.96 - 10}{0.97} = 3.05.$$

The rejection limits we find from the t-table with parameter 10. We have a one-sided test. Using 5% significance level, we look up the 5% level in the table. This gives $t_{0.05}^{[19]} = 1.812$. In this case we should reject H_0 only if $T \leq -1.812$. This is not the case here, so we have not sufficient evidence to claim that the expected value is smaller than 10.

10.7 We compute $\overline{X} = 222$ and $\overline{Y} = 192$. We then calculate

$$S = \sqrt{\frac{1}{5+6-2}\left(\sum_{i=1}^{5}(X_i - \overline{X})^2 + \sum_{i=1}^{6}(Y_i - \overline{Y})^2\right)} = 30.98,$$

which gives

$$S[\hat{\delta}] = S \cdot \sqrt{\frac{1}{5} + \frac{1}{6}} = 18.76.$$

The value of the test static is then

$$T = \frac{222 - 192}{18.76} = 1.60.$$

When the null hypothesis is true, T is t-distributed with parameter $\nu = 5+6-2 = 9$. The rejection limit for a two-sided test is then 2.26 (using 5% significance level). We keep the null hypothesis that there is no difference w.r.t. gender.

10.8 The mean value for department 1 is 131, and the mean value for department 2 is 124. A one-sided t-test in Excel returns a P-value equal to 3.06%. The difference is hence significant, and we conclude that the expected production at department 1 is probably greater than the expected production at department 2.

10.9

(a) In this case the observations are paired, and the paired test is the one that makes best use of the information. As the P-value from both tests fails to be significant, we have no sufficient evidence to claim that the expectations are different.

(b) It is hard to imagine that advertising might have a negative effect. We have hence good reason to use a one-sided test for paired observations. $H_0 : \mu_1 = \mu_2$ against $H_A : \mu_2 > \mu_1$. The P-value for this test is half the value for a two-sided test, i.e., 4%. At 5% significance level we have sufficient evidence to claim that the expected sales volume is probably greater at department 2 than at department 1.

10.10

(a) We have

$$\hat{p}_1 = \frac{190}{250}, \qquad \hat{p}_2 = \frac{147}{225}, \qquad \hat{p} = \frac{337}{475}.$$

We insert these quantities into the formula for U to get

$$U = \frac{\hat{p}_1 - \hat{p}_2}{\sqrt{\left(\frac{1}{n_1} + \frac{1}{n_2}\right)\hat{p}(1-\hat{p})}} = 2.56.$$

Since we have a two-sided test, we use the table of the standard normal distribution to look up $z_{0.025} = 1.96$. Since the observed value is greater than the rejection limit, we conclude that the two groups probably have different expectations. The P-value equals

$$2 \cdot P(U \geq 2.56) = 2 \cdot (1 - 0.9948) = 1.04\%.$$

10.11

(a) We have

$$\hat{p}_1 = \frac{52}{120}, \qquad \hat{p}_2 = \frac{75}{140}, \qquad \hat{p} = \frac{127}{260}.$$

We insert these quantities into the formula for U to get

$$U = \frac{\hat{p}_1 - \hat{p}_2}{\sqrt{\left(\frac{1}{n_1} + \frac{1}{n_2}\right)\hat{p}(1-\hat{p})}} = -1.65.$$

Since we have a two-sided test, we use the table of the standard normal distribution to look up $z_{0.025} = 1.96$. Since the observed value is within the non-rejection region, we do not have sufficient evidence to claim that the two groups have different expectations.

10.12 In the chi-square test we have $n = 500$ and $p_1 = p_2 = p_3 = p_4 = 0.25$. We then get

$$Q = \frac{(129 - 125)^2}{125} + \frac{(140 - 125)^2}{125} + \frac{(113 - 125)^2}{125} + \frac{(118 - 125)^2}{125} = 3.472.$$

When H_0 is true, then Q is chi-square distributed with parameter 3. At 5% significance level we should reject if $Q \geq 7.81$. As this is not the case here, we keep the null hypothesis. There is no sufficient evidence to claim that any of the products are more liked than the others.

10.13 In the chi-square test we have $n = 300$ and $p_1 = p_2 = p_3 = 1/3$. We then get

$$Q = \frac{(98 - 100)^2}{100} + \frac{(120 - 100)^2}{100} + \frac{(92 - 100)^2}{100} = 4.68.$$

When H_0 is true, then Q is chi-square distributed with parameter 2. At 5% significance level we should reject if $Q \geq 3.89$. As this is the case here, we reject the null hypothesis. There is sufficient evidence to claim that some of the products are probably more liked than the others.

10.14 We first write the observed numbers in the first column. Then we multiply the percentages with 1000 and write these numbers in the second column. The command =CHITEST(A1:A10;B1:B10) returns the P-value 53.90%. There is hence no reason to reject the null hypothesis.

10.15 In the chi-square test $n = 800, p_1 = 0.4, p_2 = 0.3, p_3 = 0.3$. Then

$$Q = \frac{(345 - 320)^2}{320} + \frac{(238 - 240)^2}{240} + \frac{(217 - 240)^2}{240} = 4.174.$$

When H_0 is true, then Q is chi-square distributed with parameter 2. At 5% level of significance we should reject H_0 if $Q \geq 5.99$. This is not the case here, so the test does not provide sufficient evidence that opinions have changed.

10.16 In the chi-square test $n = 400$ and

$$p_1 = 0.243, \quad p_2 = 0.213, \quad p_3 = 0.146, \quad p_4 = 0.125, \quad p_5 = 0.124, \quad p_6 = 0.149.$$

In the poll 92 people answered party A, 72 B, 68 C, 40 D, and 64 E. Then we get

$$\begin{aligned} Q &= \frac{(92 - 0.234 \cdot 400)^2}{0.234 \cdot 400} + \frac{(72 - 0.213 \cdot 400)^2}{0.213 \cdot 400} + \frac{(68 - 0.146 \cdot 400)^2}{0.146 \cdot 400} \\ &+ \frac{(64 - 0.125 \cdot 400)^2}{0.125 \cdot 400} + \frac{(40 - 0.124 \cdot 400)^2}{0.124 \cdot 400} + \frac{(64 - 0.149 \cdot 400)^2}{0.149 \cdot 400} \\ &= 10.00. \end{aligned}$$

When H_0 is true, then Q is chi-square distributed with parameter 5. At 5% level of significance we should reject H_0 if $Q \geq 11.11$. This is not the case here, so the test does not provide sufficient evidence that opinions have changed.

10.17 In the chi-square test $n = 1000$. The probability of X errors in 3 independent trials in a binomial distribution. Hence

$$\begin{aligned} P(X=0) &= \binom{3}{0} 0.06^0 0.94^3 = 0.8306, \\ P(X=1) &= \binom{3}{1} 0.06^1 0.94^2 = 0.1590, \\ P(X=2) &= \binom{3}{2} 0.06^2 0.94^1 = 0.0102, \\ P(X=3) &= \binom{3}{3} 0.06^3 0.94^0 = 0.0002. \end{aligned}$$

Then

$$Q = \frac{(829-830.6)^2}{830.6} + \frac{(163-159)^2}{159} + \frac{(6-10.2)^2}{10.2} + \frac{(2-0.2)^2}{0.2} = 18.03.$$

When H_0 is true, then Q is chi-square distributed with parameter 3. At 5% significance level we should reject if $Q \geq 7.81$. As this is the case here, we reject the null hypothesis. There is sufficient evidence to claim that some of the distribution is probably not binomial.

10.18 We first need to find the marginals. The results are shown in Table 6.

Table 6 Marginal totals

Credit rating	Unmarried	Married	Total
A	200	300	500
B	140	260	400
C	40	60	100
Total	380	620	1000

To execute the test, we also need to make a table over the expected values in each entry. Formally we use the formula $E_{ij} = \frac{A_i B_j}{n}$, but we might just as well multiply the fractions and multiply these answers with $n = 1000$. In both cases we end up with Table 7.

Now we can compute the Q-value:

$$Q = \frac{(200-190)^2}{190} + \frac{(300-310)^2}{310} + \frac{(140-152)^2}{152}$$

Table 7 Expected ratings under independence

Credit rating	Unmarried	Married	Total
A	190	310	500
B	152	248	400
C	38	62	100
Total	380	620	1000

$$+\frac{(260-248)^2}{248}+\frac{(40-38)^2}{38}+\frac{(60-62)^2}{62}$$
$$= 2.55.$$

To find the rejection limit we must use a chi-square table with parameter $\nu = (2-1)(3-1) = 2$. Using 5% significance level, the rejection limit in that table is 5.99. Our observed Q is smaller than the rejection limit, and we are unable to reject the null hypothesis stating independence. In other words we do not have sufficient evidence to claim that there is a connection between marital status and credit rating,

10.19 We first need to find the marginals. The results are shown in Table 8.

Table 8 Marginal totals

Reason	Hotel A	Hotel B	Hotel C	Total
Too expensive	50	100	150	300
Bad attractions	100	200	100	400
Bad cleaning	150	100	50	300
Total	300	400	300	1000

To execute the test, we also need to make a table over the expected values in each entry. Formally we use the formula $E_{ij} = \frac{A_i B_j}{n}$, but we might just as well multiply the fractions and multiply these answers with $n = 1000$. In both cases we end up with Table 9.

Table 9 Expected results under independence

Reason	Hotel A	Hotel B	Hotel C	Total
Too expensive	90	120	90	300
Bad attractions	120	160	120	400
Bad cleaning	90	120	90	300
Total	300	400	300	1000

Now we can compute the Q-value:

$$
\begin{aligned}
Q &= \frac{(50-90)^2}{90} + \frac{(100-120)^2}{120} + \frac{(150-90)^2}{90} \\
&+ \frac{(100-120)^2}{120} + \frac{(200-160)^2}{160} + \frac{(100-120)^2}{120} \\
&+ \frac{(150-90)^2}{90} + \frac{(100-120)^2}{120} + \frac{(50-90)^2}{90} \\
&= 138.89.
\end{aligned}
$$

To find the rejection limit we must use a chi-square table with parameter $\nu = (3-1)(3-1) = 4$. Using 5% significance level, the rejection limit in that table is 9.49. Our observed Q is far above the rejection limit, and we reject the null hypothesis stating independence. In other words there is probably a connection between the hotel that was used and the answer that was given.

10.20

(a) The null hypothesis is that there is no change in the distribution of answers, while the alternative hypothesis is that there has been a change. We should make use of a chi-square table with parameter 4, and at 5% significance level we should reject the null hypothesis if $Q \geq 9.49$.

$$
\begin{aligned}
Q &= \frac{(188-148)^2}{148} + \frac{(80-74)^2}{74} + \frac{(330-370)^2}{370} \\
&+ \frac{(92-111)^2}{111} + \frac{(50-37)^2}{37} = 23.44.
\end{aligned}
$$

Since $Q \geq 9.49$ we reject the null hypothesis, and we have sufficient evidence to claim that the customers probably have changed opinions.

(b) We should make use of a chi-square table with parameter 1, and at 5% significance level we should reject the null hypothesis if $Q \geq 3.84$.

$$
Q = \frac{(598-592)^2}{592} + \frac{(142-148)^2}{148} = 0.304.
$$

Since $Q < 3.84$, we keep the null hypothesis. We do not have evidence that the distribution of satisfied/dissatisfied has been altered. This suggests that the changes reported in (a) is due to internal changes within the two groups satisfied/dissatisfied.

(c) $\frac{X_5 - np_5}{\sqrt{np5(1-p_5}}$ is approximately standard normal under these assumptions. That gives

$$
P(X_5 \geq 50) = 1 - P(X_5 \leq 49) = 1 - G\left(\frac{49-37}{\sqrt{37 \cdot 0.95}}\right) = 1 - G(2.02) = 0.0217.
$$

If the customers have the same opinions as before, there is only 2% probability of finding as many very dissatisfied customers as we observed. There is hence reason to believe that the fraction of very dissatisfied customers has increased.

10.21 R is Bin[6,0.5]. We can find the values from a table or directly from the definition of binomial probabilities. We get

$$p_0 = 0.015625, \quad p_1 = 0.09375, \quad p_2 = 0.234375, \quad p_3 = 0.3125,$$
$$p_4 = 0.234375, \quad p_4 = 0.09375 \quad p_6 = 0.015625.$$

(b) A chi-square test can be formulated as follows:

$$H_0 : \text{The probabilities are equal to the probabilities from (a).}$$

$$H_A : \text{The probabilities are not equal to the probabilities from (a).}$$

Let X_i be the number of persons with exactly i correct answers. As test static we use

$$Q = \sum_{i=0}^{6} \frac{(X_i - 300 \cdot p_i)^2}{300 \cdot p_i}.$$

When the null hypothesis is correct, Q is approximately chi-square distributed with parameter 6. Using 5% significance level, we should reject H_0 if $Q \geq 12.6$. If we insert the observed numbers, we get $Q = 10.41$. We keep the null hypothesis, and cannot be reasonably sure that the distribution of answers are different from what we would expect if all participants were guessing the answers.

10.22

(a) $X_1 = \text{Bin}[n_1, p_1]$ and $X_2 = \text{Bin}[n_2, p_2]$.
(b) $H_0 : p_1 \leq p_2$ against $H_A : p_1 > p_2$. We insert the values and find $U = 1.51$. Since U is approximately standard normal, the P-value is given by

$$P = P(U \geq 1.51) = 1 - P(U \leq 1.51) = 1 - G(1.51) = 1 - 0.9345 = 6.5\%.$$

At 5% significance level we would keep the null hypothesis, which means that the results may be coincidental.
(c) It may happen that a company focuses funds within a particular branch, i.e., information technology. If information technology companies are doing well, all the funds will be doing well, and if the market for such companies declines, the majority of the funds will perform badly. The result of each different fund is hence strongly dependent on how the other funds are doing.

10.23

(a) A chi-square test is well suited for this situation. The null hypothesis is that the probability that a randomly chosen customer prefers product number i is given by

$$p_1 = 0.1, \quad p_2 = 0.2, \quad p_3 = 0.15, \quad p_4 = 0.3, \quad p_5 = 0.1, \quad p_6 = 0.15.$$

The alternative hypothesis is that the probabilities are not like that. As test static we use

$$Q = \sum_{i=1}^{6} \frac{(X_i - np_i)^2}{np_i}.$$

When H_0 is true, this test static is approximately chi-square distributed with parameter 5. Using 5% significance level, we should reject H_0 if $Q \geq 11.1$. The rejection region is $[11.1, \infty)$.

(b) We find

$$\begin{aligned} Q &= \frac{(28-20)^2}{20} + \frac{(42-40)^2}{40} + \frac{(25-30)^2}{30} \\ &+ \frac{(52-60)^2}{60} + \frac{(25-20)^2}{20} + \frac{(28-30)^2}{30} \\ &= 6.58. \end{aligned}$$

Since the value of Q is below the rejection limit, we keep the null hypothesis. The tendency in our data material is not sufficient strong to support a claim that opinions have changed. From the table we see that the P-value is slightly larger than 25%. (25% gives $Q = 6.63$).

10.24

(a) Any t-test takes the t-distribution as a starting point, which requires data to be approximately normal. Since the P-value is lower than the significance level, we should reject the null hypothesis. If all the requirements are satisfied, we conclude that the two departments probably have different expected production.

(b)

$$P(X \leq 125) = G\left(\frac{125 - 106.15}{\sqrt{36.87}}\right) = G(3.1) = 0.999.$$

$$\begin{aligned} P(\text{Largest} \geq 125) &= 1 - P(\text{All} \leq 125) = 1 - P(X \leq 125)^{20} \\ &= 1 - 0.999^{20} = 1.98\%. \end{aligned}$$

(c) Since the P-value is far less than the significance level, we confidently reject the null hypothesis. Our data are probably not normally distributed. This means that we cannot trust the test in (a). We hence do not have sufficient evidence to claim that the two departments have different expected production.

10.25

(a) We first find

$$S[\hat{\delta}] = \sqrt{42.71 \cdot \left(\frac{1}{8} + \frac{1}{8}\right)} = 3.27.$$

That gives

$$T = \frac{124 - 130.63}{3.27} = -2.03.$$

This is a one-sided test with 5% significance level. The parameter is $\nu = 8 + 8 - 1 = 14$, and from this t-table we find $t_{0.025}^{(14)} = 1.761$. The training has effect if $\mu_X < \mu_Y$, and we use the hypotheses $H_0 : \ \mu_X \geq \mu_Y$ and $H_A : \ \mu_X < \mu_Y$. We can reject H_0 if $T \leq -1.761$. Since this is the case, we reject the null hypothesis and claim that the training probably had effect.

(b) To compute W we sort the values in ascending order and underline the values from the first group. That gives

$$\underline{113}, \underline{118}, \underline{119}, 123, \underline{124}, 125, 126, \underline{127}, \underline{128}, 129, 130, \underline{131}, \underline{132}, 133, 139, 140.$$

To compute W we sum the positions of the underlined numbers, i.e.

$$W = 1 + 2 + 3 + 5 + 8 + 9 + 12 + 13 = 53.$$

We compute

$$\mathrm{E}[W] = \frac{1}{2} \cdot 8(8 + 8 + 1) = 68.$$

$$\mathrm{Var}[W] = \frac{1}{12}(8 \cdot 8(8 + 8 + 1) = 90.67.$$

That gives

$$Z = \frac{53 - 68}{\sqrt{90.67}} = -1.58.$$

This is a one-sided test with 5% significance level. From the table of the standard normal distribution we get $z_{0.05} = 1.6449$. The hypotheses are the same as in (a), and we should reject H_0 if $Z \leq -1.6449$. This is not the case, so we keep H_0 as we are not sufficiently sure there is an effect.

(c) We see that the two tests give opposite conclusions. If we have information that implies that data are not normally distributed, the assumptions for the t-test fails and we must disregard that result. The only valid conclusion is the one from (b).

10.26

(a)

$$\mathrm{E}[W] = \frac{1}{2} \cdot 20 \cdot (20 + 20 + 1) = 410.$$

$$\mathrm{Var}[W] = \frac{1}{12} \cdot 20 \cdot 20 \cdot (20 + 20 + 1) = 1366.67.$$

We sort the observations in ascending order and underline the observations from group 1:

$$\begin{aligned} &195, 206, \underline{210}, 211, 212, 214, 218, 219, \underline{220}, \underline{224}, \\ &\underline{227}, \underline{228}, 229, 232, \underline{235}, \underline{237}, \underline{238}, \underline{239}, 240, 241, \\ &\underline{245}, 246, 247, \underline{248}, \underline{251}, \underline{252}, 253, \underline{259}, 260, 263, \\ &264, \underline{268}, 275, 276, \underline{279}, \underline{283}, \underline{285}, \underline{286}, \underline{288}, 296. \end{aligned}$$

W is the sum of the positions of the underlined numbers, i.e.

$$\begin{aligned} W &= 3 + 9 + 10 + 11 + 12 + 15 + 16 + 17 + 18 + 21 \\ &+24 + 25 + 26 + 28 + 32 + 35 + 36 + 37 + 38 + 39 \\ &= 452. \end{aligned}$$

This gives

$$Z = \frac{452 - 410}{\sqrt{1366.67}} = 1.14.$$

Since this is a one-sided test with 5% significance level, we find $z_{0.05} = 1.6449$. We should hence reject H_0 if $Z \geq 1.6449$. As this is not the case, we keep the null hypothesis and do not have sufficient evidence to claim that the expected working time has been reduced.

(b)

$$\mathrm{E}[W] = \frac{1}{4} \cdot 20 \cdot (20+1) = 105.$$

$$\mathrm{Var}[W] = \frac{1}{24} \cdot 20 \cdot (20+1) \cdot (2 \cdot 20 + 1) = 717.5.$$

We take the numbers from group 2 and subtract the corresponding numbers from group 1. That gives

$$-21, 3, 6, -18, -12, -16, -8, -5, -14, 1,$$
$$-19, -24, -7, -2, -25, -4, -13, 15, -22, 10.$$

The next step is to sort the observation in ascending order with respect to absolute value, and then underline the negative numbers.

$$1, \underline{-2}, 3, \underline{-4}, \underline{-5}, 6, \underline{-7}, \underline{-8}, 10, \underline{-12}, \underline{-13-14},$$
$$\underline{-15}, \underline{-16}, \underline{-18}, \underline{-19}, \underline{-21}, \underline{-22}, \underline{-24}, \underline{-25}.$$

V is the sum of the positions of the underlined items:

$$V = 2+4+5+7+8+10+11+12+13+14+15+16+17+18+19+20 = 191.$$

That gives

$$Z = \frac{191 - 105}{\sqrt{717.5}} = 3.21.$$

Since this is a one-sided test with 5% significance level, we find $z_{0.05} = 1.6449$. We should hence reject H_0 if $Z \geq 1.6449$. This is true, and we hence reject the null hypothesis and claim that the expected working time has probably been reduced.

(c) The test in (b) is the one that best makes use of the given information. The observations are paired, and the test in (a) does not take this into account. There is no contradiction here. The conclusion in (a) is that we do not have sufficient evidence to reject the null hypothesis. When more precise information is given, we can execute a more refined test. We conclude that the expected working time has probably been reduced.

10.27

(a)

$$\hat{p}_1 = \frac{10}{100} \qquad \hat{p}_2 = \frac{8}{120} \qquad \hat{p} = \frac{18}{220}.$$

That gives

$$U = \frac{\hat{p}_1 - \hat{p}_2}{\sqrt{\left(\frac{1}{100} + \frac{1}{120}\right)\hat{p}(1-\hat{p})}} = 0.90.$$

We let p_1 be the probability for error before training and p_2 be the probability for error after training, In this case $H_0 : p_1 = p_2$ and $H_A : p_1 > p_2$. It is not reasonable that training of this sort will increase the probability for errors. We can hence disregard cases where $p_1 < p_2$. That means that it is legitimate to use a one-sided test in this case.

$$P\text{-value} = P(U \geq 0.90) = 1 - P(U \leq 0.90) = 1 - G(0.90) = 1 - 0.8159 = 18.41\%.$$

Since the P-value is large, there is no reason to reject the null hypothesis saying that training had no effect.

(b) It is easy to realize that training of this kind might reduce the efficiency of production, and hence a two-sided test is appropriate here.

10.28

(a) It is unreasonable that training should lead to lower production, and we can then use one-sided tests.

H_0 : Expected production is the same before and after training.

H_A : Expected production is larger after training.

(b) t-test: The P-value is large and we must keep the null hypothesis that expected production is the same as before. Training does not appear to have had effect.

The Wilcoxon test: The P-value is very small, and we reject the hull hypothesis and claim that expected production probably has increased.

(c) If we inspect to observed pairs, we see that in all cases except the last pair, production has increased after training. The last pair is very different from all the others and pulls the conclusion in the opposite direction. Either the last pair is a mistyping, or data are probably not normally distributed. In either case we should rely on the result from the Wilcoxon test. A general advantage of the Wilcoxon test over t-tests is that it is less sensitive with respect to outliers, i.e., observations that are very different from the rest.

10.29

(a) Here we have $H_0 : \mu_X \geq \mu_Y$ and $H_A : \mu_X < \mu_Y$. Using the formulas for the Wilcoxon test, we get

$$\mathrm{E}[W] = \frac{1}{2} \cdot 50 \cdot (50 + 50 + 1) = 2525.$$

$$\mathrm{Var}[W] = \frac{1}{12} \cdot 50 \cdot 50 \cdot (50 + 50 + 1) = 21{,}041.67.$$

(b) We find

$$Z = \frac{2455 - 2525}{\sqrt{21{,}041.67}} = -0.48.$$

In this case we should reject H_0 if $Z \leq -1.6449$. This is not the case here, so we keep the null hypothesis saying that training has no effect.

(c) $\mathrm{E}[V] = \frac{1}{4}50 \cdot 51 = 637.5$, $\mathrm{Var}[V] = \frac{1}{24}50 \cdot 51 \cdot 101 = 10{,}731.25$.

(d) We get $Z = \frac{604-637.5}{\sqrt{10{,}731.25}} = -0.32$. In this case, too, we should reject H_0 if $Z \leq -1.6449$. This is not the case here, so we keep the null hypothesis saying that training has no effect.

(e) After sorting we find $Z = \frac{664-637.5}{\sqrt{10{,}731.25}} = -2.64$. If this value had made sense, it would have lead to rejection. The problem is that the sorting breaks the pairing of the data, and we are not allowed to use a paired test on the sorted data.

(f) As mentioned under (e), a paired test cannot be used on the sorted data. The only valid conclusion comes from (d), which do not find sufficient evidence to claim that training had effect.

Remark The sorting in (e) will in general create strong effects. We typically get values for Z in the interval $[-25, 25]$ even when there is no effect present, and Z will not be approximately normal (under H_0) in this case. Such creative processing of data is a very serious mistake.

10.30

(a) We compute

$$S[\hat{\delta}] = S \cdot \sqrt{\frac{1}{n_1} + \frac{1}{n_2}} = 43{,}000 \cdot \sqrt{\frac{1}{5000} + \frac{1}{7000}} = 796.21.$$

$$T = \frac{312{,}000 - 310{,}000}{796.21} = 2.51.$$

Since we have a two-sided test with 5% significance level, we find $t_{0.025}^{(11,998)} = 1.96$ (with so many observations there is no difference between the t-distributions and the standard normal distribution). Since $T = 2.51 > 1.96 = t_{0.025}^{(11,998)}$, we reject the null hypothesis stating equal expected wages, and conclude that expected wages probably are different in the two regions.

(b) We compute

$$T_1 = \frac{2000 + 5000}{796.21} = 8.79, \qquad T_2 = \frac{5000 - 2000}{796.21} = 3.77.$$

In this case we find $t_{0.05}^{(11,998)} = 1.645$. Since $\min[T_1, T_2] = 3.77$,

$$\min[T_1, T_2] > 1.645 = t_{0.05}^{(11,998)},$$

and we reject the null hypothesis stating that expected wages are not equivalent, and conclude that the difference in expected wages is probably so small that it is unimportant.

Remark The exercise illustrates a general weakness of classical hypothesis testing. If we have many observations, even the slightest difference will lead to rejection of a null hypothesis stating equality. In such cases an equivalence test may be more suited to shed light on the situation. It should be noted, however, that an equivalence test is to some extent in conflict with basic principles of classical hypothesis testing where one nearly always starts out with a null hypothesis stating equality.

10.31

(a) The answer $q = 31.4$ we find from the chi-square table with parameter $\nu = 20$.

(b) The rejection limit follows from (a). We reject if

$$\frac{2 \cdot 10 \cdot \overline{X}}{10} \geq 31.4 \qquad \Leftrightarrow \qquad \overline{X} \geq 15.7.$$

Since the observed value $\overline{X} = 15$ is below the rejection limit, we keep H_0. We note that even though the observed value appears to be quite far from the expected value $\theta = 10$, this is not sufficient for rejection.

(c) By the strength of the alternative $\theta = 20$, we mean the probability of rejecting H_0 when the true value of θ is 20. We reject when $\overline{X} \geq 15.7$, and that gives

$$P(\overline{X} \geq 15.7) = P\left(\frac{2 \cdot 10 \cdot \overline{X}}{20} \geq \frac{2 \cdot 10 \cdot 15.7}{20}\right) = P(Q_{20} \geq 15.7) \approx 75\%,$$

(the closest number we find in the table is 15.5, and the strength is hence slightly smaller that 75%). To answer the last question, we must try out different values of n. If $n = 50$, we should use the chi-square table with parameter 100. We reject when $Q \geq 12.4$, and the strength of the alternative $\theta = 12.5$ becomes

$$P(\overline{X} \geq 12.4) = P\left(Q_{100} \geq \frac{2 \cdot 50 \cdot 12.4}{12.5}\right) = P(Q_{100} \geq 99.2) \approx 50\%,$$

(the closest number we find in the table is 99.3, and the strength is hence slightly above 50%).

10.32

(a) We compute

$$S[\hat{\delta}] = S \cdot \sqrt{\frac{1}{n_1} + \frac{1}{n_2}} = 2900 \cdot \sqrt{\frac{1}{15{,}000} + \frac{1}{10{,}000}} = 37.44.$$

That gives

$$T = \frac{32{,}378 - 32{,}209}{37.44} = 4.51.$$

Here we have lots of observations, and there is no difference between the t-distributions and the standard normal distribution. Hence $t^{(\nu)}_{2.5\%} = 1.96$. Since T is far above the rejection limit, we reject H_0 and conclude that the difference in expected wages is strongly significant. The wording strongly significant is sometimes used when the P-value is less than 1%, but note that strongly significant does not in any way mean the same as very important.

(b) A 95% confidence interval we find by

$$\overline{X} - \overline{Y} \pm t^{(\nu)}_{\alpha/2} \cdot S[\hat{\delta}] = 32{,}378 - 32{,}209 \pm 1.96 \cdot 37.44.$$

which gives the interval [95, 242]. We see that the difference in expected wages is quite modest even though the difference is strongly significant. In cases with many observations, confidence intervals are often more informative as they provide a clear indication of how large the difference can be expected to be.

10.33

(a)

$$\overline{X}_{\text{before}} = 1 \cdot \frac{160}{960} + 2 \cdot \frac{160}{960} + 3 \cdot \frac{160}{960} + 4 \cdot \frac{160}{960} + 5 \cdot \frac{160}{960} = 3.$$

$$\overline{X}_{\text{after}} = 1 \cdot \frac{264}{1379} + 2 \cdot \frac{310}{1379} + 3 \cdot \frac{230}{1379} + 4 \cdot \frac{115}{1379} + 5 \cdot \frac{460}{1379} = 3.14.$$

(b)

$$S[\hat{\delta}] = 1.47 \cdot \sqrt{\frac{1}{960} + \frac{1}{1379}} = 0.062, \qquad T = \frac{3 - 3.14}{0.062} = -2.25.$$

From the table of the standard normal distribution, the rejection limit at 5% significance level is -1.65. Since the observed value is less than this, we reject the null hypothesis and claim that the expected answer (whatever that might be) has increased significantly.

(c) The test in (b) is problematic. Data are not scaled; we probably do not mean that 5 (very satisfied) is 5 times better than 1 (very dissatisfied) or 25% better than 4 (somewhat satisfied). It is not even clear that the mean value has any meaningful interpretation. Overall the whole analysis is questionable.

(d) (i) Here we have $\hat{p}_1 = \frac{160}{960}, \hat{p}_2 = \frac{460}{1379}$, and $\hat{p} = \frac{160+460}{960+1379}$. Inserting these values, we find

$$U = \frac{\hat{p}_1 - \hat{p}_2}{\sqrt{\left(\frac{1}{960} + \frac{1}{1379}\right)\hat{p}(1-\hat{p})}} = -9.00.$$

The effect is strongly significant, and we conclude that there are probably more very satisfied customers than before.

(ii) Here we merge the data from answers 4 and 5. That gives

$$\hat{p}_1 = \frac{240 + 160}{960}, \qquad \hat{p}_2 = \frac{115 + 460}{1379}, \qquad \hat{p} = \frac{240 + 160 + 115 + 460}{960 + 1379}.$$

Inserting these values, we find

$$U = \frac{\hat{p}_1 - \hat{p}_2}{\sqrt{\left(\frac{1}{960} + \frac{1}{1379}\right)\hat{p}(1-\hat{p})}} = -0.015.$$

This value is well inside the non-rejection region, and there is no reason to claim that there are more satisfied customers than before.

(iii) Here we have $\hat{p}_1 = \frac{160}{960}$, $\hat{p}_2 = \frac{264}{1379}$, and $\hat{p} = \frac{160+264}{960+1379}$. Inserting these values, we find

$$U = \frac{\hat{p}_1 - \hat{p}_2}{\sqrt{\left(\frac{1}{960} + \frac{1}{1379}\right)\hat{p}(1-\hat{p})}} = -1.53.$$

Here we notice a tendency that the fraction of very dissatisfied customers has increased, but the effect is not sufficient for rejection. The result may be due to chance, and we must keep the null hypothesis stating no difference. Note that when we use one-sided tests here, we tacitly assume that more support cannot lead to more dissatisfaction. That strengthens the impression that the increase is due to chance. Strictly speaking the test in (iii) does not make sense under these assumptions.

(e) The serious problems that we pointed out with the test in (b) are not present here. Quite the contrary, these tests are credible and are clearly the right tools for handling these data.

10.34

(a)

$$\mathrm{E}[\overline{X}] = \mathrm{E}\left[\frac{1}{100}\sum_{i=1}^{100} X_i\right] = \frac{1}{100}\sum_{i=1}^{100}\mathrm{E}[X_i] = \frac{1}{100}\sum_{i=1}^{100} 489 = 489.$$

$$\mathrm{Var}[\overline{X}] = \mathrm{Var}\left[\frac{1}{100}\sum_{i=1}^{100} X_i\right] = \frac{1}{100^2}\sum_{i=1}^{100}\mathrm{Var}[X_i] = \frac{1}{100^2}\sum_{i=1}^{100} 90^2 = 81.$$

It is not necessary to show these calculations. Alternatively we can just refer to well-known principles from the book.

(b) From (a) we have $\mathrm{E}[\overline{X}] = 489$ and $\sigma[\overline{X}] = 9$. That gives

$$P(\overline{X} \le 463) = G\left(\frac{463 - 489}{9}\right) = G(-2.89) = 1 - G(2.89) = 1 - 0.9981 = 0.0019.$$

(c) From (b) we see that

$$P(\overline{X} \ge 463) = 0.9981.$$

The probability that all the 500 schools have a mean score above 463 is hence

$$0.9981^{500} = 0.386392.$$

(d) We use the equivalence

$$\text{The worst school has a result } \le 463 \Leftrightarrow \text{Not all schools have a score } > 463$$

The score has normal distribution, and hence the probability of a mean score equal to 463 is zero. That gives

$$P(\text{The worst school has a result } \le 463) = 1 - 0.9981^{500} = 61.36\%.$$

Even though a randomly selected school has very little probability of scoring 463 or less, it is very likely that at least one of the schools performs at such low level.

10.35

(a) This result is perfectly normal. If all the departments are equally good, a P-value of 4% will occur in one out of 25 cases. Since the company has 100 production departments, there is nothing strange with this value. The management should not take any action.

(b) This result is not normal. If all departments are equally good, a P-value of 0.01% will only occur in 1 out of 10,000 cases. Even when we take into account that the company has 100 production departments, this result is unusually bad. The management should take swift action and see if they are able to identify a cause for this.

(c) Independence gives

$$P\left(\min_{1\leq i\leq 100} Z_1 \leq 10\right) = 1 - P(Z_i \geq 10)^{100}.$$

We need to compute

$$\begin{aligned} P(Z_i \geq 10) &= 1 - P(Z_i \leq 10) = 1 - P(X_i \leq \ln[10]) = 1 - G\left(\frac{\ln[10] - 10}{3}\right) \\ &= 1 - G(-2.57) = G(2.57) = 0.9949. \end{aligned}$$

That gives

$$P\left(\min_{1\leq i\leq 100} Z_1 \leq 10\right) = 1 - 0.9949^{100} = 40.03\%.$$

10.36

(a) We compute $S[\hat{\delta}] = 23.23 \cdot \sqrt{\frac{1}{40} + \frac{1}{40}} = 5.19$. That gives

$$T = \frac{101.75 - 112.12}{5.19} = -2.00.$$

Rejection is decided from a t-table with parameter 78, the table with parameter 80 suggests rejection when $T \leq -1.664$. We see from the table that the P-value is about 2.5%. We are able to reject the null hypothesis, and draw the conclusion that the expected value is probably greater in group 2.

(b) If we repeat the computations from (a) using new values, we get

$$S[\hat{\delta}] = 19.91 \cdot \sqrt{\frac{1}{10} + \frac{1}{10}} = 8.90.$$

That gives

$$T = \frac{103.62 - 110.88}{8.90} = -0.82.$$

Rejection is decided from a t-table with parameter 18, and the table suggests rejection when $T \leq -1.734$. Seen in isolation, this result does not give cause for rejection.

(c) That the strength is as low as 25% means that we in 3 out of 4 cases will do a type II error, i.e., keep a wrong null hypothesis. We should hence not be surprised when the new test does not confirm the result from (a). Quite the contrary, this is something that will happen in a majority of cases. It is hence not a good idea to try to confirm the result in this way. To avoid seemingly contradictory results as this, it is important that the confirmation has sufficient strength. In our case a confirmation should build on more than 100 observations in each group. If we simply repeat the data collection in (a) with 40 observations in each group, the strength is still no more than about 65%, meaning that 1 out of 3 samples does not confirm a significant effect.

(d) If we merge the data from (a) and (b), we find

$$S[\hat{\delta}] = 22.42 \cdot \sqrt{\frac{1}{50} + \frac{1}{50}} = 4.48.$$

This gives

$$T = \frac{102.12 - 111.88}{4.48} = -2.18.$$

Rejection is decided from a t-table with parameter 98, the table with parameter 100 suggests rejection when $T \leq -1.660$. We see that the two datasets in total gives a clear rejection, and that the rejection is even clearer than in (a). It may appear contradictory that (b) in fact supports the finding in (a), but the explanation is that (b) too gives a result in the same direction as (a), i.e., $\overline{X} < \overline{Y}$.

Problems of Chap. 11

11.1 (a) Suitable. (b) Nonlinear, unsuitable. (c) Suitable. (d) No particular pairing, partly unsuitable.

11.2 We choose the points $t = 0, x = 10$ and $t = 20, x = 0$. The two point formula gives

$$x = \frac{10 - 0}{0 - 20} \cdot (t - 0) + 10 = -\frac{1}{2} \cdot t + 10.$$

11.3 Here we have $t_1 = 1, t_2 = 3, t_3 = 5, t_4 = 7$ and $X_1 = 3, X_2 = 7, X_3 = 9, X_4 = 9$. We insert those values into the formulas

$$\bar{t} = \frac{1}{4}(1+3+5+7) = 4,$$

$$\overline{X} = \frac{1}{4}(3+7+9+9) = 7,$$

$$\begin{aligned}\hat{\beta} &= \frac{1}{(1-4)^2+(3-4)^2+(3-4)^2+(7-4)^2} \\ &\cdot((3-7)(1-4)+(7-7)(3-4)+(9-7)(5-4)+(9-7)(7-4)) \\ &= \frac{1}{20}\cdot 20 = 1.\end{aligned}$$

$$\hat{\alpha} = \overline{X} - \hat{\beta}\,\bar{t} = 7 - 1\cdot 4 = 3.$$

The regression line is

$$\hat{X} = 3 + t.$$

11.4 We compute

$$S[\hat{\beta}] = \sqrt{\frac{5.70^2}{770}} = 0.205.$$

If $\beta = 0$, then

$$T = \frac{\hat{\beta}-\beta}{S[\hat{\beta}]} = \frac{2.06}{2.43} = 10.05.$$

Under H_0, T is t-distributed with parameter $\nu = 19$. In a two-sided test with 5% significance level, we should reject H_0 when

$$|T| \geq 2.093.$$

The rejection criterion is satisfied, and we claim that the effect of time t is statistically significant.

11.5 We compute

$$S[\hat{\beta}] = \sqrt{\frac{5.37^2}{340}} = 0.291.$$

If $\beta = 0$, then

$$T = \frac{\hat{\beta} - \beta}{S[\hat{\beta}]} = \frac{-0.32}{0.291} = 1.10.$$

Under H_0, T is t-distributed with parameter $\nu = 14$. In a two-sided test with 5% significance level, we should reject H_0 when

$$|T| \geq 2.145.$$

The rejection criterion is not satisfied, and we are unable to claim that time t has significant effect.

11.6

(a) When $t = 15$, then

$$\hat{X} = 78.31 - 3.01 \cdot 15 = 33.16.$$

We have

$$S[\hat{X}] = 5.81 \cdot \sqrt{\frac{1}{12} + \frac{(15-5.5)^2}{143}} = 4.91.$$

We hence estimate

$$\mathrm{E}[X] = 33.16 \pm 4.91.$$

(b) Here we compute

$$S[\hat{X} - X] = 5.81 \cdot \sqrt{1 + \frac{1}{12} + \frac{(15-5.5)^2}{143}} = 7.61.$$

The predicted value is

$$X = 33.16 \pm 7.61.$$

(c) Since the variance is unknown, we use the t-distribution with parameter $\nu = 10$. The two 95% confidence intervals hence have the limits

$$33.16 \pm 2.228 \cdot 4.91 \rightarrow [22.22,\ 44.10],$$

and

$$33.16 \pm 2.228 \cdot 7.61 \rightarrow [16.20,\ 50.12].$$

11.7

(a) When $t = 40$, then

$$\hat{X} = 64.37 + 1.81 \cdot 40 = 136.77.$$

We have

$$S[\hat{X}] = 5.76 \cdot \sqrt{\frac{1}{32} + \frac{(40 - 15.5)^2}{2728}} = 2.89.$$

We hence estimate

$$\mathrm{E}[X] = 136.77 \pm 2.89.$$

(b) Here we compute

$$S[\hat{X} - X] = 5.76 \cdot \sqrt{1 + \frac{1}{32} + \frac{(40 - 15.5)^2}{2728}} = 6.44.$$

The predicted value is

$$X = 136.77 \pm 6.44.$$

(c) Since the variance is unknown, we use the t-distribution with parameter $\nu = 30$. The two 95% confidence intervals hence have the limits

$$136.77 \pm 2.042 \cdot 2.89 = [130.87,\ 142.67],$$

and

$$136.77 \pm 2.042 \cdot 6.44 = [123.61,\ 149.92].$$

11.8 The residual is the difference between the point on the regression line and the corresponding observed value. We have $t_1 = 1$ and $X_1 = 3$.

$$\hat{X}_1 = 3 + t_1 = 3 + 1 = 4.$$

The first residual is hence

$$\hat{R}_1 = X_1 - \hat{X}_1 = 3 - 4 = -1.$$

Similarly we find

$$\hat{R}_2 = X_2 - \hat{X}_2 = 7 - 6 = 1,$$

$$\hat{R}_3 = X_3 - \hat{X}_3 = 9 - 8 = 1,$$

$$\hat{R}_4 = X_4 - \hat{X}_4 = 9 - 10 = -1.$$

11.9

(a) We see that education is strongly significant. The explanatory power is about 23%, and one year of extra education offers an increase of 1896 USD in expected wages.

(b) The four variables exhibit multicollinearity. For example is

$$prof4 = 1 - prof1 - prof2 - prof3.$$

When dummy variables are used in regression, one of the dummies must be deleted.

(c) We see that the variables practice, gender, and profession are strongly significant. Education is clearly nonsignificant, even the sign makes no sense. The explanation is multicollinearity between education and profession. This is later confirmed by the findings in (d). The reason why education is significant in (a) is not that extra education is good in itself, but it is likely that long education is needed to get work in the professions that pay more. The profession is probably the primary cause for high salary, and education fails to be significant when profession is included as explanatory variable.

(d) Since $R^2 > 90\%$, we interpret this as multicollinearity between education and profession. This suggest that we may delete education as explanatory variable.

(e) Now all explanatory variables are strongly significant. The explanatory power is 96% and has not been reduced by deleting the variable education. This is a better model.

(f) We use the model from (e), and find

$$\widehat{\text{wages}} = 14{,}924 + 506 \cdot 12 + 10{,}072 \cdot 1 = 31{,}063.$$

All the other terms are zero.

11.10

(a) Method is not a scale variable and cannot be used directly in a regression. The results here are all without meaning.

(b) Using X_1 and X_2 we have coded method via dummy variables. Contrary to (a) this is a valid construction, and the results show that time and method are both strongly significant. In addition we see that the model has explanatory power 91.5%, which is great.

(c) As mentioned above (a) is pointless and only the model in (b) carries weight. From the regression

$$\widehat{\text{production}} = 195.9 + 9.67 \cdot \textit{time} - 43.77 \cdot X_1 - 34.11 \cdot X_2,$$

we see that the coefficients in front of X_1 and X_2 are both negative. That means that maximum expected/predicted value is obtained when X_1 and X_2 are both zero. This case occurs when we use method 2. Method 2 is hence the one with the best expected/predicted value.

11.11 The histogram resembles the normal distribution, normal score is approximately a straight line, and the residuals are fairly symmetric and do not change along the axes. In total the assumptions of independent, normally distributed residuals appear to be satisfied.

11.12 The histogram does not resemble the normal distribution, the normal score is not a straight line, and the residuals exhibit noticeable trends. Everything goes wrong here, and the assumption of independent, normally distributed residuals does not appear to be satisfied.

11.13

(a) The observations do not lie in the vicinity of a straight line, the normal score is not a straight line, the histogram does not resemble the normal distribution, and the residuals have obvious trends. Conclusion: None of the standard criteria appears to be satisfied, and linear regression serves no purpose in this case.

(b) The observations lie in the vicinity of straight line, the normal score is a fairly straight line, and the residuals are fairly symmetric without noticeable trends. Residual versus fitted values is maybe not fully symmetric at the right side, but that is due to a low number of observations, and does not indicate that something is wrong. Conclusion: All the standard criteria appears to be satisfied, and a linear regression appears to make good sense.

(c) If we insert $p = 110$, we find

$$\widehat{\ln[Q]} = 8.91 - 0.914 \ln[110] = 4.61.$$

That gives

$$\hat{Q} = e^{4.61} = 100.$$

An estimate for the expectation of Q hence 100.

(d) The trick is to add and subtract $\mathrm{E}[\ln(U)]$ at the right place. Using standard rules for logarithms we get

$$\begin{aligned}\ln[Q] &= \ln(K \cdot p^{\beta} \cdot U) \\ &= \ln(K) + \ln(p^{\beta}) + \ln(U) = \ln(K) + \beta \ln(p) + \ln(U) \\ &= (\ln(K) + \mathrm{E}[\ln(U)]) + \beta \ln(p) + (\ln(U) - \mathrm{E}[\ln(U)]),\end{aligned}$$

i.e., $\gamma = \ln[K] + \mathrm{E}[\ln(U)]$ and $\epsilon = \ln(U) - \mathrm{E}[\ln(U)]$. Strictly speaking we also need to assume that $\mathrm{E}[\ln(U)] < \infty$.

(e) Since

$$\gamma = \ln(K) + \mathrm{E}[\ln(U)] \Rightarrow K = \mathrm{e}^{\gamma - \mathrm{E}[\ln(U)]} = \mathrm{e}^{\gamma - \ln[\mathrm{E}[U]] + \frac{1}{2}\sigma^2} = \frac{\mathrm{e}^{\gamma + \frac{1}{2}\sigma^2}}{\mathrm{E}[U]}.$$

The expected value is hence given by

$$\mathrm{E}[Q] = K \cdot p^{\beta} \cdot \mathrm{E}[U] = \frac{\mathrm{e}^{\gamma + \frac{1}{2}\sigma^2}}{\mathrm{E}[U]} \cdot \mathrm{e}^{\beta \ln(p)} \cdot \mathrm{E}[U] = \mathrm{e}^{\gamma + \beta \ln(p) + \frac{1}{2}\sigma^2}.$$

If we use this formula to estimate $\mathrm{E}[Q]$, we find

$$\mathrm{E}[Q] \approx \mathrm{e}^{\hat{\gamma} + \hat{\beta} \ln(110) + \frac{1}{2}S^2} = \mathrm{e}^{8.91 - 0.914 \ln(110) + \frac{1}{2} \cdot 0.2162^2} = 103.$$

11.14

(a) When data form a strictly convex profile, the data cannot be described by a straight line. Linear regression is unsuitable in such situations.

Stock prices, mutual bonds, and bank deposits usually exhibit exponential growth. When the value doubles, a percentage increase typically doubles the increase. For example, 5% growth will increase the price by 6 USD when the price is 120 USD, while the increase will be 12 USD when the price is 240 USD. This in turn will lead to exponential growth.

(b) The transformed data are fairly linear. The histogram is slightly skewed, but still acceptable. The normal score is fairly straight, and the residuals are fairy symmetric and homogeneous. There is a tendency that the residuals increase at the right side, but all in all we conclude that the standard assumptions for linear regression are satisfied.

(c) We have

$$X = \mathrm{e}^{\gamma + \beta t + \epsilon} = \mathrm{e}^{\gamma + \beta t} \cdot \mathrm{e}^{\epsilon}.$$

Since $e^{\gamma+\beta t}$ is a constant, we have

$$E[X] = E[e^{\gamma+\beta t} \cdot e^{\epsilon}] = e^{\gamma+\beta t} \cdot E[e^{\epsilon}] = e^{\gamma+\beta t} \cdot e^{1/2\sigma^2} = e^{\gamma+\beta t+1/2\sigma^2}.$$

An estimator for this is

$$\hat{X} = e^{\hat{\gamma}+\hat{\beta}t+1/2S^2}.$$

An estimate for expected value at $t = 110$ is hence

$$\hat{X} = e^{4.2332+0.017524\cdot110+1/2\cdot0.3025^2} = 496.$$

(d) The standard deviation is usually a fraction of the price. If the price falls by 5%, we expect that the change depends on the price level. If, e.g., the price is 10 USD, the price falls to 9.5 USD, while a price of 100 USD will fall to 95 USD. The change in price is 10 times larger in the latter case. If we try to predict prices far into the future, the price can be much higher than what we observe today. In such cases we expect that S, too, can be much larger. The estimate in (c) will then give a too low estimate. This only works if the underlying growth conditions are fixed. If we try to make a prediction far into the future, this assumption is probably not reasonable. In general we should seek to avoid predictions far outside where we have data.

11.15

(a) The observations are fairly linear, the histogram resembles the normal distribution, and the normal score is approximatively a straight line. The residuals are fairly homogeneous with no apparent trends. In total the standard assumptions appear to be satisfied.

(b) We have $n = 17$ observations and want to make a prediction at time $t = 18 + \frac{1}{7} = 18.14$. That gives the value

$$\text{Energy} = 242 - 7.83 \cdot 18.14 = 99.96.$$

Since we want to predict the value of X itself, we need to compute

$$S[\hat{X} - X] = S \cdot \sqrt{1 + \frac{1}{n} + \frac{(t-\bar{t})^2}{\sum_{i=1}^{17}(t_i - \bar{t})^2}}.$$

Here $S = 3.181, n = 17, \bar{t} = 18, t = 18.14$ and $\sum_{i=1}^{17}(t_i - \bar{t})^2 = 408$. That gives

$$S[\hat{X} - X] = 3.273.$$

We know that

$$T = \frac{\hat{X} - X}{S[\hat{X} - X]}$$

is t-distributed with parameter $\nu = n - 2 = 15$. We find the 2.5% level in that t-table, and find the value 2.131. The limits for a 95% confidence interval are hence

$$99.96 \pm 2.131 \cdot 3.273.$$

This gives the interval [93, 107].

(c) We see that the observations begin to exhibit an S-profile. The histogram no longer resembles the normal distribution, the normal score is somewhat shaky. The residuals have crystal clear trends. There is no support for independence and normal distribution here. The explanation is very simple, the power consumption is stabilizing to reach a minimum in late summer, after which it will begin to increase since the temperature falls as winter is approaching.

(d) Regression serves no purpose here. It is reasonable to assume that power consumption is largely periodic with a cycle of one year. Systematic deviations from this pattern can occur if the consumers change their habits. If we assume that the underlying conditions are fixed, we might suggest the same interval as in (b). If consumption changes, the interval could be different, but there is no way to tell how large it could be unless we have more information.

11.16

(a) The observations are approximatively linear, the histogram resembles the normal distribution, and the normal score is approximatively a straight line. The residuals, however, have crystal clear trends, which is not OK. The assumptions about constant variance appears to be violated here.

(b) Since the observations are relatively linear, we use the regression line to make a prediction. We predict

$$\hat{X}_{110} = 1.07 + 2.09 \cdot 110 = 230.97.$$

The standard assumptions are not satisfied here, so we cannot trust error estimates relying on the t-distribution. On the other hand, it seems as if the deviations from the regression line are relatively small. On the positive side we make a prediction in the near future, and have some reason to believe that the prediction error is moderate.

(c)

$$\begin{aligned} Y_t &= X_t - \rho \cdot X_{t-1} \\ &= \gamma + \beta \cdot t + R_t - \rho(\gamma + \beta(t-1) + R_{t-1}) \\ &= \gamma + \beta \cdot t - \rho\gamma - \rho\beta \cdot t + \rho\beta + R_t - \rho \cdot R_{t-1} \\ &= \gamma(1-\rho) + \rho\beta + (1-\rho)\beta \cdot t + \epsilon_t \\ &= a + b \cdot t + \epsilon_t, \end{aligned}$$

where a and b are constants given by

$$a = \gamma(1-\rho) + \rho\beta, \qquad b = (1-\rho)\beta.$$

Since a and b are constants, and ϵ_t are independent, normally distributed with constant variance, Y_t satisfy all the standard requirements.

(d) The observations are fairy linear even though the spread around the regression line is relatively large. The histogram resembles the normal distribution, and the normal score is a straight line. The residuals are fairly symmetric and do not change much along the axes. The standard assumptions in the regression model appear to be satisfied here.

(e) From the printout and the equation above, we get the equations

$$2.30 = \gamma(1-\rho) + \rho\beta, \qquad 0.201 = (1-\rho)\beta.$$

The value of $\rho = 0.9$ by assumption. That gives

$$2.30 = \gamma \cdot 0.1 + 0.9 \cdot \beta, \qquad 0.201 = 0.1 \cdot \beta.$$

If we multiply both equations by 10 on each side, we get

$$23.0 = \gamma + 9 \cdot \beta, \qquad 2.01 = \beta.$$

Hence $\gamma = 4.91$ and $\beta = 2.01$. Using these as estimators, we get

$$\hat{X} = 4.91 + 2.01 \cdot t.$$

Note that $\mathrm{E}[R_t] = 0$ for all t (a formal proof can be made by induction) and that γ and β are unbiased since ρ is a known constant. An unbiased predictor of X_{110} is

$$\hat{X} = 4.91 + 2.01 \cdot 110 = 226.01.$$

11.17

(a) From the printout we see that the P-value (for $\beta = 0$) is very small. We hence conclude that the sales of mobile phones probably relates to the sales of cars.
(b) The histogram somewhat resembles the normal distribution. The normal score is somewhat shaky, but still acceptable. The residuals are fairly symmetric and do not change much along the axes. With only 10 observations, we cannot expect more than this, and conclude that there is no indication of violation of the standard assumptions.
(c) From the printout we see that the explanatory power is 99.8%. Nearly all the variation in the number of car sales can be explained by the variation in the sales of mobile phones.
(d) The formula for the regression line is

$$y = 0.59694 \cdot x + 201.8.$$

If we insert $x = 150{,}000$, we find $y = 89{,}743$. In a town where the dealers sold 150,000 mobile phones, we predict 89,743 car sales. There is uncertainty in this prediction since the coefficients are uncertain. In addition we cannot be sure that the pattern of demand is the same in this town as in the others. This town is substantially larger than the towns in our dataset, and that could mean that the population has a different socioeconomic distribution. That in turn could lead to a different relation between sales of mobile phones and car sales.
(e) From a statistical point of view this is an unusually bad idea. The regression shows that there is a relation between the two quantities. That does not mean that the one causes the other. In this case there is a third variable, the number of people living in the towns, that governs the sales. The towns differ in population size and this is what causes the relation. If the car dealers want to increase car sales, they could seek to increase the population. Giving away mobile phones could have a slight goodwill effect, but is unlikely to affect the sales of cars.

11.18

(a) We see from the printout that data are nonlinear. The normal score is not too bad, but bends at the right side. The histogram is right skewed. The residuals have crystal clear trends breaking the assumption of independence and constant variance. From an economic point of view it is unreasonable to assume that the profit is linear. It is more natural to assume that it is strictly concave. In this connection we should seek to maximize profit, and a linear model is unsuitable for that purpose.

(b) If we differentiate with respect to a, b, and c, we get

$$\frac{\partial \text{error}}{\partial a} = \sum_{i=1}^{n} 2(X_i - a - bx_i - cx_i^2) \cdot -1$$

$$\frac{\partial \text{error}}{\partial b} = \sum_{i=1}^{n} 2(X_i - a - bx_i - cx_i^2) \cdot -x_i$$

$$\frac{\partial \text{error}}{\partial c} = \sum_{i=1}^{n} 2(X_i - a - bx_i - cx_i^2) \cdot -x_i^2.$$

The suggested set of equations is nothing but the first order conditions for this problem.

(c) The normal score is reasonably straight. The histogram is slightly skewed, but still acceptable. The residuals are evenly distributed around zero and do not change along the axes. All in all the standard assumptions appear to be satisfied. Expected profit is estimated by the function

$$\Pi[x] = -2482.2 + 243.275\,x - 2.003\,x^2.$$

We differentiate to find

$$\Pi'[x] = 243.275 - 4.006\,x.$$

This function has a maximum at $x = \frac{243.275}{4.006} = 60.73$. Since we can only produce an integer number of items, maximum expected profit is obtained at $x = 61$.

11.19

(a) All the three P-values are very small, and we conclude that the number of years of education is strongly significant for wages. The numbers for men and women are quite different. From the printout we see that one year of extra education increases expected income by 1371 USD for men, but only 621 USD for women. The gender difference is somewhat reduced since the constant term is higher for women. The difference 1249 USD is balanced by two years of education, and men are clearly ahead when they have more than two years of education.

(b) The model tries to explain differences in wages by the number of years of education. Many other aspects contribute to explain such differences. Two persons with the same years of education can have very different salaries. In addition to purely individual differences, the type of education clearly matters. For example, there are huge differences between financial analysts and school teachers. The majority of the variation is hence caused by effects not included in the model, and this explains the relatively moderate explanatory power.

(c) We predict the value

$$\widehat{\text{income}} = 11{,}223 + 621 \cdot 17 = 21{,}780.$$

To measure the variation we need to compute

$$M = \frac{S^2}{S[\hat{\beta}]^2} = \frac{5368^2}{73.26^2} = 5368.97.$$

This we insert into the formula

$$S[\hat{X} - X] = 5368 \cdot \sqrt{1 + 1/700 + (17 - 11.86361)^2/5368.97} = 5385.$$

We should use a t-table with parameter $\nu = 698$. When the parameter is so large, there is hardly any difference between the t-distribution and the normal distribution. The limits for a 95% prediction interval are hence given by

$$21{,}780 \pm 1.96 \cdot 5385 = \begin{cases} 11{,}225.4 \\ 32{,}334.6 \end{cases}.$$

11.20

(a) The plot shows that data to some extent can be approximated by a straight line, but there seems to be systematic deviations. The histogram seems strange, but that might be due to the resolution, and need not be a problem. The normal score could have been better, but may be acceptable. The residuals versus fitted values show tendencies of trends, while the residuals versus order of the data are OK. All in all it is somewhat shaky, maybe not totally unacceptable, but we should not have too much faith in the conclusions.

(b) This question is awkward. The problem is that there is no linear correspondence between the degrees of satisfaction. "Satisfied (5)" is, e.g., not 5 times better than "Dissatisfied (1)." The explanatory variable is not a scale variable, which makes it questionable to use linear regression in this case. If we insert the value $SL = 6$, in the regression line, we get

$$\hat{PR} = 14.40 + 14.8 \cdot 6 = 103.2.$$

That value is meaningless. Customers who are satisfied (5) appear to have about 90% probability of returning. It seems reasonable that customers who are very satisfied (6) should have an even larger probability of returning, but it is impossible to say how much larger.

(c) The residuals versus observations are OK. Residuals versus fitted values still have slight trends, but less than the first model. The curve appears to fit well with the observations, the explanatory power has increased, and all in all we seem to have a better model.

(d) No. The problem from (b) is still present. The reason is that we have no control on how much a one unit increase will affect the result. It may well happen that a third degree polynomial only makes matters worse. If we insert $SL = 6$ into the regression, we get

$$\hat{PR} = 5.710 + 40.06 \cdot 6 - 11.66 \cdot 6^2 + 1.389 \cdot 6^3 = 126.334,$$

which is even more meaningless than before.

Remark This exercise illustrates a common paradox in econometrics. When we increase the number of parameters, the explanatory power will always increase. The ability to predict, however, do not always increase. In some cases the ability to predict can be reduced. A model with lots of parameters often explains everything, but predicts nothing.

11.21

(a) The points are not well adapted to a straight line. It is not reasonable to assume a linear relationship here. A fraction (measured in percent) is always a number between 0 and 100. Sooner or later the increase must flatten out, which violates a linear model. From the diagnostic plots we see the following: The normal score is OK, but the histogram does not resemble the normal distribution, and the residuals have crystal clear trends. This suggests clear violations of the standard assumptions.

(b) If we use the model from (a) to predict the fraction of 80-year olds who have used the product, we find

$$\text{fraction in percent} = -8.12 + 1.78 \cdot 80 = 134.$$

This result makes no sense. In addition it may well happen that 80-year olds might have a completely different way of behavior than younger generations, which focuses that it might be problems using a model of this kind outside where we have observations.

(c)

$$\begin{aligned}\ln\left[\frac{f(x)}{100 - f(x)}\right] &= \ln\left[\frac{\frac{100e^{\gamma+\beta x}}{1+e^{\gamma+\beta x}}}{100 - \frac{100e^{\gamma+\beta x}}{1+e^{\gamma+\beta x}}}\right] \\ &= \ln\left[\frac{100e^{\gamma+\beta x}}{100(1 + e^{\gamma+\beta x}) - 100e^{\gamma+\beta x}}\right] \\ &= \ln[e^{\gamma+\beta x}] = \gamma + \beta x.\end{aligned}$$

(d) These printouts look much better. We see that the curve fits well with data, and that it flattens out in a convincing way. The diagnostic plots are also easier to accept as we cannot expect too much regularity with only 12 observations. All in all this looks like a good model.

(e) With this model we get a fraction (in percent)

$$f(80) = \frac{100e^{-4.31+0.135\cdot 80}}{1+e^{-4.31+0.135\cdot 80}} = 99.85.$$

It might still be a problem that 80-year olds may have a completely different behavioral pattern, but the fraction is in line with what we see in our data. In conclusion this a kind of product that everyone get to use sooner or later. We don't have much confidence in 99.8%, but that the true answer is close to 100% seems right.

11.22

(a) Yes, this is something we could expect. The intercept can be interpreted as fixed costs connected with the sales (e.g., wages for vendors), while the slope can be interpreted as marginal costs. From the plot we see that the number does not change much from week to week. It is then reasonable to assume that the fixed costs are fairly constant. The marginal costs, which, e.g., might be determined from a fixed amount per unit, also seems to be constant. If we some weeks sell very much or very little, we could see deviations from a linear relationship, but that does not seem to be the case.

(b) From the printout we see that fixed costs are

$$5212.6 + 0.0145 \cdot 500{,}000 = 12{,}477.6.$$

We find $M = \frac{193.985^2}{0.0006543^2} = 8.79 \cdot 10^{10}$. In the formulas we need the term

$$\frac{(500{,}000 - 499{,}110)^2}{M}$$

but the value is so small that we can comfortably ignore it. We find

$$S[\hat{X} - X] = 193.985 \cdot \sqrt{1 + 1/30 + 0} = 197.2.$$

We should make use of the t-table with parameter 28. From that table we find $t = 2.048$. The limits for the prediction interval are hence

$$12{,}477.6 \pm 2.048 \cdot 197.2 = \begin{cases} 12{,}073.7 \\ 12{,}881.5. \end{cases}$$

We see that the observed value is far outside a 95% prediction interval. It hence seems very likely that there is something special behind these costs.

(d) From the analysis in (c) we conclude that expenses are much higher than normal. The deviation is more than 10 standard deviations, and it seems very unlikely that this happened by coincidence. We should first check if the high reported costs are due to a typo. If that is not the case, we need to go through all the posts in search of a plausible explanation.

11.23

(a)

$$
\begin{aligned}
F[\alpha,\beta] &= \text{error}_1{}^2 + \text{error}_2{}^2 + \text{error}_3{}^2 \\
&= (\alpha+\beta-1)^2 + (\alpha+2\beta-3)^2 + (\alpha+3\beta-3)^2 \\
&= \alpha^2 + \alpha\beta - \alpha + \beta\alpha + \beta^2 - \beta - \alpha - \beta + 1 \\
&+\alpha^2 + 2\alpha\beta - 3\alpha + 2\beta\alpha + 4\beta^2 - 6\beta - 3\alpha - 6\beta + 9 \\
&+\alpha^2 + 3\gamma\beta - 3\gamma + 3\beta\gamma + 9\beta^2 - 9\beta - 3\gamma - 9\beta + 9 \\
&= 3\alpha^2 + 12\alpha\beta + 14\beta^2 - 32\beta - 14\alpha + 19.
\end{aligned}
$$

(b) We compute

$$\frac{\partial F}{\partial \alpha} = 6\alpha + 12\beta - 14 = 0,$$

and

$$\frac{\partial F}{\partial \beta} = 12\alpha + 28\beta - 32 = 0.$$

Solving this system, we find $\beta = 1$ and $\alpha = \frac{1}{3}$.

11.24

(a) We see that the plot is not linear. The normal score is acceptable, and so is also the histogram. The residuals, however, have crystal clear trends which are due to a nonlinear relationship. This case is unsuitable for linear regression.
(b) From the plot we see that data are fairly linear in the interval [3000, 7000]. The diagnostic plots are all acceptable. This case is suitable for linear regression.
(c) We use the regression from (b) and need to find maximum for the function

$$f(x) = (10{,}000 - x)(0.000232x - 0.587).$$

This function has a maximum for $x = 6265$ with value equal to 3236.

(d) From the plot we see that in the interval [0, 3000] the probability of winning the bidding is less than 10%. Since the profit is bounded by 10,000, the expected profit cannot exceed 1000 USD. In the interval [7000, 10,000], the profit cannot exceed 3000 USD. We hence conclude that in both these intervals, the best value is less than the value we found in (c).

11.25

(a) Data have a relatively large spread around the regression line, but that in itself need not be a problem. The histogram is not much different from the normal distribution. The normal score is fairly straight, and the residuals are fairly homogeneous with no apparent trends. As the number of observations are modest, we cannot expect anything better than this. We conclude that the standard conditions appear to be satisfied.
(b) Since the *P*-value is very high, we cannot reject a null hypothesis saying $\alpha = 0$. This makes sense in this situation. If the stock is close to zero and we do not fish, the change in the stock must be small. That corresponds to $\alpha = 0$. The number 0.262 is the percentage natural growth rate. If we do not fish, we expect that the stock grows by about 26% per year.
(c) We see that data seemingly have a smaller spread around the regression line and that the explanatory power has increased for 68.3% to 98.0%. This effect is purely cosmetic and do not provide any new insights. It is hardly surprising that the size of the stock affects the size of the stock the year after. A priori we expect that the explanatory power of this relation is very close to 100%. The number 98% is hence without practical value. The number 68.3% is much more informative since it says that other effects explain about one-third of the variation in our data. This information would have been lost if we only carried out the second regression. If we look at the residual plots, we see that the spread is exactly the same as before. In the first model we study the growth potential directly, while this quantity is only implicit in the second model. In the second model we only achieve to disguise the spread in the data, and the second regression is not in any way better than the first.

11.26

(a) We see that the observations are fairly linear, normal score is a straight line, the histogram is acceptable, and the residuals are homogeneous with no clear trends. The standard assumptions appear to be satisfied. The explanatory power is very high, 99.4%. *P*-value for the slope is very small, which means that price is strongly significant for demand. This is classic economic theory, demand is falling when the price increases.
(b) The spread around the regression line is larger than in (a), but that is not a problem in itself. The increased spread is reflected in the explanatory power, which is 30%, considerably less than in (a). Normal score is a straight line, the histogram is acceptable, and the residuals are homogeneous with no clear

trends. The standard conditions appear to be satisfied. Increasing the price on Extra appears to increase the demand for Superior, but the model only explains a part of the variation. This is classical economic theory, the goods are substitutes, and the demand for the one good is expected to grow when the price on the substitute increases.

(c) We assume that expected demand after Superior is $\alpha - 2.1x_1 + 0.1x_2$. When $x_2 = 50$, this gives

$$\alpha - 2.1x_1 + 0.1 \cdot 50 = (\alpha + 5) - 2.1x_1.$$

This result is consistent with (a) if $\alpha = 150$. When $x_1 = 40$, the model gives

$$\alpha - 2.1 \cdot 40 + 0.1 \cdot x_2 = (\alpha - 84) + 0.1x_2.$$

That is consistent with (b) if $\alpha = 150$. The value $\alpha = 150$ is hence the only value which makes the results consistent.

(d)

$$\begin{aligned}\text{Expected sales value} &= \text{E}[x_1 \cdot \text{Demand Superior} + x_2 \cdot \text{Demand Extra}]\\ &= x_1 \cdot \text{E}[\text{Demand Superior}] + x_2 \cdot \text{E}[\text{Demand Extra}]\\ &= x_1(150 - 2.1x_1 + 0.1x_2) + x_2(216 + 0.2x_1 - 1.9x_2).\end{aligned}$$

If we define

$$f[x_1, x_2] = x_1(150 - 2.1x_1 + 0.1x_2) + x_2(216 + 0.2x_1 - 1.9x_2),$$

then

$$\frac{\partial f}{\partial x_1} = 150 - 4.2x_1 + 0.3x_2,$$

and

$$\frac{\partial f}{\partial x_2} = 216 + 0.3x_1 - 3.8x_2.$$

Using first order conditions, we find $x_1 = 40$ and $x_2 = 60$, which gives the maximum for the function.

11.27

(a) The normal score is fairly straight. The histogram is slightly skewed, but still acceptable. The residuals have obvious trends, which is a clear violation of the standard assumptions. If we consider the price development outside the interval [30, 60], the price function is not at all linear. Even though the *P*-value for the slope is small and the explanatory power is good, we should seriously doubt if linear regression is the right tool here.

(b) If we insert $t = 80$ into the formula for the regression line, we get

$$\widehat{\text{Stock price}} = 120.985 - 0.3702 \cdot 80 = 91.37.$$

If we compare with the observed value at $t = 80$, we see that the difference is not very large. This, however, is pure luck. At best, we could use the model for predictions within the interval [30, 60], but we should not even consider using the model for predictions outside this interval. The usual formulas for confidence intervals do not apply here. In this case we have systematic problems with even using the model, and the randomness is likely to be much larger than what is suggested by the standard formulas. There is no reason to trust this prediction.

Remark The plot we used in this problem was generated by a numerical process which, by definition, was free from trends. At each time-step it was equally probable that the trend continued or was broken. Such processes will very often generate fictitious trends. When we look at the data in retrospect, it seems to be possible to exploit the trends to make lots of money. This is false, any profit from such analysis is pure luck, and on average it is impossible to find strategies that produces extra profit.

11.28

(a) The histogram is skewed, and the normal score is not a straight line. The residuals are not symmetric. In total this model seems very shaky. The explanatory power is as high as 99.3%, which suggests that the model nevertheless can be used for prediction. We should not trust the P-values since they rest on assumptions which are clearly not satisfied.

(b) Using standard rules for logarithms, we get

$$\begin{aligned}\ln(Y) &= \ln(\alpha K^{\beta_1} L^{\beta_2} \cdot \epsilon)\\ &= \ln(\alpha) + \ln(K^{\beta_1}) + \ln(L^{\beta_2}) + \ln(\epsilon)\\ &= \ln(\alpha) + \beta_1 \ln(K) + \beta_2 \ln(L) + \ln(\epsilon),\end{aligned}$$

which means that $\ln(Y)$ is a linear function of $\ln(K)$ and $\ln(L)$. The intercept is $\ln(\alpha)$ and the slopes are β_1 and β_2. The error term is $\ln(\epsilon)$. If this model is to satisfy the standard assumptions for linear regression, the error term must have normal distribution. Then it must be possible to write ϵ on the form

$$\epsilon = e^X,$$

where X has normal distribution. Such distributions are called log-normal.

(c) The histogram resembles the normal distribution. The normal score could have been better, but is still acceptable. The residuals are homogeneous and free of trends. In total this looks very good. The P-values are extremely small, and we conclude that $\ln(K)$ and $\ln(L)$ are strongly significant. This means that changes in K and L probably affects the value of Y. The relation is nonlinear (concave), which explains why we get problems in (a).

(d) From the computation in (b) we see that

$$\begin{aligned}\ln(Y/10^6) &= \ln(Y) - \ln(10^6) = \ln(\alpha) + \beta_1 \ln(K) + \beta_2 \ln(L) + \ln(\epsilon) - \ln(10^6) \\ &= \ln(\alpha) + \beta_1(\ln(K/10^6) + \ln(10^6)) + \beta_2 \ln(L) + \ln(\epsilon) - \ln(10^6) \\ &= \ln(\alpha) + (\beta_1 - 1)\ln(10^6) + \beta_1 \ln(K/10^6) + \beta_2 \ln(L) + \ln(\epsilon).\end{aligned}$$

From the printout we see directly that $\beta_1 = 0.30$ and $\beta_2 = 0.90$. Furthermore the intercept leads to the equation

$$\ln(\alpha) + (\beta_1 - 1)\ln(10^6) = -5.06822.$$

Here everything is known except $\ln(\alpha)$, and we can solve to get

$$\ln(\alpha) = -(0.30 - 1)\ln(10^6) - 5.06822 = 4.60264.$$

Hence

$$\alpha = e^{4.60264} = 99.75.$$

11.29

(a) We see that the coefficient for EdSh is positive, which means that the larger fraction that has short higher education, the better are the scores. The coefficient for EdL is negative, however, which is rather weird. None of the coefficients are significant, so we cannot claim they are important for the results. On the positive side the model explains about 50% of the variation.

The problem with this regression is multicollinearity between EdSh and EdL. This is confirmed by the second printout where EdL explains more than 90% of the variation in EdSh. That suggests that we should not use both EdSh and EdL as explanatory variables in the same model. Common practice is to delete one of the variables, but in this context we may also merge the results as we do below.

(b) This regression is much better. We have removed the problem with collinearity, and Ed is strongly significant. It seems quite clear that the fraction of the population with higher education affects the results. If we increase Ed by 10, we expect that results improve by 0.2. We see that the explanatory power is about 49%, almost the same as in (a). Taking into account that we only have 19 observations, the diagnostic plots are all OK. The normal score has a slight bend, but not more than we can accept. The residuals versus order are OK. The residuals versus fitted values are not uniform, but the plot is partly misleading since many observations have the same value. To the extent that we can see trends, those are caused by two outliers, which happen to be skewed. This is normal when we have few observations.

(c) The predicted value we find from the regression line

$$\text{predicted value} = 2.38286 + 0.0200711 \cdot 47.5 = 3.34.$$

The variation we find using the formula

$$S[\hat{Y} - Y] = S \cdot \sqrt{1 + \frac{1}{n} + \frac{(X - \overline{X})^2}{M}}.$$

In our case we have $S = 0.122724, n = 19, X = 47.5, \overline{X} = 27.86$. The value for M we find by

$$M = \frac{S^2}{S[\hat{\beta}]^2} = \frac{0.122724^2}{0.00492369^2} = 621.266.$$

Inserting these number into the formula, we get $S[\hat{Y} - Y] = 0.158761$. The limits for the prediction interval we find using a t-table with parameter $\nu = n-2 = 17$, giving $t_{2.5\%}^{(17)} = 2.11$. The limits for a 95% prediction interval are hence

$$3.34 \pm 2.11 \cdot 0.158761,$$

which rounded gives [3.0, 3.7]. The observed value, 3.3, is slightly lower than the predicted value 3.34. The value is safely near the center of the prediction interval, so we have no reason to claim that the result is significantly weaker than expected.

11.30

(a) We see that the P-value for the coefficient of Price is very low, hence Price (not unexpected) is strongly significant for demand. The explanatory power is good, about 86%. We see that the regression coefficient is negative. This means that demand falls when the price increases, which seems logical. The normal score is supposed to be a straight line; it could have been better, but is still acceptable. The histogram resembles the normal distribution and is OK. The residuals should be homogeneous and free of trends; they could have been better, but deviations probably appear as a consequence of very few observations. In total the model can be accepted.

(b) In both models we see that all the regression coefficients are significant. The explanatory power increases from 86% with linear regression, to 94% for quadratic regression, and further to 95% for cubical regression. Cubical regression is best in the sense that it offers the best fit to data, but is only slightly better than quadratic regression.

(c) Model 1: Demand $= 911.713 - 112.057 \cdot 10 \approx -209$.
Model 2: Demand $= 1281.78 - 356.953 \cdot 10 + 27.2106 \cdot 10^2 \approx 433$.
Model 3: Demand $= 1513.62 - 581.236 \cdot 10 + 84.7985 \cdot 10^2 - 4.26577 \cdot 10^3 \approx -85$.

Models 1 and 3 produce negative values, which must be wrong. Model 2 produces a positive value, but the value is much higher than the observed values at the right side of the plot. That, too, must be wrong. It is reasonable to assume that expected demand is a positive and monotonically decreasing function of price, but no polynomial has those properties over the whole real axis. Even though polynomial regression gives better fit to data, it is unsuitable for prediction outside the set where we have observations.

Table of the Binomial Distribution

Table A gives the probability $P(X = x)$ when X is a binomial distribution with parameters (n, p). Example: $n = 8, p = 0.1$ gives $P(X = 2) = 0.1488$.

Table A Binomial distribution

n	x	$p = 0.05$	$p = 0.1$	$p = 0.2$	$p = 0.3$	$p = 0.4$	$p = 0.5$
2	0	0.9025	0.8100	0.6400	0.4900	0.3600	0.2500
	1	0.0950	0.1800	0.3200	0.4200	0.4800	0.5000
	2	0.0025	0.0100	0.0400	0.0900	0.1600	0.2500
3	0	0.8574	0.7290	0.5120	0.3430	0.2160	0.1250
	1	0.1354	0.2430	0.3840	0.4410	0.4320	0.3750
	2	0.0071	0.0270	0.0960	0.1890	0.2880	0.3750
	3	0.0001	0.0010	0.0080	0.0270	0.0640	0.1250
4	0	0.8145	0.6561	0.4096	0.2401	0.1296	0.0625
	1	0.1715	0.2916	0.4096	0.4116	0.3456	0.2500
	2	0.0135	0.0486	0.1536	0.2646	0.3456	0.3750
	3	0.0005	0.0036	0.0256	0.0756	0.1536	0.2500
	4	0.0000	0.0001	0.0016	0.0081	0.0256	0.0650
5	0	0.7738	0.5905	0.3277	0.1681	0.0778	0.0312
	1	0.2036	0.3280	0.4096	0.3602	0.2592	0.1562
	2	0.0214	0.0729	0.2048	0.3087	0.3456	0.3125
	3	0.0011	0.0081	0.0512	0.1323	0.2304	0.3125
	4	0.0000	0.0005	0.0064	0.0284	0.0768	0.1562
	5	0.0000	0.0000	0.0003	0.0024	0.0102	0.0312
6	0	0.7351	0.5314	0.2621	0.1176	0.0467	0.0156
	1	0.2321	0.3543	0.3932	0.3025	0.1866	0.0938
	2	0.0305	0.0984	0.2458	0.3241	0.3110	0.2344
	3	0.0021	0.0146	0.0819	0.1852	0.2765	0.3125
	4	0.0001	0.0012	0.0154	0.0595	0.1382	0.2344
	5	0.0000	0.0001	0.0015	0.0102	0.0369	0.0938
	6	0.0000	0.0000	0.0001	0.0007	0.0041	0.0156

(continued)

Table A (continued)

n	x	$p = 0.05$	$p = 0.1$	$p = 0.2$	$p = 0.3$	$p = 0.4$	$p = 0.5$
7	0	0.6983	0.4783	0.2097	0.0824	0.0280	0.0078
	1	0.2573	0.3720	0.3670	0.2471	0.1306	0.0547
	2	0.0406	0.1240	0.2753	0.3176	0.2613	0.1641
	3	0.0036	0.0230	0.1147	0.2269	0.2903	0.2734
	4	0.0002	0.0026	0.0287	0.0972	0.1935	0.2734
	5	0.0000	0.0002	0.0043	0.0250	0.0774	0.1641
	6	0.0000	0.0000	0.0004	0.0036	0.0172	0.0547
	7	0.0000	0.0000	0.0000	0.0002	0.0016	0.0078
8	0	0.6634	0.4305	0.1678	0.0576	0.0168	0.0039
	1	0.2793	0.3826	0.3355	0.1977	0.0896	0.0312
	2	0.0515	0.1488	0.2936	0.2965	0.2090	0.1094
	3	0.0054	0.0331	0.1468	0.2541	0.2787	0.2188
	4	0.0004	0.0046	0.0459	0.1361	0.2322	0.2734
	5	0.0000	0.0004	0.0092	0.0467	0.1239	0.2188
	6	0.0000	0.0000	0.0011	0.0100	0.0413	0.1094
	7	0.0000	0.0000	0.0001	0.0012	0.0079	0.0312
	8	0.0000	0.0000	0.0000	0.0001	0.0007	0.0039
9	0	0.6302	0.3874	0.1342	0.0404	0.0101	0.0020
	1	0.2985	0.3874	0.3020	0.1556	0.0605	0.0176
	2	0.0629	0.1722	0.3020	0.2668	0.1612	0.0703
	3	0.0077	0.0446	0.1762	0.2668	0.2508	0.1641
	4	0.0006	0.0074	0.0661	0.1715	0.2508	0.2461
	5	0.0000	0.0008	0.0165	0.0735	0.1672	0.2461
	6	0.0000	0.0001	0.0028	0.0210	0.0743	0.1641
	7	0.0000	0.0000	0.0003	0.0039	0.0212	0.0703
	8	0.0000	0.0000	0.0000	0.0004	0.0035	0.0176
	9	0.0000	0.0000	0.0000	0.0000	0.0003	0.0020
10	0	0.5987	0.3487	0.1074	0.0282	0.0060	0.0010
	1	0.3151	0.3874	0.2684	0.1211	0.0403	0.0098
	2	0.0746	0.1937	0.3020	0.2335	0.1209	0.0439
	3	0.0105	0.0574	0.2013	0.2668	0.2150	0.1172
	4	0.0010	0.0112	0.0881	0.2001	0.2508	0.2051
	5	0.0001	0.0015	0.0264	0.1029	0.2007	0.2461
	6	0.0000	0.0001	0.0055	0.0368	0.1115	0.2051
	7	0.0000	0.0000	0.0008	0.0090	0.0425	0.1172
	8	0.0000	0.0000	0.0001	0.0014	0.0106	0.0439
	9	0.0000	0.0000	0.0000	0.0001	0.0016	0.0098
	10	0.0000	0.0000	0.0000	0.0000	0.0001	0.0010

Table of the Poisson Distribution

Table B gives the probability $P(X = x)$ when X is a Poisson distribution with parameter λ. Example: $\lambda = 5$ gives $P(X = 4) = 0.1755$.

Table B Poisson distribution

	λ									
x	0.1	0.2	0.3	0.4	0.5	0.6	0.7	0.8	0.9	1.0
0	0.9048	0.8187	0.7408	0.6703	0.6065	0.5488	0.4966	0.4493	0.4066	0.3679
1	0.0905	0.1637	0.2222	0.2681	0.3033	0.3293	0.3476	0.3595	0.3659	0.3679
2	0.0045	0.0164	0.0333	0.0536	0.0758	0.0988	0.1217	0.1438	0.1647	0.1839
3	0.0002	0.0011	0.0033	0.0072	0.0126	0.0198	0.0284	0.0383	0.0494	0.0613
4	0.0000	0.0001	0.0003	0.0007	0.0016	0.0030	0.0050	0.0077	0.0111	0.0153
5	0.0000	0.0000	0.0000	0.0001	0.0002	0.0004	0.0007	0.0012	0.0020	0.0031
6	0.0000	0.0000	0.0000	0.0000	0.0000	0.0000	0.0001	0.0002	0.0003	0.0005
7	0.0000	0.0000	0.0000	0.0000	0.0000	0.0000	0.0000	0.0000	0.0000	0.0001
	λ									
x	1	2	3	4	5	6	7	8	9	10
0	0.3679	0.1353	0.0498	0.0183	0.0067	0.0025	0.0009	0.0003	0.0001	0.0000
1	0.3679	0.2707	0.1494	0.0733	0.0337	0.0149	0.0064	0.0027	0.0011	0.0005
2	0.1839	0.2707	0.2240	0.1465	0.0842	0.0446	0.0223	0.0107	0.0050	0.0023
3	0.0613	0.1804	0.2240	0.1954	0.1404	0.0892	0.0521	0.0286	0.0150	0.0076
4	0.0153	0.0902	0.1680	0.1954	0.1755	0.1339	0.0912	0.0572	0.0337	0.0189
5	0.0031	0.0361	0.1008	0.1563	0.1755	0.1606	0.1277	0.0916	0.0607	0.0378
6	0.0005	0.0120	0.0504	0.1042	0.1462	0.1606	0.1490	0.1221	0.0911	0.0631
7	0.0001	0.0034	0.0216	0.0595	0.1044	0.1377	0.1490	0.1396	0.1171	0.0901
8	0.0000	0.0009	0.0081	0.0298	0.0653	0.1033	0.1304	0.1396	0.1318	0.1126
9	0.0000	0.0002	0.0027	0.0132	0.0363	0.0688	0.1014	0.1241	0.1318	0.1251
10	0.0000	0.0000	0.0008	0.0053	0.0181	0.0413	0.0710	0.0993	0.1186	0.1251
11	0.0000	0.0000	0.0002	0.0019	0.0082	0.0225	0.0452	0.0722	0.0970	0.1137
12	0.0000	0.0000	0.0001	0.0006	0.0034	0.0113	0.0264	0.0481	0.0728	0.0948
13	0.0000	0.0000	0.0000	0.0002	0.0013	0.0052	0.0142	0.0296	0.0504	0.0729
14	0.0000	0.0000	0.0000	0.0001	0.0005	0.0022	0.0071	0.0169	0.0324	0.0521
15	0.0000	0.0000	0.0000	0.0000	0.0002	0.0009	0.0033	0.0090	0.0194	0.0347
16	0.0000	0.0000	0.0000	0.0000	0.0000	0.0003	0.0014	0.0045	0.0109	0.0217
17	0.0000	0.0000	0.0000	0.0000	0.0000	0.0001	0.0006	0.0021	0.0058	0.0128
18	0.0000	0.0000	0.0000	0.0000	0.0000	0.0000	0.0002	0.0009	0.0029	0.0071
19	0.0000	0.0000	0.0000	0.0000	0.0000	0.0000	0.0001	0.0004	0.0014	0.0037
20	0.0000	0.0000	0.0000	0.0000	0.0000	0.0000	0.0000	0.0002	0.0006	0.0019
21	0.0000	0.0000	0.0000	0.0000	0.0000	0.0000	0.0000	0.0001	0.0003	0.0009
22	0.0000	0.0000	0.0000	0.0000	0.0000	0.0000	0.0000	0.0000	0.0001	0.0004
23	0.0000	0.0000	0.0000	0.0000	0.0000	0.0000	0.0000	0.0000	0.0000	0.0002
24	0.0000	0.0000	0.0000	0.0000	0.0000	0.0000	0.0000	0.0000	0.0000	0.0001

Table of the Normal Distribution—Area Table

Table C gives the area $G(z)$ under the standard normal density to the left of z. Example: $z = 1.54$ gives $G(z) = 0.9382$.

Table C Normal distribution

z	0.00	0.01	0.02	0.03	0.04	0.05	0.06	0.07	0.08	0.09
0	0.5000	0.5040	0.5080	0.5120	0.5160	0.5199	0.5239	0.5279	0.5319	0.5359
0.1	0.5398	0.5438	0.5478	0.5517	0.5557	0.5596	0.5636	0.5675	0.5714	0.5753
0.2	0.5793	0.5832	0.5871	0.5910	0.5948	0.5987	0.6026	0.6064	0.6103	0.6141
0.3	0.6179	0.6217	0.6255	0.6293	0.6331	0.6368	0.6406	0.6443	0.6480	0.6517
0.4	0.6554	0.6591	0.6628	0.6664	0.6700	0.6736	0.6772	0.6808	0.6844	0.6879
0.5	0.6915	0.6950	0.6985	0.7019	0.7054	0.7088	0.7123	0.7157	0.7190	0.7224
0.6	0.7257	0.7291	0.7324	0.7357	0.7389	0.7422	0.7454	0.7486	0.7517	0.7549
0.7	0.7580	0.7611	0.7642	0.7673	0.7704	0.7734	0.7764	0.7794	0.7823	0.7852
0.8	0.7881	0.7910	0.7939	0.7967	0.7995	0.8023	0.8051	0.8078	0.8106	0.8133
0.9	0.8159	0.8186	0.8212	0.8238	0.8264	0.8289	0.8315	0.8340	0.8365	0.8389
1.0	0.8413	0.8438	0.8461	0.8485	0.8508	0.8531	0.8554	0.8577	0.8599	0.8621
1.1	0.8643	0.8665	0.8686	0.8708	0.8729	0.8749	0.8770	0.8790	0.8810	0.8830
1.2	0.8849	0.8869	0.8888	0.8907	0.8925	0.8944	0.8962	0.8980	0.8997	0.9015
1.3	0.9032	0.9049	0.9066	0.9082	0.9099	0.9115	0.9131	0.9147	0.9162	0.9177
1.4	0.9192	0.9207	0.9222	0.9236	0.9251	0.9265	0.9279	0.9292	0.9306	0.9319
1.5	0.9332	0.9345	0.9357	0.9370	0.9382	0.9394	0.9406	0.9418	0.9429	0.9441
1.6	0.9452	0.9463	0.9474	0.9484	0.9495	0.9505	0.9515	0.9525	0.9535	0.9545
1.7	0.9554	0.9564	0.9573	0.9582	0.9591	0.9599	0.9608	0.9616	0.9625	0.9633
1.8	0.9641	0.9649	0.9656	0.9664	0.9671	0.9678	0.9686	0.9693	0.9699	0.9706
1.9	0.9713	0.9719	0.9726	0.9732	0.9738	0.9744	0.9750	0.9756	0.9761	0.9767
2.0	0.9772	0.9778	0.9783	0.9788	0.9793	0.9798	0.9803	0.9808	0.9812	0.9817
2.1	0.9821	0.9826	0.9830	0.9834	0.9838	0.9842	0.9846	0.9850	0.9854	0.9857
2.2	0.9861	0.9864	0.9868	0.9871	0.9875	0.9878	0.9881	0.9884	0.9887	0.9890
2.3	0.9893	0.9896	0.9898	0.9901	0.9904	0.9906	0.9909	0.9911	0.9913	0.9916
2.4	0.9918	0.9920	0.9922	0.9925	0.9927	0.9929	0.9931	0.9932	0.9934	0.9936
2.5	0.9938	0.9940	0.9941	0.9943	0.9945	0.9946	0.9948	0.9949	0.9951	0.9952
2.6	0.9953	0.9955	0.9956	0.9957	0.9959	0.9960	0.9961	0.9962	0.9963	0.9964
2.7	0.9965	0.9966	0.9967	0.9968	0.9969	0.9970	0.9971	0.9972	0.9973	0.9974
2.8	0.9974	0.9975	0.9976	0.9977	0.9977	0.9978	0.9979	0.9979	0.9980	0.9981
2.9	0.9981	0.9982	0.9982	0.9983	0.9984	0.9984	0.9985	0.9985	0.9986	0.9986
3.0	0.9987	0.9987	0.9987	0.9988	0.9988	0.9989	0.9989	0.9989	0.9990	0.9990

(continued)

Table C (continued)

z	0.00	0.01	0.02	0.03	0.04	0.05	0.06	0.07	0.08	0.09
3.1	0.9990	0.9991	0.9991	0.9991	0.9992	0.9992	0.9992	0.9992	0.9993	0.9993
3.2	0.9993	0.9993	0.9994	0.9994	0.9994	0.9994	0.9994	0.9995	0.9995	0.9995
3.3	0.9995	0.9995	0.9995	0.9996	0.9996	0.9996	0.9996	0.9996	0.9996	0.9997
3.4	0.9997	0.9997	0.9997	0.9997	0.9997	0.9997	0.9997	0.9997	0.9997	0.9998
3.5	0.9998	0.9998	0.9998	0.9998	0.9998	0.9998	0.9998	0.9998	0.9998	0.9998
3.6	0.9998	0.9998	0.9999	0.9999	0.9999	0.9999	0.9999	0.9999	0.9999	0.9999
3.7	0.9999	0.9999	0.9999	0.9999	0.9999	0.9999	0.9999	0.9999	0.9999	0.9999
3.8	0.9999	0.9999	0.9999	0.9999	0.9999	0.9999	0.9999	0.9999	0.9999	0.9999
3.9	1.0000	–	–	–	–	–	–	–	–	–

Table of the Normal Distribution—Percentage Points

Table D gives z such that $P(X \geq z) = a$, when X is a standard normal distribution. Example: $P(X \geq 1.6449) = 5\%$.

Table D Normal distribution

a	z	a	z	a	z
0.50	0.0000	0.30	0.5244	0.10	1.2816
0.49	0.0251	0.29	0.5534	0.09	1.3408
0.48	0.0502	0.28	0.5828	0.08	1.4051
0.47	0.0753	0.27	0.6128	0.07	1.4758
0.46	0.1004	0.26	0.6434	0.06	1.5548
0.45	0.1257	0.25	0.6745	0.050	1.6449
0.44	0.1510	0.24	0.7063	0.045	1.6954
0.43	0.1764	0.23	0.7389	0.040	1.7507
0.42	0.2019	0.22	0.7722	0.035	1.8119
0.41	0.2275	0.21	0.8064	0.030	1.8808
0.40	0.2534	0.20	0.8416	0.025	1.9600
0.39	0.2793	0.19	0.8779	0.020	2.0538
0.38	0.3055	0.18	0.9154	0.015	2.1701
0.37	0.3319	0.17	0.9542	0.010	2.3264
0.36	0.3585	0.16	0.9945	0.005	2.5758
0.35	0.3853	0.15	1.0364	0.0010	3.0902
0.34	0.4125	0.14	1.0803	0.0005	3.2905
0.33	0.4399	0.13	1.1264	0.0001	3.7190
0.32	0.4677	0.12	1.1750		
0.31	0.4959	0.11	1.2265		

Table of the Chi-Square Distribution—Percentage Points

Table E gives q such that $P(X \geq q) = a$, when X is a chi-square distribution with parameter ν. Example: $\nu = 10$ gives $P(X \geq 9.342) = 50\%$.

Table E Chi-square distribution

	a										
ν	99.9%	99.5%	99.0%	97.5%	95.0%	90.0%	87.5%	80.0%	75.0%	66.6%	50.0%
1	0.000	0.000	0.000	0.001	0.004	0.016	0.025	0.064	0.102	0.186	0.455
2	0.002	0.010	0.020	0.051	0.103	0.211	0.267	0.446	0.575	0.811	1.386
3	0.024	0.072	0.115	0.216	0.352	0.584	0.692	1.005	1.213	1.568	2.366
4	0.091	0.207	0.297	0.484	0.711	1.064	1.219	1.649	1.923	2.378	3.357
5	0.210	0.412	0.554	0.831	1.145	1.610	1.808	2.343	2.675	3.216	4.351
6	0.381	0.676	0.872	1.237	1.635	2.204	2.441	3.070	3.455	4.074	5.348
7	0.598	0.989	1.239	1.690	2.167	2.833	3.106	3.822	4.255	4.945	6.346
8	0.857	1.344	1.646	2.180	2.733	3.490	3.797	4.594	5.071	5.826	7.344
9	1.152	1.735	2.088	2.700	3.325	4.168	4.507	5.380	5.899	6.716	8.343
10	1.479	2.156	2.558	3.247	3.940	4.865	5.234	6.179	6.737	7.612	9.342
11	1.834	2.603	3.053	3.816	4.575	5.578	5.975	6.989	7.584	8.514	10.341
12	2.214	3.074	3.571	4.404	5.226	6.304	6.729	7.807	8.438	9.420	11.340
13	2.617	3.565	4.107	5.009	5.892	7.042	7.493	8.634	9.299	10.331	12.340
14	3.041	4.075	4.660	5.629	6.571	7.790	8.266	9.467	10.165	11.245	13.339
15	3.483	4.601	5.229	6.262	7.261	8.547	9.048	10.307	11.037	12.163	14.339
16	3.942	5.142	5.812	6.908	7.962	9.312	9.837	11.152	11.912	13.083	15.338
17	4.416	5.697	6.408	7.564	8.672	10.085	10.633	12.002	12.792	14.006	16.338
18	4.905	6.265	7.015	8.231	9.390	10.865	11.435	12.857	13.675	14.931	17.338
19	5.407	6.844	7.633	8.907	10.117	11.651	12.242	13.716	14.562	15.859	18.338
20	5.921	7.434	8.260	9.591	10.851	12.443	13.055	14.578	15.452	16.788	19.337
21	6.447	8.034	8.897	10.283	11.591	13.240	13.873	15.445	16.344	17.720	20.337
22	6.983	8.643	9.542	10.982	12.338	14.041	14.695	16.314	17.240	18.653	21.337
23	7.529	9.260	10.196	11.689	13.091	14.848	15.521	17.187	18.137	19.587	22.337
24	8.085	9.886	10.856	12.401	13.848	15.659	16.351	18.062	19.037	20.523	23.337
25	8.649	10.520	11.524	13.120	14.611	16.473	17.184	18.940	19.939	21.461	24.337
26	9.222	11.160	12.198	13.844	15.379	17.292	18.021	19.820	20.843	22.399	25.336
27	9.803	11.808	12.879	14.573	16.151	18.114	18.861	20.703	21.749	23.339	26.336
28	10.391	12.461	13.565	15.308	16.928	18.939	19.704	21.588	22.657	24.280	27.336
29	10.986	13.121	14.256	16.047	17.708	19.768	20.550	22.475	23.567	25.222	28.336
30	11.588	13.787	14.953	16.791	18.493	20.599	21.399	23.364	24.478	26.165	29.336
35	14.688	17.192	18.509	20.569	22.465	24.797	25.678	27.836	29.054	30.894	34.336
40	17.916	20.707	22.164	24.433	26.509	29.051	30.008	32.345	33.660	35.643	39.335
45	21.251	24.311	25.901	28.366	30.612	33.350	34.379	36.884	38.291	40.407	44.335
50	24.674	27.991	29.707	32.357	34.764	37.689	38.785	41.449	42.942	45.184	49.335
55	28.173	31.735	33.570	36.398	38.958	42.060	43.220	46.036	47.610	49.972	54.335
60	31.738	35.534	37.485	40.482	43.188	46.459	47.680	50.641	52.294	54.770	59.335

Table of the Chi-square Distribution—Continued

Table F gives q such that $P(X \geq q) = a$, when X is a chi-square distribution with parameter ν. Example: $\nu = 10$ gives $P(X \geq 18.307) = 5\%$.

Table F Chi-square distribution

	a										
ν	40.0%	33.3%	25.0%	20.0%	12.5%	10.0%	5.0%	2.5%	1.0%	0.5%	0.1%
1	0.708	0.936	1.323	1.642	2.354	2.706	3.841	5.024	6.635	7.879	10.828
2	1.833	2.197	2.773	3.219	4.159	4.605	5.991	7.378	9.210	10.597	13.816
3	2.946	3.405	4.108	4.642	5.739	6.251	7.815	9.348	11.345	12.838	16.266
4	4.045	4.579	5.385	5.989	7.214	7.779	9.488	11.143	13.277	14.860	18.467
5	5.132	5.730	6.626	7.289	8.625	9.236	11.070	12.833	15.086	16.750	20.515
6	6.211	6.867	7.841	8.558	9.992	10.645	12.592	14.449	16.812	18.548	22.458
7	7.283	7.992	9.037	9.803	11.326	12.017	14.067	16.013	18.475	20.278	24.322
8	8.351	9.107	10.219	11.030	12.636	13.362	15.507	17.535	20.090	21.955	26.125
9	9.414	10.215	11.389	12.242	13.926	14.684	16.919	19.023	21.666	23.589	27.877
10	10.473	11.317	12.549	13.442	15.198	15.987	18.307	20.483	23.209	25.188	29.588
11	11.530	12.414	13.701	14.631	16.457	17.275	19.675	21.920	24.725	26.757	31.264
12	12.584	13.506	14.845	15.812	17.703	18.549	21.026	23.337	26.217	28.300	32.910
13	13.636	14.595	15.984	16.985	18.939	19.812	22.362	24.736	27.688	29.819	34.528
14	14.685	15.680	17.117	18.151	20.166	21.064	23.685	26.119	29.141	31.319	36.123
15	15.733	16.761	18.245	19.311	21.384	22.307	24.996	27.488	30.578	32.801	37.697
16	16.780	17.840	19.369	20.465	22.595	23.542	26.296	28.845	32.000	34.267	39.252
17	17.824	18.917	20.489	21.615	23.799	24.769	27.587	30.191	33.409	35.718	40.790
18	18.868	19.991	21.605	22.760	24.997	25.989	28.869	31.526	34.805	37.156	42.312
19	19.910	21.063	22.718	23.900	26.189	27.204	30.144	32.852	36.191	38.582	43.820
20	20.951	22.133	23.828	25.038	27.376	28.412	31.410	34.170	37.566	39.997	45.315
21	21.991	23.201	24.935	26.171	28.559	29.615	32.671	35.479	38.932	41.401	46.797
22	23.031	24.268	26.039	27.301	29.737	30.813	33.924	36.781	40.289	42.796	48.268
23	24.069	25.333	27.141	28.429	30.911	32.007	35.172	38.076	41.638	44.181	49.728
24	25.106	26.397	28.241	29.553	32.081	33.196	36.415	39.364	42.980	45.559	51.179
25	26.143	27.459	29.339	30.675	33.247	34.382	37.652	40.646	44.314	46.928	52.620
26	27.179	28.520	30.435	31.795	34.410	35.563	38.885	41.923	45.642	48.290	54.052
27	28.214	29.580	31.528	32.912	35.570	36.741	40.113	43.195	46.963	49.645	55.476
28	29.249	30.639	32.620	34.027	36.727	37.916	41.337	44.461	48.278	50.993	56.892
29	30.283	31.697	33.711	35.139	37.881	39.087	42.557	45.722	49.588	52.336	58.301
30	31.316	32.754	34.800	36.250	39.033	40.256	43.773	46.979	50.892	53.672	59.703
35	36.475	38.024	40.223	41.778	44.753	46.059	49.802	53.203	57.342	60.275	66.619
40	41.622	43.275	45.616	47.269	50.424	51.805	55.758	59.342	63.691	66.766	73.402
45	46.761	48.510	50.985	52.729	56.052	57.505	61.656	65.410	69.957	73.166	80.077
50	51.892	53.733	56.334	58.164	61.647	63.167	67.505	71.420	76.154	79.490	86.661
55	57.016	58.945	61.665	63.577	67.211	68.796	73.311	77.380	82.292	85.749	93.168
60	62.135	64.147	66.981	68.972	72.751	74.397	79.082	83.298	88.379	91.952	99.607

Table of the t-Distribution—Percentage Points

Table G gives t such that $P(X \geq t) = a$, when X is a t-distribution with parameter ν. Example: $\nu = 10$ gives $P(X \geq 3.169) = 5\%$.

Table G t-distribution

	a										
ν	40.0%	33.3%	25.0%	20.0%	12.5%	10.0%	5.0%	2.5%	1.0%	0.5%	0.1%
1	0.325	0.577	1.000	1.376	2.414	3.078	6.314	12.706	31.821	63.657	318.31
2	0.289	0.500	0.816	1.061	1.604	1.886	2.920	4.303	6.965	9.925	22.327
3	0.277	0.476	0.765	0.978	1.423	1.638	2.353	3.182	4.541	5.841	10.215
4	0.271	0.464	0.741	0.941	1.344	1.533	2.132	2.776	3.747	4.604	7.173
5	0.267	0.457	0.727	0.920	1.301	1.476	2.015	2.571	3.365	4.032	5.893
6	0.265	0.453	0.718	0.906	1.273	1.440	1.943	2.447	3.143	3.707	5.208
7	0.263	0.449	0.711	0.896	1.254	1.415	1.895	2.365	2.998	3.499	4.785
8	0.262	0.447	0.706	0.889	1.240	1.397	1.860	2.306	2.896	3.355	4.501
9	0.261	0.445	0.703	0.883	1.230	1.383	1.833	2.262	2.821	3.250	4.297
10	0.260	0.444	0.700	0.879	1.221	1.372	1.812	2.228	2.764	3.169	4.144
11	0.260	0.443	0.697	0.876	1.214	1.363	1.796	2.201	2.718	3.106	4.025
12	0.259	0.442	0.695	0.873	1.209	1.356	1.782	2.179	2.681	3.055	3.930
13	0.259	0.441	0.694	0.870	1.204	1.350	1.771	2.160	2.650	3.012	3.852
14	0.258	0.440	0.692	0.868	1.200	1.345	1.761	2.145	2.624	2.977	3.787
15	0.258	0.439	0.691	0.866	1.197	1.341	1.753	2.131	2.602	2.947	3.733
16	0.258	0.439	0.690	0.865	1.194	1.337	1.746	2.120	2.583	2.921	3.686
17	0.257	0.438	0.689	0.863	1.191	1.333	1.740	2.110	2.567	2.898	3.646
18	0.257	0.438	0.688	0.862	1.189	1.330	1.734	2.101	2.552	2.878	3.610
19	0.257	0.438	0.688	0.861	1.187	1.328	1.729	2.093	2.539	2.861	3.579
20	0.257	0.437	0.687	0.860	1.185	1.325	1.725	2.086	2.528	2.845	3.552
21	0.257	0.437	0.686	0.859	1.183	1.323	1.721	2.080	2.518	2.831	3.527
22	0.256	0.437	0.686	0.858	1.182	1.321	1.717	2.074	2.508	2.819	3.505
23	0.256	0.436	0.685	0.858	1.180	1.319	1.714	2.069	2.500	2.807	3.485
24	0.256	0.436	0.685	0.857	1.179	1.318	1.711	2.064	2.492	2.797	3.467

(continued)

Table G (continued)

	a										
ν	40.0%	33.3%	25.0%	20.0%	12.5%	10.0%	5.0%	2.5%	1.0%	0.5%	0.1%
25	0.256	0.436	0.684	0.856	1.178	1.316	1.708	2.060	2.485	2.787	3.450
26	0.256	0.436	0.684	0.856	1.177	1.315	1.706	2.056	2.479	2.779	3.435
27	0.256	0.435	0.684	0.855	1.176	1.314	1.703	2.052	2.473	2.771	3.421
28	0.256	0.435	0.683	0.855	1.175	1.313	1.701	2.048	2.467	2.763	3.408
29	0.256	0.435	0.683	0.854	1.174	1.311	1.699	2.045	2.462	2.756	3.396
30	0.256	0.435	0.683	0.854	1.173	1.310	1.697	2.042	2.457	2.750	3.385
35	0.255	0.434	0.682	0.852	1.170	1.306	1.690	2.030	2.438	2.724	3.340
40	0.255	0.434	0.681	0.851	1.167	1.303	1.684	2.021	2.423	2.704	3.307
45	0.255	0.434	0.680	0.850	1.165	1.301	1.679	2.014	2.412	2.690	3.281
50	0.255	0.433	0.679	0.849	1.164	1.299	1.676	2.009	2.403	2.678	3.261
55	0.255	0.433	0.679	0.848	1.163	1.297	1.673	2.004	2.396	2.668	3.245
60	0.254	0.433	0.679	0.848	1.162	1.296	1.671	2.000	2.390	2.660	3.232
∞	0.253	0.431	0.674	0.842	1.150	1.282	1.645	1.960	2.326	2.576	3.090

Index

J. Ubøe, *Introductory Statistics for Business and Economics*, Springer Texts in Business and Economics, https://doi.org/10.1007/978-3-319-70936-9

GPSR Compliance
The European Union's (EU) General Product Safety Regulation (GPSR) is a set of rules that requires consumer products to be safe and our obligations to ensure this.

If you have any concerns about our products, you can contact us on

ProductSafety@springernature.com

In case Publisher is established outside the EU, the EU authorized representative is:

Springer Nature Customer Service Center GmbH
Europaplatz 3
69115 Heidelberg, Germany

www.ingramcontent.com/pod-product-compliance
Lightning Source LLC
Chambersburg PA
CBHW071220201125
35560CB00031B/169
9783319709352